CONSTITUTIONAL EXCLUSION

CONSTITUTIONAL EXCLUSION

THE RULES, RIGHTS, AND REMEDIES THAT STRIKE THE BALANCE BETWEEN FREEDOM AND ORDER

JAMES J. TOMKOVICZ

OXFORD
UNIVERSITY PRESS

OXFORD
UNIVERSITY PRESS

Oxford University Press, Inc., publishes works that further Oxford University's objective of excellence in research, scholarship, and education.

Oxford New York
Auckland Cape Town Dar es Salaam Hong Kong Karachi Kuala Lumpur Madrid Melbourne Mexico City Nairobi New Delhi Shanghai Taipei Toronto

With offices in
Argentina Austria Brazil Chile Czech Republic France Greece Guatemala Hungary Italy Japan Poland Portugal Singapore South Korea Switzerland Thailand Turkey Ukraine Vietnam

Published by Oxford University Press, Inc.
198 Madison Avenue, New York, New York 10016

Library of Congress Cataloging-in-Publication Data

Tomkovicz, James J.
Constitutional exclusion : the rules, rights, and remedies that strike the balance between freedom and order / James J. Tomkovicz.
p. cm.
Includes bibliographical references and index.
ISBN 978-0-19-536924-3 ((hardback) : alk. paper)
1. Due process of law—United States. 2. Criminal procedure—United States.
3. Constitutional law—United States. 4. Presumption of innocence—United States.
5. Burden of proof—United States.
I. Title.
KF4765.T66 2011
347.73'5—dc22

2010039092

Note to Readers
This publication is designed to provide accurate and authoritative information in regard to the subject matter covered. It is based upon sources believed to be accurate and reliable and is intended to be current as of the time it was written. It is sold with the understanding that the publisher is not engaged in rendering legal, accounting, or other professional services. If legal advice or other expert assistance is required, the services of a competent professional person should be sought. Also, to confirm that the information has not been affected or changed by recent developments, traditional legal research techniques should be used, including checking primary sources where appropriate.

(Based on the Declaration of Principles jointly adopted by a Committee of the American Bar Association and a Committee of Publishers and Associations.)

To Nancy, Vivian, Michelle, and Henry—my reasons, motivations, and inspirations

CONTENTS

PREFACE

Many have made substantial contributions to this examination of the constitutional rules that exclude evidence from criminal trials. The University of Iowa College of Law and the Iowa Law Foundation generously supported this project by providing the time and resources necessary to complete it. Particular thanks are due to Dean Carolyn Jones for her encouragement and confidence. Moreover, the folks at Oxford University Press deserve credit. The remarkably rapid and unqualifiedly enthusiastic response to my proposal was a source of considerable reinforcement and encouragement. The freedom to design and execute the project as I saw fit facilitated its timely and successful completion.

A project of this magnitude evolves over the course of years. Many bright and devoted law students have served as research assistants during the evolution of this text. Some were instrumental in getting the project off the ground by helping determine whether it was feasible. Others joined the effort a bit later, performing foundational research for the initial chapters. Those who came on board in the middle of the endeavor played a number of different roles. They were researchers, reviewers, and editors, and they ensured that the early momentum was not lost. A few pitched in as the manuscript was nearing completion and devoted their labors to the final stages. There can be no doubt that some research assistants made more substantial contributions than others, but I will make no effort here to describe, measure, or rank the specific accomplishments of each. Instead, I will simply acknowledge my indebtedness and express my sincere appreciation to the many who made measurable contributions to the final product. For their expert assistance, their dedication, and their service, I am deeply grateful to these outstanding research assistants: Scott Burrill, Kevin Kehe, Robert Ladd, Jonathan Landon, Benjamin Roth, Chad Skarpiak, Mikaela Shotwell, Brian Shust, and Jason Wiltfang. Each of you shares in this achievement.

Finally, I would like to pay tribute to the less concrete, but nonetheless real, contributions made by generations of Iowa law students whom I have taught and learned from. I am a teacher, and a scholar, because of you and for you. Your love of learning, your thirst for knowledge, your commitment to the rule of law, and your respectful appreciation have long been inspirations for me and for my work.

INTRODUCTION

Those with any familiarity with the American legal system know that in criminal cases the government bears the burden of proving guilt beyond a reasonable doubt.[1] This demanding standard can impede and prevent the conviction of guilty persons, thereby making it more difficult to preserve public safety. Our nation is willing to pay the costs of fidelity to the reasonable doubt standard, however, because of a fundamental aversion to imposing the stigma and more concrete consequences of criminal conviction upon the innocent. We prefer to allow some guilty persons to escape just punishment in order to minimize the risk that those who have not offended will suffer erroneous conviction.

The burden of proving guilt beyond a reasonable doubt is not a focus of this text. That requirement does, however, serve as a significant backdrop for the array of controversial constitutional rules and dictates that are the objects of concern here. When the prosecution seeks to carry its burden of proof by introducing into evidence a quantity of cocaine found by officers during a search of the accused's bedroom, the Fourth Amendment exclusionary rule may require a judge to prohibit introduction of the contraband because the bedroom search was unreasonable. If the government attempts to clear the reasonable doubt hurdle by disclosing to the jury a defendant's confession of guilt, due process or the Fifth Amendment self-incrimination privilege may require a court to prevent such disclosure because officers coerced the words from the accused or because they failed to give him *Miranda* warnings before interrogating him. The state may wish to call a witness to testify to the incriminating admissions her indicted cellmate made during casual conversations in their cell. The Sixth Amendment entitlement to the assistance of counsel, however, may require the judge to bar that witness from testifying because she was working for the state at the time of the conversations. Eyewitness identifications of the perpetrators of crimes made at pretrial lineups and at trials themselves may prove quite persuasive with jurors in satisfying the reasonable doubt standard, but due process protections against suggestive identification procedures or the Sixth Amendment guarantee of legal assistance may prevent jurors from learning of those identifications. Finally, a homicide victim may have informed officers prior to her death that her abusive

1. The reasonable doubt standard is not explicit in the text of our Constitution. However, the Due Process Clause of the Fourteenth Amendment provides that "[n]o State shall . . . deprive any person of life, liberty, or property, without due process of law." U.S. Const. amend. XIV. The Supreme Court has decided that the requirement that the prosecution prove every element of a criminal offense beyond a reasonable doubt is an element of due process. *See* In re Winship, 397 U.S. 358, 364 (1970).

former lover had threatened to kill her. When he is later accused of and tried for carrying out that threat, his Sixth Amendment entitlement to be confronted with witnesses against him may prohibit the prosecutor from calling the officers who listened to and recorded the victim's earlier account.

In all these situations, constitutional safeguards, as interpreted by the United States Supreme Court, require the exclusion of relevant, sometimes highly probative, evidence of guilt from criminal trials. Provisions enshrined in our Bill of Rights bar the prosecution from using that evidence to satisfy the invariably demanding burden of proving every element of an offense beyond a reasonable doubt. From one vantage point, this constitutional suppression of the truth is often, if not always, a serious, self-defeating, and irrational handicap to the government's commendable efforts to protect the citizenry from crime and criminals. From another perspective, these prohibitions on the introduction of evidence are essential to the preservation of vital American values reflected in an array of fundamental guarantees of liberty. These competing attitudes toward constitutional exclusion have informed, and continue to influence, United States Supreme Court decision-making and public discourse. They will permeate the analyses and explorations throughout this text.

The evidentiary constraints discussed here have engendered a variety of difficult, often divisive issues. With regard to each rule, a core question is whether it is a legitimate interpretation of the Constitution—that is, whether the Bill of Rights provision undergirding the exclusionary command really does bar evidence of guilt. Does the Fourth Amendment, whose literal terms provide only a "right . . . to be secure . . . against unreasonable searches and seizures"[2] really command that narcotics found by officers during a warrantless home search be kept from the courtroom? Does the Sixth Amendment entitlement to the assistance of counsel for one's defense really prevent the government from showing that an eyewitness to a sexual assault positively identified the accused at a lineup where he lacked a lawyer's assistance? Intertwined with the question of legitimacy is the pivotal inquiry into rationales. Why does each constitutional safeguard studied here dictate that the prosecution be prevented from offering the proof it has in hand? What purposes are served by barring the illegally found narcotics from trial? What values and objectives are promoted by suppressing evidence of the eyewitness identification made at the lineup?

In addition, most of the rules excluding evidence give rise to an array of quite specific doctrinal questions. Initially, it is necessary to define the contours and specify the breadth of each constitutional bar. Are the illegally discovered narcotics inadmissible against all persons they might incriminate? If they lead the authorities to discover additional proof of guilt, is that evidence also barred from trial? If the lineup identification cannot be introduced, may the government call the same eyewitness to the witness stand at trial to testify that the defendant is

---

2. U.S. Const. amend. IV.

the person she saw perpetrate the assault? Moreover, once the scope of a particular rule is defined, issues regarding the propriety of various possible exceptions to exclusion arise. Assuming grounds for barring evidence, are there circumstances that justify lowering the bar and allowing the government to use illegally acquired proof? What if law enforcement officers would have found the narcotics by means of a legally valid investigation if other officers had not first secured them by searching the home without a warrant? Suppose, in a case very close to the constitutional line, that officers reasonably, albeit mistakenly, believed that they did have constitutionally adequate grounds for searching a home without a warrant. Should the lineup identification be admissible if the prosecution convincingly establishes that the eyewitness to the assault had a very clear view of the crime and has a strong, confident recollection of having seen the accused commit the offense?

Most of the legal doctrines considered here are typically referred to as "exclusionary rules." This terminology is appropriate insofar as each distinct doctrine does exclude evidence the prosecution would like to introduce to establish an accused's guilt. The label is potentially misleading, however, and seriously so, to the extent that as it suggests that the rules are identical in nature or scope. In fact, both in character and in reach, there is considerable diversity in the constitutional bars to the admission of evidence that are the subjects of this book. A central objective here is to dispel misunderstandings rooted in a monolithic conception of the exclusionary rules by explaining the distinctive nature of and the underlying justifications for each constitutional principle. Accurate identification of the rules' characters and rationales should promote accurate determinations of their scope and of the appropriateness of recognizing particular exceptions to suppression. When there is dispute or ambiguity as to any of these matters, as there often is, I intend to explain and analyze all plausible views and all potentially defensible interpretations and ramifications.

Legal rules that prevent the state from using probative evidence to convict criminals have long been, and are destined to remain, controversial. This text is unique in assembling all the different suppression doctrines in one place, enabling productive comparison and contrast. Moreover, this study is timely because broad and narrow exclusionary rule questions that have serious implications for the survival of civil liberties and for the efficacy of law enforcement efforts continue to trouble and divide the United States Supreme Court. It seems most unlikely that any thoughts offered here will end the often heated arguments between critics and supporters of the exclusionary rules. However, by juxtaposing these rules and subjecting each to in-depth examination, this text may at least promote more rational, more informed scholarly and public debates. It may also provide significant assistance for judges who are faced with the responsibilities of resolving perplexing exclusionary rule issues. Their decisions play a central role in defining the balance between freedom and order struck by our Bill of Rights.

Each chapter in this text will sketch the history and nature of a specific command that evidence be excluded from trial, will address the proffered and potential constitutional justifications for that command, and will then explain and investigate doctrinal intricacies and unresolved questions. Chapter 1 explores evidentiary suppression resulting from violations of the Fourth Amendment guarantee against unreasonable searches and seizures. The Fourth Amendment prohibition is by far the most prominent and most divisive of the exclusionary rules. In modern times, it has been the subject of substantial development both in the United States Supreme Court and in the lower courts and has been the focus of numerous—and often quite exhaustive—scholarly critiques. For all these reasons, and because the Fourth Amendment rule has at times served as a model for exclusion under other constitutional guarantees, this text extensively and closely considers every aspect of the Fourth Amendment rule. Chapter 2 analyzes the bars to coerced or compelled confessions of guilt found in both the Fourteenth Amendment Due Process Clause and the Fifth Amendment privilege against compulsory self-incrimination. Chapter 3 addresses suppression resulting from violations of the protections against custodial interrogation prescribed by the *Miranda* doctrine—an outgrowth of the Fifth Amendment privilege discussed in Chapter 2. Chapter 4 discusses the last of the constitutional exclusion doctrines that target "confessions" of guilt—the *Massiah* doctrine. This doctrine, rooted in the Sixth Amendment right to the assistance of counsel, prohibits the use of statements that government agents have "deliberately elicited" from accused individuals in the absence of counsel. The subjects of Chapters 5 and 6 are a pair of minimally developed, nearly dormant, but still operational—and theoretically fascinating—rules that bar eyewitness identification evidence. The Sixth Amendment right to counsel bars eyewitness identification testimony if counsel was not present at certain types of government-conducted identification processes, and the Fourteenth Amendment Due Process Clause requires the exclusion of some identifications resulting from unnecessarily suggestive official methods. The final rule that keeps probative evidence from the courtroom, the Sixth Amendment Confrontation Clause ban on "testimonial hearsay," is the topic of Chapter 7. Although this longstanding impediment to evidence of guilt is not ordinarily categorized with the other exclusionary rules, there can be no doubt that it prohibits the introduction of potentially probative evidence and thereby hinders government efforts to prove guilt just like the doctrines studied in the first six chapters. A brief conclusion will endeavor to synthesize and summarize general lessons about constitutional exclusion that emerge from the analyses of the seven constitutional suppression doctrines explored in this text.

1. THE FOURTH AMENDMENT EXCLUSIONARY RULE

INTRODUCTION

For good reason, the descriptions and analyses of the Fourth Amendment exclusionary rule[1] in this text are somewhat more extensive and detailed than the descriptions and analyses of most of the other sources of constitutional exclusion. The Fourth Amendment rule has a long and eventful history. Moreover, because issues involving Fourth Amendment suppression have arisen with much greater frequency, judges and scholars have devoted substantially more time and effort to discussions and critiques of the Fourth Amendment rule. Myriad opinions and articles exhaustively address broad and narrow questions generated by the rule. Controversies over the legitimacy of and justifications for the Fourth Amendment suppression doctrine and disputes over the details of its operation have been legion.

Because so much ink has been spilled, the opportunities for original insights about the topics considered here are few indeed. Consequently, although I hope to offer a few new slants on some old questions and a few reflections on some unsettling new trends, most of this chapter's account of Fourth Amendment exclusion will not be novel or groundbreaking. The approach taken in this text is designed to enhance understanding of the Fourth Amendment rule in at least two respects. First, this chapter will provide a comprehensive picture of the Fourth Amendment exclusionary rule. Every significant aspect of the rule—its history, its rationales, and its many doctrinal limitations—is addressed. Second, the book will juxtapose the Fourth Amendment rule with other constitutional bases for exclusion in the hope that their differences and similarities might shed additional light on each.

A. THE BASIC FOURTH AMENDMENT RULE

The Fourth Amendment to the United States Constitution extends to "the people" a "right . . . to be secure against unreasonable searches and seizures,"

1. Generally, references to the Fourth Amendment exclusionary rule in this text are intended to encompass not only the Fourth Amendment-based rule that binds the federal government, but also the equivalent Fourteenth Amendment-Due Process Clause-based rule that constrains states. In the historical section of this chapter, however, it will be necessary to distinguish between the initial birth and evolution of the Fourth Amendment rule that dictates exclusion in federal courts and the later inception and development of the Fourteenth Amendment rule that commands exclusion in state courts.

commanding that this right "shall not be violated."[2] The exclusionary rule developed by the Supreme Court prescribes a consequence for the failure to honor this command. It declares that the government may not use evidence its agents acquire by means of an unreasonable search or seizure to prove the guilt of a defendant at trial. Narcotics found during a warrantless search of a home may be barred from a criminal prosecution. A murder weapon found in a suspect's coat pocket and the same suspect's confession made after an arrest without probable cause are inadmissible to meet the state's burden of proof. Officers may be prohibited from testifying that they found stolen laptops in the trunk of a vehicle that they towed and searched without justification.

The terse statement of the Fourth Amendment exclusionary rule in the preceding paragraph makes clear the fundamental predicate for its operation. The rule applies only if government agents acquire evidence by means of an unreasonable search or seizure. Private parties—those not acting on behalf of the government—cannot violate the Fourth Amendment, for it does not govern their conduct.[3] Thus, those conducting the search or seizure must be state actors[4] and the search or seizure must be unreasonable.[5] In addition, evidence is subject to exclusion only when it is obtained as a result of that search or seizure. If the same officers perform both an unconstitutional and a constitutionally reasonable search, objects found by means of the

---

2. In its entirety the Fourth Amendment to the United States Constitution provides: "The right of the people to be secure in their persons, houses, papers, and effects, against unreasonable searches and seizures, shall not be violated, and no Warrants shall issue, but upon probable cause, supported by Oath or affirmation, and particularly describing the place to be searched, and the persons or things to be seized." U.S. CONST. amend. IV.

3. *See* United States v. Jacobsen, 466 U.S. 109, 113 (1984); Coolidge v. New Hampshire, 403 U.S. 443, 487–90 (1971); Burdeau v. McDowell, 256 U.S. 465, 475–76 (1921).

4. One need not be an actual employee of the state to qualify. Private parties can qualify as state actors for purposes of the Fourth Amendment when they act to further governmental purposes. *See* United States v. Jacobsen, 466 U.S. 109, 113–14 (1984) (suggesting that the conduct of a private party who is "'acting as an agent of the Government or with the participation or knowledge of any government official'" can qualify as "governmental action") (quoting Walter v. United States, 447 U.S. 649, 662 (1980) (Blackmun, J., dissenting)); United States v. Hardin, 539 F.3d 404, 418 (6th Cir. 2008) (suggesting that whether a party is a state actor depends on the government's knowledge of or acquiescence in the search and the intent of the party performing the search).

5. The subject of what constitutes an "unreasonable" search or seizure is not the concern here. Suffice it to say that the developed doctrine concerning the meaning of unreasonableness is extensive.

former are excluded, but items discovered by means of the latter are admissible.[6]

This pithy statement of the Fourth Amendment rule, however, does not answer a number of other significant questions. One question is whether the rule prevents the admission of evidence not only in criminal prosecutions, but also in any other court proceedings. Does the Fourth Amendment forbid the state from using illegally discovered evidence to prove civil tax liability or to secure civil forfeiture of a home? Another is whether the rule prohibits admission against all individuals. If the unreasonable search of my automobile yields contraband narcotics, does the exclusionary rule prevent the government from using them to prove my partner's guilt? Still another is whether the rule forbids only evidence found immediately, during the unlawful search or seizure, or also extends to evidence obtained by pursuing investigative leads found during the search or seizure. If officers unreasonably seize my person and I provide information that furnishes ample probable cause for a warrant to search a warehouse where they discover incriminating weapons and find a witness willing to testify against me, are the weapons and the witness's testimony subject to suppression? Another issue is whether there are circumstances that suspend the exclusionary rule's operation and allow the government to introduce evidence it has illegally gained. Put otherwise, should the law recognize exceptions to the presumptive bar to evidence secured in violation of the guarantee against unreasonable searches and seizures? If so, when is it permissible to lower the barrier to courtroom use of illegally-acquired evidence?

All of these issues and more will be explored at length in subsequent sections of this chapter. For now, suffice it to say that the exclusionary rule is narrower and considerably more complex than one might think. It generally applies *only* in criminal trials, not in other phases of the criminal process or in civil proceedings. In addition, the rule bars use *only* against an individual who was the victim of the unreasonable search or seizure, not against any other person incriminated by the evidence. It presumptively prohibits *all* evidence with any causal connection to the illegality, not just evidence found immediately during the unlawful search or seizure, but also evidence acquired by pursuing illegally-obtained leads. On the other hand, there are several exceptions that permit the use of illegally-acquired evidence in a criminal prosecution to prove the guilt of the very individual whose Fourth Amendment right has been violated by the unreasonable search or seizure. Before considering these "nuts and bolts" questions concerning the operation of the rule, two foundational matters merit attention. The next subsection reviews the historical development of the Fourth Amendment exclusionary rule, sketching its limited origins and its gradual evolution into a

---

6. The need for causation and the relevance of a lawful independent source are explained later in this chapter. *See infra* text accompanying notes 145–55, 204–12.

much more expansive prohibition. The following subsection explores the rationales for the rule—both the currently accepted justifications and alternative, competing explanations.

B. THE ORIGIN AND DEVELOPMENT OF THE FOURTH AMENDMENT EXCLUSIONARY RULE: A BRIEF HISTORICAL OVERVIEW

The focus of this book is the current status of constitutional exclusion in the United States. My primary goal is not to explore how we got where we are, but to describe and assess the present—and perhaps try to gain a glimpse into the future. Consequently, this foundational account of the history of the Fourth Amendment exclusionary rule will be relatively brief and rudimentary.

It is generally agreed that the Fourth Amendment exclusionary rule was born nearly a century ago in the Supreme Court's unanimous 1914 opinion in *Weeks v. United States*.[7] The Supreme Court itself traces the rule to the *Weeks* decision.[8] Some have found even earlier support for the rule in the Court's landmark 1886 opinion in *Boyd v. United States*,[9] a case that involved a court order to produce an invoice for plate glass that was the subject of a forfeiture action brought by the government. Although *Boyd* did bar the government from using evidence it acquired by means of conduct that the Court deemed an unreasonable search, there are a number of reasons why that opinion cannot be read as endorsing a broad rule that requires the suppression of all evidence obtained by violating the Fourth Amendment's commands. First, the case was concerned only with "private papers," not with other types of evidence. The Court specifically indicated that it would find no constitutional impediment if property the government was entitled to possess—stolen goods, forfeited goods, or other objects that it was unlawful to possess—was at issue. Thus, any rule of exclusion contained in *Boyd* was confined to private papers and information such papers contain. Second, the Court clearly, consistently, and repeatedly relied on both the Fourth Amendment and the Fifth Amendment privilege against compulsory

---

7. 232 U.S. 383 (1914).

8. *See* Hudson v. Michigan, 547 U.S. 586, 590 (2006); United States v. Calandra, 414 U.S. 338, 347 (1974).

9. 116 U.S. 616 (1886). For authors suggesting that *Boyd* contains the roots of the Fourth Amendment exclusionary rule, see, e.g., Morgan Cloud, *Rights Without Remedies: The Court that Cried "Wolf,"* 77 Miss. L. J. 467, 478 (2007) [hereinafter Cloud, *Rights Without Remedies*]; Thomas Y. Davies, *An Account of* Mapp v. Ohio *That Misses the Larger Exclusionary Rule Story*, 4 Ohio St. J. Crim. L. 619, 622–23 (2007) [hereinafter Davies, *An Account of* Mapp]; Potter Stewart, *The Road to* Mapp v. Ohio *and Beyond: The Origins, Development, and Future of the Exclusionary Rule in Search-and-Seizure Cases*, 83 Colum. L. Rev. 1365, 1372 (1983) [hereinafter Stewart, *The Road to* Mapp].

self-incrimination. *Boyd* did not hold that the papers would have been inadmissible by virtue of the Fourth Amendment alone.

Perhaps most telling, however, is the fact that 18 years later, in *Adams v. New York*,[10] the Supreme Court read *Boyd* very narrowly indeed. In *Adams*, police raided the defendant's premises and discovered papers that were then used to convict him of possessing gambling paraphernalia. The Court held that if the papers were relevant to prove guilt they were not to be excluded from the trial, even if they had been secured by means of an unconstitutional search or seizure. *Boyd* was still good authority, but only for the proposition that the government could not compel an individual to produce papers in a forfeiture suit because that act violated "both the Fourth and Fifth Amendments."[11] According to the *Adams* Court, those two constitutional provisions "were never intended" to require the exclusion of evidence found as a result of a search or seizure.[12] Not only did the *Adams* Court interpret *Boyd* as having nothing to say about the inadmissibility of probative evidence obtained by means of an unreasonable search and seizure, it also appeared to hold that there was no Fourth Amendment exclusionary rule—that is, no mandate that evidence obtained by violating that guarantee is inadmissible at trial.

Just ten years later, the Court decided *Weeks v. United States*,[13] the landmark case generally viewed as the source of the Fourth Amendment exclusionary rule. Just as *Adams* had read *Boyd* narrowly, *Weeks* construed *Adams* stingily. Federal officers had conducted warrantless searches of Mr. Weeks's home in violation of the Fourth Amendment, finding relevant, probative evidence of his participation in a lottery enterprise. Both before and at the outset of his criminal trial, Weeks filed a petition seeking the return of his seized property. The trial judge, adhering to *Adams*, ordered the government to return only items that were not relevant to proving his guilt. The judge then allowed the prosecution to introduce illegally-obtained papers at the trial, and Weeks was convicted.

A unanimous Supreme Court agreed with Mr. Weeks's contention that refusing to order a return of the papers and permitting their use as evidence was error of constitutional magnitude. First, the Court easily concluded that the search of the accused's home without a warrant was a violation of the proscription against unreasonable searches and seizures. It then asserted that the Fourth Amendment restrained not only federal law enforcement officers, but also federal courts, and that those courts should not "sanction" efforts to secure convictions by means of unlawful searches and seizures.[14] In the Court's view, if the government could retain the letters and documents the officers had illegally obtained and could use

---

10. 192 U.S. 585 (1904).
11. *Id.* at 597.
12. *Id.* at 598.
13. 232 U.S. 383 (1914).
14. *Id.* at 391–92.

them as evidence to convict the accused, the Fourth Amendment would be "of no value, and . . . might as well be stricken from the Constitution."[15] In sum, the judge's refusal to order that the government return the items to the defendant was itself "a denial of [his] constitutional rights," and by allowing the government to "use" the evidence at "trial," the judge committed "prejudicial error."[16]

According to Justice Day, the *Adams* opinion (which he had authored) had merely decided "that a court will not in trying a criminal cause permit a collateral issue to be raised as to the source of competent testimony."[17] The controlling principle—that a "'court, when engaged in trying a criminal cause, will not take notice of the manner in which witnesses have'" gained possession of material evidence—did not apply in *Weeks* because the defendant had not asked the trial court to stop his trial and "consider the illegal means by which" evidence had been "obtained."[18] He had "made timely application to the court for an order for the return of the[] letters," both before and "at the beginning of the trial."[19] *Adams* was thus cast as a mere rule of process designed to preclude disruption of "the orderly progress of a cause."[20] When, as in *Weeks*, an aggrieved party raised a challenge at a time that did not threaten a disruption of orderly progress and proved that items of evidence were acquired through an unreasonable search and seizure, the Fourth Amendment required the government to return the items and not introduce them at trial.

Although the Court has subsequently described *Weeks* as holding that evidence obtained by means of a Fourth Amendment violation generally must be excluded from trial,[21] it is not at all clear that the Court intended to promulgate so sweeping a principle. First, it preserved the *Adams* rule that if the accused first complains that evidence was obtained unconstitutionally when the evidence is offered at trial, a court should not exclude it on that ground. Second, and probably more important, the *Weeks* opinion was concerned with, and repeatedly limited to, "letters and private documents."[22] It did not address the admissibility of other sorts of evidence—contraband, stolen goods, instrumentalities of crime, or nondocumentary items, for example. A plausible, narrow reading is that *Weeks* required the return, and therefore barred the use, only of private papers and perhaps other evidentiary items that an accused can lawfully possess.[23] The novel

15. *Id.* at 393.
16. *Id.* at 398.
17. *Id.* at 396.
18. *Weeks*, 232 U.S. at 395–96, 392 (quoting People v. Adams, 176 N.Y. 351, 358 (1903)).
19. *Id.* at 393.
20. *Id.* at 396.
21. *See* Hudson v. Michigan, 547 U.S. 586, 590 (2006); Wolf v. Colorado, 338 U.S. 25, 28 (1949).
22. *Weeks*, 232 U.S. at 393.
23. *See* Stewart, *The Road to* Mapp, *supra* note 9, at 1375.

exclusionary rule announced in *Weeks*—the unprecedented holding that an unconstitutional search or seizure can pose a bar to the government's use of competent evidence to prove guilt—might well have been intended only for certain, limited kinds of evidence. Moreover, one undoubted limitation of the suppression doctrine of *Weeks* was its confinement to evidence obtained illegally by *federal* agents offered as proof in *federal* prosecutions.

It would be 35 years before the Supreme Court would confront the issue of whether the Constitution prevented the admission in state courts of evidence found by state agents as a result of unreasonable searches and seizures. In a small number of decisions rendered during that time, the Justices refined and developed the federal exclusionary rule born in *Weeks*. *Silverthorne Lumber Co., Inc. v. United States*[24] involved the illegal seizure of papers from an office by federal agents. The trial court granted the defendant's application for return of the original papers. The court also impounded photographs and copies of the papers that the government had made. Subsequently, based on those photographs and copies, the government secured subpoenas requiring production of the original papers, and the trial court ordered compliance with the subpoenas despite finding that "all the papers had been seized in violation of" the Fourth Amendment.[25] The court then held Silverthorne and his company in contempt of court for failure to comply with the subpoenas and the order.

The Supreme Court reversed the judgment of contempt, holding that because the government had illegally seized the papers it could not use them to secure a subpoena requiring that the papers be produced. According to Justice Holmes, *Weeks* had interpreted the Fourth Amendment prohibition on "the acquisition of evidence in a certain way" to forbid the use in court of evidence that was unconstitutionally acquired.[26] The exclusionary mandate was broader, however, and dictated that illegally-acquired evidence could "not be used at all."[27] Because the government could not use the illegally secured papers to obtain the subpoenas for the original documents, the contempts based on failures to comply with those subpoenas were invalid. In *Silverthorne Lumber*, therefore, the Court expanded the suppressive reach of the Fourth Amendment exclusionary rule, holding that it not only forbade admission of evidence in the courtroom, but that it also prohibited the government's use of illegally-obtained information as a means of acquiring further evidence.[28]

---

24. 251 U.S. 385 (1920).

25. *Id.* at 391.

26. *Id.* at 392.

27. *Id.*

28. In *Silverthorne Lumber*, the government used the illegally acquired evidence as a basis for subpoenaing the *very same evidence*, but the principle enunciated by Justice Holmes was in no way tied to that fact and prohibited the use of the unconstitutionally gained information to secure any other evidence which might itself be admitted to

Just one year later, in *Gouled v. United States*,[29] the Court was confronted with two different situations. In one, a defendant first objected to the use of illegally seized papers at trial when the government sought to introduce them to prove conspiracy charges. The Court concluded that the *Adams* "rule of practice" did not prevent objection at trial if the accused raised his objection promptly after first receiving notice that the government possessed the evidence.[30] Significantly, the Court held that the stealthy search of Gouled's office had violated the Fourth Amendment, but that the admission of the papers found had violated the *Fifth* Amendment guarantee against compelled self-incrimination. The Court thereby appeared to root the exclusion of evidence obtained by an unreasonable search and seizure in the guarantee against being compelled to be a witness against oneself.[31]

Gouled also involved other papers seized under a search warrant. The defendant had raised a pretrial objection, but the trial judge had refused to return the papers and had then refused to reconsider that ruling at trial. In ruling on the admissibility of these papers, the Court asserted that the *Adams*'s pretrial objection rule needed to be applied in a way that served "the ends of justice" and could "not be allowed for any technical reason to prevail over a constitutional right."[32] The *Gouled* Court, therefore, narrowed *Adams*'s practical limitation upon the exclusionary rule and thereby expanded the scope of that rule in two respects. Where there was either no opportunity for a pretrial objection or an erroneous denial of a pretrial objection, a judge should ignore the *Adams* rule of practice, apply the *Weeks* rule *at trial*, and bar the government from introducing papers acquired in violation of the Fourth Amendment.

Finally, *Agnello v. United States*[33] involved a trial for narcotics offenses in which the trial court had allowed the prosecutor to rebut a defendant's testimony that he had never seen drugs by introducing a can of cocaine that federal agents had obtained by a warrantless, thus unreasonable, search of his bedroom. The Court declared it "well settled" that "the Fifth Amendment protects every person from

---

prove guilt. The Court also reaffirmed *Weeks*'s constrictive interpretation of *Adams* as a mere bar to "collateral inquiry into" how evidence was obtained "when the question is raised for the first time at the trial." 251 U.S. at 392.

29. 255 U.S. 298 (1921).

30. *See id.* at 305.

31. With regard to certain papers of mere "evidential value," the Court found that the means of obtaining them had violated the Fourth Amendment, while their introduction had violated the Fifth Amendment. *Id.* at 309–11. The Court's reliance on the latter guarantee is reminiscent of the reasoning in *Boyd*. In *Boyd*, however, the Court had suggested that the Fourth Amendment, at least in part, was a foundation for suppression. In *Gouled*, the reasoning of the Court appeared to tie inadmissibility *solely* to the Fifth Amendment's proscription of compulsory self-incrimination.

32. 255 U.S. at 312–13.

33. 269 U.S. 20 (1925).

incrimination by the use of evidence obtained" in violation of the Fourth Amendment, citing *Boyd*, *Weeks*, *Silverthorne Lumber*, and *Gouled* for support.[34] Consequently, the trial court had erred in allowing admission of the can of cocaine over the defendant's objection at trial. The Court thereby implicitly extended the reach of the *Weeks* doctrine beyond private papers, bringing illegally seized narcotics within the scope of the exclusionary rule. On the other hand, although *Weeks* itself had placed no reliance on the Fifth Amendment privilege, the Court once again declared *that* guarantee to be *the* basis for excluding probative evidence from courtrooms.

The government contended that the failure to apply for a return of the can before trial precluded its exclusion at trial. The Court first responded that the accused had no notice of the government's intent to introduce the can. Then, much more broadly, it asserted that when "uncontroverted facts" show an unreasonable search and seizure, "there is no reason why one whose rights have been so violated and who is sought to be incriminated by evidence so obtained, may not invoke protection of the Fifth Amendment immediately and without any [prior] application for the return of the thing seized."[35] With this observation, the Court appeared to deal a deathblow to the already eroded procedural constraint *Adams* had placed on the exclusionary rule, broadening the scope of the search and seizure exclusionary rule in the process.

In *Wolf v. Colorado*,[36] the Court finally confronted the question of whether the Constitution permitted the admission of the products of unreasonable searches and seizures by *state* officers in *state* trials. This question had not only theoretical importance, but also considerable practical significance because the vast majority of criminal prosecutions are the business of states and their courts.[37] Because the Bill of Rights provisions bind only the federal government, the question was not whether the Fourth Amendment dictates exclusion. Instead, the question was whether the Fourteenth Amendment command that no "State [shall] deprive any person of life, liberty, or property, without due process of law,"[38] required the suppression of evidence that a federal court would have to exclude under *Weeks*. Initially, the Court had to decide whether the guarantee of due process includes protection against unreasonable searches and seizures. Unanimously, the Justices

---

34. *Id.* at 33–34.

35. *Id.* at 34.

36. 338 U.S. 25 (1949).

37. *Compare* U.S. Dept. of Justice, *Prosecutors in State Courts*, 2005, at 6 (2006), *available at* http://www.ojp.usdoj.gov/bjs/pub/pdf/psc05.pdf (noting that "[i]n 2005, State court prosecutors reported closing 2.4 million felony cases and nearly 7.5 million misdemeanor cases") *with* U.S. Dept of Justice, *Federal Justice Statistics*, 2005, at 3 (2008), *available at* http://www.ojp.usdoj.gov/bjs/pub/pdf/fjs05.pdf (observing that "U.S. Attorneys . . . concluded 143,640 [cases] in 2005").

38. U.S. Const. amend. XIV.

agreed that the "security of one's privacy against arbitrary intrusion by the police—which is at the core of the Fourth Amendment—is basic to a free society," and, consequently is "enforceable against the States through the Due Process Clause."[39] Six of these Justices, however, in an opinion by Justice Frankfurter, concluded that "in a prosecution in a State court for a State crime the Fourteenth Amendment does not forbid the admission of evidence obtained by an unreasonable search and seizure."[40]

According to the majority, the questions were how to restrain "arbitrary conduct" by state officers, "what remedies" to afford for such conduct, and by what "means" the right to privacy "should be made effective."[41] The *Weeks* holding that "the Fourth Amendment" bars "the use of evidence secured through an illegal search and seizure" from a "federal prosecution," was not rooted in "explicit requirements of the Fourth Amendment," but, instead, "was a matter of judicial implication."[42] While casting no doubt on that rule, the Court identified a number of reasons that militated against imposing the same rule on the states. "[M]ost of the English-speaking world" did not suppress evidence and the states held contrary views on the need for an exclusionary rule.[43] A majority, in fact, rejected it.[44] Those states that refused to exclude evidence afforded "the right to privacy . . . other means of protection," including actions for damages against, criminal prosecutions of, and internal discipline by the police.[45] According to the Court, such remedies, which protect both the innocent and the guilty, cannot be condemned as contrary to due process if, when "consistently enforced," they are "equally effective" ways of "deterring unreasonable searches."[46]

The majority did observe that *Weeks* had "interpreted the *Fourth Amendment* to forbid the admission of [illegally secured] evidence" in a federal trial.[47] Thus, although the exclusionary rule was described as judicially implied, it was not seen as merely a rule of evidence. The *Wolf* Court characterized it as a *constitutional* mandate. Moreover, the Fourth Amendment alone dictated suppression; the support of the Fifth Amendment privilege was apparently

---

39. *Wolf*, 338 U.S. at 27–28. The Court did not clearly, unequivocally hold that *any* search or seizure that the Fourth Amendment would deem unreasonable would, if performed by state officers, deprive an individual of due process. Its language left open the possibility that *some* unreasonable searches or seizures—those that offend, but do not implicate "the core of the Fourth Amendment"—would be consistent with the due process demand. *Id.*

40. *Id.* at 33.

41. *Id.* at 28.

42. *Id.*

43. *Id.* at 29.

44. *Wolf*, 338 U.S. at 29–30.

45. *Id.* at 30, 30 n.1.

46. *Id.* at 31.

47. *Id.* at 33 (emphasis added).

thought unnecessary. On the other hand, the majority did not rule out legislative abolition of the federal exclusionary rule, asserting that "if Congress . . . were to pass a statute purporting to negate the *Weeks* doctrine," the Court would need to decide how much "respect" needed "to be accorded [to that] legislative judgment."[48] Moreover, the Court placed heavy emphasis on the efficacy of exclusion a "way of deterring unreasonable searches."[49]

Three Justices expressed the view that the exclusion of evidence from state prosecutions was the *only* effective means of protecting the due process guarantee of privacy the *Wolf* Court had recognized. In their view, it had been "perfectly clear" since *Weeks* that the only "alternative to the rule of exclusion . . . is no sanction at all."[50] Other remedies the majority cited had proven "illusory" as "positive deterrent[s] to police and prosecutors tempted to violate the Fourth Amendment."[51] Just as the Fourth Amendment commanded exclusion in federal trials, the Fourteenth Amendment required exclusion in state prosecutions.

In two cases in the early 1950s, the Court considered whether due process *ever* forbade states from introducing evidence acquired by means of illegal searches and seizures. *Rochin v. California*[52] involved a conviction based on narcotics that police obtained by pumping the defendant's stomach after he resisted officers' efforts to force his mouth open and swallowed the capsules they were seeking. After exploring the meaning of the Due Process Clause and how judges are to determine whether it is violated in specific cases, the Court concluded that the "force" involved in *Rochin* was "so brutal and so offensive to human dignity" that it "shock[ed] the conscience."[53] Relying on the doctrine that prohibited the use of coerced confessions to convict "not only because of their unreliability," but also because they "offend the community's sense of fair play and decency," the Court reversed Rochin's conviction because it had been "obtained by methods that offend[ed] the Due Process Clause."[54] The Court apparently did not believe that *Weeks* or *Wolf* had any relevance, for it mentioned neither.

Two years later, in a case involving particularly intrusive searches and particularly egregious conduct, a bare majority of the Court rejected a claim that *Rochin* dictated reversal and, instead, held that *Wolf* was controlling. In *Irvine v. California*,[55] officers broke into the defendant's home without warrants on multiple occasions, planting and repositioning equipment that enabled them to listen to the occupants' conversations for more than a month. The state

48. *Id.*
49. *Wolf*, 338 U.S. at 31.
50. *Id.* at 41–42 (Murphy, J., dissenting).
51. *Id.* at 42–43 (Murphy, J., dissenting).
52. 342 U.S. 165 (1952).
53. *Id.* at 174, 172.
54. *Id.* at 173–74.
55. 347 U.S. 128 (1954).

convicted the defendant based on incriminating conversations the officers overheard. A plurality of four Justices believed that *Rochin* was distinguishable because no matter how "obnoxious" the conduct was in *Irvine*, it did "not involve coercion, violence or brutality to the person."[56] They rejected the effort to "make inroads upon *Wolf*" by restricting it to mildly shocking searches and seizures and excluding evidence obtained by those that produce more serious shock.[57] They preferred *Wolf*'s rejection of the suppression remedy for all illegal search and seizure cases, even those involving egregious misconduct. The plurality even evinced a negative attitude toward the *Weeks* rule itself, suggesting that it had little effect in curtailing illegal searches, that it led to "the escape of guilty persons," failed to "punish" offending officers, and did "nothing to protect innocent persons who are victims of" unreasonable searches.[58] They believed that admitting evidence did not "exonerate" the officers because there were other remedies that had been ineffective in the past only because interested parties failed to make officers' offenses known.[59]

The fifth vote for affirmance came from Justice Clark who first observed that if he had been on the Court in 1949, he would have extended the *Weeks* rule to the states. Because *Wolf* was the law, he reluctantly followed it, expressing a hope, however, that "strict adherence" to *Wolf* might "produce needed converts for its extinction."[60]

Justice Frankfurter, the author of both *Wolf* and *Rochin*, penned a dissent that expressed a belief that the "aggravating conduct" in *Irvine* was sufficient to bring it within the *Rochin* rationale.[61] Although there was no "physical violence," the conduct "went far beyond a bare search and seizure" because there was "powerful and offensive control over the" lives of the home's occupants.[62] It did not matter that there was "trustworthy evidence" of the defendant's guilt because the methods used to prove his guilt "offend[ed] elementary standards of justice" and deprived him of the "fundamentally fair" trial guaranteed by due process.[63] Justice Frankfurter did not mince words, declaring that the intentional deprivation of "'constitutional rights'" effected by the officers' "'crime . . ., if subtly encouraged by failure to condemn and punish, certainly leads down the road to totalitarianism.'"[64]

---

56. *Id.* at 133.
57. *Id.* at 133–34.
58. *Id.* at 135–36.
59. *Id.* at 137.
60. *Irvine*, 347 U.S. at 138–39.
61. *Id.* at 144–45 (Frankfurter, J., dissenting).
62. *Id.* at 145–46 (Frankfurter, J., dissenting).
63. *Id.* at 148 (Frankfurter, J., dissenting).
64. *Id.* at 149 (Frankfurter, J., dissenting) (quoting Statement by Director J. Edgar Hoover of the Federal Bureau of Investigation in FBI Law Enforcement Bulletin, September 1952, p.1).

In sum, as of 1954, a majority of the Court was clearly still committed to the *Wolf* holding that due process does not generally include a principle commanding that states exclude evidence yielded by unreasonable searches and seizures. Only in egregious, extreme cases like *Rochin* and *Irvine* did the admission of evidence provoke resistance from the Justices.

After these three state cases, the Court returned to the federal exclusionary rule in *Elkins v. United States*,[65] continuing the trend of expansion that had begun prior to *Wolf*. In *Elkins*, a federal criminal prosecution, the government had probative evidence that had apparently been acquired by means of an unconstitutional search and seizure by *state* law enforcement officers.[66] Federal officers were not at all involved in the illegality. In accord with the "silver platter doctrine," which authorized the introduction in federal court of evidence illegally found by state officers,[67] the trial judge allowed the government to introduce the illegally-obtained evidence. A five-Justice majority rejected that doctrine and extended the federal exclusionary rule to evidence unlawfully obtained by state agents. Evidence secured by state officers' conduct that would violate the Fourth Amendment if performed by federal agents was deemed "inadmissible . . . in a federal criminal trial."[68]

The Court first cited the difficulties presented by having to decide whether there was adequate federal involvement in a search and seizure to trigger the *Weeks* prohibition. It then documented how *Wolf* had changed the landscape by determining that unreasonable searches and seizures by state officers did violate the Constitution. According to the majority, logic alone dictated exclusion for violations of either the Fourth or Fourteenth Amendment's commands, for in both cases the "Constitution is flouted equally."[69] Significantly, the majority recognized that the object of the exclusionary rule is "to deter—to compel respect for the constitutional guaranty in the only effectively available way—by removing the incentive to disregard it."[70] Moreover, "reason and experience" led to the

---

65. 364 U.S. 206 (1960).

66. I say apparently because the state courts had so determined. The federal trial judge and the court of appeals did not decide whether the search and seizure were unconstitutional because they believed that the evidence was admissible even if the state officers had acted unconstitutionally.

67. There was support for this doctrine in *Weeks* itself. While finding error in the failure to suppress items found by federal agents, the *Weeks* Court had approved of the admission of evidence seized by state law enforcement officers in the federal prosecution involved in that case. Weeks v. United States, 232 U.S. 383, 398 (1914). The admissibility in federal criminal proceedings of "evidence unlawfully seized by state officers apparently went unquestioned for the next thirty five years." *Elkins*, 364 U.S. at 210.

68. *Elkins*, 364 U.S. at 223.

69. *Id.* at 215.

70. *Id.* at 217

same conclusion as logic.[71] In particular, there was evidence that the exclusionary rule had not rendered law enforcement ineffective, states had increasingly adopted the suppression remedy, and the silver platter doctrine undermined "federalism" by producing "needless conflict between state and federal courts."[72] In addition, the "imperative of judicial integrity" supported exclusion because when federal courts admit evidence that state officers have illegally obtained they become "accomplices in the willful disobedience of [the] Constitution."[73]

Four Justices dissented,[74] asserting that the Court should not overturn a long-standing and previously approved rule.[75] According to the dissenters, the *Weeks* Court concluded that the interest in pressuring federal officers to obey the Constitution overcame the ordinary presumption in favor of admitting truthful evidence. Subsequent opinions had confirmed, however, that the suppression doctrine applied only if the federal government was involved in the illegal search. The dissenters believed that the majority had erred both in interpreting *Wolf* as meaning that any search that is unreasonable under the Fourth Amendment also transgresses the due process requirement, and in concluding that this premise led logically to abolition of the silver platter doctrine. According to the dissent, *Wolf*'s point was that the remedies for Fourth Amendment and due process violations were "not the same."[76] Moreover, because *Wolf* allowed state courts to admit evidence gained from unconstitutional searches by state officers, suppressing that evidence in federal trials would not significantly advance the sole justification for exclusion—to exert control over the police.

The dissent also disagreed with the majority's suggestion that its holding promoted "the wise and effective administration of criminal justice."[77] The merits of the exclusionary rule were debatable, as evidenced by the fact that state adoption of the *Weeks* rule had not been inexorable. Almost 50 years after *Weeks*, half the states still refused to follow its rule. The silver platter doctrine was "workable" and was supported by practical concerns and considerations of "comity."[78] The new suppression doctrine, according to the dissenters, would create conflicts with state criminal justice policies and would undermine the federalism interests the majority hoped to promote.

---

71. *Id.* at 222.

72. *Id.* at 221.

73. *Elkins*, 364 U.S. at 222–23.

74. *Id.* at 233 (Frankfurter, J., dissenting).

75. Justice Frankfurter noted that *Weeks* had endorsed the "silver platter doctrine" in 1914 and that in *Byars v. United States*, 273 U.S. 28 (1927), a unanimous Court that included Justices Holmes, Brandeis, and Stone had reaffirmed the rule that authorized federal courts to admit evidence unlawfully acquired by state officers. *Elkins*, 364 U.S. at 233 (Frankfurter, J., dissenting).

76. *Elkins*, 364 U.S. at 240 (Frankfurter, J., dissenting).

77. *Id.* at 241 (Frankfurter, J., dissenting).

78. *Id.* at 243–45 (Frankfurter, J., dissenting).

Abolition of the silver platter doctrine effected a notable expansion of the federal exclusionary rule. The greater significance of *Elkins*, however, was as a foundation for and a long step down the road to revolution. Just one year later, in the most significant Supreme Court decision in the history of the search and seizure exclusionary rule, the *Elkins* Court's reasoning would prove integral to the overthrow of *Wolf v. Colorado*. This history concludes with *Mapp v. Ohio*,[79] the landmark decision that extended the *Weeks* rule to state courts and launched the modern era of exclusionary rule jurisprudence described and discussed in the remainder of this chapter.

Although litigants in some post-*Wolf* cases had argued that the Court should disavow that decision[80] and the trend toward an ever-broader suppression remedy made the overturning of *Wolf* far from unpredictable, *Mapp v. Ohio* was certainly an unlikely vehicle for so dramatic a development. The issue of exclusion was peripheral, at best, in *Mapp*. Briefing and oral argument focused on another unrelated constitutional question[81] and scarcely mentioned the question of evidentiary admissibility.[82] Nonetheless, five Justices decided that *Mapp* was an appropriate vehicle for interring *Wolf* and imposing the exclusionary rule on state courts. The *Mapp* majority found an occasion to explain how *Wolf* had misinterpreted the Fourteenth Amendment and why evidentiary exclusion is, in fact, a requisite component of due process in state proceedings.

In *Mapp*, officers broke into a home without a search warrant, conducted a search, and discovered obscene materials. The authorities charged Ms. Mapp with possessing those materials. The Ohio courts refused to suppress the illegally secured evidence, a constitutionally permissible option under *Wolf*. The Supreme Court granted review and reversed, holding "that the exclusionary rule is an essential part of both the Fourth and Fourteenth Amendments" and "that all

---

79. 367 U.S. 643 (1961).

80. *See id.* at 654 (referring to the "plea made here Term after Term that we overturn [the *Wolf*] doctrine"); *see also Irvine v. California*, 347 U.S. 128, 133–34 (1954) (noting that the petitioner had argued for a limitation of *Wolf*).

81. The issue briefed and argued in the Supreme Court was whether constitutionally guaranteed "rights of free thought and expression" prevented conviction for "the *mere* knowing possession or control of obscene material." *See* 367 U.S. at 672–73 (Harlan, J., dissenting).

82. Ms. Mapp did not argue that *Wolf* should be overturned. In exceedingly terse fashion, the American Civil Liberties Union, *amicus curiae* in support of Ms. Mapp, invited the Court to resolve the case on that basis. *See* Brief for American Civil Liberties Union et al. as *Amici Curiae* Supporting Petitioner-Appellant, Mapp v. Ohio (1961) (No. 236), 1961 WL 101785, at *20; *see also Mapp*, 367 U.S. at 646 n.3 (noting that the ACLU had urged *Wolf*'s overruling during oral argument); *id.* at 674 n.5 (Harlan, J., dissenting) (citing the "short concluding paragraph" in the ACLU's brief that merely called for the Court to overturn *Wolf* without providing supporting arguments).

evidence obtained by searches and seizures in violation of the Constitution is, by that same authority, inadmissible in a state court."[83]

Justice Clark's opinion began with a foundational discussion of *Boyd* and *Weeks*, which established that the federal exclusionary rule was "constitutionally required" and that the use of illegally gained evidence to convict constituted a denial of the accused's constitutional rights.[84] *Wolf* had erred in relying on "factual considerations" that were "not basically relevant" to the constitutional inquiry, considerations whose validity had been undermined in the twelve years that followed.[85] By holding that the right to privacy granted by the Fourth Amendment was a part of due process, but that the exclusion of evidence was not, the *Wolf* Court had misread *Weeks*. *Weeks* had held that the sanction of exclusion was, in fact, "an essential part of the right to privacy" safeguarded by the Fourth Amendment.[86] Moreover, the Court had recognized that the federal exclusionary rule was "a clear, specific, and constitutionally required . . . deterrent safeguard," needed to enforce the Fourth Amendment right to privacy.[87] The recognition in *Wolf* that the Fourth Amendment right to privacy was enforceable against the states as a part of due process made it "logically and constitutionally necessary that the exclusion doctrine . . . be also insisted upon as an essential ingredient of th[at] right."[88] *Wolf* had correctly recognized the right, but had mistakenly denied "its most important constitutional privilege."[89]

In addition, a Fourteenth Amendment exclusionary rule made "very good sense" because it diminished conflict and tension between state and federal courts and law enforcement officers.[90] In response to the concern that the exclusionary rule would set criminals free, the Court cited the countervailing "'imperative of judicial integrity'" and observed that when that result did occur it was because "the law . . . sets [them] free."[91] Put otherwise, the interests in ensuring that courts upheld the law and avoided participation in unconstitutional conduct outweighed the costs of suppression. Moreover, these costs had not unduly fettered law enforcement in jurisdictions adhering to the exclusionary rule.

---

83. *Mapp*, 367 U.S. at 655, 657.

84. *Id.* at 646–48.

85. *Id.* at 651. Those "factual considerations" included the "'contrariety'" of state views on the exclusionary rule, the availability of other remedies, and that the federal rule was at times too broad and at times too narrow. *Id.* at 651–53 (quoting Wolf v. Colorado, 338 U.S. 25, 29 (1949)).

86. *Id.* at 655–56.

87. *Id.* at 648.

88. *Mapp*, 367 U.S. at 655–56

89. *Id.* at 656.

90. *Id.* at 657.

91. *Id.* at 659 (quoting Elkins v. United States, 364 U.S. 206, 222 (1960)).

Mapp divided the Court. Justice Black, one of the five Justices who favored overruling *Wolf*, wrote a separate concurrence in which he explained that he was "still not persuaded that the Fourth Amendment, standing alone," provided constitutional support for exclusion.[92] In his view, however, the Fourth Amendment and the Fifth Amendment prohibition of compelled self-incrimination together provided a "constitutional basis" for requiring the exclusion of evidence gained from unreasonable searches and seizures.[93] Justice Stewart refused to express a view on the merits of the exclusionary rule issue. Instead, he voted to reverse Ms. Mapp's conviction on an entirely different ground.[94]

Three dissenters first took issue with the *Mapp* majority's willingness to address the suppression question.[95] They believed that their Brethren had erred by going out of their way to address that issue when it had been neither briefed nor argued by the parties. The Court should have reconsidered exclusion in state courts only after the litigants had fully aired and explored the issue.[96]

The dissenters believed that *Wolf*'s understanding of due process was correct and that the decision to obligate the states to exclude evidence was constitutionally unjustified. They found none of the majority's reasons for abandoning *Wolf*'s nonexclusionary rule for state courts to be persuasive. First, *Wolf* had *not* held that due process made every detail of the Fourth Amendment's constraints upon unreasonable searches and seizures applicable to the states. It had declared only that due process encompassed the privacy protections at the *core* of that guarantee. Moreover, even if the Fourth Amendment exclusionary rule had constitutional roots, it was a mere remedy that sought to deter officers' future unconstitutionalities by penalizing past misconduct. The demands of due process did not require imposition of this remedy on the states. Indeed, the Court had exceeded its authority by requiring state courts to exclude evidence, thereby depriving states of the freedom to devise their own remedies for enforcing the Fourteenth Amendment guarantee of privacy.

---

92. *Id.* at 661 (Black, J., concurring).

93. *Mapp*, 367 U.S. at 662 (Black, J., concurring).

94. Justice Stewart concluded that the statute that was the basis for conviction infringed upon the constitutional rights of free thought and expression. *Id.* at 672 (memorandum of Stewart, J.).

95. There were actually four Justices who believed that *Mapp* was not an appropriate case for addressing the continued viability of the *Wolf* rule. Justice Stewart joined the dissenters on this point. *Id.* (memorandum of Stewart, J.).

96. In his concurrence, Justice Douglas made an effort to defend the majority's decision to reach the exclusionary rule question. He deemed *Mapp* an "appropriate case" for such a decision because the facts were a graphic illustration of the "casual arrogance of those who have the untrammeled power to invade . . . home[s] and to seize . . . person[s]" and because the "illegality of the search" and the "admissibility of the evidence" were both raised in the state court and in documents filed in the Supreme Court. 367 U.S. at 671 (Douglas, J., concurring).

The history of the search and seizure exclusionary rule has, of course, continued to unfold in the nearly 50 years since *Mapp*. This historical account is intended to provide a background for discussion of the exclusionary rule's substance. It ends with *Mapp* because with that decision the federal and state exclusionary rules reached the peak of their development. As of 1961, in both federal and state criminal prosecutions, courts were constitutionally bound to exclude evidence found by means of unreasonable searches and seizures. The subsequent evolution of the suppression doctrine is captured and reflected in the sections of this chapter devoted to describing, analyzing, and critiquing the substantive details of the present-day exclusionary rule.

C. THE LEGITIMACY OF AND THE RATIONALES FOR THE FOURTH AMENDMENT EXCLUSIONARY RULE

The Fourth Amendment exclusionary rule has long been controversial, the subject of scathing criticisms and impassioned defenses. Some challenge its legitimacy, contending that it is an unacceptable creation of the judiciary, while others find it to be a vital element of our constitutional heritage. Many have written at great length in opposition to and in support of the search and seizure suppression doctrine. The broad objectives of this text preclude an exhaustive exploration of the arguments made for and against the rule's validity. For present purposes, a brief summary will suffice.

Opponents start with the indisputable premise that the text of the Fourth Amendment does not contain an exclusionary rule.[97] It merely proscribes violations of the right against unreasonable searches and seizures and prescribes the requisites for a valid warrant; it does not specify that evidence acquired in violation of its guarantees is inadmissible in a criminal prosecution.[98] The history and background of the Fourth Amendment do not fill the breach and compensate for the lack of textual support. To the contrary, the common law of neither England nor the United States called for the exclusion of illegally discovered

---

97. *See* Akhil Reed Amar, *Against Exclusion (Except to Protect Truth or Prevent Privacy Violations)*, 20 HARV. J.L. & PUB POL'Y 457, 459 (1997) [hereinafter Amar, *Against Exclusion*]; Susan R. Klein, *Identifying and (Re)formulating Prophylactic Rules, Safe Harbors, and Incidental Rights in Constitutional Criminal Procedure*, 99 MICH. L. REV. 1030, 1048–49 (2001); Daniel Solove, *The First Amendment as Criminal Procedure*, 82 N.Y.U. L. REV. 112, 163 (2007).

98. The same is true of the textual source of the exclusionary rule in state proceedings. There is no specific mention of evidentiary suppression in the Fourteenth Amendment Due Process Clause, which provides only an assurance that states will not deprive any person of "life, liberty, or property, without due process of law." U.S. CONST. amend. XIV.

evidence from criminal trials.[99] Courts affirmatively rejected the contention that relevant evidence should be barred from trial because it was the product of an improper search.[100] The traditional recourse for a victim was instead a civil suit for damages to compensate for the injury occasioned by the unlawful search or seizure.[101]

Exclusionary rule detractors believe that because the Fourth Amendment grants no right to have the products of unreasonable searches and seizures excluded from trial, the admission of such products does not violate the Fourth Amendment.[102] They contend that it is constitutionally indefensible for judges to infer or create the suppression sanction as a means of preserving Fourth Amendment rights. The critics do not argue that judges lack authority to enforce the guarantee against oppressive searches and seizures, but object that the exclusionary rule is not a constitutionally defensible option. In their view, other sanctions such as civil damages, criminal prosecution of offending officers, and internal police discipline for unconstitutional conduct can provide adequate assurances against official misconduct. In light of these alternative enforcement mechanisms, the exclusionary rule is not only unnecessary, it reflects an indefensible policy choice. Unlike the other methods of promoting compliance with Fourth Amendment commands, by barring relevant evidence from criminal trials the suppression remedy rewards undeserving guilty persons with freedom,[103] defeats the search for the truth,[104] undercuts efforts to protect society against criminals,[105] and fails to provide any relief for those who are most deserving—innocent victims of unreasonable searches and seizures.[106] According to the anti-exclusionary rule camp, it simply makes no sense to infer that the

---

99. *See* Thomas Y. Davies, *Recovering the Original Fourth Amendment*, 98 Mich. L. Rev. 547, 624 (1999) [hereinafter Davies, *Recovering the Original*]; Alfred Hill, *The Political Dimension of Constitutional Adjudication*, 63 S.Cal. L. Rev. 1237, 1288 (1990).

100. *See* Amar, *Against Exclusion*, *supra* note 97, at 459–60; Commonwealth v. Dana, 43 Mass. 329 (1841) (noting that there was no "legal objection" against the admission of illegally seized evidence).

101. *See* Cloud, *Rights Without Remedies*, *supra* note 9, at 477; Davies, *Recovering the Original*, *supra* note 99, at 625–26.

102. *See* Amar, *Against Exclusion*, *supra* note 97, at 459; Akhil Reed Amar, *Fourth Amendment First Principles*, 107 Harv. L. Rev. 757, 790–91 (1994) [hereinafter Amar, *First Principles*]; *see also* United States v. Leon, 468 U.S. 897, 906 (1984).

103. *See* Amar, *First Principles*, *supra* note 102, at 793–94; Morgan Cloud, *Judicial Review and the Exclusionary Rule*, 26 Pepp. L. Rev. 835, 835 (1999).

104. *See* Edwin Meese III, *Promoting Truth in the Courtroom*, 40 Vand. L. Rev. 271, 274 (1987) [hereinafter Meese, *Promoting Truth*]; *see also* Hudson v. Michigan, 547 U.S. 586, 591 (2006).

105. *See* Meese, *Promoting Truth*, *supra* note 104, at 275; Stewart, *The Road to* Mapp, *supra* note 9, at 1393.

106. *Cf.* Amar, *First Principles*, *supra* note 102, at 797; Sherry F. Colb, *Innocence, Privacy, and Targeting in Fourth Amendment Jurisprudence*, 96 Colum. L. Rev. 1456, 1482 (1996).

Framers of the Fourth Amendment, who made no mention of and had no experience with evidentiary exclusion, would prefer to have that guarantee implemented by such a harmful, self-defeating, costly device. There is no basis for inferring that they would select such an unwise and misguided sanction.

Proponents of the Fourth Amendment exclusionary rule make no claim that the text of that guarantee provides explicit support. Nor do they contend that the suppression doctrine has historical credentials that predate the Bill of Rights. Some assert, nonetheless, that the exclusion of evidence discovered by means of an unreasonable search or seizure is a constitutional entitlement of one who is the victim of that search or seizure. According to one conception, exclusion is itself an essential part of the right to be secure against unreasonable searches and seizures, an essential component of the constitutional entitlement to privacy.[107] The security guaranteed is threatened *both* when officers search or arrest without adequate justification *and* when any evidence found is introduced at trial. The people have not only constitutional shelter against the initial, extra-judicial invasion of privacy or deprivation of liberty, but also a Fourth Amendment entitlement to protection from the injury inflicted when illegally-found items surface in the courtroom.[108] Privacy is breached by the warrantless home entry or the unjustified arrest, and the loss of privacy is intensified when the government makes use of what it unlawfully found in a trial.

Another conception perceives a right to exclusion that grows out of, and is required by, the constitutional entitlement not to be deprived of life, liberty, or property without due process of law.[109] Due process guarantees a fair trial, and the government violates this guarantee when it exploits unconstitutional methods of investigation in order to secure a conviction. A verdict of guilt that rests on proof that government operatives have gained in contravention of fundamental constitutional rights is the product of a fundamentally unfair proceeding. Suppression is required to preserve the entitlement to a fair trial process.

---

107. *See* Lawrence Crocker, *Can the Exclusionary Rule Be Saved?* 84 J.Crim L. & Criminology, 310, 316 (1993); Sam J. Ervin, Jr. *The Exclusionary Rule: An Essential Ingredient of the Fourth Amendment*, 1983 Sup. Ct. Rev. 283, 287 (1983); *see also* United States v. Leon, 468 U.S. 897, 935 (1984) (Brennan, J., dissenting).

108. *See* Ruth W. Grant, *The Exclusionary Rule and the Meaning of Separation of Powers*, 14 Harv. J.L. & Pub Pol'y 173, 193–96 (1991) [hereinafter Grant, *Separation of Powers*]; Yale Kamisar, *Does (Did) (Should) the Exclusionary Rule Rest on a "Principled Basis" Rather than an "Empirical Proposition"?* 16 Creighton L. Rev. 565, 594–95 (1983) [hereinafter Kamisar, *"Principled Basis"*]; Thomas S. Shrock & Robert C. Welsh, *Up from* Calandra*: The Exclusionary Rule as a Constitutional Requirement*, 59 Minn. L. Rev. 251, 257–60 (1974); *see also Leon*, 468 U.S. at 935–43 (Brennan, J., dissenting).

109. *See* Alfredo Garcia, *Toward an Integrated Vision of Criminal Procedural Rights: A Counter to Judicial and Academic Nihilism*, 77 Marq. L. Rev. 1, 17 (1993); Grant, *Separation of Powers*, *supra* note 108, at 195–96.

Those who contend that evidentiary exclusion is an inseparable part of the constitutional right against unreasonable searches and seizures conceive of that guarantee as a constraint upon government conduct both outside and within the courtroom. To them, the Fourth Amendment contains explicit prohibitions upon acquiring evidence in certain ways and logically implicit prohibitions upon the use of evidence so acquired. Because the government is forbidden from conducting unreasonable searches and seizures, it is not entitled to the possession of evidentiary items it discovers as a result. To enforce the Fourth Amendment in the present, the government must not be allowed to exploit in the courtroom any advantages gained by conducting unlawful searches and seizures. The exclusionary rule is justified because the Fourth Amendment grants accused individuals a constitutional entitlement to protection against the use of evidence at trial, which saddles the government with an obligation not to use that evidence to convict.

A second basis of support—which can either be an alternative or a supplement to the constitutional right theory of suppression—holds that the exclusion of illegally-obtained evidence is essential to ensure that agents of the government will honor the assurance against unreasonable searches and seizures.[110] If officials were allowed to use the products of unconstitutional conduct to convict, they would have powerful motivations to violate the Fourth Amendment's constraints. The exclusionary rule, which prevents such use, is considered essential to ensure that the fundamental entitlements to privacy, liberty, and property—which are the core objectives of the Fourth Amendment—are adequately protected, preserved, and respected. The object of suppression is to *deter* law enforcement from depriving citizens of their undisputed constitutional entitlements—that is, to discourage improper techniques of investigation by making them unprofitable and informing officers that they may use *only* evidence acquired by means that comply with Fourth Amendment commands.[111] According to this defense of the exclusionary rule, the aim of suppression is to enforce constitutional rights for all *in the future*, not to prevent a present violation of rights in the courtroom. The object is to ensure that the interests and values enshrined in the Fourth Amendment do not become empty promises or ephemeral entitlements.[112]

According to this conception of the exclusionary rule, alternative potential sources of deterrence—civil damages, criminal prosecution, internal discipline,

---

110. *See* Peter Arenella, *Rethinking the Functions of Criminal Procedure: The Warren and Burger Courts' Competing Ideologies*, 72 Geo. L. J. 185, 237 (1983); Grant, *Separation of Powers*, *supra* note 108, at 179–80; Stewart, *The Road to* Mapp, *supra* note 9, at 1389.

111. *See* Grant, *Separation of Powers*, *supra* note 108, at 187–88; Wayne R. LaFave, *The Fourth Amendment in an Imperfect World: On Drawing "Bright Lines" and "Good Faith,"* 43 U. Pitt. L. Rev. 307, 317 (1982); Stewart, *The Road to* Mapp, *supra* note 9, at 1395.

112. Silverthorne Lumber Co. v. United States, 251 U.S. 385, 391–92 (1920); Weeks v. United States, 232 U.S. 383, 393 (1914).

and citizen supervision, for example—are insufficiently effective.[113] Because the available alternatives do not provide officers with adequate incentives to comply with Fourth Amendment dictates, they are inadequate mechanisms for preserving the constitutional guarantee. The judiciary, entrusted with the task of preserving Bill of Rights liberties, has not only the authority, but also the obligation, to suppress evidence. Fidelity to the promises made by the Framers of the Fourth Amendment requires no less.

The third foundational premise for the exclusionary rule is intertwined with, but analytically distinct from, the constitutional right and deterrent foundations. The focus is neither on any courtroom entitlement of the victims of unreasonable searches or seizures, nor on any need to prevent future law enforcement misconduct. Instead, the object is to safeguard judicial integrity.[114] According to this view, the Fourth Amendment constrains all branches of the government, including judges.[115] When they allow the products of unconstitutional law enforcement methods to fuel the processes of guilt-innocence determination, judges participate in and sanction the illegalities perpetrated by officers.[116] When judges permit the executive branch to exploit unconstitutionally gained advantages in the courtroom, they invite disrepute and breed cynicism. To avoid these harmful consequences, judges must close the doors of their courtrooms to illegally-acquired evidence. If they fail to do so, they become complicit in a process that the Framers declared unacceptable and undermine their integrity, an invaluable commodity for the administration of justice.[117]

Despite the chorus of opposition that has pursued the exclusionary rule for decades and continues to advocate abolition, the rule survives in both federal and

---

113. Carol S. Steiker, *Second Thoughts About First Principles*, 107 HARV. L. REV. 820, 848 (1994); Stewart, *The Road to* Mapp, *supra* note 9, at 1388–89.

114. Robert M. Bloom, *Judicial Integrity: A Call for its Reemergence in the Adjudication of Criminal Cases*, 84 J. CRIM. L. & CRIMINOLOGY 462, 467 (1993) [hereinafter Bloom, *Judicial Integrity*]; Grant, *Separation of Powers, supra* note 108, at 179.

115. *See Weeks*, 232 U.S. at 391–92.

116. *See id.* at 394.

117. *See* Bloom, *Judicial Integrity, supra* note 114, at 499–501; Michael J. Daponde, *Discretion and the Fourth Amendment Exclusionary Rule: A New Suppression Doctrine Based on Judicial Integrity*, 30 MCGEORGE L. REV. 1293, 1313–14 (1999).

The judicial integrity underpinning for the exclusionary rule is similar to the premises that underlie the federal courts' supervisory power over the administration of justice. In essence, federal judges possess an authority to adopt rules that guarantee fairness in federal court proceedings beyond that mandated by any particular constitutional command. *See* Dickerson v. United States, 530 U.S. 428, 437 (2000); United States v. Payner, 447 U.S. 727, 735 n.7 (1980). The courts are thought to have an inherent interest in ensuring that the administration of justice, both in reality and in appearance, satisfies the highest standards of fair play. *See* McNabb v. United States, 318 U.S. 332, 340–41 (1943).

state prosecutions.[118] A number of current Supreme Court Justices do appear sympathetic to the abolitionists' views.[119] Nonetheless, a majority remains committed to preservation of the *Weeks-Mapp* doctrine.[120] As will be seen, the prevailing rationale for preserving the exclusionary rule is the deterrence of future Fourth Amendment violations.[121] The remainder of this section sketches the evolution over time of the Supreme Court's justifications for the suppression doctrine and describes in detail the reasoning that has come to dominate the analysis prescribed by the Court.

When it adopted the federal exclusionary rule, the *Weeks* Court did not identify the deterrence of future illegalities as an objective of the suppression doctrine.[122] The Court endorsed the "rights" rationale, indicating that a defendant who had been the victim of an improper, warrantless search had a constitutional right to bar the use of the evidence at trial and that allowing the government to introduce it as proof would itself violate the Fourth Amendment.[123] The Court

---

118. As will be seen in the sections that follow, while the cores of the federal and state exclusionary rules survive, the suppression doctrines have shrunk considerably over the past half century.

119. *See* Hudson v. Michigan, 547 U.S. 586, 591 (2006); James J. Tomkovicz, Hudson v. Michigan *and the Future of Fourth Amendment Exclusion*, 93 Iowa L. Rev. 1819, 1885–86 (2008) [hereinafter Tomkovicz, *Future of Exclusion*]; *see also* Sharon L. Davies & Anna B. Scanlon, Katz *in the Age of* Hudson v. Michigan*: Some Thoughts on "Suppression as a Last Resort,"* 41 U.C. Davis L. Rev. 1035, 1058–59 (2008).

120. Some have expressed concern that the Court seems to be headed toward abolition of the exclusionary rule. *See* Adam Cohen, *Is the Supreme Court About to Kill Off the Exclusionary Rule?*, Feb. 15, 2009, N.Y. Times, at A22; Adam Liptak, *Justices Step Closer to Repeal of Evidence Ruling*, Jan. 30, 2009, N.Y. Times, at A1. While the most recent opinions on the subject do furnish cause for concern, it seems clear that at least five current Justices would not be willing to support elimination of the suppression doctrine. *See Hudson*, 547 U.S. at 603 (Kennedy, J., concurring); *id.* at 611, 613–14 (Breyer, J., dissenting); *see also* Tomkovicz, *Future of Exclusion*, *supra* note 119, at 1832–35.

121. For a number of years after Justice Brennan left the Court, it seemed as if virtually every member of the Court might subscribe to the view that deterrence is the sole rationale for the *Weeks-Mapp* doctrine. In *Herring v. United States*, 555 U.S.____, 129 S.Ct. 695 (2009), the Court's most recent curtailment of Fourth Amendment exclusion, Justice Ginsburg, in a dissent joined by three other Justices, championed "'a more majestic conception' of the . . . exclusionary rule." 555 U.S. at ____, 129 S.Ct. at 707 (Ginsburg, J., dissenting) (quoting Arizona v. Evans, 514 U.S. 1, 18 (1995) (Stevens, J., dissenting)). The *Herring* dissenters agreed that the exclusionary rule serves an important deterrent function, but suggested that it was also an inseparable part of the Fourth Amendment's constraint on sovereign power, serving to preserve both judicial integrity and trust in the government. *Id.* (Ginsburg, J., dissenting).

122. Some language *can* be read that way, but it is a stretch to conclude that the Court had deterrence in mind. There is no specific reference to the objective of discouraging law enforcement agents from engaging in future illegalities.

123. Weeks v. United States, 232 U.S. 383, 398 (1914).

also suggested that the admission of illegally-obtained evidence would sully the judicial process and the judges who thereby "sanction[ed]" and participated in the impermissible conduct.[124] In the years that followed, the Court intimated that the Fifth Amendment privilege against compulsory self-incrimination could be the source of the constitutional right to suppress illegally discovered evidence.[125] It then backed away from that suggestion, reaffirming a Fourth Amendment-based entitlement to prevent the government from using proof gained as a result of an unreasonable search or seizure.[126] Just one year before extending the exclusionary rule to the states, the Court, without denying that defendants had a right to exclusion, supplemented the underpinnings of the exclusionary rule by acknowledging that deterrence was *an* objective of suppression and that the need for judicial integrity provided further support.[127]

Mapp v. Ohio, which required state courts to exclude the products of unreasonable searches and seizures by state officers, relied upon all three core justifications. The suppression doctrine was "an essential part of the right to privacy" that the Court already deemed to be part of the entitlement to due process.[128] It was also a "constitutionally required . . . deterrent safeguard," aimed at preventing future wrongs.[129] Finally, it furthered the "'imperative of judicial integrity'" by upholding the rule of law and ensuring that courts would not become entangled in an illegal process.[130]

By the mid-1960s, however, the emphasis began to change. The Court increasingly stressed the deterrent purpose of exclusion and referred to judicial integrity as an additional objective, while casting doubt on the view that suppression is itself a constitutional entitlement.[131] The erosion of the rights rationale over little more than a decade ultimately culminated in a declaration that no provision of the Constitution grants the party aggrieved by a search or seizure (or anyone else) a personal right to evidentiary exclusion.[132] Suppression does not remedy, repair, or compensate for constitutional wrongs officers have committed.[133] Its aim is not to prevent a further deprivation of constitutional rights in court.

---

124. *Id.* at 391–92, 394.

125. Agnello v. United States, 269 U.S. 20, 33–34 (1925); Amos v. United States, 255 U.S. 313, 315–16 (1921).

126. Go-Bart Importing Co. v. United States, 282 U.S. 344, 356–57 (1931); McDonald v. United States, 335 U.S. 451, 453 (1948).

127. Elkins v. United States, 364 U.S. 206, 217–18, 222–23 (1960).

128. Mapp v. Ohio, 367 U.S. 643, 655–56 (1961).

129. *Id.* at 648.

130. *Id.* at 659 (quoting *Elkins,* 364 U.S. at 222).

131. Professor Kamisar identifies Linkletter v. Walker, 381 U.S. 618 (1965), as the opinion which began the process of modifying the justifications for Fourth Amendment exclusion. *See* Kamisar, *"Principled Basis," supra* note 108, at 630–32.

132. United States v. Calandra, 414 U.S. 338, 348 (1974).

133. *Id.* at 347 (citing *Linkletter,* 381 U.S. at 637; *Elkins,* 364 U.S. at 217).

No Fourth Amendment deprivation can occur during trials, for that guarantee contains no courtroom rights. The evolved position rests on the premise that the *sole* right granted by the Fourth Amendment is the right not to be subjected to an unreasonable search and seizure. The suppression doctrine is designed to prevent *future* deprivations of *that* right by removing incentives for officers to violate it; preventing additional out-of-court transgressions is its singular aim.

Rejection of the premise that there is a constitutional entitlement to exclusion and acceptance of deterrence as *the* justification for the *Weeks-Mapp* rule have been the controlling themes of Supreme Court jurisprudence for well over 30 years now. The Court ostensibly recognizes judicial integrity as a supplemental foundation,[134] but has reimagined the nature of that rationale in a way that makes it entirely coextensive with deterrence. When deterrence calls for exclusion, judicial integrity does as well, but if deterrent objectives do not dictate suppression, then integrity provides no basis for barring evidence.[135] It is entirely accurate to say that deterrence has come to rule the Fourth Amendment exclusionary rule's roost.

This significant reformation of the justifications for Fourth Amendment suppression is of major theoretical importance. In addition, it has enormous practical consequences for operation of the rule. As will be seen, this reconceptualization of the suppression doctrine as a future-oriented enforcement mechanism, and not a personal constitutional right, has enabled the Court to dramatically curtail its scope. According to the Court, costly, judicially-devised remedial devices of this sort must be limited to situations that most effectively serve their objectives.[136] It is appropriate, indeed necessary, to balance the costs of exclusion to the administration of justice—that is, the lost convictions of guilty criminals—against the deterrent benefits of suppression—that is, the prevention of Fourth Amendment violations—and to exclude evidence *only* when the benefits outweigh the costs.[137] When the gains in enforcement of the Fourth Amendment's commands resulting from suppression are insufficient to justify the price paid when courts bar probative, truthful evidence from trials, the balance of interests tips against exclusion and the exclusionary rule is inapplicable. This sort of cost-benefit analysis, defensible when one understands suppression as a means of achieving adequate *future* compliance with the Constitution, would

---

134. *See* United States v. Leon, 468 U.S. 897, 921 n.22 (1984).

135. The *Leon* majority suggested that if the deterrent rationale does not dictate suppression that means a judge's decision to admit evidence will not improperly encourage officers to violate the Fourth Amendment and that judicial integrity is jeopardized only when judges provide such encouragement. *Id.*

136. *See* Stone v. Powell, 428 U.S. 465, 486–88 (1976); *Calandra*, 414 U.S. at 348.

137. *See* Herring v. United States, 555 U.S. ___, 129 S.Ct. 695, 700–01 (2009); Hudson v. Michigan, 547 U.S. 586, 591, 594–95 (2006); Stone v. Powell, 428 U.S. at 488.

have been more difficult, perhaps impossible, to justify if exclusion had remained a personal right granted by the Fourth Amendment.

The nature of the anticipated deterrent effects of exclusion—how suppression is supposed to discourage Fourth Amendment violations—merits some attention as well. The exclusionary rule does not seek to discourage future illegalities by *punishing* offending officers or anyone else.[138] In other words, its aim is not to make offending officers suffer unpleasant consequences in the hope that those officers and others will develop an aversion to conduct that leads to such consequences.[139] Instead, in suppressing valuable evidence the exclusionary rule's object is to deprive government agents of the benefits of their illegal acts. It makes unconstitutional conduct unprofitable, thereby "'removing the incentive to disregard'" Fourth Amendment restrictions.[140] If unreasonable searches and seizures do not yield evidentiary advantages in the government's efforts to prosecute and convict criminals, officers will not have motives to conduct those searches and seizures and police departments will have incentives to train officers properly. If only those searches and seizures that comply with constitutional commands produce evidence that may be used to convict the guilty, officers will have influential reasons for knowing what the Fourth Amendment requires and for abiding by those requirements.[141]

In *Mapp*, the Court described the exclusionary rule as a "*constitutionally required*" deterrent safeguard.[142] In more recent years, while eroding the underpinnings, narrowing the scope, and weakening the force of the exclusionary rule,

---

138. *See* Nix v. Williams, 467 U.S. 431, 445 (1984) (rejecting exclusion in part because it would be "punitive" to put the police in a worse evidentiary position than they would have occupied in the absence of illegal conduct).

139. This is how punishment for criminal conduct is said to "deter" future crimes by the defendant and by other members of society. *See* Kamisar, *"Principled Basis," supra* note 108, at 654 (asserting that the exclusionary rule provides "'systemic deterrence'" that is aimed at inducing police organizations to promote constitutional values rather than directly altering the conduct of individual violators) (quoting Mertens and Wasserstrom, *Foreword: The Good Faith Exception to the Exclusionary Rule: Deregulating the Police and Derailing the Law*, 70 Geo. L.J. 365, 394 (1981)); *see also* Amar, *First Principles, supra* note 102, at 797–98 (noting that the exclusionary rule is not designed to punish individual officers and deter future misconduct in the way that specific deterrence from criminal punishment deters future crime).

140. Mapp v. Ohio, 367 U.S. 643, 656 (1961) (quoting Elkins v. United States, 364 U.S. 206, 217 (1960)).

141. Of course, officers sometimes have motives other than successful prosecution of the guilty. In those cases, the exclusion of evidence will not "remove the incentive" for the illegalities and may well be a wholly ineffective deterrent. *See* Terry v. Ohio, 392 U.S. 1, 13–15 (1968). Other remedies, like civil suits, criminal prosecution, or internal departmental discipline of officers, are necessary to discourage conduct that is motivated by other objectives.

142. *Mapp*, 367 U.S. at 648 (emphasis added).

the Supreme Court has refrained from such descriptions. One explanation for the omission is that the Justices do not believe that the rule is a constitutionally mandated safeguard, but instead see it as a judicially-devised rule designed to promote constitutional conduct by the executive branch. The problem with this explanation, however, is that the Supreme Court lacks the authority to impose nonconstitutional rules on the states. It can restrict the states' authority over criminal justice matters only when their practices run afoul of the Constitution.[143] Consequently, as long as the Court requires adherence to the exclusionary rule in both federal and state courts, logic dictates that it be understood as a mandate rooted in the Fourth and Fourteenth Amendments.

Assuming that is the case, there is still another question of vital importance—whether the exclusionary rule is *the* constitutionally required deterrent mechanism or merely *a* judicially developed deterrent remedy that is constitutionally required *unless* supplanted by an alternative remedy (or remedies) that would discourage unconstitutional conduct just as effectively. Does the Constitution command evidentiary suppression in order to ensure that officers are deprived of significant incentives for illegal searches and seizures? Or does the Constitution demand *some* sanction that will sufficiently deter officers from violating Fourth Amendment commands? Would it be constitutionally acceptable to allow prosecutors to introduce all illegally-obtained evidence *if* the prospect of civil suits for damages or internal police disciplinary measures provided officers with motivations to avoid future unconstitutional conduct equivalent or comparable to those provided by the suppression doctrine? Although the Court's opinions furnish no clear answers to these questions, it seems likely that a genuinely effective alternative that did not require suppression of the truth in criminal trials would find favor with a Supreme Court majority. The failure of legislatures to implement such alternatives in the decades that have passed since *Mapp*, however, make it unlikely that the Justices will have an opportunity to decide whether the exclusionary rule is the *only* constitutionally acceptable means of securing compliance with the Fourth Amendment.[144] As a practical matter, it seems likely that the Fourth Amendment exclusionary rule, albeit a watered-down version of

143. *See* Dickerson v. United States, 530 U.S. 428, 438–39 (2000).

144. In *Hudson v. Michigan*, 547 U.S. 586 (2006), a majority of the Court eliminated the exclusionary rule as a sanction for violations of the Fourth Amendment knock-and-announce requirement. One of the bases for this decision was a declaration that the costs of exclusion exceed the deterrent benefits when officers have violated this restriction on the manner of executing a search. One of the predicates for discounting the deterrent benefits of suppression was that alternative remedies such as civil suits and police discipline already provided some motivation for officers to comply with the knock-and-announce demand. This narrow and limited reliance on the efficacy of alternative means of discouraging unconstitutional searches does not indicate that the Court would accept a claim that currently available alternative remedies, in general, have rendered exclusion constitutionally unnecessary for *any* Fourth Amendment transgression. It does, however,

its former self that may well be diluted more in the coming years, will continue to serve as *the* constitutionally mandated method of enforcing Fourth Amendment rights.

D. THE REACH OF THE FOURTH AMENDMENT EXCLUSIONARY RULE

The discussions that follow address pragmatic concerns—the details of the Fourth Amendment exclusionary rule's operation. The focus is upon the reach of the evidentiary bar that results from unreasonable governmental searches and seizures. A number of distinct questions arise with regard to the ambit of Fourth Amendment suppression. What evidence is presumptively subject to exclusion? In what sorts of court proceedings does the rule apply? Who is entitled to exclusion based on an unreasonable search or seizure? What exceptions to the rule have been and should be recognized? As will be seen, the presumptive scope of the rule is relatively broad, but the rule only applies in certain kinds of proceedings, may be asserted only by a limited set of individuals, and is riddled by a fair number of exceptions. Because of the many limitations on the exclusionary rule's reach, the government is allowed to make considerable use of evidence obtained by violating the Fourth Amendment.

1. Evidence Presumptively Subject to Suppression: The Fourth Amendment Exclusionary Rule Prohibition on Both Primary and Derivative Evidence

a. The Causation Demand The very statement of the exclusionary rule suggests its presumptive scope. The rule mandates suppression of evidence the government has acquired by means of an unreasonable search and seizure.[145] The first essential requirement for application of the exclusionary rule is, of course, an unreasonable search or seizure in violation of the Fourth Amendment. The rule then bars *only* evidence with a causal connection to that violation. It requires the suppression of evidence the government has acquired *as a result*

---

suggest some receptivity to the claim that exclusion can be supplanted by alternatives that do not impede conviction of the guilty.

145. In *Herring v. United States*, 555 U.S. ____, 129 S.Ct. 695 (2009), a slim Supreme Court majority indicated that the future could hold a somewhat dramatic restriction of the exclusionary rule's reach. The majority suggested that the rule might be deemed applicable only when officers' violations of the Fourth Amendment are "sufficiently culpable." *See id.* at 702. More specifically, the *Herring* Court indicated that suppression might not be appropriate in cases involving merely a single, isolated instance of official "negligence." *Id.* Applicability of the exclusionary rule could require proof that law enforcement had either deliberately or recklessly performed the unreasonable search or seizure. *Id.* Alternatively, proof of either gross negligence or of a recurrent pattern of negligence might be sufficient to trigger suppression. *Id.* For a discussion of *Herring*, *see infra* text accompanying notes 199–203.

of its illegal actions. According to the Supreme Court, to come within the scope of the exclusionary rule, evidence must be "in some sense *the product* of illegal governmental activity."[146] Because "but-for causality is . . . a necessary . . . condition for suppression,"[147] an individual seeking suppression must show that the unreasonable search or seizure enabled government agents to secure the contested evidence. An obvious situation in which the causation demand renders the exclusionary rule inapplicable is when officers conduct two searches, one constitutional and one unconstitutional. For example, if officers who have probable cause to search a home and a vehicle simultaneously conduct warrantless searches of each, the search of the home is unlawful, but the search of the vehicle is lawful. The unconstitutional search of the home cannot support the exclusion of any evidence found in the car because there is no causal connection between the illegality and the acquisition of the evidence.

There are other situations, however, in which the illegal conduct might appear to be connected to the discovery of the evidence, yet the causation requirement precludes suppression. The reason is that what might seem to be a single governmental act is sometimes characterized as two, separate constitutional events. In one such situation, officers conduct a search with adequate constitutional justification—that is, they have probable cause and a valid warrant—but they fail to honor some Fourth Amendment constraint upon the *manner* in which the search is carried out. The Supreme Court has been willing to treat the actual search and the improper execution method as constitutionally divisible for purposes of exclusion. If the officers in fact acquire evidence as a result of the justified search, and the illegal aspect of their conduct (i.e., the improper execution) does not contribute to the acquisition, the exclusionary rule does not apply because there is no "but-for" causal link between the unconstitutionality and the discovery of the evidence. In other words, evidence is admissible when the police would have conducted the very same lawful search "and would have discovered" the evidence whether or not they had employed the unreasonable method of carrying out that search.[148]

To illustrate, suppose officers search a home pursuant to a valid search warrant but, prior to their entry, failed to knock and announce their presence and purpose, as required by the Fourth Amendment. The "illegal *manner* of entry [is] *not* a but-for cause" of finding evidence inside the home, and the evidence is not subject to exclusion, if the officers would still have found it during the warranted home search had they given the occupants proper notice.[149] Similarly, suppose officers unnecessarily or unreasonably damage or destroy property while entering

---

146. United States v. Crews, 445 U.S. 463, 471 (1980) (emphasis added).

147. *Hudson*, 547 U.S. at 592.

148. *Id.*

149. *Id.*

a home to conduct a justified search.[150] They might, for example, use a battering ram on a door that they could open by less damaging means. This unreasonable method of carrying out the reasonable search of the home—an act that in fact constitutes an unreasonable "seizure" of the property damaged—is seen as separable from the search itself. If the unjustified damage to the home did not contribute to the discovery of the evidence during the search of the home, the exclusionary rule is inapplicable because there is no causal connection between the acquisition of the evidence and the Fourth Amendment violation.

Another situation in which the requirement of causation precludes suppression is when an apparently singular search is divisible into two separate Fourth Amendment invasions, one that is supported by adequate justification and another that is not. If the evidence is found solely as a result of the justified invasion, the exclusionary rule does not apply. Suppose, for example, that officers who are executing a valid warrant to search a home decide to bring with them a gratuitous third party such as a member of the press.[151] The lawful privacy invasion by the officers and the unreasonable privacy invasion effected by the presence of the third party are seen as distinct searches. If the unlawful search—the presence of the member of the media—does not contribute to the discovery of evidence in the home, the causation demand prevents application of the exclusionary rule.[152] The suppression remedy is unavailable because there is no "but-for" link between the violation of the Fourth Amendment and the acquisition of the evidence.

Similar reasoning governs the situation where officers fail to secure a warrant before entering a home to arrest a resident based on probable cause to believe he has committed a felony. The home entry is an unreasonable search because a warrant is necessary. The arrest of the suspect, however, is a reasonable seizure because warrantless arrests of suspected felons are constitutional if officers have probable cause. In this situation, any evidence acquired inside the home is the product of the illegal search and is subject to suppression.[153] If officers escort the arrestee outside the home, however, any evidence acquired thereafter is admissible.[154] The exclusionary rule does not reach that evidence because the unlawful search of the home and the lawful arrest of the suspect are distinct constitutional events, and evidence found after the search has ended lacks the necessary causal connection to the only illegality.[155] It is the product of the constitutionally valid seizure of the arrestee.

150. *See* United States v. Ramirez, 523 U.S. 65, 71 (1998).
151. *See* Wilson v. Layne, 526 U.S. 603, 607 (1999).
152. *Id.* at 614 n.2.
153. *See* New York v. Harris, 495 U.S. 14, 20 (1990).
154. *Id.* at 20–21.
155. *Id.* at 19.

b. The Types of Evidence Subject to Exclusion The exclusionary rule extends to tangible items.[156] Contraband narcotics, an illegal weapon, a piece of clothing connecting a defendant to a murder, a computer printout, a blood sample, and any other concrete proof is subject to suppression. Knowledge gained illegally is also subject to exclusion. Thus, the rule bars not only contraband narcotics, but also an officer's testimony that she saw drugs in the defendant's car. If a document is found by unconstitutional means, then it may not be introduced and a witness may not recount his memory of its contents. In addition, the suppression remedy reaches intangible verbal evidence, like an illegally arrested person's admission of guilt or an unconstitutionally discovered witness's report about what he knows, when that admission or report is causally connected to an unreasonable search and seizure.[157]

The exclusionary rule commands the suppression of both "primary" and "derivative" evidence. Primary evidence comprises both items seized and information gained during or as an immediate result of an illegal search or seizure.[158] Evidence is a primary product when there is no cognizable spatial or temporal distance between the illegality and its acquisition. Drugs found while searching a home without a warrant, a gun found inside the trunk of a car that was opened without probable cause, a bloody piece of clothing taken from an illegally arrested suspect, or an incriminating admission made during the illegal detention of a motorist all are primary evidence. Derivative evidence, on the other hand, is any item or information "that is the product of the primary evidence, or that is otherwise acquired as an indirect result of the unlawful search" or seizure.[159] It is evidence "derived" from some lead discovered during, or as an immediate result of, the official illegality. The lead can be primary evidence or knowledge that itself is not evidence. Thus, the consent of a person arrested illegally on the street may prompt and permit officers to search his home and discover drugs. An incriminating document gained during an unconstitutional search of an office may contain an address and other information that supports a warrant to search a warehouse where counterfeit money is found. An individual who is detained without reasonable suspicion may offer an exculpatory explanation for his presence that yields a witness who is willing to testify against him. The drugs, money, and witness's testimony are derivative products of the initial illegal searches or seizures. Even if the later conduct that produced the evidence is constitutionally valid, the evidence falls within the presumptive scope of the Fourth Amendment exclusionary rule because its acquisition is causally linked to the earlier illegality.

---

156. *See* Murray v. United States, 487 U.S. 533, 536 (1988).

157. *See* United States v. Ceccolini, 435 U.S. 268, 274–75 (1978); Wong Sun v. United States, 371 U.S. 471, 485–86 (1963).

158. *See Murray*, 487 U.S. at 536–37, 541.

159. *Id.* at 536–37.

2. Proceedings in Which the Exclusionary Rule Operates

The primary domain for operation of the exclusionary rule is the criminal trial. Evidence of guilt falling within the scope of the suppression doctrine is inadmissible in proceedings to determine guilt or innocence for a criminal offense. The rule governs trials in which the jury is the fact finder and trials in which a judge serves that role. Typically, a defendant with a Fourth Amendment claim files a pretrial motion seeking a suppression ruling before trial. A judge may decide such a motion on the papers filed or may hold an evidentiary hearing in which the accused and the prosecution present testimony and evidence relevant to the merits of the Fourth Amendment claim and to the applicability of the exclusionary rule.

The only other type of proceeding in which the Supreme Court has held the Fourth Amendment exclusionary rule operative was an action in which the government sought the forfeiture of a vehicle based on the allegation that it had been used to illegally transport liquor.[160] The government was barred from using the evidence it had acquired from an unlawful search of the vehicle to prove the illegal use that was the predicate for forfeiture. This modest extension of the exclusionary rule was rooted in the conclusion that the forfeiture proceeding, although not a criminal prosecution, was "quasi-criminal in character."[161] This characterization was justified because the proceeding "requir[ed] the determination that the criminal law ha[d] been violated" and a resulting "forfeiture [was] clearly a penalty for the criminal offense."[162]

On the other hand, the Supreme Court has refused to extend the bar to probative evidence to one pretrial phase of the criminal process—grand jury hearings—and to one post-trial proceeding that is technically not part of the criminal process, but is intimately related to the criminal process—probation revocation proceedings. Grand juries hear evidence presented by a prosecutor in order to decide whether criminal charges are warranted. If the grand jurors decide that there is sufficient evidence to justify charges, they return indictments—formal accusations of criminal offenses. In proceedings before grand juries, the government *may* ask witnesses questions based on evidence acquired by means of an illegal search because the exclusionary rule *does not apply* at this stage of a criminal prosecution.[163] In addition, the suppression remedy is not available in an administrative proceeding seeking revocation of a convicted defendant's

---

160. *See* One 1958 Plymouth Sedan v. Pennsylvania, 380 U.S. 693 (1965).

161. *Id.* at 700.

162. *Id.* at 701. Considering the age of the decision in *One 1958 Plymouth,* the subsequent erosion of the exclusionary rule, and the prevalent attitude toward excluding evidence obtained in violation of the Fourth Amendment, there is reason to wonder whether the Court would adhere to this ruling today and ample reason to believe that the Court would not extend the rule to other types of forfeiture proceedings.

163. *See* United States v. Calandra, 414 U.S. 338, 354 (1974).

release on parole based on a claim that the parolee has violated a condition of release.[164] In parole revocation proceedings, the state is free to establish an alleged parole violation with relevant evidence even though it acquired the evidence by means of an unreasonable search or seizure. The Court concluded that the risk of exclusion from a criminal trial provided sufficient deterrence and that any additional or incremental deterrence that might result from suppression in a grand jury hearing or in a parole revocation proceeding was outweighed by the costs of exclusion.

After the trial and appellate phases of a prosecution have run their course, a defendant may seek to challenge a conviction and obtain release from confinement by seeking a writ of habeas corpus.[165] In a federal habeas corpus action raising a "collateral" challenge to the validity of a state conviction,[166] a convicted defendant is barred from claiming that the judge erred in refusing to exclude evidence from his trial unless he did not have a "full and fair" opportunity to pursue his Fourth Amendment exclusionary rule claim at the trial.[167] A majority of the Supreme Court found it unjustifiable and unnecessary to allow a defendant to raise a Fourth Amendment suppression claim in a federal habeas corpus action when a state court has adequately considered the merits of the claim. According to the Court, the deterrent benefits of the prospect of exclusion could not outweigh the social costs of sustaining a valid claim for suppression at that late stage of the adjudicatory process.

The Supreme Court has also rejected extension of the exclusionary rule to two entirely civil contexts. One involved a federal civil tax action in which the evidence at issue had been seized unlawfully, but in good faith, by a state police officer.[168] The lower courts decided that the exclusionary rule barred the

---

164. *See* Pennsylvania Bd. of Prob. & Parole v. Scott, 524 U.S. 357 (1998). The Court majority observed that it had not been inclined to extend the *Weeks-Mapp* rule to any process other than criminal trials. *Id.* at 363. Although a parole revocation process is a part of the administration of criminal justice, it is not part of the process of "criminal prosecution." *See id.* at 365–66; Morrissey v. Brewer, 408 U.S. 471, 489 (1972).

165. Although a habeas corpus proceeding is nominally civil, *see* Pennsylvania v. Finley, 481 U.S. 551, 556–57 (1987); Fay v. Noia, 372 U.S. 391, 423–24 (1963), there can be no doubt that it is intimately connected to the criminal process.

166. The challenge is "collateral" because it is not raised in a direct appeal from the conviction, and, in fact, is typically brought after an accused has failed to obtain relief by means of direct review. *See Finley*, 481 U.S. at 557.

167. *See* Stone v. Powell, 428 U.S. 465, 481–82 (1976). The question in the other types of proceedings discussed in this part is whether evidence is barred *from* those proceedings. The question in *Stone* was *not* whether evidence must be excluded *from a habeas corpus action*, but, rather, whether a convicted defendant may claim in a habeas proceeding that evidence should have been excluded *from the trial* that resulted in conviction.

168. *See* United States v. Janis, 428 U.S. 433 (1976). The officer had conducted his search in good faith reliance on an invalid warrant. *Id.* at 438–39, 447.

Internal Revenue Service from using the unconstitutionally obtained evidence as a basis for a civil tax assessment. Consequently, the courts had quashed the tax assessment, granted the taxpayer's claim for a refund, and dismissed the government's counterclaim for the unpaid part of the assessment.[169] The Supreme Court reversed, holding that the suppression doctrine did not bar the use of the illegally-acquired evidence in this type of proceeding.[170] The other was a civil deportation proceeding in which the issue was whether an individual was eligible to remain in the United States.[171] The Court of Appeals had held that the exclusionary rule barred the government from using admissions obtained from the individual after he had been unlawfully detained to prove that he was ineligible to remain in the country. The Supreme Court disagreed, concluding that the exclusionary rule was not applicable in a deportation action because the costs of applying it exceeded any deterrent benefits.[172]

The Court's holdings in these two civil settings were somewhat qualified. Moreover, while the Court did declare that it "never ha[d] applied [the exclusionary rule] to exclude evidence from a civil proceeding,"[173] neither opinion asserted that the suppression doctrine could never apply in any genuinely civil action. Increased antipathy in recent cases toward any extension of the Fourth Amendment exclusionary rule, however, makes it extremely unlikely that the current Supreme Court would hold that evidence must be excluded from any truly civil proceeding.

In sum, with one narrow and dated exception, the Supreme Court has kept the exclusionary rule confined to the arena for which it was originally designed, determinations of guilt or innocence. It has consistently rejected contentions that the suppression doctrine should apply during other phases of the criminal process or in civil proceedings of any sort.

---

169. *Id.* at 439.

170. The Court's refusal to extend the exclusionary rule to federal civil tax proceedings was limited to cases in which federal agents are not involved in the illegal search. *Id.* at 436 n.3, 455 n.31.

171. *See* Immigration & Naturalization Serv. v. Lopez-Mendoza, 468 U.S. 1032 (1984).

172. Four of the five Justices who supported the holding indicated that they might reach a different conclusion *if* it were shown that INS agent violations of Fourth Amendment rights "were widespread." *Id.* at 1050. Moreover, they observed that the case before them did not involve an "egregious" constitutional violation of a sort that "might transgress notions of fundamental fairness and undermine the probative value of the evidence obtained." *Id.* at 1050–51.

173. United States v. Janis, 428 U.S. at 447.

3. The "Standing" Doctrine: A Restriction of the Individuals Entitled to Evidentiary Suppression

Ordinarily, only individuals who have suffered violations of their own rights have "standing" to claim legal relief based on those violations.[174] I have no standing, for example, to sue for damages when the government infringes on my neighbor's First Amendment right to free speech. Nor am I legally entitled to relief when my brother's home is searched without probable cause or a warrant. When the suppression of evidence was understood as an integral part of the Fourth Amendment guarantee, it surely made sense to accord standing to claim exclusion only to those who had been the victims of the unreasonable search or seizure that produced the challenged evidence. An accused individual had a constitutional entitlement not to be prosecuted on the basis of evidence found by violating his or her right to be secure against unreasonable searches or seizures.

When the Court shifted the underlying rationale for the exclusionary rule, denying the existence of a personal right to exclusion and focusing more narrowly upon the objective of deterring future illegalities, it was arguable that "standing" to raise Fourth Amendment suppression claims should be broadened to include anyone subject to prosecution on the basis of illegally-obtained evidence. If the victim of the unreasonable search was not entitled to object because suppression was her personal right, but instead was allowed to seek exclusion in order to remove incentives for any future violations, then it was arguable that someone who was not a victim of the search should be allowed to object to the illegally-obtained evidence for the very same reason. Put otherwise, if officers could use the evidence against those who were not injured by the search or seizure, it might furnish them with incentives for future violations of the Fourth Amendment. Suppression was arguably necessary to remove those incentives.

The Supreme Court, however, has rejected the contention that its modification of the exclusionary rule's justification—i.e., the elimination of the "right to exclusion" basis and the emphasis on deterrent objectives—undermined the standing limitation.[175] According to the Court, the purposes of exclusion do not dictate application of the rule whenever any additional deterrence might be achieved. The standing limitation is reconcilable with the deterrent objectives of suppression because the exclusion of the evidence at the request of individuals whose rights were violated adequately discourages future violations. Exclusion in the case of other individuals not harmed by the search or seizure itself might

---

174. There are exceptions to this norm. In situations involving some sort of impediment to victims' abilities to vindicate their own rights, third parties are sometimes allowed to seek relief for the violations of others' rights. *See* Powers v. Ohio, 499 U.S. 400, 410–11 (1991); Singleton v. Wulff, 428 U.S. 106, 115–16 (1976).

175. Alderman v. United States, 394 U.S. 165, 174–75 (1969).

promote additional deterrence—that is, the knowledge that any evidence found could not be used against those who are not victims of a search or seizure might provide further incentives to avoid illegalities. Nonetheless, any additional gain in Fourth Amendment enforcement is outweighed by the costs of suppressing the truth in the trials of those who suffered no Fourth Amendment injury.[176]

Consequently, today, as in the time before deterrent reasoning came to rule the roost, only those whose Fourth Amendment rights have been violated by an unreasonable search or seizure are legally entitled to have evidence causally linked to that violation excluded from their trials. Those who are aggrieved only because the evidence is being used to convict them, those associated with the victim of the search or seizure, and even those who were the "target" of the search or seizure—i.e., those the officers were investigating or pursuing at the time—all lack "standing."[177] "Fourth Amendment rights are *personal* rights which . . . may not be vicariously asserted."[178] The exclusionary rule extends only to those who can show that officers obtained the challenged evidence by means of an unreasonable search or seizure that violated *their* Fourth Amendment rights.

In the mid-1970s, the Court sought to eliminate "standing" terminology from the exclusionary rule discourse.[179] The Court suggested that the "standing" label was not helpful to the accurate resolution of exclusionary rule claims, but was only potentially misleading.[180] It was preferable to focus on the substantive inquiry reflected in the "standing" limitation by asking whether the individual raising an exclusionary rule claim had his or her own Fourth Amendment rights violated by the search or seizure that produced the contested evidence.[181] An individual suffers such a violation only if the search or seizure at issue: (1) infringed upon his or her own protected interests and (2) was, in fact, unreasonable. Any separate inquiry into standing should be replaced by a more direct effort to determine whether the law enforcement conduct being challenged invaded constitutionally safeguarded interests of the individual seeking exclusion.

No matter how unreasonable a search, an individual cannot suppress evidence if that search violated only another person's rights. Even if officers exploit the "standing" limitation by *deliberately* conducting an unconstitutional search in order to gain evidence against someone other than the individual injured by that

---

176. *Id.*

177. *See* Rakas v. Illinois, 439 U.S. 128, 132–36 (1978); *Alderman*, 394 U.S. at 173–75; Jones v. United States, 362 U.S. 257, 261 (1960).

178. *Alderman*, 394 U.S. at 174 (emphasis added).

179. *Rakas*, 439 U.S. at 139–40. The effort to purge the term was not entirely successful. *See* Minnesota v. Carter, 525 U.S. 83, 87–88 (1998); United States v. Payner, 447 U.S. 727, 731 (1980).

180. *Rakas*, 439 U.S. at 138–40.

181. *Id.* at 139–40.

search and do find the evidence they were seeking, that evidence is admissible to prove the guilt of the person the officers were after.[182] Thus, when Internal Revenue Service agents planned a blatantly unreasonable search of a banker's briefcase to find records incriminating bank customers, they could use those records in the customers' trials because the briefcase search did not infringe on or implicate the customers' Fourth Amendment rights.[183]

The Fourth Amendment protection against governmental *searches* is designed to protect "'reasonable expectation[s] of privacy.'"[184] As a result, a person is entitled to exclusion based upon an illegal search only when it violated his or her reasonable expectation of privacy. An individual may not suppress items found in a search of a friend's purse, for example, unless he demonstrates a sufficient connection to the purse to give him a protected privacy interest therein.[185] Standing to exclude incriminating statements made by a partner in crime and intercepted by unconstitutional electronic eavesdropping or wiretapping depends on whether the individual objecting was a party to the conversation or had a reasonable privacy expectation in the place being eavesdropped upon or wiretapped.[186]

The Fourth Amendment right not to have one's *person* unreasonably *seized* protects a personal liberty interest, while the right not to have one's *property* unreasonably *seized* shelters a proprietary or possessory interest. Therefore, a person has an entitlement to bar evidence obtained from an unreasonable seizure of a person only if that seizure infringed upon his or her own freedom. If my spouse is unlawfully arrested or if my co-conspirator is detained for investigation without justification, I lack standing to suppress evidence found as a result—drugs in the spouse's coat or an admission the co-conspirator made. Similarly, an individual may not bar evidence secured by taking possession of property unless that person had a proprietary or possessory interest in the seized object. Consequently, if the police tow a car from the street in front of my home without justification and gather evidence by close examination of its exterior, I lack standing to suppress that evidence based upon an unreasonable seizure of the car unless I have an ownership or possessory interest in the vehicle.

---

182. *Payner*, 447 U.S. at 733–34. Not only does the standing demand—i.e., the requirement that the objecting party suffer a Fourth Amendment injury from the search or seizure—prevent application of the Fourth Amendment exclusionary rule no matter how deliberately or egregiously unconstitutional the search or search, that same requirement prevents a judge from relying upon his supervisory power over the administration of criminal justice or the due process guarantee to suppress that same evidence. *Id.* at 735–37.

183. *Id.* at 731–32.

184. *See* California v. Ciraolo, 476 U.S. 207, 211 (1986) (quoting Katz v. United States, 389 U.S. 347, 360 (1967) (Harlan, J., concurring)).

185. *See* Rawlings v. Kentucky, 448 U.S. 98, 104–06 (1980).

186. *See* Alderman v. United States, 394 U.S. 165, 176 (1969).

In large part, the Supreme Court's effort to reform "standing" doctrine by eliminating that word from exclusionary rule discourse, and focusing closely and precisely on whether the individual raising a suppression claim had interests intruded upon by the search or seizure, was designed to narrow the scope of the exclusionary rule. Prior decisions under the "standing" rubric had been somewhat reflexive and categorical. In the Court's view, these decisions were sometimes overbroad insofar as they allowed some who had suffered no constitutional injury to suppress probative evidence from their trials.[187] For example, a person might have been allowed to challenge a search merely because he was lawfully present in a place searched at the time of the search,[188] or simply because his property was seized during the search.[189] A person who is merely present in a place or who simply has a possessory interest in an item located in that place, however, does not necessarily have a legitimate expectation of privacy there. In the absence of such a privacy interest, a search does not infringe on his rights. To grant him standing to suppress evidence without a constitutionally cognizable privacy interest is to extend the exclusionary rule beyond its proper bounds.

A person seeking exclusion bears the burden of showing that an allegedly unconstitutional search or seizure infringed upon his or her constitutionally protected interests. The Supreme Court has paid particular attention to standing questions involving searches of vehicles and homes, declaring that the entitlement to object to a search of a car or a home depends on whether the individual can establish that the search violated his or her legitimate expectation of privacy.[190] In the case of a vehicle, an owner or lawful possessor would ordinarily qualify. A passenger may qualify, but not on the basis of passenger status alone. A "passenger *qua* passenger," or a mere passenger, may not object to the search of a car in which he or she is riding.[191] A greater connection to the vehicle is needed to give rise to a reasonable expectation of privacy in the car. Relevant facts that could help a passenger meet the standard include, for example: repeated or frequent presence as a passenger, presence during a long-distance journey with the owner-driver, past instances of borrowing the car, or the presence of belongings stored in the car. The inquiry is always whether the totality of facts

187. *See* Rakas v. Illinois, 439 U.S. 128, 141–42 (1978).

188. *See* Jones v. United States, 362 U.S. 257, 265 (1960).

189. *See* United States v. Jeffers, 342 U.S. 48, 51–54 (1951) (declaring that a seizure of property could not be "untied" from a preceding search and holding that a defendant was entitled to exclusion based on an unreasonable search because "his property" had been seized as a result).

190. *See* Minnesota v. Carter, 525 U.S. 83, 88–91 (1998) (for homes); *Rakas*, 439 U.S. at 148–49 (for cars). A demonstration of this same interest, a reasonable or legitimate "expectation of privacy in the place searched," is a constitutionally necessary predicate to be entitled to object to the *search* of any particular *place*. *Carter*, 525 U.S. at 88; *Rakas*, 439 U.S. at 143.

191. *Rakas*, 439 U.S. at 148–49.

establishes a legitimate expectation of privacy in the vehicle. Moreover, an individual who has demonstrated a protected privacy interest in a passenger compartment may not have such an interest in a trunk or glove compartment of the vehicle and therefore may not be able to object to separate searches of those spaces. Each search must be analyzed individually to determine whether it infringed on a protected privacy interest of the specific claimant.

The Court's decisions suggest that a person can more readily gain a protected privacy interest in a home. As with vehicles, a person seeking evidentiary exclusion due to an illegal search of a home must show a legitimate or reasonable expectation of privacy in the home. An owner will typically have a sufficient privacy interest,[192] and a current resident will always have such an interest even if he or she is not present at the time of the search, pays no rent, and has no recognized *property* interest in the premises. An overnight guest has an adequate relationship to her host's home to generate a legitimate expectation of privacy in that home.[193] Moreover, it is not necessary to stay in a home overnight, for "*almost all social guests*" have Fourth Amendment privacy interests in homes, even those who are visiting for a relatively short time.[194] If an owner or resident invites a person to share the privacy of a dwelling—any dwelling, be it a mansion, an apartment, or a trailer—that person typically acquires a legitimate expectation of privacy in the dwelling and will have standing to suppress evidence acquired as a result of an illegal entry.

Mere presence in a home is not sufficient, however. Those unlawfully present cannot claim exclusion. And, like mere passengers in vehicles, some home guests who are legitimately present lack standing. Those who have "no meaningful tie[s]," but have only "fleeting and insubstantial" connections to the premises, do not possess cognizable Fourth Amendment privacy interests and may not contest illegal entries.[195] Factors relevant to determining whether a social guest

---

192. An owner who leases a home or other dwelling to others and retains no other connection to the place would not possess a legitimate expectation of privacy in the place. *See Rakas*, 439 U.S. at 143 n.12.

193. *See* Minnesota v. Olson, 495 U.S. 91, 98–100 (1990).

194. *See* Minnesota v. Carter, 525 U.S. 83, 99 (1998) (Kennedy, J., concurring) (emphasis added); *id.* at 103 (Breyer, J., concurring); *id.* at 106 (Ginsburg, J., dissenting). Because Justice Kennedy would accord standing to object to a home search to "almost all social guests" and four other Justices (Justice Breyer and the three Justices joining Justice Ginsburg's opinion) would grant standing to all social guests, it is fair to conclude that "almost all social guests" in homes are entitled to exclude evidence discovered as a result of illegal entries of those homes.

195. *See id.* at 102 (Kennedy, J., concurring). Justice Kennedy would deny standing to anyone with merely a "fleeting and insubstantial" connection. It seems clear that the four other Justices who joined the majority opinion would deny standing to anyone with so thin a connection and might even deny standing to some with stronger connections to homes. *Id.* at 90–91.

falls into the limited category of those with insufficient connections to dwellings include: the length of time the guest was present, whether the guest has been in the home before, and the reason for or purpose of the visit.[196] Thus, a mere two-hour visit would undermine, whereas a day-long visit would support, a privacy claim. The connection of a first-time visitor is more likely to be deemed insubstantial than the connection of one who has been in the home on prior occasions. Presence for a shared meal, mutual entertainment, or conversation would bolster one's assertion that he or she had an adequate nexus to a dwelling, while a visit to a home to engage in a commercial type of activity would not.

Finally, even those who have privacy interests in a dwelling generally, interests that give them standing to claim exclusion based upon unconstitutional entries, may not be entitled to object to unreasonable searches of discrete spaces within that dwelling. Suppose two individuals reside in a shared apartment. The police lawfully enter, but officers then unreasonably extend the search to one resident's bedroom or closet. The other resident who never enters that bedroom or uses that closet cannot suppress incriminating items found in the unlawfully searched bedroom or closet because she lacks a legitimate privacy expectation in the unconstitutionally searched space. Similarly, an occasional dinner guest who always stays on the ground floor of a home cannot object if officers illegally exceed the bounds of a lawful entry and search areas of the home the guest never visited. He has a legitimate privacy expectation only in the spaces within the home that an owner or resident has invited him to share.

The modern "standing" doctrine is a significant limitation on the reach of the Fourth Amendment exclusionary rule. Only a limited number of persons—perhaps merely a single individual—will be able to object to any particular unreasonable search or seizure.[197] All others—the universe of those whose constitutional rights were not infringed upon by officers—lack an essential predicate for suppressing evidence gained by unconstitutional means. These individuals cannot complain of the Fourth Amendment transgression, and, therefore, the exclusionary rule does not prevent the prosecution from using any relevant evidence to prove guilt—no matter how unconstitutional the search or seizure that led to its discovery.

---

196. *See id.*; *id.* at 102 (Kennedy, J., concurring).

197. With regard to the unreasonable *seizure* of a person, the universe of persons capable of objecting is even more limited. While a third person can gain a privacy interest in another person's home, car, or luggage, it seems inconceivable that one might have a protected liberty interest in another's person. Consequently, if the acquisition of evidence is causally linked to an unlawful arrest or detention of a particular individual, it seems virtually certain that only that individual will have "standing" to object to the unconstitutionality. Anyone else incriminated by his admissions, items found on his person, or evidence gained by following leads provided by the arrest will not be able to exclude that proof.

4. A Possible "Culpability" Limitation on the Scope of the Exclusionary Rule

An officer may violate the Fourth Amendment deliberately or accidentally. She may be reckless in carrying out an unreasonable search or seizure—aware that there is a risk of unconstitutionality. Or she may be negligent—unreasonable in believing that her conduct is proper. The officer's "culpability" or "fault" is a factor relevant to the application of at least two exceptions to exclusion.[198] Until recently, however, there was no reason to think that there might be a culpability limitation on the reach of the *Weeks-Mapp* doctrine. Barring the application of one of the defined exceptions to the exclusionary rule, evidence has been subject to suppression even if officers had no fault in crossing some Fourth Amendment line.

In *Herring v. United States*,[199] however, a majority of the Court intimated that the future might hold a general culpability restriction, declaring that "[t]o trigger the exclusionary rule, police conduct must be sufficiently deliberate that exclusion can meaningfully deter it, and sufficiently culpable that such deterrence is worth the price paid by the justice system."[200] More specifically, the Court suggested that the suppression remedy could well be confined to cases in which official transgressions of the Fourth Amendment's commands are "deliberate, reckless, or grossly negligent," or, perhaps, where the circumstances demonstrate ordinary negligence that is "recurring or systemic."[201] In fact, the issue and holding in *Herring* were quite narrow.[202] The discussion of culpability, while germane, was largely unnecessary. Although some will surely read the opinion as endorsing a prerequisite of fault for application of the suppression doctrine, that conclusion seems premature.[203] *Herring*'s reflections on the significance of culpability were, at best, nonbinding dicta, not controlling law. Whether they mature into a significant constraint upon Fourth Amendment exclusion remains to be seen.

---

198. As will be seen in the discussions later in this part, the traditional "attenuation" exception factors in the officer's culpability, and the "good faith" exception's reasonableness demand seems to rest on the notion that the exclusionary rule should not seek to deter violations of the Fourth Amendment that are not at least negligent.

199. Herring v. United States, 555 U.S. ____, 129 S.Ct. 695 (2009).

200. *Id.* at ____, 129 S.Ct. at 702.

201. *Id.*

202. The issue and holding are described in detail in the subsection on the "good faith" exceptions, later in this part.

203. In the wake of *Herring*, some have expressed fear that the Court might be intending not merely to restrict the exclusionary rule with a culpability requirement, but to do away with the rule entirely. *See* David G. Savage, *Who's Policing the Fourth Amendment?*, 95 A.B.A. J. 19 (2009); Craig Bradley, *Red Herring or the Death of the Exclusionary Rule?*, TRIAL MAGAZINE (April 2009) 52; Adam Cohen, *Is the Supreme Court About to Kill Off the Exclusionary Rule?*, Feb. 16, 2009, N.Y. TIMES, at A22.

5. Exceptions to the Fourth Amendment Exclusionary Rule

Over time, a number of "exceptions" to the Fourth Amendment exclusionary rule have evolved. These exceptions, which permit the government to introduce illegally-obtained evidence at the trial of a person whose rights were violated by the search or seizure that produced the evidence, include: the independent source doctrine; the inevitable discovery exception; the attenuation exception; the "good faith" exceptions; and the impeachment use exception. This subsection sketches the contours of and underlying reasoning for each exception.

a. The "Independent Source" Doctrine When officers discover evidence by means of an unreasonable search or seizure, but then acquire evidence not because of their illegal conduct but by distinct, legal means—a constitutionally valid search or seizure or any other conduct that does not transgress the Fourth Amendment—the exclusionary rule does not apply to the lawfully discovered evidence.[204] Prior or simultaneous unconstitutional conduct does not require the suppression of evidence obtained from such a lawful "independent source." Although it is traditional to refer to the independent source doctrine as an "exception" to the exclusionary rule, the label is actually inaccurate. The exclusionary rule, by definition, reaches only primary and derivative evidence with a "but-for" causal connection to a Fourth Amendment violation. Consequently, evidence that lacks that predicate—and, in fact, is gained by lawful conduct—does not fall within the presumptive scope of the suppression doctrine. Because the rule does not mandate exclusion, there is no need for an "exception."

The independent source doctrine, first recognized more than 90 years ago, clearly applies when the legally acquired evidence is entirely distinct from any evidence found as a result of the unconstitutional search or seizure. Consequently, if officers search a suspect's home without a valid warrant and find stolen money, then search the suspect's office with a valid warrant and find the gun used in the robbery, the gun is admissible. The doctrine also extends to situations where officers learn certain facts by illegal methods, and then subsequently learn the *very same facts* by other, legal avenues.[205] In the words of the Court, "the facts . . . obtained [illegally do not] become sacred and inaccessible. If knowledge of them is gained from an independent source they may be proved like any others."[206] The exclusionary rule does not command the suppression of evidence in these circumstances despite the fact that it "*is identical to the evidence unlawfully acquired.*"[207] Thus, if officers unconstitutionally search a home and find an incriminating letter, then find an exact copy of the very same letter during a lawful search of the individual's office, or if they learn the very same

---

204. *See* Nix v. Williams 467 U.S. 431, 443 (1984); Silverthorne Lumber Co., v. United States, 251 U.S. 385, 392 (1920).

205. Murray v. United States, 487 U.S. 533, 538 (1988).

206. *Silverthorne Lumber Co.*, 251 U.S. at 392.

207. *Murray*, 487 U.S. at 538 (emphasis in original).

information contained in the illegally-acquired letter by any other lawful method, they may testify to the facts they learned even though they are the identical facts that the officers learned unlawfully. Finally, the doctrine reaches tangible items that are once discovered illegally, but later found lawfully.[208] Suppose officers unreasonably search a home without a warrant and find a stash of contraband narcotics. Later, they conduct a lawful search of the same home with a warrant and find and seize the same narcotics. Both the knowledge that the narcotics were in the home *and* the narcotics themselves are admissible evidence *if* the second search was "a *genuinely independent* source of the information and tangible evidence at issue."[209] That search would not be independent if it had an actual causal connection to the initial, illegal search. Thus, if the officers' "decision to seek the warrant was prompted by what" they saw while present in the home illegally, it would not be independent.[210] Alternatively, "if information obtained during [the illegal] entry was presented to the Magistrate and affected his decision to issue the warrant," the second search would not be independent of the Fourth Amendment violation.[211] In both of these situations, the evidence found during the second home entry pursuant to the warrant would be causally connected to—and derivative of—the illegal first entry. For that reason, the evidence would be presumptively subject to suppression. The independent source doctrine applies *only* if a lawful search or seizure is truly independent of the unlawful search or seizure. If the lawful conduct was in some way a product or outgrowth of the unlawful conduct, the independent source doctrine is inapplicable.

The independent source doctrine rests on the premise that a proper balancing of the costs and benefits of the exclusionary rule dictates that the government not reap benefits from an illegality. By depriving the prosecution of unconstitutionally acquired evidentiary profit, the exclusionary rule removes incentives for future violations and thereby deters those illegalities. The suppression of evidence or knowledge discovered by independent lawful means would effect more than the deprivation of profit. The prosecution would be penalized by the loss of evidence that was not a net benefit of unconstitutional conduct. It would be put in a "worse position" than it would have occupied without the unreasonable search or seizure.[212] Such a penalty surely could have a deterrent impact. Officers might be even more hesitant to engage in unlawful activity if they knew that the prosecution would be unable to introduce lawfully acquired evidence. The societal costs of such a sanction, however, are thought to outweigh any additional gains in terms of motivating Fourth Amendment compliance. In sum, the

208. *See id.* at 541–42.
209. *Id.* at 542 (emphasis added).
210. *Id.*
211. *Id.*
212. Nix v. Williams, 467 U.S. 431, 443 (1984).

independent source doctrine rests on the very same reasoning that supports restriction of the exclusionary rule to evidence with a but-for causal link to an unreasonable search or seizure.

b. The "Inevitable Discovery" Exception The inevitable discovery doctrine is analytically related to, but distinct from, the independent source doctrine and is a much later development in exclusionary rule doctrine.[213] Inevitable discovery is a true exception to the Fourth Amendment exclusionary rule. It allows the state to use evidence that it did, in fact, gain illegally at the trial of an individual whose rights were violated by that illegality. To invoke the exception, the government must simply show, by a "preponderance of the evidence," that even though it did acquire the evidence at issue by means of an unreasonable search or seizure, it "ultimately or inevitably *would have* . . . discovered [that evidence] by lawful means."[214] Suppose that an officer were to illegally seize a driver as he parked in his driveway and stepped from his car. In a search of his pockets, the officer found incriminating evidence. Another officer, however, operating independently and armed with a valid warrant, was just about to arrest the man and would have done so if he had not already been unlawfully seized. The evidence found in the pocket is admissible if it is more likely than not that the second officer would inevitably have found it during a search following a lawful arrest pursuant to the arrest warrant.

There is no need to prove that the officer who violated the Fourth Amendment and discovered the evidence unlawfully did so in good faith.[215] Even if that officer acted in bad faith, knowingly or deliberately violating the Fourth Amendment in order to discover or expedite the discovery of the evidence, the exception still applies if the state can show it *would have* discovered the contested evidence by independent lawful means. In the preceding example, suppose that the first officer had deliberately seized the suspect, acting on a mere hunch and hope that he would find contraband and knowing that he did not have the objective

---

213. While the Court endorsed the independent source doctrine in 1920 in the *Silverthorne Lumber Co.* opinion, it did not sanction inevitable discovery until the 1984 opinion in *Nix*.

214. *Nix*, 467 U.S. at 444 (emphasis added). This case involved a deprivation of the Sixth Amendment entitlement to the assistance of counsel. The Supreme Court has never applied inevitable discovery in a case involving a Fourth Amendment violation. Nonetheless, the logic of the doctrine explained in *Nix*—the Court's reconciliation of the doctrine with the goal of deterrence and with the cost-benefit balancing that informs analyses of whether deterrent objectives justify suppression—makes it clear that inevitable discovery is a viable exception for evidence acquired by means of some, if not all, Fourth Amendment violations. The "preponderance" standard approved by the Court means that the state does not have to prove that it is *certain* that it would have inevitably gained the evidence by lawful means. Rather, it is sufficient to show that it is *more likely than not* that the same evidence would have been lawfully secured.

215. *Id.* at 445–46.

justification constitutionally necessary to seize a person. The fact that the second officer would have lawfully found that same contraband if the unlawful seizure and search had not transpired immunizes the contraband from suppression.

Moreover, the proximity of the illegality and the discovery of the evidence does not seem to matter. The sole case in which the Supreme Court has explained and employed the inevitable discovery exception, *Nix v. Williams*, involved "derivative" evidence that would ultimately have been found by lawful methods. The evidence at issue—information gained from analysis of the body of a murder victim—was causally linked to the official impropriety, but was not the direct, primary product of that impropriety. Instead, it was acquired indirectly, by exploiting the statements the police obtained immediately from the suspect. The logic that underlies the inevitable discovery exception, however, justifies—in fact, it dictates—application of the doctrine to primary evidence as well. Whether evidence that would have been found lawfully is derivative or primary, suppression does more than remove profit because it places the government in a worse evidentiary position. Thus, even though the narcotics found in the pocket of the illegally seized suspect are the direct and immediate fruits of the Fourth Amendment violation, they are nevertheless admissible if they would inevitably have been found by means of a lawful arrest and search.

Inevitable discovery does not necessarily apply whenever the same *item* that was illegally acquired would have been lawfully found. It is necessary to show that the same *evidence* would have been obtained lawfully. Suppose that officers instruct doctors to unconstitutionally draw a blood sample from a man properly held in custody. They discover that he has an extremely high blood alcohol level. At the time, other investigators were following leads that would inevitably have led to facts that provided the information necessary to lawfully draw a sample of that suspect's blood. To invoke the inevitable discovery exception, the state must show not only that those investigators would have conducted a lawful search for and obtained a sample of the suspect's blood. They must also prove that they would have done so *before* the alcohol level had dissipated. The fact that blood would have inevitably been acquired does not mean that the evidence—the knowledge that the suspect was intoxicated—would have been inevitably discovered. If that knowledge would not have been inevitably discovered by lawful means, it is a profit of the illegality, and suppressing it would remove an incentive for future illegal blood taking.

Some courts have required proof that the investigation that would have inevitably led to lawful acquisition of the evidence was in process or underway at the time of the illegal conduct.[216] Although the case in which the Supreme Court endorsed the inevitable discovery exception did involve an in-progress lawful

---

216. *See* United States v. Cherry, 759 F.2d 1196, 1204–06 (5th Cir. 1985); United States v. Satterfield, 743 F.2d 827, 846–47 (11th Cir. 1984).

search, the opinion did not prescribe such a requirement and the reasoning underlying the exception does not support that demand. When no alternative means of discovery was underway, it may be more difficult for a prosecutor to demonstrate that discovery was inevitable. Nonetheless, if a judge is persuaded that the state would have initiated a constitutionally valid investigative process, evidence that the process would have produced should be admissible under the inevitable discovery exception.

There is at least one instance in which it is arguable that the inevitable discovery exception should not apply even though its ordinary requirements are satisfied. According to governing interpretations of the Fourth Amendment, even if officers have probable cause to conduct a search they must *first* apply for and secure a valid search warrant from a judge. A search without a warrant is presumptively unreasonable.[217] The primary rationale for the warrant demand is to prevent overzealous, biased officers from conducting unjustified searches by demanding a predetermination of probable cause by a neutral, impartial judge. Although an after-the-fact review of a search might be able to correct an officer's erroneous probable cause assessment, that correction would come too late to repair the injury to privacy effected by the search. By ensuring judicial screening and correction before the search takes place, the warrant requirement furthers the Fourth Amendment objective of preserving privacy unless the government has reason to intrude.

On its face, the inevitable discovery exception applies to evidence found during a warrantless search if the prosecution demonstrates that officers would have found the evidence lawfully, either because they had already initiated the warrant application process and would have secured a valid warrant, or because they would have initiated the application process if they had not conducted the warrantless search. Application of the exception to situations like these, however, could defeat the important preventive purposes of the Fourth Amendment warrant requirement by providing officers with incentives to avoid spending their time securing warrants when they have (or believe they have) facts that would justify issuance of a warrant. Therefore, it is arguable that the inevitable discovery exception should not apply when it rests on the contention that a warrant that *should* have been obtained *would* have been obtained had officers not conducted an unconstitutional warrantless search. Fidelity to the warrant rule could well preclude invocation of the inevitable discovery exception in these

217. California v. Acevedo, 500 U.S. 565, 580 (1991); Katz v. United States, 389 U.S. 347, 357 (1967). While there is a general warrant requirement, there are many exceptions that permit searches conducted without warrants. *See generally* Theodore P. Metzler, et al., *Warrantless Searches and Seizures*, 89 Geo. L. J. 1084–1163 (2001).

circumstances even though the ostensible result is to deprive the government of proof it would have acquired if its agents had not acted unconstitutionally.[218]

The inevitable discovery exception is reconcilable with the prevailing logic that justifies the Fourth Amendment exclusionary rule. The rule seeks to deter officers by depriving the state of evidentiary profits that provide incentives for future Fourth Amendment violations. It aims to put the government in the same position it would have occupied had it not acted illegally.[219] If evidence would inevitably have been discovered by lawful means, suppression would, in fact, put the government in a worse position.[220] Exclusion would bar the state from introducing unconstitutionally obtained evidence that it would have been able to introduce if it had not conducted the illegal search or seizure. According to the Supreme Court, this "punitive" outcome would not be consistent with the basic design of the exclusionary rule, which aims to remove gains, not to impose penalties. It would be costly to society and unjustified by the objective of deterring future illegalities, a goal adequately achieved by ensuring that the government's wrongs do not yield evidentiary advantages.

c. The Attenuation Exception A causal connection between a Fourth Amendment violation and the acquisition of evidence is essential for application of the exclusionary rule. As the inevitable discovery exception shows, however, the suppression doctrine does not require that all evidence with a "but-for" causal connection—that is, all "products" of illegalities—must be excluded. The inevitable discovery exception allows the use of evidence that has a causal link to unlawful conduct but affords the government no evidentiary advantage. Other exceptions, however, permit the admission of evidence with a but-for connection to a violation even though its introduction does constitute a net gain for the state. These exceptions allow the government to use items discovered as a result of improper conduct even though, as far as we know, the evidence would not be in the state's hands but for that conduct. In the colorful words of the Supreme Court, not all evidence that "would not have come to light but for the illegal actions of the police" must be suppressed as the "'fruit of the poisonous tree.'"[221] The remainder of the exceptions discussed in this chapter describe situations in which products of illegalities that are in fact profits are nonetheless admissible because they are not considered tainted "fruits."

218. Some lower courts have recognized the danger to the warrant requirement posed by application of the inevitable discovery exception to situations like this. *See* United States v. Virden, 488 F.3d 1317, 1322–23 (11t h Cir. 2007); People v. Schoondermark, 717 P.2d 504, 506 (Colo. App. 1985), *rev'd*, 759 P.2d 715 (Colo. 1988).

219. Nix v. Williams, 467 U.S. 431, 443 (1984).

220. *Id.* at 447.

221. Wong Sun v. United States, 371 U.S. 471, 487–88 (1963).

The oldest of these exceptions is the traditional branch of the "attenuation exception."[222] Attenuation dates to a 1939 opinion declaring illegally-obtained evidence admissible if the causal connection between the unconstitutional acts and the acquisition of the evidence was "so attenuated as to dissipate the taint" of those acts.[223] The notion of "taint dissipation" is not particularly helpful in determining *when* evidence is admissible. It does, however, capture and reflect a belief that exclusion is inappropriate when the connection between a Fourth Amendment wrong and an item of evidence is sufficiently weak—that is, when the acquisition of the evidence is sufficiently remote from the commission of the wrong to diminish the "poisonous" impact of that wrong.

Primary evidence found during or as an immediate result of a Fourth Amendment transgression cannot, by definition, fall within the attenuation exception. The link between a violation and the discovery of primary evidence is always strong, the wrong and acquisition are always proximate. Derivative evidence may be admitted under this exception, however, if the facts demonstrate an attenuated—a "weakened" or "stretched"—connection to the illegality. One relevant variable in assessing the strength of the linkage is the amount of time that elapsed between the violation and obtainment of the evidence.[224] The longer the time, the more likely a finding of attenuation. Intervening events or circumstances also can weaken a causal chain.[225] Any additional step in the chain of events between a search or seizure and the discovery of the evidence is a potentially pertinent attenuating factor. Thus, the delivery of *Miranda* warnings between an illegal arrest and a suspect's confession[226] or the release of an illegally seized person from custody prior to his admission of guilt[227] are relevant events. Similarly, if a witness is found as a result of an unlawful search, but in an exercise of "free will" decides to provide information about the search victim's guilt or to lead the authorities to contraband, that decision is an intervening, attenuating variable.[228]

As already mentioned, the exclusionary rule reaches not only tangible, but verbal evidence. Because the social cost of barring "live witness testimony" is high and because a witness will often exercise her "free will" and choose to testify, courts should more readily find attenuation when an illegal search enables

---

222. For cases recognizing and applying the exception, see United States v. Ceccolini, 435 U.S. 268, 273–74, 279–80 (1978); Brown v. Illinois, 422 U.S. 590, 598–99, 604–05 (1975); *Wong Sun*, 371 U.S. at 487, 491.

223. Nardone v. United States, 308 U.S. 338, 341 (1939).

224. *Brown*, 422 U.S. at 603–04.

225. *Id.*

226. *Id.* at 603.

227. Wong Sun v. United States, 371 U.S. 471, 491 (1963).

228. *See, e.g.*, United States v. Ceccolini, 435 U.S. 268, 276–77 (1978).

the government to secure such testimony.[229] The testimony of a witness should be admitted when the strength of the connection would not permit an attenuation finding for other kinds of evidence—narcotics, weapons, or incriminating clothing, for example.

Another highly relevant variable is the "purpose and flagrancy" of the constitutional violation.[230] The less culpable and extreme the wrong, the stronger the case for finding attenuation. Conversely, when law enforcement officers act more culpably or vary more dramatically from governing standards, attenuation is less likely. Thus, two items of derivative evidence that are the but-for products of illegal searches with identical causal connections to those searches might well be treated differently under the attenuation exception. If the police purposefully search with no cause whatsoever, the character of their transgression would support a conclusion that time and intervening events have not dissipated the taint. On the other hand, if the officers in good faith or carelessly fall a bit short of the showing needed for a reasonable search, the same time lapse and series of intervening events might well justify admission under the attenuation doctrine.[231]

The Court has not fleshed out the logic underlying the attenuation exception in any detail. When the doctrine first arose, exclusionary rule jurisprudence was undeveloped. The focus on deterrence as the rationale for suppression was still years in the future. The traditional attenuation doctrine, however, can be reconciled with the modern premises that govern Fourth Amendment exclusion and with the dominant analytical theme. The attenuation exception does not dictate admission of either primary or unattenuated derivative evidence. Officers who violate Fourth Amendment constraints still risk losing any and all valuable evidence that has a strong enough causal link to their conduct. This prospect, it is thought, gives them ample reason for future compliance with constitutional standards. The suppression of weakly connected derivative evidence, particularly when their violation is neither culpable nor egregious, has little incremental deterrent value. The potential admission of more remote evidentiary products is not likely to provide strong, offsetting incentives for ignoring Fourth Amendment commands. Moreover, the substantial additional costs of suppression outweigh any additional deterrence produced by excluding attenuated evidence.

---

229. *See id.* at 276–78, 280 (stating that because of the free will of witnesses and the costs of suppressing live-witness testimony, "the exclusionary rule should be invoked with much greater reluctance").

230. *See Brown*, 422 U.S. at 604.

231. Law enforcement fault and the degree of variance from norms are among the factors relevant to attenuation, but are not alone determinative. Dictum in *Herring v. United States*, however, suggests that the Court could prescribe a threshold showing of culpability and/or flagrancy as a necessary precondition for application of the exclusionary rule. *See supra* text accompanying notes 199–203.

Suppose, for example, that officers carelessly, but with no culpable intent, arrest an individual without probable cause. As a result of this arrest, but after six months and a number of voluntary, cooperative decisions by individuals, they discover information that leads them to a cache of heroin belonging to the illegally arrested individual. The fact that the government is allowed to introduce the heroin at trial will probably not provide strong motivation for a similar illegal arrest in the future—particularly when the officers know that more closely connected evidence has been, and will be, barred. Officers are not likely to anticipate such remote gains and are therefore not likely to misbehave in order to reap profit of that sort. On the other hand, the impacts of exclusion on the administration of justice—the costs to efforts to prove guilt and secure public safety—are high. In fact, the price paid is just as high as it would have been if the heroin were found in an immediate search of the arrestee's pockets. In such cases, the balance of interests dictates an exception to the presumptive ban on illegally-obtained evidence.

In 2006, the attenuation exception sprouted a second branch that is entirely distinct in nature from the original doctrine. For the first time, the Court announced that "[a]ttenuation can occur" not only "when the causal connection" between the wrong and the evidence "is remote," but also "when, even given a direct causal connection, *the interest protected by the constitutional guarantee that has been violated would not be served by suppression of the evidence obtained.*"[232] What this means, apparently, is that if suppression would not somehow *remedy* or *repair* the constitutional harm inflicted by the specific violation that led to the acquisition of the evidence, the attenuation exception calls for its admission.

The Supreme Court devised this novel form of attenuation as one ground for its holding that the exclusionary rule is not available as a sanction for violations of the Fourth Amendment knock-and-announce rule.[233] Its application in that context illuminates the significance of this new development and how this alternative branch of attenuation operates. According to the Court, evidence that is the product of officers' failure to knock-and-announce before entering a home falls within the attenuation exception because the knock-and-announce rule serves three purposes. It prevents harm to "life and limb," prevents damage to property, and allows occupants to preserve their "privacy and dignity" by preparing themselves for entry.[234] Unlike some other Fourth Amendment commands, that Fourth Amendment constraint does *not* serve to protect the interest in "shielding of potential evidence from the government[]."[235] Because this is the privacy interest exclusion serves—that is, because suppression effectively

---

232. Hudson v. Michigan, 547 U.S. 586, 593 (2006) (emphasis added).

233. The Court eliminated suppression as a remedy for knock-and-announce violations in Hudson v. Michigan. *Id.* at 599.

234. *Id.* at 594.

235. *Id.* at 593.

"reshields" evidence from the state—suppression due to a knock-and-announce rule violation would not serve any of the three interests protected by that demand. This is the sole context in which the new branch of the attenuation exception has been employed to justify the introduction of illegally-obtained evidence. Its logical premises, however, seem capable of extension to violations of other Fourth Amendment rules whose purposes are not to shield evidence from the government.[236]

"Attenuation" seems like a misnomer for this alternative version of the exception. The connection between the violation and the evidence at issue can be very close and very strong. Indeed, this offshoot of the attenuation doctrine encompasses even *primary* evidence acquired as an immediate result of a Fourth Amendment violation and is unconcerned with the culpability of the officers or the egregiousness of their transgression. Considering its very different character, it is at least odd to pair it with the traditional form of the attenuation.

More important, the logic beneath this variety of attenuation seems patently inconsistent with the enduring, animating themes of modern exclusionary rule jurisprudence. The Court made no effort to justify its new creation in terms of the balance between deterrent gains and costs to the truth-finding process. Instead of focusing on how the exclusionary rule is thought to serve the interests of any guarantee it is supposed to enforce—by removing incentives and thereby discouraging officers from disregarding that guarantee *in the future*—the Court analyzed whether the exclusionary rule would protect the interests that underlie the guarantee immediately and in the present case. The problem with this approach is that, according to accepted wisdom, Fourth Amendment suppression is not designed to make reparation to the victim of the constitutional violation. It cannot and is not intended to undo the harm done outside the courtroom.[237] The privacy breached by an unreasonable search is forever lost and keeping the evidence from the trial cannot restore it. Only by implicitly endorsing an understanding of the objectives of the exclusionary rule that is entirely foreign to the conception that has long controlled suppression analysis was it possible to justify the second branch of attenuation. If there were good reasons to ignore the entrenched underpinnings of the exclusionary rule and rely on rejected logic to create an exception bearing no relationship to its longstanding counterpart with the same name, the Court did not explain them.

d. The "Good Faith" Exceptions Although it is common to refer to the next set of exceptions as the "good faith" exceptions, that label is somewhat misleading. The admissibility of evidence does not require and is not dependent on proof that officers who violated the Fourth Amendment actually did believe that their conduct was constitutional. Instead, the exceptions addressed here require a

236. *See* Tomkovicz, *Future of Exclusion*, *supra* note 119, at 1864–65.
237. *See* United States v. Calandra, 414 U.S. 338, 347–48 (1974).

showing that it was "objectively reasonable" for officers to believe that their search or seizure was lawful. This showing is a necessary, but not yet a sufficient, predicate for admissibility under these exceptions to the suppression doctrine.

The foundational, and most prominent, exception in this category was first recognized and defined by the important ruling in *United States v. Leon*.[238] The Supreme Court held that when officers search on the basis of a warrant issued by a neutral and detached magistrate, but that warrant turns out for some reason to have been invalid, *all* evidence the officers obtain as a result of their unreasonable search is admissible if they acted "in objectively reasonable reliance" on the warrant.[239] The officers' actual "subjective" beliefs or knowledge about the validity or invalidity of the warrant are not determinative.[240] The governing standard is "objective"—whether a "reasonably well trained officer" would have relied on the warrant as valid authority for the search.[241] Thus, if a warrant authorizing a search of a home for narcotics is not, in fact, supported by probable cause, but a reasonable officer could conclude that the facts that supported issuance of the warrant did satisfy this constitutional standard, the *Leon* exception requires a judge to admit any evidence acquired as a result of the illegal search of the home, both primary and derivative evidence.

Ordinarily, when officers search on the basis of a warrant, their reliance will be reasonable and evidence will therefore be admissible.[242] The *Leon* decision delineated four atypical situations, however, in which "[s]uppression . . . remains an appropriate remedy" because it is unreasonable for officers to execute a flawed warrant.[243] The first is when officers secure a warrant based on false statements made deliberately or recklessly.[244] The second involves an "issuing magistrate [who] wholly abandon[s] his judicial role," acting as an adjunct of law enforcement rather than a neutral and unbiased judge.[245] The third situation calling for

---

238. 468 U.S. 897 (1984).

239. United States v. Leon, 468 U.S. 897, 922 (1984).

240. *Id.* at 922 n.23.

241. *Id.*

242. *Id.* at 918 (asserting that exclusion will be called for only in "unusual cases" when officers act in reliance on warrants); *id.* at 922 (indicating that suppression will be rare when officers rely on warrants).

243. *Id.* at 923.

244. *Leon*, 468 U.S. at 923. In *Franks v. Delaware*, 438 U.S. 154 (1978), the Court held that if warrants are based on false statements that are made "knowingly and intentionally, or with reckless disregard for the truth," a warrant is invalid if those statements were necessary to the showing of probable cause. *Id.* at 155–56.

245. *Leon*, 468 U.S. at 923. For a warrant to be valid, it must be issued by a "neutral and detached" magistrate. *See* Shadwick v. City of Tampa, 407 U.S. 345, 350 (1972). Although the Court suggested that this second qualification on the *Leon* exception applies only when there is complete abandonment of the proper judicial role, it is arguable that suppression is in order whenever it would be objectively unreasonable for a well-trained officer to

exclusion is where it is "'entirely unreasonable'" for an officer to believe that the warrant is supported by the constitutionally necessary showing, "'probable cause.'"[246] The fourth is where a warrant is "so facially deficient," so lacking in particularity, for example, that "executing officers cannot reasonably presume it to be valid."[247]

The *Leon* "good faith" exception rests on the premise that modifying judicial behavior is *not* an appropriate objective of the exclusionary rule.[248] Evidentiary suppression is not necessary to discourage judicial mistakes and is unlikely to deter judicial errors effectively. Judges are neither inclined to violate the Fourth Amendment, nor likely to be affected by the loss of evidence, because, unlike law enforcement officers, they lack institutional biases and have no stake in the outcomes of trials. Consequently, "[t]he threat of exclusion . . . cannot be expected significantly to deter them."[249] In sum, the application of the exclusionary rule cannot be predicated on the prevention of future judicial mistakes in granting search warrants.

Law enforcement conduct is the proper target of the exclusionary rule's deterrent efforts. When officers violate the Fourth Amendment, but are acting in reasonable reliance on the authority of a warrant, however, the deterrent benefits of suppression are thought to be "marginal or nonexistent."[250] If it is reasonable for officers to believe that they are executing valid warrants, there is little chance that they will alter their behavior, for they will not foresee the consequence of suppression based on their conduct. According to the Court, only the judge, not the officer, has erred, and he is "'acting as a reasonable officer would and should act in similar circumstances. Excluding the evidence can in no way affect his

---

conclude that an issuing magistrate was neutral and detached, as is required by the Fourth Amendment.

246. *Leon*, 468 U.S. at 923 (quoting Brown v. Illinois, 422 U.S. 590, 610–11 (1975) (Powell, J., concurring)). The Fourth Amendment text commands that "no Warrants shall issue, but upon probable cause." U.S. CONST. amend. IV. The Court suggested that as long as reasonable minds could differ over the existence of probable cause, the *Leon* exception applies. *Leon*, 468 U.S. at 914. Only when a reasonable person could not mistakenly find the constitutional standard satisfied—i.e., when it is "entirely unreasonable" to conclude that probable cause was established—is the suppression sanction appropriate. *Id.* at 923.

247. *Id.* at 923. This qualification refers to cases in which the "form" of the warrant is improper in some respect, most likely because it does not comply with the Fourth Amendment's edict that warrants must "particularly describ[e] the place to be searched, and the persons or things to be seized." U.S. CONST. amend. IV.

248. The deterrent objectives of the exclusionary rule had always been framed in terms of law enforcement conduct, but the Court had not ruled out judicial errors as an appropriate aim of corrective sanctioning. *Leon* marked the first announcement that deterring future judicial errors is not an aim of the exclusionary rule.

249. *Leon*, 468 U.S. at 917.

250. *Id.* at 922.

future conduct unless it is to make him less willing do his duty.'"[251] In other words, because we can expect no more than reasonable conduct from officers, when they are reasonably mistaken about the validity of a search warrant, excluding the evidence will not produce desired deterrence. Moreover, the threat of suppression in situations when it is reasonable to believe a warrant is valid may discourage some officers from executing warrants that are, in fact, valid. This sort of deterrent overkill—discouraging reasonable searches pursuant to legitimate authority—could prove costly, impeding effective law enforcement.

Any marginal deterrence of unreasonable searches that might result from extension of the exclusionary rule to situations where officers have reasonably relied on invalid warrants "cannot justify the substantial costs of exclusion."[252] In the Supreme Court's opinion, the costs of barring probative evidence and hindering efforts to convict the guilty clearly outweigh the minimal gains in Fourth Amendment enforcement that could occur if officers refrain from executing defective warrants in close, debatable cases.

A second variety of "good faith exception" applies when officers rely on *statutes* that authorize unreasonable searches or seizures.[253] If their reliance is "objectively reasonable," that is, if an officer with reasonable knowledge of Fourth Amendment requirements could believe that the statutorily authorized search is constitutional, any evidence obtained is admissible.[254] Like judges, legislators are not appropriate targets of exclusionary rule deterrence, and when officers reasonably rely on invalid legislative enactments, the cost-benefit balance again favors an exception to the suppression doctrine. Consequently, when state lawmakers enacted a provision sanctioning warrantless "administrative searches" of motor vehicles, but granted officers excessive discretion that rendered the provision violative of Fourth Amendment constraints, evidence obtained from a vehicle search pursuant to that statute was not subject to suppression because it was reasonable for an officer to rely on the statutorily-granted authority prior to any ruling that the enactment was unconstitutional.[255]

Another variation on the "good faith" theme applies when an officer searches or seizes in reasonable reliance on a clerical error made by a judicial branch employee.[256] Suppose that, due to an oversight by an individual working for the courts, a computer record shows that an arrest warrant exists when, in fact, that warrant has been canceled. If an officer unreasonably arrests a suspect based on the erroneous information, all the evidence he finds is admissible as long as he was "acting objectively reasonably when he relied upon the . . .

---

251. *Id.* at 920. (quoting Stone v. Powell, 428 U.S. 465, 539–40 (White, J., dissenting)).
252. *Leon*, 468 U.S. at 922.
253. *See* Illinois v. Krull, 480 U.S. 340, 349 (1987).
254. *Id.* at 349, 355.
255. *See id.* at 356–60.
256. *See* Arizona v. Evans, 514 U.S. 1, 3–4 (1995).

computer record."[257] Because the source of the mistake is the judicial branch and the officer is not responsible for the constitutional error, the same balance of interests dictating the *Leon* exception justifies another exception.

A fourth type of "good faith" doctrine emerged from *Herring v. United States*.[258] According to the five-Justice majority, when *law enforcement* employees in one jurisdiction erroneously *and negligently* fail to correct the computer database to reflect that a warrant no longer exists and officers in a different jurisdiction, reasonably relying on the erroneous information in the database, arrest a suspect and find evidence, the exclusionary rule is inapplicable. Although it is the outgrowth of the other "good faith" exceptions, this latest version differs dramatically from its predecessors. It suspends the exclusionary rule even though police operatives not only made the critical mistake, but did so negligently—that is, even though the unconstitutional search or seizure is due to *objectively unreasonable* law enforcement conduct. The preceding contexts all involved mistakes by other governmental branches and reasonable care by the police who were involved. Despite the significant differences in *Herring*, the Court concluded that any deterrence that might be achieved by suppression would be more than offset by the social costs that would result.

The holding in *Herring* is restricted to situations where the law enforcement source of the information has been negligent, but the officers who conduct the unreasonable search or seizure have no fault—that is, there is no objective reason for the latter officers to believe that the search or seizure is unconstitutional. Nonetheless, the majority went out of its way to speak in broader terms and address broader issues than necessary, indicating that the exclusionary rule *might* be restricted to situations involving law enforcement culpability greater than isolated negligence. The suggestion was that the scope of the *Weeks-Mapp* rule might well be confined to situations in which the police deliberately or recklessly violate the Fourth Amendment or, at a minimum, have been grossly negligent or engaged in a pattern of systemic negligence.[259]

The reasoning in *Herring* has potentially dramatic implications for the extant "good faith" exceptions. To date, those doctrines have evolved incrementally and have been kept relatively confined. In the aftermath of the 1984 ruling in *Leon*, it seemed entirely possible that the Court might dramatically expand the exception to encompass any unreasonable search and seizure—whether or not it was based

---

257. *Id.* at 16.

258. 555 U.S. ___, 129 S.Ct. 695 (2009).

259. These broader implications of *Herring* were discussed earlier. *See supra* text accompanying notes 199–203. Future decisions will determine whether this potential culpability limitation on the exclusionary rule actually becomes a part of controlling Fourth Amendment law. For a discussion of *Herring*'s implications, see Wayne R. LaFave, *The Smell of Herring: A Critique of the Supreme Court's Latest Assault on the Exclusionary Rule*, 99 J. CRIM. L. & CRIMINOLOGY 757 (2009).

on a warrant—as long as it was "objectively reasonable" to believe that the conduct was constitutional. Much of the reasoning of *Leon* could have supported the extension to objectively reasonable mistakes about the lawfulness of warrantless searches and seizures. The Court could have reasoned that it never makes sense to expect officers to be more than reasonable, and that the costs of suppression aimed at deterring reasonable constitutional errors outweigh any benefits that might be attained.[260]

For whatever reason, the Court did not venture down that potentially revolutionary road. As a result, at the time *Herring* was decided mistakes by law enforcers—even those that might be deemed "objectively reasonable"—still triggered the exclusionary rule. The three variations on the "good faith" theme applied only when officers were reasonable and were acting in reliance on the errors of others. The premises of *Herring*, however, could foretell a sea change in exclusionary rule law. The majority's suggestion that even *negligence* by officers should not yield suppression could lead to suspension of the exclusionary rule not only when officers are the source of an unconstitutionality, but even when it would be objectively *unreasonable* to believe that their conduct complied with the Fourth Amendment. Moreover, if mere negligence by officers precludes suppression, there would no longer be reason to exclude evidence when officers' reliance on warrants, statutes, or judicial employee errors is objectively unreasonable—a result currently dictated by the standards prescribed in the "good faith" opinions. In essence, the three "good faith" exceptions would become superfluous, for it would not matter whether officers were relying on the errors of others *and* it would not matter that a reasonably well-trained officer would have realized that a search or seizure was unconstitutional. If a general demand for greater culpability than mere isolated negligence becomes a controlling premise of exclusionary rule law, it could effectively eliminate any need for "good faith" exceptions.

e. The Impeachment Use Exception To *impeach* a witness is to cast doubt on his or her credibility, to suggest that the witness's testimony is not worthy of belief. Two methods of impeachment are relevant to the instant discussion. First, a witness's credibility might be undermined by evidence that she made a statement on a prior occasion that is inconsistent with statements she made while testifying. This is sometimes known as "self-contradiction." In addition, a witness's veracity might be attacked by introducing contradictory testimony or statements from another witness or by presenting tangible evidence that refutes what the witness has asserted in court.

---

260. On the other hand, the Court could have concluded that the exclusionary rule should seek to deter even reasonable mistakes by police officers and that the cost-benefit balance favors admission only when someone other than law enforcement is the source of the unconstitutionality and officers' conduct is "largely error-free." *See* Massachusetts v. Sheppard, 468 U.S. 981, 990 (1984).

The final exception to the exclusionary rule allows the government to introduce evidence acquired as a result of an unconstitutional search or seizure to impeach a defendant's testimony.[261] Both the defendant's prior inconsistent statements and other evidence are admissible. Thus, if an unlawfully arrested suspect admits to arresting officers that he was outside a bank that was robbed, then testifies at trial that he was elsewhere, the admission to the officer may be used to impeach him. Alternatively, if an accused testifies that she did not have narcotics in her automobile, narcotics found there during an unreasonable search may be employed to cast doubt on her credibility. Because the evidence may not be used to prove the guilt of the accused in the government's "case in chief," but is admissible *only* for impeachment purposes, the judge must inform the jurors of its limited value—that is, that they may consider the evidence *only* in deciding whether to believe the defendant.[262] Moreover, the substantive value of the evidence—its tendency to prove the defendant's guilt—may not be counted in evaluating the sufficiency of the state's evidence to prove the offense charged.

The impeachment use exception allows the prosecution to introduce the illegally-obtained evidence if the defendant makes a contradictory statement during his *direct* testimony—that is, while answering the questions asked by his own lawyer who has called him as a witness.[263] It also permits the state to use the evidence to contradict testimony given during cross-examination of the defendant by the government attorney—as long as that cross-examination was "reasonably suggested" by the testimony given on direct examination.[264] Consequently, if the accused denies having incriminating clothing in his illegally searched luggage while testifying either on direct examination or when properly cross-examined by the prosecutor, the exclusionary rule does not bar the prosecutor from suggesting that the defendant did not tell the truth by showing that the incriminating clothing was found in the luggage.[265] The evidence may not be used to prove the accused's possession, but insofar as it is in tension with assertions made on the witness stand, it is admissible to erode the accused's credibility.

The foundation for this exception is, of course, cost-benefit balancing. According to the Supreme Court, suppression from the government's case in chief—i.e., the bar to substantive use of the evidence—provides sufficient

261. *See* United States v. Havens, 446 U.S. 620, 627–28 (1980).

262. *Id.*

263. *See* Harris v. New York, 401 U.S. 222, 225–26 (1971). Although this opinion involved exclusion based on a *Miranda* doctrine violation, not a Fourth Amendment wrong, the exception for impeaching direct testimony was clearly extended to the Fourth Amendment exclusionary rule in *Havens*, 446 U.S. 620.

264. *See Havens*, 446 U.S. at 627–28.

265. *Id.* at 628.

motivation for future compliance with the Constitution's commands.[266] The costs to the truth-finding process of denying the government the opportunity to use the evidence to impeach a dishonest defendant outweighs any incremental deterrence of Fourth Amendment violations that might result from precluding impeachment use.[267] A particularly weighty consideration in the balance is the special affront to the administration of justice when a defendant is allowed to perjure himself without being challenged by contradictory information in the government's hands.[268]

The exception does *not* authorize the impeachment of witnesses other than the accused. The exclusionary rule prohibits the use of unlawfully acquired evidence even for the limited purpose of casting doubt on the credibility of testimony of other defense witnesses.[269] Suppose, for example, that officers illegally arrest a suspect. He provides a description of his appearance on the day of a shooting that matches a description of the perpetrator provided by eyewitnesses and also admits that he recently changed his appearance. The government may not use the defendant's admissions to prove that he did resemble the shooter. Moreover, if the defendant calls a friend to testify that his appearance was very different from the description of the eyewitnesses, the defendant's own statements to the contrary may not be admitted to impeach his friend's testimony.[270]

The Court refused to expand the impeachment use exception to include defense witnesses because allowing the state to reap this profit would have substantially undermined the deterrent efficacy of the exclusionary rule. The costs to the truth-finding process of suppressing the impeachment evidence were not weighty enough to counterbalance the increased compliance with the Fourth Amendment that exclusion would produce.[271]

E. REFLECTIONS ON THE FOURTH AMENDMENT EXCLUSIONARY RULE

The federal rule barring evidence acquired by means of unreasonable searches and seizures is nearly a hundred years old. Its state counterpart has just reached the half-century mark. At its birth, the federal rule was remarkably uncontroversial. The state version arrived amidst considerable controversy and has faced fervent opposition ever since. In the years since *Mapp* imposed the suppression remedy on the states, the fates of the federal and state rules have

---

266. *Id.* at 627.
267. *Id.*
268. *Harris*, 401 U.S. at 224–26.
269. *See* James v. Illinois, 493 U.S. 307, 309 (1990).
270. *Id.* at 319–20.
271. *Id.* at 313–14.

been inextricably linked. Their rationales, scopes, interpretations, and contours have been identical.

The Warren Court's constitutional criminal procedure decisions have been aptly described as "revolutionary."[272] Within a relatively short span of years during the 1960s, a number of landmark rulings broadly construed many of the Bill of Rights entitlements granted to criminal defendants. The extension of the exclusionary rule to state prosecutions was a critical, integral part of that revolution. Soon after the expansive Warren Court era ended, the development of the exclusionary rule entered a new phase, a phase characterized by steady contraction. The pivotal step was modification of the exclusionary rule's constitutional underpinnings. The Supreme Court abandoned the premise that exclusion is a constitutional courtroom right, supplanting it with a virtually single-minded focus on the deterrence of future out-of-court transgressions. Every decision from that point on has rested upon a familiar, putatively empirical analysis, an assessment of whether Fourth Amendment enforcement achieved by suppression can justify the toll it exacts from our criminal justice systems. This balance of deterrent gains against social costs has long dictated the operation of the exclusionary rule.

Much more often than not, this emphasis on deterrence and this concern with the steep costs of evidentiary exclusion has restricted the reach of the *Weeks-Mapp* rule. In the vast majority of cases, this interest balancing approach has led to a conclusion that suppression is unwarranted. Although the exclusionary rule has survived, its erosion has been steady and the cumulative impact of the numerous constrictive decisions has been dramatic. The hostile, parsimonious attitude toward exclusion that has influenced analysis for nearly four decades has severely diminished its constitutional stature and reduced its practical impact.

A cynic might well see the shift to deterrence, and the denial of a constitutional right to be free from prosecution based on illegally-acquired evidence, as a manipulative effort by the rule's opponents to render it vulnerable to such erosion. Some limitations imposed upon the rule would be difficult, if not impossible, to justify if suppression were still understood as part of our Fourth Amendment entitlement. The good faith exceptions, the novel branch of attenuation, and the authorization of impeachment use, for example, might be logically indefensible if evidentiary exclusion had remained an integral part of the constitutional guarantee. The suggestion that only deliberate or culpable Fourth Amendment transgressions can justify suppression would seem implausible. Whether part of a clever scheme to destroy the rule, or the product of an honest reexamination of the doctrine's constitutional foundations, there can be no doubt

---

272. *See* Steven F. Smith, *Activism as Restraint: Lessons From Criminal Procedure*, 80 Tex. L. Rev. 1057, 1069 (2002).

that the effect of revising the exclusionary rule's justifications has been enormous.

Early in the twenty-first century, the suppression doctrine seems considerably weaker than at any point since it was first imposed on the states. Not only is it riddled with an ever-growing array of exceptions, but the Court has also suggested that its presumptive scope could be restricted to only those situations in which official violations of the Fourth Amendment are sufficiently culpable. The verbal barbs aimed at the rule have multiplied in number and increased in intensity, and virtually every occasion to consider the rule has become an occasion to hobble it. It is uncertain whether the *Weeks-Mapp* rule is destined for extinction. What is sure is that the road the Fourth Amendment exclusionary rule is traveling will render it less and less relevant as a constraint upon the government's ability to prove guilt at trial and less and less potent as a reason for law enforcement officers to respect the right of the people to be secure against unreasonable searches and seizures.

2. FIFTH AND FOURTEENTH AMENDMENT EXCLUSION OF CONFESSIONS

INTRODUCTION

This is the sole chapter addressing more than one constitutional rule of exclusion. The Fifth Amendment Self-Incrimination Privilege and Fourteenth Amendment Due Process Clause mandates to exclude certain confessions are treated together because the Supreme Court's interpretation of their meaning has resulted in essentially identical suppression doctrines. Both guarantees bar statements that the government has "coerced" or "compelled" an individual to make. There are reasons to question whether the Court's understanding of the significance of these distinct constitutional provisions is correct. There is little doubt, however, that the exclusionary rules that have emerged from the Court's interpretations of the Fifth and Fourteenth Amendment are virtually indistinguishable in content, rationales, and scope. Moreover, these constitutional restrictions on the government's introduction of evidence in criminal cases are dramatically different in nature from the Fourth Amendment exclusionary rule discussed in Chapter 1.

This chapter first sketches the basics of the Fifth and Fourteenth Amendment rules and highlights some of the most significant issues surrounding those rules. It then describes the historical development of the two constitutional doctrines, explores the rationales for suppressing evidence, and explains the reach and operation of the rules, including facets that have yet to be resolved.[1]

A. THE BASIC FIFTH AMENDMENT PRIVILEGE AND DUE PROCESS CLAUSE RULES

The Fifth Amendment Privilege Against Compulsory Self-Incrimination provides that "[n]o person . . . shall be compelled in any criminal case to be a witness against himself."[2] The Due Process Clause, contained in the Fourteenth Amendment, guarantees that no state "shall . . . deprive any person of life,

1. A different doctrine rooted in the Fifth Amendment privilege that also excludes confessions—the controversial *Miranda* doctrine—is not considered here. For good reason, that distinct constitutional exclusionary rule receives thorough, separate consideration in Chapter 3.

2. U.S. Const. amend. V.

liberty, or property, without due process of law."[3] Like the Fourth Amendment, neither constitutional command speaks directly to the question of evidentiary exclusion. Put otherwise, neither explicitly prohibits the government from introducing confessions or any other relevant evidence obtained before trial.

Nonetheless, the Supreme Court has held that both provisions bar the prosecution from using "coerced confessions"—that is, any statements that police or other government agents have forced individuals to give. The Fifth Amendment prohibition against compelling a person to be a witness against himself clearly prevents the state from pressuring a criminal defendant to take the witness stand at his own trial and disclose self-inculpatory information. That provision also requires the exclusion of an incriminating confession forced from the mind of an individual before trial because its introduction would have the same effect as requiring him to testify. Use of the statements against the defendant would constitute compulsory self-incrimination in violation of the Fifth Amendment privilege.

The essence of due process is an assurance of "fundamental fairness" in all proceedings, including criminal trials.[4] According to the Supreme Court, the use of a person's "involuntary" or "coerced" confession to prove her guilt denies fundamental fairness because American systems of criminal justice are accusatorial in nature. They demand that the government prove its case without evidence extorted from the mind of the defendant. Due process forbids the introduction of a coerced confession to secure a conviction because that is an essentially inquisitorial process, the antithesis of fundamental fairness.[5]

These two constitutional liberties, therefore, mandate the exclusion of any disclosures that government agents have "compelled" or "coerced" a person to make.[6] The prosecution may not use such disclosures to prove that person's guilt. Suppression depends on whether a statement has been made involuntarily due to pressures imposed by government agents—typically police interrogators. Voluntary confessions—those that are freely given—are admissible. There are a number of questions concerning the reach and operation of the Fifth Amendment and Due Process Clause "exclusionary rules." Some have been decided and others remain unresolved. One issue, for example, is whether confessions extorted by private parties are constitutionally objectionable. Another is whether

3. U.S. Const. amend. XIV. The Fifth Amendment contains an identical provision that prohibits the federal government from depriving any person "of life, liberty, or property, without due process of law." U.S. Const. amend. V.

4. *See* Miller v. Fenton, 474 U.S. 104, 110 (1985); Lisenba v. California, 314 U.S. 219, 236 (1941).

5. *See Miller*, 474 U.S. at 110, 116; Watts v. Indiana, 338 U.S. 49, 54–55 (1949).

6. *See* Dickerson v. United States, 530 U.S. 428, 433 (2000) ("Over time, our cases recognized two constitutional bases for the requirement that a confession be voluntary to be admitted into evidence: the Fifth Amendment right against self-incrimination and the Due Process Clause"). The Court has used the terms "coerced" and "compelled" synonymously, with no indication of any difference in meaning. *See, e.g., id.*

derivative evidence, additional proof of guilt that the government has acquired by exploiting a defendant's coerced disclosures, is subject to suppression. Still others are whether important government interests might justify an exception to the rule excluding coerced confessions, whether a statement forced from one person may be used to convict another person, whether coerced evidence that would have been discovered by legal means is barred, and whether the government may use coerced admissions for the limited purpose of impeaching a defendant's trial testimony.

A later section of this chapter explores these and other questions in detail. As will be seen, the Supreme Court has spent considerably less time and attention to details concerning the operation of the Fifth and Fourteenth Amendment suppression doctrines than it has devoted to the various facets of the Fourth Amendment exclusionary rule. The Court has never addressed some of the issues that have long been settled under the Fourth Amendment—for example, "standing" to object to another person's involuntary admissions or the admissibility of derivative evidence with an "attenuated" causal connection. Before explaining and analyzing the intricacies of these bases for constitutional exclusion, a sketch of their long, and fascinating, histories and a close examination of their underlying rationales are in order.

B. A HISTORY OF FIFTH AND FOURTEENTH AMENDMENT EXCLUSION: THE ORIGINS AND EVOLUTION OF THE DUAL CONSTITUTIONAL BARS TO COERCED CONFESSIONS

This part begins with a short description of the *preconstitutional* sources of the two exclusionary doctrines that are the subjects of this chapter. It then identifies the origins of each *constitutional* bar to involuntary confessions and traces how numerous Supreme Court opinions developed the doctrines over the course of several decades. Although each of the exclusionary rules has continued to evolve up to the present day, this historical account will end in the 1960s, when the Court promulgated two additional, significant restrictions on the admissibility of confessions.[7] The explorations and analyses of doctrinal details of the current bars to coerced confessions effectively depict the history of the Fifth and Fourteenth Amendment rules from the 1960s until the present.

1. Common Law Precursors: The "Nemo Tenetur" and "Voluntariness" Doctrines

It is generally agreed that the two constitutional rules regarding the inadmissibility of compelled or coerced statements have roots in distinct common

---

7. Those restrictions—the *Miranda* doctrine and the *Massiah* doctrine—are the topics of Chapters 3 and 4.

law doctrines. The Fifth Amendment privilege can be traced to a British doctrine known as "nemo tenetur," a safeguard against the government's use of extortionate methods to induce individuals to accuse themselves.[8] "Nemo tenetur prodere seipsum" meant that "no one is bound to bring forth (i.e., accuse) himself."[9] This prohibition, which began to emerge in the early 1700s,[10] reflected "abhorrence [to] . . . torture and coercive interrogation techniques" by the government and a determination to preserve civil liberties by providing protection against such abuses.[11] Although the "nemo tenetur" doctrine could result in the exclusion of evidence,[12] its *objective* was to condemn and prevent the government's mistreatment of individuals.[13]

The due process-coerced confession doctrine has roots in a very different source, the common law "voluntariness" doctrine.[14] This rule of evidence, which originated in a 1783 British decision,[15] forbade the use of involuntary confessions secured by private parties to prove guilt.[16] The animating concern was the unreliability of such confessions and the risks that innocent persons would be convicted by their use at trial.[17]

---

8. *See* Thomas Y. Davies, *Farther and Farther from the Original Fifth Amendment: The Recharacterization of the Right Against Self-Incrimination as a "Trial Right" in* Chavez v. Martinez, 70 TENN. L. REV. 987, 1001–02 (2003) [hereinafter Davies, *Original Fifth Amendment*]; Mark A. Godsey, *Rethinking the Involuntary Confession Rule: Toward a Workable Test for Identifying Compelled Self-Incrimination*, 93 CAL. L. REV. 465, 478–80 (2005) [hereinafter Godsey, *Rethinking the Involuntary Confession Rule*]. According to one author, the doctrine originated in "medieval European canon law." Steven Penney, *Theories of Confession Admissibility: A Historical View*, 25 AM. J. CRIM. L. 309, 314 (1998) [hereinafter Penney, *Theories of Confession Admissibility*].

9. Godsey, *Rethinking the Involuntary Confession Rule, supra* note 8, at 479.

10. *See* Penney, *Theories of Confession Admissibility, supra* note 8, at 317.

11. Godsey, *Rethinking the Involuntary Confession Rule, supra* note 8, at 480.

12. *See* Lawrence Herman, *The Unexplored Relationship Between the Privilege Against Compulsory Self-Incrimination and the Involuntary Confession Rule (Part I)*, 53 OHIO ST. L. J. 101, 159 (1992) [hereinafter Herman, *Unexplored Relationship*]; *see also* Davies, *Original Fifth Amendment, supra* note 8, at 1006.

13. *See* Godsey, *Rethinking the Involuntary Confession Rule, supra* note 8, at 478, 479–80, 481 n.83; *see also* Davies, *Original Fifth Amendment, supra* note 8, at 1001–02.

14. *See* Davies, *Original Fifth Amendment, supra* note 8, at 1022; Godsey, *Rethinking the Involuntary Confession Rule, supra* note 8, at 478, 481–82.

15. King v. Warickshall, 1 Leach 263, 168 Eng. Rep. 234 (K.B. 1783); *see* Penney, *Theories of Confession Admissibility, supra* note 8, at 320–21, 320 n.58 (observing that the first decision establishing the common law rule of exclusion was *Warickshall*, but asserting that the "voluntariness" concept antedated the decision).

16. *See* Davies, *Original Fifth Amendment, supra* note 8, at 1021–22; Godsey, *Rethinking the Involuntary Confession Rule, supra* note 8, at 482.

17. *See* Davies, *Original Fifth Amendment, supra* note 8, at 1021, 1022–23; Godsey, *Rethinking the Involuntary Confession Rule, supra* note 8, at 481–82; *see also* Herman, *Unexplored Relationship, supra* note 12, at 185–86 (referring to the risk that an innocent person

Originally, neither of these doctrines was concerned with or applied to police interrogation because the development of organized police forces and the emergence of police interrogation as an integral part of the investigatory process in criminal cases did not occur until the second half of the nineteenth century.[18] Eventually, however, courts concluded that both were pertinent to law enforcement efforts to secure admissions of guilt.

2. The Origins and Development of the Dual Constitutional Bars to Involuntary Confessions

The Supreme Court first found a constitutional basis for excluding a confession in a landmark 1897 ruling.[19] *Bram v. United States*[20] involved the killing of a ship's captain in his cabin. After the ship docked in Nova Scotia, Bram, the first officer, was taken to Boston and indicted for the murder. At his trial, the prosecution called a detective to testify to certain statements Bram made while he was in custody. Over defense counsel's objection that the statements were not "free and voluntary,"[21] the trial judge allowed the detective to recount Bram's statements.[22] Bram was convicted and sentenced to death.

In the Supreme Court, Bram contended that because the statements had not been "shown to have been voluntary,"[23] it was error to allow their admission. The Supreme Court agreed, but instead of citing the common law voluntariness doctrine, the majority found support in our Constitution's Bill of Rights. In the majority's view, the question of whether a confession was inadmissible in a federal trial because it was "not voluntary . . . [was] controlled by" the Fifth Amendment privilege against compelled self-incrimination.[24] Although the Court briefly did mention the "nemo tenetur" principle in passing, it found guidance primarily in authorities expounding the common law voluntariness doctrine.[25]

---

will suffer conviction and punishment if the government uses an unreliable compelled confession).

18. *See* Penney, *Theories of Confession Admissibility*, *supra* note 8, at 314, 322–23; *see also* Davies, *Original Fifth Amendment*, *supra* note 8, at 1030–31.

19. Prior to its reliance on the Constitution, the Supreme Court had endorsed and applied the common law rule deeming involuntary confessions inadmissible. *See* Hopt v. Utah, 110 U.S. 574 (1884).

20. 168 U.S. 532 (1897).

21. *Id.* at 533.

22. Although the statements were not particularly incriminating, they were admitted on the ground that they were relevant proof of the defendant's guilt.

23. *Id.* at 540.

24. *Id.* at 542.

25. Scholars have criticized the *Bram* Court's indefensible "conflation" of the Fifth Amendment protection against compulsion, which was a civil liberties doctrine rooted in "nemo tenetur," and the common law rule of evidence, which barred involuntary

Under the rule "existing at common law," which the Court found "embedded in the Fifth Amendment," a confession was admissible only if "'made freely, voluntarily and without compulsion or inducement of any sort.'"[26] The Court's decisions had already accepted the "general rule" that a "confession [had to] be free and voluntary, that is, not produced by inducements engendering either hope or fear."[27] According to the Court, the "test" of voluntariness was "uniform" and had to "be ascertained by the condition of mind which the causes *ordinarily* operated to create."[28] This seemed to suggest that the peculiar strengths or weaknesses of the individual confessor were not relevant considerations. Instead, the inquiry focused upon the character of the conduct that produced the confession. Moreover, because the force of the influence used or its effect upon the mind of the suspect could not be measured, a declaration had to be excluded "'if *any* degree of influence ha[d] been exerted.'"[29]

Precedents established that involuntary statements were barred if they were drawn from a defendant by a *magistrate*—i.e., a judicial officer.[30] The Court had no trouble concluding that this same bar extended to involuntary confessions resulting from *police officers'* inducements, because an officer was also undoubtedly "a person in authority."[31] Consequently, statements were involuntary and inadmissible if made in response to communications by officers that engendered either a hope of some benefit or a fear of some adverse consequence.

In *Bram*, the accused had been arrested, placed in irons, and delivered to the custody of the police. A detective had him escorted to a private office. Either while Bram was being or after he had been stripped of his clothing, the detective informed him that his "'position [was] rather an awkward one'" and that another sailor (also a suspect) claimed that he had seen Bram murder the captain. Bram replied that the other sailor "'could not have seen me,'" a denial that carried a potential "implication of guilt."[32] In the Court's view, this reply clearly could not "have been the result of a purely voluntary mental action," but instead "must necessarily have been the result of either hope or fear, or both, operating on the mind."[33] The result of the detective's words "was to produce upon [Bram's] mind the fear that if he remained silent it would be considered an admission

---

confessions out of a concern for reliability. *See* Davies, *Original Fifth Amendment, supra* note 8, at 1034–38; Godsey, *Rethinking the Involuntary Confession Rule, supra* note 8, at 485–88.

26. *Bram*, 168 U.S. at 548 (quoting Wilson v. United States, 162 U.S. 613, 623 (1896)).

27. *Id.* at 557–58.

28. *Id.* at 548 (emphasis added).

29. *Id.* at 565 (emphasis added) (quoting 3 Russ. Crimes (6th ed.) 478).

30. *Id.* at 550–51.

31. *Bram*, 168 U.S. at 551, 556.

32. *Id.* at 562.

33. *Id.* at 562.

of guilt."[34] These same words would have naturally generated an "impression" that "by denying [his guilt], there was hope of removing the suspicion from himself."[35] In this situation, Bram's answer could not be considered "wholly voluntary and in no manner influenced by the force of hope or fear[.]"[36] A person in his situation "would be impelled to speak either for fear that his failure to make answer would be considered against him, or in hope that if he did reply he would be benefited thereby."[37] Considering the facts, "taken as a whole," the statements "were not made by one who in law could be considered a free agent."[38] The use of Bram's compelled confession to secure a conviction was a "plain[] violation" of both "the letter" and "the spirit" of the Fifth Amendment guarantee.[39]

Bram was groundbreaking in more than one respect. It was the first time that the Court excluded an involuntary confession on constitutional grounds. It was also significant in concluding that the Fifth Amendment was concerned not only with formal, courtroom pressures to confess, but also with extrajudicial pressures produced by police interrogation and in interpreting the privilege against "compelled" self-incrimination to bar inculpatory admissions induced by relatively mild pressures, inducements, or influences.

Twenty-seven years later, in *Ziang Sung Wan v. United States*,[40] relying on *Bram*, the Court held that five statements secured from the accused by police interrogators were inadmissible in another federal capital murder trial. The case involved prolonged, and sometimes quite intense, interrogation of a sick suspect over a 12-day span. The interrogators held the suspect incommunicado and deprived him of sleep and medical attention. Although they kept him in custody the entire time, they did not formally arrest him until the ninth day. A doctor who examined Wan at the end of the process found him to be so ill and exhausted that he might well have confessed just "'to have the torture stopped.'"[41]

The Court of Appeals deemed the statements admissible, apparently believing that a confession was "voluntary, as a matter of law, if it was not induced by a promise or a threat."[42] In a terse opinion, the Supreme Court explained that "voluntariness is not satisfied by establishing merely that the confession was not induced by a promise or a threat," and declared that a confession is admissible "only if, it was, in fact, voluntarily made."[43] Custody and examination by

34. *Id.*
35. *Id.*
36. *Bram*, 168 U.S. at 563.
37. *Id.*
38. *Id.* at 563–64.
39. *Id.* at 564.
40. 266 U.S. 1 (1924).
41. *Id.* at 14.
42. *Id.*
43. *Id.*

the police do not necessarily render a confession involuntary, "[b]ut a confession obtained by compulsion must be excluded whatever may have been the character of the compulsion, and whether the compulsion was applied in a judicial proceeding or otherwise."[44] Because the "undisputed facts showed that compulsion was applied" here, all of the statements "should have been excluded" from the trial.[45] Although the opinion did cite *Bram* for support, it did not refer specifically to the Fifth Amendment privilege and it relied on the pre-*Bram* opinions excluding involuntary confessions on nonconstitutional grounds.

Twelve years later, in *Brown v. Mississippi*,[46] the issue was the admissibility of confessions in a *state* trial of three African-American defendants charged with murder. Law enforcement officers had hanged and brutally whipped the men and had threatened that the beatings would continue until they confessed in the precise terms dictated by the officers. The men succumbed to the torture and complied with the demands for confessions "'in the exact form and contents . . . desired.'"[47] The trial court allowed the prosecution to introduce the confessions, and the defendants were convicted and sentenced to death. The Mississippi Supreme Court did not question that the confessions "were procured by coercion," but concluded that there was no constitutional mandate to exclude them from the trial.[48]

In a path-blazing ruling, the United States Supreme Court concluded that the Fourteenth Amendment Due Process Clause prohibited the use of coerced confessions in state criminal proceedings.[49] The Court did acknowledge that in *Twining v. New Jersey*[50] it had ruled that no provision in the Constitution required states to abide by the privilege against compelled self-incrimination.[51] It reasoned, however, that the compulsion that was the domain of the privilege was not at issue in *Brown*. That guarantee is concerned with compulsion "of the processes of justice by which the accused may be called as a witness and required to testify. Compulsion by torture to extort a confession is a different matter."[52]

Although states are free to regulate their own courtroom processes, the guarantee of due process forbids them from employing a procedure that "'offends some principle of justice so rooted in the traditions and conscience of our people as to be ranked as fundamental.'"[53] A state trial "is a mere pretense," and violates

---

44. *Id.* at 14–15.
45. *Ziang Sung Wan*, 266 U.S. at 16–17.
46. 297 U.S. 278 (1936).
47. *Id.* at 282.
48. *Id.* at 280.
49. *Id.* at 286.
50. 211 U.S. 78 (1908).
51. *Brown*, 297 U.S. at 285.
52. *Id.* Certainly, this declaration was in tension with *Bram*'s premise that the pressure generated by police interrogation was a proper object of Fifth Amendment regulation.
53. *Id.* (quoting Snyder v. Massachusetts, 291 U.S. 97, 105 (1934)).

the promise of due process of law, "where the state authorities have contrived a conviction resting solely upon confessions obtained by violence."[54] The Fourteenth Amendment "requires 'that state action . . . shall be consistent with . . . fundamental principles of liberty and justice,'"[55] and the trials of the *Brown* defendants were not. In the Court's view, it was "difficult to conceive of methods more revolting to the sense of justice than those taken to procure the confessions of these [defendants], and the use of the confessions thus obtained as the basis for conviction and sentence was a clear denial of due process."[56] The convictions had been obtained by inquisitorial methods prohibited by our Constitution and were "void for want of the essential elements of due process."[57]

Brown gave birth to the due process rule that bars coerced confessions from state criminal trials.[58] For almost three decades, this rule would prove to be the *only* basis invoked by the Supreme Court to resolve involuntary confession claims. In a long string of state cases, the Court would wrestle with the seemingly intractable problem of coerced confessions, refining and explaining the due process suppression doctrine along the way.[59] The discussion that follows highlights the most significant of these decisions.

Brown was an extreme case involving physical torture and brutality. The decision in *Chambers v. Florida*[60] proved that the due process bar extended to confessions coerced by less abusive methods. Over a 5-day period, officers who

---

54. *Id.* at 286.

55. *Id.* (quoting Hebert v. Louisiana, 272 U.S. 312, 316 (1926)).

56. *Brown*, 297 U.S. at 286.

57. *Id.* at 287.

58. According to one author, there were two reasons for the Court's use of the Constitution to intervene in state criminal justice processes—the use of brutality to preserve white supremacy in the South and the widespread use of "the third degree" by police interrogators. *See* Penney, *Theories of Confession Admissibility*, *supra* note 8, at 334–36. It is fair to assume that any constraints that the Fourteenth Amendment due process guarantee imposed on the states were also imposed on the federal government by the *identical* Fifth Amendment Due Process Clause. There would seem to have been no need to invoke that part of the Fifth Amendment for federal trials, however, because *Bram* had held that the privilege against compulsory self-incrimination barred involuntary confessions from federal trials.

59. Not once during this period did the Court rest a coerced confession decision on *Bram*'s Fifth Amendment privilege foundation. It has been suggested that the Court may have recognized that the application of the privilege outside the context of formal, legal compulsion—that is, its extension to police interrogation—had been a misstep. *See* Godsey, *Rethinking the Involuntary Confession Rule*, *supra* note 8, at 490, n.134. The *Brown* Court's suggestion that compulsion by torture is not a Fifth Amendment privilege concern lends support to that thesis. On the other hand, the involuntary confession claims resolved by the Court during this period were raised by defendants convicted in state proceedings.

60. 309 U.S. 227 (1940).

were investigating a murder engaged in prolonged, "persistent and repeated questioning" of 30 to 40 African-American suspects, but obtained no confessions.[61] When the interrogations continued, 4 of the suspects, the defendants in *Chambers*, eventually confessed. The state introduced these confessions at trial, and the defendants were convicted and sentenced to death.

The Supreme Court began with an explanation of the historical origins of the due process provision, observing that it had evolved from "popular hatred and abhorrence of illegal confinement, torture and extortion of confessions" and was an "assurance against [such] ancient evils."[62] More specifically, the guarantee of due process "sprang . . . from . . . the historical truth that the rights and liberties of people accused of crime could not be safely entrusted to secret *inquisitorial* processes."[63]

In *Chambers*, there was dispute over whether there had been physical violence and mistreatment of the suspects. The Court concluded that the undisputed methods used by the officers and the circumstances surrounding the interrogation were nonetheless "calculated to break the strongest nerves and the stoutest resistance."[64] Although there had been physical abuse in *Brown*, the Court's ruling had been "based upon the fact that the confessions were the result of compulsion."[65] In *Chambers*, the uncontested facts showed the officers had also used compulsion to obtain the confessions.[66] According to the Court, due process would be a "meaningless symbol" if confessions like these could be used to secure death sentences.[67] The state's contention that its methods were "necessary" to uphold the law was unpersuasive because "[t]he Constitution proscribes such lawless means irrespective of the end."[68] Thus, *Chambers* made it clear that physical mistreatment was not necessary to support the exclusion of a confession under the Due Process Clause; compulsion generated by protracted interrogation methods was sufficient.

Lisenba v. California[69] was the next significant opinion in the development of the due process-coerced confession doctrine. There was no doubt that before he confessed the defendant had been subjected to coercive pressures—including prolonged questioning—and that his confession was used to secure a murder conviction for which he was sentenced to death. It was plausible to conclude, however, that the improper actions of the officers had not coerced the defendant

61. *Id.* at 230.
62. *Id.* at 236, 237.
63. *Id.* at 237 (emphasis added).
64. *Id.* at 238–39.
65. *Chambers*, 309 U.S. at 239.
66. *Id.*
67. *Id.* at 240.
68. *Id.* at 240–41.
69. 314 U.S. 219 (1941).

into confessing. The Court held that even though officers had engaged in illegal and coercive interrogation methods the Due Process Clause did not require exclusion unless there was a causal relationship between the coercion and the confession. Because the facts in *Lisenba* did not establish that the defendant "had so lost his freedom of action that the statements made were . . . the result of the deprivation of his free choice to admit, to deny, or to refuse to answer," the use of those statements at trial did not violate the Fourteenth Amendment.[70]

The Court provided important insights concerning the underpinnings of the due process doctrine. Prior to *Lisenba*, it was arguable that the suppression of involuntary confessions was based entirely on their untrustworthiness. Put otherwise, the primary, if not the sole, basis for the bar to coerced confessions might have been the potential unreliability of forced disclosures. The *Lisenba* Court announced that, unlike the common law involuntary confession rule, the purpose of which was "to exclude false evidence," the "aim of . . . due process is . . . to prevent fundamental unfairness in the use of evidence, whether true or false."[71] Due process is denied when a defendant does not receive "a fair trial," and "unfairness exists when a coerced confession is used as a means of obtaining a verdict of guilt."[72] Courtroom threats or promises that induced a defendant to testify against himself would violate due process.[73] In the Court's view, the same result should follow if "by resort to the same means" the state induces a defendant to make an out-of-court confession and that confession is "given in evidence" at trial.[74]

The *Lisenba* Court provided a standard for judging involuntariness—whether an individual was deprived of the "free choice to admit, to deny, or to refuse to answer"—and also made it clear that preventing inaccurate verdicts was not the sole objective of the due process suppression doctrine. A criminal trial is unfair if a confession extorted from the accused by law enforcement officers is used to convict him, even if that confession is trustworthy proof of guilt.[75] The introduction of the confession can render the trial *process* fundamentally unfair whether or not it casts doubt on the reliability of the *outcome*.

The next noteworthy development occurred in *Ashcraft v. Tennessee*,[76] a case in which a man was convicted of the murder of his wife and sentenced to 99 years in prison. The confession used against him had been secured after 36 hours of continuous, incommunicado questioning by relays of officers, investigators, and lawyers. A majority of the Court decided that this confession was "not voluntary

70. *Id.* at 241.
71. *Id.* at 236.
72. *Id.* at 236–37.
73. *Id.* at 237.
74. *Lisenba*, 314 U.S. at 237.
75. *Id.* at 236.
76. 322 U.S. 143 (1944).

but compelled," because the situation was "so inherently coercive that its very existence [was] irreconcilable with the possession of mental freedom by a lone suspect against whom its full coercive force [was] brought to bear."[77] Testimony indicating that the defendant appeared to make his admissions freely did not persuade the Justices to the contrary. In their view, the pressures brought to bear on the defendant were so potent—so "inherently coercive"—that any person subjected to them would be deprived of "mental freedom" and compelled to speak.[78] The majority cited *Bram*, suggesting that the Fifth Amendment privilege rule barring "compelled or coerced" statements in federal trials and the Fourteenth Amendment due process rule that excluded "coerced" admissions from state trials were essentially the same.[79] The majority then concluded that under *Bram*'s demanding standard, the circumstances of *Ashcraft* "preclude[d] a holding that [the defendant] acted voluntarily" when he confessed.[80]

Later that year, the Court decided *Lyons v. Oklahoma*,[81] a case involving a murder conviction and a life sentence. After being arrested, the defendant had been subjected to two interrogation sessions. He claimed that he was physically assaulted during both sessions.[82] It was undisputed that the second session, which yielded an oral admission, lasted from 6:30 one evening until 2:30 the next morning and that the interrogators had placed a pan of the murder victim's bones in the defendant's lap.[83] Officials had then taken the defendant to a penitentiary in a different town where, late that same evening, he signed a second confession.[84] He contended that this latter confession, which was introduced at his murder trial, was the result of official force. Moreover, he maintained that even if the officers used no force on the later occasion, fear generated by the way the authorities treated him during the two prior interrogations had continued to exert coercive effects that rendered the signed confession inadmissible.[85]

The Supreme Court upheld the admission of the second confession, observing that the Fourteenth Amendment does not mandate suppression simply because officers at a time prior to a confession used "forbidden inducements."[86] The question is always whether the confession at issue is voluntary, and when a confession is given "subsequently to unlawful pressures, force or threats," the voluntariness of the confession "depends on . . . the continuing effect of

77. *Id.* at 153, 154.
78. *Id.* at 154.
79. *Id.* at 154 n.9.
80. *Id.*
81. 322 U.S. 596 (1944).
82. *Id.* at 599.
83. *Id.* at 599–600.
84. *Id.* at 600.
85. *Id.*
86. *Lyons*, 322 U.S. at 603.

the coercive practices."[87] Admissibility depends upon whether the suspect possessed the "'mental freedom' to confess to or deny" guilt at the time of the confession.[88] A post-coercion confession that is given freely is admissible because the affront to due process does not lie in the grievance the accused has against the police. Rather, a "coerced confession is offensive to basic standards of justice . . . because declarations procured by torture are not premises from which a civilized forum will infer guilt."[89] There was no due process violation in *Lyons* because there was ample evidence that the earlier abuse that did occur "did not bring about the [later] confession."[90]

Five years later, in *Watts v. Indiana*,[91] another capital murder case, the Court found a Fourteenth Amendment violation in the use of a confession obtained by law enforcement authorities who held the suspect in their exclusive control and subjected him to a series of interrogations extending over several days. The Court asserted that a statement "need not be volunteered" to be voluntary, but, instead, "must be the expression of free choice," and that a confession that "is the product of sustained pressure by the police . . . does not issue from a free choice."[92] The trial use of evidence "wrench[ed]" from a suspect during pretrial detention offends "the underlying principle" of our system, which is "accusatorial" in character, not "inquisitorial."[93] Prolonged official interrogation "for the purpose of eliciting disclosures or confessions" which the authorities could not extort from an accused on the witness stand "is subversive of the accusatorial system."[94] It is, in fact, worse than the inquisitorial process our nation rejected, for "[i]t is the inquisitorial system without [the] safeguards" present in the courtroom.[95]

In *Stein v. New York*,[96] which involved murder prosecutions and death sentences, a majority of the Court found no due process violation in the admission of confessions obtained by interrogating suspects in custody. The opinion provided insights into both the premises of the Fourteenth Amendment exclusion doctrine and the circumstances that are relevant to its application. The Court clarified an aspect of the voluntariness inquiry that had not been made explicit in prior opinions—that when a defendant alleges psychological coercion,

---

87. *Id.* at 602.

88. *Id.* (quoting Ashcraft v. Tennessee, 322 U.S. 143, 154 (1944)).

89. *Id.* at 605.

90. *Id.* at 604. Dissenting Justices who disagreed with this conclusion opined that the Court's due process decisions had effectively made the privilege against self-incrimination exclusion doctrine enunciated in *Bram* applicable to the states. *Id.* at 605–06 (Murphy, J., dissenting).

91. 338 U.S. 49 (1949).

92. *Id.* at 53.

93. *Id.* at 54.

94. *Id.* at 55.

95. *Id.*

96. 346 U.S. 156 (1953).

the admissibility of a confession "depend[s] upon a weighing of the circumstances of pressure against the power of resistance of the person confessing."[97] The due process inquiry is whether the particular suspect has been forced to speak and that depends not only on the coercive pressures applied, but also on the strength of that suspect's will. "What would be overpowering to the weak of will or mind might be utterly ineffective against" one with greater powers of resistance.[98] Moreover, the Due Process Clause does not demand that a confession must be either "voluntary in the sense that" an individual "wanted to make" it or "completely spontaneous."[99] A confession is constitutionally inadmissible *only* if it has been procured by physical or psychological coercion.

As to the nature of the Fourteenth Amendment "exclusionary rule," the *Stein* majority described it as "a guarantee against conviction on inherently untrustworthy evidence."[100] A conviction based on a coerced confession violates due process "because such a confession combines . . . persuasiveness . . . with what judicial experience shows to be *illusory* and *deceptive* evidence. A forced confession is a *false* foundation for any conviction."[101] The *Stein* majority's heavy emphasis upon the reliability rationale that was the core justification for the common law coerced confession rule stood in sharp contrast with the earlier declaration in *Lisenba* that the aim of due process was not to exclude false evidence, but to prevent fundamental unfairness in the use of true or false evidence.

Spano v. New York[102] was also a murder prosecution that had yielded a death sentence. The defendant, who had some unique weaknesses, confessed after approximately 8 hours of interrogation that, ultimately, involved the use of a deceptive ploy. According to the Court, the use of his statements at trial had violated the Fourteenth Amendment because "the totality" of the circumstances—that is, both the pressures applied to the suspect and his vulnerabilities—showed that his "will was overborne."[103] The Court prefaced its analysis of the facts with a terse, but pointed assertion that unreliability was not the sole concern of due process exclusion. According to Chief Justice Warren, "[t]he abhorrence of society to the use of involuntary confessions *does not turn alone on their inherent untrustworthiness.* It also turns on the deep-rooted feeling that the police must obey the law while enforcing the law" and that the use of illegal methods to

---

97. *Id.* at 185.

98. *Id.*

99. *Id.* at 186.

100. *Id.* at 192.

101. *Stein*, 348 U.S. at 192 (emphasis added).

102. 360 U.S. 315 (1959).

103. *Id.* at 323. This voluntariness standard—one which appeared to allow considerably more pressure to confess than *Bram*'s Fifth Amendment prohibition of any inducement by way of promise or threat—would become commonplace in subsequent due process analyses.

convict criminals are as dangerous to life and liberty as the acts of the criminals themselves.[104] In other words, while the Fourteenth Amendment does provide a shield against misleading evidence that can produce erroneous convictions, it also safeguards against improper, unfair procedures that are inconsistent with our commitment to accusatorial values.

The 1960s began with a significant opinion in *Blackburn v. Alabama.*[105] A young, black defendant suffering from serious mental illness was convicted of robbery and sentenced to 20 years in prison after a trial in which the state introduced a confession made after 8 or 9 hours of interrogation. The Court used the occasion to reflect upon the nature of the voluntariness inquiry, the governing standards, and the values underlying due process exclusion.

After first observing that "coercion can be mental as well as physical, and that the blood of the accused is not the only hallmark of an unconstitutional inquisition," the Court reiterated that the determination must be based on the totality of circumstances.[106] In the circumstances of *Blackburn*, there was only a "remote" chance that his confession was "*the product of a rational intellect and a free will.*"[107] Because the totality "clearly establishe[d] that the confession most probably was not *the product of any meaningful act of volition,*" it could "fairly be characterized only as involuntary."[108]

---

104. *Id.* at 320–21 (emphasis added). The Court did not, however, reject the need for a causal connection between unacceptably coercive police methods and the confession to be suppressed. In fact, a five-Justice majority had just recently reaffirmed that requirement in *Thomas v. Arizona*, 356 U.S. 390 (1958), a capital murder prosecution in which a black suspect was lassoed around the neck once, then around the neck or shoulders a second time. *Id.* at 395–96. He subsequently made an oral confession followed by two written confessions. A trial judge found that the written confessions had both been "'procured by threat of lynch' and declared [them] involuntary," but determined that the earlier oral confession was "voluntary." *Id.* at 400. After describing the "ropings" as "[d]eplorable . . . to the spirit of a civilized administration of justice," the Court nonetheless found no due process violation in the use of the defendant's oral confession because "the undisputed facts" did not establish that his "oral statement was a product of fear engendered by" the ropings. *Id.* The oral statement was not shown to be the result of "fear" that "overbore [his] free will," but, instead, "appear[ed] to be the spontaneous exclamation of a guilty conscience." *Id.* at 402.

105. 361 U.S. 199 (1960).

106. *Id.* at 206.

107. *Id.* at 208 (emphasis added).

108. *Id.* at 211, 205 (emphasis added). These doctrinal standards seemed less demanding than the "overborne will" criterion employed in *Spano* and other decisions. In fact, the "rational intellect and free will" and "meaningful act of volition" criteria seem closer in spirit to *Bram*'s Fifth Amendment standards. During the nearly three decades that followed the advent of the due process doctrine in *Brown v. Mississippi*, the Court appeared to vacillate between more and less stringent standards—that is, between those that allowed officers to apply a considerable amount of pressure and those that tolerated very little

The Court stressed that "important human values are sacrificed whe[n] . . . the government" secures a conviction by "wring[ing] a confession out of an accused against his will."[109] Our nation insists upon means "other than inquisition" in order to further "a complex of values."[110] The constitutional bar to coerced confessions not only guards against unreliability and preserves the individual's interests in free will and rational choice, it also implements the "strong conviction that our system of law enforcement should not operate so as to take advantage of a person" by convicting him on the basis of forced disclosures.[111] *Blackburn*, thus, reinforced the belief that the due process exclusionary rule safeguards liberties and expresses our abiding devotion to an accusatorial criminal justice system.

In *Malloy v. Hogan*,[112] a 1964 decision that did not involve the admissibility of a confession, the Court addressed an issue with important ramifications for confession law: whether the Fifth Amendment guarantee against compulsory self-incrimination was a part of the due process states must provide. Over 50 years earlier, in *Twining v. New Jersey*,[113] the Court had held that "the privilege against self-incrimination is not safeguarded against state action by the Fourteenth Amendment."[114] In *Malloy*, the Court reversed course, concluding that "the Fifth Amendment's exception from compulsory self-incrimination is also protected by the Fourteenth Amendment against abridgment by the States."[115] The Court relied heavily upon a somewhat surprising understanding of the due process opinions described in this historical account.

According to the *Malloy* majority, *Twining* had "impelled" the Court to base its holding in *Brown v. Mississippi* on the Due Process Clause and to deny application of the Fifth Amendment privilege.[116] The Court, however, had "soon abandoned" the distinction between the privilege and due process in favor of an approach that tests "the admissibility of a confession in a state criminal prosecution . . . by the same standard applied in federal prosecutions

---

infringement upon suspects' free wills. *See* Penney, *Theories of Confession Admissibility*, *supra* note 8, at 360 n.309 (noting that there was a move away from *Bram* but that the standards had "vacillated" over time); *see also* Monrad G. Paulsen, *The Fourteenth Amendment and the Third Degree*, 6 Stan. L. Rev. 411, 429–30 (1954) [hereinafter Paulsen, *The Fourteenth Amendment*] (suggesting that the due process decisions were the product of two distinct constitutional standards, one concerned with trustworthiness and one concerned with police methods).

109. *Blackburn*, 361 U.S. at 206–07.

110. *Id.* at 207.

111. *Id.*

112. 378 U.S. 1 (1964).

113. 211 U.S. 78 (1908).

114. *Malloy*, 378 U.S. at 2.

115. *Id.* at 6.

116. *Id.*

since" *Bram*.[117] The *Lisenba* decision had begun the "[t]he marked shift to the federal standard in state cases," reflecting a "recognition that the American system of criminal prosecution is accusatorial, not inquisitorial, and that the . . . privilege is its essential mainstay."[118]

In applying "the policies of the privilege itself" to state proceedings, the coerced confession cases had never suggested "that a confession might be considered coerced if used in a federal but not a state tribunal."[119] The test first announced in *Bram* to implement the mandate that a "person must not [be] compelled to incriminate himself" required a confession to be "'free and voluntary.'"[120] Later, the Court adopted the very "same standard" to determine whether due process allowed the admission "of a confession in a state criminal prosecution."[121] To be admissible, a confession could "'not be extracted by any sort of threats or violence, nor obtained by any direct or implied promises, however slight, nor by the exertion of any improper influence.'"[122]

In essence, *Malloy* declared that the due process exclusionary rule, announced 28 years earlier and applied in numerous state cases, was in fact identical in nature, objectives, and governing standards to the bar imposed by the privilege against compelled self-incrimination. The stringent Fifth Amendment criteria prescribed by *Bram*—which forbade "'slight'" promises and "'any improper influence'"—controlled both federal and state proceedings.[123] Like the Fifth Amendment, the Fourteenth Amendment encompasses a "right . . . to remain silent unless [a person] chooses to speak in the unfettered exercise of his own will."[124]

Despite this conclusion that the constraints of the privilege were binding on the states, just one week after *Malloy* the Court relied exclusively on the Due Process Clause in reversing yet another state murder conviction and death sentence. The core question in *Jackson v. Denno*,[125] the final decision included in this historical sketch, was whether states could allow the trial jurors to make the constitutional voluntariness determination. After observing that the Fourteenth Amendment mandates "a reliable determination of the voluntariness of [a] confession," the Court concluded that the issue of voluntariness must be resolved by a judge or by a separate jury, not by the jury that determines guilt.[126] In resolving

117. *Id.* at 6–7.
118. *Id.* at 7.
119. *Malloy*, 378 U.S. at 10.
120. *Id.* at 7 (quoting Bram v. United States, 168 U.S. 532, 542–43 (1897)).
121. *Id.* at 7.
122. *Id.* (quoting Bram v. United States, 168 U.S. 532, 542–43 (1897)).
123. *Id.* (quoting Bram v. United States, 168 U.S. 532, 542–43 (1897)).
124. *Malloy*, 378 U.S. at 8.
125. 378 U.S. 368 (1964).
126. *Id.* at 377, 391, n.19. The Court endorsed "the orthodox rule" under which judges alone decide the voluntariness question. The Court also approved "the Massachusetts

this procedural issue, the Court observed that due process accords defendants the "right to be free of a conviction based upon a coerced confession."[127] The Constitution mandates exclusion "not only because of the probable unreliability," of such a confession, but also because of the "'important human values . . . sacrificed'" when officials force a suspect to confess and because it is necessary for police to abide by the law when enforcing the law.[128]

The same year that it decided *Malloy* and *Denno*, the Supreme Court discovered another constitutional basis for excluding confessions. In *Massiah v. United States*,[129] the Court held that the Sixth Amendment right to counsel requires the suppression of some incriminating disclosures whether or not they are voluntary.[130] Two years later, the Court decided *Miranda v. Arizona*,[131] a novel interpretation of the Fifth Amendment privilege that announced another constitutional exclusionary rule for confessions.[132] According to that ruling, a confession obtained by custodial interrogation was inadmissible unless officers took steps to counteract the pressures inherent in that setting. As will be seen, these two new constitutional bases for excluding confessions dramatically altered the landscape, changing the role and status of the two bars to coerced confessions that are the subject of the instant chapter.[133]

---

procedure," which provides for an initial judicial determination. If the judge determines that the confession was not voluntary, the confession is excluded. If the judge determines that the confession was voluntary, the confession is admitted. Jurors are authorized to make a second determination of voluntariness and to ignore a confession that they find to have been coerced. *See id.* at 378–79, 378 n.8.

127. *Id.* at 377.

128. *Id.* at 385–86 (quoting Blackburn v. Alabama, 361 U.S. 199, 206 (1960)).

129. 377 U.S. 201 (1964).

130. This Sixth Amendment exclusionary rule is the subject of Chapter 4.

131. 384 U.S. 436 (1966).

132. If the original understanding of *Miranda* had prevailed, the discussion of its exclusion doctrine would be an inseparable part of this chapter's treatment of the Fifth Amendment bar to compelled confessions. Subsequent interpretations of *Miranda*, however, have cast its rule of inadmissibility as constitutional prophylaxis that provides necessary, but overbroad, shelter for the privilege against compulsory self-incrimination. The Court has made it clear that the privilege's bar to confessions and *Miranda*'s privilege-based suppression doctrine are distinct in character, rationale, and scope. For that reason, the *Miranda* exclusionary rule merits separate discussion. It is the focus of Chapter 3.

133. The decisions in *Massiah* and *Miranda* were in part reactions to a perception that the prohibition of coerced confessions had not proven to be an effective means of controlling inappropriate interrogation techniques and preventing constitutionally infirm convictions. *See* Martin R. Gardner, *The Emerging Good Faith Exception to the* Miranda *Rule—A Critique*, 35 HASTINGS L.J. 429, 446–48 (1984) [hereinafter Gardner, *Emerging Good Faith Exception*]; Godsey, *Rethinking the Involuntary Confession Rule*, *supra* note 8, at 499 (2005). Although these two new constitutional suppression doctrines supplemented the bars

Before beginning the analysis of the current coerced confession exclusion doctrines, a brief distillation of historical patterns and themes seems appropriate. It can hardly have escaped notice that a significant number of Supreme Court decisions involved murder convictions and death sentences.[134] Moreover, a considerable number of the defendants in the cases selected for review were seriously disadvantaged in one or more ways.[135] In addition, the Court frequently found that the state courts had erred by allowing the government to introduce confessions.[136] The Supreme Court was deeply concerned that individuals of limited abilities, means, and resources were suffering severe punishment due to convictions arrived at by methods incompatible with constitutional principles of fundamental fairness.

Legally, the due process exclusion doctrine dominated. Although the Court first invoked the Fifth Amendment privilege in two federal cases, the subsequent opinions all involved application of the Fourteenth Amendment to state convictions.[137] This was, of course, a necessary consequence of the Court's initial conclusion that the dictates of the Fifth Amendment privilege did not restrict the states. Nonetheless, even after the Court reversed that ruling and held that the Fourteenth Amendment includes the same constraints imposed by the privilege, the Court has continued to use due process, not the specific dictates of the privilege, as the basis for resolving true involuntary confession claims.[138] Not once has the Court relied on the Fifth Amendment privilege in deciding whether to suppress a confession alleged to be the product of official compulsion.[139]

It is also noteworthy that during the evolution of the coerced confession doctrine the Court occasionally intimated that the exclusionary dictates of

---

to introducing confessions discussed in this chapter, the *Massiah* and *Miranda* rules did not supplant or supersede the due process and privilege rules for coerced confessions.

134. Roughly two-thirds of *all* the cases the Court reviewed were capital, and approximately five-sixths involved death or very long prison sentences.

135. Some defendants were members of disfavored minority groups, some were impoverished, some were young, some suffered from mental disabilities, and some fell into more than one of these categories.

136. By my count, the Court found error in the admission of a confession in more than four-fifths of the cases.

137. *See* Godsey, *Rethinking the Involuntary Confession Rule*, *supra* note 8, at 489–90 (asserting that the Court ignored the Fifth Amendment privilege and the *Bram* holding during the era of due process decisions and that it was unclear whether *Bram* was still good law).

138. *See* Colorado v. Connelly, 479 U.S. 157, 163 (1986); Miller v. Fenton, 474 U.S. 104, 110 (1985).

139. The Court has relied on *Miranda*'s extension of the Fifth Amendment privilege to suppress confessions that are *presumed* to be compelled, but every case involving an allegation of *actual* compulsion has been resolved on the basis of due process.

the privilege and due process were essentially the same.[140] This infrequent suggestion has emerged as the controlling position today. The due process and privilege suppression doctrines are virtually, perhaps even precisely, identical in nature and in scope.[141] Moreover, during the nearly 30 years of due process decisions, the standards for determining whether a confession was involuntary, and therefore inadmissible, became increasingly more demanding than those first announced in *Bram*.[142] Although opinions occasionally favored standards forbidding even mild pressures to confess, the general trend was toward prohibiting only those pressures sufficient to overcome the will of the particular individual.[143] Despite this movement toward an involuntariness standard that allowed interrogators to employ more pressure, the Court was also clear that physical coercion was not the sole constitutional concern—the Constitution also barred the products of psychological force.[144]

The rationales for exclusion also evolved. Although the earliest due process decisions seemed to be concerned with unreliability—that is, the risk that extorted admissions could result in convictions of innocents—subsequent opinions that focused directly on constitutional justifications made it clear that other values were implicated. In the Court's view, neither the privilege nor the due process exclusionary rule was merely a filter designed to capture untrustworthy confessions. Both assured a fundamentally fair process consistent with our nation's rejection of inquisitorial methods.[145] Before examining the details of the current constitutional rules excluding involuntary confessions, an exploration of the character of and justifications for suppression is in order.

---

140. *See, e.g.*, Malloy v. Hogan, 378 U.S. 1, 7–8 (1964); Gallegos v. Colorado, 370 U.S. 49, 51–52 (1962); Ashcraft v. Tennessee, 322 U.S. 143, 154 n.9 (1944).

141. Any possible differences, which surely are relatively minor, will be described in the analytical sections of this chapter.

142. *See* Godsey, *Rethinking the Involuntary Confession Rule, supra* note 8, at 490; Penney, *Theories of Confession Admissibility, supra* note 8, at 332–33.

143. *See* Godsey, *Rethinking the Involuntary Confession Rule, supra* note 8, at 490–91.

144. *See* Blackburn v. Alabama, 361 U.S. 199, 206 (1960); Chambers v. Florida, 309 U.S. 227, 238–40 (1940).

145. Although this historical account of the due process and privilege doctrines ends in the 1960s, these two constitutional bases for exclusion have continued to evolve in the years since the Court announced that there were two additional bases for suppressing incriminating statements. These later historical developments have not been overlooked, but have been incorporated into the descriptions and analyses of the current doctrines.

C. THE NATURE OF AND RATIONALES FOR THE DUE PROCESS AND FIFTH AMENDMENT RULES

The nature of and rationales for the constitutional bars to coerced confessions stand in marked contrast to the nature of and rationales for the Fourth Amendment exclusionary rule. This section undertakes a detailed exploration and analysis of the characters of the Fifth and Fourteenth Amendment exclusion doctrines and of the constitutional justifications on which they rest. For the most part, the two rules are discussed jointly because their natures and underpinnings are identical. Any potential differences between these two bases for constitutional exclusion are highlighted along the way.

Both the privilege against compulsory self-incrimination and the guarantee of due process grant defendants *personal constitutional rights* to have involuntary confessions excluded from their trials. When the authorities force a confession from the mind of a suspect prior to trial, then use that confession against him in court, they effectively compel him to be a witness against himself in violation of the Fifth Amendment's command. The introduction of compelled disclosures deprives the defendant of this fundamental constitutional entitlement.[146] Similarly, to use a coerced confession at a criminal trial is to deny the accused his Fourteenth Amendment right not to be deprived of life or liberty without due process. The introduction of such evidence in court is a fundamentally unfair method of securing a conviction in violation of another basic constitutional right.[147]

One of the reasons our justice system accords defendants these rights to exclude evidence is to ensure the reliability of convictions.[148] It has long been acknowledged that admissions of guilt extorted from suspects by physical abuse, threats of violence, or psychological coercion are potentially untrustworthy.[149]

---

146. *See* United States v. Patane, 542 U.S. 630, 640 (2004); Chavez v. Martinez, 538 U.S. 760, 769 (2003) (plurality opinion); Kastigar v. United States, 406 U.S. 441, 461 (1972).

147. *See* Mincey v. Arizona, 437 U.S. 385, 398 (1978); Jackson v. Denno, 378 U.S. 368, 376 (1964).

148. *See* Jackson v. Denno, 378 U.S. at 385–86 ("It is now inescapably clear that the Fourteenth Amendment forbids the use of involuntary confessions . . . because of the probable unreliability of confessions that are obtained in a manner deemed coercive. . . .").

149. *See* Rex v. Warickshall, 1 Leach 263, 263–64, 168 Eng. Rep. 234, 235 (K.B. 1783) ("[A] confession forced from the mind by the flattery of hope, or by the torture of fear, comes in so questionable a shape when it is to be considered as the evidence of guilt, that no credit ought to be given to it; and therefore it is rejected."). The common law rule was concerned exclusively with the unreliability of involuntary confessions. *See* Godsey, *Rethinking the Involuntary Confession Rule*, *supra* note 8, at 481–82. Although the Court's first decision excluding an involuntary confession under the Due Process Clause, *Brown v. Mississippi*, did not explicitly state that unreliability was the reason for suppression, some scholars have concluded that it was the primary rationale for that ruling. *See* Laurie

A suspect who is beaten, threatened with abuse, or interrogated for hours or days on end by multiple state officials in close quarters might falsely confess to end the ordeal.[150] Even lesser pressures might lead a vulnerable suspect to tell officers whatever they want to hear, whether or not it is the truth. If the assurance of fundamental fairness extended by the Due Process Clause means anything, it means that the government will not manufacture misleading evidence of guilt and then convict an innocent person based on that evidence. The extreme unfairness of depriving a person of freedom for an offense she did not commit is beyond dispute.[151] Similarly, one goal of the Fifth Amendment privilege is to guard against unreliable convictions based on untrustworthy, compelled revelations.[152] The array of values underlying that guarantee includes a commitment to avoid convicting innocent persons based on confessions that are unreliable because law enforcement brought pressures to bear that overcame suspects' abilities to resist.

Magid, *Deceptive Police Interrogation Practices: How Far Is Too Far?*, 99 MICH. L. REV. 1168, 1173–74 (2001) (suggesting concern with unreliability was *Brown*'s primary basis); Paulsen, *The Fourteenth Amendment, supra* note 108, at 414–17 (asserting that *Brown* and other early due process rulings rested mainly on a concern with the reliability of involuntary confessions).

150. *See* Stein v. New York, 346 U.S. 156, 182 (1953); Ashcraft v. Tennessee, 322 U.S. 143, 160 (1944) (Jackson, J., dissenting).

151. The Court has repeatedly observed that the aim of the Due Process Clause "'is not to exclude presumptively false evidence.'" *See* Colorado v. Connelly, 479 U.S. 157, 167 (1986) (quoting Lisenba v. California, 314 U.S. 219, 236 (1941)). This should not be understood as a declaration that the Fourteenth Amendment is not concerned with potential unreliability generated by coercion. In fact, the Court has often indicated that untrustworthiness is not the *only* reason for due process exclusion, an acknowledgment that it is among the justifications for suppression. *See, e.g.*, Jackson v. Denno, 378 U.S. 368, 385–86 (1964); Spano v. New York, 360 U.S. 315, 320–21 (1959). The observation that excluding falsehood is not the aim of due process is better understood as expressing the view that a risk of unreliability *alone* is not a constitutionally sufficient basis for suppressing evidence. The introduction of false evidence, an unreliable confession, does undermine fundamental fairness, but *only* when the government has sufficient responsibility for generating the risk of falsehood.

152. *See* Withrow v. Williams, 507 U.S. 680, 692 (1993); Michigan v. Tucker, 417 U.S. 433, 448 (1974). Scholars differ over whether reliability was originally an aim of the privilege against compelled self-incrimination. Some argue that ensuring the accuracy of the truth-seeking process was not a function of the privilege. *See* Davies, *Original Fifth Amendment, supra* note 8, at 1007; Godsey, *Rethinking the Involuntary Confession Rule, supra* note 8, at 484. Others maintain that reliability is an objective of the privilege. *See* Lawrence Herman, *Unexplored Relationship, supra* note 12, at 188; Penney, *Theories of Confession Admissibility, supra* note 8, at 314. There can be no doubt, however, that the Supreme Court considers the prevention of untrustworthiness as one of the goals of the bar to compelled, testimonial self-incrimination.

The concern with trustworthiness, however, is not the sole basis for either constitutional right that guards against conviction on the basis of an involuntary confession. Both the Fifth and Fourteenth Amendments guarantee a fair trial *process*. Both reflect an abiding dedication to an accusatorial system—one in which the government does not pressure an accused to disclose what he knows about his guilt, then use those disclosures to obtain a conviction.[153] That methodology is the essence of the inquisitorial approach rejected by our Constitution. The entitlement to fundamental fairness captured by the notion of due process assumes a system consistent with accusatorial values. These values, which include a commitment to "'fair play which dictates "a fair state-individual balance [that requires] the government to leave the individual alone . . . [and] to shoulder the entire load,"'" are also the foundation of the Fifth Amendment privilege.[154] Whether coerced confessions are true or false, they are excluded because their introduction at trial would nullify the dual constitutional guarantees of a fair accusatorial process. In sum, the constitutional rights to suppress involuntary confessions are grounded not only in the vital interest in fair outcomes, but also in the critical interest in fair procedures. Even when there is no threat of untrustworthiness, the use of a coerced confession transgresses a core principle of accusatorial system fair play.

Unlike Fourth Amendment suppression, which is purely a deterrent safeguard designed to prevent future out-of-court constitutional deprivations, evidentiary suppression under the privilege and due process guarantee is an in-court entitlement of the accused that is essential to prevent present constitutional harm. The suppression of coerced confessions probably also has future deterrent *effects*. The bars to involuntary statements surely must alter the conduct of some officers. The question is whether deterring future conduct by law enforcement officers is merely a by-product of suppression or, instead, an ancillary *objective* of exclusion.

The Supreme Court's opinions provide little insight into the legitimacy of a deterrent rationale for Fifth or Fourteenth Amendment exclusion. Although some discussions in the Court's due process opinions can be construed as suggestions that the courtroom bar to coerced confessions seeks to deter unacceptable behavior by interrogators, deterrence has not been an explicit theme of Fourteenth Amendment rulings.[155] Moreover, in large part because none of the Court's

---

153. *See* Arizona v. Fulminante, 499 U.S. 279, 293–94 (1991) (White, J., dissenting); Miller v. Fenton, 474 U.S. 104, 109–10 (1985).

154. Withrow v. Williams, 507 U.S. 680, 692 (1993) (quoting Murphy v. Waterfront Comm'n of New York Harbor, 378 U.S. 52, 55 (1964)).

155. One modern due process opinion posits, without discussion, that the suppression of a coerced confession is designed to deter official mistreatment of suspects. *See* Colorado v. Connelly, 479 U.S. 157, 166 (1986) (stating that the purpose of the exclusion of evidence obtained in violation of the Constitution is deterrence); *see also* Paulsen, *The Fourteenth Amendment*, *supra* note 108, at 420–21 (suggesting that the Court has excluded coerced

coerced confession opinions rest on the privilege, there are positively no discussions of whether Fifth Amendment exclusion rests on a deterrent rationale.[156]

It is arguable that deterrence can justify evidentiary suppression *only* when the conduct to be deterred actually violates a constitutional right. According to the Court, out-of-court compulsion to speak *never* violates the Fifth Amendment privilege because the guarantee against being compelled to be a *witness* against oneself provides protection *only in the courtroom*.[157] Suppression, therefore, would not prevent a Fifth Amendment transgression merely by discouraging officers from forcing a suspect to confess. Exclusion would "deter" an actual constitutional transgression only insofar as the compulsion that is discouraged would have produced a disclosure that would have been used at trial. In a perfect world, judges would identify and bar from trial every compelled confession. In that case, there would be no Fifth Amendment violations to deter. In the real world, however, perfection is unattainable. Forced disclosures might not be accurately identified as the products of overborne wills. By deterring officers from pressuring suspects, exclusion *could* prevent the obtainment of a coerced confession that would not have been identified. A Fifth Amendment violation that would have occurred at trial would thereby be prevented.

The due process analysis is a bit different. Although not all official coercion to confess violates the Fourteenth Amendment, extremely coercive mistreatment of a suspect can, by itself, deprive a person of liberty without due process of law.[158]

---

confessions not just to guard against erroneous convictions, but also to discourage illegal police practices).

156. There are opinions indicating that suppression of a confession under *Miranda v. Arizona*—an outgrowth of the privilege—seeks to deter failures to honor that decision's guidelines for custodial interrogation. *See* Oregon v. Elstad, 470 U.S. 298, 308 (1985); Michigan v. Tucker, 417 U.S. 433, 446–47 (1974). If that is so, then one might logically conclude that suppression under the privilege itself is designed to discourage officers from compelling suspects to admit their guilt. Recently, however, the legitimacy of a deterrent rationale for *Miranda* suppression has been called into question. *See* United States v. Patane, 542 U.S. 630, 642 (2004) (plurality opinion) (rejecting deterrence as a basis for exclusion); *id.* at 645 (Kennedy, J., concurring in the judgment) (reserving judgment on whether deterrence is a basis). This issue is discussed in detail in Chapter 3.

157. *See* Chavez v. Martinez, 538 U.S. 760, 766–73 (2003) (opinion of Thomas, J.); *id.* at 777–78 (Souter, J., concurring in the judgment). Some Justices disagreed, opining that a Fifth Amendment violation can occur at the time officers subject suspects to compelling pressures. *See id.* at 789–95 (Kennedy, J., concurring in part and dissenting in part). Some scholars believe that the majority's restrictive interpretation of the Fifth Amendment is patently incorrect. In their view, the origins and history of the privilege demonstrate that it was designed to protect individuals against governmental efforts to compel them to accuse themselves. *See* Davies, *Original Fifth Amendment*, *supra* note 8, at 998, 1000; Godsey, *Rethinking the Involuntary Confession Rule*, *supra* note 8, at 478–80, 495–96.

158. *See Chavez*, 538 U.S. at 774–75; *id.* at 779 (Souter, J., concurring in the judgment).

In other words, sufficiently harmful official misconduct can effect a Fourteenth Amendment deprivation not only when a resulting disclosure is used to convict, but also *at the time of the misconduct*.[159] If suppression motivates officers not to engage in such misconduct during future interrogations, it can deter actual constitutional transgressions prior to trial. As with the privilege, suppression might also prevent violations of the right to due process at trial by preventing the generation of coerced confessions that could be erroneously admitted.

It is also arguable that pretrial coercive conduct that does not violate the Constitution is still an appropriate goal of deterrence. One might contend that even if official coercion does not inflict a constitutionally cognizable injury, it is harmful, objectionable, and should be discouraged. If deterrence is sometimes desirable even when the targeted conduct does not deprive anyone of a constitutional right, then it might serve as an ancillary justification for the suppression of all coerced confessions.

For the most part, whether deterrence is a justification for excluding involuntary confessions is of only theoretical significance. As a practical matter, in most cases where the admission of a coerced confession is at issue, suppression will be necessary to avoid depriving the accused of Fifth and Fourteenth Amendment trial rights. Whether or not deterrence is a goal, the evidence will be excluded. There are situations, however, where a particular defendant may not be entitled to bar a disclosure—that is, where neither the right not to be compelled to be a witness against oneself nor the right to due process would be violated by the use of a forced admission. In those situations, which are surely limited in number, the appropriateness of constitutional exclusion *could* hinge on whether deterring future misconduct is a legitimate rationale for suppression.

As discussed in Chapter 1, some judges and scholars believe that the Fourth Amendment exclusionary rule is an illegitimate creation of the Supreme Court that is neither dictated nor justified by the Constitution. Such is not the case with the exclusion of coerced confessions. To be sure, some have contended that the Fifth Amendment privilege is not an appropriate foundation for suppression because the compulsion it refers to and prohibits is legal compulsion brought to bear in formal court proceedings.[160] In their view, informal, extra-legal, law

159. The standards for determining when coercive mistreatment of a suspect by itself amounts to a violation of substantive due process are murky, at best. Some Justices have suggested that it may depend on whether officers' conduct was "outrageous," *id.* at 779 (Souter, J., concurring in the judgment), while others have indicated that mistreatment violates the Fourteenth Amendment when it is "'egregious'" or "'conscience shocking.'" *Id.* at 774–75 (plurality opinion of Thomas, J.). Official mistreatment of an individual that is sufficiently injurious would violate due process whether or not it was aimed at securing or did secure a confession.

160. *See* Miranda v. Arizona, 384 U.S. 436, 510–11 (1966) (Harlan, J., dissenting). Wigmore, the preeminent authority on the law of evidence, believed that the privilege against compelled self-incrimination protected only against "legal compulsion," and

enforcement compulsion that forces a suspect to admit guilt is not governed by the Fifth Amendment privilege. Although some probably still adhere to this limiting interpretation of the privilege, the issue is no longer a subject of judicial or scholarly debate and division. The Supreme Court, without disagreement, has announced that the Fifth Amendment privilege precludes the use of coerced confessions at trial.[161] Moreover, since the Court's first due process decision in 1936, *Brown v. Mississippi*, it has been undisputed that the Fourteenth Amendment Due Process Clause forbids the use of involuntary confessions to secure convictions. Because the due process right to exclude a confession is essentially the same as the Fifth Amendment right—both bar disclosures forced from the accused's mind—whether the privilege is a legitimate foundation for suppression is of no practical significance.[162]

D. THE REACH OF THE FOURTEENTH AND FIFTH AMENDMENT RIGHTS TO EXCLUSION

This final section describes and analyzes the contours of the rights to exclusion currently granted by the Fourteenth and Fifth Amendments. The focus is first on the general scope of the rights—that is, the requirements that must be satisfied to give rise to the entitlement to suppression. After this explanation of the basics, the limitations upon the rights to exclusion are analyzed.

1. Evidence Subject to Suppression under the Due Process Clause and the Privilege against Compulsory Self-Incrimination

a. The Meaning of Involuntariness The basic exclusionary commands of the Fourteenth and Fifth Amendments are identical: both require the suppression of involuntary confessions.[163] To qualify as involuntary, a disclosure must be

---

maintained, therefore, that it did not govern the pressures brought to bear by police interrogation. *See* Davies, *Original Fifth Amendment, supra* note 8, at 1025.

161. *See* Dickerson v. United States, 530 U.S. 428, 433 (2000); Miller v. Fenton, 474 U.S. 104, 110 (1985). In *Michigan v. Tucker*, 417 U.S. 433 (1974), the Court observed that although the "language" of the Fifth Amendment might seem to restrict it to situations involving compulsion to testify at a criminal trial, the Court had not "limited" its "application" to that situation. *Id.* at 440. Instead, the Court had extended the right to other contexts, including police interrogation, in order to prevent the "inability to protect the right" at an earlier stage from rendering it "useless" at trial. *Id.* at 440–41.

162. The point is that if the Court concluded that the Fifth Amendment had no bearing on police interrogation, not a single confession that is excluded currently because it has been coerced by official pressures would become admissible. The identical due process right to exclusion would continue to mandate suppression.

163. *See Dickerson*, 530 U.S. at 433 (recognizing the dual constitutional sources for the suppression of coerced confessions); Davis v. North Carolina, 384 U.S. 737, 740 (1966) (suggesting that the due process doctrine is grounded in the policies of the privilege and

the product of coercion or compulsion. It must result from pressures that overbear the will of the individual and force him to confess.[164] The Court has definitively rejected the undemanding standard promulgated in its first constitutional confession case, *Bram v. United States*. The Constitution does not demand that a confession be wholly voluntary, uninfluenced by hope or fear. *Bram*'s bar to confessions obtained by "'"any . . . promises, however slight, [or] by the exertion of any improper influence"'" clearly "does not state the standard for determining the voluntariness of a confession" today.[165]

Subjective factors that bear upon the strength or weakness of the suspect's will are highly relevant to the determination.[166] Thus, if a suspect is young, mentally infirm, under the influence of alcohol, or has no experience with official interrogation, her will may be more easily overcome. Conversely, a suspect's high intelligence, maturity, and extensive experience with law enforcement could all weigh against a finding that her will was broken. It is important to note, however, that internal pressures *alone*, psychological compulsions that induce a person to speak involuntarily, cannot suffice.[167] Thus, if a mentally disturbed suspect hears hallucinatory commands threatening him with death if he does not confess, the decision to admit guilt is not "involuntary" for constitutional purposes. A certain amount of external coercive pressure is essential for constitutional exclusion.[168] Moreover, the necessary coercion *must* be applied by officials—that is, by persons acting for the government. Private party coercion is not a subject of constitutional concern.[169] If a relative of a crime victim were to

---

that the standard that evolved for states under the Fourteenth Amendment was essentially the same standard dictated in federal courts by the Fifth Amendment).

164. *See* Mincey v. Arizona, 437 U.S. 385, 401–02 (1978).

165. Arizona v. Fulminante, 499 U.S. 279, 285 (1991) (quoting Bram v. United States, 168 U.S. 532, 542–43 (1897) (quoting 3 H. Smith & A. Keep, Russell on Crimes and Misdemeanors 478 (6th ed. 1896))).

166. *Dickerson*, 530 U.S. at 434; Colorado v. Connelly, 479 U.S. 157, 164–65 (1986).

167. *See Connelly*, 479 U.S. at 164-65.

168. *See id.* at 165, 167. While *Connelly* made it clear that "some" coercion is needed, it left the minimal amount of external pressure necessary to render a confession coerced undefined and uncertain. It bears mention that while the Constitution does not mandate suppression, a jurisdiction could adopt an evidentiary rule barring an internally compelled admission.

The Court has acknowledged that the "hybrid quality" of the standards for determining whether a confession is constitutionally involuntary—that is, the need to determine whether a person's admission was the product of an overborne will in light of the totality of internal and external variables—complicates the inquiry. *See* Miller v. Fenton, 474 U.S. 104, 116 (1985); Culombe v. Connecticut, 367 U.S. 568, 605 (1961) (describing the standard as "amphibi[ous]"). The voluntariness inquiry has been the target of scathing criticism by scholars. *See Miller*, 474 U.S. at 116 n.4.

169. *See Connelly*, 479 U.S. at 166 (stating that private party coercion is not a due process concern); Oregon v. Elstad, 470 U.S. 298, 304–05 (1985) (asserting that official compulsion is necessary to trigger the protection of the Fifth Amendment).

torture a person until he admitted his guilt, neither constitutional guarantee would bar that confession.

b. The Restriction to Confessions The evidence presumptively subject to suppression is a confession—a suspect's disclosure of information relevant to proving her guilt.[170] Although the revelation is typically made by spoken or written *words*, it is also possible for a suspect's coerced *acts* to be subject to suppression because they reveal incriminating thoughts or knowledge.[171] Because the Fifth Amendment privilege against being compelled to be "a witness" against oneself bars *only* "testimonial" evidence,[172] the right to exclusion does not encompass either physical evidence that a person has been compelled to surrender[173] or nontestimonial actions that a person has been compelled to perform.[174] The Fifth Amendment guarantee bars only compelled disclosures—thoughts that officials have forced a person to reveal. The due process right could be different in this respect. It is not inconceivable that the Fourteenth Amendment deems it fundamentally unfair for the government to coerce the production of "nontestimonial" evidence and then use that evidence to secure a conviction. In the decided cases, however, the due process right to exclusion has also been restricted to coerced confessions.[175]

---

170. Confessions are thought to be very probative of guilt and very damaging to an accused when admitted at trial. *See Fulminante*, 499 U.S. at 292 (White, J., dissenting).

171. *See* United States v. Hubbell, 530 U.S. 27, 36 (2000).

172. *See Elstad*, 470 U.S. at 304; United States v. Wade, 388 U.S. 218, 221–22 (1967).

173. *See* Schmerber v. California, 384 U.S. 757, 764–65 (1966) (concluding that the Fifth Amendment did not prohibit the admission of a blood sample forcibly taken from a suspect).

174. *See Wade*, 388 U.S. at 222 (requiring a suspect to appear in a lineup and speak words for identification purposes does not compel a testimonial act because it does not force the revelation of knowledge).

175. In *Rochin v. California*, 342 U.S. 165 (1952), the Court did hold that a state violated due process when it convicted an accused based on the evidence forcibly pumped from his stomach because the government's "conduct . . . shock[ed] the conscience." *Id.* at 172. *Rochin*, however, was decided before *Mapp v. Ohio* determined that the evidentiary products of unreasonable searches and seizures were generally barred from state trials. Today, the methods used in *Rochin* would render evidence inadmissible under the state counterpart of the Fourth Amendment exclusionary rule. *See supra* Chapter 1, text accompanying notes 79–91. It seems unlikely that any coerced nontestimonial evidence that is not excluded by the *Mapp* rule would be subject to suppression as a matter of pure due process.

It is interesting that the historical source of the Fifth Amendment privilege—the "nemo tenetur" doctrine—*did* extend to compelled physical evidence while the source of the due process bar to involuntary confessions—the common law rule of evidence—*did not* include coerced physical evidence. *See* Davies, *Original Fifth Amendment*, *supra* note 8, at 1006, 1023.

c. The Need for a Causal Connection Implicit in the preceding description of the basic requirements for evidentiary suppression is the need for a causal connection between the requisite governmental coercion and the incriminating disclosures. An accused has constitutional entitlements not to be convicted on thoughts forced from her mind. The official pressure must, in fact, overbear the suspect's will and produce the confession.[176] A confession is admissible if interrogators use objectionably coercive methods but a suspect confesses voluntarily, not because the coercion broke his resolve and prompted him to speak against his will. There is no need that the suspect confess *at the time* the officials apply the pressures. A confession given some time after unacceptably coercive conduct may be the delayed result of the effects of that conduct on the mind of a suspect.[177] If so, the Constitution mandates exclusion. Nonetheless, it is entirely possible for coercive pressures to confess to dissipate as time passes and circumstances change, and a later disclosure may be the result of a free choice rather than an overborne will. Despite the earlier pressures to speak, such an admission is not subject to suppression as a "coerced confession."[178]

d. The Exclusion of Derivative Evidence The primary evidence that a defendant has Fifth and Fourteenth Amendment rights to suppress is always an involuntary confession obtained as a direct result of official pressures. Coerced revelations sometimes lead to the acquisition of additional evidence—incriminating physical evidence, inculpatory statements by witnesses, or successive, but voluntary, confessions by the accused herself, for example. The question here is whether such "derivative evidence" is also subject to exclusion.

The Fifth Amendment privilege-based right to exclude compelled testimonial evidence *does* encompass evidence derived from involuntary statements. According to the Court, "those subjected to coercive police interrogations have *an automatic protection from* the use of their involuntary statements (or *evidence derived from their statements*) in any subsequent criminal trial."[179] Although the

---

176. *See* Thomas v. Arizona, 356 U.S. 390, 400–02 (1958).

177. *See* Oregon v. Elstad, 470 U.S. 298, 310 (1985) (recognizing that the potential effects of actual coercion on the mind of a suspect can dissipate with the passage of time and the change of circumstances, and that a subsequent statement might be admissible because it was not the product of that coercion).

178. It is arguable, nonetheless, that a confession that is not itself coerced should be suppressed because it is an evidentiary product of the earlier coercion—that is, that there is a causal link between the coerced statement and the subsequent, voluntary disclosure. This question is addressed below.

179. Chavez v. Martinez, 538 U.S. 760, 769 (2003) (emphasis added in part); *see also* United States v. Patane, 542 U.S. 630, 644 (2004) (plurality opinion) (noting that the Court's interpretation of the Fifth Amendment "requires the exclusion of the physical fruit of actually coerced statements"); United States v. Hubbell, 530 U.S. 27, 38 (2000) (referring to "the Fifth Amendment's protection against the prosecutor's use of incriminating information derived directly or indirectly from . . . compelled testimony");

evidence forced from a suspect must initially be testimonial in nature,[180] the constitutional right to exclusion extends to nontestimonial evidence that the government acquires by exploiting coerced disclosures. The government violates a defendant's entitlement not to be convicted on compelled testimony if it uses either the coerced confession or incriminating evidence of any sort obtained as a consequence of that confession.[181] This derivative evidence bar extends to physical evidence such as drugs, firearms, or computer records. It also must reach statements and testimony given by witnesses found as a result of the compelled revelations. In addition, it would seem to require the suppression of a subsequent voluntary confession made by the coerced suspect *if* there is a causal link between the involuntary and voluntary disclosures.[182] A defendant's awareness that he has once admitted his guilt to the authorities could induce him to repeat and even embellish the contents of the initial admission.[183]

None of the Court's discussions of evidence derived from coerced confessions has involved the Fourteenth Amendment bar to coerced confessions.[184] It seems

---

Kastigar v. United States, 406 U.S. 441, 462 (1972) (recognizing that under the Fifth Amendment when a defendant establishes coercion, both "his confession and evidence derived from it become inadmissible").

180. *See Hubbell*, 530 U.S. at 34.

181. The initial, coerced statement need not be a confession in the sense that it is probative of guilt. The bar to derivative evidentiary fruits applies even if the forced disclosures themselves are not incriminating. *Hubbell*, 530 U.S. at 37.

182. It seems entirely possible that a defendant who first confesses because his will has been overborne by official pressure could freely choose to confess a second time—i.e., that a later decision to make revelations might not be coerced. The Supreme Court clearly believes a subsequent decision might be voluntary. *See Elstad*, 470 U.S. at 310–12 (noting that when a first confession is coerced circumstances may show that coercion did not carry over to a second confession).

183. This is known as the "cat out of the bag" phenomenon. A defendant who has once confessed may well confess again because he realizes that he has already "let the cat out of the bag." *See* United States v. Bayer, 331 U.S. 532, 540 (1947). The Court has refused to apply the principle to exclude successive confessions made after initial confessions obtained in violation of the *Miranda* warnings requirement. *See Elstad*, 470 U.S. at 311–14. The reasoning and holding of *Elstad*, however, are clearly limited to cases involving initial confessions that are not *actually coerced*. *See id.* at 310, 318. In a subsequent opinion, Justice O'Connor, the author of *Elstad*, observed that the Court rejected the "cat out of the bag" principle under *Miranda* as a matter of law. It had not denied that as a matter of psychological fact a defendant who has once confessed might well be inclined to confess a second time because of his awareness that he has already divulged his guilt. *See* Missouri v. Seibert, 542 U.S. 600, 627 (2004) (O'Connor, J., dissenting). There is good reason to believe, therefore, that when a genuinely coerced admission leads a defendant to make a second, voluntary confession, the defendant has a Fifth Amendment right to exclude the second confession under the derivative evidence principle.

184. In *Malinski v. New York*, 324 U.S. 401 (1945), Justice Rutledge, in dissent, indicated that the due process evidentiary bar must extend to derivative evidence, including

virtually certain, however, that the due process exclusionary right also includes derivative fruits.[185] In the first place, one of the opinions endorsing the Fifth Amendment bar to derivative evidence cites and relies on due process decisions.[186] This indicates an inclination to treat the due process and privilege rights identically insofar as derivative evidence is concerned. Moreover, in an opinion addressing Fourteenth Amendment suppression, the Court announced that "*any* criminal trial use against a defendant of his *involuntary* statement is a denial of due process of law,"[187] and that "[d]ue process . . . requires that [involuntary] statements . . . cannot be used *in any way* against a defendant at his trial."[188] The introduction of evidence gained by exploiting an involuntary statement arguably falls within the prohibition on using that statement "in any way." Finally, the Fifth Amendment derivative evidence principle rests on the premise that the trial use of the fruits of a coerced testimonial disclosure is inconsistent with the anti-inquisitorial policies and values underlying the privilege. The use of derivative evidence would seem equally irreconcilable with the accusatorial system principles that give meaning to the Due Process Clause guarantee of fundamental fairness. In sum, both the Fifth and Fourteenth Amendment rights to exclusion would seem to bar not only the coerced disclosures themselves, but also any other evidence that the government acquires as a result.

2. Proceedings in Which the Rights to Exclude Apply

The Fifth Amendment forbids compelling a person "to be a witness against himself" in "any criminal case." That provision protects against compelled self-*incrimination*; it does not provide shelter against harmful *civil* case consequences that might result from compelled testimony.[189] Similarly, the Due Process Clause

---

successive confessions. *Id.* at 422–23 (Rutledge, J., dissenting). None of the Court's due process opinions suggests that his view is misguided.

185. The original common law rule barring involuntary confessions did *not* require the exclusion of physical fruits because the sole concern of that rule of evidence was to guard against unreliability. *See* Davies, *Original Fifth Amendment*, *supra* note 8, at 1023. While involuntary statements might mislead the trier of fact, physical fruits would not. The logic of this limitation does not carry over to the due process exclusion doctrine because the constitutional objective is not merely to exclude unreliable evidence "but to prevent fundamental unfairness in the use of evidence, whether true or false." Lisenba v. California, 314 U.S. 219, 236 (1941).

186. *See* Kastigar v. United States, 406 U.S. 441, 461 n.53, n.54 (1972) (citing and relying on *Spano v. New York*, 360 U.S. 315 (1959) and *Jackson v. Denno*, 378 U.S. 368 (1964) in discussing the exclusion of evidence derived from coerced confessions).

187. Mincey v. Arizona, 437 U.S. 385, 398 (1978) (emphasis in original).

188. *Id.* at 402 (emphasis added).

189. The very terms of the Fifth Amendment clearly confine its shelter to "criminal case[s]." Thus, while the privilege prohibits adverse inferences from a defendant's refusal to testify in a criminal case, *see* Griffin v. California, 380 U.S. 609, 614 (1965), it permits such inferences in civil proceedings. *See* Mitchell v. United States, 526 U.S. 314, 328 (1999);

has been interpreted to bar the use of coerced statements in *criminal* prosecutions because of the threat to the accusatorial nature of our *criminal* justice system.[190] The Supreme Court's coerced confession decisions, therefore, accord defendants entitlements to bar coerced disclosures from criminal cases. They grant no entitlement to suppress coerced confessions from any type of civil proceeding.

The Fifth and Fourteenth Amendments require that evidence be excluded from *trials*.[191] The Supreme Court has also concluded that a *sentencing proceeding* is an integral part of a "criminal case" for Fifth Amendment purposes.[192] To compel a convicted defendant to provide testimony in a sentencing hearing that could render him liable to the "adverse consequences" of increased punishment "'clearly would contravene the Fifth Amendment.'"[193] Because the government's use of compelled pretrial disclosures for sentencing purposes would also "contravene" the privilege, the constitutional right to exclude coerced confessions must reach sentencing proceedings as well.[194]

Baxter v. Palmigiano, 425 U.S. 308, 318 (1976). A person *is* entitled to refuse to testify in a civil proceeding on Fifth Amendment grounds, but not because of the harms of a civil nature that might ensue. The reason for Fifth Amendment protection against being forced to testify in a civil case is the risk that revelations made there might be used adversely in a later criminal proceeding. *See* Lefkowitz v. Turley, 414 U.S. 70, 77 (1973).

190. Unlike the Fifth Amendment, the Fourteenth Amendment's language does not preclude application to civil proceedings. In fact, the guarantee of due process does ensure a fundamentally fair process in civil cases. *See,* e.g. Mathews v. Eldridge, 424 U.S. 319 (1976); Goldberg v. Kelly, 397 U.S. 254 (1970); *see also* Akhil Reed Amar, *Constitutional Redundancies and Clarifying Clauses,* 33 Val. U. L. Rev. 1, 19 (1998). It seems more than unlikely, however, that the due process right to exclude coerced confessions—which is inextricably tied to fundamental premises about the nature of our criminal justice system—would be extended to civil actions.

191. As noted in Chapter 1, the Supreme Court has held that in habeas corpus proceedings challenging state convictions, prisoners may not raise Fourth Amendment exclusionary rule claims unless the state court did not provide a full and fair hearing. *See* Stone v. Powell, 428 U.S. 465, 481–82 (1976). *Stone* restricts a defendant's opportunity to vindicate a claim that evidence should have been barred from his *trial*. The Court has held, however, that *Stone*'s habeas restriction does not extend to claims that state courts erroneously failed to bar confessions obtained in violation of the *Miranda* doctrine. *See* Withrow v. Williams, 507 U.S. 680 (1993). Consequently, there can be no doubt that a prisoner is entitled to raise a Fifth or Fourteenth Amendment coerced confession claim in a habeas action challenging a state conviction even if the state court did provide a full and fair hearing of the claim.

192. *See Mitchell,* 526 U.S. at 327 ("To maintain that sentencing proceedings are not part of 'any criminal case' is contrary to the law and to common sense.").

193. *Id.* at 326 (quoting Estelle v. Smith, 451 U.S. 454, 463 (1981)).

194. In *Estelle v. Smith,* 451 U.S. 454 (1981), the Court held that the *Miranda* doctrine required the exclusion of a statement from a capital sentencing proceeding. Although the *Miranda* doctrine is an interpretation of the Fifth Amendment privilege, exclusion of a confession given without proper warnings is *not* a constitutional right. If *Miranda*'s

It is arguable that the rationales for the Fifth and Fourteenth Amendment rights to exclude evidence from trials support extending those rights to other phases of the criminal process—grand jury proceedings, hearings on motions to dismiss charges, or other pretrial stages, for example. All stages might be seen as inseparable parts of a single "criminal case." On the other hand, the constitutional entitlements to suppress evidence might logically be restricted to trials and sentencing phases—that is, proceedings to determine guilt or innocence or the extent of punishment for criminal offenses—because those are the stages of the criminal process when defendants have the most at stake.[195] Because of the serious consequences faced by an accused at a trial or a sentencing hearing, evidentiary unreliability is of greatest concern and the need to adhere to accusatorial methods is most compelling.[196] For present purposes, suffice it to say that the exclusionary rights discussed in this chapter govern trials and sentencing phases of criminal cases.[197] The Fifth and Fourteenth Amendment doctrines do not apply in civil cases,[198] and it does not seem likely that the Court would find

exclusionary rule bars pretrial admissions from sentencing proceedings, there can be no doubt that the Fifth Amendment right to exclusion requires the suppression of coerced admissions from such proceedings. Moreover, in *Mitchell v. United States*, the Court made it clear that Fifth Amendment protection extends "to noncapital sentencing hearings as well." *Mitchell*, 526 U.S. at 326.

195. *See Mitchell*, 526 U.S. at 327 (explaining that "common sense" dictates extension of the Fifth Amendment to sentencing hearings because a defendant may be more "concerned" with "the severity of her punishment" than with "the proof of her guilt or innocence" and that the sentencing phase may be "most important" to a defendant); *see also id.* at 328 (indicating that a reason for granting Fifth Amendment protection in criminal, but not civil, cases is that "'the stakes are higher' in criminal cases, where liberty or even life may be at stake, and where the government's 'sole interest is to convict'") (quoting Baxter v. Palmigiano, 425 U.S. 308, 318–19 (1976)).

196. This is not to suggest that either the concern with the risk of error due to unreliability or the unfairness of an inquisitorial process are *insignificant* considerations in other phases of the criminal process. The point is that these considerations are not as compelling when the question is not guilt or innocence or the severity of the penalty, but whether a defendant should stand trial for an offense or whether a criminal charge should be dismissed.

197. Even if the Fifth Amendment privilege did apply only to trials and not to sentencing hearings—i.e., to determinations of guilt or innocence, not decisions about how much punishment a convicted defendant should suffer—the protection against compulsory self-incrimination would reach some phases labeled sentencing proceedings. Interpretations of the Sixth Amendment right to a jury trial make it clear that substance must govern over form and that constitutional rights that apply to criminal trials generally extend to almost all determinations of fact that increase the maximum penalty a defendant can receive. *See* Apprendi v. New Jersey, 530 U.S. 466 (2000); *see also* Blakely v. Washington, 542 U.S. 296 (2004).

198. The Supreme Court has held that the Fifth Amendment privilege applies to at least some nominally civil proceedings involving the forfeiture of property. The right not

them applicable to stages of the criminal process that cannot result in conviction or punishment.

3. Individuals Entitled to Exclude Coerced Confessions

The Fourth Amendment exclusionary rule is available only to those whose rights have been violated by an unreasonable search or seizure. Others lack "standing" and may not invoke the suppression sanction at their trials.[199] The question here is whether a similar limitation governs the suppression of coerced confessions. If a suspect is physically or psychologically forced to admit that his wife, best friend, and he robbed a bank, does his wife or friend also have a Fifth or Fourteenth Amendment entitlement to bar that admission from their trials?[200] There are no Supreme Court decisions directly on point—no opinions deciding whether an accused is entitled to the suppression of another person's coerced confession from her trial.[201] It seems unlikely, however, that the Court would recognize an entitlement to exclude coerced confessions made by others.[202]

The Fifth Amendment grants a right not to be compelled to be a witness against *oneself* in a criminal case. It accords the accused no entitlement to stop the government from compelling another person to furnish incriminating testimony.

---

to be compelled to be a witness against oneself governs forfeiture proceedings that "may be civil in form, [but] are in their nature criminal." Boyd v. United States, 116 U.S. 616, 634 (1886); *see also* United States v. United States Coin and Currency, 401 U.S. 715, 721–22 (1971). In those cases, the Court was willing to look past the civil label, holding the Fifth Amendment applicable because the government sought to impose penalties based on conduct constituting criminal offenses. *Boyd*, 116 U.S. at 634; *see also United States Coin and Currency*, 401 U.S. at 718, 721–22. It makes sense to extend the Fifth Amendment right to exclude coerced confessions to such proceedings. A contrary holding would elevate form over substance. To bar a coerced disclosure from a suit seeking a genuinely civil sanction, however, would be an unwarranted extension of the privilege.

199. *See supra* Chapter 1, text accompanying notes 174–97.

200. The issue here is whether due process or the privilege provides a basis for suppression. Third parties, like the wife and friend, do have a different constitutional entitlement to exclude some inculpatory confessions made by others, a right rooted in the Sixth Amendment Confrontation Clause. That right is entirely distinct from those that are the subject of this chapter. Unlike the doctrines discussed here, for example, it encompasses and forbids the use of *voluntary* confessions. However, it does not bar even a coerced confession if the confessor testifies at the defendant's trial. The Confrontation Clause exclusionary rule is the subject of Chapter 7.

201. In *Malinski v. New York*, 324 U.S. 401 (1945), Justice Rutledge expressed a belief that the due process doctrine could be invoked by a defendant to exclude a confession coerced from another person. *Id.* at 430–31 (Rutledge, J., dissenting in part).

202. Some lower courts have concluded that while the Fifth Amendment privilege does not provide a basis for excluding coerced statements by third parties, the Due Process Clause does provide an entitlement to exclude such evidence. *See* United States v. Dowell, 430 F.3d 1100, 1107 (10th Cir. 2005); People v. Badgett, 895 P.2d 877, 885–88 (Cal. 1995).

The prosecution, therefore, does not violate the privilege when it forces a third person to reveal inculpatory information about the defendant then uses that information to secure a conviction. The Fifth Amendment right to exclude involuntary confessions surely is limited to one's own statements.

The text of the Due Process Clause is more flexible and does not preclude an argument that a defendant is entitled to suppress another individual's coerced confession. The concern with potential unreliability resulting from official pressures to disclose one's thoughts would seem to be equally strong, perhaps even stronger, in the case of a third party's forced disclosures.[203] Moreover, it is arguable that the sanction of exclusion is justified by the interest in deterring coercive behavior that forces disclosures from the minds of third parties. Society's interests in discouraging official coercion are arguably weightier than the interests in discouraging mere unreasonable searches and seizures. Those interests might be sufficient to outweigh the costs suppression imposes on the truth-finding process.[204]

On the other hand, the risk of unreliability alone is an arguably inadequate basis for a constitutional entitlement to exclude coerced admissions.[205] The due process exclusionary right preserves the accusatorial process, and the predicate of past decisions is that it is inquisitorial to force a person to be the instrument of *her own* destruction. While it may be objectionable to coerce suspects to disclose what they know about others, the use of third-party disclosures to fuel the criminal process is not inconsistent with the accusatorial principles reflected in past rulings. Moreover, with regard to deterrence, it is arguable that any incremental gains in deterring the coercive conduct that produces third-party confessions are insufficient to outweigh the costs of suppression. The threat of being unable to use revelations against the third party herself may sufficiently deter official coercion.[206]

---

203. Such disclosures might be even more likely to be untrustworthy because a person might be more inclined to falsely accuse another person in response to coercive influences before he would be willing to falsely accuse himself of criminal acts.

204. Moreover, because coercion does generate risks of untrustworthiness, the costs to the truth-finding process would not seem to be as high as they are when undeniably reliable evidence is suppressed due to an unreasonable search or seizure.

205. *Colorado v. Connelly*, 479 U.S. 157, 167 (1986), indicates that unreliability is not a sufficient reason for due process suppression. *Connelly*, however, did not hold that risks of erroneous conviction resulting from government misconduct are an inadequate basis for suppression. The point of that decision was that evidentiary unreliability not attributable to the government in some way could not support exclusion under the Fourteenth Amendment.

206. Although it did not involve a coerced confession, the Court's ruling in *United States v. Payner*, 447 U.S. 727 (1980), supports the case for not according a defendant "standing" to exclude another's coerced confession. The *Payner* majority refused to suppress evidence despite the fact that government agents had egregiously and deliberately

4. Exceptions to the Exclusionary Commands of the Due Process Clause and Fifth Amendment Privilege

The Fifth and Fourteenth Amendments generally require the suppression of coerced confessions and derivative evidence from the trial of a defendant who was forced to speak. The questions considered here are whether there are any "exceptions" to the exclusionary rights contained in those two provisions—any circumstances in which evidence is admissible even though it satisfies the basic criteria for exclusion. As seen in Chapter 1, the Supreme Court has developed an extensive body of doctrine defining exceptions to the Fourth Amendment exclusionary rule. The opposite is true for the due process and privilege rules. There is precious little case law regarding exceptions to these suppression doctrines. Not a single Supreme Court ruling recognizes an exception.[207]

a. Justifiable or Necessary Coercion: The Significance of Societal Interests Officers might compel a suspect to speak in order to serve an important interest such as public safety. An individual who has refused to speak might be the only source of information that could prevent a public health crisis or avert some other life-endangering threat—a terrorist attack, for example. The harm sought to be avoided might be less extreme, but still might be weightier than any injury inflicted on a suspect by the coercive treatment. It is clear that compelling the suspect to divulge what he knows would not violate the Fifth Amendment

---

violated the Fourth Amendment to secure evidence against individuals whose rights were not violated by the search and seizure. *See id.* at 730–31, 733, 736–37. The trial judge had recognized that the Fourth Amendment standing limitation precluded application of the *Weeks-Mapp* suppression doctrine, but had held that both the guarantee of due process and the supervisory power over the administration of justice were grounds for exclusion. *See id.* at 731. The Supreme Court rejected both premises. The majority held that because the defendant was not the victim of the search and seizure, the Due Process Clause did not furnish a basis for suppression. *See id.* at 737 n.9. Similarly, today's Supreme Court, which has become increasingly hostile to the suppression of evidence from trials, might well hold that only victims of coercion are entitled to the suppression of involuntary confessions.

A plausible alternative might be to grant standing to suppress involuntary confessions to nonvictims only in those cases where the coercive mistreatment was sufficiently extreme to deprive the third-party victim of liberty without due process. The interest in deterring officers from employing egregiously coercive interrogation methods—methods that violate individuals' Fourteenth Amendment substantive due process rights—may justify an exception to the generally applicable standing restriction.

207. Although there are no recognized situations in which the government is legally entitled to use an involuntary confession against a defendant, it is possible for the unconstitutional use of such a confession at trial to constitute "harmless error." In *Arizona v. Fulminante*, 499 U.S. 279 (1991), a bare majority overturned the Court's prior conclusion that the erroneous admission of a coerced confession could not be harmless and always required reversal of a conviction. According to *Fulminante*, reversal on appeal is not required if the use of the confession against a defendant was "harmless beyond a reasonable doubt." *Id.* at 310.

privilege, a guarantee that provides only a "trial right."[208] On the other hand, pretrial mistreatment alone can violate the right to due process.[209] It is uncertain whether egregious coercion can be justified, and rendered constitutional, when it promotes countervailing societal interests. Otherwise unacceptable deprivations of liberty may be fundamentally fair when they serve important values.[210]

The question here, however, is not whether the out-of-court conduct is constitutional, but whether *trial use* of the evidentiary products of necessary or justified coercion is constitutional. The answer under the Fifth Amendment is clear because that guarantee commands, in unexceptionable terms, that no person "shall be compelled . . . to be a witness against himself."[211] Our accusatorial system makes no provision for necessary, justified, or reasonable compelled self-incrimination. Instead, it categorically denounces inquisitorial methods of conviction whether or not the methods themselves serve some important, or even a compelling, end.[212] The Fifth Amendment exclusionary right, which the Court describes as "*automatic*,"[213] is absolute and not subject to any exceptions based on the reason officers have compelled incriminating revelations.

Because the Fifth Amendment commands exclusion even if there is justification for compelling a suspect to speak, the legitimacy of an exception to the Fourteenth Amendment right is of only theoretical importance. Suffice it to say that the Due Process Clause is potentially more malleable than the privilege. It is arguable that the use of a coerced confession at trial is fundamentally fair, and therefore consistent with due process, when officers pressured disclosures to further an important or compelling societal interest. On the other hand, the same accusatorial system values that support the Fifth Amendment's categorical bar to compelled statements could dictate a similar, unqualified Fourteenth

---

208. *See* Chavez v. Martinez, 538 U.S. 760, 766–73 (2003) (opinion of Thomas, J.); *id.* at 777 (Souter, J., concurring in the judgment).

209. *See id.* at 774–75 (opinion of Thomas, J.); *id.* at 779–80 (Souter, J., concurring in the judgment); *see also supra* text accompanying notes 158–59.

210. *See id.* at 775–76 (opinion of Thomas, J.) (indicating that government interests are relevant to whether due process is violated by official interrogation that infringes upon liberty interests); *id.* at 779 (Souter, J., concurring in the judgment) (suggesting that whether due process is violated depends on whether officers' actions are "'unjustifiable by any government interest'") (quoting County of Sacramento v. Lewis, 523 U.S. 833, 849 (1998)).

211. U.S. CONST. amend. V.

212. Although they disagreed over whether a public safety need can justify the use of statements obtained in violation of the *Miranda* doctrine, the majority and the dissenters in *New York v. Quarles*, 467 U.S. 649 (1984), clearly would agree that the Fifth Amendment does not permit the use of statements that are actually coerced from the mind of a suspect even if officers resorted to coercion to preserve the public safety. *See id.* at 655 n.5, 658 n.7; *id.* at 665 (O'Connor, J., concurring in the judgment in part and dissenting in part); *id.* at 686 (Marshall, J., dissenting).

213. *Chavez*, 538 U.S. at 769 (emphasis in original).

Amendment bar. A conviction based on coerced admissions may well be fundamentally unfair, and a deprivation of the right to due process, whether or not the coercion served vital ends outside the courtroom.[214] To the extent that due process suppression ordinarily serves to deter coercive interrogation methods, one might plausibly contend that deterrence is undesirable when the information sought is essential to prevent harm of sufficient magnitude. On the other hand, if egregious coercion violates the Constitution and deprives victims of protected liberty interests even when officers employ it to prevent serious dangers or harms, the interest in deterring the unconstitutional conduct could outweigh the costs of suppression and justify the exclusion of the evidence obtained.[215]

b. "Good Faith" Coercion: The Relevance of Official Intent or Culpability The Fourth Amendment exclusionary rule has "good faith" exceptions that hinge on whether officers' conduct was "objectively reasonable."[216] In addition, the Fourth Amendment suppression sanction may be inapplicable unless an officer's unreasonable search or seizure was sufficiently "culpable"—that is, intentional, reckless, or part of a pattern of negligence.[217] The question here is whether an officer's lack of intent, absence of culpability, or objective good faith might justify exceptions to the Fifth or Fourteenth Amendment rights to exclusion. An officer may not intend to force a suspect to speak. The officer may, in fact, have been entirely unaware that the minimal (but sufficient) pressures she applied would cause a vulnerable suspect to confess involuntarily. If a suspect was profoundly, but imperceptibly, vulnerable to official pressure, it might even be objectively reasonable to believe the decision to speak was the product of free, unbroken will. In any of these situations, should a confession that was coerced be admissible?

Officers' fault is inapposite to both the privilege and due process inquiries. As already noted, the Fifth Amendment prohibition on compelled testimony is unqualified. Just as it does not permit compelled self-incrimination when officials have pressured a suspect to speak in order to further important public interests, the privilege does not allow compelled self-incrimination when officers had neither the intent to compel disclosures nor any other fault. The privilege mandates the exclusion of an involuntary confession (and derivative evidence)

---

214. *See* Chambers v. Florida, 309 U.S. 227, 240–41 (1940) (holding that due process required exclusion of compelled confessions and rejecting the argument that the "law enforcement methods" used were "necessary" because "[t]he Constitution proscribes such lawless means *irrespective of the end*") (emphasis added).

215. For arguments that both the Fifth Amendment privilege and the Due Process Clause can be interpreted to allow the introduction of coerced admissions acquired by officers who were not acting to investigate crime but were seeking to prevent a tragedy, see William T. Pizzi, *The Privilege Against Self-Incrimination in a Rescue Situation*, 76 J. CRIM L. & CRIMINOLOGY 567, 586–93, 603–06 (1985).

216. *See supra* Chapter 1, text accompanying notes 238–57.

217. *See supra* Chapter 1, text accompanying notes 198–203, 258–60.

without regard to the officer's state of mind or culpability. A "good faith" exception to the Fifth Amendment right to exclusion is indefensible.

The result under the Due Process Clause is identical.[218] Under the evolved doctrine, a confession must be excluded if the totality of circumstances establishes that it was, in fact, coerced.[219] If a suspect's disclosures are "'in fact involuntary,' . . . the absence of evidence of improper purpose on the part of questioning officers" is, quite simply, "irrelevant."[220] Unintentional or entirely faultless coercion poses the same jeopardy to Fourteenth Amendment objectives—ensuring reliability and preserving accusatorial principles—as intended or culpable coercion. Convictions based on forced disclosures are fundamentally unfair whether or not officers' coercive conduct was deliberate or blameworthy. The due process right to exclusion is not qualified by any type of "good faith" exception.[221]

c. Independent Source and Inevitable Discovery Exceptions The Fourth Amendment exclusionary rule recognizes exceptions for evidence obtained from an independent, lawful source and for illegally obtained evidence that would have inevitably been discovered by legal means.[222] The question here is whether there are analogous exceptions to the Fifth and Fourteenth Amendment coerced confession rules. Is a confession that is not the product of the coercion employed by officers admissible? May the prosecution use evidence discovered by means independent of disclosures that were coerced? If officers, by legal means, would have acquired a coerced confession or physical evidence derived from a coerced confession, is the confession or evidence admissible?

The answer to the independent source question is implicit in the causation demand discussed earlier.[223] Only coerced confessions and evidence derived from coerced confessions are barred by the Fifth and Fourteenth Amendment

---

218. Once again, the clear exclusionary mandate of the privilege means that the due process analysis has only theoretical significance. Even if a lack of fault was a basis for an exception to Fourteenth Amendment exclusion, the Fifth Amendment would still require suppression.

219. *See* Arizona v. Fulminante, 499 U.S. 279, 285–86 (1991).

220. Townsend v. Sain, 372 U.S. 293, 309 (1963) (quoting Stroble v. California, 343 U.S. 181, 190 (1952)).

221. Culpability is wholly inapposite under the Fifth and Fourteenth Amendments because the primary object of exclusion is not to penalize or motivate officers, but to ensure that defendants receive fair trials.

222. *See supra* Chapter 1, text accompanying notes 204–20.

223. As noted in Chapter 1, the "independent source" doctrine is not a true exception to the Fourth Amendment exclusionary rule because the rule presumptively bars only evidence with a causal connection to unconstitutional conduct. Similarly, because the Fifth and Fourteenth Amendment rights to exclusion encompass only coerced confessions and evidence with a causal connection to coerced confessions, the independent source doctrine is not a true exception to those rights.

exclusionary rights. If officers employ pressures but a suspect confesses voluntarily, the confession has a source independent of the coercion and is clearly admissible.[224] Moreover, if officers did coerce disclosures, other evidence they find independently of leads provided by the disclosures is admissible. The Fifth and Fourteenth Amendments bar only derivative evidence—evidence with a causal connection to the coerced confession.[225] The values that underlie the privilege and due process require no more. There is no threat of unreliability and no jeopardy to accusatorial principles when prosecutors use uncoerced statements or independently acquired evidence to convict.

The answer to the inevitable discovery question is not as clear. A forced confession that would have inevitably been given without official pressure is still coerced, and derivative evidence that officers would have gained by following lawful leads is still the product of statements forced from the defendant's mind.[226] Both the confession and the derivative evidence fall within the presumptive scope of the constitutional rights to exclusion. It seems likely, however, that the Supreme Court would deem both admissible under the inevitable discovery doctrine.

In its sole consideration of the inevitable discovery exception, *Nix v. Williams*,[227] the Court held that the exception was entirely consistent with the deterrent goals of suppression.[228] Of more importance for present purposes, the Court decided that even if exclusion under the Sixth Amendment-*Massiah* doctrine was a constitutional right,[229] evidence that would have inevitably been found by legal means would be admissible.[230] The reasoning that led to this conclusion supports a similar exception to the privilege and due process exclusionary rights.

224. *See* Thomas v. Arizona, 356 U.S. 390, 400–02 (1958).

225. *See* Kastigar v. United States, 406 U.S. 441, 460 (1972) (acknowledging that the Fifth Amendment permits the prosecution to use incriminating evidence it acquires after compelling a person to testify under a grant of immunity if it "prove[s] that the evidence . . . is derived from a legitimate source wholly independent of the compelled testimony").

226. The possibility that the prosecution will be able to sustain its burden of showing it more likely than not that a suspect who has been forced to speak would have made the same disclosures freely and voluntarily seems quite remote. Consequently, an inevitable discovery exception is unlikely to permit the admission of a coerced confession. Derivative evidence, such as contraband narcotics or a weapon discovered as a result of coerced revelations, might well fall within such an exception.

227. 467 U.S. 431 (1984).

228. *See id.* at 442–46.

229. This exclusion doctrine—rooted in the Sixth Amendment right to counsel—is the subject of Chapter 4.

230. *Id.* at 446–47. In so ruling, the Court made it clear that the inevitable discovery exception is logically reconcilable not only with exclusionary rules that are future-oriented deterrent sanctions, but also with exclusionary mandates that are defendants' personal constitutional entitlements.

According to the Justices, if the identical evidence would have been found by constitutionally legitimate methods and would have appeared at trial even if the impropriety had not occurred, then an accused has received the very same trial he would have received without that impropriety.[231] There is no unfairness involved in the use of the improperly acquired evidence at trial because the government has, in fact, gained no net evidentiary advantage from its illegitimate conduct.[232] More specifically, the Court would probably conclude that even though the prosecution introduced a confession that was coerced or a gun that was found as a result of a forced statement, the defendant's trial was indistinguishable from the trial that would have occurred without the coercion. Because the state did not *profit* in court from the compelled or coerced disclosures, the accused has suffered no harm that the Fifth or Fourteenth Amendment is intended to prevent. Because the defendant has not been disadvantaged by the involuntary statement, the unfairness that both guarantees guard against is absent.[233] The inevitable discovery exception seems consistent with the constitutional rights not to be convicted on the basis of coerced admissions. It would seem to be a legitimate exception to the Fifth and Fourteenth Amendment rights to exclusion.

d. The Attenuation Exception As noted in Chapter 1, Fourth Amendment exclusionary rule law now has two varieties of attenuation exception.[234] According to the longstanding branch of the exception, when a connection between misconduct and the acquisition of evidence is sufficiently "attenuated"—that is, indirect and weakened—derivative evidence is admissible.[235] The Supreme Court has never discussed whether a similar exception might permit the introduction of evidence derived from coerced confessions. For example, if admissions forced from a vulnerable suspect by minimally coercive methods initiated a lengthy, time-consuming investigation that led eventually to the discovery of narcotics, are those narcotics admissible at the suspect's trial? It is uncertain how the Court would resolve this issue.

The Fourth Amendment's attenuation exception is justified today in terms of cost-benefit deterrent balancing. When evidence is sufficiently attenuated from unconstitutional conduct, the costs of suppression are thought to outweigh

---

231. *See id.* at 447.

232. *See id.*

233. The trial process is neither less reliable nor more inquisitorial in character as a result of the official coercion that did occur.

234. *See supra* Chapter 1, text accompanying notes 221–37.

235. Time and intervening circumstances can attenuate causal connections, and the character of the illegality—whether it was deliberate and/or flagrant—is also pertinent to the analysis. The recently-minted, alternative branch of the Fourth Amendment attenuation doctrine seems inapplicable to the due process and privilege rights to exclusion, and, therefore, is not discussed here.

the additional deterrence that might be gained by exclusion.[236] Similar reasoning cannot support an attenuation exception to the due process and privilege doctrines because exclusion under those doctrines is a trial right, not a mere deterrent sanction designed to secure future compliance. Fifth and Fourteenth Amendment policies—in particular, the accusatorial values underlying our criminal justice systems—are arguably jeopardized whenever *any* evidentiary product of a coerced confession contributes to conviction.[237] No matter how weak or remote the connection between the coercion and the evidence, the government has reaped an advantage from forcing the accused to speak. The use of even attenuated evidence arguably renders the trial process inquisitorial because the government has fueled its case with inculpatory evidence acquired by forcing a defendant to make disclosures. According to this view, an accused has constitutional rights to suppress any and all evidentiary advantages the government gained by coercing her to reveal her thoughts.

On the other hand, the Court did endorse the attenuation exception to Fourth Amendment suppression at a time when the exclusionary rule was considered an integral part of the right against unreasonable searches and seizures.[238] This indicates a belief that the doctrine is a legitimate exception to a personal exclusionary right. It is arguable that attenuation is reconcilable with the Fifth and Fourteenth Amendment rights to exclusion because evidence with a sufficiently weak connection to official coercion poses insubstantial threats to accusatorial principles. The interest in convicting an accused based on reliable proof of guilt—and most derivative evidence, unlike a coerced confession itself, will be of unquestionable reliability—could outweigh the limited infringement upon accusatorial values and justify limiting exclusion to evidentiary fruits with a sufficiently strong connection to coerced confessions.

Nonetheless, the trial use of any evidence resulting from a coerced statement, even evidence with a remote connection, would seem to be inquisitorial. The accused suffers a disadvantage—one that might be quite serious[239]—as a

---

236. *See supra* Chapter 1, text following note 231.

237. *See* Mincey v. Arizona, 437 U.S. 385, 398 (1978) ("*any* criminal trial use against a defendant of his *involuntary* statement is a denial of due process of law") (emphasis in original).

238. When the Court first endorsed the attenuation exception in *Nardone v. United States*, 308 U.S. 338, 341 (1939), the original justifications for the Fourth Amendment exclusionary rule explained in *Weeks v. United States*, 232 U.S. 383 (1914), controlled. For a discussion of those justifications, see *supra* Chapter 1, text accompanying notes 122–26. The *Nardone* Court did not explain why or how the admission of attenuated evidence was consistent with the personal entitlement to exclude both direct and indirect products of illegalities.

239. Evidence of contraband narcotics remotely connected to coerced admissions, but highly probative of the defendant's possession and intent to deliver, for example, would surely be a major disadvantage for the defendant in the quest to avoid conviction.

consequence of thoughts forced from his mind. Neither the constitutional text nor precedent furnishes a basis for concluding that modest modification of our accusatorial approach is tolerable. The commitment to a system that requires the government to prove guilt without the aid of compelled admissions is arguably unqualified, despite the costs.[240] If so, an attenuation exception is not appropriate.

It is unclear whether the modern Court would accept an attenuation exception to the Fifth and Fourteenth Amendment exclusionary rights. The Court's increased hostility to the suppression of probative evidence might lead it to balance competing interests and permit the use of some reliable fruits. Alternatively, the Court could find the use of any advantage acquired by coercion to be irreconcilable with the fundamental nature of our criminal justice systems and the justifications for these two constitutional entitlements.

e. Impeachment Use The "impeachment use" exception to the Fourth Amendment exclusionary rule permits the government to introduce any illegally acquired evidence to cast doubt on the credibility of the defendant's trial testimony. The Court deems this exception justified because the costs of exclusion to the truth-finding process outweigh any additional Fourth Amendment compliance that might result from informing officers that even impeachment use is forbidden.[241] The Court has rejected impeachment use exceptions to both constitutional rights to exclude coerced confessions. The resulting contrast with Fourth Amendment doctrine highlights the importance of the distinction between exclusion that is aimed exclusively at preventing future violations and exclusion that is a defendant's personal trial right.

In *Mincey v. Arizona*, the Court unequivocally and emphatically held that the Due Process Clause forbids the introduction of a coerced confession not only as substantive proof of guilt, but also to cast doubt on the credibility of the accused's testimony.[242] "[A]*ny* criminal trial use" of forced disclosures to incriminate a

---

240. *Cf.* New Jersey v. Portash, 440 U.S. 450, 459 (1979) (declaring that interest balancing is "impermissible" in deciding whether coerced testimony can be used at trial).

Some Justices have described the Fifth Amendment derivative evidence bar as the product of the Court's interpretation of that provision. *See* United States v. Patane, 542 U.S. 630, 644 (2004) (plurality opinion) (stating that "it is true that the Court requires the exclusion of the physical fruit of actually coerced statements"). This might suggest a belief that the Court has the authority to make appropriate "adjustments" to the rule. Other characterizations of the derivative evidence rule, however, suggest that it is an unalterable command of the Fifth Amendment that might not be subject to Court-developed limitations. *See* Chavez v. Martinez, 538 U.S. 760, 769 (2003) (opinion of Thomas, J.) (referring to the "*automatic* protection" the Fifth Amendment furnishes against the use of "evidence derived from" involuntary confessions) (emphasis in original); *see also Patane*, 542 U.S. at 646 (Souter, J., dissenting) (asserting that "the Fifth Amendment privilege against compelled self-incrimination extends to the exclusion of derivative evidence").

241. *See supra* Chapter 1, text accompanying notes 266–68.

242. 437 U.S. 385, 398, 402 (1978).

defendant—even the limited use involved in introduction for impeachment purposes—is a violation of due process.[243] Impeachment use is impermissible because it is fundamentally unfair. The introduction of an involuntary confession for any incriminating purpose is a deprivation of the constitutional entitlement to due process of law.

Similarly, *New Jersey v. Portash* declared that impeachment use of compelled disclosures violates a defendant's Fifth Amendment privilege.[244] In categorical, absolute terms, that guarantee extends a right not to be "compelled to be a witness against [one]self." Use of a forced disclosure to erode an accused's credibility has incriminating impact—it makes him a witness against himself—and thereby denies the constitutional entitlement against compulsory self-incrimination. When an exclusionary rule that is designed solely to deter future misconduct is involved, it is necessary to balance competing interests. When "the constitutional privilege against compulsory self-incrimination in its most pristine form" is involved, as it is when statements are genuinely compelled, interest balancing is both "unnecessary" and "impermissible."[245]

E. REFLECTIONS ON THE FIFTH AND FOURTEENTH AMENDMENT RIGHTS TO EXCLUSION

The constitutional exclusion of involuntary confessions has a long history. It predates the Fourth Amendment exclusionary rule by 17 years. Well over a century ago, the Supreme Court first announced that our Constitution bars the government from using such confessions to secure convictions. In the ensuing years, the Court has identified two distinct provisions that grant to criminal defendants constitutional rights to exclude coerced confessions and derivative evidence—the Fifth Amendment privilege against compulsory self-incrimination and the Fourteenth Amendment Due Process Clause. These two bars to the use of evidence are dramatically different from the search and seizure exclusionary rule discussed in Chapter 1. While the latter began as a constitutional right, it has evolved into a deterrent safeguard against future unconstitutional conduct. From the start, the Fifth and Fourteenth Amendment coerced confession doctrines have been understood to be personal rights of the individual on trial. That understanding persists today. The admission of a coerced confession in a criminal trial violates both constitutional guarantees.

While the basic doctrines defining the scope of these exclusionary rights are relatively well-developed, the Court has not had occasion to explore or answer many issues concerning potential limitations. The extensive body of decisions

243. *Id.* at 398 (emphasis in original).
244. *Portash*, 440 U.S. at 459.
245. *Id.*

refining and cabining the Fourth Amendment exclusionary rule's operation stands in marked contrast to the small number of decisions addressing the details of the Fifth and Fourteenth Amendment rights. When issues do arise, it is vital to avoid the temptation to rely on misleading Fourth Amendment exclusionary rule reasoning rooted in the premise that no constitutional rights are at risk in the courtroom.[246] The resolution of Fifth and Fourteenth Amendment questions must instead be informed and guided by an awareness that the exclusion of evidence is essential to avoid deprivations of personal constitutional entitlements. Fortunately, the Court has demonstrated on more than one occasion that it appreciates the special character of these exclusionary rights.[247]

Dissatisfaction with the coerced confession doctrine as a tool for preserving fundamental values led the Court in the 1960s to develop two additional constitutional constraints upon law enforcement efforts to secure confessions.[248] The violation of these constraints, which are the subjects of the two chapters that follow, also may require evidentiary exclusion at trial. The more specific restrictions on law enforcement efforts to obtain inculpatory statements from suspects and accused individuals imposed by these two doctrines supplement the coerced confession doctrine, rendering it less significant as a practical matter. Nevertheless, they have not supplanted the due process and privilege limitations on interrogation practices and on the admissibility of evidence. In more than one situation, the due process and privilege rules are, and will surely remain, the sole grounds for barring evidence. Moreover, the exclusionary rights granted by the Fifth Amendment Privilege and the Due Process Clause have enduring theoretical and symbolic significance.

In addition, the modern Supreme Court's abiding antipathy toward evidentiary exclusion has led to the severe erosion of the other two bases for suppressing confessions and related evidence. It seems unlikely, however, that the Court's hostility toward suppression will diminish the constitutional entitlements to exclude coerced confessions and derivative evidence. The fact that the due process and privilege suppression doctrines are inseparable parts of core constitutional liberties gives them an immunity to erosion based on the ever-present interest in ensuring conviction of the guilty.

---

246. *See, e.g.*, Colorado v. Connelly, 479 U.S. 157, 166, 169 (1986) (intimating that deterrence-based cost-benefit balancing was relevant to the determination of whether a confession is subject to exclusion under the due process-coerced confession doctrine).

247. *See, e.g.*, United States v. Patane, 542 U.S. 630, 640, 644 (2004) (plurality opinion) (acknowledging that the Fifth Amendment right requires the exclusion of derivative physical evidence); *id.* at 646 (Souter J., dissenting); Mincey v. Arizona, 437 U.S. 385, 398 (1978) (recognizing that the use of a coerced confession, even for the limited purpose of impeachment, is a deprivation of due process).

248. *See* Gardner, *Emerging Good Faith Exception*, *supra* note 133, at 446–48; Godsey, *Rethinking the Involuntary Confession Rule*, *supra* note 8, at 499.

3. THE *MIRANDA* EXCLUSIONARY RULE

INTRODUCTION

Chapter 3 explains the *Miranda* exclusionary rule, the second of the three constitutional suppression doctrines pertaining to confessions. The *Miranda* doctrine is one of the Supreme Court's two efforts to address perceived inadequacies of the coerced confession doctrine explained in Chapter 2. Chronologically, it was the Court's second attempt to further constrain law enforcement interrogation techniques and thereby supplement the constitutional safeguards against conviction by methods inconsistent with the character of American criminal justice. *Miranda*, however, is clearly much better known and much more controversial than the Court's initial effort to augment protection two years earlier.[1] Moreover, the Supreme Court has spent considerably more time and effort examining and developing both the substantive rules and the exclusionary consequences of the *Miranda* doctrine.

The focus here is on evidentiary exclusion, not the guidelines *Miranda* announced for conducting custodial interrogations. In truth, however, the two are inseparable. It was impossible to appreciate the details of the doctrine suppressing coerced confessions without understanding the conditions that require suppression—i.e., official pressures that overcome the will of the particular individual and yield testimonial evidence. Similarly, one cannot appreciate the nuances of the *Miranda* suppression doctrine without comprehending the basic substantive criteria that require courts to exclude confessions. Consequently, the discussion necessarily includes some treatment of the rules governing the conduct of law enforcement officers.

A. THE BASIC *MIRANDA* EXCLUSIONARY RULE

The Supreme Court's decision in *Miranda v. Arizona*[2] was rooted firmly and exclusively in the Fifth Amendment Self-Incrimination Clause.[3] If the Court's

1. The Court's first attempt, in *Massiah v. United States*, 377 U.S. 201 (1964), is the subject of Chapter 4. The *Miranda* rule, in fact, is one of the "youngest" bases for constitutional exclusion. The only two bases for suppressing evidence born since *Miranda* are but one year younger. Those two doctrines, which suppress eyewitness identification evidence, are analyzed in Chapters 5 and 6.

2. 384 U.S. 436 (1966).

3. U.S. Const. amend. V.

original understanding of *Miranda* exclusion had endured, the explanation of that doctrine would not be the subject of a separate chapter. Instead, it would be an integral part of Chapter 2's discussion of the Fifth Amendment *right* to exclude compelled confessions. Because of the Court's radical reconception of *Miranda,* a subject addressed in the historical account that follows, there can be no doubt that *Miranda* exclusion is a separate and distinct, Fifth Amendment-based exclusionary *rule.*

Miranda excludes the products of "custodial interrogation."[4] It declares that incriminating disclosures made by a person subjected to official interrogation while held in custody by the authorities are inadmissible at trial *unless* officers recite certain warnings and the person voluntarily and knowingly waives her rights.[5] Consequently, if officers arrest a murder suspect and, without delivering the required warnings, ask whether she killed the victim, any admission she makes cannot be introduced to prove guilt. Moreover, if a suspect expresses a desire to remain silent or asks for the assistance of a lawyer, a confession secured thereafter is inadmissible *unless* officers abide by additional safeguards deemed necessary to respect the suspect's wishes.[6] Thus, if an individual suspected of terrorism requests a lawyer, officers immediately ask whether he will reconsider that decision, and the suspect then agrees to waive the entitlement to counsel and answers the officers' questions, his answers cannot be used to prove that he engaged in terrorism.

It has been clear from *Miranda*'s inception that inculpatory statements obtained in violation of its dictates may not be used at the interrogated suspect's trial to prove guilt. The *Miranda* Court, however, did not explore the boundaries and details of the new exclusion doctrine. For example, the Court did not discuss whether evidence found as a result of inadmissible statements was subject to suppression, whether individuals other than the suspect could claim suppression, or whether exclusion is required in any proceeding other than a criminal trial. May a cache of cocaine found in my home as a result of statements I made without warnings be used to prove that I possessed narcotics? May a business partner claim that statements inadmissible to prove my guilt for securities fraud cannot be used to prove his guilt? May prosecutors introduce my confession to a

---

4. *Miranda,* 384 U.S. at 444. *Miranda* has no application unless a statement is a product of both custody *and* interrogation. These two constructs have been defined in a number of post-*Miranda* decisions. *See, e.g.,* Berkemer v. McCarty, 468 U.S. 420 (1984) (defining custody); Rhode Island v. Innis, 446 U.S. 291 (1980) (defining interrogation).

5. *See Miranda,* 384 U.S. at 467–72, 475–76, 479.

6. *See id.* at 473–74. The restrictions on custodial interrogation following assertions of the rights to silence and counsel have been developed in subsequent decisions. *See, e.g.,* Edwards v. Arizona, 451 U.S. 477 (1981) (explaining the consequences of asserting the entitlement to have counsel present); Michigan v. Mosley, 423 U.S. 96 (1975) (explaining the consequences of asserting the right to remain silent).

sexual assault in an effort to secure an indictment from a grand jury? Moreover, the Court did not explore whether the "exceptions" to exclusion discussed in the first two chapters—inevitable discovery, attenuation, good faith, and public safety—could justify the introduction of evidence that *Miranda* would otherwise bar.[7] If officers reasonably, but erroneously, believe that a suspect is not in custody or that adequate warnings have been delivered, or if they are understandably unaware that a suspect has a mental impairment that prevents a valid waiver of rights, will incriminating answers still be excluded?

These and other issues will be explored and analyzed in the doctrinal section of this chapter. For now, suffice it to say that the scope of the *Miranda* exclusionary rule has been severely limited. It does not bar derivative evidence of any sort, only a confessing suspect can claim suppression, and its operation seems to be confined to criminal trials and sentencing proceedings. The government may use cocaine found in my home as a result of my disclosures to prove my guilt, a business partner surely has no standing to suppress my revelations about our joint fraud, and the grand jury almost certainly will be allowed to rely on my statements in deciding whether to charge me with sexual assault. Because suppression does not reach derivative evidence, there is no need for the attenuation exception and little room for the inevitable discovery exception to operate. The Court has endorsed a public safety exception, meaning that officers may question me without warnings to save a life or prevent an explosion, for example, and the prosecution may then introduce any inculpatory statements to prove my guilt. Even when a failure to warn a suspect is unjustified, prosecutors may use her incriminating statements to impeach her contradictory trial testimony. Consequently, the government can introduce my wife's admissions of involvement in terrorism to cast doubt on her credibility after she testifies at trial that she was not involved. Finally, the Court has not yet decided whether there is an exception for statements obtained as a result of unintended, good faith *Miranda* violations. Consequently, suppression is currently called for even if officers' failures are neither deliberate nor in bad faith.

One last point merits mention. Undoubtedly, the original rationales for *Miranda*'s rule of inadmissibility would have dictated different answers to some of the significant exclusionary rule questions settled by precedent. The revised understanding of the justifications for suppression has been a critical predicate for a number of restrictions on *Miranda* exclusion. The dramatic impact of the Court's modifications of *Miranda*'s constitutional underpinnings will become apparent as this chapter unfolds.

---

7. The Court did discuss whether inadmissible confessions could be used for impeachment purposes. *See Miranda*, 384 U.S. at 476–77. As will be seen, however, the Court revisited that question just five years later and reached a very different conclusion.

B. THE ORIGIN AND TRANSFORMATIONS OF THE *MIRANDA* EXCLUSIONARY RULE: A HISTORICAL ACCOUNT

In more than one sense, the history of the coerced confession exclusion doctrine recounted in Chapter 2 is also the history of *Miranda* exclusion. As already suggested, the deficiencies of that doctrine—its failure to provide guidance, consistency, and adequate protection—prompted efforts to develop clearer, more predictable constitutional safeguards. *Miranda* is a result of those efforts. In addition, originally *Miranda*'s bar to confessions was simply an extension of the Fifth Amendment right to exclude compelled testimonial disclosures. The earlier decisions recognizing that the privilege barred statements forced from a suspect's mind were *Miranda*'s ancestors. Because of the radical revision of the basis for *Miranda*'s exclusionary rule, however, the present historical account begins with *Miranda v. Arizona*. The unique rule of inadmissibility that exists today first appeared in that landmark decision.

In the opening paragraph of the majority opinion in *Miranda*, Chief Justice Warren acknowledged that evidentiary exclusion was at issue.[8] He observed that a central question raised by the case was "the admissibility of statements obtained from an individual who is subjected to custodial police interrogation."[9] In the course of a quite lengthy opinion, Warren explained that the combination of custody and interrogation engendered "inherently compelling pressures which work to undermine the individual's will to resist and to compel him to speak where he would not otherwise do so freely."[10] Because statements made in response to those inherent pressures cannot "truly be the product of his free choice,"[11] they must be considered compelled within the meaning of the Fifth Amendment privilege against self-incrimination. Officers can take steps to eliminate the pressures generated by interrogating a person in custody.[12] However, if they do not employ "adequate protective devices . . . to dispel the compulsion inherent in custodial surroundings,"[13]—a warning of rights and a voluntary and informed choice to surrender those rights, for example—any disclosures are inadmissible.[14] The *Miranda* majority believed that the use of such disclosures to

8. *Miranda* was the product of a sharply divided Court. Five Justices joined the majority opinion. Four Justices dissented, finding the ruling to be unnecessary and unjustified. *See id.* at 499 (Clark, J., dissenting and concurring in the result); *id.* at 504 (Harlan, J., dissenting); *id.* at 526 (White, J., dissenting).

9. *Miranda*, 384 U.S. at 439.

10. *Id.* at 467.

11. *Id.* at 458.

12. *See id.* at 467.

13. *Id.* at 458.

14. *Miranda*, 384 U.S. at 479. I say warnings and waiver, "for example," because the Court made it clear that effective alternative means of dispelling compulsion could render statements admissible. *See id.* at 467, 479, 490.

prove guilt would violate the right not to be compelled to be a witness against oneself. The exclusion of confessions obtained by custodial interrogation without protective measures was constitutionally necessary to prevent deprivations of the Fifth Amendment privilege.[15]

The Court was aware that the Fifth Amendment privilege had been developed in response to, and was designed to prevent, formal courtroom pressures to testify against oneself.[16] The majority concluded, however, that the threat to accusatorial system values is equivalent when law enforcement officers, in informal settings, pressure individuals to reveal their thoughts and the government then seeks to use the compelled revelations at trial.[17] The same policies that bar the state from forcing a defendant to testify at trial also prevent the state from forcing disclosures before trial, then using those disclosures to convict. Each practice violates the spirit and intent of the Fifth Amendment guarantee against compelled self-incrimination.

Although the Court did recognize that the "admissibility" of statements was a central issue,[18] the *Miranda* opinion did not separately or explicitly address evidentiary exclusion or explain the rationales for its new suppression doctrine. The reason for that is simple. *Miranda* was concerned with enforcing the Fifth Amendment right. Exclusion was not a remedy or sanction distinct from that right, but, instead, was an inseparable part of the right. By preventing the prosecution from forcing a defendant to give self-accusatory testimony, the Fifth Amendment itself erects an evidentiary bar, a right not to have a certain kind of evidence—a person's compelled thoughts—contribute to the government's case for conviction. *Miranda* merely interpreted that constitutional bar to encompass thoughts compelled from a suspect before trial by the pressures of custodial interrogation. Consequently, there was no need for a separate discussion of the reasons for excluding confessions. Any treatment of suppression as a distinct subject would have been superfluous and downright odd. In the majority's view, the Fifth Amendment, and the accusatorial values on which it rests, commanded suppression. Exclusion was an inseverable part of the privilege. At birth, *Miranda* exclusion was an integral component of the right not to be compelled to testify against oneself.[19]

---

15. *See id.* at 439, 461–62, 479, 490–91.

16. *See id.* at 458–60.

17. *See id.* at 460–66.

18. *Id.* at 439, 445.

19. The Court was explicit about this understanding of exclusion in at least one post-*Miranda* decision. *See* Orozco v. Texas, 394 U.S. 324, 326 (1969) (asserting that the use of statements "was a flat violation of the Self-Incrimination Clause of the Fifth Amendment as construed in *Miranda*"). On one occasion well after it had already disavowed the view that the introduction of statements violates the Fifth Amendment, the Court relied on the original rationale for *Miranda* suppression, inexplicably asserting that "Fifth Amendment rights were violated by the admission of" testimony based on

Before *Miranda* was five years old, however, the Court began a dramatic redesign that recast its suppression doctrine as an exclusionary rule, separate and apart from the constitutional right on which it rests.[20] *Harris v. New York*[21] was the first decision treating suppression as a remedy or sanction distinct from the Fifth Amendment right. *Miranda* had declared that statements secured by custodial interrogation without protective safeguards could not be used to impeach a testifying defendant.[22] The radical reformation of *Miranda*'s character enabled the *Harris* Court to reach a contrary conclusion and hold impeachment use permissible.[23]

The reasoning of the *Harris* majority was far from fully developed.[24] Implicit was a critical distinction between statements that are actually "coerced or involuntary" due to official pressures and statements resulting from custodial interrogation.[25] The majority saw the latter as not genuinely compelled. Unlike truly coerced statements, their "trustworthiness" is not in doubt.[26] The Court's opinion was clearly based on a rejection of *Miranda*'s fundamental premise that defendants have a Fifth Amendment right to bar disclosures made during custodial interrogation without protective measures.[27]

Harris did not offer an explicit alternative explanation for *Miranda*'s bar to the use of statements as substantive proof of guilt. If statements are not compelled and, thus, forbidden by the very terms of the Fifth Amendment, why may the prosecution not introduce them for any relevant purpose? The Court suggested, quite obliquely, that suppression served a deterrent function—that is, that an objective of excluding revelations made during custodial interrogation was to motivate law enforcement to implement the protective, compulsion-dispelling

---

statements obtained without warnings. Estelle v. Smith, 451 U.S. 454, 468 (1981). *See also* Yale Kamisar, *Foreword: From* Miranda *to ∬ 3501 to* Dickerson *to . . .*, 99 MICH. L. REV. 879, 883–85 (2001) [hereinafter Kamisar, *Foreword*] (discussing the original constitutional status of *Miranda*).

20. *See* Carol S. Steiker, *Counter-Revolution in Constitutional Criminal Procedure? Two Audiences, Two Answers*, 94 MICH. L. REV. 2466, 2522–23 (1996) (discussing how the Court turned *Miranda*'s absolute Fifth Amendment rule into an exclusionary rule like the Fourth Amendment rule).

21. 401 U.S. 222 (1971).

22. *Miranda*, 384 U.S. at 476–77.

23. *Harris*, 401 U.S. at 226.

24. Like *Miranda*, *Harris* was decided by a deeply split Court. Five Justices joined the majority opinion, while four once again dissented. *See Harris*, 401 U.S. at 226 (Black, J., dissenting); *id.* (Brennan, J., dissenting).

25. *Id.* at 224.

26. *Id.* The Court's mention of the need for the "trustworthiness of" statements to satisfy "legal standards" clearly implied that mere *Miranda* violations do not undermine trustworthiness.

27. While the rejection of this foundation for suppression was clear, it was not overt. The terse, revolutionary reasoning of the *Harris* majority left much unsaid.

devices prescribed by *Miranda*.[28] Because "sufficient deterrence flow[ed]" from preventing the prosecution from using admissions as direct proof of guilt and because barring impeachment use resulted in the unique cost of allowing a defendant to lie in court, the Court concluded that the *Miranda* exclusionary rule did not forbid impeachment use.[29] In essence, the *Harris* Court seemed to conceive of suppression as a future-oriented sanction for failures to adhere to the guidelines for custodial interrogation announced by *Miranda*. It was a mere exclusionary rule, much like the one used to enforce Fourth Amendment commands.

This reformulation of *Miranda*'s rule of inadmissibility began to flower just a few years later in *Michigan v. Tucker*.[30] The issue was whether a trial judge should have barred the testimony of a witness found as a result of statements obtained in violation of *Miranda*. The Court held that the witness could testify, but relied heavily on the significant fact that the custodial interrogation that led to the discovery of the witness occurred before the decision in *Miranda*.[31] Although the *Tucker* holding was narrow, its reasoning had enormous significance.

The Court drew a sharp distinction between actual infringements of the "right against compulsory self-incrimination" and violations of "only the prophylactic rules [*Miranda*] developed to protect that right."[32] Under *Miranda*'s suppression doctrine, statements "might be excluded at trial despite their voluntary character"[33] because the pressures of custodial interrogation without *Miranda*'s "procedural safeguards" did not amount to "genuine compulsion" of a sort "sufficient to breach the right against compulsory self-incrimination."[34] The *Tucker* majority confirmed and made explicit what *Harris* had cryptically intimated: there is no Fifth Amendment right to exclude statements obtained without *Miranda* safeguards because the introduction of such statements does not violate that guarantee. Rather than a constitutional right, exclusion under *Miranda* is a "judicially imposed consequence[]" of officers' disregard of "procedural rules."[35]

Having disavowed the original basis for exclusion, the *Tucker* majority proceeded to explore the justifications for *Miranda*'s evidentiary bar. The Court asserted that "[i]n a proper case," the deterrent "rationale" that is the justification for the Fourth Amendment exclusionary rule could support the *Miranda* rule,[36]

---

28. *Id.* at 225.
29. *Id.* at 225–26.
30. 417 U.S. 433 (1974).
31. *Id.* at 447–48.
32. *Id.* at 439.
33. *Id.* at 443.
34. *Id.* at 440, 444–45.
35. *Tucker*, 417 U.S. at 445.
36. *Id.* at 446–47. The Court did indicate that the deterrent analysis ought to be different under *Miranda* because, unlike the searches and seizures that are the target of the Fourth Amendment exclusionary rule, the conduct sought to be discouraged by *Miranda*

but rejected the notion that suppression could be justified by a concern for reliability. Statements resulting from actual compulsion are barred to guard against untrustworthiness because compulsion "might . . . cause a defendant to accuse himself falsely."[37] The same concern cannot support exclusion under *Miranda* because the pressures to speak from custodial interrogation without safeguards are not comparable to the pressures of actual compulsion.[38]

Moreover, genuinely compelled statements and evidence obtained as a result are barred for an "additional reason"—to enforce "the adversary system [principle that] requires 'the government in its contest with the individual to shoulder the entire load.'"[39] Because this principle, like trustworthiness, is jeopardized only when disclosures have actually been coerced from an individual against his will, it cannot support *Miranda*'s bar to "voluntary statements."[40]

In addition, the *Tucker* Court made it clear that because the *Miranda* exclusionary rule is a judicially-devised dictate—not a part of the Fifth Amendment's core protection—cost-benefit balancing is necessary. To determine whether suppression is required, any gains in protecting the privilege resulting from suppression must be weighed against the harm done to society's powerful interests in resolving criminal charges on the basis of all "trustworthy evidence" and effectively prosecuting criminals.[41]

In sum, *Tucker* embellished and advanced the transformation of *Miranda* exclusion begun by *Harris*. Because *Miranda* violations yield statements that are, in fact, voluntary, the Fifth Amendment is not violated when evidence obtained in violation of its custodial interrogation guidelines is admitted. Consequently, defendants have no personal right to suppression. The voluntariness of the statements means that neither trustworthiness nor the accusatorial system values that underlie the Fifth Amendment justify suppression. The only rationale the Court recognized for *Miranda* exclusion was deterrence—discouraging officers from neglecting *Miranda*'s procedural safeguards for custodial interrogation. Suppression was justified only when that interest outweighed the ever-present costs of impeding convictions of the guilty by excluding probative, reliable admissions of guilt.[42]

---

suppression does not by itself violate the Constitution. It merely transgresses "procedural rules" or "prophylactic standards" for the conduct of custodial interrogation. *Id.* at 445–46.

37. *Id.* at 449.

38. *Id.*

39. *Id.* (quoting 8 J. WIGMORE, EVIDENCE § 2251 (Chadbourne rev. 1970)).

40. *Tucker*, 417 U.S. at 450.

41. *Id.*

42. The Court rejected the claim that "'the imperative of judicial integrity'" furnishes an "independent basis" for *Miranda* exclusion. *Id.* at 450 n.25 (quoting Elkins v. United States, 364 U.S. 206, 222 (1960)). Because judicial integrity was at risk only to the extent that courts failed to adequately deter misconduct or allowed convictions based on

In two opinions in the mid-1980s, the Court continued to reform the underpinnings of the *Miranda* exclusionary rule and to restrict its scope. *New York v. Quarles*[43] announced a "'public safety' exception to the requirement that *Miranda* warnings be given *before a suspect's answers may be admitted into evidence.*"[44] If officers interrogate a suspect in custody to further the public safety, incriminating statements are not excludable despite the failure to issue warnings. This exception to *Miranda*'s bar rested on the critical distinction between actually coerced statements, which are categorically barred by the Fifth Amendment, and statements obtained in violation of *Miranda*'s "prophylactic rules."[45] Confessions resulting from violations of these "judicially imposed strictures,"[46] are "presumed" to be compelled and ordinarily are suppressed.[47] The absence of actual compulsion, however, means that the admission of such statements does not violate the Fifth Amendment's guarantee against compulsory self-incrimination.[48]

Quarles did make it clear that *Miranda* does not exclude statements whose introduction at trial would deny a suspect his Fifth Amendment right. The Court was not explicit, however, about the affirmative reasons for the bar to disclosures when public safety concerns are not present. Asserting that *Miranda*'s safeguards were designed to "reduce the likelihood that . . . suspects would fall victim to constitutionally impermissible practices"[49] in police stations and concluding that there was no reason to "penaliz[e] officers for asking . . . questions . . . crucial" to public safety,[50] the Court hinted at deterrent purposes. Ordinarily, suppression penalizes officers, inducing future compliance with safeguards that reduce the likelihood of victimization by impermissible police practices.

Even more subtly, the Court seemed to suggest that *Miranda* exclusion serves an immediate Fifth Amendment function. According to *Quarles*, the *Miranda* Court declared statements obtained during unconstrained custodial interrogation inadmissible because of a perceived need to provide "enlarged protection for the Fifth Amendment privilege."[51] Like its guidelines for custodial interrogation, *Miranda*'s evidentiary bar is a "prophylactic rule [that] protect[s] the Fifth Amendment's privilege against self-incrimination."[52] The Court seemed to

---

genuinely compelled disclosures, it was inseparable from the "more specific rationales" the Court had considered. *Id.*

43. 467 U.S. 649 (1984).

44. *Id.* at 655 (emphasis added).

45. *Id.* at 653.

46. *Id.* at 653 n.3.

47. *Id.* at 654, 655 n.5.

48. *Quarles*, 467 U.S. at 658 n.7.

49. *Id.* at 656.

50. *Id.* at 658 n.7.

51. *Id.* at 657.

52. *Id.*

suggest that *Miranda* prohibits statements obtained in a "presumptively coercive environment"[53] not simply to deter officers, but also because of the *possibility* that those statements are compelled and that their admission *could* violate the Fifth Amendment. In other words, suppression prevents potential violations.

A year later, the Court decided *Oregon v. Elstad*,[54] a case in which officers failed to warn a suspect, secured a confession by means of custodial interrogation, then subsequently complied with *Miranda*'s safeguards and obtained a second confession. According to a majority, the latter confession was not subject to suppression. The ruling, once again, was rooted in the critical distinction between actual coercion and *Miranda*'s presumption of coercion and an understanding of *Miranda*'s exclusionary rule as overbroad prophylaxis that bars more evidence than the Fifth Amendment privilege.[55] The *Elstad* reasoning, though somewhat incomplete and "opaque,"[56] suggested that *Miranda* suppression might rest upon "the twin rationales" of "trustworthiness and deterrence."[57]

More specifically, the Court appeared to believe that the unalleviated pressures of custodial interrogation create risks that revelations are compelled and, therefore, untrustworthy. By barring potentially untrustworthy statements, *Miranda*'s exclusionary rule, like the Fifth Amendment, prevents wrongful convictions based on false admissions of guilt.[58] Suppression under *Miranda* is also designed to deter future officers from failing to follow the guidelines for custodial interrogation.[59] Knowing of the bar to confessions, officers will be motivated to abide by *Miranda*'s dictates.[60]

Unlike *Tucker*, both *Quarles* and *Elstad* suggested that *Miranda* exclusion was more than a future-oriented deterrent, unable to do anything about

---

53. *Quarles*, 467 U.S. at 656.

54. 470 U.S. 298 (1985).

55. *Id.* at 304, 306, 307.

56. *Id.* at 365 (Stevens, J., dissenting).

57. *Elstad*, 470 U.S. at 308.

58. *See id.* at 307–08. It is noteworthy that the *Elstad* Court did not acknowledge any Fifth Amendment values other than trustworthiness. I admit that I have filled in considerable gaps in the Court's reasoning, inferring and fleshing out the affirmative bases for exclusion primarily from the *Elstad* majority's explanation of why the second confession, following warnings, did not have to be suppressed.

59. *See id.* at 308. Again, from the Court's declarations that deterrence did not justify suppression in *Elstad* (or in *Tucker*) I have inferred the view that it is a rationale for the exclusion that *Miranda* does command.

60. The Court also reinforced the notion that there is a distinction between the deterrent objectives of *Miranda* exclusion and the deterrent objectives of the Fourth Amendment exclusionary rule. Because the behavior sought to be discouraged—failures to comply with judicially-devised constraints upon custodial interrogation—does not itself violate the Constitution, the interest in deterrence is less potent than under the Fourth Amendment. The social costs of barring probative evidence more readily outweigh this less substantial deterrent interest. *See id.* at 306–09.

a fully-accomplished infringement upon constitutional interests. The Court seemed to believe that suppression plays a role in preventing Fifth Amendment injuries at the current trial. The holdings and the unmistakable tenors of these two opinions, however, reflected a hostility toward *Miranda* suppression and a determination to confine its scope consistent with the spirit of *Harris* and *Tucker*. The two opinions that followed indicated that a majority might be having doubts about its treatment of the *Miranda* exclusionary rule and could be preparing to reinvigorate the doctrine.

In light of the developments since *Miranda*, the ruling and reasoning in *Withrow v. Williams*[61] were nothing short of astounding. *Stone v. Powell*[62] had held that a prisoner challenging a state conviction in a habeas corpus proceeding could not raise a Fourth Amendment exclusionary rule claim if the state had accorded the claim a full and fair hearing.[63] The question in *Withrow* was whether to impose a similar constraint on *Miranda*'s exclusionary rule. A five-Justice majority held that because of important differences between *Miranda* and Fourth Amendment suppression, a *Miranda* claim can be pursued in a habeas action even if a state court has provided a full and fair opportunity to litigate the claim.[64]

According to the *Withrow* majority, Fourth Amendment exclusion aims entirely at future deterrence and can do nothing "to remedy" the completed constitutional wrong or "enhance the soundness of the criminal process by improving the reliability of evidence."[65] Although *Miranda* bars statements that have not been proven to have been involuntary, it does "safeguard[] 'a fundamental *trial* right'"—the Fifth Amendment privilege.[66] By guarding against potentially compelled confessions, *Miranda*'s suppression doctrine furthers the array of accusatorial system values that underlie the guarantee against compulsory self-incrimination.[67] Moreover, by shielding against "'the use of unreliable statements at trial'" and the risks of convicting innocent persons, it enhances the integrity of the criminal process.[68] These important functions persuaded the Court that defendants should be able to vindicate *Miranda* exclusion claims in habeas proceedings. The majority found no need to rely on deterrent objectives.[69]

---

61. 507 U.S. 680 (1993).

62. 428 U.S. 465 (1976).

63. *Id.* at 481–82.

64. *Withrow*, 507 U.S. at 688.

65. *Id.* at 691.

66. *Id.* at 690–91 (quoting United States v. Verdugo-Urquidez, 494 U.S. 259, 264 (1990)).

67. *Id.* at 691–92.

68. *Id.* at 692–93 (quoting Johnson v. New Jersey, 384 U.S. 719, 730 (1966)).

69. In essence, the majority concluded that even if a state court gave a *Miranda* exclusion claim full and fair consideration, if it erroneously resolved the claim the

The *Withrow* majority certainly did not restore the *Miranda* exclusionary rule to its original status as a personal constitutional right. Nonetheless, it recast *Miranda* suppression as a valued safeguard against the possibility that admissions made during unregulated custodial interrogation have been forced from the suspect's mind. In keeping such admissions from trial, *Miranda* prevents Fifth Amendment deprivations. The confirmation and explanation of this role in preventing immediate constitutional injury to the accused suggested that *Miranda* exclusion was more important than Fourth Amendment exclusion. The holding, reasoning, and spirit of the majority opinion signaled the possibility of a new era for *Miranda* suppression in which its vital constitutional role at trial would lead to more generous interpretations.[70]

Despite its ambiguous, even cryptic, reasoning, the Court's subsequent ruling in *Dickerson v. United States*[71] provided further reason to believe that *Miranda*'s exclusionary rule could be poised for a renaissance. *Dickerson* involved a direct challenge to *Miranda*'s survival. A lower court had ruled that because "*Miranda* was not a constitutional holding," it could be replaced by a congressional enactment mandating the admission of any voluntary statement. Seven Justices disagreed, holding that because *Miranda* was, in fact, "a constitutional decision," it could not "be in effect overruled by . . . Congress."[72] *Miranda* had not announced mere "judicially created rules of evidence and procedure [that were] not required by the Constitution."[73] Because its dictates were an interpretation and implementation of the Fifth Amendment, the lower court had erred in deciding that

---

prisoner's conviction could be the result of a Fifth Amendment deprivation. For that reason, a prisoner ought to have the opportunity to show that the state court had erred.

Four Justices emphatically disagreed with the holding and reasoning in *Withrow*. *See Withrow*, 507 U.S. at 697 (O'Connor, J., concurring in part and dissenting in part); *id.* at 715 (Scalia, J., concurring in part and dissenting in part). Justice O'Connor contended that *Miranda*'s "prophylactic remedy" of exclusion actually undermines the accuracy of verdicts by suppressing reliable evidence and that the balance of relevant interests militated in favor of extending the *Stone v. Powell* limitation to *Miranda* claims. *Id.* at 706–08, 713–14 (O'Connor, J., concurring in part and dissenting in part). She asserted that the *Miranda* rule serves as a deterrent sanction—that is, it "provides a strong incentive for the police to adopt 'procedural safeguards' against the exaction of compelled or involuntary statements." *Id.* at 702–03 (quoting Miranda v. Arizona, 384 U.S. 436, 444 (1966)). Suppression under *Miranda* "also promotes institutional respect for constitutional values." *Id.* at 703.

70. The sense a new phase might be beginning was bolstered by the majority's declaration that the dictates of *Miranda* had earned and deserve respect. *Withrow*, 507 U.S. at 695.

71. 530 U.S. 428 (2000).

72. *Id.* at 431–32.

73. *Id.* at 437.

"the protections announced in *Miranda* are not constitutionally required."[74] In fact, the *Miranda* exclusion doctrine was "a constitutional rule."[75]

Dickerson confirmed that suppression is an important trial safeguard for the Fifth Amendment privilege. The *Miranda* Court had believed that the "coercion inherent" in "modern custodial police interrogation" techniques "blur[red] the line between voluntary and involuntary statements" and "heighten[ed] the risk" of compelled self-incrimination.[76] The traditional voluntariness test—which required case-by-case determinations of whether suspects had been forced to speak—could not adequately identify compelled statements. Without additional protection against the introduction of compelled statements, there was an "unacceptably great" risk that involuntary confessions would be "overlook[ed]" and then used to convict defendants.[77] By barring potentially compelled disclosures, *Miranda*'s exclusionary rule furnished a constitutionally necessary safeguard against violation of the Fifth Amendment.[78] This conception of the role *Miranda* suppression played was entirely consistent with the generous reasoning in *Withrow*. In addition, the Court's undoubtedly deliberate decision not to describe *Miranda* as "prophylactic"[79]—a pejorative that had played a pivotal role in the erosive opinions preceding *Withrow*—suggested that a more favorable attitude toward *Miranda* suppression might have taken root.[80]

The tortuous history of *Miranda* exclusion ends nearly 40 years after it began with one final twist. In *United States v. Patane*,[81] a deeply divided Court drastically

74. *Id.* at 437–38.

75. *Id.* at 439, n.4.

76. *Dickerson*, 530 U.S. at 434–35.

77. *Id.* at. 442.

78. *Id.* at 438 (disagreeing with the Court of Appeals conclusion that *Miranda* protections are "not constitutionally required"); *id.* at 442 (referring to the fact that *Miranda*'s safeguards were developed because "something more . . . was necessary").

79. Dissenting Justice Scalia called attention to the Court's refusal to employ this term, but argued that the ruling could only be justified as the exercise of what he believed to be illegitimate authority to devise constitutional prophylaxis. *See id.* at 457, 460–61 (Scalia, J., dissenting).

80. Once again, the Court did *not* resurrect the original view of suppression as an essential part of the Fifth Amendment privilege. The *Dickerson* Court did not assert that the admission of a statement obtained in violation of *Miranda* would violate the Fifth Amendment. While exclusion was necessary because there were unacceptable risks that statements obtained in violation of *Miranda* were compelled, there was no proof that those statements were actually compelled. The Court reaffirmed the premise that *Miranda* was constitutionally overprotective insofar as it required the suppression of some statements that were not in fact involuntary and thereby unnecessarily set some guilty persons free. *Id.* at 444. In sum, the Court did not retract the pre-*Withrow* declaration that the Fifth Amendment is violated only when a statement proven to have been actually compelled is used to convict.

81. 542 U.S. 630 (2004).

limited the scope of suppression, holding that *Miranda* bars *only statements* acquired by means of custodial interrogation without safeguards; it does *not* require the exclusion of *any* derivative evidence.[82] The ruling and reasoning signaled a return of the grudging attitude toward *Miranda* suppression and a determination to severely curtail its impact.[83]

According to Justice Thomas's plurality opinion, just like the Fifth Amendment guarantee on which it is based, the *Miranda* decision was solely concerned with the trial process and not with constraining law enforcement conduct.[84] Because the *Miranda* Court had been concerned only with what happened in the courtroom, the rule barring evidence was the essence and entirety of its decision. The only "*Miranda* rule" was the declaration that certain evidence is inadmissible.[85] The "possibility of coercion inherent in custodial interrogations" had prompted the *Miranda* Court to devise a presumption of compulsion—and a suppression doctrine—to safeguard against risks that a defendant would be deprived of the Fifth Amendment entitlement.[86] Because exclusion is a "prophylactic rule[]" that "sweep[s] beyond the actual protection[]" provided by the Constitution, any extension "must be justified by [a] necessity for the protection of the actual right against compelled self-incrimination."[87] In fact, the "explicit textual protection" of the Fifth Amendment is a reason for a "strong presumption against expanding the *Miranda* rule."[88] Although *Miranda's* exclusion doctrine is a "constitutional rule," because it is a "judge-made" prophylactic it is necessary "to maintain the closest possible fit between" suppression and the right against compelled, testimonial self-incrimination that it is "designed to protect."[89] The plurality confirmed that *Miranda* suppression provides immediate protection for a fundamental trial right, but also solidified its status as a device that extends

---

82. *Id.* at 637, 641–43 (plurality opinion); *id.* at 645 (Kennedy, J., concurring in the judgment).

83. *Patane*'s significance for the future of *Miranda* exclusion is rendered somewhat murky by the split between the five Justices who agreed with the decision that confined suppression to the suspect's initial statements. Only three Justices joined the lead opinion. The other two members of the majority joined a separate concurrence. *See id.* at 644 (Kennedy, J., concurring in the judgment).

84. *Id.* at 637 (plurality opinion). Between *Dickerson* and *Patane*, the Court had ruled that the Fifth Amendment is not violated by officers' compulsion, but is a trial right that can be transgressed only when compelled disclosures are used in court. *See* Chavez v. Martinez, 538 U.S. 760, 767 (2003) (opinion of Thomas, J.); *id.* at 777 (Souter, J., concurring in the judgment).

85. *Patane*, 542 U.S. at 637, 641 (plurality opinion).

86. *Id.* at 639 (plurality opinion).

87. *Id.* (plurality opinion).

88. *Id.* at 640 (plurality opinion).

89. *Id.* at 643 (plurality opinion).

beyond the actual constitutional mandate. Narrow interpretation was essential to prevent excessive overbreadth.

The plurality then ventured into entirely new territory, declaring that the *Miranda* exclusionary rule can draw no support from a deterrent rationale. Because officers who fail to abide by *Miranda*'s guidelines for custodial interrogation do not violate the Constitution or even the *Miranda* rule, "there is . . . nothing to deter."[90] In the plurality's view, officers who conduct custodial interrogation without safeguards cause *no* cognizable harm or injury. For that reason, suppressing the confessions they obtain cannot be justified as an effort to alter future law enforcement behavior. The sole *Miranda* rule is the rule of exclusion, and the sole justification for that rule is to combat the intolerable risks of violating a defendant's right not to be compelled to be a witness against himself. The plurality sought to eliminate a predicate for suppression—deterrence—that had been recognized as a premise since the first post-*Miranda* rulings in the early 1970s.

The two concurring Justices who were part of the *Patane* majority, Justices Kennedy and O'Connor, joined none of the plurality's reasoning. Despite the brevity of their own opinion, it seems fair to say that they agreed that *Miranda* exclusion is a "rule" that reaches beyond the precise command of the Fifth Amendment to guard against "the risk of admitting into trial an accused's coerced incriminating statements against himself."[91] They did not explicitly reject the assertion that *Miranda*'s exclusionary rule has no deterrent justification, but pointedly refused to endorse that proposition. They considered it "unnecessary to decide whether" a failure to adhere to *Miranda*'s custodial interrogation guidelines "should be characterized as a violation of the *Miranda* rule itself, or whether there is '[any]thing to deter' so long as the unwarned statements are not later introduced at trial."[92] Consequently, the *Patane* ruling did not eliminate deterrence from the *Miranda* exclusionary calculus.[93]

Perhaps the most significant message of this most recent chapter of *Miranda*'s history is that the Court is determined to narrow its suppression doctrine. It is difficult to imagine any future expansion of the scope of the *Miranda* exclusionary rule beyond that which currently exists. On the other hand, it is possible that the Court will find ways to further constrain *Miranda*'s prophylactic courtroom safeguard.

---

90. *Patane*, 542 U.S. at 641–42 (plurality opinion).

91. *Id.* at 645 (Kennedy, J., concurring in the judgment). Justices Kennedy and O'Connor, the two Justices who joined the concurrence, had subscribed to this description of *Miranda* in *Dickerson*.

92. *Id.* (Kennedy, J., concurring in the judgment).

93. Three Justices explicitly endorsed deterrence as a justification for *Miranda*'s bar. *See id.* at 645 (Souter, J., dissenting).

Miranda's exclusionary rule has undergone dramatic changes since it first appeared in the mid-twentieth century. For the most part, radical modifications of the rule's very foundations have restricted its reach and impact. A bar to confessions that began as an inseparable part of the Fifth Amendment trial right was soon transmuted into an exclusionary rule designed to alter law enforcement interrogations.

For a time, it was uncertain whether suppression served any function other than deterrence, but then a second rationale emerged. *Miranda* suppression, it turned out, was also a necessary shield against intolerable risks that unregulated custodial interrogation would result in convictions based on compelled, self-incriminating statements. While *Miranda* exclusion did not regain the status of constitutional right, it became a judicially-created, but constitutionally-rooted, means of preventing deprivations of a fundamental Bill of Rights liberty. Future-oriented deterrence receded, becoming an ancillary justification for a doctrine that, unlike the Fourth Amendment exclusionary rule, provides immediate constitutional protection at trial.

Emphasis on suppression's role as a prophylactic courtroom safeguard against the risks of compelled self-incrimination has become the dominant theme. Deterrence of law enforcement conduct has clearly become a secondary rationale, at best. Some Justices have even suggested that deterrence is not an objective of *Miranda*'s exclusionary rule. With only one exception, reformulations of *Miranda*'s premises over time have diminished the scope of suppression. The currently prevailing understanding and the reaffirmation of *Miranda*'s constitutional status in *Dickerson* have not prevented further constriction of the rule. Because exclusion under *Miranda* is not part of the Fifth Amendment's core protection, but, instead, is an overbroad preventive mechanism, the Court has been resistant to efforts to expand its reach.

The details of the limits imposed on the *Miranda* rule are the subjects of the doctrinal sections of this chapter. Before turning to those matters, in-depth exploration and analysis of the rationales for and legitimacy of the *Miranda* exclusionary rule are in order. Because so much of the rule's history has revolved around the reform of its very foundations, the themes of the discussion that follows will be familiar.

C. THE RATIONALES FOR AND LEGITIMACY OF THE *MIRANDA* EXCLUSIONARY RULE

Three rationales for *Miranda*'s constitutional exclusion doctrine have played roles in its development.[94] The first premise is that suppression is an indivisible

94. For general scholarly discussions of a variety of issues surrounding the *Miranda* doctrine, see Steven D. Clymer, *Are Police Free to Disregard* Miranda?, 112 YALE L.J. 447

part of the Fifth Amendment trial right. An alternative possibility is that exclusion is not a right itself, but a safeguard necessary to counter risks of compulsory self-incrimination and prevent undetectable Fifth Amendment violations at trial. A third justification that can supplement either of the first two is deterrence—the prevention of future violations of *Miranda*'s regulations for custodial interrogation. *Miranda*'s suppression doctrine has been extremely controversial since its inception, perhaps even more controversial than the much maligned Fourth Amendment exclusionary rule. The legitimacy of each putative justification has been challenged. This section examines the meaning of the three possible rationales and assesses the arguments concerning *Miranda*'s legitimacy.

As noted earlier, *Miranda*'s evidentiary bar was initially understood to be an immanent part of the Fifth Amendment privilege. Because unconstrained custodial interrogation generates inherent pressures that force suspects to speak, any disclosures that result must be deemed compelled.[95] Introduction of these disclosures at trial would violate the Fifth Amendment command. By using the disclosures to obtain convictions, the government would effectively compel suspects to be witnesses against themselves. The Fifth Amendment guarantee prohibits the government from doing so. Exclusion implements that prohibition and preserves the privilege that is part of the bedrock of our accusatorial criminal justice system.[96]

Opponents of *Miranda* have challenged the original explanation for its rule of inadmissibility as irrational and even "preposterous."[97] In their view, the premise that the combination of custody and interrogation always or even ordinarily

---

(2002); Yale Kamisar, *Can (Did) Congress "Overrule"* Miranda?, 85 CORNELL L. REV. 883 (2000); William T. Pizzi & Morris B. Hoffman, *Taking* Miranda*'s Pulse*, 58 VAND. L. REV. 813 (2005); Stephen J. Schulhofer, *Bashing* Miranda *is Unjustified—And Harmful*, 20 HARV. J.L. & PUB. POL'Y 347 (1997); Steven J. Schulhofer, *Reconsidering* Miranda, 54 U. CHI. L. REV. 435 (1987).

95. Miranda v. Arizona, 384 U.S. 436, 457–58, 461 (1966).

96. *See id.* at 479, 490–91; *see also* Martin R. Gardner, *The Emerging Good Faith Exception to the* Miranda *Rule—A Critique*, 35 HASTINGS L. J. 429, 450–55 (1984) [hereinafter Gardner, *Emerging Good Faith*]. Although a majority of the Court soon rejected this explanation of *Miranda* suppression, for at least two decades there were members of the Court who adhered to this view. These Justices rested dissents opposing the restriction of *Miranda*'s suppression doctrine upon assertions that the Fifth Amendment privilege commanded exclusion and could not be qualified or limited by the judiciary. *See* Oregon v. Elstad, 470 U.S. 298, 347–54 (1985) (Brennan, J., dissenting); New York v. Quarles, 467 U.S. 649, 687–88 (1984) (Marshall, J., dissenting); Harris v. New York, 401 U.S. 222, 231–32 (1971) (Brennan, J., dissenting). By the 1990s, the defense of exclusion as a right seems to have disappeared. It has not reappeared in the twenty-first century. Defenders of *Miranda* suppression now rely on one of the other justifications discussed here.

97. *See* Dickerson v. United States, 530 U.S. 428, 448, 450 (2000) (Scalia, J., dissenting); *Miranda*, 384 U.S. at 534–35 (White, J., dissenting); *see also* Gerald M. Caplan, *Questioning* Miranda, 38 VAND. L. REV. 1417 (1985).

pressures suspects into speaking against their wills unless officers employ counteractive measures is indefensible as a matter of fact. In reality, many individuals subjected to custodial interrogation remain free to choose whether to make incriminating disclosures. The conclusion that the Fifth Amendment bars the testimonial products of custodial interrogation without warnings and waiver rests on a patently fallacious foundation, an unsupportable assumption about the effects of custodial interrogation on the wills of suspects. There is no right to exclude confessions obtained in violation of *Miranda* because there is no constitutional bar to voluntary disclosures. Without proof that the government has brought more pressure to bear or that a particular suspect was peculiarly vulnerable to the interrogation environment, the privilege does not bar the government from using confessions.

This challenge to *Miranda*'s original premises rests on a belief that the Fifth Amendment prohibits only testimony that is the product of a broken will, barring disclosures only when a person has succumbed to official coercion and spoken involuntarily. If these critics are right about the meaning of Fifth Amendment compulsion, if that guarantee forbids only convictions based on thoughts forced from suspects' minds, then their argument that there is no constitutional right to exclude the products of mere custodial interrogation has considerable force. The assumption that official questioning of a person who has been deprived of freedom always, or even typically, forces him to disclose his guilt involuntarily is more than questionable. It becomes all the more dubious when the definitions of custody and interrogation are taken into account. Custody occurs the moment a person is formally arrested, even in her own home in the company of sympathetic family or friends. There is no need for isolation in a police station.[98] Moreover, a single question from an officer constitutes interrogation. Prolonged, intense grilling or other oppressive tactics are unnecessary.[99]

The original conception of *Miranda* exclusion is defensible, however, if one interprets the Fifth Amendment prohibition on compelling a person to speak as more protective than the Due Process Clause bar to coerced confessions. In fact, Chief Justice Warren's majority opinion in *Miranda* appeared to rest on the premise that the Fifth Amendment forbids lesser pressures than the Fourteenth Amendment. He declared that "no statement obtained" by means of unconstrained custodial interrogation "can *truly* be the product of [the suspect's] *free choice*"[100] and asserted that "the privilege is fulfilled only when the person is guaranteed the right 'to remain silent unless he chooses to speak in the

---

98. *See* Berkemer v. McCarty, 468 U.S. 420, 434, 440–42 (1984) (holding that a formal arrest or its functional equivalent constitutes custody).

99. *See* Rhode Island v. Innis, 446 U.S. 291, 300–01 (1980) (deciding that interrogation is satisfied by either express questioning or its functional equivalent).

100. *Miranda*, 384 U.S. at 458 (emphasis added).

unfettered exercise of his own will.'"[101] The Fifth Amendment does not require coercive pressures that overbear the suspect's free will. Any infringement upon "free choice" is impermissible and any revelation that is not the result of an "unfettered exercise of . . . will" is barred.[102] If the Fifth Amendment guarantee is as expansive as the Warren Court suggested, *Miranda*'s conclusions that confessions made during custodial interrogation without safeguards are compelled and that exclusion is therefore an indivisible part of the privilege are hardly implausible. In sum, the legitimacy of the view that *Miranda* exclusion is a constitutional right is contingent on the meaning of the Bill of Rights pledge that "[n]o person . . . shall be compelled . . . to be a witness against himself."

As a historical matter, the original "rights-based" justification for *Miranda* suppression was soon interred. The Court concluded that Fifth Amendment compulsion, like Fourteenth Amendment coercion, requires pressures that overcome a individual's will. Moreover, by themselves, custody and interrogation do not generate actual compulsion, and absent actual compulsion, there can be no right to exclude disclosures. A different rationale for *Miranda* exclusion was needed.

The alternative vision that took root—and controls the discourse today—depicts *Miranda*'s inadmissibility doctrine as a constitutional exclusionary *rule*. The *Miranda* rule, however, is notably different in nature from its Fourth Amendment counterpart—a device aimed entirely at the prevention of future constitutional violations. The prevention *Miranda* seeks is in the present. It is primarily concerned with eliminating risks that the accused on trial will be denied his Fifth Amendment entitlement. It is a courtroom prophylactic that combats undetected deprivations of a fundamental trial right.[103]

The alternative rationale for *Miranda* exclusion, like the original rationale, rests on the premise that custodial interrogation contains inherent pressures to speak. These pressures give rise to a certain "likelihood" that suspects will be compelled to speak against their wills.[104] If revelations are admitted at trial, there are "unacceptably great" risks of compulsory self-incrimination in violation of

---

101. *Id.* at 460 (quoting Malloy v. Hogan, 378 U.S. 1, 8 (1964)) (emphasis added).

102. The majority also stated that their "concern for adequate safeguards to protect precious Fifth Amendment rights [was] . . . not lessened in the slightest" by the fact that they "might not find the . . . statements [in *Miranda*] to have been involuntary in traditional terms." *Id.* at 457. This provided further evidence of a belief that the Fifth Amendment prohibition of compulsion imposed greater restrictions on law enforcement than the due process guarantee against coercion.

103. The basic character of the *Miranda* rule and its sharp contrasts with the Fourth Amendment exclusionary rule are best explained in *Withrow v. Williams*, 507 U.S. 680, 691–93 (1993).

104. *See* New York v. Quarles, 467 U.S. 649, 656 (1984) (referring to "the likelihood" of suspects succumbing to "impermissible" interrogation methods in a "presumptively coercive environment").

the Fifth Amendment.[105] An evidentiary bar is a necessary constitutional prophylactic that prevents these risks from being realized. The Fifth Amendment shelter furnished by *Miranda* is "enlarged"—that is, broader than that required by the privilege's prohibition.[106] Because exclusion is a response to mere risks of compulsion, some barred statements will be the result of voluntary decisions, not overborne wills. For that reason, *Miranda*'s courtroom protection "sweeps more broadly than the Fifth Amendment itself," providing "a remedy" to some defendants who would "suffer[] no identifiable constitutional harm" from the introduction of their confessions.[107]

The natural question is whether an overbroad exclusionary rule is constitutionally justified. Why not suppress only confessions forbidden by the Fifth Amendment? A second, essential premise for the alternative explanation for *Miranda* suppression is that accurate, individualized, case-by-case assessments of actual compulsion are not possible. The judiciary cannot reliably distinguish between the products of custodial interrogation that would transgress the Fifth Amendment and those that would not. The result is a danger of overlooking and admitting compelled disclosures, thereby depriving defendants of Fifth Amendment rights.[108] A rule that encompasses a certain number of voluntary statements is necessary to prevent these deprivations. Put otherwise, the choice is between individualized assessments that under-protect the privilege and a general, bright-line evidentiary bar that overprotects. On balance, the costs of excess prevention—the loss of voluntary revelations and the legitimate convictions that might result—are justified (indeed, are necessary) to prevent the inevitable constitutional harms from the deficient shelter provided by case-by-case determinations. In essence, the *Miranda* Court concluded that an imperfect exclusionary regime was necessary to ensure adequate constitutional enforcement.

The alternative rationale for *Miranda* rests upon a cost-benefit assessment.[109] Ordinarily, the gains in safeguarding invaluable Fifth Amendment rights by suppressing risky statements are worth the price paid—the loss of valid convictions resulting from the exclusion of voluntary disclosures.[110] According to the

---

105. *See* Dickerson v. United States, 530 U.S. 428, 442 (2000) (noting that *Miranda* was based on the Court's conclusion that the due process coerced confession test "raised a risk" of overlooking forced confessions and its finding that the "risk" was "unacceptably great when the confession [was] offered . . . to prove guilt").

106. *See Quarles*, 467 U.S. at 657 (asserting that *Miranda* had decided that the costs of its evidentiary bar should be "borne in the interest of enlarged protection for the Fifth Amendment privilege").

107. *See* Oregon v. Elstad, 470 U.S. 298, 306–07 (1985).

108. *See Dickerson*, 530 U.S. at 442.

109. *See Quarles*, 467 U.S. at 656–57.

110. *See Dickerson*, 530 U.S. at 444 (citing the "disadvantage" of a "guilty defendant go[ing] free as a result" of the suppression of a voluntary statement).

prophylactic explanation of *Miranda* exclusion, the risks of compulsion resulting from custodial interrogation do not always require suppression. When suppression imposes additional costs, it is necessary to reassess the balance to determine whether these costs outweigh the constitutional benefits. Potential Fifth Amendment deprivations can be acceptable when other costs are factored in. When the price of enlarged protection is too high, *Miranda*'s logic does not dictate suppression.

Although exclusion is not a personal constitutional right of the accused, it is a "constitutional rule"—a mechanism that provides necessary reinforcement for the Fifth Amendment privilege.[111] For that reason, legislative substitutes are impermissible unless they provide equivalent protection against the risks of courtroom deprivations.[112] The degree of overbroad prophylaxis afforded by *Miranda*'s exclusionary rule is constitutionally required.

This alternative justification for exclusion reflects the exercise of a rarely used power. It rests on a belief that when circumstances pose sufficiently serious threats to fundamental liberties, the Supreme Court has not only the authority, but the constitutional obligation to devise legal tools to effectively combat the threats. In the absence of an adequate legislative response, the Justices must prescribe and enforce preventive measures. One criticism of *Miranda*'s legitimacy rejects the premise that the Supreme Court has prophylactic authority. According to this view, the Court has no authority to enlarge Fifth Amendment protection and provide more shelter than is prescribed by the Bill of Rights. The Court may only forbid government conduct that actually transgresses constitutional commands. By imposing a preventive remedy sweeping beyond what the privilege demands, the Court has arrogated to itself a power that, in our system of government, belongs to the people. That power must be exercised, if at all, by the legislative branch. The judiciary must respect the Framers' balance and may not strike a new balance simply because perfect case-by-case determinations are not possible.[113]

It is not unfair to suggest that the prevailing justification for *Miranda* exclusion is a clever, if not entirely honest, construct of Justices who found the original "rights" rationale indefensible but lacked sufficient support to overrule *Miranda*. The reconception of exclusion as an essential constitutional safeguard rooted in

---

111. *See id.* at 441, 444.

112. *See id.* at 441–44.

113. Justice Scalia's dissent in *Dickerson* develops this challenge to *Miranda* in great detail. *See id.* at 446, 454–61, 465. For scholarly discussions of the prophylactic justification for *Miranda* suppression, see Joseph D. Grano, *Prophylactic Rules in Criminal Procedure: A Question of Article III Legitimacy*, 80 Nw. U. L. Rev. 100, 106–11, 154–55 (1985); Susan R. Klein, *Identifying and (Re)formulating Prophylactic Rules, Safe Harbors, and Incidental Rights in Constitutional Criminal Procedure*, 99 Mich. L. Rev. 1030, 1071–77 (2001).

a cost-benefit balance has enabled the *Miranda* rule to survive. At the same time, it has proven to be an effective tool for dramatically curtailing the impact of *Miranda* suppression. It has been an effective foundation for compromise between those who would eliminate the *Miranda* doctrine and those who wish to preserve it, but limit its damage to legitimate law enforcement. The alternative, prophylactic predicate for *Miranda* exclusion is arguably a pragmatic, goal-driven rationalization, not a legitimate constitutional rationale.

On the other hand, the premise that the judiciary has the power, indeed the duty, to devise methods of preserving constitutional liberties when those liberties are endangered by societal change is surely not implausible. If accurate identification of constitutional violations is impractical or impossible, a somewhat overprotective approach—when the only alternative is seriously underprotective—does not run afoul of any indisputable principle about the nature of judicial authority or the character of our government. And while the skeptical explanation of the evolved rationale as a pragmatic compromise may reflect *how* the revision came about, it does not necessarily render the revision illegitimate. The prophylactic safeguard explanation of *Miranda* exclusion may well be more consistent with realities and might be a preferable way of understanding why confessions secured by unconstrained custodial interrogation must be barred.

In sum, like the original justification for *Miranda*'s constitutional exclusion doctrine, the justification that took its place has been controversial. Critics contend that it is premised on authority that the judiciary does not possess.[114] Whatever its merits, it seems virtually certain that this explanation will continue to dictate the contours of *Miranda*'s exclusionary rule.

A possible supplemental justification for *Miranda* exclusion is the dominant rationale for Fourth Amendment suppression—deterring future misconduct by officers. For good reason, deterrence has never been influential in the resolution of *Miranda* suppression issues. The question is whether it has *any* role to play—i.e., whether it is *a* logical premise for *Miranda*'s rule.

The *Miranda* opinion understood suppression as a Fifth Amendment right, and, for that reason, had no occasion to discuss whether deterrence furnished

---

114. The criticisms discussed here have been leveled by *Miranda* opponents. *Miranda*'s supporters are also quite critical of the revised justification for exclusion. They find it to be an unacceptable dilution of the constitutional foundation for *Miranda*'s rule of inadmissibility. *See* Irene M. Rosenberg & Yale L. Rosenberg, *A Modest Proposal for the Abolition of Custodial Confessions*, 68 N.C. L. Rev. 69, 82 (1989) (alleging that Court has "diluted *Miranda* by denying its constitutional base"); Charles D. Weisselberg, *Saving* Miranda, 84 Cornell L. Rev. 109, 126–30 (1998) [hereinafter Weisselberg, *Saving* Miranda] (describing the Court's departures from the original premises of *Miranda*). They would adhere to the original view that the exclusion of statements is necessary to avoid Fifth Amendment violations. *See* Weisselberg, *Saving* Miranda, *supra* at 140–87 (discussing the reasons for a return to and calling for a revival of the "original vision" of *Miranda*).

any support.[115] The deterrence rationale first appeared in the opinions that transformed the character of *Miranda* exclusion, but during this transformative process not once did the Court affirmatively assert that deterring future conduct *is* a justification for suppression or rely on deterrence as a basis for a holding.[116] There seemed to be an assumption that deterrence was an objective, but there were no explanations of the anticipated behavioral changes and why they might be desirable constitutional ends. The opinions that seemed to reinvigorate *Miranda* by explaining the important role it plays in preventing Fifth Amendment violations at trial placed no reliance on deterrence. It seemed that the role of deterrence was ancillary, at best. Finally, in the most recent of the *Miranda* suppression decisions, the legitimacy of the deterrent premise was challenged. Today, it seems entirely possible that the deterrent justification might come full circle, disappearing entirely from the *Miranda* discourse.

The analytical question is whether deterrence *should* serve as a justification for the *Miranda* exclusionary rule. Is it logical to suppress disclosures made during unconstrained custodial interrogation in order to modify the way officers conduct those interrogations? If the aim of the Fifth Amendment was not only to safeguard against conviction based on compelled disclosures, but also to prevent the harmful effects compulsion can have outside the courtroom, deterrence could be a legitimate justification for *Miranda* exclusion. Under the original understanding of *Miranda*, custodial interrogation without safeguards brings compulsion to bear upon suspects. By inducing officers to follow *Miranda*'s compulsion-dispelling guidelines—that is, to give warnings, secure waivers, and respect requests to remain silent or have counsel—the suppression of statements would prevent the constitutional harm occasioned by official pressures to speak. Under the revised conception of *Miranda*, the inherent pressures of unconstrained custodial interrogation generate intolerable risks of compulsion. By motivating officers to adhere to *Miranda*'s interrogation room prescriptions, exclusion would forestall constitutional injury in situations where unconstrained custodial interrogation would actually force suspects to speak. In either case, the *Miranda* exclusionary rule would discourage Fifth Amendment violations.

115. Although the primary goal was to enforce the privilege at trial, not to eliminate incentives for officers to conduct unregulated custodial interrogation, there are a number of indications in *Miranda* that the Court was concerned with the harmful effects prevailing interrogation practices had on suspects. *See* Miranda v. Arizona, 384 U.S. 436, 445–48, 455–58 (1966). It is possible that the Court believed that the right to exclusion would have salutary, desirable effects in interrogation rooms.

116. The closest the Court came was in *Michigan v. Tucker*, 417 U.S. 433 (1974), when the majority stated that "[i]n a proper case, [the deterrence] rationale *would seem* applicable." *Id.* at 447 (emphasis added). This was hardly a ringing endorsement of deterrence as a *Miranda* foundation.

The Supreme Court, however, has concluded that no Fifth Amendment violation can occur at the time a person is compelled to speak. The privilege is solely a trial guarantee, a right not to be convicted on compelled self-accusatory disclosures.[117] If the Court is right, then custodial interrogation cannot inflict immediate constitutional injury.[118] *Miranda*'s bar to confessions cannot deter extrajudicial violations of the privilege because that guarantee provides no protection outside the courtroom. Unlike the Fourth Amendment exclusionary rule, even if *Miranda*'s rule changes the way officers conduct investigations, there are no immediate gains in the enforcement of constitutional rights.[119]

Because the Fifth Amendment is solely a trial guarantee, *Miranda*'s exclusionary rule can deter violations only if it has impact in the courtroom. Will suppression diminish the number of judicial violations of the privilege? Will there be fewer actual or potential violations of the trial right against compulsory self-incrimination if officers are deterred from engaging in unconstrained custodial interrogation? The answers to these questions depend on whether *Miranda*'s exclusionary rule provides an effective shield against constitutionally risky evidence. If the suppression remedy, as interpreted and applied, prevents compelled revelations from reaching the courtroom, then there will be no net increase in Fifth Amendment enforcement if officers are induced not to secure those revelations in the first place. In other words, if the *Miranda* exclusionary rule already prevents courtroom violations of the Fifth Amendment by barring the use of statements at trial, the deterrent effects on law enforcement will not add anything to enforcement of the Fifth Amendment in the courtroom. There is no need to discourage the production of compelled statements if they are kept from the courtroom.

---

117. *See* Chavez v. Martinez, 538 U.S. 760, 767 (2003) (opinion of Thomas, J.); *id.* at 777 (Souter, J., concurring in the judgment).

118. Some Justices think the Court erred in concluding that the Fifth Amendment does not provide shelter against the compulsion itself. *See id.* at 790–91 (Kennedy, J., concurring in part and dissenting in part). Some scholars agree that the conclusion of the majority in *Chavez* was a constitutional error. *See, e.g.*, Thomas Y. Davies, *Farther and Farther from the Original Fifth Amendment: The Recharacterization of the Right Against Self-Incrimination as a "Trial Right" in* Chavez v. Martinez, 70 Tenn. L. Rev. 987, 1009–18, 1044–45 (2003); John T. Parry, *Constitutional Interpretation, Coercive Interrogation, and Civil Rights Litigation after* Chavez v. Martinez, 39 Ga. L. Rev. 733, 763 (2005).

119. One could argue that even if it is not unconstitutional per se, official compulsion to speak is harmful and undesirable. *Miranda* suppression would remove the incentives for, and thereby discourage, such conduct. This defense of *Miranda* exclusion has serious weaknesses. First, it is questionable whether courts have the authority to suppress evidence in order to alter conduct that comports with constitutional commands. Moreover, when the benefits of suppression are not a net increase in the enforcement of constitutional rights, it is doubtful that they can outweigh the costs of barring probative evidence of guilt.

What if *Miranda*'s bar does not effectively prevent courtroom violations, but allows prosecutors to introduce a more than negligible number of actually or potentially compelled confessions? In that case, suppression's deterrent effects on officer behavior might prevent Fifth Amendment violations at trial. If officers are motivated to follow *Miranda*'s guidelines, they will not compel some statements that the *Miranda* rule would fail to bar. There would seem to be a net gain in Fifth Amendment enforcement because some forced admissions that would have found their way into trials will not exist.

There are at least two serious flaws in this deterrent logic. First, if *Miranda*'s rule does not effectively bar compelled revelations from trials, the sensible response is to plug its holes directly by improving the courtroom efficacy of the suppression remedy. It hardly seems logical to address deficiencies in the trial protection *Miranda* provides by maintaining its flawed exclusionary rule and attempting to discourage officers from producing the risky evidence that the suppression doctrine fails to bar. Moreover, if the suppression doctrine is insufficiently effective at screening out compelled statements, there is reason to wonder whether it would effectively deter future failures to respect *Miranda*'s guidelines. The inefficacy of the exclusionary rule—that is, the fact that it allows the use of potentially compelled confessions—would provide incentives for officers to ignore *Miranda*'s constraints on custodial interrogation. An ineffective courtroom bar to compelled disclosures is likely to be an ineffective deterrent of law enforcement conduct.

In sum, the current status of deterrence as a rationale for *Miranda* suppression is murky. If the Fifth Amendment grants only a trial right—a right against being convicted based on compelled self-incriminating revelations—deterrence would not seem to be a logical justification for the *Miranda* exclusionary rule. There are no out-of-court constitutional violations to be deterred, and in-court violations of the privilege should be prevented by barring all evidence that is or is likely to be compelled. If *Miranda* suppression effectively enforces the Fifth Amendment by preventing the use of risky evidence at trial, there is no constitutional reason to care about its impact on interrogation practices.[120]

---

120. Scholars differ over the legitimacy of the deterrent rationale for *Miranda*'s exclusionary rule. *Compare* Gardner, *Emerging Good Faith*, *supra* note 96, at 467 (stating that "deterrence theory is inapposite" under *Miranda*); Arnold H. Loewy, *Police-Obtained Evidence and the Constitution: Distinguishing Unconstitutionally Obtained Evidence From Unconstitutionally Used Evidence*, 87 MICH. L. REV. 907, 925–27 (1989) [hereinafter Loewy, *Police-Obtained Evidence*] (maintaining that deterrence is an "illegitimate . . . rationale" for *Miranda* exclusion and "has no place in fifth amendment jurisprudence") *with* Erwin Chemerinsky, *Unanswered Questions*, *in* SIXTH ANNUAL SUPREME COURT REVIEW: OCTOBER 2003 TERM, at 17, 31–32, 34 (PLI Litig. & Admin. Practice, Course Handbook Series No. 3318, 2005) (contending that recent decisions "encourage police to ignore *Miranda*" and that "exclusion . . . is meant to deter violation"); William E. Hellerstein, *A Year to Remember: The Supreme Court's Fourth, Fifth, and Sixth Amendment Jurisprudence for the 2003 Term*, 20

D. THE REACH AND OPERATION OF THE *MIRANDA* EXCLUSIONARY RULE

This section describes and explores the operational details of the *Miranda* exclusionary rule. The topics considered here all pertain to a single question: What evidence does *Miranda* suppress? The first subject addressed is the presumptive scope of *Miranda*'s rule of inadmissibility. The discussion then turns to the "exceptions" to the *Miranda* rule—the doctrines that permit the admission of evidence presumptively subject to exclusion. Many of the same issues discussed in Chapters 1 and 2 are relevant under *Miranda*. These include the persons entitled to exclude evidence, the proceedings in which evidence may be suppressed, and the admissibility of derivative evidence. As will be seen, there are only two established exceptions to the *Miranda* rule. While other exceptions are possible, some of the doctrines that limit the Fourth Amendment exclusionary rule and the Fifth and Fourteenth Amendment rights to exclusion are of little or no relevance to the *Miranda* context.

1. Evidence Subject to Exclusion: The Narrow Scope of *Miranda*'s Rule of Inadmissibility

From the start, *Miranda* has prohibited the government from introducing incriminating statements obtained by means of custodial interrogation. The evidentiary bar applies *only* when the individual who made the statements was in custody at the time—that is, under formal arrest or subjected to equivalent restraints upon her freedom.[121] If officers vigorously question a person who is either free to leave or is subjected to a limited detention that is unlike an arrest, *Miranda* does not bar statements made by that person. Moreover, official interrogation is essential. Known authorities must ask express questions or employ words or acts that are equivalent to such questions.[122] If a person in a jail cell volunteers inculpatory information or responds to an officer's casual remark that generates little pressure to respond, his revelations are admissible.

Moreover, if officers comply with the safeguards announced in *Miranda* and developed in subsequent decisions—if they give adequate warnings, obtain valid waivers, and honor certain requests by suspects—statements are not excluded. Answers given by an arrestee in response to lengthy questioning in an interrogation room are admissible if officers recited warnings and the suspect decided

---

Touro L. Rev. 831, 853 (2005) (referring to "deterrence" as "the real issue" under *Miranda*).

121. *See* Berkemer v. McCarty, 468 U.S. 420 (1984).

122. *See* Rhode Island v. Innis, 446 U.S. 291 (1980); *see also* Illinois v. Perkins, 496 U.S. 292 (1990) (holding that *Miranda* governs only questioning by persons the suspect knows to be government agents).

that he was willing to respond and did not need the assistance of a lawyer.[123] *Miranda* excludes only statements that are the product of custodial interrogation that is not conducted according to that decision's compulsion-dispelling "guidelines." A Fifth Amendment presumption of compulsion and an exclusionary prophylactic are justified only when unconstrained custodial interrogation yields incriminating admissions.

Chapter 2 highlighted the fact that the Fifth Amendment is concerned with compelled "testimony"—thoughts forced from a person's mind. Although its evidentiary bar does not extend to nontestimonial evidence that the authorities force a person to surrender, it does reach nontestimonial evidence that the state has acquired as a result of compelled disclosures. Despite the fact that it is based on the Fifth Amendment, *Miranda*'s exclusionary rule does not apply to derivative evidence.[124] It reaches only *statements* secured by means of custodial interrogation and does not bar any evidence that officers gain by exploiting those statements. Consequently, if officers fail to issue warnings and question a suspect under arrest about whether she has drugs in her home, the suspect's admissions that drugs are hidden in her bedroom may not be introduced. However, the drugs that are found as a result of those admissions may be introduced, and officers may testify that they found the drugs in the suspect's bedroom. Similarly, if an unwarned suspect admits that she has conspired to commit murder with her boyfriend, her statements are excluded, but any statement or testimony by the boyfriend is entirely admissible even if it is the product of the suspect's admissions. Moreover, if officers fail to comply with *Miranda* and obtain a statement, then satisfy *Miranda* and obtain a second statement from the same suspect, the second statement is not subject to suppression as the fruit of the initial violation even if there is a causal connection to that violation.[125]

---

123. The point here is that *Miranda* does not bar evidence in this situation. As Chapter 2 makes clear, statements may be subject to exclusion under the Fifth and Fourteenth Amendments because officers actually coerced such a suspect to speak.

124. *See* United States v. Patane, 542 U.S. 630, 641–43 (2004) (plurality opinion); *id.* at 645 (Kennedy, J., concurring in the judgment).

125. *Oregon v. Elstad*, 470 U.S. 298 (1985), foreshadowed the holding in *Patane*, suggesting that *Miranda*'s exclusion doctrine might not extend to any derivative evidence. The holding in *Elstad*, however, was limited to successive confessions. According to the *Elstad* majority, a second confession obtained after compliance with *Miranda* was not subject to suppression merely because officers had obtained an initial confession without reciting warnings. The Court refused to consider the second confession a "fruit" of the first interrogation and the inadmissible confession, rejecting the argument that the second confession should be excluded because the suspect was aware that he had already "let the cat out of the bag." *Id.* at 311–12. In essence, the Court concluded that even if there was a causal link between the *Miranda* violation and the second confession—that is, even if that confession was derivative evidence obtained as a result of the failure to follow *Miranda*'s

Patane, the case in which the Court decided that derivative evidence is not within the scope of *Miranda*'s exclusionary rule, involved a failure to deliver proper warnings. There was no evidence that the failure to warn was deliberate or done in bad faith. The language and reasoning of the opinions in *Patane*, however, furnish no basis for believing that derivative evidence would be excluded if it was discovered as a result of either a different kind of *Miranda* violation or a deliberate, bad faith refusal to follow *Miranda*'s guidelines. Suppose that a murder suspect explicitly asks for a lawyer and officers purposefully ignore that request and continue to interrogate him in order to find the murder weapon or discover the identity of useful witnesses. The suspect's disclosures will be suppressed, but *Miranda*'s exclusionary rule will not bar the weapon, a forensics report that the suspect's fingerprints were on the weapon, or information provided by any witness who is found.

The reasoning underlying the conclusion that derivative evidence is admissible is far from lucid. It is firmly rooted in the conception of the *Miranda* rule as an overbroad prophylactic designed to guard against risks of Fifth Amendment violations. The Constitution commands that actually compelled statements and evidence derived from those statements must be excluded.[126] Admission would violate the Fifth Amendment privilege. Statements obtained in violation of *Miranda*, however, are not actually compelled, but are "voluntary." They are excluded to address constitutionally unacceptable risks of compulsion. To combat the likelihood of compelled testimonial self-incrimination, a prophylactic constitutional rule bars these statements from trial.[127] The scope of *Miranda*'s overprotective prevention, however, must be kept sufficiently narrow to assure a "close fit" with the core constitutional provision in which it is grounded.[128] In other words, *Miranda*'s overbroad prophylaxis—the amount of suppression beyond that mandated by the right against compulsory self-incrimination—must be kept in check. The costs of excessive exclusion are not justified by any increase in Fifth Amendment protection.

The suppression of derivative evidence would violate the "close-fit" requirement, enlarging the borders of *Miranda*'s already overprotective domain beyond what is justified by the interest in safeguarding the privilege.[129] The costs of excluding often quite reliable derivative fruits outweigh any additional constitutional enforcement gained from suppression. In the first place, derivative evidence—whether a gun, drugs, or another person's revelations—is not itself the "testimony" of the suspect. Its admission, therefore, runs absolutely no risk

---

guidelines—it was not barred from trial. *Patane* later extended this rejection of the "fruits" doctrine to all evidence obtained as a result of statements secured by *Miranda* violations.

126. *See Patane*, 542 U.S. at 640 (plurality opinion).

127. *See id.* at 636, 639 (plurality opinion).

128. *See id.* at 639–41 (plurality opinion).

129. *See id.* at 643 (plurality opinion).

of compelled *testimonial* self-incrimination—the core concern of the Fifth Amendment.[130] Moreover, because the statements that have led to the evidence are presumed to be compelled, but are actually voluntary, use of the derivative evidence cannot constitute indirect incrimination by means of *compelled* testimony.[131] Suppression of the voluntary statements provides sufficient enlarged protection for the Fifth Amendment trial right. Excessive overprotection would result from the exclusion of derivative evidence.[132]

The Fourth Amendment derivative evidence principle reflects a belief that the interest in deterring future unconstitutional law enforcement conduct justifies a presumptive bar to all causally connected products of unreasonable searches and seizures. Two alternative threads of reasoning led the Court to conclude that deterrence does not dictate a derivative evidence principle under *Miranda*. Some Justices believe that deterrence is not a rationale for *Miranda*'s exclusionary rule. Because officers who fail to adhere to *Miranda*'s custodial interrogation guidelines violate neither the Constitution nor the *Miranda* rule, there is *no* interest in deterring—that is, *no* reason to seek to discourage—similar future conduct.[133] Other Justices believe that even if deterrence is a legitimate justification for *Miranda* suppression—that is, even if one goal of suppression is to encourage future compliance with *Miranda*'s prescriptions—it cannot justify a bar to derivative evidence. Because the conduct deterred does not violate Fifth Amendment rights, any constitutional gains are less substantial and cannot outweigh the costs of suppressing ordinarily reliable derivative fruits.[134]

In sum, the presumptive scope of *Miranda*'s exclusionary rule is much narrower than the scope of the suppression doctrines discussed in the first two chapters. It bars *only* inculpatory statements and does not reach any evidence other than disclosures obtained from custodial interrogation without safeguards.

---

130. *See id.* at 637–38, 643–44 (plurality opinion).

131. *See Patane*, 542 U.S. at 643 (plurality opinion).

132. The plurality declared twice that "'[t]he exclusion of unwarned statements . . . is a complete and sufficient remedy' for any perceived *Miranda* violation." *Id.* at 641–42, 643 (plurality opinion) (quoting Chavez v. Martinez, 538 U.S. 760, 790 (2003) (Kennedy, J., concurring in part and dissenting in part)). The reasoning summarized in the text is contained in a plurality opinion joined by just three Justices. While they refused to join the plurality opinion, the two concurring Justices who were necessary for a majority ruling seemed to agree with the premises sketched here.

133. *See id.* at 641–43 (plurality opinion).

134. *See id.* at 645 (Kennedy, J., concurring in the judgment) (deeming it "doubtful that exclusion can be justified by a deterrence rationale sensitive to both law enforcement interests and a suspect's rights"). These Justices did not declare that deterrence is a *Miranda* goal. They merely assumed that it is a rationale for suppressing statements. According to these Justices, in light of the need to "accommodate[] . . . other objectives of the criminal justice system," deterrence could not support a *Miranda* ban on the fruits of statements. *Id.* at 644–45 (Kennedy, J., concurring in the judgment).

The *Miranda* doctrine permits the prosecution to convict defendants based on any other evidentiary profit it can reap from those disclosures.[135]

2. Proceedings in Which the *Miranda* Rule Bars Statements

The *Miranda* exclusionary rule bars confessions from *trials*. The Supreme Court has rejected the claim that the rule is inapplicable in trials for misdemeanor level offenses—that is, that it operates only in felony prosecutions. Statements must be excluded from all trials for criminal offenses.[136] The *Miranda* rule also requires suppression from some, perhaps all, sentencing proceedings.[137] In *Estelle v. Smith*,[138] the question was whether a psychiatrist's testimony that included conclusions based on statements obtained in violation of *Miranda* was barred from a *capital* sentencing proceeding. Because the Court could "discern no basis to distinguish between the guilt and penalty phases of [the] capital murder trial so far as . . . the Fifth Amendment privilege is concerned,"[139] it held that *Miranda* required exclusion of the testimony from the sentencing phase of the capital prosecution.[140]

---

135. For discussions of whether the *Miranda* exclusionary rule should include a derivative evidence doctrine, see Yale Kamisar, *Postscript: Another Look at* Patane *and* Seibert, *the 2004* Miranda *"Poisoned Fruit" Cases*, 2 Ohio St. J. Crim. L. 97 (2004); David A. Wollin, *Policing the Police: Should* Miranda *Violations Bear Fruit?*, 53 Ohio St. L. J. 805 (1992).

136. *See* Berkemer v. McCarty, 468 U.S. 420, 434 (1984).

137. The label of a proceeding is not determinative. The Court has ruled that some proceedings denominated sentencing hearings are, in substance, part of the trial—i.e., the determination of guilt—for purposes of the constitutional entitlements to trial by jury and proof beyond a reasonable doubt. *See* Apprendi v. New Jersey, 530 U.S. 466 (2000). The question is one of substance, not form. Any proceeding that qualifies as a trial for purposes of the jury and reasonable doubt guarantees surely would qualify as a trial for purposes of *Miranda* exclusion.

138. 451 U.S. 454 (1981).

139. *Id.* at 462–63.

140. The Court today would clearly disavow *Estelle*'s conclusion that the defendant's "*Fifth Amendment rights were violated* by the admission of [the] testimony at the penalty phase." *Id.* at 468 (emphasis added). The admission of evidence secured in violation of *Miranda* does *not* violate the Fifth Amendment, but is necessary to guard against the risks of a violation. It seems unlikely, however, that this altered understanding of the nature of *Miranda*'s exclusionary rule would cause the Court to reach a different conclusion about the application of the rule to the sentencing phase of a capital proceeding. In any case, the Court has concluded that if a defendant is not eligible for the death penalty without a further finding of fact at the sentencing stage, that stage is essentially part of the trial for Sixth Amendment jury trial purposes. *See* Ring v. Arizona, 536 U.S. 584 (2002). Even if the Court were to conclude today that *Miranda* is not applicable to sentencing proceedings, it would reach the same conclusion in *Estelle* because the capital sentencing proceeding was, in reality, a trial.

Whether *Miranda*'s bar operates in noncapital sentencing proceedings is unsettled. The holding in *Estelle,* and much of its reasoning, was tied to the capital nature of the punishment proceeding. Later, in *Mitchell v. United States,*[141] the Court decided that the Fifth Amendment privilege applies in noncapital sentencing hearings, and, consequently, that a defendant cannot be forced to testify against himself in such a proceeding.[142] Both "law and . . . common sense" dictated the conclusion that "sentencing proceedings," in general, are "part[s] of" the "'criminal case[s]'" that are the domain of the Fifth Amendment privilege.[143] *Mitchell* involved the applicability of the Fifth Amendment's protection against adverse inferences based upon a defendant's failure to testify. The question was not whether *Miranda*'s prophylactic Fifth Amendment extension required the suppression of statements. The Court could conclude that an extension of *Miranda*'s bar to sentencing hearings satisfies the "close-fit" requirement for prophylactic rules and is necessary to combat risks of unconstitutional compulsory self-incrimination. On the other hand, the Court's general antipathy toward the expansion of *Miranda*'s overprotective shield certainly could lead to a decision that the balance of interests tips against applying the suppression doctrine in noncapital sentencing hearings.

Defendants sometimes challenge their convictions by filing a petition in federal court seeking a writ of habeas corpus. One issue is whether a claim that evidence should have been excluded from trial may be raised in a habeas proceeding. Chapter 1 discussed the Supreme Court's ruling that a defendant may not raise a Fourth Amendment exclusionary rule claim in a federal habeas corpus action unless the state failed to accord his claim a "full and fair" hearing.[144] Surprisingly, the Court reached a contrary conclusion under *Miranda,* holding that a defendant may pursue a claim that a statement should have been suppressed even if the state did afford an ample opportunity to litigate that claim.[145] The majority reasoned that the dramatically different nature of the *Miranda* rule required an entirely different conclusion. Unlike the Fourth Amendment exclusionary rule, *Miranda*'s rule of inadmissibility is not a mere deterrent device designed to prevent future transgressions. It is not a costly sanction that can do nothing to prevent constitutional injury to the particular defendant on trial. Instead, it is an immediate safeguard against violation of the current defendant's fundamental Fifth Amendment "trial right." It is a remedial device that preserves

141. 526 U.S. 314 (1999).

142. *Id.* at 326.

143. *Id.* at 327.

144. *See* Stone v. Powell, 428 U.S. 465, 481–82 (1976). The issue is not whether evidence should be excluded from a habeas proceeding, but whether a claim that it should have been barred from trial can be raised in a habeas action.

145. *See* Withrow v. Williams, 507 U.S. 680 (1993).

important values underlying the privilege.[146] According to the majority, the constitutional benefits of allowing a habeas petitioner to establish that a judge erred in denying a *Miranda* suppression claim offset the costs resulting from the availability of relief at that late stage.

The Supreme Court has not considered whether the *Miranda* exclusionary rule applies in any other types of proceedings. It seems quite unlikely that its prophylactic bar would operate in any pretrial phase of the criminal process—for example, in a grand jury proceeding or a hearing on a motion to dismiss a charge. The rule is designed to guard against unacceptable risks of compulsory self-incrimination—that is, to protect defendants against being forced to assist the state's efforts to secure a conviction (or, perhaps, to increase punishment). An extension of *Miranda*'s suppression doctrine to a pretrial proceeding that cannot result in conviction or punishment would seem inconsistent with the demand for a "close fit" between that prophylactic constitutional rule and the core guarantee it is designed to protect. An adverse ruling in a pretrial proceeding may make it more likely that a defendant will ultimately be convicted, but a defendant cannot be convicted or punished more severely as a direct consequence of such a ruling. There would seem to be little or no risk of compelled testimonial self-*incrimination* from the use of statements in pretrial proceedings.

The Fourth Amendment exclusionary rule applies in certain forfeiture proceedings that are "quasi-criminal."[147] It seems unlikely that the Court would extend the disfavored *Miranda* rule to such proceedings. The Fifth Amendment guarantee in which *Miranda* is grounded is, by its terms, restricted to "criminal case[s]." While the Court might conclude that the core Fifth Amendment right not to be forced to testify reaches some nominally civil actions with sufficient connections to criminal cases, it seems likely that the Court would confine *Miranda*'s enlarged Fifth Amendment prophylaxis to cases that are genuinely criminal in character. Any risks to the core right from the use of statements in civil proceedings, even those deemed quasi-criminal, would be minimal, at best, and almost certainly insufficient to justify an expansion of *Miranda*'s overprotective prophylaxis.

Finally, the Fifth Amendment itself provides no protection in genuinely civil proceedings.[148] An individual may be forced to provide testimonial evidence that results in harmful civil consequences. *Miranda*'s suppression doctrine,

---

146. *Id.* at 691–92.

147. *See* One 1958 Plymouth Sedan v. Pennsylvania, 380 U.S. 693, 700 (1965). As observed in Chapter 1, based on its current attitude toward the Fourth Amendment exclusionary rule, the Court might well overturn this ruling were it to revisit the issue today.

148. As noted in Chapter 2, a person may have a Fifth Amendment entitlement to refuse to testify in a civil proceeding. This entitlement, however, is based on the threat that the testimony will be used in a later *criminal* case, not on any harm that could result from an adverse outcome in the civil proceeding itself.

therefore, cannot operate in civil contexts. A defendant in a civil suit seeking millions of dollars cannot rely on the *Miranda* doctrine to exclude from trial damaging statements she made as a result of unwarned official custodial interrogation.

3. "Standing" to Suppress Statements Under *Miranda*

A suspect who makes incriminating revelations as a result of custodial interrogation without safeguards has "standing" to exclude those statements from his trial. Although the issue has never reached the Supreme Court, it seems beyond question that third parties—those who did not make the statements but are incriminated by them—cannot raise *Miranda* suppression claims. Suppose that I am arrested. When questioned about a murder without being warned, I admit that the victim's wife paid me to kill him. *Miranda* bars the prosecutor from using this admission to prove my guilt, but poses no impediment to the use of that same admission to prove the wife's guilt.[149]

This conclusion follows necessarily from the nature of *Miranda*'s exclusionary rule and the right it enforces. A confession secured in violation of *Miranda* harbors risks that give rise to a presumption of compulsion. It is barred from trial because admission *might* violate the confessing defendant's right not to be compelled to incriminate *himself*. An accused person has no Fifth Amendment right against having another individual compelled to incriminate him; the government is free to coerce witnesses into testifying. Consequently, there is neither a Fifth Amendment basis for nor a need for a prophylactic safeguard against risks that statements forced from the mind of another person will be used to inculpate the defendant.

4. Exceptions to the *Miranda* Exclusionary Rule

The *Miranda* exclusionary rule presumptively bars inculpatory disclosures secured by means of custodial interrogation without safeguards from a criminal trial of the individual who made the disclosures. The Court has endorsed two exceptions which allow the introduction of statements otherwise barred—a "public safety" exception and an "impeachment use" exception. This section analyzes these and other potential exceptions to the *Miranda* doctrine.

a. The Relevance of the "Independent Source," "Inevitable Discovery," and "Attenuation" Exceptions to the *Miranda* Exclusionary Rule Three established and well-known exceptions to the Fourth Amendment exclusionary rule—independent source, inevitable discovery, and attenuation—are addressed together because they merit only brief treatment in the *Miranda* context. The independent source doctrine holds that when officers engage in unconstitutional

---

149. The Sixth Amendment Confrontation Clause may provide the wife with protection. For a discussion of that basis for constitutional exclusion, see Chapter 7.

conduct but acquire contested evidence by lawful means entirely divorced from their impropriety—that is, when there is no causal link between the conduct and the acquisition of evidence—the evidence is admissible. As noted in the discussion of the Fourth Amendment exclusionary rule in Chapter 1, the independent source doctrine is *not* a true "exception" to exclusion because a basic predicate for suppression is the need for a but-for causal connection between an official illegality and the obtainment of evidence. In independent source situations, there is no causal link because the evidence at issue has been acquired by constitutionally legitimate methods.

An earlier section highlighted the need under *Miranda* for a causal connection between unconstrained custodial interrogation and the disclosures to be suppressed. If officers conduct custodial interrogation without following *Miranda*'s guidelines, then conduct a genuinely independent session complying with the dictates of *Miranda*, statements secured in the second interrogation are admissible. As long as the second interrogation meets the compulsion-dispelling requirements prescribed in *Miranda*,[150] there is no cognizable risk of compulsion and no basis for a prophylactic presumption that dictates suppression.[151] It bears mention, however, that a failure to abide by *Miranda*'s safeguards initially *may* make compliance with *Miranda*'s requirements at a second session difficult, if not impossible. In other words, if officers do not respect the guidelines for custodial interrogations when they first interrogate a suspect, they may create impediments to satisfying the guidelines at a subsequent interrogation of that suspect.[152] In situations where that is the case, a claim that disclosures made at

---

150. From the start, *Miranda* has permitted the adoption of equally effective alternative measures to dispel the compulsion inherent in custodial interrogation. *See* Miranda v. Arizona, 384 U.S. 436, 467 (1966). The possibility of an effective substitute to protect against the risks of compulsory self-incrimination remains viable today. *See* Dickerson v. United States, 530 U.S. 428, 440–42 (2000).

151. The decision in *Oregon v. Elstad*, 470 U.S. 298 (1985), discussed earlier, illustrates this principle. Officers interrogated a suspect without warnings and obtained a statement. Soon thereafter, they questioned him again and secured additional statements. The Court considered the second session independent of the first. The officers' warnings and the suspect's waiver of rights prior to the statements made at this second interrogation were sufficient to comply with *Miranda* and render those statements admissible. In the circumstances of *Elstad*, the initial failure to warn did not prevent the officers from delivering meaningful warnings prior to the second interrogation. *See* Missouri v. Seibert, 542 U.S. 600, 614–16 (2004) (plurality opinion).

152. For example, there are circumstances in which an initial failure to warn a suspect will preclude effective warnings before a second questioning session. *See Seibert*, 542 U.S. at 616–17 (plurality opinion) (concluding that even though warnings were given before a second interrogation, they could not have effectively served their intended function because of the circumstances surrounding the initial unwarned interrogation); *id.* at 620–21 (Kennedy, J., concurring in the judgment) (agreeing that the warnings were not adequate because of the prior events). There are other circumstances in which an initial

the later interrogation are the product of an independent source would lack merit. Viewed in isolation, the second session might appear to satisfy *Miranda*'s guidelines. When the earlier events are considered, however, the second interrogation could not qualify as a lawful, independent source. The disclosures would be suppressed as the product of custodial interrogation that did not abide by *Miranda*'s safeguards.

The inevitable discovery exception allows the prosecution to introduce illegally acquired evidence if it can show, by a preponderance of the evidence, that the same evidence would inevitably have been obtained by lawful means if the illegal conduct had not occurred. In Chapter 2, I suggested that if officers could show that they would have properly secured confessions that were, in fact, coerced, those confessions might well be admissible under the inevitable discovery exception. The trial that the defendant receives in that situation is the same trial he would have received if no coercion had been applied. Because the accused is not disadvantaged by the government's objectionable conduct, he suffers no trial harm of a sort that the Fifth and Fourteenth Amendments are intended to prevent. It is arguable that in those circumstances the use of the coerced confession does not deprive the accused of any constitutional entitlement. The real problem is factual. It seems quite unlikely that the government could show that it inevitably would have secured a voluntary confession from a suspect who was forced to speak. This theoretically applicable exception probably has little practical utility.

The same reasoning should lead to a similar conclusion under *Miranda*. Although it seems quite improbable that the government could prove that it would have obtained the same disclosures if there had been no *Miranda* violation, such a showing should lead to the suspension of *Miranda*'s presumptive bar. Because statements that are subject to suppression under *Miranda* are in fact voluntary, a defendant has no Fifth Amendment right to suppression. The case for admitting a presumptively compelled disclosure that would have been properly obtained is even stronger than when actual coercion is involved. Even if the Court were to reject the inevitable discovery exception for genuinely compelled confessions, it would almost certainly conclude that the doctrine is a valid limitation on *Miranda*'s prophylactic exclusionary rule.

When officers improperly obtain incriminating statements, the inevitable discovery doctrine is most likely to be of use in justifying the introduction of derivative evidence—in particular, tangible items found due to those statements.

---

failure to satisfy *Miranda*'s dictates may hinder or prevent later compliance. A failure to respect an assertion of the right to remain silent or the right to counsel prior to an initial interrogation may preclude or impede officers' abilities to honor such an assertion before conducting a subsequent interrogation. Because this is a matter concerned with *Miranda*'s substance rather than the operation of its suppression remedy, there is no need to explore those situations at length here.

Although it is unlikely the state could show that it would lawfully have acquired incriminating statements, it is certainly conceivable that the prosecution might well demonstrate that officers would have used independent, and lawful, methods to find a gun that an unwarned suspect admitted was in his car. Because *Miranda*'s rule does not exclude derivative evidence, however, there is no need to show inevitable discovery for derivative evidence.

For the same reason, the traditional attenuation exception is inapposite to *Miranda*. By its very nature, the attenuation doctrine is applicable only to derivative evidence. Primary evidence—evidence gained as an immediate, direct result of improper conduct—cannot have a weakened or remote causal connection. Because derivative evidence is generally admissible under *Miranda*, the attenuation exception has no role to play.[153]

b. *Miranda*'s Public Safety Exception In *New York v. Quarles*,[154] the Supreme Court recognized a "'public safety' exception to the requirement that *Miranda* warnings be given *before a suspect's answers may be admitted into evidence*."[155] This exception to *Miranda*'s exclusionary rule has no Fourth Amendment analogue[156] and is not a legitimate exception to the constitutional bar to coerced confessions.[157] According to the *Quarles* majority, when officers engage in unwarned custodial interrogation that is "reasonably prompted by a concern for the public safety," a suspect's responses may be used to prove guilt at trial even though officers did not recite the *Miranda* warnings.[158] An officer's actual, "subjective" motivation is irrelevant because the standard is objective.[159] In essence, the question is whether a reasonable officer would (or perhaps could) have been motivated by a public safety concern. In *Quarles*, the officer who asked the defendant

153. The second, recently developed branch of the Fourth Amendment attenuation exception discussed in Chapter 1 requires a showing that the purpose of the Fourth Amendment rule that was violated was not to shield evidence from the government. It is difficult to see how that type of attenuation could be extended to confessions secured in violation of *Miranda*'s rules. All of *Miranda*'s safeguards are designed to prevent the authorities from obtaining compelled disclosures.

154. 467 U.S. 649 (1984).

155. *Id.* at 655 (emphasis added).

156. Under the Fourth Amendment, public safety interests may well render a search or seizure "reasonable." Because the Fourth Amendment forbids only "unreasonable searches and seizures," there would be no constitutional violation and, thus, no basis for suppression. If a search or seizure is unreasonable, the fact that officers acted to further the public safety does not support an exception to the Fourth Amendment exclusionary rule.

157. As discussed in Chapter 2, the Fifth Amendment trial right is absolute, barring compulsory self-incrimination even if officers employed compulsion to serve a compelling interest. The courtroom bar to a suspect's compelled admissions is unexceptionable. *See supra* Chapter 2, text accompanying notes 211–13.

158. *Id.* at 656.

159. *Id.*

where a firearm was located was not, in fact, concerned with the threat posed by the gun. Nonetheless, the Court concluded that his inquiry was "reasonably prompted" by a sufficient public safety concern.

A public safety exception could not have been reconciled with the original premises underlying *Miranda* suppression. The *Miranda* Court barred statements because they were compelled and their admission would violate the Fifth Amendment privilege. The Justices believed they were interpreting and implementing the categorical constitutional prohibition on the use of compelled statements. The reasons why officers engaged in unwarned custodial interrogation could not have justified an exception to that absolute bar.[160]

The public safety exception is reconcilable with the reformulated rationale for the *Miranda* rule. According to the revised understanding of *Miranda*, statements obtained without warnings are not *actually* compelled, but are, in fact, voluntary.[161] Consequently, such statements can be admitted at trial without violating the Fifth Amendment. "[T]here is no constitutional imperative" necessitating exclusion.[162] Ordinarily, a *Miranda* violation such as a failure to deliver warnings gives rise to a presumption of compulsion.[163] This presumption mandates evidentiary suppression to provide "enlarged protection" that safeguards against the "likelihood" of compulsory self-incrimination engendered by unconstrained custodial interrogation.[164] According to *Quarles*, the *Miranda* majority believed that the presumption of compulsion and the exclusion of evidence were justified because the constitutional gains from suppression—the Fifth Amendment violations prevented—outweighed the costs—the loss of some voluntary statements that are not barred by the privilege.[165] When the competing interest is not simply the decreased effectiveness of law enforcement from the loss of probative evidence of guilt, but instead is some potential harm to the public, the balance tips against suppression.[166] The interest in ensuring the safety of the public outweighs the interest in affording extra protection against threats to the Fifth Amendment and justifies suspension of the requirement that warnings be given if statements are to be admitted at trial.[167]

---

160. The *Miranda* majority made its views on this question clear, rejecting the argument that "society's need for interrogation outweighs the privilege" because "the Constitution . . . prescribed the rights of the individual . . . when it provided in the Fifth Amendment that an individual cannot be compelled to be a witness against himself." According to the Court, "[t]hat right cannot be abridged." Miranda v. Arizona, 384 U.S. 436, 479 (1966).

161. *See Quarles*, 467 U.S. at 654, 655 n.5.

162. *Id.* at 658 n.7.

163. *Id.* at 654, 655 n.5.

164. *Id.* at 656–57.

165. *Id.*

166. *Quarles*, 467 U.S. at 657.

167. According to the Court, if warnings are given in public safety situations, "suspects . . . might well be deterred from responding" and officers will not be able to

Quarles, the sole opinion in which the Supreme Court has considered *Miranda*'s public safety exception, did not resolve every question about its operation. The Court held that the exception applies to failures to warn suspects, but did not address other types of *Miranda* violations.[168] Is there a public safety exception if an officer pressures a suspect into giving an involuntary waiver of rights or ignores a suspect's assertion of the entitlement to a lawyer's assistance? The logic underlying the *Quarles* exception, rooted in *Miranda*'s prophylactic nature, suggests that the exception probably would be extended to all types of *Miranda* violations. Each of *Miranda*'s constraints, and the rule suppressing evidence obtained by violating those constraints, rests upon the very same foundation—an interest in providing enlarged protection for the Fifth Amendment privilege. Society's interest in combating a sufficiently serious threat to the public's safety would seem to outweigh the prophylactic objective that underlies every *Miranda* safeguard. Thus, if an officer ignores a request for an attorney and questions a suspect because she reasonably believes that the suspect has information that will enable her to save lives, the suspect's answers should be admissible. If a reasonable belief about danger prompts an officer to force a suspect to waive his rights, but the officer does not coerce the suspect to respond to her questions, the same result should follow.

Another question is the nature of the potential harms that qualify as public safety interests. In *Quarles*, the risk of personal injury posed by a gun that had been discarded in a supermarket qualified. Must there be a danger of serious physical injury or would other sorts of harm qualify? Suppose there was a threat that someone would molest a child in a nonviolent way or engage in consensual relations with a minor. What if the only harm was substantial property damage or serious financial loss? Suppose there was a risk of serious injury to the suspect alone—a danger, for example, that she could suffer a life-endangering drug overdose if a heroin-filled balloon she might have swallowed were to burst. Can an interest in protecting the suspect from her own actions or from perils posed by third parties qualify as a public safety interest that would allow the introduction of disclosures at trial?

Quarles involved an *imminent* threat to the public. Because there was reason to believe that a dangerous weapon had been hastily discarded in a market,

---

prevent the harms that are threatened. *Id.* It was senseless to "exclude . . . evidence" and "thus penaliz[e] officers for asking the very questions which are the most crucial to their efforts to protect themselves and the public." *Id.* at 658 n.7. Moreover, an officer would be put in an "untenable position" if he had to decide, "often in a matter of seconds," whether to warn a suspect to ensure the admissibility of statements or not warn a suspect to ensure that he could obtain necessary information. *Id.* at 657–58. In that position, an officer might understandably make a choice that would defeat the public safety.

168. The Court made it clear that if an officer were to actually coerce a statement from the suspect, a "constitutional imperative" would bar use at trial. *Id.* at 658 n.7.

immediate injury to someone was possible. Although the situations triggering the *Quarles* exception will typically threaten imminent harm, a suspect could have information about a serious danger that would be realized sometime in the distant future. An arrestee, for example, could have information concerning a possible terrorist attack planned for the following year. The question is whether the public safety exception should apply to answers officers obtain to address a danger that is not immediate. The logic of *Quarles* strongly suggests that imminence is not a requisite. According to the majority, delivery of the *Miranda* warnings can be inconsistent with public safety interests because they "might well . . . deter a suspect from responding."[169] If a suspect does not respond, officers do not obtain the information needed to prevent harm. Whether or not the harm will occur soon, warnings that discourage a response may thwart efforts to protect the public.

Two additional, unsettled matters are how likely it must be that a qualifying harm will come to pass if officers do not elicit information from the suspect, and how likely it must be that information a suspect has will help avert the danger. There may be a high probability that someone will die, a moderate likelihood, or only a small chance. Is any chance of death enough, even a minimal risk? Similarly, even if death is very likely, would a very small possibility that the particular suspect has useful information be sufficient?

The answers to these questions and any others regarding the breadth of the public safety doctrine should be guided by the reasoning underlying *Quarles*. Because the public safety exception is grounded in a balance of the interests at stake, its application should always depend on whether the interest served by questioning a suspect is sufficiently weighty to counterbalance *Miranda*'s goal of guarding against unacceptable risks to the Fifth Amendment privilege that are ordinarily posed by the products of custodial interrogation.[170]

c. A Possible "Good Faith" Exception to *Miranda* The Fourth Amendment exclusionary rule is qualified by "good faith" exceptions which permit prosecutors to use evidence when it was reasonable for the officers who conducted an unreasonable search or seizure to believe that their conduct was constitutional.[171] The Fifth and Fourteenth Amendment rights to exclude coerced confessions, on the other hand, are not and should not be qualified by any good faith exception.[172] The Supreme Court has alluded to the relevance of good faith to *Miranda* exclusion, but has never directly addressed the legitimacy of a good

---

169. *Id.* at 657.

170. For discussions of the Court's recognition of the public safety exception in *Quarles*, see Loewy, *Police-Obtained Evidence*, *supra* note 120, at 923–25; William T. Pizzi, *The Privilege Against Self-Incrimination in a Rescue Situation*, 76 J. CRIM L. & CRIMINOLOGY 567, 576–80 (1985).

171. *See supra* Chapter 1, text accompanying notes 238–60.

172. *See supra* Chapter 2, text accompanying notes 216–21.

faith limitation. Should the *Miranda* exclusionary rule apply when an officer's failure to comply with the prescribed custodial interrogation guidelines is not "culpable"? An officer might lack "subjective" fault—his neglect of the safeguards might not be intentional or even reckless. An officer might even lack "objective" fault—it might be reasonable to believe that he is complying with the guidelines. To illustrate, an officer might reasonably believe that warnings are unnecessary because his restraint of a suspect's freedom does not constitute custody or that his actions do not satisfy the standard for interrogation. An officer, for example, might reasonably believe that he has demonstrated adequate respect for a suspect's assertion of the right to remain silent or that a suspect's conduct following a clear request for counsel's assistance has demonstrated a change of heart and a desire to answer questions without assistance.

Michigan v. Tucker[173] involved an officer who failed to warn a suspect prior to an interrogation that occurred before the Supreme Court decided *Miranda*. The question was whether the testimony of a witness found as a result of statements made by the unwarned suspect had to be excluded. The Court held that suppression was not appropriate. Assuming that deterrence was a predicate for *Miranda*'s rule, the Court reasoned that it could not support suppression because "[t]he deterrent purpose of the exclusionary rule necessarily assumes that the police have engaged in willful, or at the very least negligent, conduct."[174] Consequently, when officers act "in complete good faith, . . . the deterrence rationale loses much of its force."[175] Although the holding was specifically limited to evidence gained from pre-*Miranda* interrogations,[176] this reasoning suggests that good faith—an absence of willfulness or negligence—might be a basis for suspending the *Miranda* exclusionary rule. On the other hand, the *Tucker* Court did not permit the use of the defendant's statements; exclusion was necessary despite the officer's complete good faith.[177] This suggests that the Court had no intent to suggest that a general good faith exception is valid.

In the 35 years since *Tucker*, however, the Court has neither recognized nor rejected a good faith exception to *Miranda*. In *Oregon v. Elstad*,[178] while holding that a confession did not have to be excluded, the majority asserted that it was "in no way retreat[ing] from the bright-line rule of *Miranda*" and that it did "not"

---

173. 417 U.S. 433 (1974).

174. *Id.* at 447.

175. *Id.* There could be no doubt about the "complete good faith" of law enforcement in *Tucker* because an officer could not have been expected to know of a demand for warnings that had not yet been announced.

176. *Id.* (deeming it "significant to our decision" that the failure to warn "occurred prior to the decision in *Miranda*").

177. *Id.* at 435, 450, 452 (referring to and not questioning the application of *Miranda*'s suppression doctrine to the statements themselves).

178. 470 U.S. 298 (1985).

mean to "imply that good faith excuses a failure to administer *Miranda* warnings."[179] Later, in *Missouri v. Seibert*,[180] both the plurality and Justice Kennedy, the critical fifth vote supporting suppression of a confession, did suggest that a *deliberate* effort to undermine the efficacy of *Miranda* warnings was an essential predicate for exclusion.[181] Neither, however, meant to imply that *Miranda*'s bar typically depends on official culpability. Their point was only that in successive confession contexts a bad faith effort to "undermine" *Miranda* will justify a conclusion that ordinarily sufficient warnings were ineffective—i.e., that officers had violated *Miranda*'s warnings requirement.[182]

In the absence of a clear-cut pronouncement from the Court, the prevailing rationales for suppression should guide analysis. The Fourth Amendment good faith exceptions are justified by and reconcilable with the purely deterrent purposes of the search and seizure exclusionary rule. To the extent that *Miranda*'s exclusionary rule is designed to deter future violations, logic would dictate a similar exception. *Tucker*'s suggestion that a good faith exception could be legitimate rested on the premise that deterrence was a central objective of *Miranda* suppression. After *Tucker*, however, as the Court reformulated the rationales for *Miranda* suppression, deterrence assumed, at most, a secondary role.

Today, the primary justification for the *Miranda* exclusionary rule is not to deter future violations of the custodial interrogation guidelines. Exclusion is designed to counter the risks that compelled statements will violate the defendant's Fifth Amendment trial right. It is a constitutionally necessary protection for a fundamental trial right—the right not to be compelled to be a witness against oneself. This predicate has led the Court to deny suppression when countervailing interests outweigh the risks of constitutional deprivation and when suppression would yield excessive prophylaxis. Exclusion is unjustified when the reach of the *Miranda* bar would be too broad, violating the general requirement of a "close fit" between prophylactic rules and the core rights they protect. Unlike the situation where an officer withholds warnings because of a threat to the public safety, an officer's lack of fault—the fact that his neglect was

---

179. *Id.* at 317.

180. 542 U.S. 600 (2004).

181. *Id.* at 616 (plurality opinion) (highlighting the relevance of "objective" indications that officers have employed a "strategy adapted to undermine" *Miranda*); *id.* at 622 (Kennedy, J., concurring in the judgment) (opining that warnings should be deemed ineffective and exclusion should follow when officers engage in "deliberate" attempts to "undermine" *Miranda*).

182. In *New York v. Quarles*, 467 U.S. 649 (1984), the Court asserted that there was no reason to "penaliz[e] officers for asking . . . questions" designed to further public safety interests. *Id.* at 658 n.7. The holding that suppression is not appropriate when officers have a good reason not to issue warnings does not imply that suppression is inappropriate when officers merely lack the intent to violate *Miranda* or act with a good faith belief that they are following the guidelines for custodial interrogation.

neither deliberate nor negligent—gives rise to no societal interest to counterbalance the interest in preventing compelled self-incrimination. Moreover, the admission of statements obtained by means of a good faith violation risks conviction based on words forced from an accused's mind. Exclusion would seem entirely consistent with the "close-fit" demand insofar as it avoids violations of the core guarantee against compelled, testimonial self-incrimination.

There can be no doubt that the Court has severely narrowed the *Miranda* exclusionary rule and evinced a genuine reluctance to expand that safeguard. Nonetheless, it has infringed upon the core of *Miranda*'s suppression doctrine—the bar to substantive use of a suspect's testimonial disclosures at trial—only when necessary to accommodate competing public safety interests.[183] In the absence of countervailing interests, the Court has concluded that *Miranda*'s enlarged Fifth Amendment protection is justified. When officers violate *Miranda* without fault, there are no competing interests that outweigh the need to protect the privilege. The underpinnings of *Miranda*, therefore, provide no reason to "retreat from the bright-line rule of *Miranda*" and adopt a "good faith" exception to the *Miranda* exclusionary rule.

d. The Impeachment Use Exception The first exception to *Miranda*'s exclusionary rule endorsed by the Supreme Court is the "impeachment use" exception. It allows prosecutors to introduce otherwise inadmissible statements for the limited purpose of casting doubt on the credibility of a defendant's trial testimony. In dictum, the *Miranda* Court declared that statements obtained by custodial interrogation without safeguards were inadmissible for impeachment purposes.[184] The logic underlying this ban was simple: because statements secured in violation of *Miranda*'s constraints on custodial interrogation were compelled, their use for any incriminating purpose—even the limited purpose of making an accused's testimony less believable—would violate the Fifth Amendment.[185]

Just five years after *Miranda*, in *Harris v. New York*,[186] a five-Justice majority reached a contrary conclusion, holding that the prosecution could introduce

183. *See* Dickerson v. United States, 530 U.S. 428, 443–44 (2000) (observing that the Court has consistently "reaffirm[ed] the [*Miranda*] decision's core ruling that unwarned statements may not be used as evidence in the prosecution's case in chief"). The decision in *Withrow v. Williams*, 507 U.S. 680 (1993), which allows habeas corpus petitioners to raise claims that state courts erroneously allowed prosecutors to use statements at trial, demonstrates the Court's commitment to preserving *Miranda*'s bar to the substantive use of statements to obtain convictions.

184. Miranda v. Arizona, 384 U.S. 436, 476–77 (1966).

185. *Id.* (asserting that the privilege "does not distinguish degrees of incrimination" and that statements introduced "to impeach . . . testimony at trial . . . and thus to prove guilt by implication . . . are incriminating in any meaningful sense of the word and may not be used").

186. 401 U.S. 222 (1971).

statements obtained without adequate warnings to impeach the defendant's inconsistent testimony given on direct examination. As noted in the historical account, *Harris* was the opinion that began the radical reformulation of *Miranda*'s logic and the transformation of its rule of inadmissibility from a constitutional right into a mere exclusionary rule.[187] The majority justified the creation of an impeachment use exception by first positing that statements obtained in violation of *Miranda* were voluntary, not coerced.[188] For that reason, the introduction of such statements did not violate the Fifth Amendment privilege. Their use did not jeopardize the Fifth Amendment interest in preventing convictions based on untrustworthy evidence.[189] There is no good reason to fear that the admission of statements as part of this "traditional truth-testing device[]" would mislead jurors into erroneous assessments of a defendant's credibility.[190]

The only affirmative basis for *Miranda* suppression suggested in *Harris* was to deter officers from failing to follow *Miranda*'s interrogation guidelines. Deterrence did not justify an impeachment bar for two reasons. First, "sufficient deterrence flow[ed]" from the bar to the use of the statements as substantive proof of guilt.[191] In addition, a ban on impeachment use would result in the unique cost of allowing a defendant to perjure herself without challenge.[192] The Court concluded that the cost-benefit balance that underlies deterrence-based exclusion tips against prohibiting the government from impeaching defendants.

The original explanation for permitting impeachment was terse, incomplete, and based on an apparent assumption that deterrence was the main—if not the exclusive—rationale for *Miranda* suppression. The later recognition that the primary function of the *Miranda* rule is to combat risks of compelled self-incrimination at trial, not to alter officers' future conduct, undermined *Harris*'s explanation of why an impeachment use exception is defensible. In *United States v. Patane*, the Court reaffirmed *Harris*, reiterating that neither trustworthiness concerns nor deterrence objectives can support a bar to impeachment use.[193] The Court indicated that allowing the government to cast doubt on a defendant's credibility was entirely consistent with the demand for a "close fit" between *Miranda*'s prophylactic exclusionary rule and the Fifth Amendment's core prohibition on compelled, testimonial self-incrimination.[194] *Miranda*'s effort to guard against risks of compelled self-incrimination at trial results in suppression that

---

187. *See supra* text accompanying notes 21–29.
188. *Harris*, 401 U.S. at 224.
189. *Id.*
190. *Id.* at 225.
191. *Id.*
192. *Id.* at 225–26.
193. United States v. Patane, 542 U.S. 630, 639–40 (2004) (plurality opinion).
194. *Id.* at 640 (plurality opinion).

"necessarily sweep[s] beyond the actual protections of the Self-Incrimination Clause."[195] An extension of the scope of the exclusion doctrine announced in *Miranda*—that is, the bar to substantive use of statements at trial—is justified only if "necess[ary] for the protection of the actual right against compelled self-incrimination."[196] Like a ban on substantive use of derivative evidence, a ban on the impeachment use of statements is, in the Court's view, an unjustified extension of *Miranda*'s reach and an impediment to probative evidence that is not necessary to protect the core Fifth Amendment right.[197] Such an extension would result in excessive overprotection for the privilege that would not be worth the costs to effective prosecution.

The impeachment use exception allows the government to introduce statements to undermine the credibility of testimony given by a defendant on *direct examination*. Suppose that a defendant admitted during unwarned custodial interrogation that she was sitting in a car outside a bank that was robbed. If her attorney calls her to testify and she denies that she was outside the bank, the prosecutor may not introduce her admission to prove that she was at the bank but may use it to impeach her exculpatory testimony. Because the clear inconsistency with her testimony indicates that she has not been entirely truthful, a jury may choose to disbelieve her in-court account.[198] The exception also permits the use of statements obtained by other types of *Miranda* violations. For example, a

195. *Id.* at 639 (plurality opinion).

196. *Id.* (plurality opinion). The reasoning recounted is in a plurality opinion joined by only three Justices. Two additional Justices joined a concurrence reaffirming the validity of *Harris* because "the concerns underlying [*Miranda*] . . . must be accommodated to other objectives of the criminal justice system." *Id.* at 644–45 (Kennedy, J., concurring in the judgment).

197. The merits of the Court's analysis are questionable. The conclusion in *Patane* that derivative evidence is not barred seems to be based, in part, on the view that the core of the Fifth Amendment is protection against incriminating *testimonial* evidence. The impeachment use exception allows the introduction of the accused's testimonial revelations. Moreover, the risk that compelled statements will find their way into trial is just as high as it is when the very same statements are used for substantive purposes. Perhaps the Court's conclusion rests on the premise that impeachment use of statements is not as incriminating as substantive use. As a result, any Fifth Amendment harm that might occur is less substantial. *But see* Miranda v. Arizona, 384 U.S. 436, 476 (1966) (asserting that the Fifth Amendment "does not distinguish degrees of incrimination"). Alternatively, the Court's conclusion might be rooted in the peculiar costs resulting from preventing the government from contesting a defendant's trial perjury and a belief that those costs outweigh any gains in Fifth Amendment protection resulting from suppression. The persuasiveness of these supplemental rationales is arguable.

198. The accused is entitled to have the jury instructed to use a contradictory statement only for credibility purposes, not as proof of guilt. Moreover, in assessing the sufficiency of evidence to prove guilt, a trial or appellate court may not count the statement's value as proof of guilt.

defendant may be impeached by statements obtained after the police ignored a request for counsel and initiated questioning.[199] In addition, it is virtually certain that testimony given by an accused in response to the government's proper *cross-examination* may be impeached. It is difficult to imagine a conclusion that a bar to impeachment of testimony given on cross-examination is consistent with the "close-fit requirement" imposed on *Miranda*'s prophylactic rule.[200] Thus, in the bank robbery situation, it would not matter if the defendant's testimony that she was not outside the bank was responsive to proper cross-examination by the prosecutor.

An unsettled question is whether the *Miranda* exclusionary rule permits the government to use improperly obtained evidence to impeach a *defense witness* other than the accused. Suppose that an unwarned accused admitted to interrogators that he was selling drugs on a street corner. At trial, he calls a close friend to testify that he was in her home at the time of the alleged sale. May the government use the unwarned admission to cast doubt on the truthfulness or accuracy of the friend's assertion? In *James v. Illinois*,[201] the Court refused to expand the Fourth Amendment impeachment exception to authorize the impeachment of defense witnesses. The majority's reasoning, however, was based entirely on deterrent cost-benefit balancing.[202] Considering the radically different underpinnings of *Miranda*'s exclusion doctrine, it is far from certain that the Court would prohibit the impeachment of defense witnesses. In light of the palpable determination to constrain *Miranda*'s prophylaxis, it seems quite likely that the Court would refuse to extend *Miranda*'s bar and prevent impeachment of defense witnesses. In all probability, such an expansion would be deemed irreconcilable with *Miranda*'s close-fit demand.

E. CONCLUDING REFLECTIONS UPON THE *MIRANDA* EXCLUSIONARY RULE

Although *Miranda*'s exclusionary rule is relatively young, its history has been remarkably eventful. What began as a part of the Fifth Amendment right against compulsory self-incrimination quickly evolved into a judicially-created doctrine apparently designed, at least in part, to deter future neglect of *Miranda*'s custodial interrogation guidelines. Today, the *Miranda* bar to evidence is an overbroad

---

199. *See* Oregon v. Hass, 420 U.S. 714 (1975).

200. Moreover, the Court has expanded the Fourth Amendment impeachment use exception to permit impeachment of testimony given on cross-examination. *See* United States v. Havens, 446 U.S. 620 (1980). It has been atypical for the Court to interpret the *Miranda* exclusionary rule more expansively than the Fourth Amendment rule.

201. 493 U.S. 307 (1990).

202. *See id.* at 313–20.

prophylactic mechanism designed primarily to counter risks that defendants will be deprived of the Fifth Amendment privilege at their trials. While not an integral part of the accused's personal right against compulsory self-incrimination, it is necessary protection for that right. Whether it is also a future-oriented deterrent sanction is uncertain. In fact, *Miranda*'s rule appears to be the only one of its species. The other rules described in this book are either purely deterrent safeguards designed to enforce constitutional rights by altering future law enforcement conduct[203] or integral parts of constitutional rights.[204] *Miranda* alone is an overprotective constitutional safeguard against risks that a fundamental trial right will be denied.[205]

The radical transformations of the nature of and justifications for *Miranda* suppression during the more than 40-year period since it first appeared have played a major role in shaping its contours. The result of this revolutionary process is a relatively confined exclusionary rule that allows defendants to bar from trials and at least some sentencing proceedings their own confessions obtained by custodial interrogation without adequate safeguards. No derivative evidence is subject to exclusion, no matter how closely linked it is to a confession. Moreover, a public safety exception and an impeachment use exception authorize the prosecution to introduce otherwise inadmissible confessions. While some additional exceptions are possible, it seems unlikely that many will emerge. There is little need to impose further restrictions on the already narrow *Miranda* rule. At a time when the Supreme Court seems quite hostile to most varieties of constitutional exclusion, the *Miranda* rule may be the most disfavored.

It seems unlikely that the Supreme Court will ever restore *Miranda* exclusion's status as part of the Fifth Amendment guarantee. One or two changes in Supreme Court membership, however, could restore a measure of vitality to the *Miranda* suppression doctrine by extending its prophylactic reach. It also seems unlikely that the Court will abolish the *Miranda* exclusionary rule. When the Justices had the opportunity to overthrow *Miranda* a little more than ten years ago in *Dickerson v. United States*,[206] seven voted to retain it. On the other hand, the changes in the Court's membership since *Dickerson* make it possible that

---

203. The Fourth Amendment exclusionary rule and, apparently, the Sixth Amendment right to counsel rule discussed in Chapter 4, are of this variety.

204. The Fifth and Fourteenth Amendment bars to coerced confessions, the Due Process Clause exclusion of eyewitness identification evidence described in Chapter 6, and the Sixth Amendment Confrontation Clause bar to testimonial hearsay treated in Chapter 7 are personal rights belonging to accused persons.

205. The only constitutional exclusion doctrine that might have the same nature is the Sixth Amendment bar to eyewitness identification evidence discussed in Chapter 5. The character of that evidentiary bar is uncertain.

206. 530 U.S. 428 (2000).

currently there are four Justices who would eliminate *Miranda*.[207] If so, it would take but one new Justice to overturn the infamous icon. Nonetheless, the most likely future for *Miranda* exclusion would seem to be maintenance of the status quo. Neither noteworthy expansion nor substantial contraction of the constitutional exclusion mandated by *Miranda* seems probable. Although its history has been one of dramatic change, the narrow prophylactic safeguard that has evolved is likely to remain relatively stable in the coming years.

---

207. In *Dickerson*, only two Justices—Justices Scalia and Thomas—advocated abolition. *Id.* at 461–65 (Scalia, J., dissenting). In light of his abiding hostility to *Miranda*, however, it seems likely that Chief Justice Rehnquist would have voted to abandon the doctrine if there had been four other Justices willing to do so. *See* Yale Kamisar, Dickerson v. United States*: The Case That Disappointed* Miranda*'s Critics And Then Its Supporters*, *in* THE REHNQUIST LEGACY 106, 128 (Craig Bradley ed. 2006) (maintaining that the Chief Justice "probably contributed more to the depreciation of *Miranda* than any other" Justice). He may well have joined the majority so that he could author as narrow an affirming opinion as possible. *See* Daniel M. Katz, *Institutional Rules, Strategic Behavior, and the Legacy of Chief Justice William Rehnquist: Setting the Record Straight on* Dickerson v. United States, 22 J. L. & POL. 303, 338 (2006); *see also* Kamisar, *Foreword*, *supra* note 19, at 889. Today, it is conceivable that Justice Alito (who assumed Justice O'Connor's place) and Chief Justice Roberts (who filled the Rehnquist vacancy) would join Justices Scalia and Thomas.

4. THE *MASSIAH* DOCTRINE: SIXTH AMENDMENT EXCLUSION OF CONFESSIONS

INTRODUCTION

This final chapter concerning the exclusion of confessions addresses a rule rooted in the Sixth Amendment right to the assistance of counsel.[1] This constitutional basis for suppression, generally known as the *Massiah* doctrine,[2] was the Supreme Court's first effort to compensate for the ambiguities and inadequacies of the coerced confession doctrine. It predated the much better known *Miranda* doctrine by two years. Although it was essentially dormant for the decade following *Miranda*, leading some to wonder whether it had been effectively supplanted by that decision, the *Massiah* doctrine re-emerged alive and well in a highly controversial 1977 decision.[3] A number of subsequent opinions spanning the past 30 years have reaffirmed and modified the doctrine.

Despite the resurgence of *Massiah*, the Court has devoted considerably less time and effort to discussing and developing its suppression mandate than it has to the *Miranda* rule. The great majority of *Massiah* opinions have addressed issues pertaining to the substance and scope of the pretrial right to assistance of counsel. Very few have involved "exclusionary rule" issues. In other words, most *Massiah* rulings have been concerned with whether a defendant was entitled to or deprived of counsel in a pretrial encounter with the government—not whether evidence obtained as a result of a proven deprivation of assistance should be kept from the courtroom.

The object in this chapter is to explore and explain the evidentiary consequences of pretrial deprivations of counsel, not the contours of the substantive entitlement to assistance. As in Chapter 3, however, the courtroom consequences of earlier Sixth Amendment denials cannot be severed entirely from the out-of-court entitlement at issue. One cannot fully comprehend the underpinnings and details of the suppression doctrine without a basic appreciation of the circumstances that dictate suppression—that is, the particulars of the pretrial encounters in which defendants have constitutional entitlements to legal assistance. Those particulars will serve as a foundation for the detailed discussion of exclusion.

---

1. The Sixth Amendment provides: "In all criminal prosecutions, the accused shall enjoy the right . . . to have the Assistance of Counsel for his defence." U.S. Const. amend. VI.

2. The doctrine originated in *Massiah v. United States*, 377 U.S. 201 (1964).

3. The decision referred to is *Brewer v. Williams*, 430 U.S. 387 (1977).

One other point merits mention at the outset. The first three chapters provide illustrations of the three different kinds of constitutional exclusion. The Fourth Amendment rule is essentially a deterrent of future violations of the constitutional right against unreasonable searches and seizures. In contrast, the Due Process and Self-Incrimination bars are personal constitutional rights, inseparable parts of the constitutional guarantees at issue. The *Miranda* suppression doctrine is a third variety of exclusionary rule, not a personal right of the accused but a prophylactic safeguard against risks that Fifth Amendment rights will be violated at trial. For more than four decades after the *Massiah* exclusion doctrine first appeared in 1964, its character was obscure and uncertain. There were clear indications that it was a constitutional right as well as some intimations that deterrence was an objective, perhaps *the* objective. In a highly questionable 2009 ruling, the Court finally explained its conception of the nature of this constitutional exclusion doctrine.

A. THE BASIC *MASSIAH* SUPPRESSION DOCTRINE

In *Massiah v. United States,*[4] the Supreme Court interpreted the Sixth Amendment right of accused persons to have "the assistance of counsel," a guarantee originally designed to ensure that defendants would have the aid of a trained expert at trial.[5] Prior to *Massiah,* the Court had already ruled that this trial right had to be extended to some formal courtroom phases of the criminal process occurring before trial.[6] In *Massiah,* the Court extended the Sixth Amendment right to trial assistance to certain "informal" confrontations with government agents occurring outside the judicial process.

According to the *Massiah* doctrine, after a person has been formally charged with a criminal offense,[7] he is entitled to a lawyer's assistance when a government

---

4. 377 U.S. 201 (1964).

5. *See* United States v. Ash, 413 U.S. 300, 309 (1973); *see also* James J. Tomkovicz, The Right to the Assistance of Counsel 81 (2002).

6. *See, e.g.,* White v. Maryland, 373 U.S. 59, 60 (1963) (holding that the right to counsel extended to a preliminary hearing); Hamilton v. Alabama, 368 U.S. 52, 54 (1961) (holding that a defendant had the right to counsel at an arraignment).

7. The *Massiah* Court recognized a right to counsel against deliberate elicitation following indictment for an offense. *Massiah,* 377 U.S. at 206. Subsequently, it has become clear that any formal accusation—any governmental action that qualifies as "the initiation of adversary judicial criminal proceedings," Kirby v. Illinois, 406 U.S. 682, 689 (1972) (plurality opinion)—is a predicate for attachment of the Sixth Amendment right. *See* Brewer v. Williams, 430 U.S. 387, 398 (1977). It has also become clear that the Sixth Amendment right to counsel attaches *only* upon a formal accusation by the state. *See* Rothgery v. Gillespie County, Texas, 554 U.S. 191, 197–98 (2008); Moran v. Burbine, 475 U.S. 412, 428–30 (1986).

operative—a known police officer, an undercover police officer, or an informant working for the state[8]—deliberately elicits from him incriminating statements pertaining to the charged offense. Put otherwise, deliberate elicitation of statements from an accused person is a "'critical stage[]' of the prosecution" that triggers the constitutional entitlement to counsel.[9] If the accused does not have a lawyer and has not waived the right to assistance, the government is not allowed to use any incriminating disclosures it obtains to prove that he committed the offense that was the subject of the charge.[10] For example, if a person is indicted for bank robbery and officers engage him in a conversation about that crime when he is assisted by neither retained nor appointed counsel and has not made a valid choice to forego such assistance, any admissions he makes are excluded from the bank robbery trial. Suppose instead that an arrested defendant makes an initial appearance in court where a judge informs her that she has been accused of selling narcotics and restricts her liberty by releasing her on bond.[11] Thereafter, the defendant's cellmate or a co-conspirator who has agreed to work for law enforcement converses with the defendant and tapes her incriminating disclosures. The state may not introduce those disclosures at trial to prove that the defendant sold narcotics.

In *Massiah*, the Court prohibited the federal government from using statements deliberately elicited from an indicted individual to prove guilt at trial. The Justices did not discuss the breadth of the evidentiary exclusion required by the Sixth Amendment right to counsel. One question is whether derivative evidence is suppressible. May a prosecutor introduce a weapon found as a result of the defendant's revelations to a police officer or narcotics whose location a

8. The elicitation of statements by a private person who is not involved with the state does not trigger an entitlement to counsel. Evidence of those statements is not subject to suppression under the Sixth Amendment. A private individual can qualify as a "state agent," however, even though he or she is not formally employed or compensated by the state. The question is whether the individual is acting at the instigation or behest of state officials. For discussions of the requirement of state agency, see Randolph v. California, 380 F.3d 1133, 1144 (9th Cir. 2004); Jackson v. State, 684 A.2d 745, 751 (Del. 1996).

9. *See* United States v. Henry, 447 U.S. 264, 269 (1980); *see also* Kansas v. Ventris, 556 U.S. ___, ____,129 S.Ct. 1841, 1845 (2009) (observing that the right to counsel extends to "'critical' interactions between the defendant and the State" and that "deliberate elicitation by law enforcement officers (and their agents)" qualifies).

10. As will be seen later, for Sixth Amendment purposes, some offenses other than the precise offense that is the subject of a formal accusation are considered the "same offense" as the charged offense. *See* Texas v. Cobb, 532 U.S. 162, 173 (2001). The right to counsel attaches, and the suppression sanction is applicable, for any offense that qualifies as the same offense under the standard adopted in *Cobb*. *See id.*

11. *See Rothgery*, 554 U.S. at 213 (holding that adversary proceedings have been initiated when a defendant makes a first appearance, is informed of the charges against him, and has his liberty subjected to restriction even if a prosecutor was not involved in starting the process).

cellmate elicited from the accused? One significant post-*Massiah* ruling rests on the premise that all evidence derived from a right to counsel deprivation is presumptively inadmissible and may be introduced only if it falls within an exception to the suppression doctrine. The *Massiah* Court did not consider the issue of "standing" to raise Sixth Amendment exclusion claims, and, indeed, the issue has never come before the Supreme Court. May a spouse of the accused raise a *Massiah* objection to disclosures that incriminate her? The Court has never addressed whether confessions are inadmissible in any court proceeding other than a trial of guilt or innocence. Are admissions barred from a grand jury proceeding seeking an indictment or from a post-trial sentencing hearing?

The Court has addressed two qualifications on the *Massiah* suppression doctrine—holding that both the inevitable discovery and impeachment use exceptions permit the government to introduce statements secured in violation of *Massiah*'s guarantee of counsel. Thus, DNA evidence acquired by following leads improperly obtained from the accused is admissible if the prosecutor can show that the police inevitably would have discovered the same evidence by independent lawful methods. Moreover, if an accused testifies at trial that he was out of town on the day of a robbery, a judge should admit an unconstitutionally obtained statement that he was involved in the robbery to undermine the credibility of his testimony. On the other hand, the Court has not considered whether the attenuation exception qualifies *Massiah*'s rule. May the government use a weapon found by means of a lengthy chain of investigative steps initiated by disclosures the accused made long before the weapon was discovered? The Court has held that the fact that officers were involved in a "good faith" effort to investigate an uncharged offense cannot justify the introduction of statements to prove a crime that already was the subject of a formal charge. It has not ruled, however, on whether a "public safety" interest might support an exception to the Sixth Amendment exclusionary rule—i.e., whether deliberately elicited statements may be used to prove a charged offense if officials were motivated by a public safety interest. Suppose, for example, that the police employ an informant to discover the location of a nuclear device from an accused terrorist. Are the statements the defendant made to the informant admissible at the terrorism trial because officers were attempting to counter a serious threat of harm?

The portion of this chapter devoted to doctrinal details considers all of these questions about the reach of and restrictions on *Massiah*'s Sixth Amendment suppression doctrine. Efforts will be made to assess the merits of the few answers the Court has provided and to determine how the unresolved exclusionary rule questions will and should be decided. Once again, the analyses in this chapter highlight the critical importance of the rationales for exclusion in accurately defining the contours of suppression doctrines. Chapter 3 explained how the modified explanation of *Miranda*'s evidentiary bar has sometimes led to dramatically different conclusions about the need for suppression than those that would have been dictated by the original conception of the *Miranda* rule.

The same is true under *Massiah*. The view that exclusion is a trial right—an inseparable part of the counsel guarantee—can produce starkly different answers than those yielded by the view that suppression is designed solely to discourage future counsel deprivations. Before discussing the different possible conceptions of *Massiah* exclusion, the debate over its legitimacy, and the array of operational questions I have highlighted, a sketch of the history of Sixth Amendment suppression is in order.

B. THE INCEPTION AND DEVELOPMENT OF *MASSIAH*'S SIXTH AMENDMENT EXCLUSION DOCTRINE: A BRIEF HISTORY

As explained in Chapter 3, the *Miranda* exclusionary rule first appeared in the mid-1960s. During the more than 40 years since its arrival, the Supreme Court has paid extensive attention to explaining its constitutional underpinnings and developing its doctrinal details. The results have been radical transformations of *Miranda*'s rationales and substantial alterations of *Miranda*'s scope. As is clear from the historical account in the preceding chapter, *Miranda*'s evolution has been dramatic and complicated. The *Massiah* suppression doctrine also appeared in the mid-1960s. In the decades that have followed, however, the Justices have not devoted extensive attention to either its rationales or its doctrinal standards. Until very recently, explanations of the justifications for Sixth Amendment exclusion have been sketchy or equivocal, at best, and many questions of scope and application remain unresolved today. As a result, the history of evidentiary suppression under *Massiah* is considerably less complex.

Before announcing the Sixth Amendment bar to inculpatory statements in *Massiah*, the Supreme Court had twice rejected defendants' claims that the pretrial deprivation of a lawyer's assistance required the exclusion of incriminating statements made to government agents. On another occasion, while the Justices did seem favorably disposed toward a right to counsel basis for exclusion, they found an alternative ground for decision that enabled them to avoid resolving the question of whether a denial of counsel before trial could ever be a basis for suppressing evidence of guilt.

In 1958, in both *Crooker v. California*[12] and *Cicenia v. LaGay*,[13] convicted defendants contended that state courts had denied them due process of law by allowing prosecutors to introduce confessions made after interrogators had ignored their express requests for the assistance of counsel. Although both were suspected of crimes, neither defendant had been formally charged with an offense at the time of the official questioning. The defendant in *Crooker* was not

12. 357 U.S. 433 (1958).
13. 357 U.S. 504 (1958).

represented by counsel at the time of his request, but the defendant in *Cicenia* had already retained legal assistance and his lawyer had repeatedly asked for permission to see his client.[14] In both instances, the Supreme Court rejected the constitutional challenge. According to the Justices, the Due Process Clause contained no rigid requirement that the authorities, in all circumstances, had to honor requests for counsel by suspects they sought to question.[15] Because the circumstances in neither *Crooker* nor *Cicenia* provided a basis for a due process right to confer with a lawyer, there was no constitutional bar to the use of the defendants' confessions to prove their guilt.[16]

Just a year later, in *Spano v. New York*,[17] a majority ruled that a defendant's confession was involuntary and, thus, inadmissible under the Due Process Clause.[18] Four Justices joined concurring opinions concluding that the confession was also inadmissible because the defendant had been deprived of his right to the assistance of counsel during the police interrogation.[19] These Justices found a critical distinction between the circumstances in *Spano* and those in *Crooker* and *Cicenia*. In the latter cases, the authorities "were questioning a [mere] *suspect* in the course of investigating an unsolved crime."[20] In *Spano*, however, the defendant was under indictment for murder at the time of the interrogation—that is, he had already been "formally charged with a crime."[21] Because he had become an "accused," he was clearly entitled to the assistance of counsel when the police questioned him about the murder.[22]

---

14. *See Cicenia*, 357 U.S. at 505.

15. *See Cicenia*, 357 U.S. at 508–10; *Crooker*, 357 U.S. at 440–41.

16. In *Crooker*, four Justices did dissent. They asserted that the denial of the defendant's expressed wishes for counsel's assistance in connection with the police interrogation violated his due process entitlement to consult with a lawyer in connection with pretrial questioning by the police. *Crooker*, 357 U.S. at 442 (Douglas, J., dissenting). In *Cicenia*, three Justices dissented, declaring that the defendant had been deprived of a "constitutional requirement for fair criminal proceedings" when officers placed "an insuperable barrier between" him and his retained counsel. *Cicenia*, 357 U.S. at 512 (Douglas, J., dissenting). The dissenters in both cases would have held that the Fourteenth Amendment guarantee of due process forbade the use of the confessions obtained after the defendants' requests for counsel were ignored.

17. 360 U.S. 315 (1959).

18. For a discussion of *Spano*'s place in the history of the due process-coerced confession exclusion doctrine, see *supra* Chapter 2, text accompanying notes 102–04.

19. *Spano*, 360 U.S. at 325–26 (Douglas, J., concurring); *id.* at 326–27 (Stewart, J., concurring).

20. *Id.* at 327 (Stewart, J., concurring) (emphasis added); *see also id.* at 324–25 (Douglas, J., concurring).

21. *Id.* (Douglas, J., concurring); *see also id.* at 327 (Stewart, J., concurring).

22. *Id.* at 325 (Douglas, J., concurring) ("Depriving a person, formally charged with a crime, of counsel during the period prior to trial may be more damaging than denial of counsel during the trial itself."); *id.* at 327 (Stewart, J., concurring) ("Under our system of

If these four concurring Justices were the only support for the right to counsel basis for suppressing the confession, *Spano* would have little, if any, Sixth Amendment significance. After all, four dissenting Justices had also opined that the defendant in *Crooker* was entitled to legal assistance. The difference is that in *Crooker* a majority *rejected* the right to counsel ground for suppression, while in *Spano* not a single Justice denied that the defendant had been deprived of a constitutional entitlement to counsel. Instead, the majority opinion found "it unnecessary to reach" the right to counsel claim because "use of the [coerced] confession" was "inconsistent with" due process.[23] More important, the author of the *Spano* majority opinion, Chief Justice Warren, had joined the dissent in *Crooker*. It seems clear that if he had been forced to reach the question he would have found that the deprivation of counsel required a bar to Spano's confession. In other words, at the time of *Spano* there were at least five members of the Court prepared to endorse a Sixth Amendment exclusion doctrine for confessions obtained by interrogating individuals *accused* of crimes.

Another five years passed before the Court explicitly endorsed a right to counsel exclusion doctrine. When the Justices did confront the question, they announced a rule that reached well beyond the police interrogation context involved in *Crooker, Cicenia*, and *Spano*. In *Massiah v. United States*,[24] a defendant was indicted for narcotics offenses. A man named Colson, who was also charged with the offenses, "decided to cooperate with" federal investigators.[25] He allowed the investigators to place a "radio transmitter" in his automobile, and then, while a federal agent listened in, he "held a lengthy conversation" in his car with Massiah.[26] Six Justices, relying in part on the reasoning of the concurring opinions in *Spano*, held that the defendant "was denied the basic protections of [the Sixth Amendment right to counsel] when there was used against him at his trial evidence of his own incriminating words, which federal agents had deliberately elicited from him after he had been indicted and in the absence of his counsel."[27] Because Massiah was entitled to the assistance of counsel during this encounter with a government agent, his revelations "could not constitutionally be used by the prosecution as evidence against *him* at his trial."[28]

The exclusion doctrine announced in *Massiah* commanded the suppression of inculpatory admissions secured by government agents in violation of an accused's pretrial entitlement to legal assistance. By its literal terms, the holding

---

justice an indictment is supposed to be followed by an arraignment and a trial. At every stage of those proceedings the accused has an absolute right to a lawyer's help.").

23. *Id.* at 320.

24. 377 U.S. 201 (1964).

25. *Id.* at 202–03.

26. *Id.*

27. *Id.* at 206.

28. *Id.* at 207.

of *Massiah* limited the right to assistance—and, thus, the evidentiary suppression command—to individuals formally charged with an offense. Massiah "had been indicted."[29] On the other hand, the entitlement to assistance was *not* restricted to cases in which known police officers "interrogated" accused individuals. Instead, it also extended to situations in which unknown operatives of the state "deliberately elicited" admissions from unsuspecting defendants. According to the *Massiah* majority, the protection of the right to counsel reached both direct and open interrogations *and* "'indirect and surreptitious'" efforts to secure incriminating disclosures.[30] A "defendant's own incriminating statements . . . could not constitutionally be used . . . against *him* at his trial" if they were the product of either sort of confrontation with the government.[31] Mere conversation by Massiah's co-defendant was sufficient to trigger a Sixth Amendment right to legal assistance.

Finally, while the *Massiah* majority offered no explicit discussion of the constitutional rationale for requiring the exclusion of deliberately elicited incriminating statements, the undeniable message of the Court's language and reasoning was that suppression was an indivisible part of the Sixth Amendment right to assistance. The Court did "not question" the constitutional propriety of eliciting incriminating revelations from accused persons in order to investigate crimes—either additional crimes the accused individual is suspected of committing or the involvement of other suspects in the offenses that are the subject of the pending accusation.[32] In the majority's view, such law enforcement conduct did not offend the Sixth Amendment. Rather, it was the use of the elicited

29. Dissenting Justices questioned whether the right to counsel, and thus the evidentiary exclusion mandate, would extend to situations in which an individual had not been formally charged, but had merely been arrested. *Massiah*, 377 U.S. at 212 (White, J., dissenting).

30. *Id.* at 206. Although the Court suggested that Massiah had been subjected to interrogation, *id.*, it seems clear that it was not using that term in its ordinary sense of questioning (or equivalent conduct) by known law enforcement officers (or other known state actors). The facts of the case established only that there were "conversations" between Colson and Massiah, not that he was the subject of questioning about his crimes or any conduct with coercive effects similar to direct questioning. As will be seen, later opinions have confirmed that mere deliberate elicitation—something less than interrogation—triggers the right to counsel and its exclusionary consequences. Today, the right attaches when an undercover agent merely converses with an accused person, *see* United States v. Henry, 447 U.S. 264, 271 (1980) (finding a right to counsel deprivation and requiring the exclusion of statements made when a cellmate working with law enforcers engaged in conversation with the defendant), or when officers engage in evocative conduct that does not constitute "'interrogation.'" *See* Fellers v. United States, 540 U.S. 519, 524–25 (2004) (unanimously concluding that officers need not engage in interrogation to trigger the protection of the right to counsel under *Massiah*).

31. *Massiah*, 377 U.S. at 207.

32. *Id.*

revelations in the courtroom to prove the charged offenses that was "constitutionally" forbidden.[33] A defendant "was denied . . . basic" Sixth Amendment "protections" when the prosecution "used against him at his trial evidence of his own incriminating words."[34] At its inception, like the Fifth Amendment and due process bars to coerced confessions, the *Massiah* exclusion doctrine was a defendant's personal trial right. Admission of the evidence secured before trial violated that right.

In an opinion handed down just a month after *Massiah*, the right to counsel exclusion doctrine expanded. *Escobedo v. Illinois*[35] involved the admissibility of incriminating statements made during the interrogation of a man who had been arrested for, but not formally charged with, a murder.[36] The authorities had denied numerous requests by a retained lawyer to see the suspect and numerous requests by the suspect to consult with counsel.[37] After acknowledging that Massiah had been indicted at the time his statements were elicited, the Court declared that "that fact should make no difference" because law enforcement officers were not investigating an "'unsolved crime.'"[38] Instead, Escobedo "had become the accused" and the "purpose of the interrogation was to 'get him' to confess his guilt."[39] Just like the defendants in *Spano* and *Massiah*, he needed the advice of counsel at this "critical" stage of the process where events "could certainly 'affect the whole trial.'"[40] In the majority's view, "[i]t would exalt form over substance to make the right to counsel . . . depend on whether . . . the interrogation" occurred after "a *formal* indictment," because Escobedo "had, *for all practical purposes*, already been charged with murder."[41] The assistance of a lawyer at trial would be of little value if the authorities could secure and use inculpatory admissions from a person in his position.

A number of limiting circumstances narrowed the *Escobedo* Court's actual holding. According to the majority, "no statement elicited by the police during [an] interrogation [could] be used against [a defendant] at a criminal trial" if: (1) it was obtained when "the investigation [was] no longer a general inquiry into an unsolved crime but ha[d] begun to focus on a particular suspect"; (2) if the suspect was in "custody," was subjected to "a process of interrogations," and had "requested and been denied an opportunity to consult with his lawyer"; and (3) if

---

33. *Id.*

34. *Id.* at 206.

35. 378 U.S. 478 (1964).

36. *Id.* at 485.

37. *Id.* at 480–82.

38. *Id.* at 485 (quoting Spano v. New York, 360 U.S. 315, 327 (1959) (Stewart, J., concurring)).

39. *Id.*

40. *Escobedo*, 378 U.S. at 486.

41. *Id.* (emphasis added).

"the police ha[d] not . . . warned him of his . . . right to remain silent."[42] In that situation, the individual had a Sixth Amendment entitlement to assistance and a denial required the suppression of any disclosures.[43] Despite these limiting conditions, *Escobedo* was a significant ruling. For the first time, the Court extended the right to counsel to an individual who had not been formally accused and barred probative evidence the authorities had obtained from him.[44] As in *Massiah*, the *Escobedo* Court did not explain the justification for the Sixth Amendment exclusion doctrine. Courtroom use was forbidden simply because the statements were acquired at a time when the authorities did not respect the defendant's constitutional entitlement to legal assistance.

Escobedo, the only Supreme Court decision recognizing a Sixth Amendment right to assistance prior to formal accusation and barring evidence obtained at that time, did not long survive. Just two years later, the Court indicated that the ruling was actually based upon and intended to implement the Fifth Amendment privilege against compulsory self-incrimination, *not* the Sixth Amendment entitlement to counsel.[45] In a number of subsequent decisions, the Court has made it unmistakably clear that the Sixth Amendment right never attaches prior to a formal accusation.[46] Historically, *Escobedo* was a constitutional misstep, a short-lived expansion of the right to counsel's scope and its corresponding suppression doctrine.

---

42. *Id.* at 490–91.

43. *Id.* at 491.

44. *Id.* at 490–91. Four dissenting Justices objected to this expansion. *See id.* at 492 (Harlan, J., dissenting); *id.* at 493 (Stewart, J., dissenting); *id.* at 495 (White, J., dissenting). Their reasoning and position would soon prevail.

45. *See* Johnson v. New Jersey, 384 U.S. 719, 729–30 (1966); Miranda v. Arizona, 384 U.S. 436, 465–66 (1966). A later opinion affirming the Sixth Amendment demand for a formal accusation noted that "the Court in retrospect [had] perceived that the 'prime purpose' of *Escobedo* was not to vindicate the constitutional right to counsel as such, but, like *Miranda*, 'to guarantee full effectuation of the privilege against self-incrimination.'" Kirby v. Illinois, 406 U.S. 682, 689 (1972) (quoting Johnson v. New Jersey, 384 U.S. 719, 729 (1966)). Although there are some references in the *Escobedo* opinion to the Fifth Amendment privilege, *see Escobedo*, 378 U.S. at 488, 489, 490 n.14, there can be no doubt that the majority had intended to root its decision firmly in the Sixth Amendment right to counsel provision. The later decisions that portrayed it as a precursor of *Miranda*, not a successor of *Massiah*, were revisionist, at best.

46. *See* Moran v. Burbine, 475 U.S. 412, 428–32 (1986); United States v. Gouveia, 467 U.S. 180, 187–88 (1984). This rigid doctrinal line that controls attachment of the right to the assistance of counsel is explained in more detail in the doctrinal section of this chapter. Whereas *Escobedo* rested on an insistence upon substance over form, *Escobedo*, 378 U.S. at 486, the currently controlling criterion arguably elevates form over substance. *See* Kirby v. Illinois, 406 U.S. 682, 698–99 (1972) (Brennan, J., dissenting); *see also Gouveia*, 467 U.S. at 193–97 (Stevens, J., concurring in the judgment).

Although the *Miranda* Court recast *Escobedo* as a Fifth Amendment decision,[47] nothing in that decision undermined *Massiah*'s extension of the Sixth Amendment to post-accusation pretrial encounters. Moreover, *Massiah*'s Sixth Amendment suppression doctrine for statements elicited after formal charges seemed untouched by, and capable of coexisting with, *Miranda*'s rule of inadmissibility. As the years passed, however, and the Supreme Court ignored the *Massiah* doctrine and its suppression dictate,[48] there was reason to wonder whether *Miranda* had also supplanted *Massiah*. It seemed entirely possible that the Court had reconsidered its extension of the Sixth Amendment to informal pretrial encounters between government agents and those accused of crime and had concluded that the privilege against compelled self-incrimination was the sole constitutional basis—other than due process—for excluding statements secured from an accused before trial.

Two decisions, however, one in 1977 and one in 1980, proved that *Massiah*'s pretrial extension of the right to counsel and its courtroom bar to admissions of guilt were alive and well. In *Brewer v. Williams*,[49] the Court suppressed statements made by a formally charged individual in response to an officer's "'Christian burial speech,'" conduct that the lower courts had deemed "tantamount to interrogation."[50] Then, in *United States v. Henry*,[51] the Court reaffirmed the applicability of the doctrine to statements made by an indicted prisoner during a mere conversation with a cellmate who was working for the government. Because in each case government agents had deliberately elicited disclosures from a man who had been formally accused, the Sixth Amendment forbade their use at trial.[52] The issue in each was whether the defendant had been deprived of his constitutional entitlement to assistance.[53] Once the Court decided that each defendant had been denied his Sixth Amendment right, suppression followed. Neither case involved any question or discussion about the proper scope of the *Massiah* exclusion doctrine. Neither opinion addressed the nature or underpinnings of the suppression sanction. Their historical significance was in

47. *Miranda*, 384 U.S. at 465–66.

48. In the 11 years following *Miranda*, the Court rendered but one decision relying upon the *Massiah* doctrine, an insignificant *per curiam* ruling in *Beatty v. United States*, 389 U.S. 45 (1967). For the 10-year span between 1967 and 1977, the Court did not resolve a single *Massiah* issue.

49. 430 U.S. 387 (1977).

50. *Id.* at 400.

51. 447 U.S. 264 (1980).

52. *See id.* at 270–74; *Brewer v. Williams*, 430 U.S. at 398–99.

53. In *Brewer v. Williams*, the question was whether the accused made a valid waiver of counsel. *See Brewer*, 430 U.S. at 401–06. In *Henry*, the issue was whether the circumstances showed deliberate elicitation that was attributable to the government. *See Henry*, 447 U.S. at 270.

reaffirming the *existence* of a right to counsel suppression doctrine and in reinforcing that it applied to confessions elicited either openly or surreptitiously.[54]

The *Williams* case assumed a more important role in the history of Sixth Amendment suppression when it returned to the Supreme Court seven years after its first arrival. The second time around it produced the Court's first *Massiah* "exclusionary rule" decision. In *Nix v. Williams*,[55] the issue was whether evidence obtained by means of an acknowledged right to counsel deprivation had to be suppressed. The *Williams* case involved the disappearance of a little girl. There was reason to believe the defendant was involved, sufficient reason for the state to initiate formal proceedings for abduction. When the case was first before the Supreme Court, the sole issue was whether the defendant had waived his entitlement to counsel before leading the authorities to the girl's body. A majority found inadequate evidence of a valid waiver. Because the defendant had been denied his Sixth Amendment right to counsel, his revelations of knowledge of the location of the victim had to be suppressed.[56] When the case again came before the Court seven years later, the issue was whether the prosecution could introduce derivative evidence found as a result of his improperly-obtained revelations—"evidence of the condition of" the victim's body and "the results of . . . medical and chemical tests [performed] on [her] body."[57]

The Court found that the derivative evidence was admissible, despite the fact that it had actually been obtained by means of a Sixth Amendment deprivation. According to the Justices, it fell within the confines of an "inevitable discovery exception" to the Sixth Amendment exclusion doctrine.[58] The prosecution could use this probative derivative evidence because it "inevitably would have been discovered by lawful means."[59] The factual basis for the conclusion that the body would have been found by alternative lawful means was an organized search for the victim that was in progress, but had been suspended temporarily when it was learned that the defendant might lead the authorities to the body.[60] This search was never resumed because the accused led the authorities to the location of the victim.

Initially, the *Nix* majority opinion implicitly assumed that the Sixth Amendment and Fourth Amendment exclusionary rules were similar, if not

---

54. In *Massiah*, the Court had indicated that both situations were within the scope of the doctrine by relying heavily upon and approving of *Spano*, a case involving interrogation by known officers, *see Massiah*, 377 U.S. at 204–06, and by asserting that surreptitious elicitation by an unknown government agent—the sort of conduct that had taken place in *Massiah*—was an *even more serious* imposition upon the accused. *See id.* at 206.

55. 467 U.S. 431 (1984).

56. 430 U.S. at 405–06.

57. *Nix*, 467 U.S. at 434, 437.

58. *Id.* at 440, 448.

59. *Id.* at 444.

60. *Id.* at 448–49.

identical, in nature. Citing Fourth Amendment precedents, the Court noted that the exclusionary rule requires the suppression of "the tainted 'fruit' of unlawful governmental conduct"—including "not only . . . illegally obtained evidence itself, but also . . . other incriminating evidence derived from the primary evidence."[61] It affirmed that this extension of the exclusionary rule to derivative evidentiary products, though socially costly, is "needed" to further the core objective of suppression—"to deter police from violations of constitutional . . . protections."[62] In the Court's view, the competing interests in deterring constitutional transgressions and in using probative evidence to prove guilt were "properly balanced by putting the police in the same, not a *worse*, position tha[n] they would have been in if no police error or misconduct had occurred."[63]

In sum, the reasoning in *Nix* suggested that, like the Fourth Amendment exclusionary rule, Sixth Amendment suppression is designed to deter future law enforcement improprieties; that it presumptively extends to and bars derivative evidence; that some evidence derived from counsel deprivations is nonetheless admissible; and that cost-benefit balancing informs exclusion analyses. The *Nix* Court deemed an inevitable discovery exception appropriate because it was consistent with deterrent objectives. The Justices reasoned that the costs of exclusion exceeded any speculative deterrent gains that might result from suppression.[64]

Had the *Nix* Court stopped after this apparent equation of the Sixth and Fourth Amendment suppression doctrines, it would have provided relatively clear, if questionable, insights into the character of the *Massiah* exclusion mandate. The Court, however, proceeded to entertain an alternative, or supplemental, understanding of Sixth Amendment suppression. The defendant had claimed that "unlike the exclusionary rule in the Fourth Amendment context, the essential purpose of which is to deter police misconduct, the Sixth Amendment exclusionary rule is designed to protect the right to a fair trial and the integrity of the factfinding process."[65] In essence, the defendant had maintained that the suppression of statements under *Massiah* is an inseparable part of the counsel guarantee and that cost-benefit balancing was impermissible in analyzing Sixth

---

61. *Id.* at 441.

62. *Nix*, 467 U.S. at 442–43.

63. *Id.* at 443. The Court was unanimous in its endorsement of the inevitable discovery exception. The sole disagreement had to do with the appropriate burden of proof. *See id.* at 459 (Brennan, J., dissenting) (asserting that a clear and convincing evidence standard should apply).

64. The details of the inevitable discovery doctrine and its underlying premises are explored in much greater depth in the doctrinal section of this chapter.

65. *Id.* at 446. The defendant's argument was that *Massiah* suppression was similar in nature to the due process and Fifth Amendment privilege-based suppression of coerced confessions insofar as exclusion is essential to avoid in-court violations of the underlying right.

Amendment exclusion issues.[66] The Court did not deny the validity of that conception of *Massiah*'s evidentiary bar. Instead, it decided that the admission of evidence that would have been legally acquired was entirely reconcilable with the contention that Sixth Amendment exclusion is an integral part of the counsel guarantee that serves to safeguard a defendant's entitlement to a fair trial.[67]

The Court's receptivity to the possibility that Sixth Amendment suppression is dramatically different in character from its Fourth Amendment counterpart—its refusal to endorse or reject the legitimacy of that view—created ambiguity and uncertainty about the nature and functions of the *Massiah* bar. After *Nix*, it was possible that Sixth Amendment and Fourth Amendment suppression were, in fact, identical in character—that is, that both were nothing more than deterrent safeguards, as the initial part of the *Nix* reasoning suggested. It was also possible, however, that exclusion was essential to enjoyment of the right to counsel. It was even possible that *Massiah* suppression had a dual nature and multiple functions—that it was both a future-oriented deterrent sanction and a personal trial right.[68] In sum, the Court's first foray into the underlying premises and operation of *Massiah*'s evidentiary bar—20 years after it was first announced—produced little clarity about the nature and purposes of right to counsel-based suppression. *Nix* generated considerable doubt about the character of and justifications this constitutional exclusion mandate.

The next year, the Court decided *Maine v. Moulton*.[69] *Moulton* raised a question about the scope of the *Massiah* right to pretrial assistance. More important, for present purposes, it presented a second question that afforded the Court another opportunity to address Sixth Amendment suppression. The government claimed that it was entitled to introduce a defendant's statements to prove crimes that were the subject of formal charges at the time of the elicitation *because* officers had sought the disclosures as part of a legitimate, good faith investigation of a separate, uncharged offense.[70] In essence, the contention was that there should be an exception to right to counsel exclusion for statements obtained from an

66. *Id.*

67. *Id.* at 446–47. This reasoning is explained in the doctrinal discussion of inevitable discovery. *See infra* text accompanying notes 189–95.

68. The reasoning in the bulk of the *Nix* opinion did suggest that the rule was at least partially rooted in deterrent objectives—that is, that one goal was to discourage confrontations of unassisted defendants. Nonetheless, the Court did not overtly declare that Sixth Amendment exclusion is designed to deter and did not contradict the defendant's contention that the purpose of *Massiah* exclusion is unlike the purpose of Fourth Amendment exclusion. Consequently, in a subsequent case, the Court could have announced that it had simply *assumed* that the Sixth Amendment rule was like the Fourth Amendment rule as a basis for explaining why the inevitable discovery exception is compatible with deterrent objectives.

69. 474 U.S. 159 (1985).

70. *Id.* at 178.

accused if the government had legitimate law enforcement reasons for seeking information from the defendant. A five-Justice majority rejected the claim, holding that the prosecution may not use statements to prove an offense that was the subject of a formal accusation *if* government agents gained those statements "by knowingly circumventing the accused's right to the assistance of counsel."[71] If the evidence was acquired in disregard of the accused's entitlement to assistance, the government's legitimate motivation did not matter. Good motives did not justify an exception to the rule requiring suppression from the trial of the charged offense.

Unfortunately, because the Court did not explain *why* statements had to be excluded in these circumstances, it did not dispel any of the uncertainty about the character of Sixth Amendment exclusion that *Nix* had engendered. One can find implicit support in *Moulton* for the view that exclusion is a future-oriented deterrent safeguard.[72] On the other hand, there are indications that deterrence is not the objective of Sixth Amendment suppression.[73] If deterrence was not the goal, then perhaps the object was to prevent constitutional injury in the courtroom—that is, to prevent completion of the right to counsel deprivation

---

71. *Id.* at 180.

72. The Court repeatedly indicated that a constitutional violation occurs out of court, at the time government agents secure incriminating admissions from an accused without counsel. *See id.* at 176 (stating that "the Sixth Amendment *is violated* when the State obtains incriminating statements by knowingly circumventing the accused's right to have counsel present in a confrontation between the accused and a state agent" (emphasis added)); *id.* (asserting that "it is clear that the State violated Moulton's Sixth Amendment right when it arranged to record conversations between [him] and its undercover informant"); *id.* at 180 (observing that "the State violated the Sixth Amendment by knowingly circumventing the accused's right to the assistance of counsel"). If a Sixth Amendment violation occurs at this stage, it seems likely that *a* purpose, perhaps *the* purpose, of suppression is to ensure that officers refrain from such violations in future situations.

73. The Court reaffirmed what it had suggested in *Massiah* about the propriety of post-charge efforts to secure information from accused persons in order to investigate suspected, but uncharged, criminal activities. It did not find such investigatory efforts objectionable, but instead acknowledged the legitimacy of the government's "interest in investigating new or additional crimes." *Id.* at 179. Thus, like the *Massiah* Court, the *Moulton* Court indicated that the Constitution was not concerned with or offended by such legitimate investigatory efforts—even when those efforts involved eliciting information from an accused that was relevant to the proof of already-charged offenses. *See id.* (suggesting that it was understandable and acceptable that "officials investigating an individual suspected of committing one crime and formally charged with having committed another [would] seek to discover evidence useful at a trial of either crime"). If the conduct at issue was not constitutionally offensive, but, instead, was legitimate and proper law enforcement, it seems unlikely that exclusion would (or should) be designed to discourage that conduct.

at trial. Thus, *Moulton*'s reasoning is ambiguous about the character of *Massiah*'s evidentiary bar. The majority's opinion did virtually nothing to clarify the character and underpinnings of the right to counsel exclusion doctrine.[74]

The final two *Massiah* opinions in this historical account of Sixth Amendment exclusion were both concerned with the propriety of using otherwise inadmissible statements—that is, admissions obtained in violation of the entitlement to pretrial assistance—to impeach a testifying defendant. The first involved a narrow issue and a limited ruling that again provided little insight into the *Massiah* exclusionary rule. The second, however, addressed a broader question and provided long overdue clarity about the Court's conception of right to counsel suppression.

In *Michigan v. Harvey*,[75] the Court permitted the prosecution to impeach a testifying defendant with statements that were not admissible to prove guilt because officers had obtained them in violation of the *Michigan v. Jackson*[76] branch of *Massiah*'s right to counsel doctrine. According to *Jackson*, when a defendant has invoked his right to assistance, a waiver would be "presumed invalid if secured pursuant to police-initiated conversation."[77] The Court held that a valid waiver was possible after a defendant has requested counsel *only* if the defendant initiated the conversation that led to the waiver. In *Harvey*, a majority held that impeachment use of statements obtained in violation of *Jackson* was permissible because of the unique nature of the *Jackson* rule.[78]

According to the Court, the *Jackson* branch of the *Massiah* doctrine was a "prophylactic rule . . . designed" to protect the right to counsel by ensuring that waivers are "voluntary, knowing, and intelligent."[79] Even though it was "based on the Sixth Amendment," *Jackson*'s specific limitation on law enforcement was analogous to and had "its roots" in *Miranda*'s limitations on custodial interrogation.[80] Its overprotective, prophylactic character made it unlike

---

74. Four dissenting Justices, who would have endorsed the exception to *Massiah* exclusion advocated by the government, were absolutely clear about their understanding of Sixth Amendment suppression. In their view, the Sixth Amendment "'wrong' . . . [is] 'fully accomplished' by the elicitation of comments from the defendant and 'the exclusionary rule is neither intended nor able to cure the invasion of . . . rights'" that has already occurred. *Moulton*, 474 U.S. at 191 (Burger, C.J., dissenting) (quoting United States v. Leon, 468 U.S. 897, 906 (1984)). The *Massiah* rule is "premised on deterrence of certain types of conduct by the police" and when the police are legitimately investigating uncharged offenses, the costs of exclusion outweigh any deterrent benefit and dictate the admission of the evidence obtained. *Id.* at 191–92 (Burger, C.J., dissenting).

75. 494 U.S. 344 (1990).

76. 475 U.S. 625 (1986).

77. *Harvey*, 494 U.S. at 345.

78. *Id.* at 346, 350–51.

79. *Id.* at 351.

80. *Id.* at 349–50.

deprivations of the pretrial entitlement to counsel that "violate[] the 'core value' of the Sixth Amendment's constitutional guarantee."[81]

The *Harvey* Court clearly held open the possibility that evidence obtained by violating other *Massiah* doctrine constraints—those implicating core elements of the right to counsel, not overprotective, prophylactic rules—was inadmissible even for the limited purpose of impeachment.[82] More important, although *Harvey* did make clear that the exclusion of evidence secured in violation of one branch of *Massiah* (the *Jackson* rule) was not an integral part of the right to counsel, it provided no new insights into the nature and functions of Sixth Amendment exclusion in general. It remained possible that suppression for core *Massiah* violations was necessary to avoid constitutional deprivations in the courtroom, to deter future violations of the pretrial right to counsel, or for both of those reasons.[83]

In *Kansas v. Ventris*,[84] 45 years after it first announced the *Massiah* exclusion doctrine, the Court finally provided an unambiguous, if questionable, explanation of the character of and constitutional justifications for Sixth Amendment suppression. The question in *Ventris* was whether the prosecution could use an "incriminating statement to a jailhouse informant, concededly elicited in violation of Sixth Amendment strictures, . . . to impeach the defendant's conflicting statement" at trial.[85] In a relatively brief opinion, a surprisingly large seven-Justice majority held that revelations obtained in disregard of the entitlement to pretrial assistance are generally admissible to impeach a defendant's inconsistent trial testimony.[86] The reasoning the majority employed to justify this conclusion is most significant.

The *Ventris* majority insightfully observed that whether evidence must be excluded in a particular situation can "depend[] upon the nature of the

---

81. *Id.* at 353. Four dissenting Justices disagreed with the Court's characterization of the *Jackson* rule as a prophylactic interpretation of the right to counsel. They would have barred the introduction of statements for impeachment purposes because in their view even that limited use of statements obtained in violation of *Jackson* constituted an in-court deprivation of the Sixth Amendment right. *See id.* at 361–63 (Stevens, J., dissenting).

82. *See Harvey*, 494 U.S. at 354 (stating that the Court "need not consider the admissibility for impeachment purposes of a voluntary statement obtained in the absence of a knowing and voluntary waiver of the right to counsel").

83. Two 2009 rulings robbed *Harvey* of all significance. In *Montejo v. Louisiana*, 556 U.S. ____, 129 S.Ct. 2079 (2009), the Court overruled *Michigan v. Jackson*'s prophylactic Sixth Amendment rule. Moreover, in the next, and final, case discussed in this historical section, the Court concluded that the impeachment use exception applies to all types of *Massiah* deprivations.

84. 556 U.S. ____, 129 S.Ct. 1841 (2009).

85. *Id.* at ____, 129 S.Ct. at 1844.

86. *Id.* at ____, 129 S.Ct. at 1847.

constitutional guarantee that is violated."[87] According to the Court, the Sixth Amendment's core guarantee is the entitlement to assistance at trial. The right to counsel, however, has been extended to certain pretrial "interactions" between the government and accused individuals to ensure that trial counsel is not "render[ed] . . . entirely impotent" by what has occurred prior to trial.[88] According to the *Ventris* majority, the *Massiah* Court was "equivocal" about whether the conduct of the authorities or the use of evidence at trial constituted the Sixth Amendment violation.[89] To decide whether impeachment use was permissible, it was necessary to resolve that pivotal question.

The *Ventris* Court definitively announced that "the *Massiah* right is a right to be free of uncounseled interrogation, and is infringed at the time of the interrogation."[90] According to Justice Scalia, author of the majority opinion, it was simply "illogical to say that the right is not violated until" an elicited "statement's admission into evidence" at trial.[91] There is no denial of counsel's aid when the prosecution introduces the evidence, even if the evidence makes the task of "gaining an acquittal . . . impossible."[92] Assistance can be "denied . . . [only] at the prior critical stage which produced the inculpatory evidence. . . . It is *that* deprivation which demands a remedy."[93] This conception of the *Massiah* counsel entitlement meant that the exclusion question before the Court—whether statements could be used to impeach—did "not involve . . . the prevention of a constitutional violation" in court, "but rather" a determination of "the scope of the remedy for a violation that has already occurred."[94] Fourth Amendment precedents had already struck the appropriate balance for suppression doctrines designed to deter future constitutional improprieties. According to those decisions, the costs of suppression outweigh the deterrent benefits of barring impeachment use.[95] The Court found that there was "no distinction that . . . alter[ed] the balance" and led to a different conclusion under *Massiah*'s exclusionary rule.[96]

The *Ventris* opinion was refreshingly direct and unambiguous about the nature and purposes of *Massiah*'s Sixth Amendment exclusion doctrine.

---

87. *Id.* at ____, 129 S.Ct. at 1845.

88. *Id.* at ____, 129 S.Ct. at 1845.

89. *Ventris*, 556 U.S. at ____, 129 S.Ct. at 1846. The Court quoted language in *Massiah* suggesting that the violation occurred before trial and other language indicating that the deprivation occurred at trial.

90. *Id.* at ____, 129 S.Ct. at 1846; *see also id.* at ____, 129 S.Ct. at 1846 (asserting that "[t]he constitutional violation occurs when the uncounseled interrogation is conducted").

91. *Id.* at ____, 129 S.Ct. at 1846.

92. *Id.* at ____, 129 S.Ct. at 1846.

93. *Id.* at ____, 129 S.Ct. at 1846 (emphasis in original).

94. *Ventris*, 556 U.S. at ____, 129 S.Ct. at 1846.

95. *Id.* at ____, 129 S.Ct. at 1846–47.

96. *Id.* at ____, 129 S.Ct. at 1847.

Because the right to counsel is not violated by the government's use at trial of statements obtained in disregard of the pretrial entitlement to counsel, an accused has no personal constitutional right to exclusion. The right at issue has already been denied, and the wrong fully accomplished, by the time of trial. Exclusion is not designed to either remedy the harm done or compensate the victim for a loss incurred. Rather, its object is to ensure that officers will respect defendants' entitlements to assistance in future pretrial confrontations. In sum, *Massiah*'s evidentiary bar is a mere exclusionary *rule* similar in character and purpose to the Fourth Amendment rule discussed in Chapter 1. It is not a personal trial *right* like the Fifth and Fourteenth Amendment bars to coerced confessions explained in Chapter 2.

The *Ventris* majority suggested that the *Massiah* opinion was "equivocal" about the nature of Sixth Amendment exclusion. As noted at the outset of this historical sketch, however, the dominant theme in *Massiah* was that the Sixth Amendment transgression occurred in court, when evidence was used to convict. In the years that followed, the Court had grown ambiguous, refusing to endorse a clear vision of the character of and the rationales for suppression under *Massiah*. After many years of uncertainty, *Ventris* painted a remarkably clear picture of right to counsel suppression—a picture that is the antithesis of the one posited by *Massiah*. *Ventris*'s conception of Sixth Amendment exclusion is currently controlling. It will surely shape the future of *Massiah* exclusion, dictating the answers to unresolved questions of scope and application. Before considering the few doctrinal questions that have already been answered and the many that remain unsettled, an analysis of the possible rationales for and constitutional legitimacy of Sixth Amendment suppression is in order.

C. THE JUSTIFICATIONS FOR, NATURE OF, AND LEGITIMACY OF THE *MASSIAH* SUPPRESSION DOCTRINE

As the preceding section made clear, the Supreme Court's understanding of the character of *Massiah*'s exclusion mandate remained uncertain until very recently. There were indications that the Court considered exclusion an inseparable part of the counsel guarantee and that the admission of a statement would violate the Sixth Amendment. There were also suggestions that the evidentiary bar served deterrent purposes by removing the incentive for officers to deprive defendants of assistance during future pretrial confrontations with government agents. It was possible that *Massiah* suppression had a dual nature—that it was both a courtroom right and an out-of-court deterrent. This section explores the meaning and plausibility of the alternative explanations and examines arguments over the legitimacy of Sixth Amendment suppression.

In this text, I generally consider competing justifications for the various exclusion doctrines without endorsing a particular alternative. My past and present analyses of *Massiah*, however, have persuaded me that there is only one defensible explanation for its evidentiary bar. Consequently, in this chapter I do express views about the merits of the Sixth Amendment suppression debate. It should be clear from discussions in earlier chapters that rationales have not just theoretical significance, but important practical implications for the scope and operation of exclusion doctrines. The doctrinal section that concludes this chapter explains the starkly different operational consequences of the competing rationales for Sixth Amendment suppression and explores the constrictive impact of the Court's endorsement of the deterrent justification.

One view conceives of *Massiah*'s evidentiary bar as a personal constitutional right belonging to the accused on trial. Proponents of this view believe that the introduction of a statement elicited from a formally charged individual completes the violation of the right to counsel begun during the pretrial confrontation—much like the introduction of a compelled statement completes the violation of the Fifth Amendment privilege begun by pretrial compulsion to speak. To prevent such a violation and preserve the substance of the entitlement to assistance, a defendant has a Sixth Amendment right to exclude a statement from trial.[97]

This personal right conception of exclusion rests on the following premises. The right to trial assistance is a core adversary system safeguard. It is essential to ensure a fair, balanced contest in which the accused has the expertise necessary to cope with the legal system and with the legally-trained prosecutorial opponent.[98] Counsel's role is to use all the lawful tools at his or her disposal to counter the state's efforts to convict and to protect the accused against anything that undermines the chances for acquittal.[99] One simple, yet important, function of a lawyer is to ensure that the defendant does not unwisely aid the prosecution by admitting guilt at trial. If a prosecutor, for example, were to try to induce a defendant to take the witness stand and make incriminating disclosures, an effective lawyer should advise against that damaging course of action.[100]

---

97. *See* Kansas v. Ventris, 556 U.S. ___, 129 S.Ct. 1841, 1847–48 (2009) (Stevens, J., dissenting); Michigan v. Harvey, 494 U.S. 344, 362–63 (1990) (Stevens, J., dissenting); Stephen J. Schulhofer, *Confessions and the Court*, 79 Mich. L. Rev. 865, 889 (1981) [hereinafter Schulhofer, *Confessions and the Court*]; James J. Tomkovicz, *Saving* Massiah *From* Elstad: *The Admissibility of Successive Confessions Following a Deprivation of Counsel*, 15 Wm. & Mary Bill Rts. J. 711, 751–54 (2007) [hereinafter Tomkovicz, *Saving* Massiah].

98. *See* United States v. Ash, 413 U.S. 300, 307–09 (1973); James J. Tomkovicz, *The* Massiah *Right to Exclusion: Constitutional Premises and Doctrinal Implications*, 67 N.C. L. Rev. 751, 753–54 (1989) [hereinafter Tomkovicz, Massiah *Right to Exclusion*]; James J. Tomkovicz, *An Adversary System Defense of the Right to Counsel Against Informants: Truth, Fair Play, and the* Massiah *Doctrine*, 22 U.C. Davis L. Rev. 1, 39–41 (1988) [hereinafter Tomkovicz, *Adversary System Defense*].

99. *See* Tomkovicz, *Adversary System Defense*, *supra* note 98, at 40–42.

100. *See* Tomkovicz, Massiah *Right to Exclusion*, *supra* note 98, at 766.

When the Sixth Amendment was adopted, the sole confrontation between the accused and the government was at trial.[101] The subsequent development of pretrial phases of the criminal process in which the state confronts an accused—both formal, courtroom events and informal events outside of court—engendered a risk that the government could take advantage of an uncounseled individual prior to trial and diminish, if not destroy, the chances for acquittal.[102] To permit the state to exploit an unaided accused's vulnerabilities prior to trial and then use the evidentiary advantages gained at trial would be to allow circumvention of the most critical adversary system protection our Bill of Rights affords.[103] An entitlement to pretrial counsel is necessary to preserve the ability of trial counsel to effectively fulfill the central responsibility of defending against the state's efforts to convict. If officials, by interactions with an unassisted defendant before trial, were able to induce admissions, and then were permitted to use them at trial, the effects on the fairness of the adversarial process would be identical to the effects of similar, surely impermissible, uncounseled confrontations of the defendant in the courtroom.[104]

The real value of having assistance *at trial* is protection against the injurious effects of ill-advised disclosures. The guarantee of counsel is an entitlement to advice and aid that can help prevent that sort of damage. A violation of that guarantee is realized when the accused is denied assistance *and* suffers harm as a consequence. When the denial of assistance occurs prior to trial, the use of evidence obtained at trial inflicts the very harm counsel is designed to prevent and completes the constitutional deprivation.[105] To permit the use of evidence is to deny the protection that the right is intended to afford. Like the Fifth Amendment guarantee against compulsory self-incrimination, the promise of counsel is designed to safeguard against harm at trial. Like pretrial compulsion, a pretrial denial of a lawyer's aid can only begin the violation of the trial right. The violation is completed when the sort of injury the right to counsel is intended to prevent is inflicted—conviction based on advantages the government acquires from

---

101. *See Ash*, 413 U.S. at 309–10; Tomkovicz, Massiah *Right to Exclusion, supra* note 98, at 754; Tomkovicz, *Adversary System Defense, supra* note 98, at 11.

102. *See Ash*, 413 U.S. at 310–11; Martin R. Gardner, *The Sixth Amendment Right to Counsel and Its Underlying Values: Defining the Scope of Privacy Protection*, 90 J. Crim. L. & Criminology 397, 401–03 (2000); Tomkovicz, Massiah *Right to Exclusion, supra* note 98, at 754.

103. *See* Tomkovicz, Massiah *Right to Exclusion, supra* note 98, at 766–67.

104. *See id.*

105. *See* Schulhofer, *Confessions and the Court, supra* note 97, at 889; Tomkovicz, Massiah *Right to Exclusion, supra* note 98, at 767. In the words of the *Massiah* majority, a defendant is "denied the basic protections of [the counsel] guarantee when there [is] used against him at his trial evidence of his own incriminating words . . . deliberately elicited from him . . . in the absence of his counsel." Massiah v. United States, 377 U.S. 201, 206 (1964).

an imbalanced confrontation. When evidence appears at trial and contributes to conviction, that injury is inflicted and a trial is thereby rendered unfair.[106]

Another possible justification for Sixth Amendment suppression is deterrence. The deterrent rationale holds that exclusion is a constitutional sanction designed to prevent future uncounseled confrontations by the state prior to trial. Deterrence can serve as an additional justification—one that coexists with and supplements the personal right rationale for suppression. On the other hand, it can constitute the sole basis for exclusion—an alternative to the conception of suppression as an integral part of the right to counsel that is necessary to prevent Sixth Amendment violations at trial.

The argument that deterrence is a supplemental justification first concedes that exclusion is necessary because the Sixth Amendment is violated when a statement elicited without counsel is introduced at trial. One view is that there is *also* a constitutional transgression at the time the state elicits admissions from an unaided defendant. Because the right to counsel encompasses an entitlement to have advice and expertise and a defendant confronted without counsel is deprived of that entitlement, constitutional injury occurs at the time of the pretrial engagement, not only when evidence obtained is used to convict. Suppression is needed to discourage officers from conducting the encounters that cause such extrajudicial injury and thereby violate the Sixth Amendment.

Another view is that deterrence is a supplemental justification for suppression even though the Sixth Amendment cannot be violated by a pretrial confrontation without the use of evidence in court. According to this view, it is necessary and desirable to discourage officers from conducting uncounseled confrontations because the evidentiary products may erroneously find their way into trials as a result of incorrect judicial determinations that confrontations did not involve deprivations of the right to assistance. For example, a judge might erroneously find that an informant passively received information from a charged defendant or that the accused validly waived his right to assistance during questioning by officers. In such cases, the statements that are introduced will violate the right to counsel at trial. To the extent that a meaningful threat of suppression discourages officers from arranging pretrial interactions with charged individuals in the absence of counsel, it will prevent the acquisition of some statements that might otherwise have been improperly admitted at trial. In sum, suppression prevents violation of the current defendant's right by barring the evidence from his trial. It also prevents violations of future defendants' trial rights by ensuring that some evidence that might be used against them never comes into existence.

---

106. *See* James J. Tomkovicz, *The Truth About* Massiah, 23 U. Mich. J. L. Reform 641, 674–76 (1990) [hereinafter Tomkovicz, *Truth About* Massiah]; Tomkovicz, Massiah *Right to Exclusion, supra* note 98, at 767.

If courts accurately identify pretrial deprivations of counsel and exclude from trials the statements those deprivations produce, there is no need to deter the acquisition of those statements as a secondary, supplemental safeguard against their use at trial. Put otherwise, if judges rarely err in determining whether the use of disclosures at trial would violate the right to counsel, it is not necessary to deter the confrontations yielding such disclosures in order to prevent their erroneous admission. Deterrence still might play a constitutionally desirable, even necessary, supplemental role, however, by eliminating other kinds of improper prosecutorial advantages gained from uncounseled confrontations.[107] Law enforcement, for example, may learn information from leads furnished by an uncounseled admission that has been barred. This information may enable the prosecution to build a more convincing case or shore up weaknesses that defense counsel might otherwise exploit at trial. These unseen, possibly imperceptible, advantages are arguably offensive to the adversary system fair play principles that undergird the guarantee of counsel. If the object of legal assistance is to ensure a fair, balanced contest—in part by preventing the government from enhancing the case for conviction by taking advantage of unaided, vulnerable defendants—then any prosecutorial advantage that makes acquittal less likely imperils the substance of the Sixth Amendment guarantee. By deterring uncounseled interactions, suppression can prevent the government from reaping these illegitimate benefits and can guard against the resulting erosion of the right to trial assistance.[108]

As noted, another view sees deterrence as an *alternative* justification for Sixth Amendment suppression—that is, as the *sole* rationale for excluding evidence. This understanding of *Massiah*'s evidentiary bar rests on the premise that the Sixth Amendment is *not* violated when evidence is used at trial.[109] The only transgression, the sole deprivation of constitutional rights, occurs at pretrial encounters with uncounseled defendants when government agents deliberately elicit statements.[110] This conception of *Massiah*'s underpinnings assumes that the constitutional harm is complete when the defendant is confronted without assistance.[111] The later use of any disclosures at trial—when counsel is present—does not violate the Sixth Amendment because the accused is, quite simply, not deprived of legal assistance at that time.[112] A prohibition on use is necessary, but

---

107. *See* Tomkovicz, *Saving* Massiah, *supra* note 97, at 756.

108. *See* Tomkovicz, Massiah *Right to Exclusion*, *supra* note 98, at 756, 772 n.120.

109. *See* Kansas v. Ventris, 556 U.S. ____, 129 S.Ct. 1841, 1846 (2009); Brewer v. Williams, 430 U.S. 387, 421, 424–26 (1977) (Burger, C.J., dissenting).

110. *See Ventris*, 556 U.S. at ____, 129 S.Ct. at 1846.

111. *See id.*

112. The argument against the position that exclusion is a part of the Sixth Amendment right and that violation occurs when evidence is introduced rests on a belief that the pretrial entitlement is either denied or respected at the time counsel's aid is needed.

only to discourage officers from future violations of the Sixth Amendment entitlement to counsel. If officials could use the fruits of pretrial transgressions to convict, they would have potent incentives to deny assistance. Exclusion removes those incentives by depriving them of the evidentiary advantages obtained and thereby deters them from arranging the imbalanced encounters the Bill of Rights forbids.

A contrary position is that deterrence cannot serve as either a supplemental or alternative justification for Sixth Amendment suppression.[113] According to this view, the elicitation of information from an uncounseled defendant is not, by itself, a deprivation of the right to counsel because the accused suffers no harm the Sixth Amendment was designed to prevent. It is not the government's investigatory, evidence-gathering efforts that offend the Constitution, but the use of the products of those efforts to convict. If the government's pretrial conduct does not violate the Constitution, there is no need to suppress significant proof of guilt in an effort to deter that conduct. Deterrence is a particularly inappropriate justification for exclusion if the conduct that would be discouraged is helpful to legitimate efforts to effectively prosecute uncharged crimes or to apprehend individuals not yet captured.[114] If *Massiah* exclusion is justified, the sole reason is to prevent constitutional violations at trial.

So far, the discussion has been premised on an assumption that exclusion is constitutionally legitimate. The arguments advanced are efforts to identify the logical foundations for its legitimacy. Some have contended, however, that neither the personal trial right nor the deterrence rationale can justify Sixth Amendment exclusion. They believe that there is, in fact, no defensible

---

If an accused has counsel, the right is respected. If the accused is deprived of assistance at that time, the deprivation—and the Sixth Amendment violation—is completed then and there. If counsel is present and assisting at trial, then there can be no deprivation of counsel at trial. There may be an impediment to trial counsel's efficacy due to the pretrial denial because the government may possess probative, even devastating, disclosures, *see Ventris*, 556 U.S. at ____, 129 S.Ct. at 1846 (acknowledging that "overwhelming" evidence gained from pretrial denial might render trial counsel's "job of gaining an acquittal . . . impossible" and thereby make trial "assistance . . . not worth much"), but an accused who has a competent lawyer who is not restricted in performing trial functions suffers no violation of the right to assistance in the courtroom. *Id.* (asserting that because trial counsel is present "the accused continues to enjoy the assistance of counsel").

113. *See* Michigan v. Harvey, 494 U.S. 344, 362–63 (1990) (Stevens, J., dissenting); Schulhofer, *Confessions and the Court*, *supra* note 97, at 889; Tomkovicz, *Saving* Massiah, *supra* note 97, at 751; Tomkovicz, Massiah *Right to Exclusion*, *supra* note 98, at 770–71.

114. To the extent that deterrence might serve to prevent erroneous decisions to admit evidence or to prevent the government from profiting in nonevidentiary ways at trial, faithful enforcement of the Sixth Amendment right to suppression will have the *effect* of discouraging officers from conducting uncounseled confrontations. Even if deterrence is not an *aim* of exclusion, the prevention of Sixth Amendment harm that *results* from exclusion might be salutary.

constitutional foundation for the *Massiah* suppression doctrine.[115] This argument rests on the premise that *Massiah*'s pretrial extension of the Sixth Amendment right to counsel is itself invalid.[116] When the government seeks to elicit information prior to trial, the accused is confronted with neither legal questions nor a legally-trained adversary.[117] There is no danger that any revelations will be coerced or unreliable as a result of the interaction with government agents.[118] A lay accused has no need for legal assistance because the dangers and harms that a lawyer is supposed to prevent are not present in the encounters *Massiah* governs. The defendant is capable of handling the situation on his own, and any revelations he makes are not the result of any sort of unfairness by the state.[119]

If one accepts the premise that the Court erred in extending the right to counsel to governmental efforts to elicit incriminating revelations from defendants, clearly the *Massiah* exclusionary rule cannot be justified. Because an accused has no entitlement to assistance in the informal encounters the *Massiah* doctrine addresses, there can be no constitutional violation from the trial use of any statements made. The argument that exclusion is a right assumes that the deliberate elicitation of disclosures from an unaided accused is the beginning of a constitutional transgression and maintains that the use of disclosures at trial completes the transgression. If an accused has no right to legal aid during the confrontation, then use cannot complete a Sixth Amendment violation. Moreover, if there is no need for and no right to counsel's assistance during the pretrial confrontation, there is no reason to seek to deter the state's pretrial conduct by denying the state the evidentiary advantages it gained from that confrontation. From the Constitution's standpoint, the interaction with the accused is an entirely permissible investigatory effort, not conduct to be discouraged by a suppression sanction.

---

115. United States v. Henry, 447 U.S. 264, 289, 296 (1980) (Rehnquist, J., dissenting); Massiah v. United States, 377 U.S. 201, 208, 213 (1977) (White, J., dissenting).

116. *See Henry*, 447 U.S. at 290 (Rehnquist, J., dissenting); *Massiah* 377 U.S. at 209 (White, J., dissenting). *See generally* H. Richard Uviller, *Evidence From the Mind of the Criminal Suspect: A Reconsideration of the Current Rules of Access and Restraint*, 87 COLUM. L. REV. 1137, 1154–95 (1987).

117. *See Henry*, 447 U.S. at 292–94 (Rehnquist, J., dissenting); *Massiah*, 377 U.S. at 210–11 (White, J., dissenting).

118. *See Henry*, 447 U.S. at 294 (Rehnquist, J., dissenting); *Massiah*, 377 U.S. at 211 (White, J., dissenting); *but see* Schulhofer, *Confessions and the Court*, *supra* note 97, at 890 (observing that the fact the evidence is reliable "is wholly beside the point" for purposes of Sixth Amendment exclusion because its use "taints the judicial proceedings in a fundamental way").

119. *See Henry*, 447 U.S. at 294 (Rehnquist, J., dissenting); Tomkovicz, *Truth About* Massiah, *supra* note 106, at 676.

After 45 years of uncertainty about the rationale for *Massiah* exclusion, the Supreme Court finally spoke with definitive clarity. According to *Kansas v. Ventris*,[120] an accused has no Sixth Amendment trial right to exclusion. The right to counsel is violated only at the time government agents confront an unaided defendant, not when incriminating statements are used at trial. The constitutional wrong begins and ends at the time the accused is denied counsel's aid. Evidentiary suppression is not necessary to avoid violation of the present defendant's rights at trial, but only to deter investigators from conducting the imbalanced pretrial encounters the Sixth Amendment prohibits. Because the objective is to discourage future transgressions, cost-benefit balancing like that employed to determine the applicability of the Fourth Amendment exclusionary rule must inform Sixth Amendment analyses.

In my view, this justification for *Massiah*'s evidentiary bar is seriously flawed. On more than one occasion, I have explained at length the logic of the view that Sixth Amendment exclusion is an integral part of the right to counsel.[121] Nothing in *Ventris* refutes that logic, despite the Court's assertion that it is "illogical to say that the right [to counsel] is not violated" until admission of a statement at trial.[122] I remain convinced of the merits of that view. It is plausible to see Fourth Amendment transgressions as fully accomplished at the time of a pretrial search or seizure. If the objects of that provision are to protect privacy and liberty interests, injuries are complete at the time of the unreasonable search or seizure. It is defensible to conclude that the trial use of evidence gained from an illegal search or seizure does not inflict further Fourth Amendment injury.[123] It is difficult to

---

120. 556 U.S. at ____, 129 S.Ct. 1841 (2009).

121. *See* Tomkovicz, *Saving* Massiah, *supra* note 97, at 751–55; Tomkovicz, *Truth About* Massiah, *supra* note 106, at 671–76; Tomkovicz, Massiah *Right to Exclusion*, *supra* note 98, at 765–72.

122. *Ventris*, 556 U.S. at ____, 129 S.Ct. at 1846. It is no more illogical to suggest that the counsel violation takes place at trial than it is to suggest that a Fifth Amendment privilege violation occurs when compelled revelations are used at trial, not when they are forced from the mind of the defendant, a position the Court clearly endorses. *See* Chavez v. Martinez, 538 U.S. 760, 767 (2003). The core reason for extending the Sixth Amendment right to *trial* assistance to *pretrial* encounters with the government is to prevent officials from engaging in forbidden trial conduct before trial begins and then using the advantages gained from that conduct to inflict the sort of injury that would be prevented by trial counsel were the government to engage in that conduct at trial. Pretrial counsel surely is not a mere "process" right that provides no shelter against the substantive disadvantages of confrontations held without assistance. Those disadvantages ripen *at trial*, not before.

123. The contrary position is also defensible. *See* United States v. Leon, 468 U.S. 897, 933–35 (1984) (Brennan, J., dissenting) (maintaining that an individual's Fourth Amendment entitlement to "security" against an unreasonable search or seizure is infringed upon both by the search or seizure and by the use of evidence to convict).

see, however, how a pretrial encounter can effect a complete Sixth Amendment deprivation. At the pretrial confrontation itself, the accused does not suffer the type of harm that legal assistance is designed to prevent. The injury—and thus, the completion of the constitutional wrong—can occur only at trial. The purpose of the constitutional guarantee of legal assistance is to ensure a fair trial.[124] The fairness of the trial is jeopardized when the evidence secured from an unaided, unequipped lay defendant fuels the government's efforts to secure a conviction.[125]

To treat Sixth Amendment suppression as analogous to the Fourth Amendment exclusionary rule is to misinterpret the Bill of Rights in a way that threatens the vitality of the right to counsel's assistance. The vision of exclusion that animated the original *Massiah* opinion—that the Sixth Amendment is not offended by efforts to elicit information from accused persons but does forbid the *use* of deliberately elicited statements against a defendant at trial—was sound. To describe *Massiah*'s suppression doctrine as a mere exclusionary rule or a future-oriented incentive scheme does grave disservice to an essential adversary system safeguard that is a fundamental trial right.[126] The Sixth Amendment suppression mandate should be understood as a vital part of the personal entitlement to counsel that the Bill of Rights extends to those accused of crime.

---

124. *See* Strickland v. Washington, 466 U.S. 668, 684–85 (1984).

125. The logic in *Strickland*—the landmark ruling on the showing needed for Sixth Amendment "actual ineffectiveness" claims—would seem to provide potent support for this reasoning. Utterly unreasonable performances by defense counsel—those that qualify as "deficient" for constitutional purposes—do not constitute violations of the Sixth Amendment unless "prejudice" results from the deficiency. *See id.* at 692. Prejudice is defined as a certain likelihood of harm to the accused's chances for acquittal. *See id.* at 693–94. Moreover, at least one of the reasons that some types of Sixth Amendment deprivations do not require an accused to prove prejudice is that prejudice is the likely result of those deprivations. *See id.* at 692. The point is that the Court has indicated that even when there is an absence of meaningful assistance at the trial itself, a Sixth Amendment deprivation does not occur until the lack of assistance damages the defendant's chances for a good trial result. In the Court's view, the fairness of a trial is not undermined by the mere denial of assistance, but by the effect such a denial has on the outcome of the trial. *See id.* at 685–86, 691–92.

126. *See* Schulhofer, *Confessions and the Court, supra* note 97, at 889 (asserting that *Massiah* exclusion is "not merely a prophylactic device" and that it is "not intended to deter any pretrial behavior"); Tomkovicz, *Saving* Massiah, *supra* note 97, at 751–55; Silas Wasserstrom & William J. Mertens, *The Exclusionary Rule on the Scaffold: But Was it a Fair Trial?*, 22 AM. CRIM. L. REV. 85, 179 (1984) (suggesting, prior to *Ventris*, that the Court "deprecate[s]" the *Massiah* rule by "relegating it to the same low level" as the Fourth Amendment exclusionary rule).

D. THE SCOPE AND OPERATION OF THE *MASSIAH* EXCLUSIONARY RULE

As in prior chapters, this subsection examines the pragmatic, operational details of Sixth Amendment exclusion—both its presumptive reach and the exceptional situations in which evidence that qualifies for exclusion is nonetheless admissible. The effort here is to identify the evidence that *Massiah* bars. Many of the specific issues addressed were also discussed in connection with the doctrines that were the subjects of the first three chapters. Only a few of the questions regarding the breadth of *Massiah* exclusion have been settled, while several remain unresolved. The recent determination that Sixth Amendment suppression is a deterrent sanction, not a constitutional right, provides a foundation for confident predictions about the resolution of the undecided issues.

1. Evidence Subject to Exclusion: The Presumptive Reach of Sixth Amendment Suppression

The *Massiah* doctrine excludes from a trial a defendant's inculpatory statements or admissions—oral or written, verbal or nonverbal.[127] Words spoken by the defendant, a letter or e-mail she composed, or a nod or any other sort of communicative conduct could all qualify for suppression. To fall within *Massiah*'s domain, however, an agent of the government must have deliberately elicited the "statements" from an accused person.

The concept of deliberate elicitation has never been fully explained or defined.[128] While the word "deliberate" suggests an actual intent to draw admissions from the accused, the Court has never required proof that officials or their recruits had the purpose of inducing revelations.[129] The government agent confronting the accused must engage in some sort of *active* elicitation. In the Court's

---

127. According to *Massiah*, "the defendant's own incriminating statements . . . could not constitutionally be used by the prosecution as evidence against *him* at his trial." Massiah v. United States, 377 U.S. 201, 207 (1964). The evidence need not be a confession of guilt as long as it is relevant evidence of use to the prosecution in convicting the accused.

128. The Court's exploration of the meaning of "deliberate elicitation" stands in marked contrast to its treatment of "interrogation"—the conduct *Miranda* regulates. The Justices have provided a definition of interrogation and have addressed several issues pertaining to the meaning of that term. The opinions provide few insights into the conduct *Massiah* regulates. *See* James J. Tomkovicz, *Reaffirming the Right to Pretrial Assistance: The Surprising Little Case of* Fellers v. United States, 15 Wm. & Mary Bill Rts. J. 501, 524–30 (2006) [hereinafter Tomkovicz, *Reaffirming the Right*].

129. In undercover informant cases, the Court has held that it is sufficient that the government agents responsible for enlisting the informant "intentionally creat[ed] a situation likely to induce" the accused to disclose information, United States v. Henry, 447 U.S. 264, 274 (1980), or "'must have known'" that their informant would take affirmative

words, there is no deliberate elicitation, and, thus, no right to assistance, unless the agent "took some action . . . to elicit incriminating remarks."[130] Merely engaging in conversation with an accused can be sufficient action,[131] but "merely listening" to an accused's disclosures is inadequate.[132] Actively elicited admissions are subject to exclusion, while passively received revelations are outside the Sixth Amendment bar. Although active conduct is required, it is clear that the government agent need not engage in "interrogation," as that term is defined by the *Miranda* doctrine.[133] Interactions with an accused that do not create the pressures to respond required by *Miranda*'s Fifth Amendment scheme, but do prompt an accused to make inculpatory disclosures, are a sufficient basis for suppressing those disclosures under *Massiah*.[134] In this respect, *Massiah*'s Sixth Amendment bar reaches evidence that is beyond *Miranda*'s reach.

No matter how actively the government elicits statements, they are inadmissible only if the individual has been formally accused at the time.[135] Because the right to counsel attaches only after "the initiation of adversary judicial proceedings" against a person by the government,[136] there is no Sixth Amendment predicate

---

steps to elicit information from the defendant. Maine v. Moulton, 474 U.S. 159, 174, 176 n.12 (1985).

130. Kuhlmann v. Wilson, 477 U.S. 436, 459 (1986).

131. *See Henry*, 447 U.S. at 270–71; *Massiah*, 377 U.S. at 203, 207. No proof of the informant's intent to elicit has been required. The Court seems to assume that elicitation is the object of conversing with the accused.

132. *See Wilson*, 477 U.S. at 459.

133. *See* Fellers v. United States, 540 U.S. 519, 524 (2004). In *Fellers*, a unanimous Court, after years of confusing the issue, finally made it clear that the minimum conduct necessary to trigger Sixth Amendment scrutiny and exclusion is different from—something "less" than—the minimum conduct needed to trigger *Miranda*'s application. *See id.* at 523–24; Tomkovicz, *Reaffirming the Right*, *supra* note 128, at 509, 520. Unfortunately, in *Montejo v. Louisiana*, 556 U.S. ___, 129 S.Ct. 2079 (2009), and in *Kansas v. Ventris*, 556 U.S. ____, 129 S.Ct. 1841 (2009), the majority again relapsed into the misleading habit of referring to *Massiah*'s Sixth Amendment doctrine as a constraint upon "interrogation." *See Montejo*, 556 U.S. at ____, 129 S.Ct. at 2085–86; *Ventris*, 556 U.S. at ____, 129 S.Ct. at 1845–46.

134. The conduct that is the concern of *Miranda*'s Fifth Amendment-based constraints and *Massiah*'s Sixth Amendment-based restrictions is not identical because the "policies" that underlie these two different constitutional provisions—the interests they protect and the harms they are designed to avoid—are "distinct." *See* Rhode Island v. Innis, 446 U.S. 291, 300 n.4 (1980). The Fifth Amendment is concerned with the unfairness resulting from convictions based on information compelled from the mind of the defendant, whereas the Sixth Amendment is concerned with the unfairness that is the result of an imbalanced clash of adversaries—that is, a confrontation in which the government takes advantage of an inferior, unaided accused.

135. *See* Moran v. Burbine, 475 U.S. 412, 428–30 (1986).

136. *See id.* at 432; United States v. Gouveia, 467 U.S. 180, 187 (1984); *see also* Illinois v. Perkins, 496 U.S. 292, 299 (1990).

for excluding statements drawn from an individual prior to that point in time.[137] Consequently, if a suspect is arrested for an offense, placed in a cell, and a government informant actively engages him in conversation or even questions him, his revelations are not subject to exclusion.

Moreover, even when statements are actively elicited after a formal accusation, a right to counsel violation can occur, and exclusion is in order, only if the elicitor is a government agent at the time he or she prompts the accused's disclosures. Because the right to counsel is a protection against imbalanced confrontations between the state and the defendant, the Sixth Amendment does not constrain private parties—those who have not been enlisted or induced to act on behalf of the government. Thus, its exclusion doctrine does not reach the products of private party conduct.[138] If the neighbor of a person already charged with sexual misconduct with children takes it upon himself to learn the truth about the accusations, and, after befriending the accused, induces him to confide the details of his wrongdoing, anything the defendant reveals is admissible.

The requirement that one be "accused" at the time of the elicitation gives rise to a further restriction on the presumptive scope of exclusion. The right to counsel is "offense-specific."[139] Statements that a government agent has deliberately elicited from an accused individual are inadmissible at the trial of offenses that were the subject of formal charges at the time of the elicitation. They are not, however, subject to exclusion from the trial of offenses not charged at the time.[140]

---

137. If the Court's view that the right to counsel cannot attach before formal accusation is correct, then neither a personal right nor a deterrent justification could support Sixth Amendment-based exclusion of statements elicited prior to accusation. Because the suspect had no right to counsel during the pretrial encounter, the use of evidence at trial could not complete a Sixth Amendment violation. Because there is no constitutional deprivation prior to trial, there is no impermissible conduct to be deterred.

138. The suppression of statements obtained by a private party could not be justified by either predicate for Sixth Amendment exclusion. The Sixth Amendment surely provides no right not to be convicted on the basis of evidence obtained by means of confrontation by a private party. Moreover, because such a confrontation threatens no constitutionally-protected interest, deterrence can provide no justification for suppression.

139. *See* Texas v. Cobb, 532 U.S. 162, 167–68 (2001).

140. There is one important qualification upon this limitation. Offenses that qualify as the "same offense" for purposes of the Fifth Amendment Double Jeopardy Clause also qualify as the same offense for Sixth Amendment right to counsel purposes. *See id.* at 173. An offense is considered to be formally charged, and the right to counsel attaches, if any offense that qualifies as "the same" under the double jeopardy standard has been formally charged. It is noteworthy, however, that even identical statutory offenses are *not* the same if they are offenses against separate sovereigns. If the federal government charges an individual with manufacturing methamphetamine, the right to counsel does not attach for an identical state offense based on the very same conduct. Statements deliberately elicited in the absence of counsel would not be admissible to prove the federal offense, but

It does not matter that the uncharged offense is "'factually related'" to the charged offense in time, place, or nature.[141] Consequently, the very same disclosure may well be barred from the trial of one crime, but admissible in the trial of another related offense.[142] To illustrate, suppose that someone broke into a home, sexually assaulted a resident, and then killed her. A suspect was arrested and formally charged with burglary, whereupon the government recruited his cellmate to secure information. By conversation and direct inquiries, the cellmate secured admissions that the defendant was involved in the burglary. The prosecutor may not use those admissions to prove the burglary, but may use them insofar as they are relevant to proving the sexual assault and the homicide.[143]

The admissibility of evidence at trials of uncharged offenses is more easily reconciled with a conception of exclusion as an integral component of the right to assistance. If one is entitled to counsel only for formally charged offenses,[144] and if statements were suppressed because their use to convict completes a Sixth

---

could be used by the prosecution to prove the state crime. *See* Daniel R. Dinger, *Successive Interviews and Successful Prosecutions: The Interplay of the Sixth Amendment Right to Counsel and the Dual Sovereignty Doctrine in a Post-*Cobb *World*, 40 TEX. TECH. L. REV. 917, 955–56 (2008).

141. *See Cobb*, 532 U.S. at 168.

142. In a joint trial of more than one offense, the Sixth Amendment might bar use of a statement to prove one offense, but not to prove a different offense. A defendant might argue in such a case that the offenses should be tried separately because jurors could not be expected to follow a limiting instruction telling them that they may use the statement only as proof of one offense and not as proof of the other.

143. In the hypothetical situation in the text, none of the offenses would qualify as "the same" because each requires proof of an additional fact that the others do not require. *See id.* at 173. To illustrate when an offense would be the "same" as a charged offense, although not identical, suppose an offender were to attack a victim in order to steal his wallet. After he is arrested and formally charged with simple assault on the victim, an officer deliberately elicited disclosures that undermined the defendant's alibi for the crime. Those statements are inadmissible at both the simple assault trial and at a trial for assault with intent to rob the victim because the latter offense is the "same" for purposes of the right to counsel as the simple assault. All of the elements needed to prove the assault are also elements needed to prove the assault with intent to rob. Put otherwise, a conviction of simple assault does not require the proof of any fact that is not also needed to convict for assault with intent to rob. Because of the formal charge for simple assault at the time the disclosures were elicited, the statements are not admissible to prove either offense.

144. The "offense specific" limitation on the scope of the right to pretrial assistance is debatable. It is arguable that once the government has formally accused an individual of any offense, the right to assistance should extend to all offenses that are "'closely related to'" or "'inextricably intertwined with'" that offense. *See id.* at 186 (Breyer, J., dissenting). If that position were adopted, the breadth of the *Massiah* suppression doctrine would be considerably greater. Statements would be inadmissible to prove all offenses closely related to or inextricably intertwined with the offense that was the subject of a formal accusation at the time the statements were made.

Amendment deprivation by inflicting the constitutionally objectionable harm, it would make perfect sense not to exclude evidence from the trial of an offense for which the accused had no entitlement to assistance at the time the government prompted him to speak. From a deterrent standpoint, however, it is arguable that it is necessary to suppress revelations from the trials of *all* related or foreseeable offenses even though the accused had no right to counsel for those offenses when he made the revelations. Because the elicitation is a constitutional wrong with regard to the charged offense, the prospect of admissibility at the trial of other crimes could provide a potent incentive for officers to violate the Sixth Amendment in future cases. To prevent pretrial right to counsel violations, it is arguably necessary to bar evidence from the trial of all offenses with a sufficiently close relationship to a charged offense.

The determination that statements are admissible in the trials of offenses not yet charged at the time of elicitation predates the ruling that Sixth Amendment suppression is solely a deterrent safeguard, not a constitutional right. The Court will surely find its conclusion reconcilable with *Massiah*'s underpinnings by relying on the cost-benefit reasoning that has become commonplace in defining the contours of Fourth Amendment exclusion. The substantial social costs of suppressing statements from trials of offenses that involved no pretrial deprivation of counsel—uncharged offenses—will be deemed to outweigh the marginal, incremental, or speculative deterrent benefits of barring the evidence from those trials.

Disclosures in response to deliberate elicitation are the primary evidence the *Massiah* exclusionary rule forbids.[145] In *Nix v. Williams*,[146] the Court made it clear that the *Massiah* doctrine also bars derivative evidence—evidence the government obtains by pursuing leads provided by statements. According to *Nix*, "the exclusionary rule applies not only to the illegally obtained evidence itself, but also to other incriminating evidence derived from the primary evidence."[147] Extension of the suppression remedy to "the fruit of unlawful police conduct . . . is needed to deter police from violations of constitutional . . . protections."[148] The "illegally obtained [primary] evidence" in *Nix* was the accused's revelation of the

---

145. Although unlikely, it is conceivable that tangible items could be considered the primary evidentiary product of a Sixth Amendment transgression. For example, if an officer or informant asks a defendant what he has in his pocket and the defendant reaches in and extracts illegal narcotics, it is arguable that both the revelatory act—the disclosure—and the narcotics themselves are the immediate products of the uncounseled interaction.

146. 467 U.S. 431 (1984).

147. *Id.* at 441. Although the Court relied on Fourth Amendment precedent for this premise, it clearly intended to adopt "[t]he doctrine requiring courts to suppress evidence as the tainted 'fruit' of unlawful governmental conduct" as a governing principle for Sixth Amendment suppression. *See id.*

148. *Id.* at 442–43.

location of a homicide victim's body.[149] The "other incriminating evidence derived from the primary evidence" was forensic proof acquired by examining the body.[150] The Court found the presumptively excludable forensic evidence admissible only because it fell within an exception to the exclusionary rule.

As is true under the Fourth Amendment, any type of evidence can qualify as a derivative fruit of the original illegality. Tangible items, such as drugs and weapons, are subject to exclusion if they are discovered due to improperly elicited admissions. Intangible evidence gained by pursuing leads supplied by an accused—for example, an officer's testimony about what he learned or a witness's report about the defendant's activities—can also be barred by the Sixth Amendment suppression doctrine. Insofar as it reaches derivative evidentiary products of inadmissible statements, *Massiah*'s exclusion doctrine is considerably broader than the *Miranda* suppression rule. The latter, it will be recalled, bars only the statements obtained by custodial interrogation conducted in violation of *Miranda*'s guidelines and allows the introduction of all derivative evidence.[151]

A causation requirement qualifies the Sixth Amendment exclusionary rule. As under the Fourth Amendment, evidence must have a "but for" causal connection to the unconstitutional official conduct. Suppression is in order only if the evidence at issue "'is in some sense the product of illegal government activity.'"[152] An accused's incriminating statements must, therefore, be secured *as a result of* a government agent's deliberate elicitation. If the agent engages in elicitation but the defendant's admissions are not responsive to that elicitation, they should not be suppressed.[153] Moreover, unless there is a demonstrated causal connection between improperly elicited revelations and evidence claimed to be the fruit of those revelations, exclusion is inappropriate. A defendant must show that the state would not have the contested evidence *but for* the deprivation of counsel that prompted the accused's disclosures.

---

149. *Id.* at 441.

150. *Id.*

151. *See supra* Chapter 3, text accompanying notes 124–35.

152. *Nix v. Williams*, 467 U.S. 431, 444 (1984) (quoting United States v. Crews, 445 U.S. 463, 471 (1980)).

153. Although the Court in *Kuhlmann v. Wilson*, 477 U.S. 436 (1986), did not base its holding on the lack of causation between the government informant's acts and the defendant's disclosures, the facts might have sustained such a conclusion. In that case, the informant made some potentially evocative remarks to the accused, but the accused did not make incriminating revelations until after his brother paid him a visit and revealed that family members "were upset because they believed that" he had committed murder. *Id.* at 440. In such a situation a court might conclude that the Sixth Amendment exclusionary rule does not apply because the revelations were the product of the brother's visit and not the result of the informant's conduct.

The decision to characterize *Massiah*'s suppression doctrine as a future-oriented safeguard analogous to the Fourth Amendment exclusionary rule makes it virtually certain that the Court will continue to endorse the view that the Sixth Amendment rule bars both statements and any derivative evidence causally connected to the uncounseled elicitation. The alternative conception of Sixth Amendment suppression—that it is an inextricable part of the counsel guarantee and a personal right belonging to the accused—would dictate the same conclusion. The personal right rationale for exclusion rests on the premise that constitutional injury occurs when the prosecution uses the products of an imbalanced pretrial encounter to convict an accused who was denied counsel. Any trial advantage the government gains as a result of a pretrial deprivation of assistance denies the accused the protection that the Sixth Amendment is intended to furnish. Consequently, causally-linked primary and derivative fruits would also fall within the scope of a Sixth Amendment right to exclusion.[154]

2. Proceedings in Which the Sixth Amendment Bars Evidence

Like all suppression doctrines, the *Massiah* exclusionary rule bars the government from introducing evidence in criminal *trials*.[155] Trials always have been and always will be the primary, if not exclusive, domain for Sixth Amendment exclusion. It was noted in Chapter 3 that *Miranda*'s exclusion doctrine applies to trials for every level of criminal offense. Because *Miranda* enforces the Fifth Amendment prohibition on compulsory self-incrimination "in all criminal cases," there is no basis for distinguishing between serious and petty offenses.[156]

On the other hand, despite the fact that the Sixth Amendment right to counsel textually governs "*all* criminal prosecutions,"[157] the Supreme Court has held that an indigent's right to appointed assistance *at trial*, the source and foundation of the pretrial right defined by the *Massiah* doctrine, does not extend to trials for misdemeanors that do not result in "actual imprisonment."[158] This limitation of the right to state-funded assistance could well mean that if an indigent defendant is charged with a misdemeanor at the time the government elicits

---

154. *See* Tomkovicz, Massiah *Right to Exclusion*, *supra* note 98, at 782 (discussing why derivative evidence would be subject to exclusion if Sixth Amendment suppression was an integral part of the right to counsel).

155. *See* United States v. Henry, 447 U.S. 264, 274 (1980); Massiah v. United States, 377 U.S. 201, 207 (1964).

156. *See supra* Chapter 3, text accompanying note 136.

157. U.S. Const. amend. VI (emphasis added).

158. *See* Scott v. Illinois, 440 U.S. 367, 373–74 (1979). It is unclear whether a court could deny a defendant the opportunity to be represented by retained counsel in a misdemeanor case where the actual punishment imposed does not trigger a right to appointed assistance. If so, then the same rule would govern the situations *Massiah* regulates and disclosures would not be subject to exclusion even if the state denied an accused the opportunity to have a retained lawyer at a pretrial encounter.

disclosures without counsel, the prosecution may use those disclosures at the trial of that offense if a conviction does not result in a sentence involving jail time. It seems plausible that if the accused has no right to *trial* assistance in that situation, he has no right to *pretrial* assistance and the elicitation of revelations without appointed counsel does not constitute a violation of the Sixth Amendment guarantee. Without a deprivation of the assistance that the Sixth Amendment guarantees, there is no predicate for exclusion.[159]

The result is not as clear when evidence obtained in violation of the right to assistance is offered at a trial in which the accused is not entitled to assistance. Indigent defendants charged with and tried for felonies have the right to an appointed lawyer's assistance no matter what penalty is imposed upon conviction.[160] Suppose a defendant who lacks funds is charged with a felony, is denied assistance, and a state agent then elicits statements. Is exclusion required if the state seeks to introduce the statements at a subsequent trial for a misdemeanor that qualifies as the "same offense" if conviction will not result in a sentence that includes prison time?[161] If the *Massiah* suppression doctrine was an integral part of the right to counsel, one might contend that because there is no right to assistance at the trial itself, the use of the elicited revelations at trial cannot violate the right to counsel. Because Sixth Amendment suppression is a deterrent safeguard, however, it is arguable that exclusion from the misdemeanor trial is necessary to discourage officers from violating a felony defendant's right to pretrial assistance in the future. On the other hand, one could contend that the threat of excluding the defendant's statements from a trial for the felony that was charged at the time of the elicitation—and was the offense for which trial was likely and anticipated at the time of the elicitation—provides officers with sufficient incentives to honor future felony defendants' rights to appointed pretrial assistance. The incremental deterrence gained by suppressing the evidence from a misdemeanor trial for a crime that is the same offense as the charged felony could be deemed insufficient to justify the costs of suppression. In sum, it is

159. This certainly follows from the deterrent rationale for exclusion, which holds that suppression follows constitutional violations because it is designed to discourage future conduct of that nature. It also would follow from a personal right rationale. If an accused has no right to assistance prior to trial, the use of disclosures at trial cannot cause the sort of injury that completes a constitutional wrong.

160. *See* Nichols v. United States, 511 U.S. 738, 743 n.9 (1994).

161. For example, an indigent defendant initially charged with a form of aggravated assault might ultimately be tried for simple assault. Because the simple assault is included in the aggravated assault, the right to counsel attached for both offenses when the defendant was charged with the aggravated assault. *See supra* text accompanying notes 139–43. On the other hand, one might contend that the right to appointed counsel did not attach for the misdemeanor simple assault if the accused is ultimately tried for and convicted of that offense and receives a sentence that does not entail actual imprisonment. If, in retrospect, the right did not attach, there is no basis for exclusion.

uncertain whether the Sixth Amendment bars a statement elicited in violation of an indigent felony defendant's right to assistance if the prosecution offers the statement at a trial in which the accused has no constitutional entitlement to appointed counsel's assistance. The deterrent rationale for Sixth Amendment exclusion could support either outcome.[162]

The Supreme Court has never had occasion to decide whether the Sixth Amendment suppression doctrine applies in any other types of court proceedings. Because the Court has characterized the Sixth Amendment exclusionary rule as a future-oriented deterrent safeguard, not a personal right of the accused, it seems virtually certain that the Court would find that the *Massiah* suppression doctrine ordinarily operates only in those proceedings where the Fourth Amendment's deterrent sanction operates.

The Court has never decided whether either the Fourth Amendment or Sixth Amendment exclusionary rule requires that evidence be barred from *sentencing proceedings*. If a process labeled a sentencing proceeding is, in substance, part of the determination of guilt or innocence for an offense under the "jury trial" doctrine of *Apprendi v. New Jersey*[163]—that is, if it qualifies as a criminal *trial* under that line of authority—both the Fourth and Sixth Amendment evidentiary bars would apply. On the other hand, it is far from clear that deterrent exclusionary rules would be extended to true *sentencing* proceedings—that is, phases of the process whose function actually is to determine the appropriate punishment for a conviction.[164] The Fifth Amendment right to exclusion and *Miranda*'s prophylactic Fifth Amendment exclusionary rule apply in sentencing proceedings because the purpose of those rules is to prevent constitutional deprivations in the courtroom. In the Court's view, the protection against being forced to incriminate oneself extends beyond trials and constrains decisions concerning the severity of the consequences for committing a crime.[165]

---

162. This theoretically interesting issue is probably of limited practical significance. Situations involving attachment of a pretrial right to appointed assistance, but no Sixth Amendment right to appointed assistance at trial, are likely to be quite rare.

163. 530 U.S. 466 (2000). The landmark ruling in *Apprendi* held that even though a jurisdiction labels a post-trial process a sentencing proceeding, if the process involves the determination of a fact, other than the existence of "a prior conviction[,] . . . that increases the penalty for a crime beyond the prescribed statutory maximum," for constitutional purposes that proceeding is a trial for a more serious offense and the fundamental guarantees of trial by jury and proof beyond a reasonable doubt are applicable. *Id.* at 409.

164. Proceedings in which a judge chooses a sentence at or below the statutory maximum that is authorized by a jury verdict are, for constitutional purposes, sentencing proceedings. Such proceedings are not trials even if the judge makes findings of fact to support her choice of sentence. *See* Blakely v. Washington, 542 U.S. 296, 308–09 (2004); *Apprendi*, 530 U.S. at 481–82.

165. *See supra* Chapter 2, text accompanying notes 189–98; *see supra* Chapter 3, text accompanying notes 136–43. As noted in Chapter 3, whether *Miranda*'s bar applies in

Because the Sixth Amendment right to trial counsel also extends to sentencing proceedings, an accused is entitled to have legal assistance during a sentencing process.[166] The question here, however, is whether a suppression sanction that is designed to deter pretrial counsel deprivations applies in sentencing proceedings. The issue is debatable. The Court could conclude that the close relationship between trial and sentencing and the benefits for law enforcement of using illegally acquired evidence to enhance sentences suggest that exclusion would have substantial deterrent value that outweighs the costs of barring relevant evidence from sentencing phases. On the other hand, the Court could strike the Sixth Amendment balance in favor of admission, reasoning that a bar to use at the trial furnishes sufficient motivation for officers to avoid denying counsel in future cases. Any additional deterrent benefits from a bar to sentencing use could be deemed insufficient to justify ignoring evidence that will enable a judge to ascertain the appropriate punishment for a crime. As is typically the case, once one moves beyond the core ban imposed by a deterrence-based exclusionary rule—the suppression of evidence from the prosecution's case-in-chief in a criminal trial of a defendant whose rights were violated—interest-balancing analysis can justify either suppression or admission.

Long ago, the Court held that the Fourth Amendment exclusionary rule applies in a nominally civil proceeding to forfeit property because it was, in fact, "quasi-criminal" in nature.[167] Forfeiture was based on a determination that there had been a criminal offense, and the Court thought it clear that the forfeiture imposed was a penalty for that offense. The discussion of this holding in Chapter 1 indicated that the Court might not reaffirm it today and would certainly not extend its reach.[168] As long as this Fourth Amendment ruling retains force, Sixth Amendment suppression should also be required in quasi-criminal forfeiture actions. If the objective of deterring unreasonable searches and seizures dictates suppression, the similar objective of deterring right to counsel deprivations would seem to require exclusion.

The decision to cast *Massiah* exclusion as a mere deterrent safeguard would almost certainly lead the Court to follow Fourth Amendment precedents and conclude that the Sixth Amendment exclusionary rule does not operate in either grand jury proceedings or administrative processes to revoke a prisoner's release

---

noncapital sentencing proceedings is uncertain. *See supra* text accompanying notes 141–43.

166. *See* Gardner v. Florida, 430 U.S. 349, 358 (1977); Mempa v. Rhay, 389 U.S. 128, 137 (1967); *see also* JAMES J. TOMKOVICZ, THE RIGHT TO THE ASSISTANCE OF COUNSEL 110–12 (2002).

167. *See* One 1958 Plymouth Sedan v. Pennsylvania, 380 U.S. 693, 700 (1965).

168. *See supra* Chapter 1, note 162.

on parole.[169] Similarly, like the Fourth Amendment exclusionary rule, the Sixth Amendment's evidentiary bar surely does not extend to civil tax assessment or deportation proceedings.[170] While the Court has denied the applicability of the search and seizure exclusionary rule in these two civil contexts, but has never categorically ruled that it cannot apply in *any* civil action, the tenor of recent decisions strongly indicates a lack of receptivity to a claim for exclusion in any sort of civil case.

Finally, there is the question of whether a petitioner in a habeas corpus challenge to a state conviction can raise a claim that a trial judge erred in failing to exclude evidence obtained in violation of the Sixth Amendment. In *Stone v. Powell*,[171] the Court held that a convicted defendant may not vindicate a Fourth Amendment exclusionary rule claim in a federal habeas corpus action—that is, he is not entitled to raise a claim that a judge erred in refusing to suppress evidence from his trial—unless the state failed to provide "an opportunity for full and fair litigation of" that claim.[172] In *Withrow v. Williams*,[173] however, the Court reached the opposite conclusion for *Miranda* suppression claims. In a federal habeas action, a defendant may pursue a claim that a judge erred in refusing to exclude statements from a state trial because they were obtained in violation of *Miranda*'s constraints on custodial interrogation even if the state court provided an adequate opportunity to litigate that claim.[174]

Had the Court adhered to the original understanding of *Massiah*'s exclusion doctrine as an integral part of the right to counsel, Sixth Amendment suppression claims would be treated like *Miranda* suppression claims. Defendants convicted in state trials would surely be able to vindicate such claims in federal habeas proceedings.[175] The *Withrow* Court refused to apply the *Stone v. Powell* bar to *Miranda* claims because exclusion under *Miranda*, while not a right in itself, is a safeguard against risks that a fundamental trial right will be violated. If the admission of evidence obtained in violation of *Massiah* actually violated the Sixth Amendment (and suppression, therefore, was a personal constitutional entitlement of the accused), there would be even more reason to reject the *Stone v. Powell* limitation. The cost-benefit reasoning underlying *Stone*'s restriction of

---

169. For a discussion of the pertinent Fourth Amendment exclusionary rule rulings, see *supra* Chapter 1, text accompanying notes 163–67.

170. For a discussion of the pertinent Fourth Amendment exclusionary rule rulings, see *supra* Chapter 1, text accompanying notes 168–73.

171. 428 U.S. 465 (1976). For a discussion of the *Stone v. Powell* decision, see *supra* Chapter 1, text accompanying note 166.

172. *Id.* at 494.

173. 507 U.S. 680 (1993).

174. *See id.* at 688, 691–95. For a discussion of the *Withrow* decision, see *supra* Chapter 3 text accompanying notes 145–46.

175. For a more complete discussion, see Tomkovicz, Massiah *Right to Exclusion*, *supra* note 98, at 789–92.

habeas relief is firmly rooted in the future-oriented deterrent justification for Fourth Amendment suppression and the fact that no personal right of the defendant is jeopardized by the use of evidence against him at trial. Cost-benefit analysis has no application to exclusion doctrines necessary to prevent immediate constitutional deprivations in the courtroom. When a habeas claimant asserts a right to exclusion, there is no reason to limit his opportunity to seek collateral relief.[176]

The Court, however, has rejected the view that *Massiah* suppression is a personal right and has cast it as a mere deterrent of future wrongs that is cut from the same cloth as the Fourth Amendment exclusionary rule. For that reason, the *Stone v. Powell* restriction on raising Fourth Amendment exclusion claims in collateral attacks on convictions surely must apply with equal force to Sixth Amendment suppression claims. *Stone*'s premise is that the costs of allowing Fourth Amendment suppression claims in habeas proceedings ordinarily outweigh any deterrent benefits resulting from the threat of exclusion. *Kansas v. Ventris*[177] made it clear that the same cost-benefit interest-balancing that informs Fourth Amendment exclusion analyses also informs Sixth Amendment assessments.[178] Thus, it seems certain that the Court would hold that a habeas petitioner may raise a Sixth Amendment suppression claim only when a state court has denied him a full and fair chance to litigate that claim.[179]

In sum, the primary domain for the *Massiah* suppression doctrine's operation is the trial. It *could* apply to true sentencing proceedings and *might* dictate

---

176. *Stone* and *Withrow* are the only Supreme Court decisions involving the availability of evidentiary exclusion claims in habeas challenges to state convictions. When the government has sought the extension of *Stone*'s jurisprudential bar to other sorts of constitutional claims, the Court has been quite unreceptive. In *Jackson v. Virginia*, 443 U.S. 307, 323 (1979), the Court held that a habeas claimant could pursue a due process-based contention that the evidence supporting his conviction was insufficient, and in *Rose v. Mitchell*, 443 U.S. 545, 563 (1979), the Court concluded that a habeas petitioner could raise an equal protection-based claim of racial discrimination in the selection of a grand jury foreman. Of greatest relevance to the discussion in the text is *Kimmelman v. Morrison*, 477 U.S. 365 (1986). The *Kimmelman* Court rejected the government's argument that *Stone* barred a claim that counsel was ineffective in failing to seek evidentiary suppression under the Fourth Amendment. *Id.* at 374–75. Even though the petitioner's challenge was ultimately based on the merits of a Fourth Amendment exclusionary rule claim, his core assertion was that his lawyer's poor performance had denied him the Sixth Amendment right to effective assistance. *Kimmelman* deemed *Stone* inapplicable to a claim that an accused had been denied his constitutional entitlement to the assistance of trial counsel. If suppression under *Massiah* was an indivisible part of that very same guarantee, *Stone* could not govern a habeas claim that a state judge had erred in refusing to exclude evidence.

177. *See supra* text accompanying notes 84–96.

178. Kansas v. Ventris, 556 U.S. ____, ____, 129 S.Ct. 1841, 1846–47 (2009).

179. *See* Brewer v. Williams, 430 U.S. 387, 426–28 (1977) (Burger, C.J., dissenting).

exclusion in some quasi-criminal forfeiture actions. It seems quite unlikely to operate in any other phases of the criminal process or in any civil proceedings. Moreover, in federal habeas corpus actions, defendants ordinarily will not be able to challenge state convictions on the ground that a trial judge erroneously denied a *Massiah* suppression claim.

3. "Standing" to Raise a Sixth Amendment Exclusion Claim: The Individuals Entitled to *Massiah*'s Suppression Remedy

The Supreme Court has never addressed the question of standing to raise a Sixth Amendment exclusionary rule claim.[180] Suppose that an individual accused of robbery responds to deliberate elicitation by government agents with disclosures that incriminate both herself and her accomplice. May the accomplice seek suppression of those statements from her robbery trial under the *Massiah* doctrine? Undoubtedly, just as a defendant may not claim that the violation of another person's Fourth Amendment rights requires the suppression of illegally-obtained evidence from her trial,[181] she may not bar evidence on the ground that it is the fruit of violating a third person's right to counsel. The deterrent objectives of excluding evidence under *Massiah* cannot justify the costs of barring probative evidence from the trial of a defendant who was not deprived of counsel in the pretrial encounter that produced the evidence. Only the accused who makes the uncounseled revelations is entitled to suppression. Suppression in third parties' cases could yield some incremental deterrent gains—the government might be even more hesitant to elicit information if it could not use that information against anyone. Nonetheless, the threat of barring the statements from the trial of the person most likely to be incriminated—the accused who made the revelations—furnishes adequate deterrence. The social costs of thwarting prosecutions by excluding probative admissions made by someone other than the defendant on trial outweigh any additional benefit in terms of encouraging future respect for the right to the assistance of counsel.[182] A standing limitation undoubtedly restricts the availability of *Massiah*'s suppression sanction.

---

180. For a discussion of standing, see Tomkovicz, Massiah *Right to Exclusion, supra* note 98, at 774–75. According to one scholar, issues of standing rarely arise because defendants whose statements are at issue do have standing and because the protection afforded by the Sixth Amendment Confrontation Clause against the use of another person's out-of-court statements typically discourages the government from trying to introduce such statements. *See* Carol S. Steiker, *Counter-Revolution in Constitutional Criminal Procedure? Two Audiences, Two Answers*, 94 MICH. L. REV. 2466, 2526 (1996) [hereinafter Steiker, *Counter-Revolution*].

181. For a discussion of the Fourth Amendment issue, see *supra* Chapter 1, text accompanying notes 174–97.

182. Chapter 7 discusses in detail a different constitutional basis that an accused *may* rely upon to suppress statements made by other individuals—the Sixth Amendment Confrontation Clause.

It bears mention that the same result would follow from recognition of a Sixth Amendment right to suppression. In fact, a right to counsel exclusion doctrine rooted in the premise that admission completes a deprivation of counsel would provide an even more persuasive foundation for the standing limitation. Only those who were denied assistance at a pretrial confrontation with the government could suffer a right to counsel deprivation by the trial use of statements to secure a conviction. When the statements are used to convict another defendant, that conviction is *not* the product of an imbalanced, unfair adversarial encounter that the defendant had with the state. The *Massiah* right reflects a fundamental principle of adversary system fair play—that our system does not permit the government to secure convictions by taking advantage of inferior criminal defendants, but, instead, guarantees defense attorneys to ensure fair contests between roughly equal opponents. The values and policies underlying the right to the assistance of counsel are not threatened when the evidentiary harm to a defendant is the result of the state exploiting another person's vulnerabilities.

In sum, the *Massiah* exclusionary rule is certainly limited by a standing restriction that entitles only those who disclose information in response to deliberate elicitation to suppress the disclosures and any derivative evidence obtained from those disclosures. Both the deterrent basis that justifies Sixth Amendment suppression and the competing view that sees exclusion as a constitutional right support the standing requirement. A defendant may exclude statements from his trial *only* if those statements are the product of a violation of his personal pretrial entitlement to assistance.[183]

4. Exceptions to the *Massiah* Exclusionary Rule

The question here is whether there are "exceptions" to the rule excluding from trials uncounseled statements deliberately elicited from an accused and the derivative products of those statements. The Court has recognized the legitimacy of a few exceptions—the independent source doctrine, the inevitable discovery exception, and the impeachment use exception. It has rejected one type of good faith exception. It has not considered the validity of an attenuation exception, whether an analogue of *Miranda*'s *Elstad* doctrine governs successive confessions, or the plausibility of a public safety exception parallel to *Miranda*'s. This section explores the settled and unsettled issues concerning the admissibility of evidence presumptively barred by *Massiah*'s Sixth Amendment exclusionary rule.

---

183. Even though the original *Massiah* ruling seemed to be premised on a right to exclusion, not on deterrent reasoning, the Court implicitly acknowledged the appropriateness of a standing limitation, declaring that it was holding only that a defendant's improperly elicited statements could not be "used . . . against *him* at his trial." Massiah v. United States, 377 U.S. 201, 207 (1964) (emphasis in original).

a. The Independent Source and Inevitable Discovery Doctrines The independent source doctrine and inevitable discovery exception are closely related. Both limit the scope of the Sixth Amendment exclusionary rule.[184] The independent source doctrine provides that even if officers deliberately elicit information from an accused in violation of the right to counsel, evidence obtained from a lawful source that is entirely independent of the illegal conduct is admissible.[185] The discussion of this doctrine in Chapter 1 observed that the rule allowing the admission of evidence from an independent lawful source is not a true exclusionary rule exception. The Sixth Amendment exclusionary rule, like its Fourth Amendment counterpart, reaches only evidence with some causal connection to unconstitutional conduct—in this case, to a pretrial deprivation of legal assistance. Evidence admissible under the independent source doctrine has no causal link to any illegal conduct that has occurred and, thus, is not presumptively subject to exclusion.[186] There is, therefore, no need for an "exception" to the suppression doctrine.

Whether evidence is identical to, similar to, related to, or different from illegally gained evidence, if it is the product of a lawful, independent source it is outside the ambit of the *Massiah* exclusionary rule. The illegally-obtained evidence may be the primary product or a derivative fruit of a right to counsel violation. Evidence that is independently and lawfully acquired is admissible.

Thus, if officers improperly elicit admissions of guilt and the accused has made identical admissions in an e-mail to a friend sent before the officers' impropriety, the e-mail admissions, if found by legal means, are admissible. If narcotics found in the defendant's office as a result of uncounseled, inadmissible disclosures are also found by officers executing a valid search warrant that was obtained entirely apart from the unconstitutional pretrial encounter with the accused, those narcotics are admissible. Ordinarily, it would be difficult for a prosecutor to show that statements an accused made *after* officers have initially engaged in improper elicitation were genuinely independent of that impropriety. Judges should presume that a connection exists, and the government should bear the burden of showing that later disclosures were in no sense a product of the earlier illegal conduct.[187] It is entirely possible, however, for derivative

---

184. *See* Nix v. Williams, 467 U.S. 431, 443–48 (1984). While *Nix* held that the inevitable discovery exception applies to the Sixth Amendment exclusionary rule, the Court assumed the applicability of the independent source doctrine because both rest on the same logical premise—that the government is not to be "put in a *worse* position" than it would have been in had it not acted illegally. *See id.* at 443 (emphasis in original). For a discussion of these two qualifications on the Sixth Amendment suppression doctrine, see Tomkovicz, Massiah *Right to Exclusion*, *supra* note 98, at 776–80.

185. *Nix*, 467 U.S. at 443.

186. For a fuller discussion, see *supra* Chapter 1, text accompanying notes 204–12.

187. In the hypothetical situation discussed earlier, the e-mail admissions were made *before* the illegal conduct and, thus, were clearly unconnected to that conduct. Situations

evidentiary fruits of *Massiah* transgressions—in particular, tangible evidence like contraband, weapons, incriminating clothing, or stolen goods discovered from information in improperly elicited statements—to also be acquired by lawful means and to qualify for admission under the independent source doctrine.[188]

The inevitable discovery exception, sometimes referred to as the "'hypothetical independent source'" doctrine,[189] was first recognized in *Nix v. Williams*, a case involving Sixth Amendment suppression. In *Nix*, in the absence of counsel and without a valid waiver of assistance, officers elicited statements from an accused that enabled them to find the body of a murder victim. Because of the Sixth Amendment violation, the defendant's statements could not be used at trial.[190] The question was whether evidence gained from examination of the body was admissible because a lawful search of the area where the body was found was underway and would have led the authorities to the body and to the evidence even if the accused had not revealed the body's location. The Court held that the evidence was admissible under the inevitable discovery exception to the Sixth Amendment exclusionary rule.[191]

Unlike the independent source doctrine, the inevitable discovery exception permits the prosecution to use evidence that is, in fact, causally connected to illegal conduct. Consequently, it is a genuine exception to the Sixth Amendment exclusionary rule. It applies when the government shows, by a preponderance of the evidence, that it *would have* acquired the unlawfully obtained evidence by independent legal means. The evidence that would have been found is admissible even if the unconstitutional conduct was the product of a deliberate, bad faith

---

where an accused has made *prior* untainted revelations would probably be rare. When an accused makes inculpatory admissions *after* officers have unconstitutionally induced him to make initial admissions, it is probable that the unconstitutional conduct contributed in some way to the subsequent revelations. For a discussion of the "cat out of the bag" presumption and the relevance of a psychological connection between an initial confession and a successive confession, see *infra* text accompanying notes 201–12.

188. *Murray v. United States*, 487 U.S. 533 (1988), made it clear that the *very same evidentiary items* that are found during an illegal search can qualify for admission because they were also found by means of a subsequent legal search. For the subsequent discovery to truly be independent of the earlier illegality, two factual predicates are necessary. Officers must not have relied on illegally discovered facts to justify the legal search *and* their decision to conduct the lawful search must not have been prompted by the earlier illegal discoveries. *Id.* at 542. There is every reason to believe that the very same evidence found as a result of a *Massiah* violation could qualify for admission under the independent source doctrine if the prosecution were to establish that there was no connection between the earlier violation and the subsequent acquisition of the evidence.

189. *See Nix*, 467 U.S. at 438.

190. In *Brewer v. Williams*, 430 U.S. 387 (1977), the Court ruled that those statements were barred by *Massiah*'s suppression rule. *Id.* at 397–401, 407 n.12.

191. *See Nix*, 467 U.S. at 448, 449–50.

decision to violate the Constitution.[192] According to the Supreme Court, the exclusionary rule achieves its deterrent aims by ensuring that the government is put in "the same [evidentiary] position" it would have occupied absent the illegality.[193] It seeks to discourage illegalities by depriving the government of illegally gained profits, thereby removing the incentives for future wrongs. Because it would put the government in a worse position than it would have occupied without the illegality, the exclusion of evidence that would inevitably have been found by lawful means—like the suppression of evidence gained from an independent lawful source—would be "formalistic, pointless, and punitive."[194] Consequently, evidence that would inevitably have been discovered lawfully falls within an exception to the Sixth Amendment exclusionary rule.

When the Court endorsed the inevitable discovery exception, the nature of *Massiah*'s evidentiary bar was still unsettled. The *Nix* Court reasoned that inevitable discovery is consistent with a deterrent justification because it does not allow the government to reap any unwarranted profits from deprivations of counsel. Now that it is clear that the Sixth Amendment exclusionary rule is a deterrent safeguard, there can be no doubt about inevitable discovery's legitimacy. Even if the Court had ruled that the use of uncounseled statements at trial completes the constitutional violation and that Sixth Amendment suppression is a part of the right to counsel, the inevitable discovery exception (and its independent source cousin) would still be valid. In *Nix*, the Court did entertain the possibility that Sixth Amendment exclusion was a constitutional entitlement and concluded that the admission of evidence that would have been acquired lawfully was entirely consistent with that conception of the *Massiah* bar. Illegally acquired evidence that would have been found lawfully would have been introduced at a defendant's trial even if the illegality had not occurred. Consequently, when the government is permitted to introduce that evidence, the accused receives the very same trial he would have received absent the imbalanced pretrial confrontation. In that situation, although the government does deny the accused assistance, it reaps no advantage and the accused suffers no harm. Use of the evidence does not, in fact, inflict the sort of injury—an increased risk of conviction due to an imbalanced adversarial contest—that the Sixth Amendment guards against. Therefore, when the prosecution uses evidence that would have been inevitably discovered, the Sixth Amendment violation is not completed and a defendant is not denied the fair trial protection that is *Massiah*'s essence.[195]

---

192. *Id.* at 445–46.

193. *Id.* at 443.

194. *Id.* at 445.

195. The *Nix* Court also suggested that the trustworthiness of the process was not called into question by the admission of the evidence found from examining the victim's body because the deprivation of assistance did not "impugn the reliability of the evidence in question." *Id.* at 446–47. While that is true, it seems beside the point. Even if the body

In sum, both the independent source and inevitable discovery doctrines are accepted limitations on *Massiah*'s Sixth Amendment exclusionary rule and are reconcilable with any justification for that evidentiary bar. The government may introduce primary or derivative evidence that satisfies the simple requirements for either exception.

b. The Attenuation Exception The attenuation exception to constitutional exclusion has developed entirely in the Fourth Amendment arena. Although the Court has never considered whether it is a viable exception to Sixth Amendment suppression, the recent declaration that the *Massiah* rule is similar to the *Weeks-Mapp* doctrine in both nature and objectives makes it virtually certain that the time-honored branch of the attenuation doctrine will qualify *Massiah*'s bar.[196]

The traditional attenuation exception holds that presumptively barred derivative evidence is admissible if the causal connection between the unconstitutional conduct and the acquisition of the evidence is sufficiently remote or weak.[197] In general, evidence with any causal connection to official illegality is subject to suppression. The "taint" of the government's wrong can be "dissipated" by factors that attenuate that connection. If the connection is attenuated, the evidence is admissible. The underlying rationale is that the threat of suppressing the closely linked evidentiary products furnishes sufficient incentives for officers to avoid future constitutional violations. The social costs of exclusion outweigh any additional deterrent benefits gained by suppressing evidence with a remote connection. Although the attenuation exception permits the government to reap some profit from its impermissible acts, and in that respect is unlike the independent source or inevitable discovery doctrines, any incentives for future improprieties these evidentiary gains furnish are thought to be insubstantial. For that reason, suppression would contribute only marginally to the enforcement of

---

would not have been discovered by lawful means, the evidence acquired would not have been rendered unreliable by the unconstitutional means of discovery. Moreover, the personal right conception of Sixth Amendment exclusion posits that legal assistance guards against *any* evidentiary advantages gained from imbalanced confrontations—including advantages resulting from reliable evidence. The *Massiah* entitlement to pretrial assistance has never been seen as a mere safeguard of the accuracy of the trial process. Fortunately, this misleading reliance on the reliability of the evidence admitted does not undermine the remainder of the Court's logic. The fact that the admission of evidence under the inevitable discovery exception does not result in a different trial from the one that would have transpired without a counsel deprivation is reason enough to find the exception logically compatible with a personal right rationale for suppression.

196. The focus here is on the longstanding attenuation exception, not the highly questionable, newly-minted branch of the exception the Court announced in *Hudson v. Michigan*, 547 U.S. 586, 593 (2006). For an analysis and critique of this variety of attenuation, see *supra* Chapter 1, text accompanying notes 232–37.

197. For more details about the attenuation exception, see *supra* Chapter 1, text accompanying notes 221–31.

the underlying constitutional guarantee. The harm that suppression inflicts on the search for truth at trial counterbalances any benefit and justifies admission of the attenuated evidence.

More specifically, evidentiary products of pretrial right to counsel deprivations should not be considered suppressible fruits of the poisonous tree if the time that elapsed between the uncounseled pretrial confrontation and the acquisition of the evidence, the events and circumstances intervening between that confrontation and the acquisition, and the character of the constitutional transgression sufficiently weaken the causal link.[198] Suppose that an informant, against the good faith instructions of law enforcement officers (who did not expect, but should have expected, him to ignore those instructions), actively converses with an indicted cellmate about his involvement in a murder. The informant then conveys the defendant's disclosures to the authorities. Following leads provided by those revelations, the authorities, over the course of many months and a host of investigative steps, find a murder weapon bearing the accused's fingerprints and discover a witness who will willingly testify in a way that undermines the defendant's alibi. Although the weapon and testimony both have a "but for" connection to the Sixth Amendment violation, the government could justify their introduction by arguing that the months that elapsed and the investigatory steps needed to uncover the evidence, coupled with the witness's exercise of free will and the authorities' lack of intent to elicit admissions in the absence of counsel,[199] attenuated the connection to the illegality and dissipated its taint.

Similarly, officers might visit a terrorism suspect at his home and make remarks that qualify as deliberate elicitation, unaware that a prosecutor has filed formal charges that very morning. The defendant's responses to the remarks then spur a three-week investigation that yields incriminating documents and recorded conversations in the possession of third parties who freely surrender them. The length of the investigation, the voluntary surrender of the evidence by the third parties, and the unintended nature of the Sixth Amendment deprivation could support admission of the evidence under the attenuation exception to *Massiah*'s bar.[200]

---

198. In Fourth Amendment precedents, the Court has identified time, intervening circumstances, and the character of the illegality as relevant variables. *See* Brown v. Illinois, 422 U.S. 590, 603–04 (1975). Any other factor that weakens or stretches the causal link between the wrong and the acquisition is potentially relevant.

199. Under the developed doctrine, objective proof that the authorities "must have known" that their informant would take steps to secure information suffices to establish a Sixth Amendment violation. *See* Maine v. Moulton, 474 U.S. 159, 174, 176 n.12 (1985); United States v. Henry, 447 U.S. 264, 271 (1980). There is no need to prove that they intended the elicitation by the agent in violation of the accused's right to assistance.

200. In this section, I have analyzed the applicability of the "traditional" branch of the attenuation exception. Chapter 1 discussed an alternative, quite distinct branch of the

The legitimacy of an attenuation exception would be questionable if the Court had concluded that the admission of evidence obtained in violation of *Massiah* completes the Sixth Amendment violation by allowing the government to profit at trial from its pretrial confrontation with a vulnerable, unassisted accused. It is arguable that no matter how weak the connection between the denial of assistance and the discovery of evidence, and no matter how innocent the imbalanced encounter, permitting the government to have any trial advantage that is the product of the uncounseled confrontation offends Sixth Amendment values and denies a measure of the very protection the guarantee of counsel is intended to afford. A constitutional right rationale for *Massiah* exclusion would probably preclude any exception to suppression that allows the state to fuel its case with the evidentiary profits of denying assistance.

Although there are no Supreme Court decisions on the subject, there is every reason to believe that an attenuation exception limits the current Sixth Amendment exclusionary rule. The details and operation of that exception will surely be informed by Fourth Amendment precedents that have explained its logic and refined its contours.

c. The Application of the *Elstad* Doctrine to Successive Confessions Chapter 3 explained the special restriction on the scope of *Miranda*'s exclusionary rule announced in *Oregon v. Elstad*.[201] *Elstad* confronted the issue of whether a successive confession obtained in compliance with *Miranda* might be suppressed as the product of an earlier *Miranda* violation that yielded an inadmissible confession. Officers interrogated a suspect in custody without reciting the requisite warnings and secured an initial confession. They subsequently provided effective warnings before again interrogating the suspect and securing a second confession. A majority of the Court concluded that, under *Miranda*, the successive confession was not subject to exclusion as the product or fruit of the first, unwarned session.[202] The Justices reasoned that neither of the two ostensible

---

attenuation exception that the Court promulgated in a relatively recent Fourth Amendment decision. *See supra* Chapter 1, text accompanying notes 232–37. That alternative variety of attenuation authorizes the admission of even closely connected evidentiary products if suppression will not serve the purpose of the Fourth Amendment command that was violated. The questionable underlying premise is that exclusion is called for only if the objective of a constitutional rule is to shield evidence from the government. This very different attenuation exception would seem to have no relevance to the Sixth Amendment context which, unlike the Fourth Amendment, does not involve different kinds of rules with different constitutional objectives. The right to assistance defined by the *Massiah* doctrine seems to be uniformly concerned with preventing the government from acquiring damaging revelations from an accused. Suppression would always serve the information-shielding purpose of the restrictions imposed by the Sixth Amendment.

201. *See supra* Chapter 3, text accompanying notes 54–60 and notes 125, 151.

202. Oregon v. Elstad, 470 U.S. 298, 308–09, 317–18 (1985).

purposes of *Miranda*'s exclusion doctrine dictated suppression of the second confession.

One objective of *Miranda*'s exclusionary rule is to combat risks that involuntary statements will be used at trial to convict defendants in violation of the Fifth Amendment privilege. This objective cannot justify suppression of the second confession because the circumstances surrounding the giving of that confession do not support a presumption of compulsion. First, proper warnings were given prior to the confession.[203] In addition, any psychological pressures to confess brought to bear by the suspect's knowledge that he had already revealed his guilt did not qualify as the official compulsion forbidden by the Fifth Amendment. They were the result of the suspect's "voluntary disclosure of a guilty secret," not governmental coercion to speak.[204] For these reasons, exclusion of the successive confession was not necessary to guard against risks that its introduction would effect a Fifth Amendment deprivation.

The *Elstad* Court also reasoned that exclusion of the second, properly obtained confession was not necessary to serve any deterrent objectives underlying the *Miranda* suppression doctrine. In the first place, *Miranda*'s bar induces compliance with prophylactic constraints upon custodial interrogation. For example, it motivates officers to give warnings. The *Miranda* exclusionary rule does not prevent the violation of genuine constitutional rights.[205] Consequently, the benefits of any deterrence achieved by exclusion are less significant than the gains yielded by encouraging officers to respect actual constitutional commands. Moreover, the connection between an initial, unwarned confession and a successive confession obtained after warnings and a waiver is inherently attenuated. Any causal link between the two rests in the psyche of the suspect and is premised on the suspect's awareness that he has "let the cat out of the bag."[206] Although this awareness may induce him to repeat what he has already revealed, any connection is speculative, at best, and is insufficiently strong to justify suppression.[207] Together, the nature of the potential benefits and the relative weakness of the connection diminish the deterrent value of suppressing a successive confession. Suppression of the initial confession provides officers with a reason to warn suspects in future cases. Any additional deterrence gained by suppressing the second confession is outweighed by the costs of barring probative, voluntary admissions of guilt.[208]

---

203. *Id.* at 310–11, 314.

204. *Id.* at 312.

205. *Id.* at 306–07.

206. *Id.* at 311.

207. *Elstad*, 470 U.S. at 312–14.

208. I have fleshed out and filled in some of the logical gaps in the somewhat cryptic reasoning offered by the *Elstad* Court.

The question here is whether the reasoning that supported the *Elstad* rule for successive confessions applies when the source of the initial confession is a Sixth Amendment violation, not a neglect of *Miranda*'s Fifth Amendment constraints. Suppose an officer or an informant deliberately elicits an inculpatory statement in violation of the right to counsel. A second inculpatory statement is then secured from the accused by constitutional means. Should the latter statement be immune from suppression, as it would be under *Miranda*? Critical distinctions between the nature of the *Miranda* and *Massiah* evidentiary bars suggest that *Elstad*'s logic and its rule are not transferable and that a presumption of exclusion should extend to successive confessions in the Sixth Amendment context. Moreover, this conclusion follows whether one accepts the deterrent conception or a personal right conception of Sixth Amendment suppression.

According to the Court, Sixth Amendment suppression is a future-oriented deterrent sanction. The objective is to deter violations of a fundamental constitutional *right*—the right to the assistance of counsel. Consequently, a primary reason for not applying the Fourth Amendment fruit of the poisonous tree doctrine under *Miranda*—that a failure to honor *Miranda*'s restrictions is not a violation of the Constitution—is inapplicable to *Massiah* exclusion. The other basis for the *Elstad* Court's conclusion that deterrence did not justify the suppression of a successive confession was a suggestion that the causal connection between the two confessions was weak or nonexistent. In a subsequent opinion, however, Justice O'Connor, the author of *Elstad*, made it clear that the Court had not questioned the existence of a psychological connection between successive confessions. It had rejected the "cat out of the bag" presumption as a basis for exclusion under *Miranda not* because that presumption was *factually* invalid, but instead because it was a *constitutionally* insufficient basis for exclusion.[209] In other words, the nature of *Miranda*'s bar to confessions had prompted the *Elstad* majority to reject the presumption as a matter of law, not as a matter of fact.

This reasoning is also inapposite to *Massiah*'s very different constitutional exclusionary doctrine. In the Sixth Amendment context, if there is a causal link between an initial confession obtained in violation of the right to counsel and a successive, legally-obtained confession—a link supplied by the "cat out of the bag" effect—the derivative evidence principle dictates exclusion of a successive confession. Because it is a product of the initial constitutional deprivation, the confession must be suppressed to eliminate an incentive for future denials of counsel.

Of course, if the connection between the initial wrong and the acquisition of the evidence at issue—the successive confession—is sufficiently attenuated, the successive confession will be admissible under the attenuation exception to the derivative evidence bar. Fourth Amendment precedent has established, however,

209. *See* Missouri v. Seibert, 542 U.S. 600, 627 (2004) (O'Connor, J., dissenting).

that voluntariness alone is *not* a sufficient attenuating variable.[210] The connection between the illegality and the acquisition may be strong despite a voluntary choice to make the successive statement. Voluntariness is a relevant attenuating factor when the object of exclusion is to prevent violations of actual constitutional rights, but it is not a per se basis for finding attenuation. While the voluntariness of a confession is of critical concern under *Miranda*, the primary purpose of which is to prevent compelled self-incrimination, it cannot be determinative under *Massiah*'s deterrence-based exclusionary rule.

Even if the Court had deemed *Massiah* exclusion a personal right of the accused, a necessary step to avoid the completion of a counsel deprivation at trial, *Elstad*'s *Miranda*-based reasoning would not support the admission of successive confessions.[211] The object of a Sixth Amendment right to exclusion would be to protect an accused against conviction based on *any* confession obtained as a result of an uncounseled confrontation. Because the aim would be to safeguard against injuries resulting from the adversarial imbalance during the government's encounter with the accused, this protection, unlike the Fifth Amendment shelter afforded by *Miranda*, would extend to both voluntary and involuntary confessions. A voluntary confession obtained by taking advantage of an unaided defendant would threaten the kind of adversary system injury that is the Sixth Amendment's concern. As long as there was a causal link between a denial of counsel and a successive confession—and the presumptive psychological connection would provide that link—an accused would have a Sixth Amendment right to bar that confession from trial.[212]

In sum, because of the differences in the character of *Miranda* and *Massiah* suppression, it would be irrational to extend the *Elstad* doctrine to the Sixth Amendment context. A successive confession obtained properly after the government has secured an initial confession in violation of the defendant's right to counsel should be presumptively barred by the derivative evidence principle governing *Massiah* suppression. Such a confession should be admissible *only* if it falls within a defensible exception to the Sixth Amendment rule.

---

210. *See* Brown v. Illinois, 422 U.S. 590, 601–02 (1975).

211. For a thorough exploration of why *Elstad*'s exemption of successive confessions from exclusion under *Miranda* is logically inapplicable to a Sixth Amendment suppression doctrine that is understood to be an essential part of the right to counsel, see Tomkovicz, *Saving* Massiah, *supra* note 97, at 757–62.

212. If the government could show that there was no connection—that the confession came, in fact, from a source entirely independent of the counsel denial—the confession would be admissible. Because there is a basis for presuming a psychological connection, and because ordinarily the prosecution must show that evidence acquired *after* unconstitutional conduct is the product of a lawful, independent source, the government would have the burden of establishing that a successive confession is not the profit of a denial of counsel.

d. "Good Faith" Exceptions This section addresses two different species of "good faith" exception to the *Massiah* exclusionary rule. The Supreme Court has considered, discussed, and rejected one variation on the good faith theme.[213] The legitimacy of the other kind of good faith doctrine remains uncertain.

An earlier section of this chapter explained the "offense specific" nature of the *Massiah* right to counsel.[214] This characterization of the right to pretrial assistance captures an important limitation—that an individual is entitled to assistance *only* for offenses that have been the subject of a formal accusation. Consequently, a person may well have a right to counsel for one criminal offense, but not for another. Deliberate elicitation violates the Sixth Amendment with respect to the charged crime, but not with respect to the uncharged crime. The very same official conduct might be both a denial of a fundamental Bill of Rights guarantee and a commendable investigative effort.[215] In *Maine v. Moulton,*[216] the government argued that when officials are engaged in a legitimate, good faith effort to investigate an uncharged offense, evidence they obtain should be admissible to prove not only the uncharged offense, but also the offense that is the subject of a formal accusation. In essence, the claim was that there should be an exception to the Sixth Amendment exclusion doctrine when officials elicit inculpatory admissions from a formally accused person *if* the actual motivation for their conduct was the acquisition of evidence concerning an offense for which charges were not pending. Their investigation could be designed to secure proof that the accused committed another offense or to gain proof that other uncharged individuals were involved in the offense that is the subject of the accusation against the defendant.

In *Moulton,* a majority rejected this proposed exception. The Court held that if the ordinary criteria for a Sixth Amendment violation were satisfied—that is, if a government agent deliberately elicited admissions from a person accused of an offense—the evidence obtained was not admissible to prove that offense despite the government's legitimate investigative motives. The Justices observed that when the government "seek[s] evidence pertaining to pending charges, . . . [its] investigative powers are limited by the Sixth Amendment rights

---

213. For a discussion of the good faith exception addressed by the Court, see Tomkovicz, Massiah *Right to Exclusion, supra* note 98, at 783–86.

214. *See supra* text accompanying notes 139–44.

215. The Court has never suggested that the violation of the right to assistance with respect to the offense that is the subject of a formal accusation renders the investigative efforts to secure evidence about the uncharged offense somehow improper. To the contrary, it has approved of the effort to secure evidence that will enable effective prosecution of the offense for which the right to counsel has not attached. *See* McNeil v. Wisconsin, 501 U.S. 171, 175–76 (1991); Moran v. Burbine, 475 U.S. 412, 431 (1986); Maine v. Moulton, 474 U.S. 159, 179–80 (1985).

216. 474 U.S. 159 (1985).

of the accused."[217] Despite their commendable objectives, when officials confront an uncounseled defendant they deprive him of his Sixth Amendment entitlement with respect to the charged offense. The proper investigatory motive for the conduct does not nullify the constitutional violation occasioned by the imbalanced adversarial encounter with the accused. According to the Court, recognition of an exception to the *Massiah* doctrine would "invite[] abuse by law enforcement personnel in the form of fabricated investigations and [would] risk[] evisceration of the Sixth Amendment."[218] The "likelihood of *post hoc* rationalizing"—that is, of asserting that there were legitimate investigative motives after the fact—prompted the majority to adopt a "more realistic view of police investigations, and . . . accept that dual purposes may exist whenever police have more than one reason to investigate."[219]

In sum, the Court refused to endorse the proposed good faith exception for two reasons. First, legitimate motives do not prevent the constitutional injury to an uncounseled defendant that results from pretrial encounters. In addition, such an exception could generate incentives for officials to make false claims about their motives that could do serious damage to the pretrial entitlement to assistance *Massiah* affords. The threats to the Sixth Amendment right to counsel posed by this variety of "good faith" exception were too great. To preserve the right to pretrial assistance, the Court decided that admissions elicited from an unassisted accused could not be used to prove a charged offense even if officers were engaged in a good faith investigation of an uncharged crime.[220]

The Court's rejection of the proposed exception to *Massiah*'s suppression doctrine can easily be reconciled with a Sixth Amendment right to exclusion. Evidence obtained by taking advantage of an unaided defendant cannot be admitted to prove a charged offense because no matter what the reason for confronting the accused, use of the evidence at trial would complete the Sixth Amendment wrong and inflict the harm that counsel is meant to prevent. Once the adversarial process has commenced, the government may not secure convictions by means of imbalanced encounters with unaided defendants. Good motives do not justify deprivations of the fundamental right to the assistance of counsel.

The *Moulton* Court's rejection of the good faith doctrine is somewhat more difficult to reconcile with the deterrent premises for *Massiah* suppression

---

217. *Id.* at 179–80.

218. *Id.* at 180.

219. *Id.* at 180 n.15.

220. Four Justices would have accepted the government's proposed exception. In their view, there was no Sixth Amendment violation involved in the acquisition or use of statements regarding a formally charged offense if officials obtained them while engaged in the good faith investigation of an uncharged offense. *See id.* at 181, 184–86 (Burger, C. J., dissenting).

endorsed by the Court. The Court has approved investigative efforts aimed at securing proof of uncharged offenses despite the fact that the target of these efforts has been accused of another offense. If officials gain evidence while engaged in the proper performance of their duties, seeking proof needed to enforce laws that have been broken, why should courts seek to deter their conduct by suppressing that evidence? Exclusion may cause them to forego their responsibilities and neglect their duty to protect society. The only defensible explanation for a deterrent sanction must rest on the premise that officers simultaneously engage in valid investigative efforts and undesirable transgressions of the Sixth Amendment when they deliberately elicit revelations from an accused in order to obtain evidence concerning an uncharged offense. To suspend the suppression sanction during the trial of the charged offense would be to eliminate incentives to honor the right to counsel in similar future cases. Because we want officials to respect defendants' Sixth Amendment entitlement, and because the good faith exception would erode motives for such respect, it is an unacceptable restriction upon *Massiah*'s evidentiary bar. The good faith, separate investigation exception would even create positive motives to "fabricate" and "rationalize" in cases where officials did not have proper motives at the time they elicited admissions. These consequences would surely erode the Sixth Amendment guarantee. Thus, the Court's rejection of the good faith, legitimate investigation exception can be squared with the deterrent objectives of Sixth Amendment exclusion.[221]

There is another possible variety of good faith exception, one that is analogous in character to the Fourth Amendment good faith exceptions. The Supreme Court has never had occasion to address its legitimacy. The issue is whether there should be an exception to the Sixth Amendment exclusionary rule when officers obtain disclosures in violation of the *Massiah* right to counsel if a reasonable officer could have believed that she was not violating that right. Should evidence be admissible when the government improperly elicits admissions from an uncounseled accused, but it was reasonable to believe that there was no deprivation of counsel?

---

221. Although it is possible to reconcile the Court's rejection of the good faith exception with the deterrent justification for *Massiah* suppression, there are some difficulties doing so. If officers who are investigating separate, uncharged offenses are engaging in the responsible performance of their obligations to protect society, then it seems odd to discourage them from doing so. That will, however, be the inevitable consequence of suppression designed to deter counsel deprivations in situations where officers simultaneously violate the pretrial promise of counsel while pursuing information about uncharged offenses. A suppression doctrine premised on the view that a Sixth Amendment deprivation only occurs upon the use of evidence at trial can more comfortably accommodate both the accused's interest in a fair adversarial process and society's interest in encouraging officers to pursue legitimate investigations.

Because *Massiah*'s doctrinal requisites—the circumstances that constitute a denial of the pretrial right to assistance—are few in number and relatively clear, the opportunities for reasonable mistaken beliefs about whether an encounter violates the Sixth Amendment would seem to be limited.[222] Still, an officer might reasonably be unaware that an individual has been formally charged with a particular offense and therefore might understandably believe that the person is not yet entitled to assistance at the time he elicits information.[223] An agent might reasonably conclude that the few words spoken during an encounter with a charged defendant did not constitute "deliberate elicitation" and, thus, that the encounter was not a critical stage of the prosecution entitling the defendant to assistance.[224] Officers might even have a reasonable basis for believing that an accused knowingly and voluntarily waived his right to counsel under circumstances falling just short of satisfying the controlling standards for the valid surrender of this constitutional right. On the other hand, it seems unlikely that government officials could be reasonably mistaken in situations where they are charged with deliberate elicitation by their informants.[225] In those settings, an informant's acts are attributable to the government when officials either intentionally create or knowingly exploit an opportunity to confront the defendant without counsel.[226] The government cannot disavow responsibility for an

222. This stands in dramatic contrast to the opportunities for officers to have reasonable, mistaken beliefs about compliance with the numerous, less clear Fourth Amendment standards dictating whether searches or seizures are unreasonable. *See* Steiker, *Counter-Revolution, supra* note 180, at 2526 (suggesting that the good faith question rarely arises under *Massiah* because the Sixth Amendment doctrine seems to contain a culpability standard).

223. The basis for a mistaken belief could be a misunderstanding or ignorance concerning the facts or it might be uncertainty about the legal significance of a particular event—that is, whether the steps taken by the authorities amount to the initiation of adversarial proceedings necessary to convert a suspect into an accused and trigger attachment of the right to counsel. The latter, however, is unlikely because there are few ambiguities about what constitutes a formal accusation.

224. The Court has never provided a clear or comprehensive definition of "deliberate elicitation," the conduct that constitutes a critical stage of the prosecution and entitles an accused to assistance. It is clear that mere conversation by an informant is sufficient, *see* United States v. Henry, 447 U.S. 264, 271 (1980), while passive listening is not. *See* Kuhlmann v. Wilson, 477 U.S. 436, 456 (1986). However, it is uncertain, for example, whether a nod of an informant's head coupled with a word or two would suffice. Officers' conduct need not rise to the level of "interrogation," *see* Fellers v. United States, 540 U.S. 519, 524 (2004), but whether a few comments are sufficient is arguable.

225. There could still be a reasonable mistake about whether the defendant had been formally charged. The question considered here is whether officials could reasonably believe that an encounter between an accused and the informant did not violate an accused's Sixth Amendment right.

226. Maine v. Moulton, 474 U.S. 159, 176, 180 (1985); *Henry*, 447 U.S. at 274.

informant's affirmative elicitation of information from an accused if it "'must have known'" that the informant would take steps to elicit such information.[227] If this standard is satisfied—that is, if the circumstances show that the government must have known what the informant would do—the government could hardly claim that it was reasonable to believe that there was no deprivation of counsel. If officials must have known their informant would elicit disclosures, they could not reasonably believe that the confrontation was consistent with the Sixth Amendment entitlement to assistance.

In those probably rare situations where a reasonable mistake about a *Massiah* violation is plausible, it is likely that the Court would recognize an exception to the Sixth Amendment exclusionary rule. The good faith exceptions to the Fourth Amendment suppression doctrine rest on cost-benefit balancing. According to the Court, in situations where officers violate constitutional rights, but it is reasonable to believe that they have acted constitutionally, the costs of exclusion outweigh any possible deterrent benefits. Initially, the Fourth Amendment exceptions were confined to situations in which the constitutional errors were made by actors other than law enforcement officers—judges, legislators, and court employees, for example—and officers acted in reasonable reliance on those errors. More recently, however, the Court has indicated that an exception to the exclusionary rule is justified when officers themselves are the source of reasonable mistakes. Because *Massiah*'s Sixth Amendment exclusion doctrine also rests on a deterrent foundation, that same cost-benefit assessment would justify good faith exceptions to Sixth Amendment suppression identical to those that qualify the Fourth Amendment rule. The trend toward expansion of the good faith doctrine under the Fourth Amendment suggests that evidence would be admissible, despite denials of the pretrial right to counsel, whenever it was reasonable for officers to believe that they were not acting in violation of the Sixth Amendment guarantee.[228]

A different conclusion would follow if the Sixth Amendment suppression doctrine was understood as an integral part of the right to counsel guarantee. According to that view, the use of evidence at trial completes the constitutional wrong, inflicting the harm that the assistance of counsel is designed to prevent. The entitlement not to be convicted on the basis of the evidentiary products

---

227. *Moulton*, 474 U.S. at 176 n.12.

228. In the Fourth Amendment arena, the Court has even suggested that unreasonable mistakes by officers should not lead to suppression. In *Herring v. United States*, 555 U.S. ____, ____, 129 S.Ct. 695, 702 (2009), the Court indicated that deterrent cost-benefit balancing favors the admission of evidence unless officers' unconstitutional conduct is deliberate, reckless, or part of a pattern of recurrent negligence. *Id.* A similar threshold culpability criterion could be imposed on the *Massiah* suppression doctrine. For an analysis of the implications of *Herring*, see *supra* Chapter 1, text accompanying notes 199–203.

of imbalanced adversarial confrontations would seem to mandate exclusion whether or not officers reasonably believed that the accused was not deprived of his constitutional entitlement during a pretrial encounter. The protection that this fundamental constitutional guarantee extends cannot be contracted by the reasonable beliefs of government officials. An accused has an entitlement to assistance and to enforcement of that entitlement by suppression, even if the government officials who conducted an uncounseled pretrial confrontation lacked fault. In sum, this variety of good faith exception is legitimate only because the Court characterized Sixth Amendment suppression as a deterrent safeguard, not a constitutional right.

e. A Possible Public Safety Exception Does a reasonable belief that confronting an unassisted defendant is necessary to serve an important public safety interest justify an exception to the *Massiah* exclusionary rule? Suppose officers induce a formally charged individual to make admissions because they reasonably believe it is necessary to save a kidnap victim's life. Instead, assume that agents who reasonably believe that an accused person possesses critical information needed to defeat a terrorist plot recruit an informant to elicit that information from the defendant. The question these hypotheticals raise is whether the prosecution should be entitled to use deliberately elicited admissions to prove an offense that was the subject of a formal accusation *if* the motive for the elicitation was the prevention of a serious public safety threat. Under the prevailing rationale for Sixth Amendment suppression, the answer to this issue seems debatable.[229]

As discussed in Chapter 3, *Miranda*'s exclusion doctrine is qualified by a public safety exception. Even though officers have not warned a suspect of her rights prior to custodial interrogation, a confession is admissible if the questions asked were reasonably prompted by a public safety concern.[230] This exception is firmly rooted in the unique nature of and justifications for *Miranda*'s evidentiary bar. The question is whether a similar exception can be reconciled with *Massiah*'s very different rule and premises. The issue is similar, but not identical, to the question of whether an exception is warranted when officers are motivated by a good faith investigation of a separate offense. The noteworthy difference between the two situations is that the interest at stake—the prevention of some serious public danger—is weightier than the general societal interest in proving

---

229. The question has never reached the Supreme Court, perhaps because it is relatively unlikely that a need for information to defeat a public safety threat will develop *after* the government has formally charged an accused with an offense. If the threat occurs before formal charges, there would be no right to counsel and no basis for Sixth Amendment exclusion. *See* Joseph W. Yockey, *The Case for a Sixth Amendment Public-Safety Exception After* Dickerson, 2004 U. Ill. L. Rev. 501, 531–35 (2004).

230. *See supra* Chapter 3, text accompanying notes 154–70.

uncharged offenses. For that reason, a different resolution of the cost-benefit balance might be appropriate.

If Sixth Amendment suppression were part of the right to counsel—a necessary safeguard against completion of the constitutional deprivation begun by an unaided pretrial confrontation—the answer to the public safety question would be clear. Under the Fifth Amendment, truly compelled revelations may never be used to convict a defendant no matter how serious the need to force disclosures. A public safety exception to the guarantee against compulsory self-incrimination is unacceptable because that guarantee is unqualified.[231] The prohibition on conviction based on thoughts forced from one's mind is absolute. The balance struck by the Bill of Rights is not subject to modification by the judiciary. Because the Sixth Amendment right to trial counsel is also unqualified, a public safety exception seems irreconcilable with a right-based suppression doctrine. The government may not suspend the fundamental adversary system guarantee of assistance because doing so would better enable it to protect the public. A conviction cannot be fueled by the products of a constitutionally forbidden confrontation at or before trial because there is no exception to the adversary system principle of fair play reflected in the Sixth Amendment. The right to counsel, like the Fifth Amendment privilege, cannot be diluted by judicial interest-balancing.[232]

The Supreme Court, however, has decided that Sixth Amendment exclusion is not a personal trial right, but, instead, is a safeguard needed to ensure respect for and to enforce the pretrial right to assistance.[233] It is a forward-looking deterrent sanction, the application of which hinges on cost-benefit balancing.[234] Based on this characterization of the *Massiah* suppression doctrine, the validity of a public safety exception is arguable.

On the one hand, if officials know that there are no evidentiary consequences of uncounseled confrontations reasonably believed necessary to promote public safety, the incentives they would otherwise have to avoid such confrontations would be vitiated. *Massiah*'s pretrial right to assistance would be seriously undermined, perhaps eviscerated, in those situations. Deprivations of the Sixth Amendment entitlement to counsel would become routine. It is arguable that the need to exclude evidence to discourage such deprivations outweighs the

231. *See supra* Chapter 2, text accompanying notes 208–13.

232. According to the right-based view of suppression, there would be no constitutional problem with officers inducing an accused to make revelations necessary to protect the public. The pretrial encounter itself would not violate the Sixth Amendment. Officers would be free to carry out their protective functions, but would know that any evidence they acquired in violation of the *Massiah* constraints would be inadmissible at the trial of a charged offense. It would, of course, be admissible to prove uncharged offenses that are tied to the public safety threat.

233. *See* Kansas v. Ventris, 556 U.S. ____, ____, 129 S.Ct. 1841, 1846–47 (2009).

234. *Id.*

admittedly high costs of exclusion.[235] If the right to pretrial assistance is an unqualified right—if an accused is entitled to the protection of counsel even in situations where the public safety is endangered—then it would seem indefensible to suspend all efforts to enforce that right by recognizing a categorical public safety exception.[236]

A public safety exception would eliminate the ordinary incentives not to conduct imbalanced encounters with defendants. The arguments favoring such an exception rest on the premise that the cost-benefit balance supports complete suspension of the suppression sanction in public safety contexts. In the first place, any deterrence of *Massiah* violations achieved by suppression is arguably less significant because of the nature of the right being enforced. According to the prevailing understanding, the pretrial right to counsel granted by *Massiah* doctrine exists entirely apart from the trial and is not an integral part of the adversary system entitlement not to be convicted on the basis of an imbalanced confrontation. A violation of this right is fully accomplished at the time information is elicited.[237] One can plausibly contend that this pretrial entitlement to assistance is not of the same fundamental stature as the core right to assistance at trial. When an accused is deprived of trial counsel, there is an increased risk of conviction in violation of adversarial system principles of fair play. When pretrial assistance is denied, there is simply a risk that a vulnerable accused will be induced to make incriminating disclosures to the government. If the pretrial right is less valuable because the harms it guards against are not as serious, any deterrent gains from suppression are less important and not as weighty in the cost-benefit balance. Evidentiary exclusion protects future accused persons against pretrial exploitation by the government, but does not further the fairness of the trial itself.[238]

---

235. The social costs in these situations are high because they include not only impairments of the ability to convict guilty defendants but also impediments to efforts to protect the public from imminent dangers. The argument in the text rests on the premise that these social costs are the price we must pay for an essential Bill of Rights liberty, the Sixth Amendment right to assistance.

236. Perhaps other exceptions to the *Massiah* bar might be more generously applied in public safety situations because of the additional costs involved. As long as some deterrent threat exists, additional deterrent gains could be more readily outweighed by the potential public injuries occasioned by discouraging officers from eliciting information from an accused.

237. *See Ventris*, 556 U.S. at ____, 129 S.Ct. at 1846.

238. The reasoning here has similarities to reasoning employed by the Supreme Court to narrow the *Miranda* exclusion doctrine. Because suppression under *Miranda* deters violations of prophylactic constraints upon custodial interrogation, not deprivations of Fifth Amendment rights by police officers, the interest in deterring official misconduct is less substantial. *See* Oregon v. Elstad, 470 U.S. 298, 306, 308–09, 318 (1985) (indicating

Moreover, the Framers of the Bill of Rights guaranteed a right to trial assistance that they deemed essential to fair courtroom processes. They did not contemplate a right to pretrial assistance because the government did not confront accused persons prior to trial at the time.[239] The cost of the trial right they provided was impairment of the state's ability to convict accused persons. It seems unlikely that in prescribing the right to trial assistance they would have considered the countervailing interest in preventing public safety threats.[240] The pretrial extension of the right to assistance, however, can impede official efforts to prevent immediate, and serious, threats to public safety. The Framers struck a balance that provided an unqualified right to assistance at trial. When faced with the more compelling interests involved in public safety situations, they might have decided that the benefits of assistance were not worth the costs. As a consequence, they might have restricted the right to pretrial assistance, suspending its enjoyment when the public safety is endangered. The point is that the Sixth Amendment might not reflect the Framers' views of the significance of public safety costs.

In addition, it is arguable that little deterrence of pretrial counsel deprivations would be gained by exclusion in public safety situations. Officers who believe that information is necessary to prevent a serious public safety threat are unlikely to be deterred by the threat of suppression. The reasons to ignore the counsel guarantee are powerful and the exclusion sanction may be powerless to counteract those reasons in the vast majority of public safety cases. Suspending the exclusionary rule would do little to undermine enforcement of the pretrial right to assistance. Application of the suppression sanction would discourage few, if any, deprivations. Thus, suppressing evidence might well be an ineffective gesture that cannot produce deterrent gains sufficient to offset the social costs of excluding probative evidence.[241]

In sum, a public safety exception to the *Massiah* exclusionary rule could be deemed consistent with the deterrent objectives of that rule.[242] Whether the

---

that the Fourth Amendment fruits doctrine does not extend to *Miranda* contexts because suppression does not deter official violations of constitutional rights).

239. *See* United States v. Ash, 413 U.S. 300, 309–10 (1973); United States v. Wade, 388 U.S. 218, 224 (1967).

240. Of course, the Framers probably would have taken into account the long-term costs to the public safety inherent in impeding the conviction of guilty, dangerous defendants. They are not likely to have considered the more imminent threats to the public safety that might also be at stake in pretrial encounters with defendants.

241. If a deterrent sanction is impotent in public safety situations, there would be no public safety costs from suppressing evidence. The only costs resulting from exclusion would be the typical costs to the courtroom search for truth. Without measurable deterrent gains, however, those costs could not be justified.

242. Although the currently prevailing conception of the *Massiah* right supports this analysis, in my view, the arguments in support of a public safety exception highlight the

Supreme Court will strike the balance of interests in favor of endorsing such an exception remains to be seen.

f. Impeachment Use of the Products of *Massiah* Violations The final issue concerning the scope of *Massiah*'s exclusion doctrine is the propriety of an impeachment use exception. In *Kansas v. Ventris*, an opinion that is central to this discussion and analysis of the operational details of Sixth Amendment suppression, the Court confronted that question. The specific issue was whether the prosecution is allowed to impeach the direct testimony of an accused with statements secured by an informant in violation of the *Massiah* counsel guarantee. A seven-Justice majority held that impeachment use is constitutionally permissible.[243] The Court observed that whether otherwise inadmissible evidence can be used "for purposes of impeachment depends upon the nature of the constitutional guarantee that is violated."[244] If the justification for suppression is that trial use of excluded evidence would violate the Constitution, as is the case with the Fifth Amendment bar to compelled disclosures, then impeachment use is forbidden.[245] On the other hand, if suppression is not necessary "to avoid violation of [a] substantive guarantee" in court, but, instead, is a "deterrent sanction" designed to prevent future constitutional transgressions outside the courtroom, the balance of relevant interests can justify impeachment use.[246] To decide whether evidence obtained in violation of *Massiah* could be used to impeach defendants, the Court had to identify the nature and objectives of the Sixth Amendment right to pretrial assistance and its evidentiary bar.

The original understanding reflected in *Massiah* itself—that evidence was inadmissible because use at trial completed the Sixth Amendment violation—would have required a bar to impeachment use. The government would not be allowed to impeach an accused with deliberately elicited revelations because such use would violate the counsel guarantee.[247] If the Sixth Amendment stood as a safeguard against the harms inflicted by conviction based on the fruits of

---

logical weaknesses in the Court's understanding of the *Massiah* entitlement to counsel and its evidentiary bar. As already indicated, I find irrational the notion that the pretrial extension of assistance is designed to protect against the immediate consequences of unaided encounters and is not concerned with guarding against consequences at trial—enhanced risks of conviction—flowing directly from those encounters.

243. 556 U.S. ____, ____, 129 S.Ct. 1841, 1847 (2009). For a pre-*Ventris* analysis of impeachment use, see Tomkovicz, Massiah *Right to Exclusion*, *supra* note 98, at 787–89.

244. *Ventris*, 556 U.S. at ____, 129 S.Ct. at 1845.

245. *Id.*

246. *Id.*

247. The analysis would be similar to that which led to the conclusion that impeachment use of coerced statements is constitutionally impermissible. Impeachment use of coerced statements is forbidden because their introduction for even that limited purpose violates both due process and the privilege against compulsory self-incrimination. *See supra* Chapter 2, text accompanying notes 241–45.

imbalanced pretrial confrontations, it would afford shelter against the damage done by the use of those fruits to cast doubt on an accused's credibility. Although the constitutional injury from impeachment would not be as severe as it is when statements are introduced as substantive proof of guilt, it would still be the sort of injury the Sixth Amendment prohibits. No incriminating use of improperly elicited statements could be reconciled with a personal right to exclusion rooted in the Sixth Amendment guarantee of assistance.[248]

The *Ventris* Court, however, rejected the contention that *Massiah* exclusion is a personal right necessary to ensure "the prevention of a constitutional violation" at trial.[249] According to the majority, "the *Massiah* right is a right to be free of uncounseled interrogation, and is infringed at the time of the interrogation."[250] The Court deemed it "illogical to say that the right is not violated until . . . the . . . admission into evidence" of a statement secured by means of that confrontation. Rather, "[t]he assistance of counsel [is] denied . . . at the prior critical stage which produced the inculpatory evidence" and "[i]t is *that* deprivation which demands a remedy."[251] The Sixth Amendment deprivation occurs and is completed at the time of the pretrial confrontation.[252]

Because exclusion under *Massiah* is a sanction for a fully accomplished transgression, a device designed to discourage future uncounseled confrontations, cost-benefit balancing is appropriate.[253] The Court found "no distinction" in the Sixth Amendment context "that would alter the balance" already struck under the Fourth Amendment and *Miranda* exclusionary rules.[254] A bar to impeachment "would add little appreciable deterrence" because the statements are already excluded for substantive purposes and because officers are not likely to be motivated by the "exceedingly small" chance that the evidence "would be of use for impeachment."[255] Moreover, the costs to the truth-finding process and to the integrity of the trial from barring impeachment of a defendant's testimony by prior contradictory statements outweighed the "'speculative possibility'" that

---

248. *See Ventris*, 556 U.S. at ____, 129 S.Ct. at 1848 (Stevens, J., dissenting); Michigan v. Harvey, 494 U.S. 344, 355 (1990) (Stevens, J., dissenting); *see also* Tomkovicz, Massiah *Right to Exclusion, supra* note 98, at 767, 787–89.

249. *Ventris*, 556 U.S. at ____, 129 S.Ct. at 1846.

250. *Id.* Inexplicably, after a unanimous Court in *Fellers v. United States*, 540 U.S. 519, 524 (2004) took great pains to unravel the confusion created by prior references to "interrogation" in *Massiah* opinions, in *Ventris*, Justice Scalia more than once referred to the conduct that is the concern of *Massiah* as "interrogation." *Ventris*, 556 U.S. at ____, 129 S.Ct. at 1845–46.

251. *Ventris*, 556 U.S. at ____, 129 S.Ct. at 1846 (emphasis in original).

252. *Id.*

253. *Id.*

254. *Id.* at ____, 129 S.Ct. at 1847.

255. *Id.*

some right to counsel violations would be deterred.[256] In sum, once the Court decided that *Massiah* exclusion was analogous in character to Fourth Amendment suppression, the same reasoning that supported an impeachment use exception for the search and seizure exclusionary rule dictated an identical exception for the Sixth Amendment rule.

Ventris involved the use of statements an undercover informant elicited to impeach a defendant's direct examination testimony. The exception recognized clearly extends to statements elicited by known officers. Moreover, because the Court found no distinction between the Sixth and Fourth Amendment contexts, it would surely permit the government to impeach testimony a defendant gives in response to proper cross-examination by the government.[257] If the prosecutor has induced the testimony by legitimate questioning of the accused, improperly-obtained inconsistent pretrial statements may be used to cast doubt on the testimony's credibility. Moreover, just as the Fourth Amendment permits the state to use illegally-obtained tangible evidence to contradict a defendant's trial testimony, tangible items barred from trial by the Sixth Amendment derivative evidence principle may be introduced to call an accused's veracity into question.[258] Finally, as long as the Court adheres to the view that evidence obtained in violation of the Fourth Amendment may *not* be used to impeach *a defense witness*,[259] there is every reason to believe that it will similarly restrict the scope of the Sixth Amendment impeachment use exception. Consequently, if an alibi witness testifies at trial that the defendant was on a trip with her at the time of an alleged robbery, the defendant's uncounseled admission that he was present at the scene of the robbery may not be used to cast doubt on the credibility of the alibi witness's inconsistent courtroom account.

The impeachment use exception provides a final, graphic illustration of how much the rationales for constitutional exclusion matter. Because *Massiah* exclusion has been cast as a mere deterrent sanction, not an essential part of the entitlement to assistance, the government will have considerable opportunities

---

256. *Ventris*, 556 U.S. at ____, 129 S.Ct. at 1847 (quoting Oregon v. Hass, 420 U.S. 714, 723 (1975)). A particularly weighty consideration in the balance was the cost of having to "allow[] perjurious statements [at trial] to go unchallenged." *Id.* Allowing impeachment use of illegally obtained evidence serves "'the need to prevent perjury and to assure the integrity of the trial process.'" *Id* at 1846 (quoting Stone v. Powell, 428 U.S. 465, 488 (1976)).

257. *See* United States v. Havens, 446 U.S. 620, 627–28 (1980) (allowing the fruits of a Fourth Amendment violation to be used to impeach responses to cross-examination). For a discussion of the contours of the Fourth Amendment impeachment use exception, see *supra* Chapter 1, text accompanying notes 261–71.

258. *See Havens*, 446 U.S. at 623, 628 (allowing impeachment use of tee shirts illegally found in defendant's luggage).

259. *See* James v. Illinois, 493 U.S. 307, 319–20 (1990). There is reason to suspect that if the Court were to revisit this issue today it might not reach the same conclusion.

to place evidence secured in violation of the pretrial counsel guarantee before jurors.[260] Had the Court adopted the *Massiah* Court's vision of Sixth Amendment suppression—that "[t]he use of ill-gotten evidence during any phase of criminal prosecution does damage to the adversarial process—the fairness of which the Sixth Amendment was designed to protect"[261]—then it would have concluded that impeachment use, like substantive use, was an impermissible deprivation of the right to counsel.

E. CONCLUDING REFLECTIONS UPON *MASSIAH*'S SIXTH AMENDMENT EXCLUSIONARY RULE

Like the Fourth Amendment exclusionary rule, the Fifth and Fourteenth Amendment bars to coerced confessions, and *Miranda*'s bar to confessions, the Sixth Amendment exclusion doctrine began as an inseparable part of the constitutional right on which it is based. At its inception, the bar to deliberately elicited disclosures was thought necessary to avoid violation of the right to the assistance of counsel. The radical transformation of the *Miranda* rule commenced within 5 years of its arrival.[262] The conversion of the *Mapp* rule into a mere deterrent safeguard began less than a decade after it appeared.[263] The *Massiah* bar, however, did not lose its status as a constitutional right until quite recently.[264] Because the Supreme Court neither reaffirmed nor disavowed the original conception, the status and objectives of Sixth Amendment suppression were uncertain during the first 45 years of its existence. It was possible that the Court would ultimately remain faithful to the right-based understanding of *Massiah*'s exclusion doctrine.

In 2009, faced with the issue of whether statements obtained in violation of *Massiah* could be used for impeachment purposes, the Court was forced to explain the nature of right to counsel exclusion. Unfortunately, the Justices chose

---

260. The jurors must be given limiting instructions informing them that they are not allowed to use the evidence as substantive proof of guilt, but may use it only for its relevance to the defendant's credibility. Moreover, in deciding whether there is sufficient evidence to sustain a conviction, the substantive value of this evidence does not count.

261. *Ventris*, 556 U.S. at ____, 129 S.Ct. at 1848 (Stevens, J., dissenting).

262. *See* Harris v. New York, 401 U.S. 222 (1971).

263. *See* Alderman v. United States, 394 U.S. 165 (1969). It is true that the Fourth Amendment right to exclusion in federal court originated in 1914, in *Weeks v. United States*, 232 U.S. 383 (1914), and retained its elevated constitutional status for over 50 years. Because the vast majority of criminal prosecutions occurred in state courts during that time, however, the federal search and seizure rule had little practical impact. After the rule was extended to the states in *Mapp v. Ohio*, 367 U.S. 643 (1961), its days as an integral part of the Fourth Amendment were numbered.

264. *See Ventris*, 556 U.S. at ____, 129 S.Ct. at 1846.

to disavow *Massiah*'s original character and to demote it from constitutional right to mere deterrent sanction. This inadequately explained, logically indefensible characterization of the Sixth Amendment's evidentiary bar surely will dictate the resolution of future issues involving its operation and contours. It is more than unlikely that the Court will correct its misstep and restore the status of *Massiah*'s exclusion doctrine. On the other hand, having declared that the suppression sanction plays a significant role in preventing future uncounseled confrontations, it seems unlikely that the Court will abolish the Sixth Amendment bar.

There are a number of undecided questions concerning the reach of the *Massiah* exclusionary rule. The Court has never addressed whether Sixth Amendment exclusion claims are cognizable in habeas corpus challenges to state convictions, whether a standing limitation governs, whether the traditional attenuation exception applies, whether "good faith" violations of the right to counsel dictate suppression, whether successive confessions should be barred, whether a public safety exception is legitimate, or whether improperly gained statements may be used to impeach defense witnesses. Because the nature and purposes of Sixth Amendment exclusion are identical to the nature and purposes of Fourth Amendment exclusion, the cost-benefit balancing analysis that has led the Court to impose numerous restrictions on the *Weeks-Mapp* rule will surely yield similar constraints upon the *Massiah* rule. When faced with Sixth Amendment suppression questions in future cases, the Court is likely to favor admissibility, concluding that the weighty social costs of barring deliberately elicited revelations and their evidentiary products outweigh additional deterrent benefits resulting from suppression. Resolutions that could not be reconciled with a conception of exclusion as an indivisible part of the right to counsel will be deemed entirely compatible with the deterrent objectives the Court has endorsed.

5. SIXTH AMENDMENT EXCLUSION OF EYEWITNESS IDENTIFICATIONS

INTRODUCTION

The next two chapters both address constitutional doctrines that dictate the suppression of a particular category of evidence—eyewitness identifications. As the discussions will show, these two exclusionary rules have the briefest, least complicated histories of all of the constitutional suppression mandates analyzed in this text. Moreover, the Supreme Court's explanations of their underpinnings, contours, and details have been considerably less extensive. Unlike the exclusion doctrines discussed in earlier chapters, the constitutional bars to eyewitness identification evidence have not generated ongoing controversy. For a number of reasons, they are not currently the topics of debate and division among judges or legal scholars.[1]

The subject of this chapter is the Sixth Amendment exclusion of eyewitness identifications based on the right to counsel. Like the *Massiah* rule discussed in Chapter 4, which declares statements inadmissible when obtained by means of pretrial encounters with defendants in the absence of counsel, this doctrine bars certain eyewitness identifications secured as a result of pretrial confrontations of accused individuals in the absence of counsel. However, unlike *Massiah*, which has been the subject of continual development up to the present day, the Sixth Amendment suppression mandate that is the topic of this chapter stopped evolving over 30 years ago. Moreover, while the Supreme Court has recently clarified the foundational premises of the *Massiah* mandate, the constitutional justifications for right-to-counsel-based exclusion of eyewitness identification evidence remain quite opaque. Of the five Supreme Court opinions that resolve issues concerning the right to counsel and eyewitness identification evidence, only two

---

1. The perils engendered by the use of eyewitness identification evidence are still a subject of much concern to commentators. *See* Amy Luria, *Showup Identifications: A Comprehensive Overview of the Problems and a Discussion of Necessary Changes*, 86 Neb. L. Rev. 515 (2008) [hereinafter Luria, *Showup Identifications*]; Sandra Guerra Thompson, *Beyond a Reasonable Doubt? Reconsidering Uncorroborated Eyewitness Identification Testimony*, 41 U.C. Davis L. Rev. 1487 (2008) [hereinafter Thompson, *Reconsidering Identification Testimony*]; Gary L. Wells & Eric P. Seelau, *Eyewitness Identification: Psychological Research and Legal Policy on Lineups*, 1 Psychol. Pub. Pol'y & L. 765 (1995) [hereinafter Wells & Seelau, *Eyewitness Identification*]. The constitutional exclusion doctrines, however, are seldom the focus of concern or discussion today.

devote any time to exclusionary rule issues.[2] The other opinions focus upon the scope of the pretrial entitlement to counsel that is the basis for suppressing identification evidence.

The focus here is on evidentiary exclusion, not on the underlying constitutional right to the assistance of counsel. However, as prior chapters have made clear, one cannot intelligently discuss and analyze evidentiary suppression without a basic understanding of the foundational right that dictates inadmissibility. The breadth of the suppression sanction is intimately and inseparably linked to the breadth of the right to legal assistance. Consequently, the discussion that follows will describe the pretrial contexts that trigger an entitlement to assistance and thereby furnish a predicate for evidentiary suppression.

After a cursory description of the exclusionary rule, this chapter will recount the brief history of Sixth Amendment suppression of identifications. The discussion will then turn to the potential rationales for exclusion and will assess the legitimacy of suppressing identifications of defendants made in the absence of counsel. The chapter will close with an examination of the limited number of operational details that have emerged from the Court's infrequent encounters with this exclusion doctrine and with analyses of the propriety of various restrictions that might be imposed.

A. THE BASIC SIXTH AMENDMENT BAR TO EYEWITNESS IDENTIFICATION EVIDENCE

Chapter 4 discussed the Supreme Court's 1964 extension of the Sixth Amendment right to trial counsel to "informal" pretrial confrontations in which government agents deliberately elicit statements from accused persons. Three years later, in *United States v. Wade*,[3] the Court identified an additional "informal" pretrial context that justified another extension of the constitutional entitlement to the assistance of counsel. According to the *Wade* doctrine, as developed in later cases, an individual who is the subject of a formal criminal accusation[4] is entitled to legal assistance when the government conducts a lineup (or other identification

---

2. These two opinions are *United States v. Wade*, 388 U.S. 218 (1967) and *Gilbert v. California*, 388 U.S. 263 (1967), the landmark decisions that first recognized an entitlement to counsel in identification contexts and announced an exclusion doctrine rooted in that entitlement.

3. 388 U.S. 218 (1967).

4. *Wade* involved a lineup that took place after the defendant had been indicted. In *Kirby v. Illinois*, 406 U.S. 682 (1972), a plurality of the Court declared that the Sixth Amendment entitlement to assistance at identification procedures attaches *only* "at or after the initiation of adversary judicial criminal proceedings." *Id.* at 689 (plurality opinion). Later, this bright line of demarcation gained majority endorsement. *See* Moore v. Illinois, 434 U.S. 220, 226–27 (1977). Prior to formal accusation, when an individual is

procedure at which the accused is physically present) designed to secure an eyewitness's identification of the person she observed engaging in criminal conduct. In the Court's view, a pretrial confrontation of the accused for identification purposes is "a critical stage of the prosecution."[5] For that reason, the Sixth Amendment guarantee of assistance at trial extends to such a confrontation.[6] The government violates this fundamental constitutional entitlement when it confronts an accused in the absence of counsel,[7] unless the accused has knowingly and voluntarily waived the entitlement to a lawyer's aid.[8]

If the defendant does not have either retained or appointed counsel at such an encounter and has not relinquished the right to such assistance, a witness's statement identifying him as the person she saw committing the charged crime is inadmissible at trial to prove the defendant's guilt. Suppose, for example, that a man who has been arraigned for a rape is placed in a lineup with four other men. When asked if they see the offender, the rape victim and a bystander indicate that the defendant was the perpetrator. The prosecution may not use these identifications to establish that the defendant was the rapist if he was not assisted by counsel at the lineup and did not choose to forego assistance. Alternatively, assume that a woman who has been indicted for selling cocaine is brought by the police into the presence of an informant who purchased the narcotics. The informant asserts that she is, in fact, the woman who sold him drugs. If counsel was not present and the woman made no choice to relinquish her right to counsel, the informant's assertion must be excluded from trial.

As will be seen, the Court has narrowed the circumstances giving rise to a right to assistance, thereby limiting the situations that dictate suppression. The exclusion doctrine itself, however, has undergone virtually no development since it was first announced in 1967. From the start, identifications made at sessions involving a denial of assistance—the immediate products of the uncounseled confrontation—have been *per se* excluded.[9] The prosecution is barred from introducing such evidence. In addition, a limited derivative evidence principle has applied since the inception of the doctrine. If a witness identifies a defendant at a pretrial session conducted in violation of the Sixth Amendment, a subsequent identification of the accused by the same witness is presumptively subject to suppression.[10] The government may not use a later identification, even if the accused has assistance at the time it is made, unless it proves by clear and convincing

---

still a mere suspect, there is no right to counsel at any identification confrontation arranged by government officials. *See infra* text accompanying notes 57–67, 142–46.

5. *See Wade*, 388 U.S. at 237.

6. *See id.*

7. *See Moore*, 434 U.S. at 231–32; *Kirby*, 406 U.S. at 683 (plurality opinion).

8. *See Wade*, 388 U.S. at 237.

9. *See Gilbert*, 388 U.S. at 272–73; *Wade*, 388 U.S. at 240 n.32.

10. *See Wade*, 388 U.S. at 240–41.

evidence that the "origin" or "source" of that identification was independent of the pretrial identification procedure.[11] In essence, the prosecution must show that the witness's subsequent identification was based upon observations of the accused at the scene of the crime, and was not the result of seeing him at the uncounseled identification procedure.[12] Thus, in the earlier hypothetical situations, once a rape victim and bystander have identified an accused rapist at an unconstitutional lineup, the government may not call either witness to identify the defendant from the witness stand at the rape trial. Such in-court identification testimony by the witnesses must be suppressed unless the prosecution demonstrates it is not the product of seeing the defendant at the pretrial lineup. Similarly, once an informant has indicated that the woman presented to him was the person who sold him cocaine, any later identification of that woman by the informant before or at the trial is barred, even if the woman has counsel at that later time. To introduce a subsequent identification, the prosecution must show that it was based on the informant's memory of the sale. In effect, the state must rebut a presumption that an earlier identification process is, in fact, the basis for any subsequent identification by the same witness.

In the few pertinent opinions since *Wade*, the Supreme Court has not addressed a single facet of the scope or details of the exclusionary rule's operation. It has addressed none of the exclusionary rule questions that have been resolved for other suppression mandates. Consequently, we do not know whether the *Wade-Gilbert* exclusionary rule is limited by a standing limitation, whether it operates only at trial or in other settings, whether other types of evidence derived from an improper identification are subject to suppression, and whether any of the exceptions recognized in other contexts—attenuation, inevitable discovery, good faith, public safety or exigency, or impeachment use—constrain the operation of this Sixth Amendment suppression doctrine. The final section of the chapter will explore these topics. However, because they are of limited significance, they will not receive the depth of treatment accorded them in previous chapters. An account of the history of the *Wade-Gilbert* exclusionary rule and an exploration of the underlying premises for and the constitutional legitimacy of this Sixth Amendment evidentiary bar will precede this doctrinal exploration.

B. THE ORIGINS AND DEVELOPMENT OF RIGHT TO COUNSEL SUPPRESSION OF EYEWITNESS IDENTIFICATIONS

The two constitutional bars to eyewitness identification evidence—the Sixth Amendment rule discussed here and the due process rule that is the subject of

11. *See id.* at 240–42.
12. *See id.* at 240.

Chapter 6—are the last-born of the seven suppression doctrines addressed in this text. They arrived on the same day in 1967, the year after *Miranda* had declared certain confessions inadmissible on Fifth Amendment grounds, and three years after *Massiah* had first found a Sixth Amendment foundation for excluding incriminating statements. Moreover, it is interesting and noteworthy that these two doctrines, quite unlike any of the other constitutional bases for exclusion, both reached full maturity within a decade of their birth. The Supreme Court has not decided a single case dealing with either basis for eyewitness identification suppression since 1977, and there are no signs of any interest in the subjects.

Prior to 1967, eyewitness identification evidence was not subject to constitutional control. The only sources of restriction on admissibility were nonconstitutional rules of evidence. The primary means of combating risks of injustice posed by eyewitness identification evidence were adversarial confrontation of witnesses in the courtroom and arguments to jurors regarding the deficiencies and worth of the evidence.[13] The Warren Court was troubled by the inherent unreliability of eyewitness identification evidence and the increased risks of injustice from suggestive identification procedures that could mislead witnesses. The Justices were aware of serious miscarriages of justice resulting from such evidence.[14] A majority concluded that the Constitution contained two distinct restrictions upon its admissibility. The first constraint was the Sixth Amendment right to the assistance of counsel.

In *United States v. Wade*,[15] an FBI agent had arranged a lineup that included the defendant after he had been indicted for conspiracy to rob a bank. The agent did not notify Wade's appointed lawyer of the lineup. Two bank employees identified Wade as the bank robber. These pretrial identifications were not introduced at trial, but the two employees pointed to Wade from the witness stand "when asked . . . if the robber was in the courtroom."[16] The Court's opinion opened with a forthright acknowledgment that the central issue was the admissibility of this testimony. Specifically, the "question [was] whether courtroom identifications of an accused at trial are to be excluded from evidence because the accused was exhibited to witnesses before trial at a post-indictment lineup conducted for

---

13. *See* Stovall v. Denno, 388 U.S. 293, 299–300 (1967); *see also* Fredric D. Woocher, *Did Your Eyes Deceive You? Expert Psychological Testimony on the Unreliability of Eyewitness Identification*, 29 STAN. L. REV. 969, 989 (1977).

14. The perils of injustice engendered by eyewitness identification that troubled the Warren Court remain a part of our criminal justice system and are of continuing concern to commentators. *See, e.g.*, Luria, *Showup Identifications*, *supra* note 1; Thompson, *Reconsidering Identification Testimony*, *supra* note 1; Wells & Seelau, *Eyewitness Identification*, *supra* note 1.

15. 388 U.S. 218 (1967).

16. *Id.* at 220.

identification purposes without notice to and in the absence of the accused's appointed counsel."[17]

At the outset, the Court rejected a claim that the government had violated Wade's Fifth Amendment privilege against compelled self-incrimination.[18] It then turned to the "contention that the courtroom identifications should have been excluded because the lineup was conducted without notice to and in the absence of his counsel."[19] To resolve that contention, the Court first had to decide whether the Sixth Amendment right to assistance extended to the pretrial lineup in which Wade had participated.

The majority asserted that evolutionary changes in the processes of criminal justice since adoption of the Bill of Rights had generated "critical confrontations of the accused by the prosecution at pretrial proceedings."[20] Because such confrontations "might well settle the accused's fate and reduce the trial itself to a mere formality," the Court had previously recognized that the Sixth Amendment entitlement to trial assistance had to be extended "to 'critical' stages of [criminal] proceedings."[21] A number of cases stood for the "principle that in addition to counsel's presence at trial, the accused is guaranteed that he need not stand alone against the State at any stage of the prosecution, formal or informal, in court or out, where counsel's absence might derogate from the accused's right to a fair trial."[22] As at trial, a lawyer's help at critical pretrial confrontations "assure[d] that the accused's interests [would] be protected consistently with our adversary theory of criminal prosecution."[23] Consequently, a stage was critical and triggered an entitlement to assistance if "counsel is necessary to preserve the ... basic right to a fair trial as affected by [the] right meaningfully to cross-examine ... witnesses ... and to have effective assistance of counsel at the trial itself."[24] More specifically, to decide whether counsel was necessary it was essential "to

---

17. *Id.* at 219–20.

18. *Id.* at 221–23. Forcing Wade to stand in the lineup and to speak words allegedly spoken by a robber for purposes of identification did compel his involvement in the production and acquisition of incriminating evidence that was used to secure a conviction. The Fifth Amendment, however, does not prohibit the government from compelling every kind of incriminating evidence from an accused and then using that evidence to convict. It forbids the government from compelling an individual "to give evidence having testimonial significance"—that is, to "disclose ... knowledge he might have." *Id.* at 222. According to the Court, the actions the government required Wade to perform did not force him to furnish "testimonial" evidence, and the government did not use anything Wade said or did in the lineup to secure a conviction. *Id.* at 222–23.

19. *Id.* at 223.

20. *Wade*, 388 U.S. at 224.

21. *Id.*

22. *Id.* at 226.

23. *Id.* at 227.

24. *Id.*

analyze whether potential substantial prejudice . . . inheres in the particular confrontation and [to assess] the ability of counsel to help avoid that prejudice."[25]

In the majority's view, confrontations for purposes of identification engender potential substantial prejudice for several reasons. First, eyewitness identifications of suspects are "'proverbially untrustworthy.'"[26] Put otherwise, inaccuracies of perception and memory often led to "mistaken identification."[27] Second, identification processes harbor risks of intentional and unintentional suggestion that can mislead a witness into making an erroneous identification.[28] Third, once a witness has chosen a suspect, he is unlikely to change his mind. Consequently, "'the issue of identity may . . . for all practical purposes be determined'" at the pretrial confrontation.[29] Finally, the "difficulty in depicting what transpires" at confrontations for identification purposes—that is, impediments to "reconstruct[ing] the manner and mode of . . . [the] identification for judge or jury"—severely hampers the defense's ability to expose any deficiencies in the process or any "unfairness that occurred."[30] This "may deprive [the defendant] of his only opportunity meaningfully to attack" an identification witness's "credibility,"[31] undermining the "right of cross-examination which is an essential safeguard to [the] right to confront the witnesses against him."[32] The substantial prejudice that results is the product of both the "dangers inherent in eyewitness identification and the suggestibility inherent in the context of the pretrial identification."[33] Moreover, a lawyer's presence at an identification process "can often avert prejudice," not only by ensuring effective cross-examination at trial and thereby providing an "assurance of accuracy and reliability," but also by preventing "unfairness" and lessening "the hazards of eyewitness identification" at the pretrial identification confrontation.[34] For all these reasons, the *Wade* Court had "little doubt that . . . [a] post-indictment lineup [is] a critical stage of the prosecution" at which a defendant is entitled to the assistance of counsel granted in the Sixth Amendment.[35]

25. *Wade*, 388 U.S. at 227.

26. *Id.* at 228.

27. *Id.*

28. *Id.* at 229.

29. *Id.*

30. *Wade*, 388 U.S. at 230–32.

31. *Id.* at 232.

32. *Id.* at 235.

33. *Id.* at 235; *see also* Felice J. Levine & June Louin Tapp, *The Psychology of Criminal Identification: The Gap from* Wade *to* Kirby, 121 U. Pa. L. Rev. 1079, 1130 (1973) [hereinafter Levine & Tapp, *Psychology of Criminal Identification*].

34. *Wade*, 388 U.S. at 235–36.

35. *Id.* at 236–37. The majority noted that "substitute counsel might . . . suffice where notification and presence of the suspect's own counsel would result in prejudicial delay." *Id.* at 237. Although ordinarily the Sixth Amendment right is an entitlement to assistance from one's "own counsel," in this context "substitute counsel's presence may eliminate

Having concluded that the essential predicate for evidentiary exclusion was present—that is, that the Sixth Amendment guaranteed an accused person an entitlement to legal assistance at lineups and similar identification procedures—the Court had to decide whether evidence like that introduced at Wade's trial—the in-court identifications by the bank employees who had participated in the uncounseled lineup—should be subject to suppression.[36] The majority concluded that if the sanction of exclusion was "limited solely to . . . testimony concerning identification at the" pretrial confrontation, "the right to counsel" would be rendered "empty."[37] Because a subsequent identification by a witness—a courtroom identification, for example—is often the product of an earlier pretrial identification, and because "counsel's presence at" a pretrial procedure "would equip him to attack not only the lineup identification but the courtroom identification as well," to limit "the impact of violation of the right to counsel to exclusion of evidence only of [the] identification at the lineup itself" would be to "disregard[] a critical element of that right."[38] For these reasons, the Court declared that a courtroom identification by a witness who has made an earlier identification at a pretrial confrontation would not be admissible unless the government "establish[ed] by clear and convincing evidence that the in-court identification [was] based upon observations of the suspect other than the lineup identification."[39] A judge must suppress a courtroom identification unless, after "consideration of various factors,"[40] she finds that the prosecution has shown clearly and convincingly that the "in-court identification[] ha[s] an . . . origin"

---

the hazards which render the lineup a critical stage for the presence of [a defendant's] *own* counsel." *Id.* at 237 n.27 (emphasis added). In addition, the majority observed that "[l] egislative or other regulations . . . which eliminate the risks of abuse and unintentional suggestion at lineup proceedings and the impediments to meaningful confrontation at trial may also remove the basis for regarding [a] stage as 'critical.'" *Id.* at 239. In that case, an accused would have no right to counsel, and there would be no Sixth Amendment basis for excluding any identification.

36. The Court did not have to address exclusion of an identification made *at* a pretrial confrontation conducted without counsel because the bank employees' lineup identifications of Wade were not introduced by the prosecutor at his trial. The companion decision to *Wade*, *Gilbert v. California*, *see infra* text accompanying notes 43–56, discussed the exclusion of identifications made at uncounseled pretrial sessions.

37. *Wade*, 388 U.S. at 240.

38. *Id.* at 241.

39. *Id.* at 240.

40. *Id.* at 241. The factors include: the quality of the witness's opportunity to observe the accused at the time of the crime, whether there is a discrepancy between an earlier description of the accused by the witness and the actual appearance of the accused, whether the witness identified another person before the pretrial confrontation, whether the witness identified a picture of the accused before the pretrial confrontation, whether the witness failed to identify the accused on a prior occasion, and the length of time between the alleged crime and the pretrial identification. *Id.*

or a "source" that is "independent" of the improperly conducted identification procedure.[41]

In sum, the revolutionary decision in *Wade* discerned and imposed a novel constitutional constraint upon the admissibility of eyewitness identification evidence. After deciding that pretrial confrontations for identification were critical stages of the criminal process that justified extension of the Sixth Amendment right to trial counsel, the Court concluded that deprivations of that right required evidentiary exclusion. *Wade* held that courtroom identifications made by witnesses who participated in and identified defendants at pretrial encounters conducted without counsel were barred unless their origin was independent of the constitutionally improper pretrial sessions.[42]

In *Gilbert v. California*,[43] a companion opinion issued with *Wade*, the Court fleshed out the exclusionary consequences of the new right-to-counsel doctrine. *Gilbert* was a capital case in which a number of witnesses identified the defendant at a lineup at which he was not assisted by counsel. Some identified him as the perpetrator of an armed robbery and murder for which he was ultimately tried and convicted.[44] One identified him as the resident of an apartment where incriminating evidence was found.[45] Several more witnesses identified the accused as the perpetrator of other robberies.[46] At trial, witnesses made in-court identifications and also testified that they had identified Gilbert at the lineup.[47] During the penalty stage of the proceedings, when the issue was whether the accused should be sentenced to death, several witnesses identified the defendant in connection with the other robberies and also reported "that they [had] identified Gilbert at the lineup."[48]

---

41. *Id.* at 242.

42. Like all of the Warren Court's major rulings dictating the exclusion of evidence on constitutional grounds—*Mapp v. Ohio*, *Miranda v. Arizona*, and *Massiah v. United States*, discussed in Chapters 1, 3, and 4, respectively—the ruling in *Wade* was controversial. One dissenting Justice agreed with the decision to extend the right to counsel, but maintained that the Court lacked the authority to prescribe the exclusionary rule it announced for courtroom identifications. *See Wade*, 388 U.S. at 248–49 (Black, J., dissenting in part and concurring in part). Three other Justices asserted that the Court had erred both in extending the right to counsel to lineup confrontations, *see id.* at 252–53, 258 (White, J., dissenting in part and concurring in part), and in "propound[ing] a broad constitutional rule barring use of a wide spectrum of relevant and probative evidence." *See id.* at 250–51 (White, J., dissenting in part and concurring in part).

43. 388 U.S. 263 (1967).

44. *Id.* at 269.

45. *Id.* at 269–70.

46. *Id.* at 270.

47. *Id.* at 269–72.

48. *Gilbert*, 388 U.S. at 270, 272.

Relying on *Wade*, the Court first concluded that because the defendant was entitled to counsel at the lineup, it was error to allow introduction of the *courtroom* identifications "without first determining that they were not tainted by the illegal lineup but were of independent origin."[49] The majority then considered the witnesses' guilt and penalty phase testimony that they had identified Gilbert *at the lineup*. Because that "testimony [was] the direct result of the illegal lineup," the Court ruled that the prosecution was "not entitled to an opportunity to show that [it] had an independent source."[50] Unlike later identifications, those made at the very confrontations involving a denial of assistance were subject to "a per se exclusionary rule."[51] A strict, unqualified suppression sanction for such evidence was needed "to assure that law enforcement authorities will respect the accused's constitutional right to the presence of his counsel."[52] Because of the "hazards to a fair trial which inhere in lineups . . . the desirability of deterring the constitutionally objectionable practice [had to] prevail over the undesirability of excluding relevant evidence."[53] In addition, exclusion was required because evidence of the pretrial identification would "enhance the impact of [an] in-court identification on the jury and seriously aggravate [any] derogation . . . of the accused's right to a fair trial."[54]

In sum, *Gilbert* enhanced understanding of the evidentiary consequences of depriving an accused of the Sixth Amendment entitlement explained in *Wade*. Evidence of pretrial identifications made at official confrontations of the accused for identification purposes were categorically excluded. Lineup identifications themselves were inadmissible at trials and during capital sentencing proceedings.[55] This strict sanction was essential both to provide a sufficient incentive for officials to honor the right to counsel and to prevent the types of prejudice to the right to a fair trial that were the foundation for the *Wade* decision.[56]

---

49. *Id.* at 272.
50. *Id.* at 272–73.
51. *Id.* at 273.
52. *Id.*
53. *Gilbert*, 388 U.S. at 273.
54. *Id.* at 273–74.
55. *Id.* at 272–73.
56. The Court noted that the out-of-court identifications were "hearsay" and that jurisdictions had split over whether they were admissible under the rules of evidence. *Id.* at 272 n.3. Because the Sixth Amendment Confrontation Clause forbids the admission of certain types of hearsay, both pretrial identifications barred by the right-to-counsel doctrine and others that are not subject to the right-to-counsel exclusionary mandate (because they predated formal charges, because they were not the result of physical confrontations with the accused himself, or because the accused waived his right to assistance) may be barred by the guarantee of confrontation. This separate constitutional exclusionary rule is discussed in Chapter 7.

Five years passed before the Court decided *Kirby v. Illinois*.[57] The evidence at issue was a robbery victim's pretrial identification of the two defendants and his courtroom testimony that they were the men who had robbed him.[58] The pretrial identifications occurred at a showup confrontation between the victim and the defendants at the police station after the defendants were arrested, but before they had been formally charged with the robbery.[59] The question was whether "the *Wade-Gilbert* per se exclusionary rule" should be extended "to identification testimony based upon" a confrontation "that took place *before* the defendant had been . . . formally charged with any criminal offense."[60]

The Justices noted that the "*Wade-Gilbert* exclusionary rule" was rooted in "the right to counsel contained in the Sixth . . . Amendment[]."[61] This right, they asserted, "attaches *only* at or after the time that adversary judicial proceedings have been initiated against" an individual.[62] Because that point in time is "the starting point of our whole system of adversary criminal justice," the juncture at which "a defendant finds himself faced with . . . prosecutorial forces . . . and immersed in the intricacies of [the] law," it "marks the commencement of the 'criminal prosecutions' to which alone the explicit guarantees of the Sixth Amendment are applicable."[63] The plurality refused "to import into a routine police *investigation* an absolute constitutional guarantee historically and

57. 406 U.S. 682 (1972).

58. *Id.* at 685–86.

59. *Id.* at 684–85. A showup is an identification procedure involving the presentation of a single person to the eyewitness, whereas a lineup presents the witness with a number of persons. It is clear that the *Wade* right to counsel applies in both settings.

60. *Id.* at 684. The main opinion in *Kirby* was joined by only four Justices, a plurality of the Court. Justice Powell provided the fifth vote for the result in a one-sentence declaration that he "would not extend the *Wade-Gilbert* per se exclusionary rule." *Id.* at 691 (Powell, J., concurring in the result). Later, *Kirby*'s formal charge threshold for attachment of the right to counsel did gain the support of a majority of the Justices. *See* Moore v. Illinois, 434 U.S. 220, 226–27, 231 (1977).

Although the plurality opinion in *Kirby* asserted more than once that it was deciding whether the "per se exclusionary rule" was applicable, *see Kirby*, 406 U.S. at 684, 690, in fact the question was whether any exclusionary sanction—either the *per se* rule of *Gilbert* or the presumptive rule of *Wade*—would bar identifications when a confrontation occurs before formal charges. Both exclusionary rules announced in 1967—*Gilbert*'s *per se* bar of identifications made at pretrial confrontations and *Wade*'s presumptive bar to subsequent identifications—were at issue in and addressed by *Kirby*. The plurality opinion was inaccurate and potentially misleading insofar as it used the phrase "per se exclusionary rule" to refer to *Wade*'s holding "that no 'in-court identifications' are admissible in evidence if their 'source' is a lineup conducted in violation of" the right to counsel. *See id.* at 683.

61. *Kirby*, 406 U.S. at 688.

62. *Id.* (emphasis added).

63. *Id.* at 689–90.

rationally applicable *only* after the onset of formal prosecutorial proceedings."[64] The premise of *Wade* was that defendants were "'entitled to counsel at any "critical stage *of the prosecution*" and that a *post-[charge]* lineup [was] such a "critical stage." ' "[65] Consequently, the exclusionary rule announced in those decisions did not bar any testimony concerning or resulting from an identification occurring "before the commencement of any prosecution."[66]

Despite the plurality's emphasis on the applicability of the exclusionary sanctions announced in *Wade* and *Gilbert*, *Kirby* was *not* an exclusionary rule opinion. The sole issue was the breadth of the entitlement to counsel recognized in *Wade*, and the conclusion was that the Sixth Amendment right did not attach prior to *formal* charges. That conclusion did have the *effect* of limiting the scope of evidentiary suppression, but only because the Sixth Amendment permits uncounseled confrontations prior to formal accusation. In the absence of a constitutional deprivation, there is no predicate for an evidentiary bar. *Kirby* did not focus on the sanctions mandated by *Wade* and *Gilbert*. It did not decide that identification evidence was admissible even though the government had deprived a defendant of counsel, and it did not address pragmatic or operational details of the Sixth Amendment exclusionary rule. Moreover, the plurality opinion did not contain a single hint about the rationales or justifications for that rule. The only concern of the brief opinion was the breadth of the constitutional guarantee that was the predicate for the *Wade-Gilbert* exclusionary mandates.[67]

Just one year later, in *United States v. Ash*,[68] the Court further limited the scope of the right to counsel recognized in *Wade*. The identification at issue in *Ash* occurred after the defendant had been indicted for robbery. Consequently, the accused's right to counsel had attached. The eyewitness, however, had not identified the defendant after viewing him in person.[69] Instead, he had been shown an

---

64. *Id.* at 690 (emphasis added).

65. *Id.* (emphasis added).

66. *Kirby*, 406 U.S. at 690. The plurality maintained that the sole constitutional protection against risks of unfairness posed by pre-charge identification procedures was the Due Process Clause's shelter against unnecessarily suggestive processes. *Id.* at 690–91. That protection is the subject of Chapter 6.

67. Four Justices disagreed with the plurality's conclusion regarding attachment of the *Wade-Gilbert* right to counsel. They reasoned that the potential prejudice to a fair trial that *Wade* relied upon as a basis for extending the Sixth Amendment to lineups was also inherent in identification processes conducted before formal charges. *See Kirby*, 406 U.S. at 695–98 (Brennan, J., dissenting); *id.* at 705 (White, J., dissenting). For a scholarly criticism of the attachment limitation, see Joseph D. Grano, Kirby, Biggers, *and* Ash: *Do Any Constitutional Safeguards Remain Against the Danger of Convicting the Innocent?*, 72 MICH. L. REV. 717, 726–30 (1974) [hereinafter Grano, Kirby, Biggers, *and* Ash].

68. 413 U.S. 300 (1973).

69. *Id.* at 303.

array of five color photographs and had identified Ash by selecting his picture. [70] Although counsel for Ash was not present when the witness viewed the photos, the judge allowed the government to introduce the pretrial photographic identification at Ash's robbery trial.[71] The question was "whether the Sixth Amendment grants an accused the right to have counsel . . . whenever the Government conducts a post-indictment photographic display . . . for the purpose of allowing a witness to attempt an identification of the offender."[72] Put otherwise, the issue was whether a photographic identification process is a critical stage of the prosecution that entitles an accused to legal assistance. If not, there was no basis for excluding the witness's identification of Ash, but if so, the photographic identification was *per se* inadmissible.

The Court devoted considerable time to an exploration of the history of the right to counsel. One lesson gleaned from that history was that "the core purpose of the counsel guarantee was to assure 'Assistance' at trial, when the accused was confronted with both the intricacies of the law and the advocacy of the public prosecutor."[73] An untrained layperson's inabilities to cope with these legal intricacies and prosecutorial advocacy were the reasons for recognizing the right to a trained lawyer.[74] Over time, criminal justice processes evolved, generating "pretrial events" that involved confrontations "by the procedural system, or by [the] expert adversary, or by both" that "might appropriately be considered to be parts of the trial itself."[75] Recognizing that the right to legal assistance could become "less than meaningful if it were limited to the formal trial itself,"[76] the Court had extended the right to certain pretrial settings. Such expansion of the Sixth Amendment guarantee had been deemed appropriate, however, "*only* when new contexts . . . present[ed] the same dangers that gave birth initially to the right itself."[77] In other words, the Court had found a right to assistance justified only when a pretrial event involved legal complexities or confrontation by a prosecutor that engendered a need for a lawyer "to act as a spokesman for, or advisor to, the accused," "to remove the disabilities of the accused," or "to compensate for the [accused's] deficiencies."[78] Consequently, "the test utilized" to decide whether an event is a critical prosecutorial stage necessitating an extension of the Sixth

70. *Id.*
71. *Id.* at 303–04.
72. *Id.* at 300–01.
73. *Ash*, 413 U.S. at 309.
74. *Id.* at 307–09.
75. *Id.* at 310.
76. *Id.*
77. *Id.* at 311 (emphasis added).
78. *Ash*, 413 U.S. at 312–13.

Amendment is "whether the accused require[s] aid in coping with legal problems or assistance in meeting his adversary."[79]

According to *Ash*, the *Wade* Court did not extend the right to counsel to lineups because of "the dangers of mistaken identification," but, rather, because a "lineup constituted a trial-like confrontation" at which assistance was needed "to preserve the adversary process by compensating for advantages of the prosecuting authorities."[80] *Wade* deemed counsel necessary "to render 'Assistance'" to the accused and "counterbalanc[e] any 'overreaching' by the prosecution."[81] The Court had *first* decided that "a lineup constituted a trial-like confrontation requiring counsel."[82] Only then did the Court assess the prejudice and risks of mistaken identification and conclude that the "lack of scientific precision and inability to reconstruct" what occurred at a lineup meant that counsel at trial could not serve as a substitute for counsel at the pretrial confrontation.[83]

Therefore, the lower court had erred in deciding that the right to counsel reached photographic display identification processes *because* dangers of mistaken identification like those at lineups also exist when a witness identifies a photograph.[84] The pertinent question was whether a photo display is a trial-like confrontation of the accused involving legal questions and an expert prosecutor. Because "the accused . . . is not present at the time of the photographic display," there is, in fact, "no possibility . . . that [he] might be misled by his lack of familiarity with the law or overpowered by his professional adversary."[85] The assistance of counsel "would not . . . produce equality in a trial-like adversary confrontation," but, instead, would "produce confrontation at an event that previously was not analogous to an adversary trial."[86] Because a photographic

---

79. *Id.* at 313.

80. *Id.* at 314.

81. *Id.*

82. *Id.*

83. *Ash*, 413 U.S. at 314–16. This was, at best, a creative reading of *Wade*'s reasoning, and, at worst, a major revision of the original logic that supported extension of the right to counsel. It might have been better for the *Ash* Court to explain that the *Wade* majority had reached the right result for the wrong reasons and to admit that it was replacing the original foundation for the pretrial right with a new foundation that was more consistent with the traditional role and understanding of counsel. For criticism of the *Ash* majority's reading of *Wade*, see *id.* at 326, 338–44 (Brennan, J., dissenting).

84. *Id.* at 314.

85. *Id.* at 317.

86. *Id.* In the last part of its opinion, the *Ash* majority observed that "[e]ven if [it was] willing to view the counsel guarantee . . . as a generalized protection of the adversary process, [it] would be unwilling" to recognize a right to counsel at photo arrays. *Id.* According to the majority, the defense's equal access to photographic identification displays "remove[s] any inequality in the adversary process . . . and . . . fully satisfies the historical spirit of the Sixth Amendment's counsel guarantee." *Id.* at 319. The majority's concession that defense counsel might have a broader purpose—i.e., that the entitlement to assistance might be a

identification process does not meet the traditional test for extending the right to counsel to pretrial events, "the Sixth Amendment does not grant the right to counsel at photographic displays conducted by the Government for the purpose of allowing a witness to attempt an identification of the offender."[87]

In sum, the *Ash* Court limited the right to counsel recognized in *Wade* to identification procedures involving the physical presence of the accused—what are sometimes called "corporeal" identification procedures.[88] The right to assistance exists to ensure that a lay defendant is not disadvantaged by his inability to cope with legal complexities or prosecutorial expertise. The "function of the lawyer" is to "remove disabilities of the accused" and to "compensate for [his] deficiencies."[89] If an accused is not actually present at an identification session, he cannot possibly need expert assistance to enable him to cope with legal questions or prosecutorial authorities.

Ash constituted a significant development in the history of the right to counsel doctrine that is the focus of this chapter. Like *Kirby*, however, *Ash* revolved around the breadth of the pretrial right to legal assistance during official identification processes. The Court's decision to narrow the circumstances justifying a Sixth Amendment entitlement limited the situations in which a constitutional violation can occur.[90] Although this limitation had the *effect* of contracting the

---

"generalized protection of the adversary process"—evinced some doubt about the narrow conception of counsel's roles that supported its holding. Moreover, the notion that defense counsel's access to photographic processes eliminated "any inequality" ignored *Wade*'s concern that an initial erroneous identification has prejudicial impact on a witness's psyche likely to carry over to any subsequent identification.

87. *Id.* at 321. Three Justices disagreed with the Court's reasoning and holding. They believed that *Wade*'s reasoning concerning the irreparable risks to an accused's interest in a fair trial posed by pretrial identification procedures applied with at least equal force to photographic displays. *See id.* at 332–38 (Brennan, J., dissenting). They would have extended the right to counsel to identification processes that did not involve the accused's physical presence. *Id.* at 329, 344.

For scholarly criticism of the *Ash* opinion, see Grano, Kirby, Biggers, *and* Ash, *supra* note 67, at 764–73. Professor Grano finds it somewhat surprising that the first retreat from the revolutionary rulings of the Warren Court was in the eyewitness identification arena. Unlike other expansive interpretations of constitutional guarantees pertinent to the criminal process—*Mapp* and *Miranda*, for example—the *Wade-Gilbert* doctrine was designed to protect the innocent from wrongful conviction. *See id.* at 722. In his view, decisions like *Ash* and *Kirby*, which diminished the scope of the protection afforded by *Wade* and *Gilbert* and increased the risks of wrongful conviction, did not promote the objectives of the war on crime. *Id.* at 722.

88. *See* Moore v. Illinois, 434 U.S. 220, 228 (1977).

89. *Ash*, 413 U.S. at 312–13.

90. There is evidence that law enforcement authorities employ photographic identification procedures that do not trigger an entitlement to counsel a large majority of the time. *See* Wells & Seelau, *Eyewitness Identification*, *supra* note 1, at 784 (noting that recent data

reach of the *Wade-Gilbert* suppression sanction,[91] neither the reasoning of nor the conclusions in *Ash* focused on the character, objectives, or operational details of the Sixth Amendment exclusionary rule. The opinion did little to enhance understanding of this suppression doctrine.

The development of Sixth Amendment exclusion of eyewitness identification evidence ended just ten years after it began. The 1977 decision in *Moore v. Illinois*,[92] nearly 35 years ago, is the Supreme Court's most recent word on the right to counsel in identification contexts and the inadmissibility of evidence obtained as a result of denying that right. Unlike *Kirby* and *Ash*, the ruling in *Moore* did not diminish the reach of the *Wade-Gilbert* entitlement. Instead, it reaffirmed the core guarantee and the original rules regarding evidentiary exclusion.

In *Moore*, a rape victim identified the defendant at a preliminary hearing held to determine whether to bind him over to the grand jury and to set bail.[93] Specifically, after the accused's name was called and he was led before the bench and informed of the charges against him, the judge called the victim to the bench.[94] He asked her "whether she saw her assailant in the courtroom, and she pointed at" the defendant.[95] At the time, the defendant had no lawyer and the court did not offer appointed counsel.[96] A pretrial motion to suppress this identification from trial was denied "on the ground that the prosecution had shown an independent basis for the victim's identification."[97] The trial judge allowed the prosecution to introduce the victim's identification of the accused from the preliminary hearing and also allowed the victim to identify the defendant in the courtroom as "the man who had raped her."[98]

The Court first reviewed *Wade*'s holding that an accused is entitled to counsel at "a pretrial corporeal identification" after indictment.[99] According to the Justices, a lawyer who is present at such a confrontation "can serve" both the accused's and the government's "interests by objecting to suggestive features" of the procedure, thereby preventing unfairness and diminishing the dangers.[100]

---

indicate that approximately three-fourths of the identification procedures are photo arrays, that one-fourth are corporeal lineups, and that counsel is present at fewer than one in four identification processes).

91. It is certainly possible that hostility to evidentiary exclusion and a desire to contract the Sixth Amendment suppression sanction were underlying motivations for the Court's strained, revisionist reading of *Wade*'s logic.

92. 434 U.S. 220 (1977).

93. *Id.* at 222–23.

94. *Id.* at 222.

95. *Id.* at 223.

96. *Id.*

97. *Moore*, 434 U.S. at 223.

98. *Id.*

99. *Id.* at 224.

100. *Id.* at 225.

The *Moore* Court pointedly observed that *Wade* and *Gilbert* had "also considered the admissibility of evidence derived from a corporeal identification conducted in violation of the . . . right to counsel," and then described the distinct exclusionary rules announced in *Wade* and *Gilbert*.[101] The Court highlighted the two premises *Gilbert* had offered as justifications for the *per se* ban on an identification made at an uncounseled pretrial session—that is, both the damage to the defendant's right to a fair trial and deterrence.[102]

The defendant in *Moore* contended that *Gilbert* forbade the admission of the "uncounseled corporeal identification" made at the preliminary hearing "without regard to whether there was an 'independent source' for it."[103] The Court agreed, rejecting three grounds for concluding that the accused had not been entitled to counsel at the time of the victim's identification. According to the Court, the contention that *indictment* was necessary could not "be squared with *Kirby*," which had held that the Sixth Amendment right attaches upon any "'initiation of adversary judicial criminal proceedings.'"[104] In *Moore*, the filing of the victim's complaint and the conduct of the preliminary hearing clearly marked the point of attachment.[105]

The suggestion that the defendant had no right to assistance because the victim viewed him in "a one-on-one identification procedure" and not in "a lineup" was also misguided.[106] To restrict the Sixth Amendment entitlement to lineups would have been inconsistent with *Wade*, which "clearly contemplated that counsel would be required" at both multi-person lineups and at one-person showups.[107] Moreover, to impose such a restriction would have been illogical because the "risks of mistaken identification" of concern in *Wade* were "generally . . . thought" to be "greater" in "a one-on-one identification."[108]

Finally, the fact that the identification took place "in the course of a judicial proceeding" was no reason to suspend the Sixth Amendment. *Wade*'s reasoning applied "with equal force" to the judicial setting in *Moore* because the confrontation was extremely suggestive and counsel could have prevented "some or all of [the] suggestiveness" in the way the defendant was presented to the victim.[109]

The Court was "unpersuaded" that the identification procedure in *Moore* was distinguishable from those employed in *Wade* and *Gilbert*.[110] Moore's "Sixth

---

101. *Id.* at 225–26.
102. *Moore*, 434 U.S. at 226.
103. *Id.* at 228.
104. *Id.*
105. *Id.* at 228–29.
106. *Id.* at 229.
107. *Moore*, 434 U.S. at 229.
108. *Id.*
109. *Id.* at 229–30.
110. *Id.* at 231.

Amendment rights were violated by a corporeal identification conducted after the initiation of adversary judicial criminal proceedings and in the absence of counsel."[111] Under *Gilbert*, the prosecution could not "buttress its case-in-chief" with the "identification made in violation of the accused's Sixth Amendment rights, even if it [could] prove that the pretrial identification had an independent source."[112] Moore was undoubtedly "entitled to the benefit of the strict [exclusionary] rule of *Gilbert*."[113]

The *Moore* Court refused to further shrink the scope of the Sixth Amendment right to assistance at pretrial identification confrontations. More important, for purposes of this discussion, the Court reaffirmed the exclusionary regimes announced in 1967. It is particularly noteworthy that the Justices did not reconsider or qualify the strict, categorical ban on "the prosecution's exploitation at trial of evidence derived directly from [a right to counsel] violation."[114] The *Moore* Court left unscathed this inflexible bar to identifications that might be both probative and critical for conviction.

C. THE JUSTIFICATIONS FOR AND LEGITIMACY OF SIXTH AMENDMENT EXCLUSION OF EYEWITNESS IDENTIFICATION EVIDENCE

Previous chapters have made it quite clear that there are two primary justifications for evidentiary suppression.[115] Exclusion may be an inseparable part of the right at issue, necessary to avoid a present constitutional deprivation that would occur in court by admission of the evidence at trial. Alternatively, exclusion can be a necessary deterrent sanction—a means of discouraging future violations of rights outside the courtroom. The two justifications are not mutually exclusive; suppression can be grounded in both rationales.[116]

---

111. *Id.*

112. *Moore*, 434 U.S. at 231.

113. *Id.* at 231–32.

114. *Id.* at 232.

115. *See* Arnold H. Loewy, *Police-Obtained Evidence and the Constitution: Distinguishing Unconstitutionally Obtained Evidence from Unconstitutionally Used Evidence*, 87 Mich. L. Rev. 907, 907 (1989) [hereinafter Loewy, *Police-Obtained Evidence*] (observing that exclusion can be rooted in one of two theories—deterring unconstitutional law enforcement methods in the future or enforcing a present procedural right—and that the former focuses on obtainment of the evidence while the latter focuses on its use in court).

116. A third potential rationale for constitutional exclusion is the preservation of "judicial integrity," the notion that judges are tainted when they allow evidence acquired by unconstitutional means to fuel the processes of justice. *See* Mapp v. Ohio, 367 U.S. 643, 659 (1961). This rationale, discussed *supra* Chapter 1, text accompanying notes 114–17, is clearly not a significant premise for any constitutional exclusionary rule today.

The Supreme Court's discussions of the justifications for and objectives of Sixth Amendment exclusion of eyewitness identification evidence have been minimal. There are indications, however, that suppression is both a forward-looking deterrent safeguard and a present trial right. According to *Gilbert*, a categorical bar to identifications made at uncounseled lineups was necessary because only a *per se* rule of exclusion could "be an effective sanction to assure that law enforcement authorities [would] respect the . . . right to . . . counsel at the critical lineup."[117] The "desirability of *deterring* the constitutionally objectionable practice [had to] prevail over the undesirability" of exclusion.[118] Moreover, the Court has asserted that a denial of counsel at a critical pretrial confrontation for identification purposes is itself a violation of the accused's Sixth Amendment entitlement.[119] If so, it is logical and fully consistent with other constitutional exclusion doctrines to deem suppression necessary to remove incentives for future deprivations.[120]

The majority opinion in *Gilbert* also indicated that the *per se* rule it announced was "buttressed" by the fact that introduction of an identification made at an uncounseled session would "aggravate [the] derogation . . . of the accused's right

117. Gilbert v. California, 388 U.S. 263, 273 (1967).

118. *Id.* (emphasis added); *see also Moore*, 434 U.S. at 226; Stovall v. Denno, 388 U.S. 293, 297 (1967); Grano, Kirby, Biggers, *and* Ash, *supra* note 67, at 790–93 (assuming that deterrence is a goal of *Wade-Gilbert* suppression).

119. *See Moore*, 434 U.S. at 231–32; Kirby v. Illinois, 406 U.S. 682, 683 (1972); *see also* Joseph D. Grano, *Prophylactic Rules in Criminal Procedure: A Question of Article III Legitimacy*, 80 Nw. U. L. Rev. 100, 121 (1985) (maintaining that under *Wade* an actual violation of the Sixth Amendment right occurs at the uncounseled lineup). The premises for pretrial extension of counsel posited in *Ash*—that a lawyer is supposed to play the same roles in trial-like pretrial confrontations that he plays at trial—would also seem to support the view that a Sixth Amendment violation occurs when an accused is denied counsel at a pretrial encounter.

120. Even if violation of the right to counsel—that is, an actual constitutional deprivation—does not occur at the uncounseled pretrial confrontation, deterrence can serve as an important objective of suppression. In *Stovall v. Denno*, an opinion issued the same day as *Wade* and *Gilbert*, the Court had to decide whether the right-to-counsel holdings in those two cases would apply retroactively. In resolving that issue, the Court observed that the object of the *Wade* and *Gilbert* "exclusionary rules" was "to deter law enforcement authorities" from conducting uncounseled identification procedures. *Stovall*, 388 U.S. at 297. According to the Court, a "conviction which rests on a mistaken identification is a gross miscarriage of justice." *Id.* The *Wade-Gilbert* exclusion doctrine "minimiz[ed]" the risks of unfair trials by discouraging officials from conducting processes that might yield mistaken identifications. *Id.* If those identifications are not produced, they cannot cause justice to miscarry. The *Wade* and *Gilbert* exclusionary rules, thus, seek to deter pretrial confrontations in order to "avoid[] unfairness at the trial," and "are justified by the need to assure the integrity and reliability of our system of justice." *Id.* at 298–99.

to a fair trial."[121] Moreover, *Wade*'s extension of the right to counsel to pretrial lineups rested firmly on the premise that a primary objective of the right to the assistance of counsel was to ensure that the accused received a fair trial.[122] The Court's repeated emphasis of this foundation for recognizing a pretrial entitlement to assistance, coupled with explicit assertions that the failure to exclude in-court identifications following lineups would "render the right to counsel an empty one" and would "disregard[] a critical element of that right,"[123] indicate that the Warren Court believed suppression was necessary to avoid violation of the Sixth Amendment at trial.[124]

In sum, the two opinions that are the source of the Sixth Amendment evidentiary bar indicate that exclusion is both a personal trial right belonging to the accused and a deterrent safeguard designed to prevent future out-of-court deprivations of assistance.[125] The remainder of this section explores and analyzes the significance, logic, and legitimacy of these two justifications, ventures a prediction about how the modern Supreme Court would justify suppression, and critiques the plausibility of the rationale that would probably prevail.

The view that exclusion is an inseparable part of the constitutional entitlement to assistance starts with a conception of the function and purpose of trial counsel. As the Supreme Court has said in more than one context, the Sixth Amendment right to a lawyer's assistance exists to ensure that defendants receive fair trials.[126] By contesting the prosecution's evidence and making use of specific Bill of Rights guarantees—for example, the right to confront adverse witnesses and the right to call supportive witnesses and present other evidence—lawyers make essential contributions to the fairness of our adversary system.[127] Perhaps most important,

---

121. *Gilbert*, 388 U.S. at 273–74; *see also Moore*, 434 U.S. at 226.

122. United States v. Wade, 388 U.S. 218, 226–27 (1967).

123. *Id.* at 240–41.

124. *See also* Loewy, *Police-Obtained Evidence*, *supra* note 115, at 931–33 (suggesting a constitutional right rationale for *Wade-Gilbert* exclusion and asserting that as a consequence an alternative to exclusion would not be constitutionally legitimate).

125. The third opinion in the Supreme Court's trailblazing identification trilogy, *Stovall v. Denno*, emphasized the deterrent objective of *Wade-Gilbert* exclusion and explained how deterring uncounseled identification processes can ensure fair trials in future cases. *See supra* note 120. Although the reasoning in *Stovall* is not inconsistent with the view that exclusion is also a personal Sixth Amendment trial right of the accused who seeks to suppress identification evidence, the Court did *not* specifically endorse that alternative rationale. A recognition that defendants have the right not to be convicted on the basis of identifications stemming from uncounseled encounters could have made it more difficult for the *Stovall* Court to strike the balance of interests against retroactive application of the *Wade* and *Gilbert* rulings.

126. *See* Strickland v. Washington, 466 U.S. 668, 684–85 (1984); United States v. Cronic, 466 U.S. 648, 658 (1984); *Wade*, 388 U.S. at 226–27; Gideon v. Wainwright, 372 U.S. 335, 344 (1963).

127. *See Cronic*, 466 U.S. at 653–57; Powell v. Alabama, 287 U.S. 45, 69 (1932).

the promise of legal assistance ensures that trials arrive at "just results"[128]—that is, it provides an essential safeguard against convicting innocent persons.[129] If the prosecution called a witness to identify the accused at trial, defense counsel would be expected to effectively cross-examine the witness, exploring deficiencies in the witness's testimony by testing and questioning the accuracy of her perception and memory. Counsel would also be expected to expose and explore any suggestion that might have misled the witness into inaccurately identifying the accused. By playing this role and contesting the state's evidence, a lawyer would promote a fair adversarial process and diminish the risks that the trial would result in an unjust conviction based on mistaken identification. In sum, the core Sixth Amendment guarantee of legal assistance at trial furthers the accused's entitlement to a fair process that produces a fair result.

When the Bill of Rights was adopted, confrontations between the government and the accused—including any identification witness "testimony"—occurred solely at trial. Later evolution of criminal justice processes produced pretrial confrontations between defendants and identification witnesses. These confrontations generated identification "testimony" harboring the same potential risks and deficiencies as trial testimony. Perception or memory deficiencies or suggestive influences might prompt the witness to mistakenly select the accused. Although counsel will be present at trial to challenge the witness's accusation, his absence from the critical pretrial encounter could significantly undermine his efficacy. Counsel could not observe and address weaknesses in the witness's perception or memory and could not observe and highlight for the jury any suggestion that occurred at the pretrial confrontation. Deficiencies or influences that might have produced a mistaken identification could not be recreated and, consequently, they could not be exposed at trial. Moreover, having selected the defendant before trial, the witness herself might be unjustifiably confident that he was the perpetrator and less willing to entertain doubts or alternative explanations for her choice. Put simply, counsel could not effectively fulfill the roles he is expected to play at trial. He would be handicapped, unable to explore deficiencies in the witness's capacities, to prevent or reveal suggestive influences, or to make effective use of the vital tool of cross-examination.

The introduction of the witness's out-of-court identification or in-court testimony resulting from the pretrial encounter inflicts the kinds of fair trial harm that the right to counsel is supposed to guard against. The admission of risky evidence that cannot be contested effectively threatens both the fairness of the adversarial process and, more importantly, the accuracy of the verdict. Suppression is necessary to counter these threats and to preserve the substance of the right to trial assistance. If identifications resulting from uncounseled

---

128. *Strickland*, 466 U.S. at 685.

129. *See Gideon*, 372 U.S. at 345.

pretrial confrontations were not barred, the government would be able to circumvent the protection trial counsel affords and inflict the kinds of harm trial counsel is empowered and expected to combat. To maintain the value of the right to legal assistance, accused individuals must be accorded a Sixth Amendment right to exclude such identification evidence.

The right to exclusion justification for the Sixth Amendment bar to identifications is plausible, but not indisputable. One basic challenge to the right-based understanding of *Wade-Gilbert* suppression rests on the premise that an accused has no right to counsel at pretrial confrontations for identification purposes. According to this view, the *Wade* Court made a fundamental mistake in extending the Sixth Amendment guarantee to this informal evidence-gathering stage.[130] A second challenge concedes that defendants have a right to counsel, but maintains that the sole Sixth Amendment deprivation occurs at the pretrial encounter when counsel is not present. According to this critique, it makes no sense to declare that an accused's right to counsel is violated at trial if he has an unhindered lawyer assisting him at that time.

Dissenters in *Wade* challenged the majority's creation of a new constitutional exclusion doctrine.[131] A primary basis for their challenge was a belief that the majority had erred in concluding that an accused has a Sixth Amendment entitlement to assistance at a post-indictment lineup.[132] The dissenters disagreed with the majority's extension of the right to counsel because they did not share the majority's concerns about official suggestion, did not agree that the results of suggestion would necessarily be inaccurate identifications, did not believe that official misconduct had "unavoidable" and "undiscoverable impact on the trial," and were unwilling to assume that juries or judges provided insufficient safeguards against the risks of police conduct at pretrial identification proceedings.[133] Moreover, the dissenters doubted that the administration of justice would be "measurably improved by inserting defense counsel into the investigative processes of police departments."[134] In their view, defense counsel could impair a state's interest in "the prompt and efficient enforcement of its criminal laws."[135]

---

130. As will be pointed out, this view also supports a challenge to the deterrent foundation for the *Wade-Gilbert* exclusion doctrine. If there is no right to assistance at a pretrial confrontation for identification purposes, there would arguably be no reason to discourage officials from conducting confrontations in the absence of counsel.

131. *See Wade*, 388 U.S. at 250 (White, J., dissenting in part and concurring in part).

132. Three years earlier, Justice White, the author of the *Wade* dissent expressing this view, had maintained that the Court's decision to recognize a Sixth Amendment right to assistance when the government deliberately elicits disclosures from an accused was an unjustified expansion of the right to counsel. *See* Massiah v. United States, 377 U.S. 201, 209 (1964) (White, J., dissenting).

133. *Wade*, 388 U.S. at 251–53 (White, J., dissenting in part and concurring in part).

134. *Id.* at 254 (White, J., dissenting in part and concurring in part).

135. *Id.* at 255 (White, J., dissenting in part and concurring in part).

Moreover, because of the unique role defense lawyers play in our adversary system, a right to assistance at identification procedures would not necessarily enhance the "reliability of identification testimony," but might well "have precisely the opposite result."[136] In sum, the *Wade* dissenters concluded that the primary objective of the majority—avoiding unjust convictions resting on unreliable eyewitness testimony—did not justify recognition of a right to counsel or a constitutional entitlement to exclude evidence secured in counsel's absence.

The second critique of the personal right conception of Sixth Amendment suppression of eyewitness identification evidence acknowledges that defendants have a right to assistance in the critical confrontations defined by the evolved *Wade* doctrine. According to this view, however, this right to counsel is either honored or violated at the pretrial encounter. A Sixth Amendment deprivation is completed when the government confronts the accused without assistance. A defendant who has a lawyer's assistance at trial is not denied his Sixth Amendment entitlement. The mere introduction of unconstitutionally obtained evidence at trial cannot prevent effective legal representation at that time. If suppression is appropriate, the purpose is not to prevent a constitutional wrong in the courtroom. The only possible justification for an evidentiary bar is to discourage officials from denying the pretrial right to assistance in future critical confrontations with defendants.[137]

This challenge to the constitutional right justification for *Wade-Gilbert* suppression posits that deterrence is the only rationale for the bar to identification evidence. Exclusion is a judicially-created, constitutionally justified sanction that removes officials' incentives for denying counsel in corporeal identification processes following formal charges. If evidence were not suppressed, officers and

---

136. *Id.* at 256–59 (White, J., dissenting in part and concurring in part).

137. This argument borrows directly from the Supreme Court's reasoning in *Kansas v. Ventris*, which held that Sixth Amendment exclusion under *Massiah* is a deterrent safeguard, not a personal right. *See supra* Chapter 4, text accompanying notes 84–96. The Court has asserted that the right to counsel is denied and that the Sixth Amendment is violated by the conduct of a pretrial identification procedure without assistance. *See* Moore v. Illinois, 434 U.S. 220, 231–32 (1977) and Kirby v. Illinois, 406 U.S. 682, 683 (1972). While these declarations do not preclude the possibility that Sixth Amendment violations occur both before and at trial, they might support the view that deterrence is the sole reason for barring identification evidence. Professor Grano endorsed this position. *See* Grano, Kirby, Biggers, *and* Ash, *supra* note 67, at 790–93. Moreover, in his view, the denial of counsel at a lineup is "*malum prohibitum*" because it "invades no inherent right" and "only becomes significant upon the introduction of evidence at trial." *Id.* at 793. Consequently, the interest in deterring counsel deprivations is not as potent or weighty as the interest in deterring conduct that actually violates a constitutional guarantee—an unreasonable search or seizure, for example. *Id.* at 790–93. This analysis led Professor Grano to conclude that the *Wade-Gilbert* exclusion doctrine could and should be limited. For an explanation of his reasoning, see *id.* at 793–97.

prosecutors too often would deprive defendants of the fundamental adversary system right to legal assistance during such critical stages of their prosecution.

One view is that the personal right premise is the only possible justification for the *Wade-Gilbert* rules. According to this position, deterrence cannot serve as a foundation for suppressing evidence because a pretrial confrontation without counsel cannot effect a complete constitutional deprivation that necessitates a sanction. The contrary view holds that a constitutional deprivation occurs only outside the courtroom and that the single legitimate basis for barring evidence is deterrence. There is a plausible argument that both premises undergird the exclusion doctrine—as *Wade* and *Gilbert* seem to suggest. Suppression can be understood as both a personal trial right and a deterrent safeguard because constitutional wrongs occur at both stages of the process. An accused suffers a deprivation of his *process* right to an adversarial battle between equals when he is denied assistance at the pretrial confrontation. He suffers a deprivation of the *substantive* benefits of assistance when a risky identification based on an uncounseled process contributes to his conviction.

One might also contend that even though the realization of a constitutional deprivation and the completion of a Sixth Amendment violation do not occur until harm is inflicted by the use of evidence in court, deterrence is nonetheless a desirable goal or consequence of suppression. By barring evidence, and thereby diminishing the number of uncounseled confrontations, the Sixth Amendment exclusion doctrine prevents unreliable eyewitness identifications from being made. Some mistaken identifications that would have been made at the uncounseled encounters might have been erroneously, and unconstitutionally, admitted at trial. A judge, for example, might mistakenly conclude that an accused was not entitled to or had waived assistance or might err in finding an independent source for a courtroom identification that was, in fact, the product of the questionable pretrial identification. To the extent that suppression discourages conduct that could yield evidence threatening constitutional injury, it would guard against judicial errors that occasion Sixth Amendment deprivations at trial. In sum, a sufficient risk of erroneous judicial rulings could support a deterrent justification for *Wade-Gilbert* suppression even if a pretrial denial of counsel alone does not constitute a complete Sixth Amendment wrong.

In my view, if the Court's expansion of the right to counsel to reach pretrial identification processes is legitimate, then suppression must be understood as a personal trial right. The harms that were the concern and foundation of the *Wade* and *Gilbert* opinions do not occur until evidence is used to secure convictions. An uncounseled pretrial lineup or showup begins, but does not complete, a deprivation of the right to assistance, the purpose of which is to ensure a fair *trial*. It is only the use of the evidentiary products of an unequal adversarial encounter to fuel the trial process that jeopardizes interests in a fair result obtained by means of a fair process. If I am correct, then suppression is not needed to deter actual constitutional violations at pretrial confrontations.

A deterrent justification for the *Wade-Gilbert* bar is defensible only if there is need to discourage the creation of evidence that judges might erroneously admit. I am doubtful that the risk of such errors can justify deterrence-based suppression. If judges adequately identify the evidence that threatens Sixth Amendment harm at trial, deterrence cannot support the *Wade-Gilbert* suppression regime.

If the current Supreme Court were to address the issue, I would expect it to adopt the opposite view and hold that deterrence alone justifies exclusion. This illogical premise is indefensible as the sole justification for *Massiah*'s Sixth Amendment exclusionary rule.[138] Nonetheless, the Court has ruled that *Massiah*'s evidentiary bar is a cost-benefit-based deterrent safeguard directed toward future wrongs, not a constitutional right.[139] Even though the concern with unreliability that underlies the Sixth Amendment entitlement to counsel in identification contexts is different from—and perhaps more compelling than—the premises supporting *Massiah*'s pretrial right to counsel against deliberate elicitation of disclosures, it seems highly unlikely that the Court would discern different premises for the *Wade-Gilbert* exclusion doctrine. No matter how irrational, I would expect the Court to endorse the purely deterrent rationale for the *Wade-Gilbert* suppression rule. The Court's abiding hostility to the exclusion of potentially probative evidence and the fact that a deterrent foundation based on cost-benefit balancing readily leads to limitations on the scope of suppression would surely prompt the Justices to hold that the Sixth Amendment-based exclusion of eyewitness identification evidence is solely and entirely a deterrent sanction designed to remove incentives for future pretrial right to counsel denials.

D. THE SCOPE AND OPERATION OF THE *WADE-GILBERT* EXCLUSION DOCTRINE

This section describes the practical details of the Sixth Amendment bar to eyewitness identification evidence. The first subject addressed is the presumptive scope of the exclusionary rule. After describing the reach of the suppression doctrine, I explore the potential qualifications and limitations upon its application. Because few of the doctrinal issues that could arise have been settled by precedent, and because many of the questions considered are unlikely to arise with any frequency, the discussions here may be somewhat more cursory than the corresponding sections of prior chapters. Because the rationales for exclusion remain uncertain, I examine the doctrinal implications of both a personal right justification and a deterrent foundation.

---

138. *See supra* Chapter 4, text accompanying notes 121–26.

139. *See* Kansas v. Ventris, 556 U.S. ___, ___, 129 S.Ct. 1841, 1845–47 (2009).

1. Suppressible Evidence: The Presumptive Scope of Right-to-Counsel Exclusion of Identification Evidence

The *Wade-Gilbert* doctrine bars from trial an eyewitness identification made after a witness has observed an accused person at an uncounseled confrontation arranged by the government.[140] A witness might declare at an official lineup or showup that the defendant is the individual she saw committing an offense. Instead, she might assert that the accused was present at a particular location at a specific time—perhaps the vicinity of an offense—or that she saw him in the company of another individual—perhaps the actual perpetrator of an offense. All of these identifications would be subject to suppression. In addition, although the question has not been addressed by the Supreme Court, it seems likely that a witness's identification of a defendant's voice after hearing him speak at a government-arranged encounter would also qualify for exclusion under *Wade-Gilbert*. Thus, a declaration that a particular defendant's voice is the voice of the individual who committed an offense or sounds like the voice that issued a threat, command, or instructions probably should be suppressed.

As discussed earlier, an identification made at a session that does not involve the physical presence of the accused is not excludable.[141] Consequently, a witness's selection of a defendant from a videotape or a still picture of a lineup, her identification of the accused's photograph that was displayed individually or as part of a group, or her assertion that a voice she heard on tape is the same voice she recalls hearing at a crime scene or on some other pertinent occasion would not come within the Sixth Amendment's exclusionary dictates. Only identification evidence generated at "corporeal" identification procedures conducted by government officials is inadmissible.

For the right to counsel to attach at a corporeal identification session, and, consequently, for evidentiary exclusion to be a possibility, the accused must be formally charged with an offense at the time of the identification.[142] Moreover, as

---

140. This assumes, of course, that the accused did not validly waive his entitlement to assistance. Moreover, because only the state can deprive an accused of counsel, only identifications made at government-arranged encounters are subject to suppression. An assertion that a witness makes upon encountering the defendant by chance on the street or in a restaurant, or upon viewing the accused at the insistence of a private party, would not be subject to exclusion on Sixth Amendment grounds. There is no constitutional predicate for excluding eyewitness identifications made at confrontations with defendants for which government agents bear no responsibility.

141. *See* United States v. Ash, 413 U.S. 300, 317 (1973); *see also supra* text accompanying notes 84–91.

142. *See* Kirby v. Illinois, 406 U.S. 682, 688–90 (1972) (plurality opinion); *see also supra* text accompanying notes 58–67. Any type of formal charge will suffice for attachment of the Sixth Amendment right to assistance of counsel. "Attachment occurs when[ever] the government has used the judicial machinery to signal a commitment to prosecute." Rothgery v. Gillespie County, 554 U.S. 191, 211 (2008).

noted in Chapter 4, the right to counsel is "offense-specific."[143] Consequently, an eyewitness identification is subject to exclusion only from a trial for an offense that was the subject of formal charges at the time it was made. Suppose that a defendant is identified in connection with a robbery that has already been the subject of an indictment, but the identification is relevant proof of another offense for which adversarial judicial proceedings have not been initiated—perhaps an assault on a police officer that occurred while fleeing the scene of the robbery. The identification is admissible at the trial for the assault because the right to counsel had not attached for that offense at the time of the pretrial confrontation.[144]

The restriction of the exclusion sanction to trials of crimes that were the subject of formal charges at the time an identification was made is entirely consistent with an understanding of *Wade-Gilbert* suppression as an integral part of the Sixth Amendment right to counsel.[145] If a person has no right to assistance at a pretrial encounter, the trial use of evidence acquired at that encounter cannot deprive him of the substance of the Sixth Amendment's protection. There is no infidelity to the adversary system principle that forbids conviction based on imbalanced confrontations with defendants if the evidence used to convict is not the product of a confrontation at which the Sixth Amendment affords an entitlement to equalizing expertise.

Whether the formal charge requirement and the offense-specific constraint are reconcilable with a deterrent justification for *Wade-Gilbert* exclusion is debatable. If officers violate an accused's right to counsel for a charged offense at a pretrial identification confrontation, suppressing the evidence from the trial of

---

143. *See* Texas v. Cobb, 532 U.S. 162, 164, 167–68 (2001); *see also supra* Chapter 4, text accompanying notes 139–44.

144. Although no Supreme Court decisions address the "offense-specific" nature of the *Wade-Gilbert* right to pretrial assistance, there can be no doubt that the limitation, developed in the *Massiah* arena, is applicable here. It bears mention that the right to counsel, and, thus, the *Wade-Gilbert* exclusion doctrine, are applicable to some offenses that are not themselves the subject of formal charges. As the discussion of the "offense-specific" limitation in Chapter 4 pointed out, the right to counsel attaches not only for a formally charged offense but also for any offense qualifying as the "same" offense for purposes of the Fifth Amendment Double Jeopardy Clause. *See supra* Chapter 4, note 140. Consequently, in the example in the text in which the defendant was charged with robbery at the time of the identification, a witness's identification would not be admissible to prove "robbery with a firearm" or "robbery causing bodily harm." For constitutional purposes, the latter offenses are "the same" as robbery because robbery does not require proof of any fact that does not also have to be proven for those offenses.

145. This analysis assumes that the formal charge prerequisite for attachment of the right to counsel is a valid interpretation of the Constitution. While accepted by the Supreme Court, the legitimacy of that threshold criterion is not undisputed. *See* James J. Tomkovicz, *An Adversary System Defense of the Right to Counsel Against Informants: Truth, Fair Play, and the* Massiah *Doctrine*, 22 U.C. DAVIS L. REV. 1, 63–71 (1988).

both that offense and also any uncharged offenses would surely promote respect for the entitlement to counsel in future confrontations. Officials would have greater incentives to avoid counsel deprivations if they could not profit at *any* future trial. Allowing the use of identification evidence to fuel convictions for offenses not charged at the time of the pretrial session can furnish incentives for future denials of assistance. On the other hand, the cost-benefit assessment that always informs deterrent analysis can support the exclusionary rule restriction at issue. The threat that an identification will be barred from the trial of a charged offense provides a potent reason for officials to avoid counsel denials. This threat may well furnish sufficient incentives for officers to comply with the Sixth Amendment. Any additional, incremental deterrence that would result from a fear that identification evidence will also be barred from trials of uncharged crimes is arguably insufficient to outweigh the social costs occasioned by suppressing the evidence from those trials.[146]

Eyewitness identifications made at uncounseled confrontations with an accused are the primary evidence the *Wade-Gilbert* rule excludes. A strict, *per se* exclusionary rule governs identification evidence that is the direct, immediate product of the pretrial counsel deprivation.[147] The bar to derivative identification evidence is less strict. Subsequent identifications by a witness who has previously identified an accused at an uncounseled procedure—both courtroom identification testimony and any additional identifications of the accused outside the courtroom—are presumptively inadmissible as the fruits of the initial session.[148] Thus, if a rape victim identifies her assailant at a post-accusation showup conducted without defense counsel, the victim's later identification of the defendant at a lineup in counsel's presence, her subsequent choice of the accused's picture from a photographic array at which the accused has no entitlement to counsel, and her assertion from the witness stand at trial that the accused was her attacker are all inadmissible. Once a witness has viewed and selected an accused at a

146. As previous chapters have made clear, this is precisely the sort of cost-benefit reasoning that has led to restrictions on the scope of other deterrence-based exclusionary rules. In deciding whether the cost-benefit balance favors admission at trials of uncharged offenses, it would be useful to know how often an identification that is both the product of an uncounseled confrontation and is relevant to proving a charged offense is also relevant to prove an uncharged crime. If identification evidence is often valuable not only in proving charged offenses, but also in proving uncharged offenses, the prospect of use at trials for the latter offenses might furnish potent incentives for denying counsel. Suppression could yield Sixth Amendment benefits outweighing the social costs.

147. *See* Gilbert v. California, 388 U.S. 263, 272–73 (1967). All ways of presenting the out-of-court, uncounseled identification to the fact finder are barred. Thus, the prosecutor may not play a recording of the identification, may not have a witness recount her own identification, and may not have a police officer repeat the witness's identifying words or describe her accusatory actions.

148. *See* United States v. Wade, 388 U.S. 218, 239–41 (1967).

corporeal procedure, there is a presumption that later identifications by that witness are based on the mental image formed at the earlier session.[149] An accused need not establish a causal connection between the initial identification and any later identification made by that witness.

The bar to derivative identification evidence is consistent with both possible predicates for the *Wade-Gilbert* exclusion doctrine. Assume first that suppression is a personal trial right. If the Sixth Amendment bar rests on the premise that the admission of identification evidence inflicts the sort of adversarial harm that legal assistance is designed to guard against and thereby completes the deprivation of counsel, then successive identifications must be excluded because they jeopardize the integrity of the trial process in the same ways that identifications made at a pretrial confrontation without assistance jeopardize the trial process.[150] There is every reason to believe that the same infirmities requiring suppression of the primary evidence—the identification made at the pretrial encounter—also infect subsequent identifications and that the same impediments to challenging the accuracy of the initial identification prevent adequate exposure of the deficiencies in later identifications. If a witness's abilities to identify the accused at a lineup are weak and the official confrontation suggests that the witness should choose the defendant, a lawyer who was not present cannot adequately reconstruct the weaknesses or the suggestive influences. He cannot effectively cross-examine the witness and expose any untrustworthiness that might exist in an identification the witness has made in the wake of the pretrial encounter. Just like the admission of the initial identification, the prosecution's use of a witness's later identification threatens to undermine and erode the protection the counsel guarantee affords. Therefore, a Sixth Amendment *right* to exclusion must encompass successive identifications by a witness who participated in an uncounseled pretrial process.

Assume now that deterring future deprivations of assistance justifies the Sixth Amendment's suppression of eyewitness identification evidence.[151] A deterrent rationale also dictates the presumptive exclusion of derivative identifications. Successive identifications by witnesses who first participate in unconstitutional sessions are the profit of, and are likely to be perceived as the profit of, the official confrontation that deprived the accused of his Sixth Amendment entitlement.

---

149. As was discussed in the historical account and will be further explained below, later identifications that have independent sources are admissible. *See supra* text accompanying notes 36–42; *infra* text accompanying notes 173–76.

150. This assumes that it makes sense to presume a psychological connection between an identification a witness makes at a pretrial confrontation without counsel and a later identification made by the same witness—that is, that the later identification is, in fact, the product of the imbalanced encounter.

151. As discussed earlier, deterrence may be a second predicate for exclusion or it could be the sole basis for suppression.

The ability to use such identifications to prove guilt would furnish clear, powerful incentives for conducting future identification procedures without counsel. Suppression is necessary to remove this incentive. It puts the government in the same evidentiary position it would have occupied had it not violated the defendant's right to assistance. Just as cost-benefit balancing dictates a Fourth Amendment bar to derivative evidence, it supports a Sixth Amendment bar to derivative evidence under the *Wade-Gilbert* doctrine.[152]

The Supreme Court has addressed only derivative identification evidence—later identifications by witnesses who first identified defendants at uncounseled confrontations. Whether other sorts of derivative evidence are barred by the *Wade-Gilbert* rule is uncertain. Although it is unlikely, the government might acquire other kinds of evidentiary fruits from improper identifications. For example, a witness's pretrial assertion that the defendant was a perpetrator might be an essential part of a probable cause showing supporting a search warrant for the defendant's home or office, and the execution of that warrant could yield probative evidence that is causally linked to the improper identification procedure. Alternatively, a defendant identified at a police station showup might protest, shifting blame to a third person previously unknown to the authorities. When questioned, the third person might provide incriminating evidence or testimony against the defendant. Unlike successive identifications by a single witness, there is no reason to assume that any other type of evidence in the government's hands is the product of an uncounseled identification. To justify suppression, an accused would clearly have to show that "but for" the confrontation without counsel the government would not have acquired the challenged evidence. No exclusionary rule extends to evidence lacking a causal connection to the constitutional wrong that is the basis for a suppression claim. Causation is necessary. The question here is whether the demonstration of a causal link between an uncounseled identification and derivative evidence other than a successive identification should give rise to a presumption of inadmissibility.

If *Wade-Gilbert* suppression is a personal constitutional right, a bar to other kinds of derivative evidence might not be justified. Unlike an identification made at an uncounseled session or a subsequent identification by the same witness,

152. One could argue that the loss of primary evidence is sufficient to deter and that there is no need for a costly bar to derivative evidence as well. The Court has rejected such reasoning in the Fourth Amendment context. In fact, such a limitation has been adopted only when the object of deterrent enforcement is not to prevent actual constitutional violations, but to discourage the breach of mere prophylactic guidelines. *See supra* Chapter 3, text accompanying notes 124–35. When the objective of a deterrent suppression sanction is to prevent violations of actual constitutional rights, the Court has found a derivative evidence bar justified. Assuming that deterrence is a premise of *Wade-Gilbert* exclusion, that premise would almost certainly be grounded in the view that uncounseled corporeal identification procedures are themselves violations of the Sixth Amendment right to the assistance of counsel.

tangible evidence—drugs or weapons, for example—or a third person's testimony acquired as a result of an uncounseled confrontation poses no threat to the reliability or accuracy of the trial process. The *Wade* Court concluded that primary and derivative eyewitness identification evidence jeopardized the fairness of trials because it had inherent infirmities and was easily distorted by suggestion, and because counsel who was not present at the identification procedure could not effectively expose the sources of untrustworthiness and protect the defendant against the risks of erroneous conviction resulting from misidentification. Those reasons are inapposite when derivative evidence other than identifications is at issue. The unreliability of an initial identification does not carry over to and infect drugs, weapons, or third-party testimony about the defendant's guilt. If the perils eyewitness identifications pose and counsel's inability to guard against unfair outcomes resulting from misidentifications are essential predicates for a Sixth Amendment right to exclusion, there is no reason to extend that right to derivative evidence that is trustworthy and does not threaten the fairness of the trial.

There is an argument to the contrary, a logical basis for extending a right-based *Wade-Gilbert* rule to non-identification derivative evidence. If the government acquires derivative evidentiary fruits by confronting an accused without assistance, those fruits are the harvest of an imbalanced contest—a clash between the government and an inferior accused that violates a fundamental premise of adversary system fair play. When they are introduced at trial, the accused suffers harm to his chances for a favorable verdict—harm directly traceable to a critical confrontation conducted in violation of the Sixth Amendment mandate that the government not exploit the weaknesses of an unassisted accused. It is arguable that an accused is denied the benefits of counsel when the derivative evidence contributes to conviction whether or not it jeopardizes the reliability of the outcome. The trial is arguably unfair because the process that enabled the government to convict the accused was inconsistent with the fundamental adversary system principle that an accused is entitled to equalizing counsel in post-accusation clashes with the state.[153]

In contrast, a deterrent justification for *Wade-Gilbert* suppression clearly dictates a bar to other types of derivative evidence. The Fourth Amendment and *Massiah* exclusionary rules, whose objectives are to deter future pretrial deprivations of constitutional rights, presumptively reach all evidence with causal connections to the initial illegalities. All evidence gained by means of official misconduct can furnish incentives for future wrongs. The presumptive bar to derivative evidence is designed to remove those incentives and ensure respect

153. This reasoning is similar to the case that can be made for a right to exclusion under *Massiah*. *See supra* Chapter 4, text accompanying notes 98–106. The reasoning in *Wade*, which was tightly tied to risks of unreliability and unfair outcomes, furnishes no explicit support for this fair process rationale for a right to exclude derivative evidence.

for constitutional rights. Deterrent objectives require the government to be put in the same position it would have occupied without the unconstitutional conduct, not a better position. The suppression of any evidentiary products acquired as a result of uncounseled corporeal identification processes is necessary to achieve that end.[154]

In sum, the Sixth Amendment exclusion doctrine extends to any eyewitness identification made at a post-accusation identification session arranged by officials and involving the presence of the accused and the absence of counsel. It also bars a subsequent identification by a witness who identifies an accused at such a session and may bar other kinds of derivative evidence. The suppression mandate applies only at trials of offenses that were the subject of formal accusations at the time of the improper confrontation. Evidence is admissible to prove offenses that were not charged at the time of the uncounseled identification session—offenses for which the right to counsel had not attached.

2. Proceedings in Which the *Wade-Gilbert* Suppression Doctrine Operates

As with all constitutional exclusionary doctrines, the primary forum for operation of the Sixth Amendment bar to eyewitness identification evidence is the criminal trial. *Wade* involved the government's introduction of evidence at the trial of a robbery for which the defendant had been indicted at the time of the challenged lineup. Subsequent Supreme Court opinions have all considered whether evidence had to be excluded from a trial. The Court's language explicitly bars identification evidence from "trial."[155]

---

154. It merits mention that causation is necessary and *presumptively* sufficient to justify suppression. The presumption can be overcome for derivative evidence. Evidence with a causal connection—evidence that does in fact put the government in a better position—might be admissible under an exception to the rule excluding derivative evidence. Possible exceptions are explored in later subsections.

155. *See* Gilbert v. California, 388 U.S. 263, 272 (1967); United States v. Wade, 388 U.S. 218, 219, 239–40 (1967). Chapter 4 discussed the Supreme Court's holding that indigent defendants have no Sixth Amendment right to appointed assistance at trials of misdemeanor offenses not resulting in sentences of "actual imprisonment." *See supra* Chapter 4, text accompanying notes 157–59. Like *Massiah*'s pretrial extension of the right to trial counsel, the *Wade-Gilbert* entitlement to assistance at corporeal identification processes surely does not include a right to appointed assistance at confrontations after an indigent individual is formally charged with a misdemeanor offense that would entail no right to appointed *trial* assistance. Whether *Wade-Gilbert* exclusion is a right or a deterrent remedy, if a defendant has no right to pretrial assistance at an identification procedure, then any identification made would be admissible at his trial. If an accused was charged with an offense that triggered a right to appointed assistance, but was ultimately tried for an offense that did not give rise to a right to appointed assistance at trial, the question of suppression is somewhat more complicated. The answer could depend on the justification for suppression, a matter still subject to some debate. The thorough discussion and analysis of questions regarding the applicability of the *Massiah* exclusion doctrine in misdemeanor

Gilbert involved the use of identification evidence not only at trial, but also in a capital sentencing proceeding. The Court held the rule of inadmissibility extended to that sentencing proceeding.[156] Today, a capital sentencing process—the stage at which a fact finder determines whether a defendant convicted of a capital offense should receive a sentence of death or life imprisonment—will usually, if not always, be considered part of the trial for constitutional purposes. Moreover, under the landmark ruling in *Apprendi v. New Jersey*,[157] some other proceedings that jurisdictions label "sentencings" are, for purposes of constitutional guarantees, trials that determine guilt or innocence for offenses. Although the *Apprendi* line of authority has addressed the application of the Sixth Amendment entitlement to trial by jury and the due process requirement of proof beyond a reasonable doubt, any "sentencing proceeding" that qualifies as a trial under *Apprendi* surely would be a trial for purposes of the Sixth Amendment right to counsel. The *Wade-Gilbert* bar to identification evidence would govern and require suppression in such proceedings.[158]

In true sentencing proceedings, it is unclear whether the *Wade-Gilbert* bar would apply. The Sixth Amendment right to the assistance of counsel in all criminal prosecutions does extend to the sentencing phase.[159] Consequently, if exclusion is an integral part of the entitlement to counsel, then a prohibition on the use of improperly obtained identifications in sentencing proceedings would be necessary to avoid a constitutional violation in the courtroom. However, if suppression is merely a deterrent sanction designed to prevent future deprivations at pretrial confrontations, the application of the *Wade-Gilbert* exclusionary rule to true sentencing proceedings is uncertain. The deterrent benefits of suppression from a sentencing phase might justify the additional social costs of barring the government from using evidence at that stage. On the other hand, suppression from the trial alone might be sufficient to achieve deterrent ends. The price of preventing use to ensure an appropriate sentence might be too high to justify any additional enforcement of the pretrial right to counsel resulting from suppression at that post-trial stage.[160]

---

trials where no right to counsel exists seems directly and fully relevant to the *Wade-Gilbert* setting. *See supra* Chapter 4, text accompanying notes 157–62.

156. None of the Court's other Sixth Amendment identification cases have involved the use of evidence at a sentencing or in any other phase of the criminal process.

157. 530 U.S. 466 (2000).

158. For a discussion of the same issue in the *Massiah* context, see *supra* Chapter 4, text accompanying note 163.

159. *See* Gardner v. Florida, 430 U.S. 349, 358 (1977); Mempa v. Rhay, 389 U.S. 128, 137 (1967); *see also* James J. Tomkovicz, The Right to the Assistance of Counsel 110–12 (2002).

160. For a fuller discussion of the sentencing use implications of a deterrent justification for Sixth Amendment exclusion, see *supra* Chapter 4, text accompanying notes 164–66, which analyzes the same issue in the *Massiah* context.

The still controlling, although questionable, holding that the Fourth Amendment exclusionary rule applies in nominally civil forfeiture proceedings deemed "quasi-criminal"[161] should extend to the *Wade-Gilbert* rule. If the *Wade-Gilbert* rule is founded on deterrent premises, the logic that requires application of the Fourth Amendment exclusionary rule also would dictate Sixth Amendment suppression.[162] Moreover, if the Sixth Amendment bar to identifications is a constitutional entitlement of the accused, that personal right not to be prosecuted on the basis of evidence secured by means of an uncounseled confrontation should govern in forfeiture proceedings deemed "quasi-criminal" because they essentially involve the imposition of penalties for a criminal offense.

In addition, if the *Wade-Gilbert* bar is ultimately cast as a mere deterrent safeguard, as I predict, the Fourth Amendment holdings that evidence need not be suppressed in grand jury proceedings, administrative processes for parole revocation purposes, and genuinely civil proceedings would surely be applicable.[163] Even if the bar to eyewitness identification evidence is an inseparable element of the accused's Sixth Amendment entitlement to counsel, the same conclusions would seem to follow. An accused's explicit right to assistance "in all criminal prosecutions" does not extend to the grand jury stage, to parole revocation proceedings, or to civil lawsuits.

The final issue in this section is whether a defendant may raise a *Wade-Gilbert* suppression claim in a habeas corpus challenge to a state conviction. The question is whether the Fourth Amendment restriction announced in *Stone v. Powell* applies in this context.[164] *Stone* barred Fourth Amendment exclusionary rule claims in federal habeas proceedings unless the state has denied the accused a full and fair opportunity to litigate his claim. The reasoning was rooted entirely in the cost-benefit analysis that controls the scope of deterrence-based constitutional exclusionary sanctions. If *Wade-Gilbert* rests solely on a deterrent foundation, the *Stone* limitation should govern.[165] If the Sixth Amendment bar is a personal trial right essential to prevent completion of the constitutional violation in court, *Stone*'s constraint on a defendant's ability to pursue collateral relief is inapplicable. In cases involving efforts to vindicate actual constitutional rights, the Court has consistently refused to extend *Stone*'s limit on habeas relief.[166]

---

161. *See supra* Chapter 1, text accompanying notes 160–62.

162. See *supra* Chapter 4, text accompanying notes 167–68, for a similar conclusion regarding *Massiah*'s Sixth Amendment exclusionary rule.

163. *See supra* Chapter 1, text accompanying notes 163–73; *see also supra* Chapter 4, text accompanying notes 169–70.

164. For a discussion of this limitation, see *supra* Chapter 1, text accompanying notes 164–66.

165. See *supra* Chapter 4, text accompanying notes 177–79, for a similar conclusion with regard to the *Massiah* bar.

166. See *supra* Chapter 3, text accompanying notes 144–46, for a discussion of the Court's refusal to extend *Stone* to *Miranda* exclusion claims because the *Miranda* bar,

In sum, the *Wade-Gilbert* rule's primary territory is the criminal trial. It might also function in genuine sentencing processes and a narrow category of forfeiture proceedings. It probably does not require exclusion in any other phases of the criminal process or in any civil proceedings. Whether defendants may bring federal habeas claims based on the Sixth Amendment exclusion doctrine depends on its character, a matter not definitively resolved.

3. "Standing" to Seek the Exclusion of Eyewitness Identifications: The Persons Entitled to Bar Evidence

A defendant identified at a post-accusation pretrial corporeal identification procedure without counsel has "standing" to suppress that identification and derivative evidentiary fruits. The Supreme Court has not addressed whether another individual can exclude such evidence from his trial. It seems relatively unlikely that an eyewitness identification of one individual would prove to be incriminating evidence against a different individual. It is possible, however, that a witness's assertion that one man committed a robbery could constitute circumstantial evidence that the man's close business associate or family member was involved in the offense. Moreover, when one person is charged and tried as an accomplice in the commission of an offense, the prosecution must prove that another person, the alleged "principal," did in fact commit the crime. Consequently, an eyewitness identification of a principal secured in violation of the Sixth Amendment could be essential evidence in the prosecution of a putative accomplice. Finally, derivative evidence found as a result of an uncounseled identification of one person—contraband, incriminating records, or forensic evidence, for example—might prove useful in the prosecution of someone other than the identified individual. The question is whether a defendant who was not the person identified at the uncounseled confrontation can rely on the denial of counsel at that confrontation as a basis for suppressing evidence from his trial.

It seems clear that such a defendant would lack "standing" to complain about the denial of another person's right to counsel. Because he is not entitled to exclusion under *Wade-Gilbert*, the evidence is admissible at his trial. This result follows no matter what rationale supports Sixth Amendment suppression. If evidentiary exclusion is a personal trial entitlement, it is because the right to counsel forbids the conviction of a defendant by exploiting advantages gained by confronting *him* before trial without legal assistance. A right to exclusion would belong solely to an accused who is denied counsel at the pretrial confrontation. Use of the evidence against a third person cannot complete a constitutional

---

while not itself a constitutional right, is a safeguard against the deprivation of a fundamental Fifth Amendment trial right. For a discussion of the Court's unwillingness to apply *Stone* to situations where defendants are seeking to enforce their constitutional rights, see *supra* Chapter 4, note 176.

transgression at trial because that individual suffered no deprivation of assistance at a critical pretrial clash with the state.

If the *Wade-Gilbert* suppression doctrine is not a right but is rooted solely in deterrence, the result would be no different. The very same cost-benefit reasoning that has led the Supreme Court to deny third-party standing to raise Fourth Amendment exclusionary rule claims dictates an identical conclusion in this context.[167] There is little doubt that exclusion could have deterrent benefits. The suppression of identification evidence and its fruits from the trials of defendants not identified would provide additional motivations for officers not to confront defendants without counsel. Nevertheless, the Court would surely conclude that excluding the evidence from the trials of identified defendants provides sufficient motivation to respect Sixth Amendment rights and that the additional costs of excluding potentially probative evidence from the trials of third parties would outweigh any incremental deterrence that might result from granting third-party "standing."[168]

In sum, as a practical matter, questions of "standing" to raise *Wade-Gilbert* exclusion claims are likely to arise only in very rare cases. As a logical and theoretical matter, it is virtually certain that a "standing" limitation confines the operation of the Sixth Amendment suppression doctrine, restricting its benefits to defendants who are identified at uncounseled pretrial confrontations.

4. Exceptions to the *Wade-Gilbert* Suppression Doctrine

This final section discusses exceptions to the Sixth Amendment bar to eyewitness identification evidence and its fruits. The "independent source" doctrine is the sole "exception" addressed by the Supreme Court. After reviewing the breadth and significance of that doctrine, this section considers the plausibility of other exceptions like those that qualify constitutional exclusion mandates discussed in earlier chapters.

a. The Independent Source Doctrine and the Inevitable Discovery Exception In general, when officers engage in improper conduct, and the evidence the prosecution wishes to introduce is not the product of that conduct, but, instead, was acquired by lawful means, the evidence is admissible.[169] From the inception

167. *See supra* Chapter 1, text accompanying notes 174–78.

168. For similar reasoning regarding "standing" to exclude evidence under *Massiah*'s Sixth Amendment suppression doctrine, see *supra* Chapter 4, text accompanying notes 180–83.

169. For a thorough explanation of the "independent source" doctrine in the Fourth Amendment context, where it has been fully developed, see *supra* Chapter 1, text accompanying notes 204–12. As noted in this earlier discussion, although the "independent source" doctrine is sometimes referred to as an "exception" to an otherwise applicable exclusionary rule, that characterization is inaccurate. Because a basic predicate for exclusion is the necessity for a causal connection between an illegality and the acquisition of

of the *Wade-Gilbert* suppression rule, evidence with an "independent source"—evidence that is not the product of an uncounseled identification session, but has an origin independent of that session—has been admissible. This subsection explains the Sixth Amendment's independent source "exception" and analyzes whether the related inevitable discovery exception might also be applicable.

In *Gilbert*, the Court made it clear that any identification that is the direct result of an improper confrontation of an unassisted accused cannot be admitted under the independent source doctrine.[170] By definition, an identification that is the direct result of the improper encounter with the accused cannot have a lawful independent source.[171] Consequently, it is barred by a *per se* rule of exclusion—a categorical sanction designed to guarantee respect for the pretrial right to counsel.[172]

While the immediate products of the pretrial impropriety are forbidden, any subsequent identification by the same witness can be admitted if the prosecution shows, by clear and convincing evidence, that the identification has an independent source or origin.[173] As noted earlier, a successive identification by a witness is presumed to be a derivative product—a "fruit"—of an identification made at the pretrial confrontation. Nonetheless, if the state can show that the witness identified the accused on the later occasion because of a recollection of perceptions or observations at a time and place other than the prior uncounseled

---

evidence, there is no need to "except" lawfully acquired evidence from suppression. Evidence obtained by lawful means does not qualify for exclusion in the first place.

170. This would include not only identifications made at and during the improper session, but also those occurring after the session has ended, if they are, in fact, direct products of the identification process. Thus, if a witness for any reason waited an hour or a day before telling an officer that a person displayed to him was in fact the perpetrator of a crime, that assertion after the confrontation could not be admitted under the independent source doctrine.

171. *See* Gilbert v. California, 388 U.S. 263, 272–73 (1967) (observing that because the identification at the pretrial confrontation "is the direct result of the illegal" conduct, the government is "not entitled to an opportunity to show that [it] had an independent source"). In *Moore v. Illinois*, 434 U.S. 220, 231 (1977), the Court declared that "even if it [could] prove that [an uncounseled] pretrial identification had an independent source," the prosecution "cannot buttress its case-in-chief by introducing evidence" of that identification. The suggestion in *Gilbert* seems to be that the circumstances make it factually impossible to prove an independent source for such evidence. *Moore*, on the other hand, suggests that even though a prosecutor might, as a matter of *fact*, show that a pretrial identification had an independent source, as a matter of *law* such a showing cannot justify admission of the identification.

172. *See Gilbert*, 388 U.S. at 273.

173. The *Wade* majority imposed this abnormally high "clear and convincing evidence" burden of proof on the government. *See* United States v. Wade, 388 U.S. 218, 240 (1967). The ordinary burden of proof for questions pertaining to evidentiary suppression is the "preponderance of the evidence" standard.

identification procedure, it may introduce the later identification.[174] "[V]arious factors" are relevant to the independent source inquiry, including the witness's "prior opportunity to observe the alleged criminal act," whether there is a "discrepancy between" a witness's earlier description and the accused's "actual description," whether the witness identified someone else earlier, whether the witness identified the accused "by picture" on an earlier occasion, whether the witness failed "to identify the defendant" earlier, and how long a period of time elapsed "between the alleged act and the . . . identification" at issue.[175] The government's object is to demonstrate, for example, that a victim of a sexual assault chose a defendant's photograph from an array of photographs or identified him at trial as the perpetrator based on recollections of the assault itself. Clear and convincing proof that an eyewitness identification originated independently of the uncounseled confrontation overcomes the presumption that it was the product of the right-to-counsel deprivation and requires a court to admit the evidence.[176]

The Court has not decided whether the independent source doctrine might apply to other sorts of derivative evidence. A defendant might provide a factual basis for concluding that contraband, evidence of a crime, or a witness's inculpatory trial testimony was acquired as a result of an identification made at an uncounseled confrontation. If the government established, to the contrary, that it had gained the evidence by lawful independent means—that is, that there was no causal link between the denial of counsel and its possession of the evidence—surely it should be permitted to introduce that evidence. Whether the *Wade-Gilbert* exclusion doctrine is a constitutional right or a deterrent safeguard, it cannot justifiably bar evidence whose origin is not the illegal pretrial confrontation. The introduction of lawfully-gained evidence cannot complete a violation of the right to counsel because it is not the yield of an imbalanced

---

174. This assumes, of course, that the later identification did not itself result from a process in which the accused was denied the right to counsel.

175. *Wade*, 388 U.S. at 241.

176. In *Wade*, several Justices suggested that the government would not be able to meet the burden the majority had imposed. *See id.* at 248 (Black, J., dissenting in part and concurring in part) (asserting that the independent source "determination . . . is practically impossible"); *id.* at 251 (White, J., dissenting in part and concurring in part) (suggesting that the clear and convincing evidence standard imposes a "heavy burden" that is "probably an impossible one" to satisfy). In fact, lower courts have frequently found that the government has satisfied its burden and have allowed the introduction of successive identifications by witnesses who first made identifications at uncounseled corporeal identification sessions. *See* Grano, Kirby, Biggers, *and* Ash, *supra* note 67, at 722, 792; Levine & Tapp, *Psychology of Criminal Identification*, *supra* note 33, at 1083; Charles A. Pulaski, Neil v. Biggers: *The Supreme Court Dismantles the* Wade *Trilogy's Due Process Protection*, 26 STAN. L. REV. 1097, 1099–1100 (1974). The task of overcoming the presumption of suppression has proven to be far from "impossible."

pretrial encounter. Moreover, because the suppression of evidence with an independent source would put the government in a worse position than it would have occupied without its impropriety, a need for deterrence would not support exclusion. The deterrent objective of constitutional exclusionary rules dictates that the government should be put in the same position it would have occupied absent its wrong—that is, that evidentiary profit is to be eliminated. Deterrent objectives do not authorize suppression that penalizes the government by putting it in a worse evidentiary position.[177] Moreover, the government probably needs only prove an independent source for the evidence by "a preponderance of the evidence," not by "clear and convincing" proof.[178]

In sum, evidence with an independent lawful source is admissible. For *identifications* made by witnesses who first made inadmissible identifications, the government must show the independent source by clear and convincing evidence. For other types of evidence, a demonstration that it is more likely than not that the evidence was obtained from an independent source probably suffices.

The "inevitable discovery" doctrine is related to the "independent source" doctrine, but is a genuine exception to exclusionary rules. While the independent source doctrine applies to evidence that has in fact been found lawfully, the inevitable discovery exception permits the admission of evidence that *has been* acquired by improper methods but *would have been* found lawfully. This exception permits the introduction of evidence that is presumptively inadmissible because it was illegally acquired if the prosecution demonstrates that government agents would inevitably have acquired the evidence by lawful methods had

177. Because the premises underlying this reasoning were fully explored in the Fourth Amendment context, where they have in fact been developed, the discussion here is somewhat cursory. For the more complete discussion, see *supra* Chapter 1, text accompanying notes 204–12.

178. The ordinary burden of proof in suppression litigation is the "preponderance of the evidence" standard. *See* Nix v. Williams, 467 U.S. 431, 444 n.5 (1984). To justify admission, the government has only to show that it is more likely than not that the factual predicate for an exception to exclusion exists. Thus, the government can satisfy the independent source doctrine by showing merely that it is more likely than not that the evidence it seeks to introduce was lawfully acquired. While the special (and controversial) clear and convincing evidence standard for subsequent identifications could be extended to other kinds of evidence allegedly derived from *Wade-Gilbert* right to counsel violations, it is very likely that this uniquely high burden of proof would be limited to independent source inquiries for *identification* evidence. Because there is a reason to assume a psychological connection between an initial identification and a subsequent identification by the same witness, it makes sense to impose a higher standard that demands clearer proof of genuine independence. *See Nix*, 467 U.S. at 444–45 n.5 (rejecting a contention that the clear and convincing evidence standard should govern inevitable discovery inquiries and highlighting the special reasons that the higher standard is justified for independent source inquiries involving successive identifications).

they not employed the unlawful methods. This doctrine would seem to have very limited relevance to the *Wade-Gilbert* eyewitness identification bar.

It seems unlikely, if not impossible, that a prosecutor could demonstrate that an eyewitness identification made at an uncounseled pretrial confrontation would have been lawfully acquired if the improper pretrial encounter had not occurred. Moreover, to safeguard the right to counsel at corporeal confrontations, there is a *per se* ban on use of the direct fruits of improper sessions. If the government may not show that such an identification actually had a lawful independent source, surely it could not introduce such an identification by showing that it would been acquired through a lawful process—even if such a showing were factually possible.

A subsequent identification by a witness who has identified a defendant at an uncounseled encounter may be introduced if it is shown by clear and convincing evidence to have an independent source. If a prosecutor cannot make that showing, it seems impossible that she could show clearly and convincingly that the same identification would have been acquired by lawful means. The factors and variables relevant to an independent source showing would also seem relevant to an inevitable discovery inquiry. If those factors do not establish that a witness did in fact recall a memory independent of the tainted lineup or showup, they surely would fail to establish that she would have recalled such a memory and made an untainted identification. If the pertinent variables prove an actual independent source for a subsequent identification, there would be no need to establish that an identification would inevitably have been gained by lawful means. Consequently, the inevitable discovery exception seems entirely inapplicable to initial and subsequent identification evidence that falls within the scope of the *Wade-Gilbert* bar.

However, the inevitable discovery exception might apply to other kinds of derivative evidence. The government might show that tangible items which are the products of an uncounseled lineup—contraband, stolen goods, or inculpatory evidence, for example—would have been found legally had they not been found as a result of the lineup. A lawful search that would have unearthed the items might have been in progress at the time they were found. Moreover, testimony or statements given by a witness who is discovered because of an improper pretrial identification might be admissible under the inevitable discovery exception. For example, the government might demonstrate by a preponderance of the evidence that an ongoing lawful investigation would have led to the witness and that she would have willingly provided the same testimony or statements. Because this type of derivative evidence is rarely acquired as a result of improper identification confrontations, the opportunities to invoke the inevitable discovery doctrine are surely infrequent.

The inevitable discovery exception would be legitimate no matter what the underpinnings of the *Wade-Gilbert* rule. The Supreme Court's sole endorsement of the exception was in a case involving *Massiah*'s Sixth Amendment exclusionary rule. The Court reasoned that the inevitable discovery exception was consistent with a deterrent justification for exclusion because a refusal to recognize the exception would put the government in a worse position than it would have occupied without the improper conduct. The Court also found the exception compatible with a personal right justification because the accused receives the very same trial he would have received if the impropriety had not occurred.[179] The same reasoning supports an inevitable discovery exception to the *Wade-Gilbert* suppression doctrine whether it is a deterrent sanction, a personal trial right, or both.

b. The Attenuation Exception The traditional attenuation exception allows the prosecution to introduce evidence when the government's improper conduct is sufficiently remote from the acquisition of the evidence—that is, when variables stretch or weaken the causal connection between the official impropriety and the evidence. By definition, the doctrine can apply only to derivative evidence. Primary evidence—the evidence discovered as an immediate, direct result of the official transgression—cannot satisfy the criteria for application of the attenuation exception because there is a close, strong causal connection. Consequently, identifications made during uncounseled encounters cannot qualify for admission under the attenuation exception.

It is uncertain whether derivative identification evidence—identifications made by witnesses who participated in unconstitutional confrontations—might be admissible under the attenuation exception. If Sixth Amendment exclusion of eyewitness identifications is grounded exclusively in deterrence, a premise that I believe the Court would misguidedly endorse, the attenuation exception could apply to subsequent identifications. If a substantial period of time passed between the initial identification and the later one, if significant events intervened, and if the failure to honor the right to counsel was a good faith error or oversight—not a deliberate, purposeful deprivation—a court might logically conclude that the costs of suppressing the identification outweigh the deterrent benefits of exclusion.[180]

On the other hand, if the suppression of subsequent identifications by witnesses who participated in unconstitutional confrontations is a personal right necessary to avoid denials of the right to counsel and to ensure fair trials, the attenuation doctrine is probably inapplicable. As long as the later identification is the product of the earlier one, its admission would seem to inflict the sort of injury the Sixth Amendment is designed to prevent. No matter how remote the

---

179. For a more thorough discussion of the Court's reasoning, see *supra* Chapter 4, text accompanying notes 189–95.

180. The reasoning would be identical to the reasoning underlying the Fourth Amendment attenuation exception for derivative evidence and the same factors would be relevant to the attenuation inquiry. For a thorough discussion of the Fourth Amendment exception, see *supra* Chapter 1, text accompanying notes 222–31.

connection between a pretrial identification and a later courtroom identification, if there is a causal link—that is, if the government gained the subsequent identification because it confronted an unaided defendant before trial—the accused should have a personal right to bar the state from exploiting its impropriety by using the derivative identification to secure a conviction.

The same analysis applies to other types of derivative evidence the government acquires as a result of an uncounseled pretrial identification session. If suppression is rooted entirely in deterrent objectives, when the state shows sufficient attenuation of the causal connection, the cost-benefit balance favors admission. However, if exclusion under *Wade-Gilbert*, including the bar to derivative evidence, is part of the Sixth Amendment guarantee—a trial protection that is necessary to prevent completion of a counsel deprivation—then an attenuation showing cannot justify admission. Trial use of evidence obtained by denying counsel would violate the Sixth Amendment even if its acquisition was remote from the pretrial confrontation and the causal connection was weak. If the government profits in any way at trial from its failure to honor the right to assistance at the pretrial session, the accused suffers an adversarial disadvantage of the sort the right to counsel was designed to prevent.

c. **"Good Faith" Exceptions** The Supreme Court has never entertained the possibility that the *Wade-Gilbert* exclusion doctrine might be qualified by a "good faith" exception. Two different scenarios that might support good faith exceptions are conceivable. First, while engaged in a legitimate investigation of an uncharged offense the government might conduct a pretrial corporeal identification procedure that yields incriminating evidence regarding a charged offense for which the right to counsel had already attached. The question is whether the legitimate motive—the investigation of a crime for which no right to assistance had attached—justifies allowing the prosecution to introduce the evidence to prove the charged offense. Second, government agents might reasonably believe that an identification procedure does not deny an accused's right to counsel. They might make a good faith mistake about whether an uncounseled identification procedure deprives a defendant of the entitlement to assistance defined by *Wade* and its progeny. The question is whether the lack of culpability on the part of the officials is a reason to suspend the ordinarily applicable exclusionary sanction.

In *Maine v. Moulton*, the Supreme Court rejected a legitimate, good faith investigation exception to *Massiah*'s Sixth Amendment exclusionary rule.[181] The Court ruled that if government agents deliberately elicit statements from an unassisted defendant, the state may not introduce those statements to prove a charged offense even though the elicitation was part of a legitimate, good faith

181. *See* Maine v. Moulton, 474 U.S. 159, 178–80 (1985). For a detailed examination of the holding in and reasoning of *Moulton*, see *supra* Chapter 4, text accompanying notes 69–74, 216–21.

investigation of an uncharged crime for which the accused had no entitlement to counsel. There were two reasons why commendable investigatory motivations of investigating officers did not justify an exception to *Massiah*'s suppression doctrine.[182] First, legitimate investigatory motives do not prevent the constitutional injury occasioned by confronting an unassisted accused prior to trial. In addition, recognition of a good faith, legitimate investigation exception to *Massiah*'s bar could endanger the right to pretrial assistance by creating positive incentives for false claims about official motives.

It seems unlikely that a pretrial identification confrontation arranged to investigate an uncharged offense would yield an identification of an accused relevant to proving a different offense that was not the subject of a formal accusation. If officers haul a suspect before an eyewitness to a just-committed bank robbery, the odds that the witness will identify the suspect as the perpetrator of another robbery for which he had been indicted seem minimal, at best. The chances of such an occurrence would seem higher if the charged and the uncharged offenses occurred in the same vicinity around the same time. Suppose a defendant is accused of attempting to kill a police officer who approached him near the scene of a sexual assault minutes after it occurred. In order to investigate the assault, which is not yet the subject of formal charges, officers place him in a lineup and a witness identifies him as the person she saw running from the scene of the assault. This identification could prove relevant to showing that the defendant had attempted to kill the officer, for it places him in the vicinity near the time of the latter offense.

In a situation like this, the identification is the result of an officially-arranged pretrial confrontation of the accused individual in the absence of counsel—a corporeal identification process that triggers a Sixth Amendment right to assistance. Moreover, the identification is probative of the offense for which an accusation was pending. Does the fact that the identification was part of a legitimate, good faith effort to investigate an uncharged offense justify use of the evidence to prove the charged offense? Put otherwise, is an exception to the *Wade-Gilbert* exclusion doctrine appropriate when officers who arrange an identification procedure to investigate an uncharged offense obtain identification evidence that can help prove a charged offense?

Whether the suppression of identification evidence is a deterrent sanction or a personal trial right, the reasoning that led to rejection of this good faith exception under *Massiah* supports an identical result under *Wade-Gilbert*. There are no distinctions between *Massiah*'s Sixth Amendment bar to statements and *Wade-Gilbert*'s Sixth Amendment ban on identifications that dictate a different conclusion.

---

182. The statements could be used to prove the uncharged offense because their elicitation did not violate the defendant's right to counsel for that offense. For the charged offense, however, the statements were inadmissible because the accused was deprived of counsel at a critical stage of his prosecution.

Despite legitimate investigatory motives, pretrial confrontations of accused persons without counsel deny a Sixth Amendment entitlement. The good faith of officials does not preclude or mitigate the constitutional injury, and an exception could induce officers to falsely claim they were pursuing a legitimate investigation when they gained the evidence that helps prove the charged offense.

If right-to-counsel exclusion of identification evidence is designed solely to deter future deprivations, the cost-benefit balance tips against a legitimate, good faith investigation exception here just as it did in the *Massiah* context. If Sixth Amendment suppression of identifications is a personal trial right of the accused, the case against the proposed exception is even stronger. The fact officers were engaged in a well-motivated investigation of a different offense can furnish no basis for depriving a defendant of the trial protection the Sixth Amendment extends to those who have been formally charged with crimes.

The other possible variety of "good faith" exception is the sort that qualifies the Fourth Amendment exclusionary rule.[183] The issue is whether evidence is admissible if officials violate the *Wade* entitlement to assistance in "objective good faith." This exception would apply if officials deny counsel at a corporeal identification procedure but reasonably could have believed that they had not denied the defendant his Sixth Amendment entitlement. Because a limited number of well-defined criteria govern this right to counsel, there are probably fewer opportunities for reasonable mistakes about the *Wade-Gilbert* entitlement than there are concerning the *Massiah* entitlement to counsel.[184] Nonetheless, "good faith" errors are possible. For example, an official might reasonably but erroneously believe that an individual was not yet formally accused of an offense at the time of a confrontation. Similarly, those conducting an identification procedure might have reasonable grounds for mistakenly concluding that an accused validly waived counsel. In these probably rare cases, should identification evidence be exempt from exclusion?

The answer depends on the nature of the *Wade-Gilbert* exclusion doctrine. If the sole justification for suppression is to discourage future counsel deprivations at pretrial identification confrontations, an exception would be warranted. The cost-benefit reasoning that supports the Fourth Amendment good faith exception dictates the same exception to *Wade-Gilbert*'s Sixth Amendment bar.[185] Deterrent gains resulting from suppression in cases of reasonably mistaken deprivations of the right to pretrial assistance would be deemed marginal, at best. The social costs of such suppression, however, would be substantial—more

---

183. For a discussion of the Fourth Amendment exception, see *supra* Chapter 1, text accompanying notes 238–60.

184. For a discussion of this type of good faith exception to the *Massiah* Sixth Amendment exclusionary rule, see *supra* Chapter 4, text accompanying notes 213–28.

185. See *supra* Chapter 1, text accompanying notes 250–52, for a discussion of the Fourth Amendment cost-benefit balance.

than sufficient to counterbalance any benefits. There is no basis for believing the Court would treat a sanction designed only to prevent future denials of assistance differently from the sanction that seeks to prevent unreasonable searches or seizures. Sixth Amendment exclusion of identifications would almost certainly be qualified by this kind of good faith exception. Evidence would be admissible when it was objectively reasonable for officials to believe that an unconstitutional identification procedure comported with the Sixth Amendment guarantee of counsel.[186]

If *Wade-Gilbert* exclusion is instead a personal right that belongs to the current accused—an essential measure to avoid the Sixth Amendment harm at trial—a good faith, reasonable mistaken belief exception is unjustified. Whether officers are culpable or innocent in conducting uncounseled identification confrontations, the accused suffers constitutional injury in the courtroom when the government introduces evidence obtained as a result of a pretrial confrontation without assistance. Denials of the guarantee of counsel violate the Sixth Amendment regardless of the fault of government officials. Thus, if the exclusion of identification evidence is an inseparable part of the right to trial assistance, exclusion is essential to avoid a denial of the right even if it is reasonable to believe that the accused has not been deprived of his *Wade-Gilbert* entitlement.

In sum, situations justifying the application of either sort of good faith exception are likely to be very rare. It seems unlikely that the Court would endorse a legitimate, good faith investigation exception to the *Wade-Gilbert* bar. If Sixth Amendment suppression, like the Fourth Amendment and *Massiah* rules, proves to be purely deterrent in nature, a reasonable mistaken belief exception seems valid. If it is a constitutional trial right, that exception is unjustified.

d. Possible Public Safety or Exigency Exceptions It seems somewhat more probable that the facts surrounding uncounseled identification confrontations could support a "public safety" or "exigency" exception to Sixth Amendment exclusion.[187] The likelihood of such a scenario, however, is limited by the threshold requirement for attachment of the right to counsel—an initiation of adversary judicial proceedings. Public safety needs and exigencies requiring prompt identifications are much more likely to arise prior to formal charges, while an individual is a mere suspect who is not entitled to assistance.

While they are related, there is a distinction between an exception based on public safety and one based on exigency. Both are premised on an assertion that

---

186. If deterrence is the singular objective here, it is even possible that the Court would qualify the Sixth Amendment exclusionary rule with a threshold culpability requirement similar to the incipient culpability demand developing under the Fourth Amendment exclusionary rule.

187. New York has apparently endorsed an "exigent circumstance" exception to right to counsel based exclusion of identification evidence. *See* Nathan R. Sobel, Eyewitness Identification: Legal and Practical Problems 113 (Dee Pridgen ed., 2d ed. 2007).

some important public interest justified the conduct of an identification procedure without counsel. The justification might be that counsel could obstruct any identification or that the delay required to secure a lawyer's presence would prevent timely identification. They are distinctive insofar as they rest on different types of public interest—that is, different varieties of harm that might result from honoring the entitlement to counsel.

A public safety exception would apply when knowledge of an individual's identity would assist efforts to prevent some serious harm or injury to one or more members of the public. Officers might need to identify a kidnapper to save a victim's life. They might need to know a terrorist's identity to prevent an explosion or hijacking. They might need to identify a large-scale drug dealer to prevent the distribution of dangerous narcotics to children. Harm might or might not be imminent, but the exception would only apply if it was reasonable for an officer to conclude that compliance with the counsel requirement would cause a sufficiently serious injury to the public.[188]

One theoretical basis for the admission of evidence in a public safety situation would be a limitation upon the right to counsel, rather than an exception to the exclusion doctrine. One might argue that unlike the Sixth Amendment right to assistance of counsel *at trial*, which is unqualified,[189] the pretrial right to counsel recognized by *Wade* and its progeny does not extend to confrontations serving sufficient public safety concerns. In essence, the contention would be that an accused's interest in having counsel at that critical stage is less substantial, less important, less critical, less fundamental than the interest in having counsel at the trial, and that it is outweighed by a significant enough public safety interest. If an accused has no entitlement to assistance because of the countervailing interest in preventing serious harm, then neither a deterrent nor a constitutional right foundation could support exclusion. There would be no wrongful action by officials, thus nothing to deter. Because there would be no pretrial deprivation of an entitlement to counsel, there could be no violation of the Sixth Amendment by the use of identification evidence against the accused at trial.

The contrary argument begins with the premise that the pretrial entitlement to assistance is an extension of the Sixth Amendment guarantee that is necessary to avoid erosion of the right to assistance at trial. This threat of erosion is the result of evolutionary changes in the processes of criminal justice—in particular, the development of significant pretrial phases. Because the pretrial extension of

---

188. The exception would be analogous to the public safety exception recognized under the *Miranda* exclusion doctrine. For a discussion of that exception, see *supra* Chapter 3, text accompanying notes 154–70.

189. Indigent defendants have no right to *appointed* assistance when tried for misdemeanor level offenses if they are not sentenced to a term of incarceration. For a discussion of this limitation, see *supra* note 155; *see also supra* Chapter 4, text accompanying notes 157–62.

the right to assistance is inseparable from the trial right, and because it is essential to the fairness of the trial, it is neither inferior nor less fundamental. Consequently, a public safety need cannot justify denying an accused the safeguard of counsel in critical pretrial confrontations for identification purposes.[190]

It is unclear whether the Court would so limit the right to pretrial assistance. *Wade* suggested that there were "[n]o substantial countervailing policy considerations" that could outweigh the need for counsel to ensure a fair trial.[191] The "policy considerations" the Court had in mind, however, were the ordinary interests in securing identification evidence that would help the state convict criminals. The *Wade* majority did not consider a situation involving a serious threat to an important public safety interest. Moreover, the modified understanding of the right to pretrial assistance reflected in *United States v. Ash* might indicate a willingness to treat pretrial assistance as distinguishable from, and possibly less fundamental than, the right to trial counsel. *Ash* rests on the premise that the right to counsel reaches pretrial identification processes because the accused needs a "spokesman" and an "advisor" during these "trial-like" pretrial confrontations to protect against adversarial injuries that might occur then and there, not because the special hazards of misidentification engendered by pretrial identification processes can undermine the substance of the trial

---

190. One might also contend that because identification sessions without counsel produce unreliable evidence—that is, because they harbor serious risks of misidentification—they would not, as a practical matter, serve the interest in preventing public safety threats. Identification of the wrong person would not help officials save a kidnap victim or thwart terrorism, but might lead to oppressive treatment of an innocent individual. According to this argument, the presence of counsel would only improve the government's ability to combat a public safety threat because a lawyer would ensure a more reliable identification. On the other hand, uncounseled confrontations are not always misleading. They may well result in correct identifications that help officials prevent harm. The absence of a lawyer may increase the risks of error, but it does not ensure misidentification. Moreover, if counsel assumes an active role in the conduct of the identification process, there are certainly instances in which she might prevent the government from securing an identification needed to deal with a serious threat. This argument does run contrary to the *Wade* majority's assumption that a lawyer's presence would do more good than harm, because identifications resulting from procedures with counsel are generally more reliable than those resulting from uncounseled procedures. The *Wade* Court, however, struck a balance for the ordinary case, not for situations in which the well-being of the public is in serious danger. When added to the risk that counsel might be counterproductive, the interest in protecting the public safety could tip the scales against a right to assistance.

191. United States v. Wade, 388 U.S. 218, 237 (1967). The Court did indicate that in situations where there is a need for a prompt identification "substitute counsel" might satisfy the Sixth Amendment. In other words, countervailing interests might be a reason to deny an accused the usual entitlement to his own personal lawyer. *See id.*

counsel guarantee.[192] This understanding of counsel could permit a restriction of pretrial assistance that would not be possible were the trial right at stake.

If the pretrial right to counsel extends to public safety situations, the question is whether evidence should be admissible when officers deny that right. If exclusion is a constitutional entitlement of the accused—a personal Sixth Amendment trial right—then a public safety exception is clearly unjustifiable. The Sixth Amendment right to counsel is unqualified. An accused has the right not to be convicted on the basis of an imbalanced adversarial process in which he has not been accorded the equalizing protection of a trained lawyer. The government cannot suspend that entitlement because of important countervailing public interests. This is not to say that officials are forbidden from conducting identification procedures without counsel to protect the public safety. If a right to counsel violation is completed *only* upon introduction of evidence at trial, a plausible position, the state would be free to confront the accused without assistance and use information gained to protect the public. It would not run afoul of the Constitution unless it used that information to convict.[193]

If suppression in this setting is purely a deterrent, concerned only with preventing future wrongs, it is still difficult to justify a public safety exception to the Sixth Amendment exclusionary rule. The exception would rest on cost-benefit balancing. The reasoning would be that ordinarily the balance of interests favors suppression. However, when the harm to the public caused by deterring officers from conducting uncounseled lineups to gain necessary information is added to the cost side of the scales, the balance tips in favor of admission. Costs then outweigh gains. The problem with this reasoning is that if the very same public safety interests do not justify a restriction of the right to pretrial assistance, it is difficult to see why they should justify a suspension of efforts to enforce and preserve that right. A deterrent objective rests on the premise that the Sixth Amendment is violated when a pretrial confrontation occurs. If the pretrial assistance of counsel is a fundamental right that cannot be denied because of a public safety threat, then the interest in deterring violations of that right is not outweighed by harms to the public safety.

In sum, the Supreme Court could conclude that public safety interests justify a narrowing of the scope of the right to assistance at pretrial confrontations

---

192. *See* United States v. Ash, 413 U.S. 300, 310–12 (1973). Although this is a plausible reading of *Ash*, it may not be the only defensible interpretation. The *Ash* Court might have meant that an accused needs a spokesman and advisor in pretrial trial-like encounters to protect him at that time *and* to ensure that the ultimate battle at trial is fair.

193. This would be analogous to the protection afforded by the privilege against self-incrimination. That Fifth Amendment safeguard does not prevent the government from compelling an individual to disclose evidence it needs or desires to serve one of its interests. It merely forbids the government's use of compelled disclosures against such an individual in the courtroom. *See* Chavez v. Martinez, 538 U.S. 760, 766–67 (2003).

for identification purposes. However, if the Court were to conclude otherwise, it is difficult to justify a public safety exception to the *Wade-Gilbert* exclusion doctrine.

An exigency exception would be narrower than a public safety exception. It would apply when there was a compelling need for an immediate identification by a particular eyewitness. A witness could be at imminent risk of dying or lapsing into a coma. If she does not have an immediate opportunity to identify the accused, she might never have a chance to do so, and a guilty defendant might go free as a result. The public interest at stake is the need for evidence both to ensure that a perpetrator is brought to justice and to protect the public against future harms that perpetrator might inflict.

Again, the Court could conclude that an accused has no right to counsel when the need for a timely identification prevents the government from honoring that entitlement. The interests in ensuring that a witness has an opportunity to speak and in providing the state an opportunity to have the witness's testimony could outweigh a pretrial right deemed less fundamental than the right to trial assistance. As noted earlier, the *Wade* Court found "[n]o substantial countervailing policy considerations" justifying the denial of counsel.[194] In addition, the Court addressed the possible need for expedition by suggesting that an accused's right to counsel might be satisfied by the presence of *any* lawyer—that is, there might be no need for the defendant's personal retained or appointed lawyer to be present.[195] Thus, the Court indicated that it might be unreceptive to denying the right to counsel based on exigencies.[196] Moreover, on the same day it decided *Wade* and *Gilbert*, the Court addressed a situation involving the necessity for an immediate confrontation for purposes of identification and held that exigency does limit the due process right against evidence produced by suggestive identification procedures.[197] The Court suggested no similar limitation upon the right to assistance. Still, neither *Wade* nor *Gilbert* involved exigencies, and none of the later opinions actually raised the issue. It remains possible, though by no means certain, that the Court would restrict the right to counsel in such situations. Without a right to assistance, there would be no predicate for exclusion.

If exigent circumstances are not a legitimate ground for denying counsel, it seems unlikely that they could support an exemption from the Sixth Amendment

194. *Wade*, 388 U.S. at 237.

195. *See id.*

196. In addition, if substitute counsel is sufficient, the number of situations in which the state could justify conducting an identification procedure without counsel would be limited. The government would have to show that the need for an expedited identification process made it infeasible to arrange for the presence of *any* lawyer.

197. *See* Stovall v. Denno, 388 U.S. 293, 301–02 (1967) (holding that there is a due process bar to the use of identifications resulting from "unnecessarily suggestive" processes and concluding that the suggestive procedure used in the case was necessary).

suppression doctrine. Evidentiary exclusion that is part of the unqualified right to counsel cannot be denied in order to serve law enforcement needs. Countervailing interests do not justify a deprivation of the right. Moreover, a deterrence-based suppression sanction should not be suspended if it is designed to enforce a constitutional right that is a defendant's Sixth Amendment entitlement despite competing, compelling law enforcement needs.

e. Impeachment Use of Eyewitness Identification Evidence Inadmissible eyewitness identification evidence might prove useful to impeach a defendant's trial testimony or the testimony of a defense witness. An accused might deny participation in a bank robbery or an arson, or a friend might furnish an alibi, testifying that the accused was with her at the time of these offenses. A lineup identification of the defendant as the robber or arsonist, or as being near the scene of either offense at the relevant time, would contradict the trial testimony, casting doubt on the accused's or the friend's credibility. The question is whether such limited use of identification evidence barred from the prosecution's case-in-chief—that is, inadmissible as substantive proof of guilt—would be constitutionally acceptable. May a barred lineup identification be used for the narrow purpose of assisting a jury assess a witness's credibility when it is relevant to such an assessment?

The Supreme Court has not addressed impeachment use, and the dearth of cases involving Sixth Amendment suppression of eyewitness identification evidence makes it unlikely that an occasion to do so will arise. Nonetheless, opinions regarding the propriety of an impeachment use exception to other constitutional exclusion doctrines can provide a firm foundation for confident analyses of the issues. If the *Wade-Gilbert* bar is a personal trial right of the accused and is essential to avoid a Sixth Amendment violation in the courtroom, the use of an identification to impeach either the accused or a defense witness would be impermissible. Whether used as substantive proof of guilt or to cast doubt on witness credibility, the evidence will assist the government in its efforts to convict. By contributing to the accused's conviction—and erosion of the credibility of a defendant or his witnesses certainly makes conviction more likely and acquittal less likely—impeachment use inflicts the kind of adversary system harm that is the basis for recognizing a right to exclusion. Although impeachment use may be less harmful than substantive use, it is still injurious. It brings to fruition at trial a constitutional deprivation begun at the uncounseled pretrial confrontation.[198] It results in the same sort of trial unfairness that is the basis for understanding *Wade-Gilbert* as an integral part of the right to counsel guarantee.

---

198. The analysis is the same as it is for the right to exclude coerced confessions extended by due process and the privilege against compulsory self-incrimination. Any use of the evidence, even limited impeachment use, is a constitutional transgression. *See supra* Chapter 2, text accompanying notes 241–45.

If the Court were to follow the misguided, but likely, course of casting Sixth Amendment suppression as a purely deterrent safeguard aimed entirely at preventing future wrongs, the result would be different. The Court has declared that the use of illegally acquired evidence to impeach a defendant's testimony given either on direct or cross-examination is entirely consistent with the cost-benefit balancing underlying the Fourth Amendment's purely deterrent sanction.[199] Similarly, the classification of *Massiah*'s exclusionary rule as a mere future-oriented deterrent led the Court to authorize the use of barred disclosures to impeach an accused's trial testimony.[200] The same analysis leads to the same conclusion for a deterrence-grounded *Wade-Gilbert* rule.

However, the Court has refused to allow the use of evidence obtained in violation of the Fourth Amendment to impeach defense witnesses other than the defendant. The balance of costs and benefits militates against expanding the Fourth Amendment impeachment use exception to reach defense witnesses.[201] One might contend that the pretrial right to assistance enforced by *Wade-Gilbert* exclusion is less fundamental than the Fourth Amendment's protection and, therefore, that a ban on impeaching defense witnesses yields less weighty deterrent benefits. As a result, the cost-benefit balance might be thought to favor admission. It seems somewhat unlikely, however, that the Court would view the pretrial right to assistance as inferior to the protection against unreasonable searches and seizures.[202] If it is as important to enforce the right to counsel as it is to enforce the right against unreasonable searches and seizures, then the *Wade-Gilbert* doctrine, like the Fourth Amendment suppression rule, would prohibit the impeachment of defense witnesses with the products of unconstitutional pretrial confrontations.

In sum, like several other possible limitations, the propriety of an impeachment use exception to Sixth Amendment exclusion hinges on the underlying nature of evidentiary suppression. A constitutional right premise leads to a quite different outcome than a deterrent foundation. The validity of an impeachment use exception to *Wade-Gilbert* suppression is uncertain because the nature of this exclusion doctrine remains in doubt.

---

199. See *supra* Chapter 1, text accompanying notes 261–68, for a detailed discussion of the reasoning that would dictate the same result here.

200. See *supra* Chapter 4, text accompanying notes 243–56, for a thorough explanation of the reasoning that led to this result under *Massiah*.

201. For a discussion of this limitation on impeachment use, see *supra* Chapter 1, text accompanying notes 269–71.

202. If anything, the Court has suggested that Fourth Amendment rights may be less important than fair trial protections like the right to counsel. *See* Schneckloth v. Bustamonte, 412 U.S. 218, 239–43 (1973).

E. CONCLUSIONS ABOUT SIXTH AMENDMENT EXCLUSION OF EYEWITNESS IDENTIFICATIONS

The Sixth Amendment right to counsel doctrine excluding eyewitness identification evidence is among the least developed of the exclusionary rules in every respect. The historical development of the doctrine was exceedingly brief. It first appeared in 1967, and the last time the Supreme Court addressed the subject was in 1977—just 10 years later and nearly 35 years ago. In *United States v. Wade* and *Gilbert v. California*, the companion opinions which gave birth to this suppression mandate, the Supreme Court addressed the justifications for excluding evidence. Those opinions indicate that at its inception the rule was viewed as both a present trial right belonging to individual defendants and a deterrent sanction designed to prevent state agents from denying counsel to future defendants. In three subsequent opinions that focused primarily upon the scope of the pretrial right to assistance that is the basis for evidentiary exclusion, the Court provided precious little insight into the character of the suppression remedy. In light of the dramatic changes in the Court's attitude toward exclusionary rules during the past four decades, there is reason to wonder whether the original understanding of this rule's foundations and rationales would survive. Suffice it to say there is uncertainty today about the underpinnings of the Sixth Amendment bar to eyewitness identifications.

In addition to its modest history and the exceedingly limited attention to its justifications, the *Wade-Gilbert* exclusionary rule has undergone minimal doctrinal development. All we know is that there is a *per se* bar to initial identifications and a presumptive bar to derivative identifications. The Court has revealed no other details about the presumptive reach of this evidentiary bar and has addressed no exceptions other than the "independent source" qualification for successive identifications, which was explained thoroughly in *Wade* and never again revisited. I have explored the possibility of extending to the *Wade-Gilbert* setting a number of the exceptions discussed, and sometimes adopted, in other exclusionary rule contexts. I have explained arguments for and against extending these exceptions to this rule and have highlighted, once again, how much depends on the governing rationale for suppression. In sum, the doctrinal structure of the Sixth Amendment's eyewitness identification exclusionary rule is skeletal. The few known details about its operation contrast dramatically with the richer doctrinal development of the rules discussed in the preceding chapters.

Moreover, it seems entirely unlikely that further development will occur. Cases involving disputed *Wade-Gilbert* issues are rare indeed. There is little chance that the Supreme Court will have opportunities to address unsettled questions. Moreover, because this constitutional exclusion doctrine has little pragmatic impact—prosecutors rarely have their cases threatened by the bar to evidence it poses—there is no reason to believe that the definition of its contours will rise to the top of the Court's agenda. If the Supreme Court were to revisit

Wade-Gilbert, its general hostility toward evidentiary suppression would probably lead to the endorsement of a misguided deterrence rationale rooted in cost-benefit balancing. This justification for suppression would harbor the potential to restrict the doctrine's scope in ways it has confined the reach of other doctrines. That potential, however, will almost certainly not be realized. The *Wade-Gilbert* doctrine is theoretically significant. It has provided important insights into the nature of the Sixth Amendment right to counsel. Nonetheless, its Sixth Amendment exclusionary rule is a harmless, nearly dormant bar to evidence that is unlikely to be reawakened.

6. DUE PROCESS EXCLUSION OF EYEWITNESS IDENTIFICATIONS

INTRODUCTION

The preceding chapter explored Sixth Amendment-based exclusion of eyewitness identification evidence. This chapter addresses and analyzes the second constitutional basis for suppressing identifications—the Fourteenth Amendment Due Process Clause bar to identification evidence resulting from unnecessarily suggestive government methods.[1] There are noteworthy similarities between the two constitutional prohibitions on the introduction of identification evidence. The objective of both is the same—to prevent erroneous convictions of innocent individuals based on mistaken eyewitness identifications.[2] Both have relatively short histories which began on the same day in 1967 and ended a mere 10 years later.

---

1. The Fourteenth Amendment due process guarantee actually constrains only *state* officials. In *federal* court proceedings, the rule addressed here is grounded in the Fifth Amendment provision that ensures due process of law.

2. Eyewitness identification evidence is notoriously unreliable, but is influential with juries. *See* Charles A. Pulaski, Neil v. Biggers: *The Supreme Court Dismantles the* Wade *Trilogy's Due Process Protection*, 26 Stan. L. Rev. 1097, 1097 (1974) [hereinafter Pulaski, *Court Dismantles*]; Benjamin E. Rosenberg, *Rethinking the Right to Due Process in Connection with Pretrial Identification Procedures: An Analysis and a Proposal*, 79 Ky. L.J. 259, 260 (1991) [hereinafter Rosenberg, *Rethinking the Right*]. Procedures used by officials to secure identifications from witnesses can exacerbate the dangers by misleading witnesses into erroneously identifying innocent individuals. *See* Pulaski, *supra*, at 1098; Gary L. Wells & Eric P. Seelau, *Eyewitness Identification: Psychological Research and Legal Policy on Lineups*, 1 Psychol. Pub. Pol'y & L. 765, 787 (1995) [hereinafter Wells & Seelau, *Psychological Research*]. When used at trial, identification evidence engenders serious risks that individuals will be convicted of crimes they did not commit. *See* Pulaski, *supra*, at 1098. In fact, identification evidence has been called "the single largest factor contributing to false convictions." Wells & Seelau, *supra*, at 787; *see also* Noah Clements, *Flipping a Coin: A Solution for the Inherent Unreliability of Eyewitness Identification Testimony*, 40 Ind. L. Rev. 271, 271 (2007) [hereinafter Clements, *Flipping a Coin*] (describing misidentification as "the leading cause of wrongful convictions in the United States"). The Supreme Court's decision to provide constitutional protection—both right to counsel and due process safeguards—was an effort to reduce, if not eliminate, the exacerbating effects of official suggestion and thereby prevent miscarriages of justice. *See* Amy Luria, *Showup Identifications: A Comprehensive Overview of the Problems and a Discussion of Necessary Changes*, 86 Neb. L. Rev. 515, 543–44 (2008) [hereinafter Luria, *Showup Identifications*] (arguing that "justice" is "better served by suppressing . . . identification evidence" secured by improper procedures because "far fewer innocent individuals will be wrongly incarcerated" and the

Moreover, neither has been the subject of extensive consideration or development by the Supreme Court. As with the *Wade-Gilbert* rule discussed in Chapter 5, there are relatively few significant rulings pertaining to the due process rule, and the Supreme Court has prescribed few doctrinal details. As will be seen, there are some noteworthy differences between the counsel and due process exclusion doctrines. First, the Court has been clear about the underlying premises of Fourteenth Amendment suppression. In the Court's view, the evidentiary bar is a trial right which belongs to an accused individual. Second, the due process right to exclusion does not include a *per se* bar to identification evidence. Despite a defendant's demonstration that the government employed a questionable, risky pretrial process, the prosecution might well be able to use any and all identifications made by witnesses subjected to that process.

In 1967, there was reason to believe that the right to counsel bar to identifications would afford the primary protection against misleading eyewitness identification evidence.[3] However, the subsequent imposition of two significant restrictions on the scope of the counsel entitlement—the formal accusation demand[4] and the need for an accused's physical presence[5]—severely limited the practical impact of the *Wade-Gilbert* doctrine and its evidentiary bar.[6] As a result, the importance of the due process entitlement—which governs identification procedures both before and after the initiation of formal charges and applies to both corporeal and noncorporeal methods—has increased.[7]

As with all prior chapters, the focus here is on the evidentiary exclusion that is constitutionally required. As noted, the due process bar is a personal constitutional right belonging to the accused on trial. Moreover, it is clear that the right to due process is violated *only* in the courtroom, *not* at the time officials acquire identification evidence.[8] Consequently, a discussion of this suppression doctrine entails

---

authorities will continue "to pursue the 'real outlaw[s]'") (quoting Manson v. Brathwaite, 432 U.S. 98, 127 (1977) (Marshall, J., dissenting)).

3. *See* Welsh S. White & James J. Tomkovicz, Criminal Procedure: Constitutional Constraints Upon Investigation and Proof 807 (6th ed. 2008).

4. *See supra* Chapter 5, text accompanying notes 61–66, 142–44.

5. *See supra* Chapter 5, text accompanying notes 88–89, 141.

6. *See* Pulaski, *Court Dismantles*, *supra* note 2, at 1102.

7. *See id.* at 1103. The *relative* significance of the due process doctrine has increased as a result of the suffocating constraints on the purview of the counsel guarantee. The *absolute* significance of the due process safeguard is another matter. Rulings that have limited the conditions dictating due process-based suppression have reduced the protection afforded by that guarantee as well. *See* Rosenberg, *Rethinking the Right*, *supra* note 2, at 261 (maintaining that later decisions "considerably weakened the right to due process" in this area, rendering it "little more than a dead letter [that] affords criminal defendants almost none of the protections . . . originally intended").

8. In this respect, the due process exclusion doctrine is different from almost all of the rules discussed in the preceding five chapters—including the due process guarantee

exploration of the breadth of the constitutional right itself. An introductory sketch of the due process rule will be followed by an account of its history. Thereafter, I offer a complete analysis of both the potential and the recognized justifications for suppression and consider the legitimacy of the current due process bar. Finally, I describe the contours of the doctrine in detail, explaining its presumptive reach and a number of qualifications that have been or may be recognized.

A. THE BASIC DUE PROCESS CLAUSE BAR TO EYEWITNESS IDENTIFICATION EVIDENCE

After deciding in *Wade*[9] and *Gilbert*[10] that an accused was entitled to legal assistance at a lineup following indictment and that identifications made by a witness at the lineup and thereafter were subject to suppression if officials failed to respect that entitlement, the Court immediately announced a second, independent constitutional safeguard against potentially unreliable identification evidence. In *Stovall v. Denno*,[11] the Court recognized due process protection against official identification procedures that are "unnecessarily suggestive and conducive to irreparable mistaken identification."[12] Over the next 10 years, this doctrine developed into a presumptive bar to any identification made by a witness at an unnecessarily suggestive pretrial identification process arranged by the government *and* to any subsequent identification—most commonly, an in-court identification—made by the same witness. A subsequent identification is presumed to be a derivative product of an initial identification that results from official suggestion conveyed to the witness. Derivative identifications are presumptively barred because they harbor the very same risks of misidentification as the initial identification—risks engendered by the government's suggestive technique.

Suppose, for example, that witnesses to a bank robbery report that the robber was short, dark-skinned, and long-haired. The police arrest a relatively short, dark-complected individual with long hair, then conduct a lineup involving the arrestee and five tall, light-skinned men with crew cuts. When witnesses hesitate, officers ask them to focus closely on suspect number three, the arrestee.

---

against coerced confessions. The use of coerced confessions in court violates due process, but officials can also violate due process when they subject individuals to coercive treatment outside the courtroom. *See supra* Chapter 2, text accompanying notes 158–59. Insofar as the only violation of constitutional rights occurs at trial, the due process bar to eyewitness identification is like the Fifth Amendment Privilege bar to compelled statements and the Sixth Amendment Confrontation Clause bar to hearsay discussed in Chapter 7.

9. United States v. Wade, 388 U.S. 218 (1967).

10. Gilbert v. California, 388 U.S. 263 (1967).

11. 388 U.S. 293 (1967).

12. *Id.* at 301–02.

Identifications of the arrestee made by witnesses at this lineup are excluded because the lineup was needlessly "suggestive." Some facets of the process—the appearances of the participants and the verbal indication that the witness should pay particular attention to the arrestee—could have induced or influenced the witnesses to select the arrestee whether or not he was the person observed at the robbery. There is no apparent reason why the suggestion was necessary—that is, officers could have found other participants with physical features similar to the arrestee's and had no need to urge hesitant witnesses to focus on him. Identifications are barred even if the accused has not been formally charged, has the assistance of counsel, or has validly waived legal assistance. Due process protection against misidentification yielded by unnecessary suggestion governs official identification processes held at any time and is quite independent of the entitlement to legal assistance. In addition, any later identification of the defendant by a witness who identified him at the improperly conducted lineup is also subject to suppression as derivative evidence.

Suppose, that investigators show a witness to a major drug transaction a single photo of the defendant, and ask whether he recognizes her. The witness identifies the woman in the photograph as the central figure in the drug deal. Later, when asked to identify the dealer at the defendant's trial in federal court, the witness points to the defendant. The photographic identification is excludable because the process was suggestive—it involved a single picture and no other choices. Moreover, it was unnecessarily suggestive because there is no evidence that officials could not have obtained and displayed other, somewhat similar pictures. The subsequent courtroom identification is subject to suppression because it is presumed to be a derivative product of the suggestive photo session.

However, all of these eyewitness identifications—the lineup identifications of the alleged robber, the photographic identification of the supposed drug dealer, and any courtroom identifications—could be admissible at trial to prove guilt. If the government shows, by a preponderance of the evidence, that any identification made was "reliable," the evidence may be introduced to prove guilt. In essence, the government must show that the identification was the product of a witness's recollection of crime scene perceptions of the culprit's appearance rather than the result of the unnecessarily suggestive method.[13] Suppose, for example, that the prosecution establishes that a witness had a particularly good opportunity to observe a criminal at the time of the crime, the lineup or photographic identification took place soon after the observations before the witness's memory has dimmed, the witness's description of the culprit matched the

---

13. The "reliability" inquiry and the pertinent factors are essentially the same as the "independent source" inquiry for right to counsel suppression of identification evidence and the factors bearing on that inquiry. *See supra* Chapter 5, text accompanying notes 173–76.

appearance of the individual identified, and the witness was confident in the accuracy of her identification. In these circumstances, a judge may well conclude that it is more likely than not that the witness selected the defendant at the lineup, chose the photograph, or will identify the accused at trial on the basis of memories of the crime, not because of the improper influences of the identification procedure. If so, the judge should refuse to exclude the identification evidence under the Due Process Clause.

In the limited number of decisions since 1967, the Supreme Court has addressed no other issues concerning the reach or operation of the due process entitlement to bar identification evidence. None of the specific exclusionary rule issues considered in earlier chapters has come before the Court. For example, the Justices have never considered whether a "standing" limitation governs, whether due process exclusion is confined to criminal trials, whether other types of derivative evidence are subject to suppression, whether inevitable discovery, attenuation, or good faith exceptions are appropriate, or whether evidence inadmissible for substantive purposes may be used to impeach witnesses. The final section of this chapter will discuss these questions and others, predicting likely resolutions when possible and highlighting competing arguments for any genuinely debatable issues.

B. THE BIRTH AND DEVELOPMENT OF THE DUE PROCESS BAR TO EYEWITNESS IDENTIFICATION EVIDENCE

As noted at the outset of the historical account in Chapter 5, the Supreme Court revolutionized the legal landscape of eyewitness identification processes on a single day in 1967.[14] Before the trilogy of eyewitness identification opinions handed down on June 12, 1967, there was no constitutional regulation of the methods used to secure this often crucial evidence of guilt. After that day, official identification procedures were constrained by both the Sixth Amendment right to counsel and the Fourteenth Amendment guarantee of due process. More important, for present purposes, two new exclusion doctrines posed barriers to the government's use of eyewitness identification evidence. *Wade* and *Gilbert* promulgated the right to counsel doctrine. *Stovall v. Denno*,[15] the third opinion in the triad, gave birth to the due process constraint.

---

14. For a brief discussion of the predicates for the Court's revolutionary decisions constitutionalizing eyewitness identification processes, see *supra* Chapter 5, text accompanying notes 13–14.

15. 388 U.S. 293 (1967).

In *Stovall*, the Behrendts, a married couple, were stabbed during an attack in their home.[16] While Mr. Behrendt died of his wounds, Mrs. Behrendt survived.[17] The next day, Mrs. Behrendt, who was seriously injured, had "major surgery to save her life."[18] That same day, the police arrested Stovall on the basis of evidence found at the Behrendts' home.[19] The following day, five officers and two members of the prosecutor's staff escorted him to Mrs. Behrendt's hospital room.[20] Stovall, who was the lone African-American in the room and did not have a lawyer present, was handcuffed to one of the officers.[21] After an officer asked him to repeat words used by the attacker for purposes of "'voice identification,'" Mrs. Behrendt identified him as the attacker.[22] At trial, she testified to this identification and also identified him in the courtroom.[23] A jury convicted Stovall of murder and he was sentenced to death.[24]

The Supreme Court first addressed Stovall's contention that his conviction should be reversed because he was entitled to the assistance of counsel at the hospital room confrontation. The Court concluded that the decisions in *Wade* and *Gilbert*—the first recognitions of such a right—were not retroactive. The right to counsel at identification confrontations extended only to *Wade, Gilbert,* and "all future cases" involving confrontations *after* the date of those decisions.[25] Because Stovall's hospital room confrontation had occurred well before that date, he was not entitled to counsel and the identifications were not suppressible on Sixth Amendment grounds.

The defendant also "claim[ed] that . . . the confrontation conducted in" the hospital room "was so unnecessarily suggestive and conducive to irreparable mistaken identification that he was denied due process of law."[26] According to the Court, this was "a recognized ground of attack upon a conviction independent of any right to counsel claim."[27] The Court acknowledged that the method

---

16. *Id.* at 295.
17. *Id.*
18. *Id.*
19. *Id.*
20. *Stovall,* 388 U.S. at 295.
21. *Id.*
22. *Id.*
23. *Id.*
24. *Id.*
25. *Stovall,* 388 U.S. at 296. The Supreme Court has subsequently modified its approach to deciding whether constitutional rulings are "retroactive." The modern approach is reflected in *Griffith v. Kentucky,* 479 U.S. 314 (1987) and *Teague v. Lane,* 489 U.S. 288 (1989).
26. *Stovall,* 388 U.S. at 301–02.
27. *Id* at 302. For support, the Court cited a single Court of Appeals opinion. This effortless, "almost casual[]" recognition that the Due Process Clause regulates identification processes was, in fact, a "novel" and quite significant ruling. *See* Rosenberg, *Rethinking*

used in this case was suggestive, highlighting that "[t]he practice of showing suspects singly to persons for the purpose of identification . . . ha[d] been widely condemned."[28] Nonetheless, there was no due process violation here. According to the Court, a due process claim "depends on the totality of the circumstances surrounding" an identification confrontation.[29] In *Stovall*, an "immediate hospital confrontation was imperative" because the victim was hospitalized after life-saving surgery and doctors did not know "'how long [she] might live.'"[30] The officers who were responsible for "'identifying the attacker'" needed to act immediately, and a "'police station line-up'" was not possible because the victim could not come to the jail.[31] Officers, therefore, "'followed the only feasible procedure and took [the defendant] to the hospital room.'"[32] Despite the official suggestion, there was no due process violation because the procedure employed was necessary.[33]

The relevant part of the *Stovall* opinion was exceedingly terse. The Court devoted a mere two paragraphs to the due process issue.[34] The Justices did not discuss the justification or rationale for due process concern with unnecessarily suggestive procedures. Perhaps it seemed obvious that the objective was to

---

the Right, *supra* note 2, at 264–65. It was the first time the Supreme Court had given any indication that such constitutional protection existed. *See id.*

28. *Stovall*, 388 U.S. at 302.

29. *Id.*

30. *Id.* (quoting Stovall v. Denno, 355 F.2d 731, 735 (2d. Cir. 1966)).

31. *Id.* In addition, Mrs. Behrendt was "'the only person in the world who could possibly exonerate Stovall.'" *Id.*

32. *Stovall*, 388 U.S. at 302 (quoting Stovall v. Denno, 355 F.2d 731, 735 (2d. Cir. 1966)).

33. The Court's analysis is questionable. An expeditious hospital room confrontation may well have been necessary, but the degree of suggestion present may have been avoidable. There is reason to wonder whether it would have been feasible to have more than one African-American male present, whether it was imperative that Stovall be the only person visibly handcuffed to an officer, and whether officers needed to ask whether he was the attacker instead of asking whether the victim recognized the attacker among those present in her room. Some suggestion was probably unavoidable, but it is far from certain that the process had to be so intensely suggestive. The risk of mistaken identification might have been lower if the officers had used a method less likely to induce the witness to choose the accused.

34. Justice Black disagreed with the analyses of both issues. He would have deemed *Wade* and *Gilbert* retroactive and would have held that Stovall was entitled to the protection of counsel at the hospital room confrontation. *Stovall*, 388 U.S. at 303–04 (Black, J., dissenting). Moreover, he would not have recognized a due process safeguard. In an analysis of the issue more than twice as long as the majority's discussion, he described the majority's holding "that the Due Process Clause [gave] it power to bar" eyewitness identification "testimony" as "an arbitrary, wholly capricious action." *Id.* at 306 (Black, J., dissenting).

prevent the unfairness of erroneous convictions.[35] Moreover, there was not a hint of why suggestive procedures that are necessary, and the risks of misidentification they entail, are compatible with the goals of due process. Finally, while it may have been implicit that a valid due process claim would require the suppression of eyewitness identification evidence, there was no explicit reference to an exclusionary sanction comparable to those prescribed by *Wade* and *Gilbert*.[36]

Less than a year later, the Court confronted another due process issue in *Simmons v. United States*.[37] The morning after a bank robbery, FBI agents showed snapshots of Simmons to five bank employees, and each identified him as "one of the robbers."[38] Later, when some of the employees were again shown pictures of Simmons, they identified him a second time.[39] At trial, the government did not introduce any of the pretrial photo identifications, but did have the employees identify the defendant from the witness stand.[40] Simmons was convicted of armed robbery. In the Supreme Court, he claimed that "his pretrial identification . . . was . . . so unnecessarily suggestive and conducive to misidentification as to deny him due process of law."[41] "[I]n light of the totality of surrounding circumstances," the Court found his claim "untenable."[42]

The Court first observed that law enforcement's improper use of photographs to secure identifications "may sometimes cause witnesses to err in identifying criminals."[43] Even proper photographic identification procedures could harbor risks of "incorrect identification," and suggestive procedures can "increase[]" that danger and heighten the "chance of misidentification."[44] A witness who errs initially is likely to remember "the image of the photograph rather than of the person actually seen," a phenomenon that "reduc[es] the trustworthiness of [any]

---

35. The Court also might have felt that its discussion of the concerns underlying its decision to interpose right to counsel protection in *Wade* and *Gilbert* was sufficient.

36. In one of the most thorough analyses of the due process doctrine, Professor Charles Pulaski asserts that "*Stovall* . . . indicated that the use of evidence obtained" by means of an "'unnecessarily suggestive'" procedure "would violate due process" and "condemned eyewitness testimony obtained from" certain kinds of "pretrial identification proceedings." Pulaski, *Court Dismantles*, *supra* note 2, at 1103 (quoting Stovall v. Denno, 388 U.S. 293, 302 (1967)). Indeed, it is difficult to imagine any "sanction" for unnecessarily suggestive identification techniques other than evidentiary suppression. Nevertheless, because the Court found no due process problem in *Stovall*, it could avoid specifying the remedy contemplated.

37. 390 U.S. 377 (1968).

38. *Id.* at 380.

39. *Id.* at 382.

40. *Id.*

41. *Id.* at 381.

42. *Simmons*, 390 U.S. at 383.

43. *Id.*

44. *Id.*

subsequent . . . identification" by that witness.[45] Despite the inherent "hazards," the Court was "unwilling to prohibit [the] employment" of photographic identification.[46] Instead, it would find a due process violation and set aside a "conviction[] based on eyewitness identification at trial following a pretrial identification by photograph . . . only if the photographic identification procedure was so impermissibly suggestive as to give rise to a very substantial likelihood of irreparable misidentification."[47]

The facts in *Simmons* did not satisfy this standard because it "was essential for the FBI agents swiftly to determine" whether their investigation of the robbery was "on the right track."[48] There was no suggestion that the identification procedure used was "unnecessary . . . in this instance."[49] In addition, there was "little chance that the procedure utilized led to misidentification of Simmons."[50] The witnesses had ample opportunities to observe Simmons at the scene; they viewed the photos a day after the robbery; they saw six different photographs which were primarily group shots; they observed the pictures while alone and not in the company of the other witnesses; and there was no indication that officials suggested in any way that they suspected any person in the photos.[51] All five witnesses identified Simmons and all confirmed their identifications at a subsequent photo display and at trial, and, when cross-examined none of them evinced "any doubt."[52] This combination of circumstances left "little room for doubt that the identification of Simmons was correct," despite an identification procedure that may have been "short of the ideal."[53] For that reason, "the identification procedure used was not such as to deny Simmons due process of law."[54]

---

45. *Id.* at 383–84.

46. *Id.* at 384.

47. *Simmons*, 390 U.S. at 384.

48. *Id.* at 385. According to the Court, the "justification" for the photographic "method of procedure" the officers used "was hardly less compelling" than the justification for the hospital room showup in *Stovall*. *Id.*

49. *Id.* at 384. In the words of the *Simmons* standard, the identification method was not *impermissibly* suggestive. Although the Court was not explicit initially about how the photographic showings to the bank employees were suggestive, it later specified the reasons for concern. According to the Justices, photograph procedures are inherently less reliable than in-person methods, and in *Simmons* the agents showed too few photos, the pictures contained too few individuals, and the agents displayed "proportionally" too many "pictures of" the defendant. *Id.* at 386 n.6. The Court did not explain why these suggestive features were necessitated by any exigencies.

50. *Id.* at 385.

51. *Id.*

52. *Simmons*, 390 U.S. at 385.

53. *Id.* at 385–86.

54. *Id.* at 386. Justice Black dissented once again. Declaring Simmons's due process claim "frivolous," he reiterated the view that the Court lacked authority to bar eyewitness

As in *Stovall*, the *Simmons* Court did not explicitly advert to or discuss evidentiary exclusion. A suppression sanction, however, was implicit in the assertion that the Constitution would require a conviction to be set aside if it were based on an identification resulting from an impermissibly suggestive session. It is noteworthy that *Simmons* was concerned only with a witness's courtroom identification following an earlier identification at a suggestive pretrial procedure. The standard announced and the analysis that led to a finding of no due process violation were limited to derivative identification evidence, and did not apply to identifications made *during* suggestive procedures. Moreover, the Court's reliance on two apparently independent and sufficient reasons for finding no due process deprivation created some ambiguity. The initial conclusion that the photographic methods were necessary could have ended the analysis. The Justices proceeded, however, to announce a second reason for rejecting the due process claim. Despite the potential for misidentification generated by the photographic displays, the facts surrounding the crime scene observations and the witnesses' identifications provided powerful evidence that they had accurately identified Simmons.[55]

---

identifications based on the suggestiveness of police methods. *Id.* at 395–96 (Black, J., concurring in part and dissenting in part).

55. According to the Court, the standard announced in *Simmons* "accord[ed] with [its] resolution of a similar issue" in *Stovall. Simmons*, 390 U.S. at 384. One critic has argued that even though the Justices did not "recognize [a] conceptual conflict," the *Simmons* standard, in fact, "represented a new formulation" prescribing "a very different inquiry" than *Stovall* in two "significant" respects. Pulaski, *Court Dismantles, supra* note 2, at 1107–09. First, *Simmons* required a defendant to show "'a very substantial likelihood' that the identification procedure irreparably tainted the witness'[s] ability to identify the true offender." *Id.* at 1108. In addition, it "attributed critical importance to the nature and extent of the witness'[s] ability to observe the offender at the scene" and found no due process violation "not because the display was unsuggestive, but because" the witnesses "were very probably correct." *Id. Stovall* understood due process as concerned with evidence obtained by "outrageously suggestive" and "potentially prejudicial means," while *Simmons*, in contrast, saw the focus and "true concern" of due process as "the factual unreliability of the identification evidence obtained, not the potential unreliability of the identification procedure used." *Id.* at 1109. For similar critiques, see Evan J. Mandery, *Due Process Considerations of In-Court Identifications*, 60 ALB. L. REV. 389, 393–94 (1996); Rosenberg, *Rethinking the Right, supra* note 2, at 266–67.

This criticism may be warranted. *Simmons* may have retracted some of the protection that *Stovall* promised. However, the differences between the opinions might instead reflect the evolution of a doctrine that was the subject of exceedingly minimal development when it first appeared less than a year earlier. *Stovall* decided that no due process deprivation resulted from the use of either an identification made at a suggestive procedure or a subsequent courtroom identification if the procedure was necessary. Without addressing the admissibility of a pretrial identification made during a suggestive process, *Simmons* indicated that due process does not bar a later courtroom identification if there is sufficient reason to believe that misidentification—the core Fourteenth Amendment concern—did not occur. Seen in this light, *Simmons* did not contradict or contract any

Just one year later, the Court addressed another due process challenge to identification evidence. In *Foster v. California*,[56] the day after an armed robbery of a Western Union office, one of the robbers turned himself in and reported that Foster was one of his accomplices.[57] The police arrested Foster, then summoned the office manager—the sole witness—to view a three-man police station lineup.[58] Foster, who was six or seven inches taller than the two other men in the lineup, wore a leather jacket that resembled one worn by one of the robbers.[59] When the manager could not positively identify Foster, he asked for and was granted the opportunity to meet with him in an office, but remained "uncertain whether [Foster] was one of the robbers."[60] Seven to ten days later, the manager observed a second lineup consisting of five men. Foster was the only individual who appeared in both lineups.[61] Upon viewing this lineup, the manager was "'convinced' [Foster] was the man."[62] At trial, he testified to this pretrial identification and identified the defendant in court, and Foster was convicted.[63]

Relying on the standard prescribed in *Stovall*, the Supreme Court found a due process violation.[64] The Justices acknowledged that the reliability of eyewitness identifications is ordinarily for the jury to determine. The "teaching" of the pathbreaking 1967 decisions, however, was that some "procedures leading to an eyewitness identification may be so defective as to make the identification *constitutionally inadmissible* as a matter of law."[65] *Foster* "present[ed] a compelling example of unfair lineup procedures" that were so defective they required evidentiary exclusion.[66] First, the defendant's height and jacket singled him out at the initial lineup.[67] After the witness expressed uncertainty, the police arranged "a one-to-one confrontation"—a presentation of the accused alone to the witness.[68] When the witness was still "tentative," officers arranged yet another lineup a week or more later in which the defendant was the only recurrent participant.[69] The "suggestive elements" in this sequence of events

protection extended by *Stovall*, but, instead, began to flesh out the exclusionary consequences of suggestive identification procedures.

56. 394 U.S. 440 (1969).
57. *Id.* at 441.
58. *Id.*
59. *Id.*
60. *Id.*
61. *Foster*, 394 U.S. at 441–42.
62. *Id.* at 442.
63. *Id.* at 441–42.
64. *Id.* at 442–43.
65. *Id.* at 442–43 n.2 (emphasis added).
66. *Foster*, 394 U.S. at 442.
67. *Id.* at 442–43.
68. *Id.* at 443.
69. *Id.*

"made it all but inevitable that [the manager] would identify [the accused] whether or not he was in fact 'the man.'"[70] Because the authorities effectively told the witness repeatedly that Foster was the robber, their methods "so undermined the reliability of the eyewitness identification as to violate due process."[71]

Despite its brevity, the *Foster* majority opinion was significant. For the first time, the Court explicitly recognized that the Due Process Clause required the exclusion of some eyewitness identification evidence. Moreover, the failure to distinguish between the identification made at the improper lineup and the subsequent in-court identification seemed to confirm what *Simmons* intimated—that a due process derivative evidence principle could bar successive identifications by witnesses subjected to deficient procedures.[72] *Foster*'s exclusive reliance on the defects in the processes might have indicated that when the methods were extremely suggestive there was no reason to consider the reliability of any identifications made.[73] On the other hand, it is far from certain that the Court meant to preclude the possibility of admitting an identification, despite extreme improprieties, if a witness's opportunity to observe and other factors demonstrated that it was probably correct.[74] Finally, *Foster* was the first (and remains the *only*) case in which the Supreme Court found a violation of the due process protection against official identification procedures and reversed a conviction on that basis.[75]

In 1970, for the fourth straight year, the Court confronted a due process challenge to an identification procedure. In *Coleman v. Alabama*,[76] a man who had parked his car along a highway to change a flat tire was approached by three men and shot twice.[77] Approximately two months later, the victim observed a police station lineup.[78] He "spontaneously" identified one of his attackers "before

---

70. *Id.*

71. *Foster*, 394 U.S. at 443. For the third time, Justice Black expressed opposition to the due process doctrine and its exclusion of eyewitness testimony, maintaining that it posed a serious threat to the concept of trial by jury. *See id.* at 446–51 (Black, J., dissenting).

72. While the cryptic nature of the *Foster* opinion did create some unclarity about whether subsequent courtroom identifications were subject to exclusion, *see id.* at 445 (Black, J., dissenting), in light of the earlier opinion in *Simmons*, it seems preferable to understand *Foster* as endorsing a derivative evidence principle that rendered subsequent identifications presumptively inadmissible.

73. *See* Pulaski, *Court Dismantles*, *supra* note 2, at 1110.

74. *See id.* at 1111; *see also* Rosenberg, *Rethinking the Right*, *supra* note 2, at 269 (contending that like *Stovall* and *Simmons*, *Foster* generated considerable ambiguity about when the jury could and could not receive evidence and when procedures were sufficiently suggestive to bar the admission of evidence obtained).

75. *See* Neil v. Biggers, 409 U.S. 188, 197 (1972); Pulaski, *Court Dismantles*, *supra* note 2, at 1110.

76. 399 U.S. 1 (1970).

77. *Id.* at 4.

78. *Id.* at 3.

the formal lineup even began."[79] He then identified another assailant at the lineup, but before the assailant spoke "words used by the attackers."[80] At trial, the victim identified the two defendants as his attackers and they were convicted of assault with intent to murder.[81]

The defendants claimed that "the lineup was so unduly prejudicial as fatally to taint [the victim's] in-court identification[s]."[82] The issue was whether the Fourteenth Amendment barred these courtroom identifications as the product of an improperly suggestive lineup. A plurality of the Justices[83] ruled that the courtroom identifications were admissible because there was no error in the finding that they "did not stem from an identification procedure . . . 'so impermissibly suggestive as to give rise to a very substantial likelihood of irreparable misidentification.'"[84] The Justices did not determine whether the lineup had been fairly conducted.[85] Instead, they based their conclusion on evidence that the victim's identifications of the men were "entirely based upon observations at the time of the assault and not at all induced by the conduct of the lineup."[86] There was no "evidence that anything the police said or did prompted [the] virtually spontaneous identification[s] of [the defendants] among the lineup participants as the proceeding got under way."[87] The contentions that the defendants were the only participants required to speak words lacked merit because there was evidence that the victim identified them "before either said anything."[88] If the pretrial identifications were not the product of the lineup, then no matter how suggestive it might have been, due process could not bar the courtroom identifications.

Coleman was a terse opinion with limited significance. Still, it did confirm what *Simmons* had suggested—that subsequent identifications by witnesses subjected to "impermissibly suggestive" methods *could be* barred by a derivative evidence principle. The *Coleman* plurality concluded that the in-court identifications

---

79. *Id.* at 5.

80. *Id.*

81. *Coleman*, 399 U.S. at 3.

82. *Id.* at 4.

83. Only four Justices joined the part of the opinion resolving this question. None of the other Justices, however, save Justice Black—who again objected to the legitimacy of the *Stovall* doctrine, *see id.* at 13 (Black, J., concurring)—disagreed with the plurality's analysis of the due process claims.

84. *Id.* at 5 (quoting Simmons v. United States, 390 U.S. 377, 384 (1968)).

85. The defendants alleged that they were the only men required to speak the words used by the attackers, but a detective asserted that all participants in the lineup spoke the words. *Id.* at 6. In addition, Coleman alleged that he had been "unfairly singled out to wear a hat," but the Court found nothing to suggest "he was required to do so." *Id.*

86. *Coleman*, 399 U.S. at 5–6.

87. *Id.* at 6.

88. *Id.*

were admissible because they "did not stem from" a tainted lineup. This furnished a basis for arguing that successive identifications by a witness who was exposed to suggestive influences were admissible because the witness was, in fact, recalling memories of crime scene observations, not memories of the lineup. On the other hand, the *Coleman* plurality did not rule that the courtroom identifications lacked a connection to an impermissibly suggestive lineup because the witness had ignored the suggestive influences at the lineup and recalled his original perceptions. Instead, the conclusion that the courtroom testimony was "entirely based on observations at the time of the assault" rested on evidence that there was no causal connection between the pretrial identifications themselves and the lineup.[89]

After *Coleman*, more than two years passed before the Court considered another case involving due process protection against official identification methods. *Neil v. Biggers*[90] involved a sexual assault of a victim by a young man who had broken into her home. During the seven months after the crime, despite several opportunities to view suspects in lineups and showups both at the police station and in her home and to review between 30 and 40 photographs, the victim identified no one.[91] Police officers then summoned her to the station to observe the defendant who was being held on a different charge.[92] Because they could find no other individuals matching his "unusual physical description," the police did not arrange a lineup.[93] Instead, two detectives walked Biggers past the victim.[94] At her request, he was directed to repeat words spoken by her assailant, and when he did so the victim identified him, saying that she had "'no doubt.'"[95] This station-house identification was introduced at trial, and the defendant was convicted of rape.[96]

The question was whether the "identification and the circumstances surrounding it failed to comport with due process requirements."[97] More specifically, the constitutional issue was whether the "due process protection against

---

89. *Id.* at 5–6. One commentator has observed that *Coleman* not only weakened the due process entitlement extended by *Stovall*, but also produced confusion about that entitlement. The confusion was the product of the Court's failure to address and resolve a critical question—"whether the purpose of the [due process] right was to guarantee the reliability of eyewitness identifications or to protect against abusive procedures." Rosenberg, *Rethinking the Right*, *supra* note 2, at 272.

90. 409 U.S. 188 (1972).

91. *Id.* at 194–95.

92. *Id* at 195.

93. *Id.*

94. *Id.*

95. *Biggers*, 409 U.S. at 195.

96. *Id.* at 189. There was "controversy" over whether the victim also identified the accused in the courtroom as well. *Id.* at 198 n.5.

97. *Id.* at 196.

the admission of evidence deriving from suggestive identification procedures" dictated the exclusion of the rape victim's pretrial identification of the accused.[98] The majority began its analysis by focusing on "the relationship between suggestiveness and misidentification."[99] Previous opinions had established "that the primary evil to be avoided" by the due process doctrine, "is 'a very substantial likelihood of irreparable misidentification.'"[100] Evidence produced by "unnecessarily suggestive" methods is barred because those methods gratuitously "increase the] chance of misidentification."[101] Ultimately, "[i]t is the likelihood of misidentification which violates [the] right to due process," and requires the exclusion of evidence.[102] Therefore, the constitutional "standard for determining" the admissibility of any identification—both one made during a pretrial confrontation and one made later—must be tied to and reflect the likelihood that it is mistaken.[103]

The Court acknowledged that prior decisions were unclear about whether "unnecessary suggestiveness alone requires the exclusion of [identification] evidence."[104] It was still uncertain whether the prosecution could ever introduce an identification made at a pretrial session that unjustifiably involved sufficient suggestion to generate a very substantial likelihood that an observer would be induced to misidentify a participant.[105] It remained possible that initial

---

98. *Id.*

99. *Id.* at 198.

100. *Biggers*, 409 U.S. at 198 (quoting Simmons v. United States, 390 U.S. 377, 384 (1968)).

101. *Id.*

102. *Id.*

103. *Id.* Even though *Simmons* had developed the "'very substantial likelihood of irreparable misidentification' . . . standard for determining whether an in-court identification would be admissible in the wake of a suggestive out-of-court identification, with the deletion of 'irreparable' [that standard] serves equally well as a standard for the admissibility of testimony concerning the out-of-court identification itself." *Id.* (quoting Simmons v. United States, 390 U.S. 377, 384 (1968)).

104. *Id.* at 198–99. None of the precedents had *clearly* decided that any identification evidence could be introduced when a witness initially identifies a suspect at an unnecessarily suggestive procedure. *Stovall* and *Simmons* had involved necessary suggestion. *Foster* had mandated exclusion. *Coleman* had described the identifications as spontaneous and not the result of the lineup.

105. For that matter, it was not certain that a *subsequent* identification by a witness who made such an initial identification could ever be admitted. While *Simmons* did allow the introduction of a courtroom identification following an apparently suggestive photographic procedure, the Court relied in part on necessity in deciding that the in-court identification was admissible. *See supra* text accompanying notes 48–49. Nonetheless, the sole concern in *Biggers* was the admissibility of a pretrial identification—what the Court referred to as "evidence of unnecessarily suggestive confrontations." *Biggers*, 409 U.S. at 199.

identifications were governed by a *per se* bar analogous to the Sixth Amendment bar to identifications made at confrontations conducted without counsel.[106]

The *Biggers* Court refused to impose a *per se* ban on the pretrial identification in that case, concluding that the victim's identification of her assailant did not have to be suppressed despite unnecessary official suggestion.[107] According to the Court, the only "purpose of a strict rule barring evidence of unnecessarily suggestive confrontations would be to deter the police from using a less reliable procedure where a more reliable one may be available."[108] Deterrence was not an appropriate objective because the procedure that produced the evidence at issue in *Biggers* had occurred before *Stovall*—that is, at a time when there was no reason to believe suggestiveness was a constitutional concern.[109]

Consequently, the question was whether the identification of the accused "was reliable" despite the official suggestion.[110] Put another way, admissibility depended on whether that identification entailed a sufficient "likelihood of misidentification."[111] The Court identified a number of factors relevant to the assessment. Because these factors, on balance, supported a finding that there was "no substantial likelihood of misidentification" by the victim, the introduction of her identification of the defendant at trial did not violate due process.[112]

---

106. *See supra* Chapter 5, text accompanying notes 170–72.

107. The Court agreed that the authorities could have made a better effort to construct a fair, nonsuggestive lineup, observing that "the police did not exhaust all possibilities in seeking persons physically comparable to" the defendant. *Biggers*, 409 U.S. at 199.

108. *Id.* According to the Court, an absolute prohibition on use would not rest on "the assumption that in every instance the admission of [such] evidence . . . offends due process." *Id.* Put otherwise, a categorical bar would exclude some trustworthy, accurate identifications which could not deprive a defendant of due process because they could not undermine the fairness of the trial's outcome.

109. *Id.* In other words, even assuming that a *per se* exclusionary rule was needed to deter improper processes in future cases, a failure to suppress a pre-*Stovall* identification could not undermine the deterrent efficacy of a strict bar for procedures conducted after *Stovall*. The narrow ruling in *Biggers* offered no incentives for officers seeking post-*Stovall* identifications. It did not promise any profit from unnecessary suggestion.

110. *Id.*

111. *Id.*

112. *Biggers*, 409 U.S. at 201. Briefly, the Court concluded that the time the victim was in her attacker's presence, the lighting conditions, her direct and intimate observations of him, and the fact that she was a practical nurse and a victim of rape afforded "an unusual opportunity to observe and identify her assailant" and suggested a high degree of attention on her part. *Id.* at 200–01. Moreover, she had provided a "more than ordinarily thorough" description of the attacker and was certain of her identification. *Id.* at 200. The fact that a long time—seven months—elapsed between the crime and the identification "would [have been] a seriously negative factor," but for the fact that she had a good "record for reliability." *Id.* at 201. The victim made no previous identification despite many opportunities and "had previously resisted" the inherent "suggestiveness . . . in a showup." *Id.*

Despite the limited reach of its holding, *Biggers* was a significant step. For the first time, the Court made an effort to clarify the purposes of the *Stovall* due process doctrine and made a potentially significant contribution to the development of that doctrine by specifying and applying the factors relevant to reliability assessments. Moreover, the Justices highlighted the tension between two distinct conceptions of due process exclusion. The first option was a deterrence-based rule that barred evidence whenever the government's pretrial conduct generated a sufficient risk of mistaken identification and erroneous conviction.[113] The alternative possibility was a rule requiring individualized analysis of the evidence produced by an improper procedure and dictating exclusion only when a particular identification harbored sufficient risks of misleading a jury. If the totality of facts demonstrated a sufficient likelihood that the witness had selected the accused based on memories of the crime and that the potentially corruptive suggestion had not in fact induced her to choose the defendant, the Fourteenth Amendment did not mandate suppression.[114] The Court endorsed the latter approach, but *only* for pre-*Stovall* procedures.[115] It did not decide whether due process protection against misidentification would be enforced by a *per se* rule in cases where officers conducted unnecessarily suggestive processes after the Court had announced the Due Process Clause constraints.

Five years later, *Manson v. Brathwaite*[116] presented an opportunity to resolve that important question. Because *Brathwaite*, decided nearly 35 years ago, is the Supreme Court's last encounter with due process suppression of eyewitness identification evidence, it is the final chapter in this historical account. It is also, by far, the most significant ruling since the due process doctrine first appeared.

---

113. In essence, this approach called for an objective assessment of the suggestive potential of the identification procedure in the abstract. It was unconcerned with whether the particular witness's identification was likely to have been corrupted by the suggestive features of the process.

114. *See* Wells & Seelau, *Psychological Research*, *supra* note 2, at 783 (observing that the underlying premise of *Biggers* is that if the reliability factors are positive "then suggestive procedures are unlikely to have significantly influenced the identification" that was made).

115. *See* Pulaski, *Court Dismantles*, *supra* note 2, at 1116, 1120 (criticizing the Court's choice of a "permissive interpretation" that focused on the reliability of the evidence rather than the reliability of the procedure used and thereby "reduced the due process test to a handy device by which courts [could] legitimately overlook suggestive confrontations"); Wallace W. Sherwood, *The Erosion of Constitutional Safeguards in the Area of Eyewitness Identification*, 30 How. L.J. 731, 770 (1987) [hereinafter Sherwood, *Erosion of Safeguards*] (disapproving of the Court's shift from "a determination of the intrinsic reliability of the identification procedures to a determination of the probable accuracy of an identification in a particular case").

116. 432 U.S. 98 (1977).

In *Brathwaite*, an undercover officer and an informant went to an apartment to purchase heroin.[117] At police headquarters, the officer described the seller to another officer.[118] Because this officer suspected the seller might be Brathwaite, he retrieved a photograph and placed it in the undercover officer's office.[119] Upon returning to his office two days later, the undercover officer found the photo and identified Brathwaite as the man "from whom he had purchased the narcotics."[120] More than a month later, Brathwaite was arrested and charged with possessing and selling heroin.[121] The pretrial photographic identification was admitted at trial and the officer "also made a positive in-court identification" of the accused.[122] The jury found him guilty of both charges.[123]

In the Supreme Court, the government conceded that the identification process employed "'was suggestive [because only one photograph was used] and unnecessary.'"[124] The issue, therefore, was whether "testimony concerning a suggestive and unnecessary identification procedure" conducted after *Stovall* had to be excluded from trial or could be admitted if it was shown to "possess[] sufficient aspects of reliability."[125] Lower courts had adopted two disparate approaches in answering this question.[126] The "per se approach . . . require[d] exclusion of the out-of-court identification evidence, without regard to reliability, whenever it has been obtained through unnecessarily suggest[ive] confrontation procedures."[127] The other, "more lenient" approach allowed the introduction of any identification made at an unnecessarily suggestive session if the identification "possesse[d] certain features of reliability."[128]

The Court discerned three relevant criteria for deciding which approach was constitutionally preferable. The first was compatibility with the fundamental objective of constitutional safeguards against identification procedures—a "concern that the jury not hear eyewitness testimony unless that evidence has aspects of reliability."[129] The majority acknowledged that both approaches shield against

---

117. *Id.* at 99–100.

118. *Id.* at 101.

119. *Id.*

120. *Id.*

121. *Brathwaite*, 432 U.S. at 101.

122. *Id.* at 102. These identifications were "the 'sole evidence'" of the defendant's guilt. *Id.* at 107.

123. *Id.* at 102.

124. *Id.* at 109 (brackets in original).

125. *Id.* at 106.

126. *Brathwaite*, 432 U.S. at 110.

127. *Id.* Under this approach, subsequent identifications were admissible if shown to be "reliable." *Id.* at 110 n.10. The *per se* approach had received the unanimous approval of scholars and had been endorsed by prominent federal judges. *See id.* at 111.

128. *Id.* at 110.

129. *Id.* at 112.

unreliable evidence. The *per se* rule, however, went "too far" by "automatically and peremptorily" keeping some reliable "evidence from the jury."[130] In essence, its exclusionary impact was overbroad. The second variable was deterrence—whether an approach would discourage the future use of suggestive procedures. The majority conceded that a *per se* ban would have a "more significant deterrent effect."[131] However, "the totality approach" would also "influence . . . police" to avoid "unnecessarily suggestive procedures" because officers would still have reason to "fear that their actions [could] lead to the exclusion of identifications as unreliable."[132] The third relevant factor was an approach's "effect on the administration of justice."[133] By preventing the trier of fact from receiving "reliable evidence," the *per se* rule could occasionally result "in the guilty going free," and its "rigidity" could "make error by the trial judge more likely."[134] Because the *per se* option prescribed a potentially "Draconian sanction"—an "inflexible rule[] of exclusion" that risked "frustrat[ing] rather than promot[ing] justice"—the effect on the administration of justice factor favored the totality analysis.[135] In evaluating the merits of the competing exclusionary rules, the majority pointedly observed that because a suggestive procedure "does not in itself intrude upon a constitutionally protected interest," identification evidence that is acquired is not "derive[d] from a constitutional violation."[136]

Brathwaite reasoned that the concern of the Fourteenth Amendment Due Process Clause is "fairness," and that the *Stovall* doctrine promotes fairness by "protecting an *evidentiary* interest."[137] Its aim is to prevent the prosecution from fueling its case with evidence that poses serious threats of misleading jurors and unfairly convicting innocent persons.[138] For this reason, "reliability is the linchpin in determining the admissibility of identification testimony."[139]

---

130. *Id.*

131. *Brathwaite*, 432 U.S. at 112.

132. *Id.* In addition, officers would realize that suggestive procedures could lead jurors to discount identifications. The interest in convicting guilty defendants would furnish a supplemental reason to avoid unnecessarily suggestive methods. *Id.* at 112 n.12. *But see* Pulaski, *Court Dismantles*, *supra* note 2, at 1114 (arguing that the totality approach "provides no real incentive to the police to avoid suggestive procedures").

133. *Brathwaite*, 432 U.S. at 112.

134. *Id.*

135. *Id.* at 113. Justice Marshall, in a dissent joined by Justice Brennan, maintained that the Court had erroneously evaluated all three of the criteria upon which it relied in choosing the totality approach. *See id.* at 125–28 (Marshall, J., dissenting).

136. *Id.* at 113 n.13. This important foundational premise was apparently relevant in assessing the weight of both the deterrence and the effect on the administration of justice criteria.

137. *Id.* at 113 (emphasis added).

138. *See Brathwaite*, 432 U.S. at 117 (Stevens, J., concurring).

139. *Id.* at 114. Because the Court prescribed no higher burden of proof, the government need only demonstrate reliability by a preponderance of the evidence. In other

Finally, the Court endorsed the factors *Biggers* had identified for assessing reliability—"the opportunity of the witness to view the criminal," his "degree of attention, the accuracy of his prior description," his "level of certainty," and the length of "time between the crime" and the identification.[140] The *Brathwaite* majority, however, noted that the "corrupting effect of the suggestive identification itself" must also be "weighed" in the balance.[141] An application of these criteria to the facts of *Brathwaite* led the Court to find the undercover officer's identification of the defendant's photograph reliable and to conclude that its admission did not entail "'a very substantial likelihood of irreparable misidentification.'"[142]

---

words, the prosecution need only establish that it is more likely than not that the witness's identification was reliable despite the unnecessary suggestion.

Justices Marshall and Brennan disagreed with these foundational premises. In their view, *Stovall* had recognized a right to a "fundamentally fair" identification *process*, a "due process right . . . to be free from" unnecessarily suggestive procedures that "was enforceable by exclusion at trial of evidence" obtained at such procedures. *Id.* at 120–21 (Marshall, J., dissenting). *Simmons* had established a different due process test that hinged on "the reliability of the identification," but it governed *only* subsequent identifications by witnesses. *Id.* at 122–23 (Marshall, J., dissenting). By "eras[ing] the distinction" and making reliability determinative for identifications made *during* flawed procedures, the Court had "ignore[d]" the principle "that an unnecessarily suggestive pretrial confrontation itself violates due process." *Id.* at 123–24 (Marshall, J., dissenting).

140. *Id.* at 114.

141. *Id.* The Court made it clear that independent evidence of the defendant's guilt is *not* relevant to the reliability inquiry. *Id.* at 116 (observing that the fact that the defendant was arrested at the same apartment where the sale took place "plays no part in our [reliability] analysis"). The inquiry is not whether the eyewitness identification at issue *correctly* identified the actual perpetrator of a crime. Rather, it is whether the identification was the product of the witness's crime scene observations and memory, and not the result of the influence of the official suggestion.

142. *Id.* at 116 (quoting Simmons v. United States, 390 U.S. 377, 384 (1968)). The Court believed that virtually all of the factors favored admission: the duration of the transaction, the proximity to the seller, and the lighting conditions created a decent opportunity for the officer to view the seller; an officer engaged in detecting narcotics traffickers would have paid close attention to the seller; his description was sufficiently detailed and matched the defendant; he was certain of his identification; and the identification was made soon after the crime. *Id.* at 114–16. These indicia that the officer had the "ability to make an accurate identification" were not "outweighed" by the suggestiveness of the procedure. *Id.* at 116. Although it was a single photo display, there was "little pressure" on the officer "to acquiesce in the suggestion" because he viewed the photo while alone in his office in a situation that did not involve "urgency." *Id.*

Justices Marshall and Brennan disagreed with the majority's reliability evaluation. They concluded that the officer's abilities to accurately identify the seller were much weaker and that the procedure used was much more corruptive and likely to produce error. *Id.* at 129–36 (Marshall, J., dissenting). In their view, the majority had granted the police "license to convict the innocent" in a case where there was "compelling evidence"

Theoretically and doctrinally, *Brathwaite* is by far the most significant decision in the evolution of the due process exclusion doctrine. The opinion resolved a long-unanswered practical question—whether the prosecution ever may use identifications obtained directly from constitutionally objectionable processes. By holding that a one-size reliability standard fits all identifications—both those made initially during flawed processes and any successive identifications by the same witness—the Justices narrowed the protection afforded by due process.[143] In addition, for the first time, the Court explored the underpinnings of the *Stovall* doctrine, explaining the nature and objectives of this constitutional exclusion command. According to the majority, the due process bar is a trial safeguard, a protection against unfair convictions resulting from eyewitness identification evidence corrupted by gratuitous official suggestion.

Due process-based exclusion of eyewitness identifications had the humblest of beginnings in *Stovall*—an exceptionally terse, yet revolutionary, opinion recognizing the possibility of due process protection against misleading identification procedures. However, that landmark ruling revealed little about the character and contours of this new constitutional shelter, providing but a barebones standard. The doctrine then developed uncertainly, ambiguously, and by small increments in a sequence of four decisions spanning a four-year period. Finally, the story of due process suppression came to a close—a mere 10 years after it began—in another major ruling. The opinion in *Brathwaite* not only brought the curtain down on the doctrine's evolution, it contributed more to our understanding of the theory and operation of this constitutional exclusion mandate than all of the prior opinions combined. The next section explores the Court's vision of the nature of and justifications for the due process bar, explaining competing understandings challenging that vision and highlighting uncertainties that still remain.

---

of "'a very substantial likelihood of misidentification.'" *Id.* at 132, 135 (Marshall, J., dissenting).

143. The Court thereby established a considerably less protective exclusionary scheme for identifications made at demonstrably suggestive sessions than the one it had prescribed for identification processes where the only proven deficiency is the absence of counsel. If an identification procedure is not suggestive at all, but the authorities do not respect an accused's entitlement to counsel, any identification made at that time is categorically inadmissible. *See supra* Chapter 5, text accompanying notes 170–72. For criticisms of the Court's rulings narrowing the scope of due process suppression, see Pulaski, *Court Dismantles*, *supra* note 2, at 1120 (asserting that the *Biggers* reliability analysis "dismantled the . . . protections" provided by *Stovall*); Rosenberg, *Rethinking the Right*, *supra* note 2, at 261 (maintaining that *Brathwaite* and prior decisions "considerably weakened the right to due process," turning it into "little more than a dead letter").

C. THE NATURE OF AND RATIONALES FOR THE DUE PROCESS BAR TO EYEWITNESS IDENTIFICATION EVIDENCE

As is the case with all constitutional exclusion doctrines, the rationales and justifications for the due process bar to eyewitness identification evidence are of critical importance. This section explains the prevailing conception of the rule's underpinnings, sketches competing perspectives and ambiguities, and then ventures a prediction about the future of this suppression doctrine.

One important question for any constitutional exclusion doctrine is whether a violation of the underlying right occurs before trial, when evidence is acquired; at trial, when evidence is introduced; or at both stages of the process. The language in a number of the initial due process decisions suggested that official methods of gathering identification evidence threatened constitutional rights—that is, that Fourteenth Amendment violations could occur at the time of improper identification procedures.[144] None of the early decisions, however, focused on the question of when due process rights were in jeopardy or on the rationales supporting suppression.[145] When the Court finally trained its gaze upon these matters, it concluded that the *Stovall* doctrine involves a violation of rights *only* when an identification is admitted into evidence at trial. An accused can suffer a deprivation of life, liberty, or property without due process of law *only* at the time the prosecution introduces identification evidence in order to secure a conviction.[146] Whether or not the individual is physically present and participating, an unnecessarily suggestive identification procedure alone cannot deprive him of due process.[147]

Because due process violations occur when the government uses evidence against a defendant, the Fourteenth Amendment bar is no mere exclusionary

---

144. *See,* e.g., Foster v. California, 394 U.S. 440, 442 (1969); Simmons v. United States, 390 U.S. 377, 386 (1968); Stovall v. Denno, 388 U.S. 293, 302 (1967). The phrasing in one of the right to counsel identification decisions also suggested that a due process violation could occur prior to trial, at the time of the identification process. *See* Kirby v. Illinois, 406 U.S. 682, 690–91 (1972) (plurality opinion).

145. *See* Rosenberg, *Rethinking the Right, supra* note 2, at 271–72 (suggesting that the opinions from *Stovall* through *Coleman* generated "confusion" because they did not address "the purpose" of the due process right at issue); *id.* at 265 (observing that the "terseness" of *Stovall*'s "enunciation of the right to due process [made it] hard to discern the rationale or theoretical basis for the new right").

146. The Supreme Court's assertion that the due process exclusion of eyewitness identification evidence protects "an *evidentiary* interest," *Brathwaite,* 432 U.S. at 113, was a clear declaration that the constitutional guarantee is threatened only by the use of evidence in court.

147. Some Justices dissented from this view, concluding that due process rights were violated at the time of unnecessarily suggestive procedures. *Id.* at 120–22, 124 (Marshall, J., dissenting).

"rule" designed to sanction a pretrial impropriety. It is unmistakably a personal right to suppression that belongs to an accused on trial. Suggestive procedures can create a serious likelihood of misidentification. The use of an identification that is the product of suggestive procedures to secure a conviction gives rise to an unacceptable risk that an innocent person will be found guilty and deprived of life, liberty, or property. Due process guarantees "fundamental fairness,"[148] and an inaccurate conviction of an innocent individual resulting from official evidence-gathering methods is a patently unfair outcome. If the Fourteenth Amendment forbids anything, it forbids substantively unjust verdicts that are the consequence of improper governmental processes. Put otherwise, a criminal defendant has a constitutional entitlement not to be wrongfully convicted because of distortion of the fact-finding process attributable to misleading identification procedures. For these reasons, the Fourteenth Amendment erects a barrier to identifications that are the product of unnecessarily suggestive techniques.[149]

Even though no completed constitutional rights violation can occur until the use of identification evidence at trial, the due process opinions indicate that suppression also serves deterrent objectives. Exclusion is necessary not only to prevent courtroom deprivations of due process rights, but also to discourage the authorities from employing unnecessarily suggestive identification techniques in future investigations.[150] Unjustifiably suggestive processes that generate risks of convicting innocent persons are undesirable, and the suppression sanction seeks to prevent officers from employing such processes.[151] Although the

---

148. *See* Pennsylvania v. Finley, 481 U.S. 551, 557 (1987) (stating that "fundamental fairness [is] mandated by the Due Process Clause"); Lisenba v. California, 314 U.S. 219, 236 (1941) (declaring that "[t]he aim of . . . due process is . . . to prevent fundamental unfairness in the use of evidence").

149. It seems clear that the character of the evidentiary exclusion mandated under *Stovall* is not like the bar to confessions erected by *Miranda*'s interpretation of the Fifth Amendment privilege. *See supra* Chapter 3, text accompanying notes 103–12. Although risks of erroneous conviction are the impetus for the due process bar, suppression under the Fourteenth Amendment is a right necessary to prevent *actual* constitutional violations that would occur if the evidence were introduced. Due process suppression is prophylactic insofar as it prevents unfair trials, but it is not an overbroad, judicially-created safeguard designed to provide enlarged protection against mere risks of due process violations. It is not similar in nature to *Miranda*, but instead resembles the due process and Fifth Amendment rights to preclude the use of coerced confessions—rights that guard against risks of inaccurate outcomes resulting from false coerced confessions. *See supra* Chapter 2, text accompanying notes 146–52.

150. *See Brathwaite*, 432 U.S. at 112; Neil v. Biggers, 409 U.S. 188, 199 (1972).

151. The Court recognized a deterrent foundation for the Sixth Amendment right to counsel bar to eyewitness identification evidence when it first announced that exclusion doctrine in *Wade* and *Gilbert*. *See supra* Chapter 5, text accompanying notes 117–20. The Court did not mention the deterrent premise for due process suppression until *Biggers*

opinions assume a deterrent objective, they do not explain why deterrence is necessary or desirable.[152] That question is explored in the analysis that follows.

There has been almost no dissent from the conclusion that the due process fairness guarantee is concerned with the accuracy of trial outcomes and that a bar to identifications produced by unnecessarily suggestive procedures is essential to enforce this guarantee.[153] Some critics maintain that the Court's conception of this constitutional right is too narrow, and that the focus on unfair, inaccurate outcomes alone does not fully capture the content of the entitlement to due process of law. They perceive an additional, and quite distinct, foundation for a Fourteenth Amendment right to bar identification evidence from criminal trials. In their view, the due process exclusion doctrine not only guarantees an outcome uncorrupted by suggestion, it also ensures procedural fairness. The use at trial of identifications obtained by unnecessarily suggestive techniques jeopardizes the fairness of the verdict *and* renders the process of adjudicating guilt unfair.[154] To ensure a fair trial consistent with the entitlement to procedural due

---

and *Brathwaite*, decisions handed down well after the Fourteenth Amendment exclusion doctrine first appeared. Prior to those opinions, the Court paid no attention to the nature of due process exclusion.

152. The *Brathwaite* Court made it clear that unnecessarily suggestive methods, unlike unreasonable searches and seizures, do not themselves violate constitutional rights. *Brathwaite*, 432 U.S. at 113 n.13. There is reason to wonder why deterrence is a justification for suppression when the conduct to be deterred does not inflict constitutional injury on anyone, and harm to constitutional trial rights is prevented by barring evidence from the courtroom. Later in the discussion, I speculate upon possible explanations for the supplemental deterrent rationale in this context.

153. Put otherwise, there has been virtually no criticism of the Court's conclusion that while the assessment of eyewitness identification evidence is ordinarily a matter for juries, "procedures leading to an eyewitness identification may be so defective as to make the identification *constitutionally inadmissible* as a matter of law." Foster v. California, 394 U.S. 440, 443 n.2 (1969) (emphasis added). As noted in the historical account, one Justice did disagree with the recognition of a due process exclusion doctrine. In the early decisions, Justice Black consistently dissented, opining that the Court had no authority to bar eyewitness identification evidence under the Fourteenth Amendment and maintaining that any risks of misidentification caused by suggestive influences were for the jury to evaluate. *See, e.g., Foster*, 394 U.S. at 446–47 (Black, J., dissenting); Simmons v. United States, 390 U.S. 377, 395 (1968) (Black, J., concurring in part and dissenting in part); Stovall v. Denno, 388 U.S. 293, 304–06 (1967) (Black, J., dissenting). Since Justice Black's departure, not a single member of the Court has challenged the legitimacy of the due process entitlement. Moreover, I have not discovered any scholarly critiques opposing the recognition of a due process right against the use of some identification evidence.

154. The argument parallels one of the rationales for due process and Fifth Amendment-based exclusion of coerced confessions. The bar to coerced confessions rests in part on the risk that coercion may lead to a false confession that produces an erroneous conviction. Quite apart from that risk, the suppression of coerced confessions also reflects a process right not to be convicted on the basis of thoughts forced from one's mind even if those

process, eyewitness identifications made at unnecessarily suggestive pretrial sessions must be excluded.[155]

There seems to be general agreement that due process suppression is a necessary deterrent measure. Justices and scholars alike agree that by threatening the loss of identification evidence, the due process exclusion sanction serves the important function of discouraging unnecessarily suggestive identification methods.[156] Dissenting Justices and a number of critics have argued that the Court's refinements of the due process doctrine have undercut the deterrent efficacy of exclusion and that a more generous sanction is necessary to provide meaningful deterrence.[157]

---

thoughts are not false and misleading. Accusatorial principles hold that it is procedurally unfair to use extorted admissions to convict a defendant. *See supra* Chapter 2, text accompanying notes 153–54.

155. For scholarly commentary reflecting this criticism, see Felice J. Levine & June Louin Tapp, *The Psychology of Criminal Identification: The Gap from* Wade *to* Kirby, 121 U. Pa. L. Rev. 1079, 1079 (1973) [hereinafter Levine & Tapp, *Psychology of Identification*]; Pulaski, *Court Dismantles, supra* note 2, at 1113–14; Rosenberg, *Rethinking the Right, supra* note 2, at 261–62, 276, 290–91, 303–04. It is also arguable that adequate protection of the *substantive* due process right to an accurate outcome requires a broader right to suppression than the one defined by the current doctrine. According to this view, it is not possible for a court to accurately determine whether an identification is reliable—i.e., whether it is the product of a witness's memory of observations at the crime scene or of the government's misleading suggestion. Consequently, due process protection against intolerable risks of erroneous conviction must encompass a right to exclude *all* identifications made at unnecessarily suggestive identification processes. *See* Joseph D. Grano, Kirby, Biggers, *and* Ash: *Do Any Constitutional Safeguards Remain Against the Danger of Convicting the Innocent?*, 72 Mich. L. Rev. 717, 781–82 (1974) [hereinafter Grano, Kirby, Biggers, *and* Ash] (maintaining that the Court's due process rulings do not adequately protect against mistaken identifications and fail to eliminate unacceptable risks of convicting the innocent); Luria, *Showup Identifications, supra* note 2, at 542–43; Sherwood, *Erosion of Safeguards, supra* note 115, at 748–49.

156. The *Brathwaite* majority deemed deterrent efficacy one of the three factors relevant to deciding between the *per se* and totality approaches to the suppression of identifications made at unnecessarily suggestive sessions. *See Brathwaite*, 432 U.S. at 112. Not a single member of the Supreme Court has ever suggested that the sole purpose of due process exclusion is to prevent violation of the accused's rights at trial and that deterrence cannot serve as a rationale. Commentators routinely accept the deterrent premise as well. *See, e.g.*, Luria, *Showup Identifications, supra* note 2, at 543; Pulaski, *Court Dismantles, supra* note 2, at 1114; Rosenberg, *Rethinking the Right, supra* note 2, at 305; Sherwood, *Erosion of Safeguards, supra* note 115, at 770.

157. *See Brathwaite*, 432 U.S. at 125 (Marshall, J., dissenting); Pulaski, *Court Dismantles, supra* note 2, at 1114 (contending that the approach adopted by the Court "provides no real incentive to the police to avoid suggestive procedures"); Rosenberg, *Rethinking the Right, supra* note 2, at 305 (arguing that the reliability standard does not provide sufficient deterrence and that, in fact, officers "have nothing to lose by conducting a suggestive pretrial procedure"); Sherwood, *Erosion of Safeguards, supra* note 115, at 770 (suggesting that the

In my view, a due process right to bar the evidentiary products of suggestive identification procedures is firmly grounded in legitimate constitutional concerns. Suggestive official identification methods generate serious, constitutionally cognizable risks of inaccurate verdicts that result in unjust deprivations of life or liberty.[158] It is more than defensible to conclude that when such risks of injustice are the product of government conduct that serves no legitimate objective, due process extends an entitlement to bar the evidence harboring those risks.

The Court's position that the fairness of a trial's outcome is the *sole* concern of the due process protection against identification procedures and the only basis for a right to exclusion is defensible. The contention of critics that the fairness of the process leading to conviction is a critical due process concern that provides

---

Biggers approach will not effectively deter suggestive methods, but "will have the opposite result").

Justice Marshall also disagreed with the *Brathwaite* majority's conclusion that improper identification processes do not by themselves violate constitutional rights. In his view, "*Stovall* . . . established a due process right of criminal suspects to be free from confrontations that . . . are unnecessarily suggestive." *Brathwaite*, 432 U.S. at 120 (Marshall, J., dissenting); *see also id.* at 121 (Marshall, J., dissenting) (quoting language in *Stovall* suggesting that a due process violation occurred "'in the conduct of a [pretrial] confrontation'") (emphasis omitted). The majority discerned no pretrial deprivation of rights and, consequently, deemed irrelevant the "considerations" that dictate the "exclusion of evidence deriving from a constitutional violation." *Id.* at 113 n.13. Because he believed that pretrial identification processes did violate the right to due process, Justice Marshall undoubtedly considered deterrence to be a more important consideration. *See id.* at 120 (Marshall, J., dissenting) (asserting that the pretrial right to be free of suggestive identification confrontations established in *Stovall* "was enforceable by exclusion at trial . . . of the constitutionally invalid identification").

Justice Marshall's position seems strained and finds no support in scholarly critiques of the due process doctrine. While participating in and being identified at a suggestive pretrial identification session could induce anxiety, embarrassment, humiliation, or even fear, it is hard to believe that official conduct causing these kinds of psychological harms infringes upon protected Fourteenth Amendment liberty interests. After all, only egregious forms of official coercion tread upon due process values. *See supra* Chapter 2, text accompanying notes 158–59, note 159. Moreover, Justice Marshall made his argument that suggestive pretrial processes violate the Fourteenth Amendment in *Brathwaite*, a case involving a noncorporeal identification procedure. It seems implausible that a suggestive photographic display occasions *any* immediate constitutional injury to a person depicted in a photograph.

158. Identification evidence is uniquely perilous and a particularly appropriate subject for constitutional regulation because it is inherently untrustworthy and particularly susceptible to distortion by suggestive influences and because juries find it persuasive. *See supra* note 2. "[A] system historically dedicated to protecting the innocent from wrongful conviction cannot tolerate [the] gratuitous risks" of unjust verdicts injected into trials by identifications resulting from suggestive techniques. *See* Grano, Kirby, Biggers, *and* Ash, *supra* note 155, at 782.

an additional foundation for the entitlement to suppression is also plausible. The latter position can find support by analogy to the coerced confession doctrine. The due process bar to coerced confessions seeks to avoid unjust outcomes based on false admissions of guilt. However, that Fourteenth Amendment exclusion doctrine is independently rooted in a concern with unfair processes. Conviction by means of an incriminating admission forced from an accused violates due process whether or not the admission is false because the trial is fundamentally unfair. It might seem logical to conclude that the two due process rights to exclude evidence must serve the same fairness goals.

On the other hand, the fair process aspect of the coerced confession doctrine rests on a well-established, fundamental principle residing at the very core of American criminal justice systems. A basic premise of our accusatorial systems is that it is unfair for the government to force an individual to disclose his thoughts and to use those thoughts to secure a conviction.[159] The Fifth Amendment ban on compulsory self-incrimination gives that principle explicit expression. This principle furnishes a persuasive foundation for the conclusion that an adjudication of guilt fueled by a coerced confession is a fundamentally unfair process no matter how accurate the verdict.

The admission of identification evidence surely does not threaten the fair process values reflected in the Fifth Amendment Self-Incrimination Clause because identification procedures involve no compulsory revelation of testimonial evidence.[160] The question is whether there is another principle that can support the contention that the use of an eyewitness identification produced at a suggestive identification procedure undermines the fundamental fairness of the trial process. Suggestive procedures might implicate the fundamental adversary system principle that entitles criminal defendants to confront their accusers at trial. This principle finds explicit expression in the Sixth Amendment guarantee that "[i]n all criminal prosecutions, the accused shall enjoy the right . . . to be confronted with the witnesses against him."[161] The confrontation right includes an entitlement to cross-examine witnesses.[162] Suggestive identification procedures arguably render cross-examination ineffective by exposing a witness to influences that distort his or her testimony but cannot be accurately

---

159. *See* Miranda v. Arizona, 384 U.S. 436, 460 (1966); *see also* Withrow v. Williams, 507 U.S. 680, 691–92 (1993); Doe v. United States, 487 U.S. 201, 212–13 (1988).

160. In *United States v. Wade*, the Court made it clear that neither the compulsion to participate in a lineup nor the compulsion to speak words for identification purposes jeopardizes Fifth Amendment values because neither involves the compelled production of "'testimonial'" evidence. United States v. Wade, 388 U.S. 218, 221–23 (1967).

161. U.S. Const. amend. VI. This provision is known as the Sixth Amendment "Confrontation Clause."

162. *See* Chambers v. Mississippi, 410 U.S. 284, 294–95 (1973); Pointer v. Texas, 380 U.S. 400, 401, 403–04 (1965).

reconstructed and probed at trial. Suggestive processes can impede the efficacy of cross-examination at trial by inducing a witness to believe incorrectly and unalterably that the person selected at the misleading pretrial process is the perpetrator seen at the crime scene. Such a witness might well be impervious to effective cross-examination at trial.[163]

A related argument is that suggestive procedures impair the efficacy of the adversary system entitlement to the effective assistance of counsel.[164] If suggestive procedures generate devastating evidence of guilt that juries find persuasive, and if that evidence cannot be effectively countered at trial because of both the unknown nature of the suggestive influences and witnesses' tendencies to become convinced of the correctness of pretrial identifications, a lawyer's efforts to defend an accused may be seriously handicapped. Thus, the animating spirit of the counsel guarantee could provide additional support for the view that the use of an eyewitness identification made at an unnecessarily suggestive session renders a trial *process* unfair.

Finally, even apart from the adversary system principles reflected in the guarantees of confrontation and counsel,[165] it is arguable that the trial process is unfair because the government has engaged in conduct that creates gratuitous risks of potentially harmful misidentification. One might consider a trial procedurally unfair—contrary to the essence of due *process*—because it involves the introduction of evidence acquired by official actions that engender unjustified and avoidable possibilities of corrupting the accurate ascertainment of guilt. The contention is that the Due Process Clause guarantee of fairness reaches beyond other principles and provisions, and that it is simply and fundamentally unfair for the government to conduct criminal prosecutions in this manner.[166]

Unless one rejects the Court's view that suggestive pretrial identification procedures do not violate constitutional rights, the deterrent reasoning typically used to justify exclusionary rules cannot support the due process bar. Even if suppression does discourage officers from employing unnecessarily suggestive

---

163. *See Wade*, 388 U.S. at 229, 235. The Sixth Amendment Confrontation Clause bar to testimonial hearsay provides some protection against witnesses' pretrial identifications. The contours and limits of that constitutional exclusion doctrine are the subject of Chapter 7, *infra*. The argument here is that the values underlying the confrontation right might inform and support a procedural due process right to exclusion.

164. *See* McMann v. Richardson, 397 U.S. 759, 771 n.14 (1970) (stating that "the right to counsel is the right to the effective assistance of counsel").

165. It is arguable that the fair process values underlying the Confrontation Clause are adequately protected by that guarantee's bar to hearsay evidence explained in Chapter 7, and that the fair process interests sheltered by the right to counsel are sufficiently safeguarded by the *Wade-Gilbert* suppression rule described in Chapter 5, *supra*. If so, perhaps it is inappropriate to rely on those values and interests to give content to the Fourteenth Amendment guarantee of fair process.

166. *See* Rosenberg, *Rethinking the Right*, *supra* note 2, at 261–62, 290–91, 297.

methods, it does not prevent any pretrial deprivations of the entitlement to due process.[167] If deterrence does not prevent pretrial violations of constitutional rights, and if the only threat to due process comes from the use of eyewitness identification evidence in the courtroom, there is reason to wonder whether suppression can be justified by an interest in deterring unnecessarily suggestive identification processes.

If judges are capable of accurately identifying evidence that threatens to undermine the fairness of trials—evidence that harbors intolerable risks of misidentification—then deterrence would seem to be an illogical rationale for suppression. As long as judges bar all identifications that are the product of suggestive techniques, there would be no net constitutional benefit from discouraging future officers' use of such techniques. The entitlement to due process would be fully preserved by interdicting the evidence at the doors of courtrooms.[168]

It is arguable, however, that courts cannot (or will not) accurately identify all identification evidence with government-generated, constitutionally intolerable risks of misidentification. In that case, deterrence of improper pretrial methods can provide additional shelter for the trial right to due process and can serve as a supplemental justification for suppression. By discouraging officers from using unnecessarily suggestive techniques in future cases, the threat of exclusion would prevent the production of potentially mistaken, unreliable evidence that might not be detected and barred from trial. For example, a judge might incorrectly decide that a suggestive process was necessary, that insufficient suggestion was present, or that an identification made by a witness was reliable despite the official suggestion. If exclusion deters officers from conducting suggestive identification sessions, some identifications that would have been improperly admitted at trials will never be made. Violations of the right to due process at trial will thereby be prevented, and there will be a net gain in Fourteenth

167. The view that a constitutional transgression occurs at the time of an unnecessarily suggestive lineup or photo identification seems implausible and has garnered little support. If a constitutional deprivation did occur at that time, the case for deterrence would be more persuasive than it is in other contexts. The gains from deterring improper methods would be the actual enforcement of rights, while the costs would be the loss of evidence of questionable probative value. In the Fourth Amendment and Sixth Amendment-*Massiah* contexts, there is no reason to question the probative value of the evidence suppressed, and yet the deterrent benefits of suppression are thought to outweigh the costs of suppression. In light of the potential unreliability of identifications yielded by suggestive procedures, the cost-benefit assessment would favor exclusion even more in the due process context.

168. The same reasoning would apply even if due process includes not only a right to fair outcomes, but also a right to fair processes. As long as judges barred the use at trial of all identifications threatening that process entitlement, deterrence of the improper sessions could produce no additional protection.

Amendment enforcement. In sum, if deterrence has a legitimate role in this context—as the Court and scholars have assumed—its function is as a backstop, a supplemental safeguard against mistaken identifications that might have slipped past the due process barrier at trial.[169]

The Supreme Court has not addressed a single *Stovall* doctrine issue in more than 30 years. It seems quite unlikely that the Court will show renewed interest in this constitutional exclusion mandate in the foreseeable future.[170] Should the Court revisit the due process bar, it would almost certainly reaffirm that no constitutional injury occurs prior to trial and that suppression enforces a courtroom right of the accused. The Justices might well reconsider whether deterrence provides any justification for suppression and could conceivably conclude that there is insufficient need to deter unnecessarily suggestive identification methods because the courtroom bar adequately safeguards the due process right to a fair trial.

D. THE REACH AND OPERATION OF DUE PROCESS SUPPRESSION OF EYEWITNESS IDENTIFICATIONS

Having set the stage with the background and foundations of due process exclusion of eyewitness identifications, it is time to examine the operational details. The presumptive scope of the suppression mandate in criminal trials is relatively well-defined by the Court's decisions. Beyond that, however, there are numerous uncertainties. Most of the doctrinal questions considered in preceding chapters have not been the subject of any consideration in this context. These include whether the bar operates outside criminal trials, who has standing to suppress evidence, and whether the exceptions to other exclusionary rules are applicable. The certainty that due process exclusion is a personal trial right provides a solid foundation for analyzing these issues. The somewhat uncertain force of the deterrent rationale can complicate the analysis.

---

169. In addition, even if a judge's decision concerning the suggestiveness of a method or the reliability of an identification is accurate, it remains possible that the witness was misled by the modest suggestion that did exist or that the witness's identification was incorrect, even though the evidence established, more likely than not, that it was reliable. To the extent that suppression might deter officers from engaging in *any* suggestion—because of the risks that a judge will find it to be too much suggestion and will be unwilling to find an identification reliable—it could provide additional shelter for constitutional interests otherwise left unprotected.

170. The lower courts decide few cases involving due process questions and there are no issues of real import yet to be resolved.

1. Evidence Subject to Exclusion: The Presumptive Scope of the Fourteenth Amendment Bar

The *Stovall* exclusion mandate forbids the introduction of eyewitness identification evidence produced at a government-arranged identification process that is unnecessarily suggestive.[171] The likelihood that an identification is unreliable is not by itself a basis for Fourteenth Amendment suppression. The potential untrustworthiness must have roots in official acts. Without governmental responsibility for the risk of inaccuracy—and, thus, the prospect of convicting an innocent person—there is no basis for due process concern.[172] Suppose, for example, that an elderly witness with poor eyesight observed a fleeing assassin for mere seconds in dim light and under extremely stressful and distracting conditions. The witness's identification of a suspect at a fairly conducted lineup or a neutral, nonsuggestive photographic display is not subject to due process-based suppression.[173] An accused must show that officials employed methods that might have improperly influenced a witness to select him.

The degree of suggestion is also important.[174] A defendant must establish that the suggestiveness of the methods used generated a high enough probability of

---

171. Every sort of identification is subject to suppression under this doctrine. A witness's identification of a live human being, a moving or still picture or a sketch of a person, or a recording of an individual's voice could be barred due to unnecessary suggestion. The two limitations that constrain right to counsel suppression of identification evidence—the need for the physical presence of the accused and the formal accusation demand—do not limit the scope of Fourteenth Amendment exclusion. Moreover, an identification might be excluded even if an accused had or validly waived the assistance of counsel. *See* Pulaski, *Court Dismantles*, *supra* note 2, at 1103 (asserting that, unlike Sixth Amendment exclusion, "due process protection is comprehensive in scope"—applicable "to all identification procedures").

172. The requirement of governmental suggestion is analogous to the requirement of official coercion as a basis for due process suppression of a confession. Just as private-party coercion that induces a confession is not a basis for suppression, private-party suggestion that influences a witness to identify a defendant cannot support exclusion. *See supra* Chapter 2, text accompanying note 169 (discussing the holding in *Colorado v. Connelly*). In the Supreme Court's view, a trial is unfair for Due Process Clause purposes *only* when the evidentiary problem has a source in pretrial conduct of a government agent.

173. When it is not the product of some official action, the unreliability of identification *evidence* is solely a matter for the mechanisms of the adversary process—counsel and cross-examination—to combat and for the jury to evaluate. Even if evidentiary unreliability is not the result of official conduct, there is some constitutional protection against the unreliability of a *verdict* based upon such evidence. The Due Process Clause requires that a conviction be supported by sufficient evidence of guilt beyond a reasonable doubt. *See* Jackson v. Virginia, 443 U.S. 307, 315–16, 317–18 (1979).

174. The Supreme Court has never defined "suggestion" for identification process purposes. *See* Rosenberg, *Rethinking the Right*, *supra* note 2, at 283. For a discussion of the meaning of suggestion, see *id.* at 298–303.

misidentification to raise due process concerns. From the start, the Court's phrasing has indicated that exclusion is not called for simply because some suggestion was present. There is some threshold degree or intensity of suggestion that is needed to support a due process claim. However, the amount of suggestion necessary to justify exclusion is unclear.[175] According to the Court, the method used must be "*so* unnecessarily suggestive and conducive to irreparable mistaken identification" that it "denie[s] due process."[176] Alternatively, the suggestion must be sufficient to give rise to "'*a very substantial likelihood* of irreparable misidentification.'"[177] Thus, if the defendant were slightly taller than the other participants in a lineup, but otherwise there was nothing that singled her out, or if the photograph of the accused was a bit brighter than the others in a 100-photo array, but nothing else highlighted her picture, the suggestion might well be too mild to support a suppression claim. The suggestion must be potent enough to engender a "very substantial likelihood" of misleading a witness into erroneously selecting the accused.[178]

The suggestion must also be "unnecessary," but ordinarily a defendant need not prove a lack of necessity. After an accused shows sufficient suggestiveness, a prosecutor wishing to defeat a suppression claim must respond with evidence that the suggestion was unavoidable—that is, that there was some sufficiently weighty reason why it had to use a suggestive technique. Perhaps the time pressures created by the risk that an injured witness might die or lose consciousness made it infeasible to construct a fairer, more neutral lineup.[179] Logically, the question is not whether it was necessary to secure an identification quickly, but whether the need to act with expedition made it impractical to employ a method that did not create a substantial likelihood of misidentification. There may be reasons other than time that necessitate a suggestive process. Perhaps the defendant's appearance is so unique or so distinctive that it was not practicable, despite ample time, to assemble photographs of individuals more like the accused.

---

175. *See id.* at 269 (highlighting the Court's failure to clarify "what procedures were 'so defective'" that they implicated due process and what procedures "were, although defective, not so egregious as to bar the jury from receiving the evidence that they produced").

176. Stovall v. Denno, 388 U.S. 293, 301–02 (1967) (emphasis added).

177. *See* Manson v. Brathwaite, 432 U.S. 98, 116 (1977) (quoting Simmons v. United States, 390 U.S. 377, 384 (1968)) (emphasis added); Neil v. Biggers, 409 U.S. 188, 197 (1972) (quoting Simmons v. United States, 390 U.S. 377, 384 (1968)) (emphasis added).

178. Again, there is an analogous aspect of the due process-coerced confession doctrine. It seems certain that some official pressures to confess are insufficient to trigger exclusion and that some undefined threshold amount of coercion is required before due process protection applies. *See supra* Chapter 2, note 168 & accompanying text.

179. The exigencies that demand swift efforts to identify a suspect might even make it infeasible to conduct any lineup—i.e., to present more than one individual to a witness. *See, e.g.*, *Stovall*, 388 U.S. at 302 (deeming it necessary to present the defendant alone to the victim).

To complete the investigation and apprehend an offender, officials had no reasonable alternative other than the suggestive array they used. Any basis for concluding that suggestive influences could not be avoided—that is, that the government employed as fair a process as could reasonably be expected under the particular circumstances—might establish necessity and eliminate the foundation required for due process suppression.[180]

If unnecessary suggestion is established, any identification made as an immediate result of the suggestive process is subject to suppression.[181] Consequently, neither a witness nor an officer may testify that the witness chose the accused at a lineup or selected the defendant's picture. Moreover, once a witness is led by suggestive influences to make an initial identification, it is assumed that a later identification is the result of the initial suggestion and choice—even if it is not made in a suggestive setting.[182] The presumed psychological connection means that any subsequent identification of the accused by the same witness before or at trial is considered "derivative" of the corruptive method. Due process bars such derivative identifications for the same reasons it bars the primary identification. If the subsequent identification is the product of the earlier improper influences, it jeopardizes the Fourteenth Amendment right to a fair, accurate outcome by injecting into the trial a gratuitous and unacceptable likelihood that the defendant will be misidentified and erroneously convicted. Moreover, if a later identification is a derivative product of the earlier impropriety, it is profit that must be eliminated to remove a potent incentive for future improprieties.

While both primary and derivative identifications are suppressible, there is no categorical bar to either—that is, no *per se* prohibition on use at trial. The government can avoid exclusion by showing, by a preponderance of the evidence, that a particular identification is "reliable."[183] The prosecution must establish that,

---

180. For analysis of both the nature of the necessity criterion and the reasoning that might justify refusing to suppress identifications when it is necessary to use suggestive methods, see *infra* text accompanying notes 214–19.

181. *See Brathwaite*, 432 U.S. at 114 (recognizing that an identification that is the immediate product of an unnecessarily suggestive procedure is admissible only if it is shown to be reliable).

182. *See* Coleman v. Alabama, 399 U.S. 1, 5 (1970) (implicitly recognizing the need to find that an in-court identification "did not stem from an" unnecessarily suggestive pretrial identification process); *Simmons*, 390 U.S. at 384 (acknowledging a need to determine whether due process is violated when a witness who has been exposed to an impermissibly suggestive pretrial procedure makes an identification "at trial").

183. *See Brathwaite*, 432 U.S. at 114; Neil v. Biggers, 409 U.S. 188, 199 (1972). Although the Court did not specify the preponderance standard for reliability determinations, that is the controlling burden of proof in suppression proceedings. The sole exception to that norm is the clear and convincing evidence standard adopted for independent source determinations under *Wade*'s right to counsel bar to derivative identification evidence. *See* United States v. Matlock, 415 U.S. 164, 178 n.14 (1974). The *Brathwaite* Court did not

despite the serious potential for misidentification, the suggestion did not prompt the witness to choose the accused. In essence, the object is to show that the evidence lacked a basic requisite for every constitutional exclusion doctrine discussed in the preceding chapters—a causal connection to the government's improper acts. The government must demonstrate that the influences that were present did not lead the witness to identify the accused, but, instead, that the identification was the product of an independent source—the witness's recollection of observations made at the crime scene or elsewhere.[184]

It is conceivable, albeit unlikely, that other kinds of evidence might be acquired as a result of an identification made at an unnecessarily suggestive session. A witness's selection of the defendant could lead to interviews of acquaintances who divulge knowledge implicating him in an attempted rape. Moreover, an identification made by a witness could result in searches of the defendant's home, office, vehicle, person, or belongings. For example, suppose that a single photo display prompts a witness to accuse a suspect of parking a vehicle filled with explosives in a crowded city. The identification leads to the arrest of the suspect and to searches of his pockets and desk drawers incident to that arrest. In addition, the witness's identification, when combined with other evidence, furnishes the probable cause needed for a warrant to search the suspect's garage for explosives. Any evidence found during any of these searches—evidence of the attempted bombing or any other offense—would be derivative of the suggestive method. There would be a "but for" causal connection because the single photo display yielded the identification which, in turn, provided the justifications for the searches.

Whether this sort of derivative evidence would fall within the presumptive scope of *Stovall*'s due process doctrine is uncertain. The primary rationale for suppression—the risk of an unfair outcome due to misleading evidence—is entirely inapposite and cannot support a derivative evidence principle for non-identification evidence. However, the deterrent premise could justify exclusion. The evidence found is profit reaped from the unnecessary suggestion and might provide incentives for future suggestive methods. On the other hand, it seems relatively unlikely that officials would be motivated by the seemingly rare situations in which suggestive identifications result in the acquisition of other types of derivative evidence. For that reason, it is arguable that suppression would produce little deterrence. Moreover, the conduct deterred does not violate constitutional rights, but simply generates later risks of due process violations.

---

impose that higher standard despite the virtually identical natures of the reliability determination and *Wade*'s independent source inquiry.

184. Close examination of this aspect of the due process exclusion doctrine appears in the "independent source" subsection, *infra* text accompanying notes 201–07. Although the Supreme Court does not refer to the reliability inquiry as an independent source determination or classify it as an "exception" to due process exclusion, that is its true nature.

Therefore, any gains are not as substantial as those that result when suppression prevents pretrial conduct that actually violates a constitutional guarantee.[185] Finally, the cost to the fact-finding process of suppressing reliable nonidentification evidence is higher than the cost of suppressing potentially mistaken eyewitness identifications. All of these considerations could tip the balance against a derivative evidence principle.[186]

In sum, the Fourteenth Amendment bar extends to eyewitness identifications generated by any official method that is unnecessarily suggestive enough to give rise to a very substantial likelihood of misidentification. It also forbids introduction of a subsequent identification by a witness who identifies an accused at the suggestive session. While the issue has not been resolved, given the premises for suppression it seems quite unlikely that due process exclusion bars other kinds of derivative evidence.

2. Proceedings in Which Due Process Excludes Evidence

The goal of Due Process Clause regulation of eyewitness identification is to ensure fair *trials*—to preclude gratuitous government-generated risks of inaccurate convictions. The primary, and probably the exclusive, arena for suppression is the criminal trial—i.e., courtroom proceedings to determine an accused's guilt or innocence. The precedents clearly focus on trials alone.[187] None has involved any other type of proceeding.[188]

---

185. The Fourth Amendment exclusionary rule and the Sixth Amendment-*Massiah* exclusionary rule, for example, aim to deter actual constitutional deprivations. In *Manson v. Brathwaite*, 432 U.S. at 98, the Court asserted that the same considerations that militate in favor of exclusion when pretrial conduct violates constitutional guarantees do not apply in this context because unnecessarily suggestive identifications do not violate any constitutional rights. *Id.* at 113 n.13. The Court almost certainly meant that deterrence does not have the same force as a justification for due process exclusion.

186. In addition, in *Brathwaite*, the Court acknowledged that a *per se* exclusionary rule had greater deterrent effect. *See id.* at 112. Nonetheless, because such a rule could result in the excessive suppression of reliable identification evidence, the majority opted for a case-by-case approach thought to adequately discourage officers. *See id.* The way in which the Court struck the cost-benefit balance in *Brathwaite* (in a situation involving evidence that might be untrustworthy), coupled with a general increase in hostility to the exclusion of undeniably reliable evidence in other contexts, *see, e.g.*, Herring v. United States, 555 U.S. ____, 129 S.Ct. 695 (2009); Hudson v. Michigan, 547 U.S. 586 (2006); United States v. Patane, 542 U.S. 630 (2004), furnish additional bases for a prediction that the Court would reject a derivative evidence principle for nonidentification evidence acquired as a result of suggestive identification methods.

187. *See Brathwaite*, 432 U.S. at 99; Neil v. Biggers, 409 U.S. 188, 193, 201 (1972); Foster v. California, 394 U.S. 440, 442 (1969); *Simmons*, 390 U.S. at 381, 384; Stovall v. Denno, 388 U.S. 293, 295 (1967).

188. The Fourth Amendment exclusionary rule has been applied to technically civil, but "quasi-criminal," forfeiture proceedings. *See supra* Chapter 1, text accompanying

It is uncertain whether a defendant could succeed with an effort to keep evidence from a true sentencing proceeding after conviction—that is, a hearing to determine punishment, not guilt.[189] The guarantee of due process reaches sentencing hearings, regulating and constraining what the government may and may not do at that phase of the criminal process.[190] On the other hand, the demands of due process in a sentencing proceeding, where the severity of the punishment is at issue, are not as stringent as at trial.[191] For example, a judge can base a sentence on a fact found merely by a preponderance of the evidence. The due process requirement of proof beyond a reasonable doubt is inapplicable.[192]

A bar to the use of identification evidence in sentencing proceedings is defensible. An accused's interest in avoiding a sentence that is unjustifiably severe because it is based on an erroneous eyewitness identification *could* justify application of the due process rule. Suppose a defendant is being sentenced for a bank robbery. The judge considers identifications of him as the perpetrator of two other violent bank robberies—identifications that could not be admitted at trials for those robberies without violating due process. The judge sentences the defendant to 50 years in prison rather than the 20 years that she would have imposed based on the conviction alone. It is arguably unfair to have deprived the defendant of 30 additional years of freedom on the basis of the questionable identification evidence.

On the contrary, it is arguable that the risks of error engendered by suggested identifications pose intolerable threats to fundamental fairness only when they undermine the accuracy of guilt-innocence determinations. A sentencing judge

---

notes 160–62. The similarities to a criminal trial could support a conclusion that the due process bar should apply to this narrow category of civil cases.

189. As discussed earlier, some processes that are labeled sentencing proceedings are criminal trials for purposes of the jury trial guarantee. *See supra* Chapter 5, text accompanying notes 157–58. There can be no doubt that these proceedings are also guilt-innocence determinations for purposes of the due process bar to identification evidence. The discussion here is concerned with true sentencing proceedings—those that do not trigger application of the jury trial guarantee or the reasonable doubt standard.

190. *See* Gardner v. Florida, 430 U.S. 349, 358 (1977) (plurality opinion); Williams v. New York, 337 U.S. 241, 252 n.18 (1949).

191. Higher standards of due process are called for at trial because stakes are higher in guilt-innocence determinations than in determinations of the amount of punishment to be imposed.

192. In criminal trials, the Fourteenth Amendment demands that the prosecution prove every element of a crime beyond a reasonable doubt. *See* In re Winship, 397 U.S. 358, 364 (1970). In sentencing proceedings, proof of facts by a preponderance of the evidence suffices. *See* McMillan v. Pennsylvania, 477 U.S. 79, 91 (1986). A thorough discussion of the differences in the demands of due process in sentencing proceedings is beyond the scope of this chapter. The stark burden of proof difference suffices to illustrate that a sentencing proceeding can be considered fundamentally fair even though the risk of error is higher than what is constitutionally tolerable in a trial.

may well be capable of assessing the probative value of identification evidence and giving it the weight it deserves, if any, in exercising her discretion to ascertain a sentence appropriate for the offender and the offense. The government's interest in offering all potentially relevant evidence could be controlling when the sole question is the amount of punishment needed and deserved. One could reasonably conclude that there is insufficient reason to expand the constitutional bar to the questionable identification evidence.

The Fourth Amendment exclusionary rule does not govern grand jury hearings, parole revocation proceedings, or civil lawsuits.[193] Reliance on questionable identification evidence could be considered unfair because it injects risks that grand jury or parole revocation processes might lead to unjustified charges or erroneous deprivations of liberty. A civil verdict might be distorted, and a defendant might suffer an unjustified financial loss or some other undeserved civil penalty, if a fact finder was influenced by a mistaken identification. Nonetheless, it seems unlikely that the Supreme Court would extend the *Stovall* doctrine to these contexts. Despite the fact that due process exclusion is a constitutional *right* that guards against unfair outcomes and not a mere deterrent safeguard, the Justices would probably refuse to apply the due process bar to these other processes. The stakes in these proceedings and the harms suffered if error occurs are not comparable to those involved in determinations of guilt or innocence for criminal offenses.

The final question is whether a convicted defendant may seek habeas corpus relief on the ground that a trial judge erroneously rejected his due process suppression claim. *Stone v. Powell* severely restricts a habeas claimant's ability to succeed with a Fourth Amendment exclusionary rule claim to cases where a state denied the defendant a full and fair hearing.[194] *Stone*'s reasoning is deeply rooted in the fact that Fourth Amendment exclusion is entirely a forward-looking deterrent sanction that vindicates no trial rights. That logic is wholly inapposite when a constitutional right to exclude evidence is at issue. The ability to vindicate the right to due process by bringing a habeas corpus challenge to a trial court's decision to admit eyewitness identification evidence is vitally important and would not be qualified by the *Stone v. Powell* doctrine.[195]

---

193. *See supra* Chapter 1, text accompanying notes 163–73. The discussions of other constitutional exclusion doctrines in this text have generally concluded that it is unlikely the Supreme Court would extend their scope to those sorts of proceedings. *See supra* Chapter 2, text accompanying notes 189–90, 195–98; *supra* Chapter 3, text accompanying notes 147–48; *supra* Chapter 4, text accompanying notes 169–70; *supra* Chapter 5, text accompanying note 163.

194. *See* Stone v. Powell, 428 U.S. 465, 481–82 (1976).

195. For a similar conclusion with regard to the Fifth and Fourteenth Amendment rights not to be convicted on the basis of coerced confessions, see *supra* Chapter 2, note 191. As observed in that note, the Court's refusal to extend the *Stone* restriction on habeas relief to claims involving *Miranda*'s prophylactic exclusion doctrine makes it certain that

In sum, it seems quite probable that the infrequently invoked due process exclusion doctrine would not be broadened to reach any proceedings other than criminal trials. In a petition for a writ of habeas corpus, however, a defendant should prevail—even though the state provided a full and fair hearing of his suppression claim—by demonstrating that the Fourteenth Amendment barred an eyewitness identification from his trial.

3. "Standing" to Claim Due Process Exclusion: The Persons Entitled to Bar Eyewitness Identifications

A person on trial for a crime is entitled to exclude evidence that a witness identified him as a result of an unnecessarily suggestive procedure. The question here is whether a third party—someone other than the individual identified—has "standing" to raise a due process suppression claim. Although an unnecessarily suggestive method will not often produce identification evidence that incriminates someone other than the person identified, an identification of one person will occasionally have probative value at the trial of a third party.

Perhaps the most likely scenario is when a person is accused of aiding and abetting another's commission of an offense. Liability as an accomplice requires proof that the person aided was a "guilty principal."[196] The prosecution must establish beyond a reasonable doubt that the alleged accomplice somehow furthered another individual's commission of the crime charged. Consequently, an eyewitness identification of one individual as the principal—the person who actually performed the criminal act—could be relevant, even essential, proof at the trial of an accomplice. Moreover, derivative nonidentification evidence—contraband or incriminating documents, for example—might also furnish proof of a third person's guilt.[197]

Suppose, for example, that a witness shown a single photograph declares that she is certain that the woman depicted is the person she saw set fire to a building. A search warrant based on this identification uncovers incriminating letters in the woman's apartment. When the woman's boyfriend is tried for arson for having assisted her by driving her to the scene and serving as a lookout, the government may wish to introduce both the witness's identification of the

---

the *Stone* doctrine would not impede a habeas claim that a trial judge had erroneously denied a personal constitutional right to suppress evidence.

196. *See* United States v. Jones, 425 F.2d 1048, 1056 (9th Cir. 1970); Edwards v. United States, 286 F.2d 681, 683 (5th Cir. 1960); WAYNE R. LAFAVE, CRIMINAL LAW 728 (5th ed. 2010).

197. Derivative evidence other than identifications could incriminate a third party as the principal in the commission of an offense. For example, contraband or a weapon found in the home of the individual identified might be linked to another individual who is subsequently charged with possession or manufacture of the contraband or with using the weapon to commit a homicide.

woman as the arsonist and the letters to prove the boyfriend's liability as an accomplice to the arson. The woman has standing to raise a due process objection to all of the evidence that qualifies for due process suppression. The question is whether the boyfriend can bar the evidence from his trial. The answer is debatable.

The Court could conclude that only those who are identified due to unnecessarily suggestive sessions suffer a due process violation when a potentially misleading identification is introduced in court. According to this view, a defendant suffers no due process deprivation at trial unless the pretrial procedure created a likelihood that *she* would be misidentified. A third person lacks "standing" to suppress an identification because there is no threat to his entitlement to due process when the identification evidence is used against him in court. The Supreme Court has held that only the "victim" of a flagrantly unreasonable search has standing to claim that due process requires the suppression of evidence.[198] Similarly, it might decide that only the "victim" of an unnecessarily suggestive procedure can seek suppression of an eyewitness identification.

There are logical arguments, however, that support the opposite conclusion. The due process danger in identification contexts is that an avoidable, government-generated risk of error might produce an unfair, inaccurate outcome—the conviction of an innocent individual. A potentially mistaken identification gives rise to the same risk of error whether introduced against the person identified or a third party. If an alleged principal is erroneously accused by a witness, the putative accomplice could be convicted of aiding a person who did not commit the offense. An essential element of complicity in the crime—the guilt of the person aided—could be inaccurately determined. Consequently, it is arguable that a defendant may object to the government's use of an identification of any person resulting from an unnecessarily suggestive process. The accused would have standing to raise his own due process entitlement to a fair trial, an entitlement jeopardized when the state uses any identification evidence with a sufficiently serious risk of error to convict him.[199]

It is uncertain which position would prevail. The primary justification for suppressing eyewitness identification evidence seems to support standing for

---

198. *See* United States v. Payner, 447 U.S. 727, 731–35 (1980).

199. The Court's conclusion in *United States v. Payner*, 447 U.S. 727 (1980), that only the victim of an egregiously unreasonable search can raise a due process suppression claim is distinguishable from the due process claim involved here. In the Court's view, in search contexts, the due process violation occurs at the time of the search—the pretrial conduct that yields the evidence. Introduction of the evidence at trial does not violate a constitutional right. In identification contexts, however, the constitutional violation occurs only at trial, not during the identification session. Moreover, untrustworthiness and unfair verdicts are not concerns that dictate the exclusion of the evidentiary products of illegal searches, no matter how flagrantly illegal those searches. To the contrary, these are the core concerns underlying due process suppression of identification evidence.

anyone who might be harmed at trial by the evidence. The danger of inaccurate conviction is not limited to cases in which misidentifications corrupt the accuracy of the trial of the person identified. Unlike most exclusionary rules, the due process doctrine bars evidence because of a fundamental concern with its trustworthiness and the injustice that could result from its use at trial. A familiar refrain in other contexts is that *suppression* undermines the search for truth. In this setting, however, *admission* might well threaten truth, and *suppression* is designed to promote it. Nonetheless, the Supreme Court's general hostility toward exclusion has made it reluctant to expand notions of standing. Despite the important differences in the nature and goals of due process suppression, it is possible that the Court's resolution of the standing issue would be guided and influenced by the same antipathy and skepticism that has led to limitations upon standing to assert other exclusionary claims.[200]

The issue is much simpler for derivative nonidentification evidence. Assuming that such evidence is subject to due process exclusion, only those individuals subjected to the identification procedure that led to acquisition of the evidence should be able to object. The sole logical rationale for suppressing such evidence would be deterrence. The evidence does not threaten the interest in a just outcome by injecting a risk of inaccuracy into a trial. When deterrence justifies suppression, the cost-benefit balance favors a standing limitation even when the pretrial conduct actually violates constitutional rights. The case for a standing limitation is even stronger when the pretrial conduct that supports the exclusion claim—an unnecessarily suggestive identification method—violates no constitutional command.

4. Exceptions to *Stovall*'s Due Process Suppression Doctrine

There are no Supreme Court decisions addressing "exceptions" to the due process exclusion mandate. However, two qualifications on the basic doctrine—the necessity criterion and the reliability inquiry—mirror exclusionary rule exceptions considered in earlier chapters. Analyses of these two facets of the due process rule and brief explorations of the legitimacy of other possible exceptions follow.

a. The Independent Source Doctrine and the Inevitable Discovery Exception I have previously observed that the independent source doctrine is not a true exception to exclusionary rules, even though it is often so described. Because a foundational predicate for the operation of every suppression doctrine is a "but

200. The Fourteenth Amendment suppression doctrine for identification evidence has not been immune from the hostility to exclusion that typically leads to the narrowing of exclusion mandates. *See* Manson v. Brathwaite, 432 U.S. 98, 112–13 (1977) (taking a less expansive approach to due process suppression in part because of hostility to "Draconian" exclusionary rules that defeat the search for truth).

for" causal connection between the evidence at issue and official impropriety,[201] evidence that is the product of an independent, lawful source does not qualify for exclusion. Such evidence is admissible because the government has obtained it legally. Whether a constitutional bar is a deterrent safeguard, a personal trial right, or both, the justifications for exclusion do not extend to evidence with an independent source.[202]

Due process presumptively bars eyewitness identification evidence if an accused proves that the method used was sufficiently suggestive and the government does not demonstrate necessity for the suggestion. However, the presumption is overcome, and the evidence is admissible, if the prosecution shows that an identification is reliable. The reliability determination hinges on an assessment of various factors, including the witness's initial opportunity to observe the crime, his degree of attention, the accuracy of prior descriptions, his level of certainty, the length of time between the observations and the identification, and the degree or intensity of the suggestive influences employed.[203] Suppose that an accused was identified at a lineup in which his distinctive appearance—his height, weight, and coloration, for example—made him the *only* individual resembling the person a witness claims to have seen sitting in a car outside a bank at the time of a robbery. The lineup identification and an in-court identification by the witness are admissible if the prosecution establishes, for example, that the witness was just a few feet away from the person in the car for several minutes in broad daylight, that she stared intensely at his unique features,

---

201. Sometimes the pretrial conduct that is the source of evidence violates constitutional rights. That is the case with unlawful searches and seizures, sufficiently egregious coercion to confess, and deprivations of the pretrial right to counsel defined by the *Massiah* doctrine. Sometimes the pretrial conduct that yields the evidence does not itself transgress the Constitution. That is the case with compulsion to speak that is not intense enough to violate due process, *Miranda* violations, and unnecessarily suggestive identification procedures. It bears mention that unlike the doctrines discussed in the first six chapters, the Confrontation Clause bar to testimonial hearsay discussed in Chapter 7 does *not* hinge upon proof of a causal connection between improper official pretrial conduct and the acquisition of the evidence excluded.

202. For an in-depth discussion of the independent source doctrine, see *supra* Chapter 1, text accompanying notes 204–12.

203. *Brathwaite*, 432 U.S. at 114. For criticism of the reliability inquiry, see Rosenberg, *Rethinking the Right*, *supra* note 2, at 275–76, 280 (maintaining that science has shown that the factors prescribed in *Biggers* and *Brathwaite* are not valid indicators of reliability and that there are too many relevant variables "to be encapsulated in a single, easily stated and applied standard"); Wells & Seelau, *Psychological Research*, *supra* note 2, at 785 (arguing that while the factors "do not strongly clash with the scientific evidence," their "value" is diminished because they "are only weakly related to . . . accuracy," they "ignore other considerations that can be more important . . . determinants of eyewitness identification accuracy," and their assessment is "confounded by other factors in complex but important ways").

subsequently gave a detailed description that corresponds closely to the accused's appearance, was supremely confident in her identification, and made the lineup identification just a day after the observations outside the bank.[204]

The reliability assessment that lowers the presumptive evidentiary bar is in fact a determination of whether the witness selected the accused because of the governmental suggestion or because of her memory of earlier perceptions.[205] Suggestive processes have the potential for distorting influence. The reliability inquiry ascertains whether that potential was realized in the identifications made. The object is to decide whether suggestion led a witness to choose the accused, or whether, instead, she identified him because she recalled observations made at an initial encounter with him at the scene of a crime. The reliability assessment is essentially a determination of whether an eyewitness identification had an "independent source"—whether it is traceable to undesirable official conduct that risks misidentification or to perceptions and memories with no causal connection to that conduct.[206]

The reliability criterion is reconcilable with the nature and objectives of due process suppression. The primary object of Fourteenth Amendment exclusion is to protect a defendant's right to a fair outcome undistorted by official influences. Evidence that is truly the product of the witness's independent recollections poses no threat that the verdict will be distorted by governmental suggestion. To the extent that deterrence is also a goal, evidence that is reliable is not the profit of official impropriety and, therefore, needs not be suppressed to remove the incentive for future misconduct. Exclusion would put the government in a worse

---

204. The degree of suggestion in the identification procedure is a factor that counts against reliability. The more intense the suggestion, the greater the evidence needed to meet the government's burden of demonstrating that the witness has identified the accused based on independent remembered perceptions. I have deliberately created a hypothetical situation here in which the reliability showing is overwhelming. The demonstration that a witness chose the defendant because of her independent memory of past observations need not be this powerful. Reliability has to be established merely by a preponderance of the evidence—i.e., more likely than not.

205. *See Brathwaite*, 432 U.S. at 122 (Marshall, J., dissenting).

206. There will be a causal connection between the identification process and the identification made because the identification will in fact be the result of that process. However, a showing of reliability establishes the lack of a causal link between the suggestive aspects of the process and the witness's identification. Consequently, there is no connection between the official impropriety and the evidence.

Insofar as the government has the burden of demonstrating reliability after an accused proves unnecessary suggestion, the reliability determination operates just like the traditional "independent source" doctrine. An individual seeking to suppress evidence must first demonstrate official impropriety and the acquisition of evidence that appears to be causally connected. To satisfy the classic independent source doctrine, the prosecution must respond with proof that there was in fact no such link—i.e., that the origin of the evidence was not the impropriety established.

position than it would have occupied without its misconduct, a consequence deemed undesirable.[207]

There can be no doubt that if other kinds of derivative evidence are suppressible under the due process rule, proof of an independent source would justify admission of that evidence.[208] If the accused were to demonstrate a reason for believing that the discovery of contraband in his vehicle was causally linked to an earlier identification, a prosecutor's demonstration that the identification played no part in finding the contraband would dictate admission. As noted earlier, the only plausible rationale for the suppression of nonidentification evidence is deterrence. The Court has found the independent source doctrine entirely consistent with deterrent objectives.[209]

The "inevitable discovery" doctrine is a genuine exception to exclusionary rules. It permits the introduction of evidence with a causal connection to an illegality if the prosecution shows by a preponderance of the evidence that the government would have acquired the same evidence by lawful means. It is unlikely

---

207. *See* Nix v. Williams, 467 U.S. 431, 443 (1984) (explaining that the deterrent goals of exclusion dictate the government be put in the same, not a worse evidentiary position than it would have occupied absent the improper conduct).

Some critics argue that the reliability inquiry is not compatible with the right to due process at trial and undermines the deterrent efficacy of the due process exclusion doctrine. In their view, the government should not have any opportunity to introduce identifications made *at* unnecessarily suggestive sessions based on a putative demonstration of reliability. *See* Pulaski, *Court Dismantles, supra* note 2, at 1113–14, 1020–21; Sherwood, *Erosion of Safeguards, supra* note 115, at 748–49, 770. If one believes that it is inherently impossible to tell whether a witness is recalling independent memories or succumbing to suggestion, *see* Rosenberg, *Rethinking the Right, supra* note 2, at 293 (stating that "one can hardly be confident of the independence of" identifications made after a witness has been exposed to suggestion), the reliability inquiry does imperil the due process entitlement to a fair result. *See* Grano, Kirby, Biggers, *and* Ash, *supra* note 155, at 781–82 (arguing that "the chaotic due process decisions" do not provide adequate protection against misidentification and the risk of convicting innocent persons); Luria, *Showup Identifications, supra* note 2, at 542–43 (calling for a *per se* bar to identifications because courts cannot accurately determine reliability of an identification if suggestion is present). In addition, if one suspects that judges are inclined to find reliability and that officials are aware of that inclination, the deterrent impact of exclusion is likely to be diluted. *See* Rosenberg, *Rethinking the Right, supra* note 2, at 305 (asserting that the reliability test does not provide sufficient deterrence because judges routinely admit evidence and the police therefore "have nothing to lose" as a result of unnecessary suggestion).

208. The "reliability" label is not appropriate to describe the independent source inquiry for nonidentification evidence. The independence of nonidentification evidence does not depend on psychological processes divorced from official suggestion. Instead, it hinges on a showing that the government did not discover the evidence because of leads from an identification subject to suppression, but found it by using independent, lawful investigatory methods.

209. *See supra* Chapter 1, text accompanying note 212.

to apply to eyewitness identification evidence secured by unnecessarily suggestive processes. The same variables that govern the reliability-independent source inquiry would be relevant to the inevitable discovery determination. Both depend upon the strength of a witness's capacities to make an identification and, thus, the improbability that her choice was influenced by the suggestion. If the prosecution cannot show that the witness in fact identified the defendant reliably—i.e., based on independent recollections of her observations—then it is hard to imagine how it could establish that the witness *would have* made a proper, untainted identification had the suggestion not occurred. In other words, if an identification was not the product of independent psychological processes, it cannot be shown that it *would have been* the product of such processes.

It is conceivable that the government could prove that derivative nonidentification evidence would have been legally discovered even though it was unlawfully obtained. Assume that the search of a vehicle resulted from probable cause based on an eyewitness identification subject to suppression. At the time, other officers were in the process of seeking a warrant for the same vehicle based on evidence unconnected to the identification. These officers would have carried out a search pursuant to the warrant very soon, finding the same contraband found by the officers who searched the vehicle. That contraband would be admissible under the inevitable discovery exception. The only logical premise for due process exclusion of derivative nonidentification evidence is deterrence, and the inevitable discovery exception is consistent with deterrent goals because it does not allow the state to reap evidentiary profit from its wrong.[210]

In sum, the reliability inquiry for identification evidence is essentially an independent source determination. An eyewitness identification is exempt from suppression if a witness selects an accused based on her own abilities, not because of the government's suggestive influences. On the other hand, because the inevitable discovery exception seems to overlap with the independent source doctrine in this area, there is no logical room for an inevitable discovery exception for eyewitness identification evidence.

b. An Attenuation Exception It also seems unlikely that the traditional attenuation exception could support the admission of any otherwise excludable eyewitness identification evidence. Attenuation first appeared as an exception to the Fourth Amendment exclusionary rule. It does not apply to primary evidence—evidence acquired as the immediate result of governmental misconduct. Instead, it permits the introduction of derivative evidence that is in fact the product of an illegality. The prosecution must show that the connection between the official misconduct and the derivative evidence is sufficiently weak—that is, that the acquisition of the evidence was sufficiently remote from the improper actions that made acquisition possible. Consequently, identifications that are made

210. *See supra* Chapter 1, text accompanying notes 219–20.

during, or as an immediate result of, unnecessarily suggestive methods cannot be attenuated from the official wrong. Only subsequent identifications by the same witness—identifications that are presumed to be the delayed results of the suggestive methods—could conceivably qualify.

However, the underlying premises of due process suppression militate strongly against the application of the attenuation exception even if the factors ordinarily pertinent to attenuation analysis are favorable. For example, suppose that a witness makes an identification at a police station lineup that was unnecessarily suggestive, although the suggestion was neither flagrant nor deliberate. Many months, even years, later, after a number of significant intervening events have occurred, the same witness again identifies the defendant.[211] If this later identification is not proven to be reliable—i.e., if the reliability factors do not contradict the presumption of a very substantial likelihood of misidentification—then the concerns that support due process suppression are fully applicable. The mere fact that the government behavior was not particularly culpable, that a long time elapsed before acquisition, and that many events transpired in the interim do not respond to the concern that underlies the due process right to exclusion—that government-created inaccuracy will yield an erroneous conviction. Put otherwise, an identification that a witness makes after she has first identified the accused at a suggestive session is either the product of the suggestion or the product of the witness's independent perceptions and memories. If it is the result of the suggestive procedures, then even though its acquisition is distant or attenuated from the initial impropriety, an accused's right to a fair trial dictates suppression. As long as there is a causal link between unnecessarily suggestive influences and an eyewitness identification, the Fourteenth Amendment should bar admission.[212]

---

211. The variables deemed relevant to traditional attenuation analysis are the passage of time, the intervention of significant events, and the character of the misconduct. *See supra* Chapter 1, text accompanying notes 224–31.

212. Other kinds of derivative evidence, if normally subject to suppression, should be admitted if the connection between the improper identification process and the acquisition of that evidence is attenuated. As noted more than once, if that sort of derivative evidence is suppressible under the *Stovall* doctrine, it is solely for deterrent ends. Cost-benefit balancing supports an attenuation exception to exclusionary rules that are designed to deter future pretrial misconduct, and not to enforce present trial rights. *See supra* Chapter 1, text following note 231. Suppose, for example, that officials, in good faith, conduct an identification session that is just barely suggestive enough to meet the due process standard. Six months later, an identification made at that session is used as an essential part of the probable cause showing needed for an arrest warrant. The suspect is arrested and a search of his pockets produces contraband. Because the "but for" causal connection between the suggestive identification process and the contraband is arguably attenuated by the passage of time and the nonegregious character of the impropriety, the contraband could be admissible at trial.

c. A Public Safety or Exigency Exception The issue here is whether potentially unreliable products of suggestive procedures are admissible because a threat to the public safety or some other need justified the failure to use neutral, nonsuggestive procedures. The premise is not that suggestive methods might further important goals. The potential for misidentification inherent in suggestion is generally considered to be unproductive.[213] It is arguable, however, that interests in acting promptly could preclude nonsuggestive techniques. Some sufficiently weighty reason why officers need to secure an immediate identification may support the use of otherwise unacceptable methods.

The constitutional question is whether the use of potentially misleading products of such methods at trial is consistent with due process. The answer has been clear since *Stovall*, the first due process decision. Therein, the Supreme Court prescribed threshold requirements for due process suppression that still govern today. Evidence is subject to exclusion *only* if the government employs *unnecessarily* suggestive processes.[214] Thus, if an important enough interest precludes the employment of a less suggestive method, the Fourteenth Amendment does not bar a resulting identification.

Although framed in terms of the criteria that must be met to establish a due process claim, the effect of the requirement that suggestion be unnecessary is the same as a public safety or exigency exception to the due process exclusion doctrine. When the government establishes a need to use otherwise unacceptable techniques, the evidentiary products—eyewitness identifications that are potentially untrustworthy—are admissible to prove guilt.[215] Thus, if a victim of a brutal attack is likely to die soon and the only way of obtaining her identification of the perpetrator is the undeniably suggestive display of a single suspect or photograph, an identification made by the victim may be introduced at trial. If law enforcement officers cannot be expected to do better, they will not lose the evidence produced.

It is arguable that the Due Process Clause should prohibit conviction based on potentially unreliable identifications even though there was a pressing need

---

213. In fact, suggestive identification processes are said to be counterproductive insofar as they may induce law enforcement officials to prosecute an innocent individual and to allow the guilty (and possibly dangerous) perpetrator of the crime to remain at large. *See* Manson v. Brathwaite, 432 U.S. 98, 127–28 (1977) (Marshall, J., dissenting).

214. *See* Stovall v. Denno, 388 U.S. 293, 301–02 (1967). *Stovall* not only prescribed the requirement that suggestion be unnecessary, it rejected the defendant's due process claim based on a finding of necessity. *See supra* text accompanying notes 26–33.

215. Ordinarily, the government has the burden of proving that presumptively excludable evidence falls within an exception to an exclusionary rule. Even though the due process bar requires unnecessary suggestion as a predicate for suppression and does not frame necessity as a criterion for exempting evidence from exclusion, the government would seem to have not only the obligation to raise the issue of necessity, but also the burden of proving that suggestive methods were in fact necessary.

to identify a suspect and less suggestive techniques were infeasible. After all, the necessity for the suggestion does not diminish the likelihood of misidentification and the ultimate risk of an unfair verdict.[216] According to this reasoning, it is always unfair to convict an innocent person; no amount of "necessity" can justify that outcome. Officials may use suggestive identification techniques to serve investigatory purposes and may follow any leads they obtain. However, they may not use the unreliable fruits of misleading techniques in court without depriving an accused of due process.

The Supreme Court has never explained the logic underlying its contrary conclusion that identifications are admissible when suggestion is necessary. It is easy to reconcile the necessity criterion with a deterrent rationale. When officers have justification for employing suggestive methods, their conduct is desirable, not something to be discouraged. Reconciling the necessity criterion with the primary rationale for due process suppression—the prevention of unfair trials—is a bit more difficult.

The necessity criterion appears to be based on the notion that it is fundamentally unfair to use potentially mistaken eyewitness identification evidence that threatens to produce an inaccurate trial outcome *only* when the likelihood of error is the result of *unjustified* official distortion—that is, only when government agents have acted improperly. The Fourteenth Amendment's concern is not simply unfair outcomes, but unfair outcomes that are the result of unfair processes. When potential untrustworthiness is the product of official suggestion justified by necessity, there is no constitutional foundation for exclusion because officials have not behaved unfairly. Because there is justification for the suggestion, the identification process is fair. The due process guarantee does not bar admission of the evidence when the risk of erroneous conviction is not the product of improper governmental conduct.[217]

---

216. The exigencies that make suggestion necessary could even increase the likelihood of misidentification by inducing officers who need information to pressure witnesses into a particular selection. *Cf.* New York v. Quarles, 467 U.S. 649, 684–85 (1984) (Marshall, J., dissenting) (suggesting that in a situation in which officers are motivated by public safety concerns the likelihood of coerciveness may be even greater).

217. Although the Fourteenth Amendment may not bar the potentially misleading identification evidence when suggestion is necessary, it still provides some protection against the danger of unfair conviction. If the evidence presented by the prosecution at trial is insufficient—if no reasonable person could find guilt beyond a reasonable doubt based on that evidence, *see* Jackson v. Virginia, 443 U.S. 307, 315–16, 317–18 (1979)—the Due Process Clause requires a trial judge to enter a judgment of acquittal and requires an appellate court to reverse a conviction. *See id.* at 317, 318 n.11, 319 n.12. Moreover, following the entry of a trial court's judgment of acquittal based on insufficient evidence or an appellate court reversal on that ground, the Fifth Amendment guarantee against double jeopardy forbids retrial. *See* Burks v. United States, 437 U.S. 1, 10–11, 18 (1978).

The Court has not addressed the meaning or breadth of necessity. Clearly, there must be some reason why officials cannot be reasonably expected to employ nonsuggestive (or less suggestive) methods. The most likely reason would be time pressure—some exigency that demands swift action. However, it is conceivable that another reason could preclude neutrality. For example, a person's appearance might be so idiosyncratic that others resembling him simply cannot be found. One issue is the sorts of law enforcement interests that can qualify as necessity. A serious enough danger that a witness will become incapacitated and unable to identify or exonerate a suspect is sufficient.[218] Any similar necessity to act or lose the ability to apprehend and prosecute a guilty, possibly dangerous individual must qualify.[219] It seems certain that a need to secure an identification to prevent a threat to public safety would constitute necessity. Thus, a sufficient risk that an explosive device will be detonated, that a kidnap victim will die, or that a child will be abused could justify suggestiveness. In general, any interest relied upon to support the use of a suggestive method ought to be sufficiently important to outweigh the unfairness—the serious risk of an erroneous conviction—occasioned by the introduction of an identification resulting from that method.

In sum, the Due Process Clause mandates exclusion only when government agents employ *unnecessarily* suggestive identification methods. When investigatory demands or public safety threats preclude nonsuggestive processes, the *Stovall* doctrine does not bar the evidentiary products.

d. A "Good Faith" Exception "Good faith" exceptions to exclusion doctrines permit the introduction of evidence when officials engage in improper pretrial conduct, but it was objectively reasonable to believe that their acts were proper. There are few possibilities for objectively reasonable mistakes regarding the propriety of unnecessarily suggestive identification procedures. Officers might mistakenly, but reasonably, believe either that suggestive procedures were necessary or that the procedures they used were not sufficiently suggestive to trigger due process concern. The question is whether eyewitness identifications should be admissible in situations involving objectively reasonable mistakes.

The argument in favor of a "good faith" exception to due process exclusion is that the use of an unnecessarily suggestive identification method is not culpable

---

If an eyewitness identification that is the product of necessary suggestion is the only evidence of guilt, the evidence might well be insufficient for due process purposes.

218. This was the necessity that sufficed in Stovall v. Denno, 388 U.S. 293 (1967). *See supra* text accompanying notes 30–33.

219. Perhaps if an offense was too petty or minor, the interest in identifying an individual might not justify the use of a potentially mistaken identification at trial. On the other hand, while the government interest in identification is not as weighty when the offense is not serious, the harm to an accused from erroneous conviction is also less significant.

when officials reasonably could believe that there was either necessity or insufficient suggestion. Because the officials lack fault, use of the evidence they obtain does not render the trial unfair. I find this argument unpersuasive, however, and would reject a good faith exception. Evidence is admissible when suggestion is necessary because there is in fact some justification for the official acts that generated the risks of misidentification. In that situation, the government's interest in securing an identification counterbalances a defendant's interest in a fair outcome. In contrast, when officers are reasonably mistaken about the propriety of their techniques, there is no actual justification for taking the chance of convicting an innocent person. Although the mistake is understandable, there was no reason to generate the likelihood of misidentification. The absence of fault seems an inadequate basis for accepting otherwise unacceptable risks of unjust conviction.[220]

e. Impeachment Use of Eyewitness Identification Evidence At a trial for a bank robbery, a defendant might offer an alibi defense, testifying that he was in another place at the time of the alleged robbery. He might call an acquaintance to support his alibi claim. An eyewitness identification of the defendant as the robber could impeach the defendant's or acquaintance's alibi testimony by contradicting it, thereby casting doubt on its credibility. The question is whether an identification that is inadmissible to prove guilt because it is the product of an unnecessarily suggestive procedure is admissible for impeachment purposes.

The Fourteenth Amendment bars identification evidence because the potential untrustworthiness that results from suggestive methods undermines the fairness of a trial by threatening an inaccurate outcome. Evidence ordinarily is less incriminating when used to impeach a witness rather than to prove guilt. It furnishes no affirmative support for the state's case, but, instead, diminishes the efficacy of the accused's defensive efforts. Nonetheless, impeachment use is incriminating—it makes conviction more likely. It may even prove to be a critical component of the prosecution's effort to persuade jurors of guilt beyond

---

220. The reasons for rejecting a good faith limitation on this due process exclusion doctrine are similar to those that led to the same conclusion with respect to the due process bar to coerced confessions. *See supra* Chapter 2, text accompanying notes 216–21.

A good faith exception would be a legitimate qualification of a due process bar to derivative nonidentification evidence. If such evidence is subject to Fourteenth Amendment suppression, the sole rationale is deterrence. When deterrence is the basis for exclusion, the cost-benefit balance has been found to favor the admission of evidence gained by conduct that actually violates constitutional rights if officers were reasonably mistaken about the propriety of their actions. *See supra* Chapter 1, text accompanying notes 236–57. Surely the balance favors admission here. Because the conduct to be deterred does not even violate the Constitution, any benefits from suppression are less substantial. In fact, the most recent Fourth Amendment exclusionary rule jurisprudence suggests that even negligent errors by officers might justify suspension of an exclusionary rule based solely on deterrence. *See supra* Chapter 1, text accompanying notes 199–203, 258–60.

a reasonable doubt. If the identification evidence used to suggest that a witness is testifying falsely or inaccurately is itself unreliable, jurors might be misled into discounting the witness's testimony. They may refuse to entertain doubts that a witness's testimony would otherwise raise.[221] The character of the unfairness is the same as when the government introduces unreliable identification evidence as proof of guilt—the outcome of the trial might be unjust because of the gratuitous distortion of evidence resulting from official identification methods.

Consequently, an impeachment use exception to the due process exclusion doctrine is unjustified. Fourteenth Amendment suppression of eyewitness identification evidence is an integral part of the personal entitlement to a fundamentally fair trial. The bar is rooted in a concern with the corruptive effects of such identification evidence on the verdict. The same reasoning that bars substantive use requires rejection of an impeachment use exception. The identification evidence should be inadmissible to impeach the defendant and any defense witness.[222]

E. CONCLUSIONS ABOUT THE DUE PROCESS BAR TO EYEWITNESS IDENTIFICATION EVIDENCE

Like Sixth Amendment right to counsel exclusion of eyewitness identification evidence, the Due Process Clause suppression doctrine has limited practical importance. Both evidentiary bars are essentially dormant. Neither has been considered by the Supreme Court in nearly 35 years, and lower courts only occasionally confront issues involving either constitutional exclusion doctrine.

---

221. Because jurors find eyewitness identifications particularly persuasive, the incriminating impeachment potential of this type of evidence may be greater than for other kinds of impeachment evidence.

222. Similar logic has led to the conclusion that impeachment use of coerced confessions is barred by due process. *See supra* Chapter 2, text accompanying notes 242–43.

Even if it is barred from the government's case-in-chief, nonidentification evidence found as a result of improperly suggestive identification processes should be admissible to impeach the defendant and perhaps even defense witnesses. The use of improperly obtained evidence to impeach a defendant is legitimate if the exclusionary rule at issue is based solely on deterrent objectives because the cost-benefit balance is thought to favor admission of the evidence for this limited purpose. *See supra* Chapter 1, text accompanying notes 261–68. When the conduct to be deterred violates a constitutional guarantee, however, the use of illegally-acquired evidence to impeach *other defense witnesses* has been found impermissible. *See supra* Chapter 1, text accompanying notes 269–71. Because improper identification methods do not violate constitutional rights, the cost-benefit balance might well support the use of derivative nonidentification evidence to impeach defense witnesses.

Nonetheless, from a theoretical standpoint, they are fascinating and significant landmarks on the constitutional exclusion terrain.

Due process exclusion is unique in character. The objectionable law enforcement conduct that dictates suppression does not itself violate constitutional rights. Because it is the use of evidence at trial that violates the Fourteenth Amendment, the primary justification for exclusion is to prevent in-court deprivations of due process. Although deterrence of flawed identification procedures does serve as an ancillary rationale, the Court has never explained why deterrence is necessary or desirable in this context.

In addition, doctrinal development has been sparse. During the ten-year span that the Supreme Court showed interest, relatively few details emerged. It is clear that successive identifications are subject to a derivative evidence bar, but it is entirely uncertain whether other kinds of derivative evidence are suppressible. Any identification evidence that is presumptively barred because of unnecessarily suggestive methods can be introduced if the government demonstrates that it is reliable. Despite an objectionable pretrial method, both immediate and subsequent identifications are admissible if they are the products of an independent source—the witness's perceptions and memories of an earlier encounter with the individual identified—and not the fruits of the suggestive influences. In addition, the threshold requirement that suggestion be "unnecessary" effectively adopts a "public safety" or "exigency" exception to due process exclusion. When the government has a sufficient need to use suggestive methods, no evidence is barred. None of the other doctrinal qualifications developed in other exclusionary contexts—standing, inevitable discovery, attenuation, good faith, and impeachment use—have been considered in this setting. I have done my best to project how those questions might properly be resolved.

No one has ever suggested that the Supreme Court's two constitutional efforts to regulate the abuses and reduce the perils of official identification procedures would remedy all of the problems that eyewitness identification evidence poses for our criminal justice systems. The Supreme Court's first venture into the area in 1967 resulted from a recognition that eyewitness identifications were a major source of miscarriages of justice—that misidentifications too often produced convictions of innocent persons. More than 40 years later, those concerns are still potent.[223]

The risks of injustice are in large part due to the inherent untrustworthiness of eyewitness identification that results from the limits of human capabilities and the willingness of jurors to credit questionable identification evidence. The Sixth and Fourteenth Amendment exclusion doctrines were not designed to address those sources of risk. Their focus was the increased risk injected by

223. *See* Clements, *Flipping a Coin*, *supra* note 2, at 272–78; Luria, *Showup Identifications*, *supra* note 2, at 518–20.

distorting official procedures. Moreover, the protective promise of the constitutional regulatory efforts has been diluted by later rulings restricting the reach of both evidentiary bars.

It is quite unlikely that the Supreme Court will show renewed interest in either doctrine. There is no reason to expect a renaissance of activity that will expand the constitutional shelter and furnish additional safeguards against the enduring threats to justice from eyewitness identification evidence. Any legal remedies for the problems that persist will have to come from other sources.[224]

224. Regulations that provide meaningful constraints on the conduct of identification procedures and rules of evidence that authorize more extensive courtroom exploration of the infirmities that plague identification testimony have long been possible options for combating the dangers. *See, e.g.*, Luria, *Showup Identifications*, *supra* note 2, at 547–51; Rosenberg, *Rethinking the Right*, *supra* note 2, at 297–314.

7. CONFRONTATION CLAUSE EXCLUSION OF HEARSAY

INTRODUCTION

This final chapter analyzes the bar to hearsay evidence rooted in the Sixth Amendment Confrontation Clause,[1] an exclusionary rule with a number of unique facets. Perhaps the most significant is that this constitutional exclusion doctrine, unlike every other suppression mandate studied in this text, is not based on official misconduct. In fact, there may be no governmental involvement in the production or acquisition of the suppressed evidence. Instead, the evidentiary bar depends upon and is defined by the nature of the evidence that the government wishes to introduce.[2] For that reason, all of the Supreme Court decisions pertaining to the relationship between the Confrontation Clause and hearsay are "exclusionary rule" decisions—that is, all are directly concerned with the scope and contours of evidentiary suppression.[3]

The identification evidence doctrines considered in the two preceding chapters are the newest exclusionary rules, have not been the subject of Supreme Court attention for nearly 35 years, and have little practical impact today.[4] In contrast,

1. The Confrontation Clause of the Sixth Amendment provides: "In all criminal prosecutions, the accused shall enjoy the right . . . to be confronted with the witnesses against him." U.S. Const. amend. VI.

2. This difference is reflected in the doctrine's location in law school curricula. The first six exclusion doctrines treated in this text are addressed in "Criminal Procedure" courses devoted to the study of constitutional limitations on police practices. The Sixth Amendment's exclusion of hearsay is considered in "Evidence" courses that are primarily concerned with the nonconstitutional rules that dictate the admissibility of evidence in court.

3. For most of the other doctrines discussed in this text, many Supreme Court opinions center around the details of the official actions that are the bases for suppression. Thus, for example, most Fourth Amendment opinions address when searches and seizures are unreasonable, most *Miranda* decisions explore the prophylactic constraints upon custodial interrogation, and most *Massiah* opinions deal with the nature of the pretrial clashes that implicate the Sixth Amendment right to counsel.

4. In fact, most of the constitutional impediments to prosecution evidence described in the preceding chapters are modern developments. The *Miranda* exclusion doctrine discussed in Chapter 3, the *Massiah* exclusionary rule discussed in Chapter 4, and both the *Wade-Gilbert* and *Stovall* bars to identification evidence discussed in Chapters 5 and 6 are all products of the Warren Court's 1960s revolution in criminal procedure. Only the Fourth Amendment exclusionary rule and Fifth and Fourteenth Amendment exclusion of

the evidentiary bar discussed in this chapter is the oldest constitutional exclusion doctrine,[5] was the subject of a landmark 2004 Supreme Court opinion that revolutionized the controlling standards and led to four refining rulings in the five years that followed, and has considerable practical significance in criminal prosecutions.

The natures of and rationales for the suppression doctrines addressed in previous chapters are often controversial, debatable, and even uncertain. In contrast, there is little, if any, dispute or ambiguity regarding the character of and justifications for the Sixth Amendment constraint on the prosecution's use of hearsay. The breadth of the bar is a topic of some division, but the legitimacy of and necessity for Confrontation Clause suppression are, and long have been, generally accepted by Justices and legal scholars. There is no question that the suppression dictate discussed here is an essential, inseparable part of the confrontation right and that deterrence is entirely irrelevant.

After a brief synopsis of the current understanding of Sixth Amendment regulation of hearsay evidence, an account of the lengthy history of this regulation will describe the different understandings of earlier times. A thorough discussion of the nature of and justifications for this suppression doctrine will follow. The chapter will close with a detailed examination of the doctrinal details of the Confrontation Clause bar to hearsay—both its presumptive reach and any accepted and potential limitations on its operation. Because this suppression mandate does not rest upon official misconduct, some of the issues considered in earlier chapters merit no consideration here. Other operational issues that are uniquely relevant in this context take their place. The functional details of this suppression doctrine further reflect its distinctive character.

A. A BASIC SKETCH OF THE CONFRONTATION CLAUSE BAR TO HEARSAY

The Sixth Amendment Confrontation Clause requires the suppression of a certain, limited kind of evidence. It bars "hearsay" offered by the prosecution to prove an accused's guilt. Hearsay is typically defined as an out-of-court statement that is offered to prove the truth of the matter asserted therein. The requirement that the statement be made "out-of-court" means that an assertion made from the witness stand at the current trial cannot be hearsay. A statement made at any other time, even one made in another courtroom proceeding, can qualify as

---

coerced confessions predate the 1960s, and the most noteworthy aspect of the Fourth Amendment rule—its extension to state proceedings in *Mapp v. Ohio*—was a 1961 development.

5. As will be seen in the history section, the Supreme Court first recognized a Confrontation Clause bar to hearsay evidence nearly 20 years before it discerned a constitutional bar to coerced confessions. *See infra* text accompanying notes 11–13.

hearsay because it was made "outside" the current court proceeding. Typically, a statement may be verbal or nonverbal, but the declarant (the maker of the statement) must intend to assert something—i.e., to express or communicate some belief. Thus, verbal or nonverbal conduct that is not intended to assert anything cannot constitute hearsay. Moreover, a verbal or nonverbal statement that does assert a belief is not hearsay if it is not offered at trial to prove the truth of that assertion, but instead is offered for some other relevant purpose.[6]

The Supreme Court has recognized a crucial distinction between "testimonial" and "nontestimonial" hearsay. The Sixth Amendment requires the exclusion of *only* testimonial hearsay. Nontestimonial hearsay is beyond the reach of the Confrontation Clause.[7] Moreover, only testimonial hearsay itself is excludable. No evidentiary products of testimonial hearsay are subject to suppression even if the actions of government agents produced the barred testimonial hearsay. Thus, if interrogating officers prompt testimonial assertions from a witness that lead them to discover tangible evidence—contraband, stolen goods, or incriminating clothing, for example—the Sixth Amendment may well forbid admission of the witness's assertions, but it does not prevent the introduction of the nonhearsay evidentiary fruits.

An accused is presumptively entitled to suppress any testimonial hearsay from his trial if the declarant does not testify at that trial. However, if the declarant does testify at the trial and the accused has an adequate opportunity to cross-examine her about her hearsay, the Confrontation Clause does not impede the prosecution's use of that hearsay. Moreover, there are three situations in which the Sixth Amendment exclusion doctrine does not (or may not) bar testimonial hearsay even though the declarant does not testify. First, if the declarant is unavailable to testify *and* the accused had an adequate prior opportunity to cross-examine her, the prosecution may introduce her otherwise barred testimonial hearsay. Second, if the accused has engaged in wrongful conduct that rendered the declarant unavailable to testify at trial, the "forfeiture by wrongdoing" doctrine lifts the presumptive bar to testimonial hearsay. Finally, testimonial hearsay that qualifies as a "dying declaration" may fall within a historically-rooted exception to the Sixth Amendment suppression doctrine.

Because the current approach to the Sixth Amendment-hearsay relationship is the product of a revolutionary 2004 ruling, there are a number of interesting

---

6. The object here is a simple introductory summary. The definition of hearsay is a complicated and sometimes confusing topic. The full doctrinal discussion later in this chapter contains additional details and insights into what constitutes hearsay evidence.

7. The Court has provided some insights into the meaning of this determinative distinction, but has not yet furnished a comprehensive definition of the "testimonial hearsay" category. Consequently, the boundary between the two remains somewhat unclear. A more complete discussion of the testimonial-nontestimonial dichotomy appears later in this chapter. *See infra* text accompanying notes 264–90.

and significant unresolved doctrinal issues. The pivotal role the concept of "testimonial" hearsay plays in determining the scope of suppression makes the definition of that term vital. The Court has already addressed the question on more than one occasion, but the definitional task is unfinished. Other issues include when a prior or current opportunity to cross-examine a testimonial hearsay declarant is constitutionally adequate; when a declarant is unavailable for Sixth Amendment purposes; whether the ban on testimonial hearsay is limited to criminal trials; whether there is a "dying declaration" exception, and, if so, what hearsay statements qualify; and whether testimonial hearsay may be used to impeach defense witnesses. These questions, and others, are analyzed in depth in the doctrinal section of this chapter. As in earlier chapters, I describe the historical development of and discuss the nature of and justifications for Confrontation Clause exclusion before detailing the doctrine.

B. A HISTORY OF THE CONFRONTATION CLAUSE BARRIER TO HEARSAY: THE BIRTH AND DEVELOPMENT OF SIXTH AMENDMENT EXCLUSION

As already noted, this final constitutional exclusion doctrine has the deepest roots. Only one other constitutional exclusion doctrine began in the nineteenth century—the bar to coerced confessions.[8] The Supreme Court first recognized a Confrontation Clause barrier to prosecution evidence in 1878.[9] This history begins with that seminal decision and concludes with the radical revision of Sixth Amendment exclusion more than 125 years later in two early twenty-first century rulings. The account is divided into three phases that reflect changing understandings of the relationship between the Confrontation Clause and hearsay. The first phase covers the initial century of development—from 1878 to 1980. During that period, almost all of the decisions involved prior testimony of witnesses, and the Court's opinions evinced an ad hoc approach rather than a general doctrinal scheme. The second phase begins in 1980 with a landmark ruling,[10] and ends a quarter of a century later with the demise of the approach launched by that ruling. During that relatively short period, a number of decisions refined the governing doctrine. The final phase, which began in 2004, documents only the origins of the revolutionary doctrine that controls today. Although they are part of the ongoing history of this exclusion doctrine, subsequent opinions fleshing out the new framework are addressed only in the doctrinal section.

---

8. That suppression mandate made its first appearance in *Bram v. United States*, 168 U.S. 532 (1897), shortly before the dawn of the twentieth century.

9. *See* Reynolds v. United States, 98 U.S. 145 (1878).

10. *See* Ohio v. Roberts, 448 U.S. 56 (1980).

1. From 1878–1980: The First Century of Confrontation Clause Exclusion

Reynolds v. United States[11] was the first Supreme Court opinion to consider a Confrontation Clause challenge to the admission of hearsay. The question was whether the admission of a witness's testimony given in an earlier trial for the very same offense—bigamy—violated the Sixth Amendment.[12] The Court acknowledged that the prosecution's use of this evidence did implicate "the right to a trial at which [the accused] should be confronted with the witnesses against him,"[13] but observed that a defendant "cannot complain" about the use of "competent evidence" in place of live testimony "if a witness is absent by his own wrongful procurement."[14] Because the record contained sufficient evidence that the defendant had wrongfully kept the witness away from trial, the testimony from the first trial was constitutionally admissible in the subsequent trial.[15] Despite the limited scope of the *Reynolds* opinion, the Court's recognition that the admission of testimony from an earlier trial could violate the confrontation entitlement was an important initial step.

Seventeen years passed before *Mattox v. United States*[16]—generally considered the first significant Supreme Court discussion of the relationship between the Confrontation Clause and hearsay.[17] In a third trial for first-degree murder,[18] the government had introduced a reporter's notes of the testimony of two

---

11. 98 U.S. 145 (1878).

12. *Id.* at 158.

13. *Id.*

14. *Id.* An accused who "voluntarily keeps the witnesses away . . . cannot insist on [the] privilege" of confrontation granted by the Sixth Amendment and cannot "assert that his constitutional rights have been violated" when the witness's "evidence is supplied in some lawful way." *Id.*

15. The Court also noted that "[t]he accused was present at the time the testimony was given [in the first trial], and had full opportunity of cross-examination." *Id.* at 161. However, the earlier discussion of the wrongful procurement doctrine did not indicate that a prior opportunity for cross-examination of the witness's testimony was essential to avoid a Sixth Amendment deprivation.

16. 156 U.S. 237 (1895).

17. *See* Thomas J. Reed, Crawford v. Washington *and the Irretrievable Breakdown of a Union: Separating the Confrontation Clause from the Hearsay Rule*, 56 S.C. L. Rev. 185, 192 (2004) [hereinafter Reed, *Irretrievable Breakdown*] (stating that "*Mattox* is the foundation for all modern Confrontation Clause law"). According to one author, *Mattox* marked the beginning of the Court's "'exclusionary thinking'" about the relationship between the Confrontation Clause and hearsay. John G. Douglass, *Beyond Admissibility: Real Confrontation, Virtual Cross-Examination, and the Right to Confront Hearsay*, 67 Geo. Wash. L. Rev. 191, 199 (1999) [hereinafter Douglass, *Beyond Admissibility*].

18. A conviction in the first trial was reversed, and a second trial ended with a hung jury. *Mattox*, 156 U.S. at 251 (Shiras, J., dissenting).

now-deceased witnesses who had testified in the first trial.[19] The accused challenged the admission of this hearsay evidence.

According to the Court, the "primary object" of the guarantee of confrontation "was to prevent depositions or ex parte affidavits . . . being used . . . in lieu of a personal examination and cross-examination of the witness in which the accused has an opportunity, not only of testing the recollection and sifting the conscience of the witness, but of compelling him to stand face to face with the jury in order that they may look at him, and judge by his demeanor upon the stand and the manner in which he gives his testimony whether he is worthy of belief."[20] The Court observed that Mattox had been "deprived of the advantage of th[e] personal presence of the witness before the jury" when the notes of prior testimony were read into evidence. It concluded, however, that the "valuable" benefits afforded by the "general rule[]" of confrontation "must occasionally give way to considerations of public policy and the necessities of the case."[21] The constitutional guarantee of confrontation was not absolute. In some situations, the societal interest in convicting a guilty defendant—i.e., "the rights of the public"—could outweigh the protections afforded the accused—i.e., could justify the introduction of hearsay in the absence of an opportunity to confront the witness at the trial.[22]

The Court cited an "exception" to the Sixth Amendment right that allowed "the admission of [unconfronted] dying declarations"—an exception that was based on the need "to prevent a manifest failure of justice" and the fact that the circumstances that give rise to dying declarations "remove all temptation to falsehood."[23] There was "equal if not greater reason for admitting [a dead witness's] statements . . . made under oath" in a prior trial.[24] A "criminal . . . once . . . convicted by the testimony of a . . . witness" should not escape justice "because death has closed the mouth of that witness."[25] Moreover, the introduction of the prior *testimony* preserves the "substance" of the confrontation entitlement because the defendant "once had" the opportunity to see "the witness face to face" and to "subject[] him to the ordeal of a cross-examination."[26]

19. *Id.* at 240. The majority indicated the testimony was given in "the former trial," *id.*, but the dissent specifies that it was given at "the first trial." *Id.* at 251 (Shiras, J., dissenting).

20. *Id.* at 242–43.

21. *Id.* at 243.

22. *Id.*

23. *Mattox*, 156 U.S. at 243–44.

24. *Id.* at 244.

25. *Id.* at 243.

26. *Id.* at 244. *See* Douglass, *Beyond Admissibility*, *supra* note 17, at 200 (observing that the Court "focused on . . . procedural rights" in *Mattox*, that "[t]he right of cross-examination [was] the heart of the opinion," and that the "admissibility" of hearsay "rested upon satisfaction of the basic procedural right of cross-examination").

At the turn of the century, the Court decided two cases involving the government's introduction of hearsay in violation of the Confrontation Clause—*Kirby v. United States*[27] and *Motes v. United States*.[28] In *Kirby*, at a trial for receipt of stolen property, the prosecution introduced a record of convictions of three other men to prove that the property at issue had in fact been stolen.[29] The Court concluded that the right to be confronted with witnesses, a "fundamental guarantee[] of life and liberty," barred the use of the convictions against the defendant.[30] The Sixth Amendment forbade proof of facts "against an accused . . . except by witnesses who confront him at the trial, upon whom he can look while being tried, whom he is entitled to cross-examine, and whose testimony he may impeach."[31] Because the prosecution had established a "vital fact" in *Kirby* "without . . . any proof whatever by witnesses confronting the accused," the defendant had been denied his constitutional right.[32]

In *Motes*, a conspiracy prosecution, the trial judge allowed the government to introduce a codefendant's "written statement" that had been made under oath "in a preliminary examination before [a] United States Commissioner."[33] Although the defendants in *Motes* had been represented by counsel who had the opportunity to and did cross-examine the codefendant on their behalf,[34] the admission of the written statement violated the Sixth Amendment.[35] According to the Court, there were "recognized exceptions to the general rule"[36] of confrontation at trial for sworn testimony that an accused had an opportunity to cross-examine in an earlier proceeding *if* a witness died, became insane or too ill to testify, or if the accused kept the witness away from the trial.[37] *Motes* did not come within any of these exceptions because the witness's absence was attributable "to the negligence of the prosecution."[38]

Sixty-six years passed before the next significant ruling in *Pointer v. Texas*.[39] In a state prosecution for robbery, after establishing that the alleged victim had

---

27. 174 U.S. 47 (1899).

28. 178 U.S. 458 (1900).

29. *Kirby*, 174 U.S. at 49–50, 53.

30. *Id.* at 55.

31. *Id.*

32. *Id.* at 55–56. The Court again highlighted the existence of an "exception" to the Sixth Amendment for unconfronted and unconfrontable "dying declarations." *Id.* at 61.

33. *Motes*, 178 U.S. at 467; *see also id.* at 469–70.

34. *Id.* at 468.

35. *Id.* at 471.

36. *Id.* at 474.

37. *Id.* at 472.

38. *Motes*, 178 U.S. at 474.

39. 380 U.S. 400 (1965). The only intervening opinion of any relevance is *Diaz v. United States*, 223 U.S. 442 (1912). *Diaz* involved a right of confrontation granted by "the Philippine Civil Government Act," not the Sixth Amendment confrontation entitlement.

moved to another state and did not intend to return, the government had introduced a transcript of testimony he had given at a preliminary hearing. The accused, who was not represented by counsel at the hearing, had not tried to cross-examine the victim. A critical threshold issue was whether the Sixth Amendment guarantee of confrontation was "made applicable to the States by the Fourteenth Amendment" Due Process Clause.[40] The Court observed that the right to confront adverse witnesses at trial includes an entitlement to cross-examine them, a valuable means of "exposing falsehood and bringing out the truth."[41] Its inclusion in the Sixth Amendment "reflects the belief of the Framers" that confrontation is "a fundamental right essential to a fair trial."[42] For these reasons, the Court concluded that the "right of an accused to confront . . . witnesses . . . is . . . made obligatory on the States by the Fourteenth Amendment."[43]

The second question in *Pointer* was whether the Sixth Amendment had been violated. According to the Court, "a major reason" for the confrontation right "is to give a defendant . . . an opportunity to cross-examine the witnesses against him."[44] Although there were "situations" in which hearsay could be admitted without an opportunity for confrontation and cross-examination at trial,[45] *Pointer* did not involve such a situation. The absent victim's preliminary hearing testimony might have been admissible if the defendant "had been given a complete and adequate opportunity to cross-examine" him at a "full-fledged [pretrial] hearing" where he was "represented by counsel."[46] Because he lacked counsel's assistance at the preliminary hearing, Pointer had no such opportunity, and, as a result, the "use of the transcript to convict [him] denied" his "constitutional right" of confrontation.[47]

The primary significance of the *Pointer* decision was the extension of the confrontation guarantee to state trials. Because the vast majority of criminal

---

Id. at 449. The Court held that by introducing a record of prior proceedings, the accused himself had "waived his right of confrontation as to [the] testimony" contained in that record. *Id.* at 452–53. Oddly, the Court characterized *Reynolds*—which involved forfeiture of the confrontation right—as a recognition that the Sixth Amendment right "may be waived." *Id.* at 452.

40. *Pointer*, 380 U.S. at 401. As has been noted in earlier chapters, Bill of Rights liberties do not apply directly to the states. Those provisions constrain only the federal government. The Fourteenth Amendment explicitly regulates the actions of the states.

41. *Id.* at 404.

42. *Id.* This belief was "nearly unanimous[ly]" shared by the judiciary. *Id.* at 405.

43. *Id.* at 403.

44. *Id.* at 406–07.

45. *Pointer*, 380 U.S. at 407. The Court cited "dying declarations" and "testimony of a deceased witness who . . . testified at a former trial" as examples. *Id.*

46. *Id.*

47. *Id.* at 407–08.

prosecutions are conducted by states, this ruling had enormous practical import.[48] The Court's intimation that there might be additional situations in which a witness's absence would permit the use of hearsay statements made in earlier proceedings was also momentous.[49]

On the same day, the Court also decided *Douglas v. Alabama*.[50] In a trial for assault with intent to commit murder, the prosecutor had called a codefendant (who had already been convicted of the same offense) to testify. When the codefendant asserted his Fifth Amendment privilege and refused to comply with a court order to testify, the prosecutor was allowed to cross-examine him by reading a confession that incriminated Douglas.[51] This violated the Sixth Amendment because Douglas had been unable to cross-examine the codefendant about accusations in that confession which furnished "crucial" evidence of Douglas's guilt.[52]

Douglas constituted an important recognition that hearsay statements made outside judicial proceedings could be barred by the Confrontation Clause. In prior cases, the prosecution had introduced hearsay statements made under oath in formal judicial proceedings of some sort. In *Douglas*, the reading of the codefendant's signed confession made him a witness against the accused and triggered constitutional protection.

Barber v. Page[53] marked the third state case and the fifth opinion in a row in which the Court found that the government's use of hearsay clashed with the Confrontation Clause. In an armed robbery prosecution, the prosecutor read a transcript of preliminary hearing testimony by a codefendant who was now in a federal prison in another state. The defendant's counsel had not cross-examined the codefendant at the hearing.[54] After recounting the historical purposes of the Confrontation Clause described over 70 years earlier in *Mattox*,

---

48. *See* Douglass, *Beyond Admissibility*, *supra* note 17, at 202 (noting that the Court had "few opportunities to consider hearsay under the Confrontation Clause" in the 70 years after *Mattox*, but that "[t]he pace quickened after *Pointer*" extended the guarantee to state prosecutions); Reed, *Irretrievable Breakdown*, *supra* note 17, at 193 (asserting that "[f]or more than sixty years after *Mattox*, criminal defendants were . . . convicted using unsworn hearsay statements by absent witnesses" and that in "federal practice, the exclusionary rule following from the Confrontation Clause lay virtually dormant until the 1960s").

49. The specific suggestion was that testimony at a *preliminary hearing* given by a witness who had *left the jurisdiction* might be "analogous" to testimony at a former *trial* given by a *dead* witness. *See Pointer*, 380 U.S. at 407.

50. 380 U.S. 415 (1965).

51. *Id.* at 416–17.

52. *Id.* at 419. Although the reading of the codefendant's statement was "not technically testimony," to the jurors it "may well have been the equivalent" and they "might [have] improperly infer[red] that the statement had been made and that it was true." *Id.* In addition, there was "no suggestion" that the codefendant's "refusal to answer was procured" by Douglas. *Id.* at 420.

53. 390 U.S. 719 (1968).

54. *Id.* at 720.

the Court acknowledged "an exception to the confrontation requirement where a witness is unavailable and has given testimony at previous judicial proceedings against the same defendant which was subject to cross-examination by that defendant."[55] This general exception, rooted in "necessity," was "justified" because the "right of cross-examination initially afforded provides *substantial compliance* with the purposes" of confrontation.[56] The Court cautioned that the confrontation guarantee "may not be dispensed with . . . lightly."[57] Consequently, "a witness is not 'unavailable' for purposes of the . . . exception . . . unless the prosecutorial authorities have made a good-faith effort to obtain his presence at trial."[58] In *Barber*, the state did not meet that requirement because it had merely ascertained that the witness was in prison and had done nothing to bring him to the trial.

According to the Court, the "right to confrontation is basically *a trial right*."[59] It affords accused individuals the chance to cross-examine witnesses *at trial* and to have the jury observe their "demeanor" *at that time*.[60] An earlier opportunity to cross-examine a witness at a preliminary hearing may "satisf[y]" the constitutional guarantee when a witness is "actually unavailable," but because the witness was not shown to be unavailable here, there was no basis for dispensing with the right to confront him at trial.[61]

Barber seems significant in two respects. It explored the meaning of and highlighted the demanding nature of the "unavailability" criterion. Perhaps more important, it confirmed the existence of a *general* exception to the guarantee of confrontation at trial for prior testimony of an unavailable witness that the accused had an adequate opportunity to cross-examine. The exception described was not limited to *dead* witnesses and testimony from earlier *trials*.

Two years later, *California v. Green*[62] broke the string of rulings finding denials of the confrontation entitlement. The opinion would prove to be the first in a series of three early 1970s decisions that laid the foundation for development of a general doctrinal framework. In *Green*, the trial judge permitted a prosecutor to read the preliminary hearing testimony of a minor who also testified at the defendant's trial for selling marijuana.[63] The minor admitted giving the contested testimony at the preliminary hearing, but proved uncooperative on the witness

---

55. *Id.* at 722.
56. *Id.* (emphasis added).
57. *Id.* at 725.
58. *Barber*, 390 U.S. at 724–25.
59. *Id.* at 725 (emphasis added).
60. *Id.*
61. *Id.* at 725–26.
62. 399 U.S. 149 (1970).
63. *Id.* at 152.

stand, claiming that he could not remember the events he had previously recounted.[64]

The Court found two distinct bases for rejecting the defendant's Sixth Amendment claim. It recognized explicitly that the issue was the relationship between "hearsay" and the Confrontation Clause.[65] The Justices acknowledged that the rule of evidence barring hearsay and the Sixth Amendment "protect similar values," but denied that the "Confrontation Clause" overlapped completely with or was a mere codification of the hearsay rule and its exceptions.[66] Prior decisions proved that the Constitution could be violated even though the rules of evidence were not and that the guarantee of confrontation might not be offended by evidence that did violate the hearsay rule.[67] The Confrontation Clause had grown out of a practice of using "ex parte affidavits or depositions" to convict, as a means of "denying . . . the opportunity to challenge [an] accuser in a face-to-face encounter in front of the trier of fact."[68] Because the Sixth Amendment was "primarily . . . aimed at the failure to call the witness to confront personally the defendant at his trial," the "literal right to 'confront' the witness *at the time of trial* . . . forms the core of the values" underlying the right.[69]

For these reasons, "the Confrontation Clause is not violated by admitting a declarant's out-of-court statements" when he testifies at the trial and is "subject to full and effective cross-examination" at that time.[70] When a declarant testifies at the trial, the protections that were lost at the time he made his statement are "regain[ed]."[71] He "must now affirm, deny, or qualify the truth of the prior statement" under oath; he is presently subject to "full and effective cross-examination;"[72] and, even though "some demeanor evidence . . . is forever lost" because the jurors could not observe the witness at the time he made the

64. *Id.*

65. The previous decisions did deal with hearsay evidence—assertions by individuals that had been made outside the current trial and had been admitted for their truth. However, previously the Court had not expressly acknowledged that the general issue involved was the relationship between "hearsay" and the Sixth Amendment guarantee—that is, whether and when hearsay evidence is barred by that provision.

66. *Id.* at 155.

67. *Id.* at 155–56.

68. *Green*, 399 U.S. at 156.

69. *Id.* at 157 (emphasis added).

70. *Id.* at 158. According to the Court, a comparison of "the purposes of confrontation with the . . . dangers in admitting an out-of-court statement" supported that conclusion. *Id.*

71. *Id.*

72. *Id.* at 159. The Court denied "that belated cross examination can never serve as a constitutionally adequate substitute for [contemporaneous] cross-examination." *Id.* Where a witness testifies in a manner inconsistent with his prior statement, as in *Green*, there is no danger that falsehood has hardened and become resistant to attack, and the inconsistency itself may even enhance the efficacy of the defendant's attack. *Id.* The Court was not

statement, the jury can "observe and evaluate his demeanor" when he now responds to inquiries about his prior statement.[73] In sum, "where the [hearsay] declarant is . . . present to testify and to submit to cross-examination . . . the admission of his out-of-court statements *does not create a confrontation problem.*"[74]

As mentioned, the *Green* Court found a second, independent basis for concluding that the Sixth Amendment had not been violated. The minor had testified at the preliminary hearing under oath and subject to cross-examination. His testimony would have been admissible if he had died or was otherwise unavailable because there would have been "substantial compliance with the purposes behind the confrontation requirement."[75] It was "untenable" to find that the Constitution allows use of earlier testimony when the declarant does not appear, but bars it when the declarant is present and subject to cross-examination.[76] The state had "made every effort to [secure] live testimony," and whether the witness testified consistently or inconsistently, claimed memory loss or his Fifth Amendment privilege, or "simply refused to answer" questions, the Confrontation Clause did not prevent the prosecution's reliance "on his prior testimony to prove its case."[77]

"convince[d] . . . that contemporaneous cross-examination before the ultimate trier of fact is [significantly] more effective than subsequent examination." *Id.* at 161.

73. *Green*, 399 U.S. at 160.

74. *Id.* at 162 (emphasis added). The Court noted that no prior decision required a bar to hearsay statements of a testifying witness. To the contrary, the precedents supported admission in that situation. *Id.* at 161. The Court did qualify its initial holding in *Green* a bit. It ruled that an adequate opportunity for "full cross-examination at trial" would prevent the exclusion of prior testimony, at least when a declarant who has given inconsistent testimony concedes making the earlier statements. *Id.* at 164. The Court also raised doubts about the conclusion that the accused had an adequate opportunity to cross-examine the minor at the trial. In considering other hearsay statements made by the minor, the Court indicated that his "apparent lapse of memory" might have deprived the accused of a constitutionally adequate opportunity to confront him at trial. *Id.* at 168–69, 169 n.18.

75. *Id.* at 166. This was the case as long as the witness's unavailability was not the state's fault. *Id.*

76. *Id.* at 166–67.

77. *Id.* at 167–68. The discussion of this second basis for finding no unconstitutionality is a bit confusing. Some of the reasoning suggests that the prior opportunity for cross-examination is a justification for permitting the use of the earlier statements when a witness is unavailable *or* when a witness testifies at the trial and is subject to cross-examination. The better view, which also finds support in the Court's reasoning, is that the testimony is admissible if the witness *does testify* because the present opportunity to cross-examine him satisfies the confrontation guarantee. On the other hand, the testimony is admissible if the witness *is unavailable to testify* because there is a need to admit it and the prior opportunity affords "substantial compliance" with the Sixth Amendment's goals. In *Green*, either the witness's memory lapse did not thwart the opportunity for adequate

Green's recognition that an adequate opportunity to cross-examine a declarant at trial can eliminate any Confrontation Clause bar to hearsay that would otherwise exist was an important development in Sixth Amendment exclusion.[78] Moreover, the second ground for the Court's decision confirmed the validity of a *general* exception for unavailable witnesses' prior testimony that the accused had an earlier opportunity to cross-examine.

The same year, the Court decided *Dutton v. Evans*,[79] the second Confrontation Clause decision in which the hearsay at issue did not originate in a formal testimonial setting. At a trial for the murder of three police officers, the government called an inmate to testify that a codefendant had made a remark implicating Evans. The Court held that the Sixth Amendment did not bar introduction of the codefendant's remark.

A plurality of four Justices observed that the confrontation issue arose because the codefendant's hearsay was a basis for the jury "to infer" that he "had implicitly identified Evans as the perpetrator of the murder."[80] In their view, "there was no denial of the right of confrontation as to [the] question of identity" because the statement was not an "express assertion about past fact;" the codefendant's "personal knowledge" of the murders was "abundantly established" and "cross-examination" could not have shown otherwise; and "the possibility" of "faulty recollection [was] remote in the extreme."[81] Moreover, "the circumstances" surrounding the remark provided "reason to suppose that [he] did not misrepresent Evans'[s] involvement."[82] He "had no apparent reason to lie," made the statement spontaneously, and "it was against his penal interest"—three "indicia of reliability . . . widely viewed as determinative" of whether juries can receive hearsay without "confrontation of the declarant."[83]

---

cross-examination at the trial or it did prevent effective cross-examination. In the latter case, he was unavailable to testify and there was a need to use the earlier testimony which the defendant had an opportunity to cross-examine. *See id.* at 168 n.17 (noting that memory lapse is a basis for unavailability under the hearsay rules).

78. This is one respect in which the Constitution and evidence law are not congruent. In general, evidence law does *not* suspend the hearsay ban merely because a declarant testifies and can now be cross-examined. The absence of oath, contemporaneous cross-examination, and an opportunity to see demeanor at the time the statement was made justify a general bar to out-of-court statements even when the source of those statements testifies at trial. For a discussion of the evidence rule that bars statements by a testifying witness and its justifications, see GRAHAM C. LILLY, AN INTRODUCTION TO THE LAW OF EVIDENCE § 6.4 (3d ed. 1996).

79. 400 U.S. 74 (1970).

80. *Id.* at 88.

81. *Id.* at 88–89.

82. *Id.* at 89.

83. *Id.*

The plurality described "the mission of the Confrontation Clause" as ensuring "the accuracy of the truth-determining process in criminal trials by assuring that 'the trier of fact [has] a satisfactory basis for evaluating the truth of [a hearsay] statement.'"[84] Evans was able to confront the inmate who related the codefendant's remark, and "the possibility that cross-examination" of the codefendant could have shown that his remark was "unreliable was wholly unreal."[85]

The reasoning of the *Dutton* plurality provided a foundation for the majority decision in the next case, *Mancusi v. Stubbs.*[86] *Mancusi*, the third consecutive case in which the Court rejected a Sixth Amendment challenge to hearsay and the final decision of the pre-*Roberts* era, involved a prosecution for first-degree murder, assault with intent to murder, and kidnapping. Convictions obtained at a first trial were reversed on appeal, and, at a retrial, the judge permitted the government to read the first trial testimony of a victim who had moved to a foreign country. Because there was support for the finding that the witness was unavailable to testify at trial,[87] the constitutionality of the admission of the testimony turned on the "adequacy of [the witness's] examination at the first trial."[88]

Relying on *Dutton* and *Green*, the Court asserted that its "concern ha[d] been to insure . . . 'indicia of reliability' . . . and to 'afford the trier of fact a satisfactory basis for evaluating the truth of the prior statement.'"[89] When a witness is unavailable to testify, "his prior testimony must bear . . . 'indicia of reliability'" of the sort cited in *Dutton*.[90] In this case, because the defendant had "an adequate opportunity to cross-examine [the witness] at the first trial, and counsel" took advantage of the opportunity, there were "sufficient 'indicia of reliability'" and the trier had a "'satisfactory basis for evaluating the [hearsay's] truth.'"[91]

Mancusi endorsed the notions that the Confrontation Clause was primarily concerned with ensuring reliability and that a judicial determination that hearsay statements had sufficient "indicia of reliability" could justify the admission of the statements even though the defendant had no opportunity to confront

---

84. *Evans*, 400 U.S. at 89 (quoting California v. Green, 399 U.S. 149, 161 (1970)).

85. *Id.* As noted, this reasoning was endorsed by only four Justices. Justice Harlan concurred in the result based on an entirely different understanding of the role of the Confrontation Clause in the regulation of hearsay evidence. *See id.* at 93–100 (Harlan, J., concurring in the result). Four dissenters did not agree with the plurality's reasoning, asserting that the result reached by the majority was "completely inconsistent with recent opinions of [the] Court" regarding the protection afforded by the Confrontation Clause. *Id.* at 100 (Marshall, J., dissenting).

86. 408 U.S. 204 (1972).

87. *Id.* at 212–13.

88. *Id.* at 213.

89. *Id.* (quoting Dutton v. Evans, 400 U.S. 74, 89 (1970) and California v. Green, 399 U.S. 149, 161 (1970)).

90. *Id.*

91. *Mancusi*, 408 U.S. at 216 (quoting Dutton v. Evans, 400 U.S. 74, 89 (1970)).

the declarant at *any* time. Significantly, the Court characterized prior cross-examination as *one means* of demonstrating reliability and providing the trier with a basis for judging truthfulness, not as a *necessary* foundation for admitting hearsay. This dramatically expanded the exception to confrontation at trial for prior statements by unavailable witnesses.[92] Apparently, hearsay was not to be excluded if a declarant was unavailable and if there were sufficient indications that her hearsay was "reliable."

2. From 1980–2004: The Rise and Fall of the *Roberts* Framework

Dutton and *Mancusi* set the stage for *Ohio v. Roberts*[93]—one of the most significant decisions in the history of Confrontation Clause regulation of hearsay. *Roberts* involved a prosecution for forgery and possession of stolen credit cards. The victim's daughter, who had been involved in a relationship with the accused, testified at a preliminary hearing and was questioned by defense counsel, but did not appear for trial. The trial court permitted the state to introduce a transcript of her preliminary hearing testimony. The Supreme Court could have ruled narrowly, upholding the admission of the testimony because the declarant was unavailable and the accused had an adequate opportunity to cross-examine her at the preliminary hearing. Instead, the Court undertook an exploration of the relationship between the Sixth Amendment and hearsay and announced a general doctrinal approach to govern future determinations.

Justice Blackmun began the majority opinion by observing that both the history of and the policies underlying the Sixth Amendment—in particular its "preference for face-to-face confrontation at trial"—made clear that it "was intended to exclude some hearsay."[94] The Confrontation Clause grants the accused an opportunity to cross-examine a witness in front of the jury, affording a vitally important "means of testing [the] accuracy" of a witness's testimony.[95] An "absence of proper confrontation at trial 'calls into question the ultimate "integrity of the fact-finding process."'"[96] Past decisions recognized that "competing interests"—interests in effective law enforcement and in appropriate rules of evidence—could justify "dispensing with confrontation at trial," but the Court had not sought to "'map out a theory . . . that would determine the validity

92. As described in precedent, the exception required a prior opportunity to cross-examine the hearsay declarant.

93. 448 U.S. 56 (1980).

94. *Id.* at 63.

95. *Id.* at 63–64.

96. *Id.* at 64 (quoting Chambers v. Mississippi, 410 U.S. 284, 295 (1973) (quoting Berger v. California, 393 U.S. 314, 315 (1969))).

of all'" exceptions to the hearsay rules.[97] Nonetheless, the precedents did reflect "a general approach to the problem."[98]

Because "face-to-face accusation" is preferred, the "Sixth Amendment establishe[d] a rule of necessity."[99] Usually, "the prosecution must either produce, or demonstrate the unavailability of, the declarant" in order to introduce her hearsay.[100] Put otherwise, ordinarily trial confrontation can be denied *only* if an inability to produce the declarant at trial makes such denial necessary.

Moreover, even when unavailability is shown, there is a second critical consideration. Because the Sixth Amendment's "underlying purpose [is] to augment accuracy in the factfinding process by ensuring . . . an effective means to test adverse evidence," hearsay evidence can be introduced "only" when it is "marked with [sufficient] trustworthiness."[101] If hearsay is trustworthy, then, despite a lack of confrontation, "'there is no material departure from the reason of the general rule.'"[102] In other words, trustworthy hearsay is constitutionally admissible because it does not threaten the objective of the Sixth Amendment—accurate fact finding.[103]

In sum, *Roberts* decided that if a declarant cannot be cross-examined at trial, "the Confrontation Clause normally requires a showing that he is unavailable" and then allows admission of his hearsay "only if it bears adequate 'indicia of reliability.'"[104] The Court prescribed two ways of demonstrating the requisite indicia of reliability. The government could establish either that "the evidence falls within a firmly rooted hearsay exception" or that the hearsay has its own "particularized guarantees of trustworthiness."[105] Without one of these showings, hearsay "evidence [had to] be excluded."[106]

---

97. *Id.* at 64–65 (quoting California v. Green, 399 U.S. 149, 162 (1970)).

98. *Roberts*, 448 U.S. at 65.

99. *Id.*

100. *Id.* The Court cited *Dutton* for the proposition that a showing "of unavailability . . . is not always required." *Id.* at 65 n.7. According to Justice Blackmun, *Dutton* had decided that an available witness did not have to be produced because "the utility of trial confrontation [was] remote." *Id.*

101. *Id.* at 65.

102. *Id.* (quoting Snyder v. Massachusetts, 291 U.S. 97, 107 (1934)).

103. The Court relied on *Dutton*, *Mancusi*, and *Green* to support the conclusions that "'indicia of reliability'" are required *and* that they can substitute for actual confrontation because the purposes of the Sixth Amendment are adequately protected. *See Roberts*, 448 U.S. at 65–66.

104. *Id.* at 66.

105. *Id.*

106. *Id.*

In *Roberts*, the government had demonstrated the declarant's unavailability.[107] Moreover, it was not necessary to "undertake a particularized search for 'indicia of reliability'" because the declarant's preliminary hearing testimony fell within the firmly rooted "prior-testimony exception" to the hearsay rule.[108] Because both doctrinal demands were satisfied, the Confrontation Clause did not require exclusion.

There is no understating the significance of *Roberts*. Although the Court purported to merely discern and explain a general approach developed in earlier decisions,[109] in fact it took a major step forward in defining the scope of the Confrontation Clause bar to hearsay evidence. *Roberts* rested on the premise that all hearsay was subject to Sixth Amendment scrutiny—that the declarants of all out-of-court assertions could qualify as "witnesses against" the accused. Even though the Sixth Amendment accords the accused an unqualified entitlement "to be confronted with" such witnesses, the Court found no absolute ban on unconfronted hearsay. When the inability to produce a declarant at trial generates a need to dispense with confrontation, trustworthy hearsay could be admitted because it posed little threat to the ultimate goal of the confrontation guarantee—accurate verdicts based on reliable evidence.

On this analytical foundation, the Court erected a two-pronged doctrinal test, normally demanding unavailability—to establish need—and always requiring reliability—to ensure accuracy. The Court's thorough explanation of the interplay between the Confrontation Clause and hearsay, and its effort to prescribe a comprehensive doctrinal framework for assessing the constitutional admissibility of hearsay evidence, were major accomplishments. *Roberts* was an undeniable landmark, a turning point in the history of Confrontation Clause exclusion.

---

107. *Id.* at 75–76. The Court reaffirmed that the government must make a "good-faith effort" to secure a declarant's presence, but added that "futile act[s]" are not necessary. *Id.* at 74.

108. *Roberts*, 448 U.S. at 72, 73 n.12. The Court did not have to decide whether "the mere opportunity" for prior cross-examination was sufficient because there had been "significant cross-examination" of the witness at the preliminary hearing. *Id.* at 70. It refused to treat cross-examined testimony at a preliminary hearing differently from cross-examined testimony at an earlier trial of the same case because both had "guarantees of trustworthiness." *Id.* at 72–73. According to the Court, "no inquiry into [the] 'effectiveness'" of earlier cross-examination was necessary except in "extraordinary cases." *Id.* at 73 n.12. If an inquiry into efficacy was generally required, "the principal objective of generally validating the prior-testimony exception" would be frustrated. *Id.*

109. Initially, the Court asserted that "a general approach to the problem [was] discernible" in its precedents. *Id.* at 65. Later, the Court reviewed a number of competing approaches to the relationship between hearsay and confrontation and "reject[ed] the invitation to overrule a near-century of jurisprudence." *Id.* at 68 n.9. According to Justice Blackmun, one reason for rejecting alternatives was "the Court's demonstrated success in steering a middle course." *Id.* For some reason, the Court seemed determined to downplay the historic nature of the *Roberts* decision.

Moreover, there was unanimity. All nine Justices endorsed the *Roberts* framework and the conception of the Sixth Amendment on which it rested.[110] For the next quarter of a century, the Court would devote its efforts to addressing issues raised by and refining the details of the *Roberts* doctrine.[111]

The first occasion to address a significant issue raised by *Roberts* arrived six years later, in *United States v. Inadi*.[112] In a trial for narcotics offenses, the government introduced hearsay statements of the defendant's co-conspirator without demonstrating that he could not testify. The sole "question [was] whether the Confrontation Clause require[d]" a showing that "a nontestifying co-conspirator is unavailable to testify, as a condition for admission of [his] out-of-court statements."[113] In a decision with far-reaching implications for the unavailability criterion, the Court concluded that no such showing was necessary.

According to the *Inadi* majority, *Roberts* had not announced a generally applicable unavailability requirement.[114] Instead, the *Roberts* Court had narrowly ruled that unavailability must be shown when the government seeks to introduce "testimony from a prior judicial proceeding."[115] There were "good reasons" not to demand unavailability as a condition for admitting co-conspirator hearsay statements.[116] Unlike prior testimony, co-conspirator hearsay has evidentiary

---

110. The three dissenters' only disagreement with the majority opinion was with the conclusion that the government had met its burden of demonstrating the declarant's unavailability. *Id.* at 77–82 (Brennan, J., dissenting).

111. For critiques of the *Roberts* doctrine, see Akhil Reed Amar, *Sixth Amendment First Principles*, 84 Geo. L.J. 641, 647, 690–92 (1996) [hereinafter Amar, *First Principles*]; Douglass, *Beyond Admissibility*, *supra* note 17, at 193–97, 204–11; Richard D. Friedman, *Confrontation: The Search for Basic Principles*, 86 Geo. L.J. 1011, 1013–31 (1998) [hereinafter Friedman, *Confrontation*]; Jerome C. Latimer, *Confrontation After* Crawford*: The Decision's Impact on How Hearsay Is Analyzed Under the Confrontation Clause*, 36 Seton Hall L. Rev. 327, 335–37, 419 (2006) [hereinafter Latimer, *Confrontation After* Crawford]; Reed, *Irretrievable Breakdown*, *supra* note 17, at 201–02.

112. 475 U.S. 387 (1986). One year earlier, in *Tennessee v. Street*, 471 U.S. 409 (1985), the Court decided that the use of a codefendant's confession for a nonhearsay purpose "raise[d] no Confrontation Clause concerns." *Id.* at 414. In essence, because the confession was not used to prove the truth of the codefendant's assertions, he was not a "witness" for Sixth Amendment purposes. *Id.* The sole witness at trial was the sheriff who testified to the content of the confession and was subject to cross-examination. *Id.* at 411–12, 414. The Court was satisfied that the trial judge's limiting instructions adequately countered any Sixth Amendment threat from the risk that jurors might misuse the confession for hearsay purposes. *Id.* at 414–15.

113. *Inadi*, 475 U.S. at 388.

114. *See id.* at 392.

115. *Id.* at 393. Whether this was a faithful reading of *Roberts* is debatable. There were some signs in *Roberts* that unavailability was a general norm and other indications that it might not be.

116. *Id.* at 394.

value "that cannot be replicated" by live testimony, and "it is extremely unlikely that [a co-conspirator's] in-court testimony will recapture the evidentiary significance of statements made when the conspiracy was operating."[117] Moreover, because an unavailability requirement would yield "little, if any, benefit"[118] while imposing a "significant" and "substantial burden on the entire criminal justice system,"[119] the balance of interests weighed against it. Consequently, *Inadi* held that "the Confrontation Clause does not embody" an unavailability requirement for co-conspirator hearsay.[120]

Inadi's interpretation of the unavailability criterion was important. By reading *Roberts* narrowly and independently assessing the merits of an unavailability requirement for co-conspirator hearsay, the Court endorsed a case-by-case approach. Perhaps more important, the analysis and conclusion in *Inadi* suggested that a failure to demonstrate the unavailability of a hearsay declarant would rarely require the exclusion of hearsay. If *Inadi* meant what it seemed to mean—a greatly diminished role for the unavailability criterion—then the presumptive entitlement to confront hearsay declarants at trial could be suspended more often, even in situations where it was entirely possible for the government to honor that entitlement.

The Court's next two interpretations of the *Roberts* doctrine addressed the reliability demand. In *Lee v. Illinois*,[121] a bare majority of five Justices found a Confrontation Clause violation in a trial judge's reliance on portions of a codefendant's confession as substantive evidence against the accused in a double

117. *Id.* at 395.

118. *Inadi*, 475 U.S. at 396. The Court reasoned that if a co-conspirator is either unavailable or available and at trial, his hearsay statements could be "introduced anyway"—thus, nothing would be excluded unless the government did not produce an available witness. *Id.* In addition, it seemed unlikely that a requirement of unavailability would "produce much testimony" furthering the "'truth-determining process'" because some available declarants would be subpoenaed by one of the parties even if unavailability was not a constitutional prerequisite. *Id.* at 396–97 (quoting Dutton v. Evans, 400 U.S. 74, 89 (1970)).

119. *Id.* at 398–99. According to the majority, an unavailability demand would "add[] another avenue of appellate review" and would require prosecutors to identify, locate, and ensure the continuing availability of all co-conspirator declarants "even if neither" party "wished to examine [them] at trial." *Id.*

120. *Id.* at 399–400. Two dissenters, Justice Marshall and Justice Brennan, disagreed with the majority's interpretation of *Roberts*, opining that it had adopted a general unavailability requirement that was supported by sound constitutional reasoning. *Id.* at 402–03 (Marshall, J., dissenting). In their view, application of that demand to co-conspirator hearsay statements would further Sixth Amendment objectives by subjecting unreliable co-conspirator statements to confrontation and cross-examination at trial. *Id.* at 404–11 (Marshall, J., dissenting).

121. 476 U.S. 530 (1986).

murder trial.[122] The Court observed that the guarantees of confrontation and cross-examination "promote . . . society's interest . . . in an open and even contest," ensuring "the perception as well as the reality of fairness" and serving "symbolic goals."[123] However, these guarantees are "primarily . . . functional," designed to "promote[] reliability" and "advance the pursuit of truth in criminal trials" by requiring witnesses to testify under oath, in the presence of jurors who can observe their demeanor, and subject to cross-examination by the accused.[124]

Lee illustrated the "danger" the Confrontation Clause guards against because the defendant's conviction was "based, at least in part, on presumptively unreliable evidence"—the accusatory "arrest statements of a codefendant."[125] Moreover, the facts surrounding the confession did not rebut the ordinary presumption that such hearsay is unreliable.[126] The Court rejected the suggestion that the confession fell within a firmly rooted hearsay exception—the exception for declarations against penal interest—because "[t]hat concept defines too large a class for meaningful Confrontation Clause analysis."[127] By characterizing the hearsay in *Lee* as "a confession by an accomplice which incriminates a criminal defendant,"[128] *Lee* evinced a hesitant, somewhat cautious, approach to the "firmly rooted" mode of establishing reliability and avoiding Sixth Amendment exclusion.[129]

The opinion in *Bourjaily v. United States*,[130] however, indicated that *Lee*'s conservative approach to the "firmly rooted hearsay exception" criterion might not be destined to prevail. *Bourjaily* involved the use of hearsay statements made by a co-conspirator who did not testify at the defendant's narcotics conspiracy trial.[131] The question was whether the *Roberts* reliability requirement had

---

122. *Id.* at 539.

123. *Id.* at 540.

124. *Id.*

125. *Id.* at 541, 543.

126. *Lee*, 476 U.S. at 543–45.

127. *Id.* at 544 n.5.

128. *Id.*

129. *See* Friedman, *Confrontation*, *supra* note 111, at 1019 (maintaining that *Lee* "reflect[ed] unwillingness . . . to accept the full implications" of *Roberts*'s firmly rooted hearsay exception doctrine and a recognition that hearsay within a firmly rooted exception might still violate the Confrontation Clause). Four dissenting Justices believed that the confession had "adequate 'indicia of reliability'" to satisfy the Sixth Amendment. *Id.* at 551 (Blackmun, J., dissenting). They asserted that the "hearsay exception for declarations against interest is firmly established," and that there were additional circumstances in *Lee* that made the codefendant's confession sufficiently reliable. *Id.* at 551, 552–57 (Blackmun, J., dissenting).

130. 483 U.S. 171 (1987).

131. *Id.* at 174, 182.

been satisfied. A majority concluded that the unconfrontable statements were admissible.[132]

Chief Justice Rehnquist explained that the *Roberts* doctrine, which "as a general matter . . . required . . . both . . . unavailability . . . and . . . 'indicia of reliability,'" was a means of "accommodat[ing] . . . competing interests"—the Confrontation Clause "goal" of limiting the kind of evidence that could be used to convict a defendant and society's "interest in accurate factfinding."[133] The co-conspirator exception to the hearsay rule was more than "a century and a half" old and had been "repeatedly reaffirmed."[134] Because it was "steeped in [the Court's] jurisprudence," it was "firmly enough rooted" to satisfy the *Roberts* standard.[135] Consequently, any statement that fell within the evidence rules exception for co-conspirator hearsay could be admitted without offending the Confrontation Clause.[136] There was no need to demonstrate that such a statement had "independent indicia of reliability."[137]

Bourjaily evinced an expansive attitude toward the "firmly rooted hearsay exception" method of demonstrating the reliability required to dispense with confrontation at trial—an attitude that contrasted sharply with the careful approach evident in *Lee*.[138] There was an unmistakable suggestion that any evidence law exception with a lengthy pedigree and consistent adherence by the judiciary would qualify as "firmly rooted" and would lower the Confrontation Clause barrier to hearsay. The Court's analysis indicated that there was no need to examine whether an exception is grounded in the premise that qualifying hearsay is reliable or trustworthy.[139]

---

132. *Id.* at 181–82.

133. *Id.* at 182. After the reasoning and ruling in *Inadi*, it was somewhat strange for the Court to describe unavailability as a "general" requirement of the Sixth Amendment.

134. *Id.* at 183.

135. *Bourjaily*, 483 U.S. at 183.

136. *Id.* at 183–84. While the decision was restricted to hearsay within the exception for co-conspirator statements incorporated in the Federal Rules of Evidence, *Bourjaily* undoubtedly meant that comparable state law exceptions for co-conspirator statements would also qualify as firmly rooted.

137. *Id.* at 182.

138. *Lee* had tersely dismissed the notion that a presumptively unreliable variety of hearsay could escape the Confrontation Clause bar because it fell within a firmly rooted hearsay exception. *See* Lee v. Illinois, 476 U.S. 530, 544 n.5 (1986). Because the *Bourjaily* opinion explored the meaning of the "firmly rooted" criterion in more depth, there was reason to believe that it might more accurately reflect the breadth of that branch of the *Roberts* doctrine.

139. While the vast majority of hearsay exceptions do rest on that premise, the coconspirator exception does not. The primary bases for the co-conspirator hearsay exception are a questionable "agency" rationale—i.e., a notion that each conspirator is responsible for what his fellow agents do and say—and a "need" rationale—i.e., a belief that coconspirator statements are often essential proof for the prosecution. *See Bourjaily*, 483

In *United States v. Owens*,[140] the Court returned to a critically important question discussed at length in *California v. Green*—whether and when the hearsay statements of *testifying* declarants are subject to exclusion. *Owens* involved a prosecution for assault with intent to commit murder. While in the hospital, the victim had identified the defendant as his attacker. At trial, he "testified that he clearly remembered" identifying the accused "as his assailant," but he did not identify the accused from the witness stand because "he could not remember seeing his assailant."[141] The trial judge ruled that the hospital room identification was admissible to prove the accused's guilt, and the Supreme Court concluded that the Confrontation Clause did not require exclusion.

The majority declared that the Sixth Amendment furnished only an *opportunity* for the accused to cross-examine adverse witnesses effectively. It did not assure that he would be able to *use* this opportunity effectively—that is, to undermine these witnesses in whatever ways he wished.[142] Put otherwise, the Sixth Amendment does not guarantee "successful cross-examination."[143] According to the Court, there is no denial of the requisite opportunity when the government introduces a statement reflecting a witness's "past belief . . . and he is unable to recollect the reason for that past belief" because, even though "the foundation for the belief . . . cannot effectively be elicited," there are "other means of impugning" it.[144]

The pretrial statement identifying the accused was clearly hearsay because it was introduced to prove what it asserted—that the accused was the assailant.[145] That hearsay was admissible, whether or not it satisfied the *Roberts* reliability requirement, because a showing of reliability is necessary *only* when an accused

U.S. at 188–90 (Blackmun, J., dissenting); *see also* Ben Trachtenberg, *Coconspirators, "Coventurers," and the Exception Swallowing the Hearsay Rule*, 61 HASTINGS L.J. 581, 583–85 (2010). The *Bourjaily* dissenters asserted that the coconspirator hearsay exception should not qualify as firmly rooted because the "exemption has never been justified primarily upon reliability or trustworthiness grounds and its reliability safeguards are not extensive." *Bourjaily*, 483 U.S. at 200–01 (Blackmun, J., dissenting). In their view, such hearsay should escape the Confrontation Clause ban only if the government shows "'particularized guarantees of trustworthiness'" for the statements at issue. *Id.* at 201–02 (Blackmun J., dissenting) (quoting Ohio v. Roberts, 448 U.S. 56, 66 (1980)).

140. 484 U.S. 554 (1988).

141. *Id.* at 556.

142. *Id.* at 559.

143. *Id.* at 560.

144. *Id.* at 559.

145. *See Owens*, 484 U.S. at 560. Although the Federal Rules of Evidence classified the statement as nonhearsay, *id.* at 561, the identification in *Owens* satisfied the traditional definition of hearsay. *Id.* at 562. *Owens* indicates that whether a statement is hearsay—and, therefore, subject to Sixth Amendment exclusion—depends on the traditional definition of that term, not on a jurisdiction's classification of the statement. The question is whether the statement is an assertion that is offered to prove the truth of what it asserts.

does not have an opportunity for cross-examination of the declarant *at trial.* No reliability assessment is necessary "when a hearsay declarant is present . . . and subject to unrestricted cross-examination" at the trial.[146] As the Court had "recognized in [*California v.*] *Green,* the traditional protections of the oath, cross-examination, and opportunity for the jury to observe the witness'[s] demeanor satisfy the constitutional requirements" in cases when hearsay declarants appear and testify at trial.[147]

The *Owens* Court's reaffirmation of the principle that there is no constitutional bar to hearsay when a declarant testifies at trial and an accused has an adequate opportunity for cross-examination was noteworthy. Both the declaration that the Sixth Amendment ensures only an *opportunity* for effective cross-examination, and the conclusion that a loss of memory regarding the subject matter of hearsay does not preclude such an opportunity, were significant insights.

In *Idaho v. Wright,*[148] an accused was prosecuted for sexually abusing his young daughter. For the second time since *Roberts,* the Court found a constitutional deprivation because a trial court refused to exclude hearsay that lacked sufficient indicia of reliability. After the trial judge determined that the child was incapable of testifying,[149] he relied on the state's "residual hearsay exception" to admit hearsay statements the child had made to a doctor.[150] A five-Justice majority found that the Sixth Amendment barred the hearsay, and reversed the accused's convictions.

The Court first concluded that the "residual . . . exception" to the hearsay rule was "not a firmly rooted hearsay exception for Confrontation Clause purposes."[151]

146. *Id.* at 560.

147. *Id.* In *Green,* the Court had declined to decide whether a memory lapse undermined the adequacy of an accused's opportunity to cross-examine the hearsay declarant. *Id.* at 557–58. It resolved that question in *Owens*—at least for the situation in which a declarant remembers making a hearsay statement but does not recall the underlying events. It is possible that a more severe loss of memory—for example, if a declarant recalled nothing about an incident or about making an earlier statement concerning the incident—might render the accused's opportunity for cross-examination constitutionally inadequate. It is clear that the mere fact that a declarant appears on the witness stand is not enough. "[L]imitations on the scope of examination by the trial court or assertions of privilege" not to testify on a matter "by the witness may undermine the process to such a degree that meaningful cross-examination" is not possible. *Id.* at 561–62. In those situations, the *Green* principle would not permit admission of the witness's hearsay, and the government would have to establish that the hearsay was sufficiently reliable to be admitted without confrontation at trial.

148. 497 U.S. 805 (1990).

149. *Id.* at 809. The "parties agreed" with the judge's view that the child could not communicate what she knew to the jury. *Id.*

150. *Id.* at 811.

151. *Id.* at 817.

According to the majority, the admissibility of hearsay within a firmly rooted exception rests upon deference to "longstanding judicial and legislative experience in assessing the trustworthiness of certain types of" hearsay.[152] The residual exception is designed to "accommodate[] ad hoc instances in which statements *not otherwise falling within a recognized hearsay exception* might nevertheless be sufficiently reliable" to be admitted.[153] Its very nature precludes classifying it as firmly rooted. "[A]lmost by definition," statements within the residual exception "do not share the same tradition of reliability that supports the admissibility of statements under a firmly rooted hearsay exception" and "'must be excluded'" unless they have "'particularized guarantees of trustworthiness.'"[154]

Particularized guarantees of trustworthiness "include only those that surround the making of the statement and that render the declarant particularly worthy of belief."[155] A statement is sufficiently reliable to dispense with the protection of confrontation at trial only if "the declarant's truthfulness is so clear . . . that the test of cross-examination would be of marginal utility"[156]—that is, only if the hearsay statement itself is "so trustworthy that adversarial testing would add little to [its] reliability."[157] Without a showing that "rebut[s] the presumption that a hearsay statement is not worthy of reliance at trial, the Confrontation Clause requires exclusion."[158]

The *Wright* majority highlighted a number of factors that bear upon whether a "child declarant [is] particularly likely to be telling the truth."[159] Most significant was the Court's conclusion that independent "evidence corroborating the truth of a hearsay statement may [not] properly support a finding that the statement bears 'particularized guarantees of trustworthiness.'"[160] The Justices ultimately

---

152. *Id.* The Court asserted that statements within "firmly rooted hearsay exception[s]" are constitutionally acceptable without confrontation based on a belief that they are "so trustworthy that adversarial testing would add little to their reliability." *Id.* at 820–21.

153. *Wright,* 497 U.S. at 817 (emphasis added).

154. *Id.* at 817–18 (quoting Lee v. Illinois, 476 U.S. 530, 543 (1986)). The majority asserted that if it deemed the residual hearsay exception "firmly rooted," then "virtually every codified hearsay exception would assume constitutional stature, a step th[e] Court ha[d] repeatedly declined to take." *Id.*

155. *Id.* at 819.

156. *Id.* at 820.

157. *Id.* at 821.

158. *Wright,* 497 U.S. at 821.

159. *Id.* at 822. The nonexhaustive list of factors included spontaneity, repetition, the declarant's mental state, a child's use of unexpected terminology, and absence of a motive to fabricate. *Id.* at 821–22.

160. *Id.* at 822. If corroborating evidence could be relied upon to establish reliability, a statement that itself was "presumptively unreliable" could be deemed reliable, and admitted into evidence, "by bootstrapping on the trustworthiness of other evidence"—a "result" that would be "at odds" with an accused's constitutional entitlement to confront a witness unless confrontation would have "marginal utility." *Id.* at 823. The majority believed that

concluded that the Confrontation Clause barred the child's hearsay accusations in *Wright* because they lacked adequate guarantees of trustworthiness.[161]

Wright enhanced understanding of both prongs of the *Roberts* "indicia of reliability" requirement. The Court's explanation of the rationale for the "firmly rooted hearsay exception" doctrine—that "longstanding judicial and legislative experience" reflects a positive judgment about the trustworthiness of hearsay falling within such an exception—provided potentially useful guidance for implementing that criterion.[162] Moreover, the disputed conclusion that corroborative evidence is irrelevant to establishing "particularized guarantees of trustworthiness" restricted the availability of that alternative.[163]

In the closing decade of the twentieth century, the Justices twice considered the Sixth Amendment's bar to hearsay in noteworthy opinions that rang down the curtain on the *Roberts* era. The first was *White v. Illinois*,[164] another sexual abuse prosecution in which a nontestifying child-victim's hearsay accusations to her mother, a babysitter, and two medical professionals were admitted. The central question was whether unavailability was a pre-condition for admission.

At the outset, the Court made clear that *Inadi* had rejected a general unavailability requirement.[165] Moreover, *Inadi* had rejected the contention that unavailability needed to be shown for coconspirator hearsay statements based on

---

if cross-examination could be useful, the Confrontation Clause bars a hearsay statement unless an accused has the opportunity to cross-examine the declarant.

161. *Id.* at 826–27. Four dissenting Justices thought that there was "no constitutional justification for" the conclusion that corroborating evidence cannot support the reliability of a hearsay statement, and that "[i]t is a matter of common sense" that "one of the best ways to determine whether what someone says is trustworthy is to see if it is corroborated by other evidence." *Id.* at 828 (Kennedy, J., dissenting). In their view, the corroborating evidence, coupled with the circumstances surrounding the making of the child's statements in *Wright*, gave "rise to a legitimate argument that admission of the statements did not violate the Confrontation Clause." *Id.* at 834 (Kennedy, J., dissenting).

162. The Court cast no doubt on *Bourjaily*'s conclusion that the co-conspirator hearsay exception was firmly rooted. Still, there was some undeniable tension between *Wright*'s explanation of the constitutional logic underlying the firmly rooted exception criterion—that those exceptions reflect positive judgments about the reliability of the hearsay they encompass—and the fact that the primary justification for the co-conspirator exception has never been the trustworthiness of co-conspirators' hearsay statements.

163. *But see* Douglass, *Beyond Admissibility*, *supra* note 17, at 217–19 (criticizing *Wright*'s "test for 'reliability' . . . [as] simply too vague to effectively limit any court . . . inclined to admit a hearsay statement under the law of evidence" and as "too malleable to have much of an effect" as "an exclusionary rule that purports to establish a constitutional barrier against unreliable hearsay").

164. 502 U.S. 346 (1992).

165. *Id.* at 353–54. *Inadi* had "understood" *Roberts* as making a showing of unavailability "necessary . . . only when the challenged out-of-court statements were made in the course of a prior judicial proceeding." *Id.* at 354.

"two factors"—that the hearsay had "evidentiary significance" that in-court testimony would not have and that the "little benefit" produced by an unavailability requirement was offset by the likely "substantial . . . burdens" it would impose.[166] Those factors "appl[ied] with full force" in *White* because the child's "spontaneous declarations" and her statements made to obtain medical care had "substantial probative value . . . that could not be duplicated" at trial and a demand for proof that the child was unavailable would "have few practical benefits while imposing pointless litigation costs."[167]

The Court focused briefly on the reliability question as well, declaring that there was "no doubt" that the two hearsay exceptions involved in *White*—the "spontaneous declarations" and "statements made for purposes of medical diagnosis or treatment" exceptions—were "'firmly rooted.'"[168] The former was "at least two centuries old" and was "currently recognized" by the federal system and "nearly four-fifths of the States," while the latter was also included in the federal evidence rules and was "equally widely accepted among the States."[169]

White confirmed that proof of a declarant's unavailability would rarely be required to avoid Sixth Amendment suppression[170] and indicated that both longevity and wide acceptance were relevant to firmly rooted hearsay exception determinations.[171] While significant, these insights were not the most important contributions *White* made to Confrontation Clause jurisprudence. The government had argued that the *Roberts* approach was fundamentally misguided and that a "narrow reading of the Confrontation Clause" rooted in its limited historical purpose would be preferable.[172] Although the majority rejected that contention as "foreclosed by our prior cases,"[173] two concurring Justices were receptive to the contention that neither the text nor the history of the Confrontation

---

166. *Id.* at 354–55.

167. *Id.* at 355–57.

168. *Id.* at 355–56 n.8.

169. *White,* 502 U.S. at 355–56 n.8.

170. The reasoning in *Inadi* and *White* suggested that unavailability would be required only for former testimony and, perhaps, for other hearsay that has no evidentiary significance that cannot be duplicated by trial testimony. Other than former testimony, there are few types of hearsay statements that are admissible under the rules of evidence but lack any special evidentiary value.

171. Moreover, the Court's classification of the "statements for medical purposes" exception based on wide acceptance alone showed that a centuries-long history was not essential. *See* Douglass, *Beyond Admissibility, supra* note 17, at 208–09 (arguing that the "standards" governing the firmly rooted hearsay exception criterion "show[ed] little concern for reliability" and were instead driven by history and that, as a result, the controlling "test [was] so generous that virtually all recognizable hearsay exceptions have passed").

172. *White,* 502 U.S. at 352.

173. *Id.* The Court deemed it "too late" for "reexamination" of its "approach" to the relationship between hearsay and the Sixth Amendment—the roots of which were in the 1895 decision in *Mattox. Id.* at 353.

Clause supported the *Roberts* doctrine.[174] They proposed an alternate "formulation" said to be more consistent with the history and purposes of the Sixth Amendment.[175] While this radical minority position seemed innocuous at the time, later it would prove to be an initial step toward revolution.

Lilly v. Virginia,[176] the final opinion of the *Roberts* era, involved a capital murder prosecution. The trial judge had allowed the state to introduce an accomplice's confession that contained some statements implicating the accomplice and others incriminating the defendant. The accomplice, who was also the defendant's brother, was unavailable to testify because he asserted his Fifth Amendment privilege against compulsory self-incrimination and refused to testify at trial. A majority of the Justices agreed that the admission of his confession violated the Sixth Amendment, but no reasoning attracted majority support.[177]

Justice Stevens observed that because "'[t]he central concern of the Confrontation Clause is to ensure the reliability of the evidence . . . by subjecting it to rigorous testing . . . before the trier of fact,'" when the prosecution attempts to use an unavailable declarant's hearsay to prove guilt "courts must decide whether the Clause permits the government to deny the accused his usual right to force" a witness to undergo cross-examination.[178] The plurality noted that the Court had recently rejected the contention that the Sixth Amendment governs only the abuses that led to the confrontation guarantee, but pointed out that even under that narrow conception of the Confrontation Clause, the confession in *Lilly* would be barred.[179]

Turning to the *Roberts* framework, Justice Stevens first announced that whether a statement "fall[s] within a firmly rooted hearsay exception . . . is a question of federal law,"[180] then observed that an exception is firmly rooted if "'longstanding . . . experience'"[181] established that its foundation was so solid that "'admission of virtually any evidence within [it] comports with the "substance of

174. *Id.* at 358–63 (Thomas, J., concurring in part and concurring in the judgment).

175. *Id.* at 365 (Thomas, J., concurring in part and concurring in the judgment). They contended that the proposed alternative was also consistent with "virtually all" of the Court's pre-*Roberts* decisions. *Id.* (Thomas, J., concurring in part and concurring in the judgment).

176. 527 U.S. 116 (1999).

177. Only four Justices joined Justice Stevens's lead opinion, and one of the four expressed serious qualms about the *Roberts* doctrine's interpretation of the Sixth Amendment. *See id.* at 140–42 (Breyer, J., concurring).

178. *Lilly*, 527 U.S. at 123–24 (plurality opinion) (quoting Maryland v. Craig, 497 U.S. 836, 845 (1990)).

179. *Id.* at 124–25 (plurality opinion).

180. *Id.* at 125 (plurality opinion).

181. *Id.* at 126 (plurality opinion) (quoting Idaho v. Wright, 497 U.S. 805, 817 (1990)).

the constitutional protection.'""[182] For an exception to qualify, "[e]stablished practice . . . must confirm that statements . . . within [that] category of hearsay inherently 'carr[y] special guarantees of credibility' essentially equivalent to, or greater than, those produced by" cross-examination.[183] The hearsay exception for statements against penal interest—at issue in *Lilly*—includes three distinct "categories" of statements.[184] The confession at issue fell into the third category—a statement by one participant in a crime that inculpates an accomplice and is used by the government to prove the latter's guilt.[185] The "practice of admitting" this sort of statement under a hearsay exception was "of quite recent vintage."[186] "Most important," insofar as this type of statement is an effort by a declarant to shift or spread blame to another, it is "inherently unreliable" and threatens the truth-finding process.[187] Adversarial testing by cross-examination would promote reliability.[188] For all these reasons, the plurality concluded that "accomplices' confessions that inculpate a criminal defendant are not within a firmly rooted exception to the hearsay rule."[189]

In addition, the confession in *Lilly* did not have "particularized guarantees of trustworthiness."[190] Evidence corroborating the truth of the declarant's accusations about his brother was irrelevant, and the circumstances surrounding the confession raised questions about its reliability.[191] These factors "militate[d] against

---

182. *Id.* (plurality opinion) (quoting Ohio v. Roberts, 448 U.S. 56, 66 (1980) (quoting Mattox v. United States, 156 U.S. 237, 244 (1895))).

183. *Lilly*, 527 U.S. at 126 (plurality opinion) (quoting White v. Illinois, 502 U.S. 346, 356 (1992)).

184. *Id.* at 127 (plurality opinion).

185. The other two categories are self-inculpatory admissions introduced against a declarant himself and statements of third parties offered by a defendant to exculpate himself. *See id.* at 127 (plurality opinion).

186. *Id.* at 130 (plurality opinion).

187. *Id.* at 131 (plurality opinion).

188. *See Lilly*, 527 U.S. at 133 (plurality opinion).

189. *Id.* at 134 (plurality opinion).

190. *Id.* at 136 (plurality opinion). The plurality believed that there was no need for an appellate court to defer to the conclusions of a trial judge in deciding whether there were guarantees of trustworthiness. *Id.* at 136–37 (plurality opinion). It also issued a "cogent reminder" that it is "highly unlikely that the presumptive unreliability" of blame-shifting or blame-spreading confessions could "be effectively rebutted when the statements are" of a sort that concerned the Framers of the Sixth Amendment—"that is, when the government is involved in the statements' production, and when the statements describe past events and have not been subjected to adversarial testing." *Id.* at 137 (plurality opinion).

191. Because the accomplice was "in custody," was suspected of being involved in and knowing about serious crimes, and his confession was made "under the supervision of governmental authorities" in response to "leading questions" and without "contemporaneous cross-examination," he "had a natural motive . . . to exculpate himself." *Id.* at 139 (plurality opinion). Another factor that weighed against reliability was that the declarant was "under the influence of alcohol" when he confessed. *Id.* (plurality opinion).

finding that his statements were so inherently reliable that cross-examination would have been superfluous."[192] Consequently, "admission of the untested confession . . . violated [the defendant's] Confrontation Clause rights."[193]

Although all nine Justices agreed that the judgment affirming the admission of the confession had to be overturned, they split over the reasons why reversal was justified. Six Justices showed no inclination to depart from the *Roberts* framework, but differed about its meaning and application.[194] Thus, *Lilly* did not advance the *Roberts* doctrine.

In fact, the movement seemed to be in the opposite direction. Three Justices now voiced sympathy with the view that *Roberts* was a misguided interpretation of the relationship between the right to confront witnesses and hearsay evidence. They suggested that there was a need for serious reform that would respect the text and history of the Sixth Amendment.[195] Moreover, not only did the overt hostility to *Roberts* increase, but the four Justices who joined the plurality opinion highlighted the implications of the suggested reforms more than once.[196] While *Roberts* survived with the endorsement of a majority, *Lilly* left it somewhat less stable.[197] The assaults that began in *White* and intensified in *Lilly* would

---

192. *Id.* (plurality opinion).

193. *Lilly*, 527 U.S. at 139 (plurality opinion).

194. Three of the six contended that the Court should not foreclose the possibility that a statement against penal interest could qualify as within a firmly rooted hearsay exception. *See id.* at 146 (Rehnquist, C.J., concurring in the judgment). These Justices also disagreed with the principle that appellate courts owed no deference to trial judge decisions when assessing guarantees of trustworthiness. *Id.* at 148–49 (Rehnquist, C.J., concurring in the judgment).

195. Justices Scalia and Thomas adhered to the position they had endorsed in *White*. *See Lilly*, 527 U.S. at 143 (Scalia, J., concurring in part and concurring in the judgment); *id.* at 143–44 (Thomas, J., concurring in part and concurring in the judgment). Justice Breyer joined the plurality opinion of Justice Stevens because there was no "need" to "reexamine the current connection between the Confrontation Clause and the hearsay rule in this case." *Id.* at 142 (Breyer, J., concurring). Nonetheless, he wrote a separate opinion raising serious questions about the legitimacy of the *Roberts* approach. *Id.* at 140–43 (Breyer, J., concurring).

196. *See Lilly*, 527 U.S. at 125, 130–31, 137 (plurality opinion). These references to the implications of the proposal to severely narrow the reach of the Confrontation Clause did not disapprove of that proposal, but, instead, used it to provide further support for the plurality's reasoning.

197. *See* Reed, *Irretrievable Breakdown*, *supra* note 17, at 212, 215–16 (asserting that *Lilly* evinced an "'irretrievable breakdown' between the Confrontation Clause and the hearsay rule" and that it "virtually guaranteed a reexamination of *Roberts* the next time a Confrontation Clause case came before the Court"); *see also* Douglass, *Beyond Admissibility*, *supra* note 17, at 194–95 (contending that *Roberts* had produced "an exclusionary rule" that "might have reached the end of its useful life" because it barred "a slice of hearsay so thin" that exclusion was "little more than a theoretical possibility"); Friedman, *Confrontation*, *supra* note 111, at 1013, 1015 (asserting that *Roberts* had become "unstable" and that

prove fatal the next time the Court resolved a conflict between the Confrontation Clause and hearsay.

3. From 2004 Into the Future: The *Crawford* Revolution

Five years after *Lilly* revealed the cracks in the *Roberts* doctrine's foundation, and just a few years after the turn of the century, the Court decided it was time to demolish the old structure and supplant it with a radically different approach. In *Crawford v. Washington,*[198] the Court announced a dramatic reconception of the Confrontation Clause bar to hearsay.[199]

Crawford involved a trial for assault and attempted murder in which the prosecution called the defendant's wife as a witness. When the defendant prevented her from testifying by asserting his marital privilege, the trial judge allowed the government to introduce the wife's inculpatory tape-recorded statement to the police during an interrogation conducted shortly after the alleged crime. The defendant contended that the Confrontation Clause barred his wife's statement.

In an opinion joined by seven Justices, Justice Scalia highlighted the ambiguity of the Sixth Amendment text. The "'witnesses'" that an accused has a "'right . . . to be confronted with'" could refer only to "those who actually testify at trial, [to all] whose statements are offered at trial, or [to] something in-between."[200] To resolve this textual unclarity, he turned to history, concluding that in both England and America the recognition of a confrontation entitlement was a response to a particular abuse—the government's examination of witnesses before trial and the introduction of their pretrial statements "in lieu of live testimony."[201] According to the Court, the historical record "support[ed] two inferences about the meaning of the Sixth Amendment."[202] The first pertained to the *scope* of that provision. Specifically, history showed that "the principal evil" targeted by the Confrontation Clause was the abusive "civil-law mode of criminal procedure," which allowed the "use of ex parte examinations as evidence against the accused."[203] This historical "focus" supported the Court's longstanding view that the Confrontation Clause governs not only "in-court testimony," but at least

---

the Court had "retreated" from "the unavailability and reliability requirements"); Richard D. Friedman, *Grappling with the Meaning of "Testimonial,"* 71 Brook. L. Rev. 241, 273–74 (2005) [hereinafter Friedman, *Meaning of "Testimonial"*] (suggesting that because *"Roberts* did not articulate a doctrine worthy of respect, . . . manipulation was inevitable").

198. 541 U.S. 36 (2004).

199. Prior to the *Crawford* decision, some scholars had advocated doctrinal reforms like the one adopted in *Crawford. See, e.g.,* Amar, *First Principles, supra* note 111, at 691–97; Friedman, *Confrontation, supra* note 111, at 1025–43.

200. *Crawford,* 541 U.S. at 42–43.

201. *See id.* at 43–49.

202. *Id.* at 50.

203. *Id.*

some out-of-court hearsay statements.[204] However, because the use of some types of hearsay "bears little resemblance to the . . . abuses" that concerned the Framers, history also "suggest[ed] that not all hearsay implicates the Sixth Amendment[]."[205]

Armed with these historical lessons, the Court returned to the constitutional text, finding additional support for the view that the Sixth Amendment regulates only some kinds of hearsay. The word "'witnesses'" is a reference to those "who 'bear testimony,'" which is "typically '[a] solemn declaration or affirmation made for the purpose of establishing or proving some fact.'"[206] Thus, the "constitutional text" confirmed the first historically-based inference, "reflect[ing] an especially acute concern with a specific type of out-of-court statement"—i.e., "a formal statement to government officers."[207] Together, history and the text indicated that "even if [the Confrontation Clause] is not solely concerned with testimonial hearsay, that is its primary object."[208]

The "second proposition" supported by the historical record related to the *content* of the Sixth Amendment's protection. History taught "that the Framers would not have allowed admission of testimonial statements of a witness who did not appear at trial unless he was unavailable to testify, and the defendant had had a prior opportunity for cross-examination."[209] The text of the Sixth Amendment contains no "open-ended exceptions from the confrontation requirement," and "is most naturally read as a reference to the right of confrontation at common law."[210] Therefore, it "incorporates" the two "necessary[] condition[s]" that the common law prescribed for admitting testimonial hearsay without trial confrontation—"unavailability and a prior opportunity to cross-examine."[211]

---

204. *Id.* at 50–51. Justice Scalia maintained that if the guarantee was restricted to individuals who actually testify at trial the Sixth Amendment would be "powerless to prevent even the most flagrant inquisitorial practices" that had been the impetus for a right to confront adverse witnesses. *Id.* at 51.

205. *Crawford*, 541 U.S. at 51.

206. *Id.* (quoting 2 N. WEBSTER, AN AMERICAN DICTIONARY OF THE ENGLISH LANGUAGE (1828)).

207. *Id.*

208. *Id.* at 53. *Crawford*'s interpretation of the Sixth Amendment was informed almost exclusively by the history and text of the Confrontation Clause rather than the values and objectives of that provision. At one point, the Court did indicate that there were sound reasons for a focus on safeguards against testimonial hearsay. According to Justice Scalia, the "[i]nvolvement of government officers in the production of testimony with an eye toward trial presents unique potential for prosecutorial abuse." *Id.* at 56 n.7.

209. *Id.* at 53–54.

210. *Crawford*, 541 U.S. at 54.

211. *Id.* at 54–55. At common law, a prior opportunity to cross-examine the declarant was "dispositive, and not merely one of several ways to establish reliability." *Id.* at 55–56. The only "deviation" from the common law rule "involve[d] dying declarations," for which

According to *Crawford*, the Court's Confrontation Clause decisions had "been largely consistent" with the "two principles" inferred from the historical record,[212] but the "rationales" for those decisions had not been "faithful to the original meaning of" the Sixth Amendment.[213] The *Roberts* framework for excluding hearsay "depart[ed] from the historical principles . . . in two respects." [214] First, its scope was "too broad" because it governed not only testimonial hearsay of the kind that was of historical concern, but also hearsay that was "far removed from the core concerns of the Clause."[215] Second, its evidentiary bar was "too narrow" because it allowed the admission of testimonial hearsay "upon a mere finding of reliability."[216]

The Court set aside the problem of excessive breadth, finding it unnecessary to "definitively resolve" whether the Confrontation Clause applies at all to non-testimonial hearsay.[217] It then held that "the excessive narrowness" of *Roberts*—its tolerance of testimonial hearsay "based on a mere judicial determination of reliability"—was a misinterpretation of the Confrontation Clause.[218] *Roberts* had erred in "replac[ing] the constitutionally prescribed method of [ensuring] reliability"—the procedural guarantees of confrontation and cross-examination—"with a wholly foreign" method—a "mere judicial determination of reliability."[219]

---

there was an undisputed "exception" allowing testimonial hearsay to be introduced despite the absence of a prior cross-examination opportunity. *Id.* at 56 n.6. The Court refused to decide whether that exception is a part of the Sixth Amendment, noting that if it "must be accepted on historical grounds, it" would be a unique, one-of-a-kind exception. *Id.*

The quotation in the text specifies the conditions for admitting testimonial hearsay without confrontation at trial. The Court explicitly reaffirmed the important principle of *California v. Green* and *United States v. Owens*—that when a "declarant appears for cross-examination at trial," there are no Confrontation Clause "constraints at all on the use of his prior testimonial statements." *Crawford*, 541 U.S. at 60 n.9. The Court also reaffirmed that the Confrontation "Clause . . . does not bar the use of testimonial statements for purposes other than establishing the truth of the matter asserted"—i.e., that exclusion is mandated *only* when an out-of-court statement is introduced *for hearsay purposes. Id.*

212. *Id.* at 57–59, 60. The sole case with a result that was "arguably in tension with the rule requiring a prior opportunity for cross-examination" of testimonial hearsay was *White v. Illinois. Id.* at 58 n.8.

213. *Id.* at 60.

214. *Id.*

215. *Crawford*, 541 U.S. at 60.

216. *Id.* By doing so, the *Roberts* approach "fail[ed] to protect against paradigmatic confrontation violations." *Id.*

217. *Id.* at 61.

218. *Id.* at 61–62.

219. *Id.* at 62. According to the Court, denying confrontation based on the reliability of hearsay "is akin to dispensing with jury trial because a defendant is obviously guilty" and "is not what the Sixth Amendment prescribes." *Id.* The Justices "lack[ed] authority to" supplant the Framers' "categorical constitutional guarantee[] with [an] open-ended

For testimonial hearsay to be admissible, the Confrontation Clause "demands what the common law required: unavailability and a prior opportunity for cross-examination" of the declarant.[220] In other words, the Sixth Amendment *excludes* testimonial statements in the absence of "confrontation"—"the only indicium of reliability sufficient to satisfy constitutional demands."[221]

The Court ventured some insights into the meaning of the critical term "testimonial,"[222] but deliberately avoided "any effort to spell out a comprehensive definition."[223] The statements of Crawford's wife clearly qualified as "testimonial," and, although she was unavailable to testify, the accused had not had the "opportunity to cross-examine her."[224] Consequently, the admission of her incriminating statements violated the Sixth Amendment.[225]

As mentioned, because nontestimonial hearsay was not at issue in *Crawford*, the Court did not determine whether *Roberts*'s overbreadth was also constitutional error—that is, whether the Confrontation Clause regulates nontestimonial hearsay at all.[226] Just two years after *Crawford*, in the companion cases of

---

balancing test[]" of its own creation. *Id.* at 67–68; *see* Friedman, *Confrontation*, *supra* note 111, at 1031 (asserting that "[b]alancing tests" of the sort *Roberts* prescribed "are not very good protectors of rights").

220. *Crawford*, 541 U.S. at 68. The Court "accept[ed]" the validity of one other "exception" to the guarantee of confrontation at trial—the "forfeiture by wrongdoing" exception. *Id.* at 62. That doctrine is rooted in reasoning that is "very different from" that underlying *Roberts* because it "extinguishes confrontation claims on essentially equitable grounds" and "does not purport to be an alternative means of determining reliability." *Id.*

221. *Id.* at 69. Only two Justices, Chief Justice Rehnquist and Justice O'Connor, refused to participate in the overthrow of *Roberts*. They believed that the majority's new doctrine was "no better rooted in history than our current doctrine," *id.* at 69 (Rehnquist, C.J., concurring in the judgment), and cited additional reasons why they preferred the *Roberts* framework. *Id.* at 73–76 (Rehnquist, C.J., concurring in the judgment).

222. *See id.* at 51–52.

223. *Id.* at 68.

224. *Id.* Earlier in the opinion, the Court had concluded that "[p]olice interrogations bear a striking resemblance to examinations by justices of the peace in England" that were the object of historical concern, and that statements yielded by police interrogation, therefore, "fall squarely within" the category of "testimonial hearsay." *Id.* at 52–53. The contested statements were the product of such an interrogation.

225. *See Crawford*, 541 U.S. at 68.

226. Although the Court specifically reserved the question of *Roberts*'s overbreadth, *see id.* at 61, it strongly suggested an answer. *Crawford*'s account of history indicated that nontestimonial hearsay was beyond the Confrontation Clause's reach. Moreover, near the end of the majority opinion, Justice Scalia declared that for "nontestimonial hearsay," it would be "wholly consistent with the Framers' design to afford the States flexibility" to develop "hearsay law" by "exempt[ing] such statements from Confrontation Clause scrutiny altogether." *Id.* at 68. It was not difficult to forecast what the Court would ultimately decide about the reach of the confrontation entitlement and its exclusionary mandate.

Davis v. Washington and *Hammon v. Indiana*,[227] the Court declared that "[o]nly [testimonial] statements . . . cause [a] declarant to be a 'witness' within the meaning of the Confrontation Clause" and that "[i]t is the testimonial character of [a] statement that separates it from other hearsay that . . . *is not subject to the Confrontation Clause*."[228] Because the "limitation" to testimonial hearsay "clearly reflected in the text of the constitutional provision . . . mark[s] out not merely its 'core,' but its perimeter," the Court held that nontestimonial hearsay is not subject to Sixth Amendment exclusion.[229] Thus was the *Crawford* revolution completed.

Crawford and *Davis* made monumental contributions to the history of Confrontation Clause regulation of hearsay evidence. More than 125 years after the its first decision on the subject, the Court announced that the Sixth Amendment bar was restricted to testimonial hearsay and that other hearsay was governed solely by the rules of evidence. Moreover, the Court corrected an error about the substance of the Constitution's protection that first appeared in *Dutton v. Evans* and was fully embraced in *Ohio v. Roberts*—that testimonial hearsay was not subject to exclusion if a judge found it sufficiently reliable to dispense with confrontation and cross-examination. *Roberts* had misconstrued the Sixth Amendment's regulatory impact on hearsay that falls within the Sixth Amendment's reach. For testimonial hearsay, an accused has a procedural entitlement to *confrontation*. For available witnesses, there is a right to confrontation at trial. For unavailable witnesses, there is an exception to trial confrontation, but only if there was a prior opportunity for confrontation. Absent confrontation at some time, testimonial statements are barred.[230]

This historical account ends with the beginning of the *Crawford* revolution. The evolution of the new doctrine in the opinions issued since *Crawford* is an undeniable part of Confrontation Clause history. Nonetheless, because *Crawford* is the present—today's framework defining Sixth Amendment exclusion—the contributions of its progeny are discussed in the section of this chapter devoted to doctrinal details.

---

227. 547 U.S. 813 (2006).

228. *Id.* at 821 (emphasis added).

229. *Id.* at 824.

230. For commentary supportive of the Court's decision to abandon *Roberts* and supplant it with the radically different framework prescribed by *Crawford*, see Friedman, *Meaning of "Testimonial," supra* note 197, at 270–74; Latimer, *Confrontation After* Crawford, *supra* note 111, at 329, 419. For criticisms of *Crawford*, see Thomas Y. Davies, *Not "The Framers' Design": How the Framing-Era Ban Against Hearsay Evidence Refutes the* Crawford-Davis *"Testimonial" Formulation of the Scope of the Original Confrontation Clause*, 15 J.L. & Pol'y 349, 351–55, 369–73, 433–34, 465 (2007) [hereinafter Davies, *Not "The Framers' Design"*]; Myrna Raeder, *Remember the Ladies and the Children Too*, 71 Brook. L. Rev. 311, 311–18, 320–25, 338 (2005) [hereinafter Raeder, *Remember the Ladies*]; Reed, *Irretrievable Breakdown*, *supra* note 17, at 222–28.

C. THE NATURE OF AND JUSTIFICATIONS FOR CONFRONTATION CLAUSE EXCLUSION OF HEARSAY

In contrast to the lengthy account of the history of Confrontation Clause exclusion of hearsay, the following discussion of the nature and justifications for this constitutional exclusion doctrine is relatively brief. The reasons for the brevity are that the character of and rationales for Sixth Amendment suppression are clear and undisputed.[231] There is some debate concerning the breadth of this constitutional bar, but virtually no controversy over its legitimacy. In other words, there is general agreement that the Sixth Amendment stands as a barrier to some government hearsay evidence in criminal cases. Differences center around the contours of that barrier—that is, how much and what kind of hearsay the Confrontation Clause governs.

Although the "text" of the Confrontation Clause "says nothing of excluding a witness's testimony,"[232] the exclusion of hearsay evidence is an integral part of the right that provision grants—a necessary means of preventing deprivations of the entitlement to confront adverse witnesses.[233] The Confrontation Clause, one of several fair trial guarantees contained in the Sixth Amendment,[234] provides that "[i]n all criminal prosecutions, the accused shall enjoy the right . . . to be confronted with the witnesses against him."[235] This right entitles a criminal defendant to insist that those who provide evidence against him will do so in his presence and in the presence of the jury,[236] and that they will take an oath and

231. Unlike Supreme Court opinions concerning other constitutional exclusion doctrines, the Confrontation Clause hearsay opinions do not discuss the nature of the evidentiary bar or its justifications in any depth. The Justices have not disagreed about these foundational premises.

232. Douglass, *Beyond Admissibility*, *supra* note 17, at 224.

233. From very early on, the Supreme Court implicitly recognized that exclusion was essential to prevent circumvention of the confrontation entitlement. *See* Douglass, *Beyond Admissibility*, *supra* note 17, at 199 (asserting that the Court's "'exclusionary thinking'" dates to its first case involving the relationship between hearsay and the Sixth Amendment confrontation right in the late nineteenth century).

234. Others include the right to a speedy and public trial, the right to trial by jury, the right to be informed of an accusation, the right to compulsory process for obtaining favorable witnesses, and the right to the assistance of counsel. "The Sixth Amendment includes a compact statement of the rights necessary to a full defense . . . [that] are basic to our adversary system of criminal justice." Faretta v. California, 422 U.S. 806, 818 (1975).

235. U.S. Const. amend. VI.

236. *See* Ohio v. Roberts, 448 U.S. 56, 63–64 (1980); California v. Green, 399 U.S. 149, 157 (1970); Barber v. Page, 390 U.S. 719, 721 (1968); Mattox v. United States, 156 U.S. 237, 242, (1895); *see also* Friedman, *Confrontation*, *supra* note 111, at 1011 (stating that the Confrontation Clause ensures that "witnesses [will be] brought 'face-to-face'" with the accused).

submit to cross-examination by the defense.[237] Each of these entitlements serves to promote fairness—to ensure that trials arrive at just outcomes by means of fair processes.[238] The primary objective is to promote the accuracy and reliability of verdicts, preventing the unfairness of convicting innocent individuals.[239] A witness who must face a defendant and swear to tell the truth is more likely to be careful, accurate, and truthful.[240] Juror observations of a testifying witness

---

237. *See* Crawford v. Washington, 541 U.S. 36, 61 (2004) (noting that the Sixth Amendment guarantee of confrontation "commands" that the reliability of evidence "be assessed in a particular manner: by testing in the crucible of cross-examination"); Lee v. Illinois, 476 U.S. 530, 540 (1986) (asserting that the guarantee of confrontation insures witnesses testify "'under oath'" and forces them "'to submit to cross-examination'") (quoting California v. Green, 399 U.S. 149, 158 (1970)); *Roberts*, 448 U.S. at 64 (observing that the Sixth Amendment contemplates cross-examination which affords the accused the opportunity to "'test[] the recollection and sift[] the conscience of the witness'") (quoting Mattox v. United States, 156 U.S. 237, 242–43 (1895)); Douglas v. Alabama, 380 U.S. 415, 418 (1965) (stating that "a primary interest secured" by the Confrontation Clause "is the right of cross-examination"); Pointer v. Texas, 380 U.S. 400, 406–07 (1965) (pointing out that "a major reason underlying the . . . confrontation rule is to give a defendant . . . an opportunity to cross-examine the witnesses against him"); *see also* Friedman, *Confrontation*, *supra* note 111, at 1011 (observing that the Sixth Amendment "also comprehends the right" to have witness testimony given "under oath" and "subject . . . to cross-examination" and that the Supreme Court has treated the right to a "'face-to-face'" encounter "as secondary to [the] right of cross-examination").

In the rare situations in which the Supreme Court has held that a witness may testify outside the physical presence of an accused, the witness still must take an oath, testify under the observation of the jury, and submit to cross-examination by the defense. *See* Maryland v. Craig, 497 U.S. 836 (1990) (holding that child witnesses may sometimes testify outside the physical presence of the accused); Illinois v. Allen, 397 U.S. 337 (1970) (holding that a judge can sometimes physically remove an accused who engages in misbehavior from the courtroom during witness testimony). Thus, all of the safeguards except face-to-face confrontation with the accused are preserved.

238. Early on, the Court characterized the confrontation right as "[o]ne of the fundamental guarantees of life and liberty . . . found in the [S]ixth [A]mendment." Kirby v. United States, 174 U.S. 47, 55 (1899). Later, in deciding that the right was binding on the states as a matter of due process, the Court observed that the Framers believed "that confrontation was a fundamental right essential to a fair trial in a criminal prosecution" and "an essential and fundamental requirement for the kind of fair trial which is this country's constitutional goal." *Pointer*, 380 U.S. at 404–05.

239. *See Lee*, 476 U.S. at 540 (describing the right to confront witnesses as "primarily a functional right that promotes reliability in criminal trials"); Dutton v. Evans, 400 U.S. 74, 89 (1970) (plurality opinion) (stating that the "mission of the Confrontation Clause is to advance . . . the accuracy of the truth-determining process in criminal trials"); *see also* Amar, *First Principles*, *supra* note 111, at 688 (asserting that "confrontation is designed to promote the truth").

240. *Green*, 399 U.S. at 158–59 (describing how the oath requirement promotes truth and accuracy); *see also* Amar, *First Principles*, *supra* note 111, at 688–89 (contending that

provide useful clues that enable better assessments of the witness's accuracy and honesty.[241] Cross-examination may be the most critical element in ensuring fair, accurate outcomes and avoiding undeserved convictions.[242] It enables an accused to question and challenge a witness in the presence of the jury, to probe her veracity, to explore the integrity and foundations of her perceptions and memory, and to clarify what she means by her account.[243] In sum, each element of the confrontation entitlement contributes to the substantive fairness of a criminal prosecution, furthering the accuracy of adjudications of guilt.

Moreover, each of the confrontation mechanisms—face-to-face confrontation with the accused in the jury's presence, oath, and cross-examination—is a component of fair *process* in our adversarial system of justice.[244] The entitlement to face one's accusers in the courtroom, to have them confronted with the prospect of perjury charges should they testify falsely, and to have them make accusations

---

confrontation "may discourage deliberate perjury" and "by simply allowing" an accused to hear witness testimony "may help an innocent defendant to figure out where [a] witness might be mistaken").

241. *See Lee*, 476 U.S. at 540 (asserting that by enabling the jury to observe a witness's demeanor, confrontation is a "mechanism[]" that "advance[s] the pursuit of truth"); *Roberts*, 448 U.S. at 64 (suggesting that the need to testify in the jury's presence is an important "means of testing accuracy"); *Green*, 399 U.S. at 158 (suggesting that the jury's opportunity to observe a witness's demeanor aids its assessment of credibility).

242. *See Pointer*, 380 U.S. at 404 (stating that "probably no one . . . would deny the value of cross-examination in exposing falsehood and bringing out the truth in the trial of a criminal case" and that it is "'one of the safeguards essential to a fair trial'") (quoting Alford v. United States, 282 U.S. 687, 692 (1931)); 5 JOHN HENRY WIGMORE, A TREATISE ON THE ANGLO-AMERICAN SYSTEM OF EVIDENCE § 1367 (3d ed. 1940) (calling cross-examination "the greatest legal engine ever invented for the discovery of truth").

243. *See* Crawford v. Washington, 541 U.S. 36, 61 (2004) (stating that "testing in the crucible of cross-examination" is the prescribed manner for securing the "ultimate goal" of the Confrontation Clause—"to ensure reliability of evidence"); *Lee*, 476 U.S. at 540 (noting that "'forc[ing] the witness to submit to cross-examination'" is a "mechanism[]" that "advance[s] the pursuit of truth in criminal trials") (quoting California v. Green, 399 U.S. 149, 158 (1970)); *Roberts*, 448 U.S. at 63–64 (observing that cross-examination affords an accused the opportunity to "'test[] the recollection and sift[] the conscience of the witness,'" an important "means of testing accuracy" and ensuring "'the ultimate "integrity of the fact-finding process"'") (quoting Mattox v. United States, 156 U.S. 237, 242–43 (1895) and Chambers v. Mississippi, 410 U.S. 284, 295 (1973)).

244. *See Lee*, 476 U.S. at 540 (asserting that confrontation "promote[s] . . . society's interest in having the accused and accuser engage in an open and even contest in a public trial" and "ensur[es] that convictions will not be based on the charges of unseen and unknown—and hence unchallengeable—individuals"); *see also* Friedman, *Confrontation*, *supra* note 111, at 1028 (maintaining that the Confrontation Clause "right . . . has a life of its own" because granting "the accused the right to confront . . . witnesses . . . is a fundamental part of the way we do judicial business" which we "should adhere to . . . even if . . . it does not help accurate factfinding").

under the watchful eyes of the citizens who will decide the accused's fate all further the interest in fundamentally fair procedures. In addition, the opportunity to cross-examine a witness about her accusations—to participate in the adjudicatory process, to have a chance to contest charges and reveal untruths, and to play a role in determining one's fate—is a vital element of a fair adversarial trial process.[245]

Hearsay consists of an assertion of fact made outside the courtroom that is introduced into a trial by means of another person's testimony or some tangible record for the purpose of proving the truth of the assertion. If a police officer testifies that a neighbor of the defendant told her that the defendant set fire to a home, or if the neighbor gave the police a written or tape-recorded statement to that effect, and the testimony, writing, or recording is introduced to prove that the defendant did set the fire, the evidence is hearsay. The source of this accusation, the neighbor, was not under oath at the time of the accusation, did not face the accused at that time, could not be observed by the jurors, and was not subject to questioning by the defendant at the time. Consequently, none of the tools for arriving at accurate outcomes are available and none of the mechanisms that constitute a fair procedure are present.

The exclusion of hearsay evidence is an essential part of the confrontation right because the admission of hearsay to prove guilt would circumvent the fair trial protections the Sixth Amendment affords, thereby defeating the fair trial objectives it is designed to achieve. Under the Confrontation Clause, a witness may report what she knows about an accused's guilt only if she takes an oath, makes the report in the defendant's and jury's presence, and can be cross-examined about that report. The admission of hearsay evidence denies these fundamental entitlements. It deprives an accused of the substantive and procedural fairness that is his constitutional entitlement. Because the government's use of hearsay evidence can violate the accused's constitutional right to confront the source of the hearsay, the accused has a constitutional right to suppress that evidence.

The right to exclusion need not be specified in the constitutional text because it is inherent in the nature and goals of the confrontation guarantee. The suppression of hearsay is a logical necessity, an essential component of the entitlement to confront witnesses. Moreover, the Sixth Amendment bar to hearsay is no mere "exclusionary rule." It is a personal trial right belonging to the accused individual, an indivisible part of the fundamental constitutional entitlement to confront adverse witnesses.[246]

---

245. The right to confront witnesses also plays a "symbolic" role, promoting not only the reality but also the appearance of justice. *See Lee*, 476 U.S. at 540.

246. The Supreme Court recognizes that the admission of hearsay evidence would violate the Sixth Amendment guarantee, an implicit acknowledgment that suppression is an inextricable and unavoidable part of the confrontation right. *See* Davis v. Washington,

Deterrence of official misconduct, a central or secondary justification for most, if not all, other constitutional exclusion mandates, plays absolutely no role in the Confrontation Clause's exclusion of hearsay.[247] The Sixth Amendment bar to hearsay evidence is not designed to discourage or modify unconstitutional, unacceptable, or risky official conduct. Hearsay that is not the product of any official conduct at all may threaten the right to confront witnesses, and, therefore, be subject to exclusion. If a witness to a crime who is not known to the authorities e-mails her account of the offense to a prosecutor or police officer to furnish proof against an accused at trial, that hearsay is barred. In such cases, there is no official conduct to deter, but a courtroom right to enforce.

Moreover, even if official actions are the source of the hearsay evidence, those actions themselves cannot violate the Sixth Amendment because the right to confront witnesses can be denied only at trial, when unconfronted witness testimony reaches the jury.[248] There is nothing unconstitutional, or even undesirable, about official efforts to discover and document a witness's account of a crime. Thus, there is absolutely no threat of constitutional deprivation when a prosecutor interviews a prospective witness or when officers interrogate someone with knowledge of an offense. That conduct alone cannot undermine the fairness of a trial.

In fact, efforts to discourage the conduct that generates hearsay evidence that the Sixth Amendment forbids would ordinarily be not just unproductive, but counterproductive. Society wants officials to investigate allegations and prepare

---

547 U.S. 813, 832 n.6 (2006) (asserting that "the trial *use* of . . . testimonial [hearsay] statements . . . offends" the Sixth Amendment) (emphasis in original); Lilly v. Virginia, 527 U.S. 116, 139 (1999) (concluding that the admission of a codefendant's confession "violated" the defendant's "Confrontation Clause rights"); *Lee*, 476 U.S. at 531, 531, 546 (stating that the issue was whether a judge's reliance on "the codefendant's confession violated . . . rights as secured by the Confrontation Clause" and holding that a "conviction[] supported by" an unconfronted codefendant's confession "violate[d] the constitutional right of confrontation"); *see also* Friedman, *Meaning of "Testimonial," supra* note 197, at 261–62 (stating that Sixth Amendment violations occur "when a testimonial statement is *admitted at trial* against an accused without his being afforded an opportunity to confront the witness" and that "the *court* . . . commits the violation by deciding to admit the statement notwithstanding the lack of confrontation") (emphasis in original).

247. There has never been the slightest hint in a single Supreme Court opinion that deterring government conduct is a justification for Sixth Amendment exclusion of hearsay.

248. *See Davis*, 547 U.S. at 832 n.6 (stating that "[t]he Confrontation Clause in no way governs police conduct, because it is the trial *use* of, not the investigatory *collection* of . . . testimonial statements which offends that provision") (emphasis in original); Friedman, *Meaning of "Testimonial," supra* note 197, at 261 (observing that the prosecutorial "authorities do not violate the [Confrontation] Clause when they take a statement behind closed doors from a witness" because Sixth Amendment violations occur only when the "statement is *admitted at trial*") (emphasis in original).

for criminal prosecutions by finding out and documenting what witnesses know—that is, by acquiring probative evidence that will constitute hearsay if used at trial. The official acts that generate the hearsay that *can* violate the Sixth Amendment at trial may well be desirable, responsible efforts to enforce the law and bring offenders to justice.[249]

In sum, in this context deterrence is not needed to prevent actual violations of constitutional rights (or risks of violations of constitutional rights) by those who acquire hearsay evidence.[250] The confrontation right at issue can be amply protected—indeed it must be protected—by preventing the use of the evidence in court. Furthermore, any effort to deter official conduct that generates hearsay evidence would be misguided. It could discourage officials from fulfilling important investigative and prosecutorial responsibilities.

Justices and critics challenge the very legitimacy of some constitutional exclusion doctrines, contending that the bars to probative evidence of guilt have no foundations in the provisions said to support them. No member of the current Supreme Court believes that the Sixth Amendment bar to hearsay is illegitimate or that it is anything other than an inseparable part of the trial right to be confronted by witnesses.[251] Moreover, scholars and commentators do not contest

---

249. *See* Friedman, *Meaning of "Testimonial," supra* note 197, at 261 (noting that we "*expect* the police to take confidential statements" and that "often they would be derelict in their investigatory duty if they did not do so") (emphasis in original).

250. There is an argument that deterrence might accomplish some good. Judges might err in deciding whether hearsay is barred by the Sixth Amendment and might admit hearsay that violates the confrontation right. If officers do not engage in the acts that produce such hearsay, the evidence will not be available for trial use, and violations of defendants' rights at trial cannot occur. Deterrence could prevent the production of this hearsay evidence and, therefore, the unconstitutionalities occasioned by its admission at trials. The potential gains from deterrence, however, cannot justify the losses that would result if officials were discouraged from interviewing and questioning witnesses. On balance, deterrence is clearly undesirable because of the importance of having officers and prosecutors investigate offenses and thoroughly prepare for trials.

251. In fact, throughout the history of this exclusion doctrine only one Justice has challenged the propriety of suppression. Justice Harlan once endorsed Wigmore's extreme view—the view that the Sixth Amendment does not proscribe hearsay, but merely prescribes the procedure required when the rules of evidence demand that a witness give her testimony in the courtroom. *See* Dutton v. Evans, 400 U.S. 74, 94–95 (1970) (Harlan, J., concurring in the result). This was a dramatic change from a position he had taken earlier the same year—that the prosecution is forbidden from introducing hearsay to convict an accused when a declarant is available to testify. *See* California v. Green, 399 U.S. 149, 186–87 (1970) (Harlan, J., concurring). The Court has consistently rejected the Wigmore-Harlan view that the Confrontation Clause does not command the exclusion of any hearsay evidence, considering that narrow interpretation of the provision inconsistent with its background and objectives. *See* Crawford v. Washington, 541 U.S. 36, 50–51 (2004); Ohio v. Roberts, 448 U.S. 56, 63 (1980); *see also* White v. Illinois, 502 U.S. 346, 359–60 (1992)

the propriety of barring hearsay evidence or the premise that the Sixth Amendment bar is a command implicit in and a component of the accused's right to confront witnesses.[252]

Both the now-disfavored view that the Confrontation Clause regulates all hearsay evidence and the currently prevailing position that only testimonial hearsay triggers Sixth Amendment scrutiny have been the subjects of considerable criticism. Before the *Roberts* approach was narrowed by *Crawford*, both Justices and scholars challenged its breadth. In their view, the Court had mistakenly construed the Sixth Amendment's reach as coextensive with the scope of the rules of evidence—i.e., as concerned with all out-of-court assertions used at trial to prove the truth of the beliefs asserted.[253] In their view, not all hearsay was a matter of constitutional concern.

Crawford and *Davis* vindicated these critics' perspectives, holding that the Sixth Amendment's regulatory ambit was markedly narrower, encompassing—and excluding—only hearsay that is "testimonial." This new, less expansive interpretation of the Confrontation Clause right to exclusion has not

---

(Thomas, J., concurring in part and concurring in the judgment); Amar, *First Principles*, *supra* note 111, at 696 (asserting that the Court has "rightly seen that the word 'witness' must go beyond those who take the stand in the flesh," and must extend to some "out-of-court declarations").

252. There is an exception. One scholar has voiced considerable opposition to the view that the Confrontation Clause includes an exclusionary command. *See* Douglass, *Beyond Admissibility*, *supra* note 17, at 226 (contending that even if hearsay declarants are witnesses, "it does not follow that the Confrontation Clause is designed to exclude hearsay from criminal trials"); *id.* at 232 (stating that there are "sound reasons . . . to read the Confrontation Clause as a right to challenge, but not to exclude, hearsay"). Professor Douglass has argued at great length that the Court's misguided vision of the Confrontation Clause as a provision that commands the exclusion of hearsay evidence has prevented the exploration of ways in which that guarantee can ensure that hearsay from witnesses who do not testify is subjected to confrontation through other means and has diminished the value of the Sixth Amendment guarantee. *See id.* at 194 (arguing that "[m]odern confrontation-hearsay law is about everything but confrontation"); *id.* at 197 (maintaining that the "choice of an exclusionary rule . . . for protecting the confrontation right . . . preempt[s] the use of any alternative means of protecting it"); *id.* at 219 (suggesting that the "choice of exclusion as a remedy changes and limits the substance of the right"); *id.* at 220 (asserting that the Sixth Amendment "exclusionary rule has contributed to . . . shrinkage" of the confrontation right).

253. *See*, e.g., *White*, 502 U.S. at 364–65 (Thomas, J., concurring in part and concurring in the judgment); Amar, *First Principles*, *supra* note 111, at 691–92 (disputing the Court's view that all hearsay implicates the Confrontation Clause and contending that it had "wrongly conflated the word 'witness' in the Confrontation Clause with the somewhat different idea of" a hearsay declarant); Friedman, *Confrontation*, *supra* note 111, at 1015–16 (criticizing the Court's understanding of the scope of the Sixth Amendment guarantee, in particular the assumption that all hearsay declarants qualify as witnesses within the meaning of the Confrontation Clause and advocating "a narrower reading").

gone unchallenged. In *Crawford* itself, two Justices challenged the Court's restrictive reading of history, expressing a preference not to abandon the *Roberts* approach.[254] In the aftermath of the *Crawford* revolution, some scholars have also questioned its legitimacy, favoring the view that the Sixth Amendment is concerned with more than just testimonial hearsay.[255] On the other hand, some Justices have contested *Crawford*'s vision of the Confrontation Clause's scope—as developed in later opinions—as excessively *broad*, contending that it gives that provision a larger scope than is justified.[256]

In sum, although there is disagreement over its breadth, the Sixth Amendment bar to hearsay has long been, and remains, an integral part of an accused's fundamental entitlement to confront adverse witnesses. The rationale for this constitutional suppression mandate is elementary. Because the admission of hearsay would violate the confrontation guarantee, an accused has a personal trial right to exclude it. Deterrence, however, plays no part—not even an ancillary role—because the suppression mandate is rooted in the nature of the evidence and its threats to the fairness of trials, not in the means by which it is acquired.

D. THE SCOPE AND OPERATION OF THE SIXTH AMENDMENT RIGHT TO EXCLUDE HEARSAY

This final section addresses the presumptive scope of the Confrontation Clause hearsay ban and the limitations on its operation. Some issues considered in prior chapters are discussed here—for example, the kind of evidence that is excludable, whether derivative evidence is barred, the types of proceedings in which hearsay may be suppressed, and "standing" to seek exclusion. Because of the nature of and premises for the Sixth Amendment bar, the analysis of "exceptions" focuses on subjects not addressed in earlier chapters. Exceptions relevant in other settings—independent source, inevitable discovery, attenuation, good faith, and public safety—are inapposite here. Other exceptions that are uniquely pertinent to this doctrine—unavailability and a prior opportunity to cross-examine, forfeiture by wrongdoing, and dying declarations—are of

---

254. *See Crawford*, 541 U.S. at 69–72 (Rehnquist, C.J., concurring in the judgment).

255. *See, e.g.*, Davies, *Not "The Framers' Design," supra* note 230, at 351–54; 433–34; Raeder, *Remember the Ladies, supra* note 230, at 321–22; Reed, *Irretrievable Breakdown, supra* note 17, at 227. Other scholars believe that the currently prevailing understanding of the Sixth Amendment's reach is constitutionally valid. *See, e.g.*, Friedman, *Meaning of "Testimonial," supra* note 197, at 274; Latimer, *Confrontation After* Crawford, *supra* note 111, at 419.

256. *See* Davis v. Washington, 547 U.S. 813, 835–38 (2006) (Thomas, J., concurring in the judgment in part and dissenting in part); *see also* Melendez-Diaz v. Massachusetts, 557 U.S. ____, ____, 129 S.Ct. 2527, 2543–44, 2550–52 (2009) (Kennedy, J., dissenting).

central importance. The permissibility of impeachment use of hearsay evidence does merit attention here.[257]

1. The Evidence Subject to Suppression: Unconfrontable Testimonial Hearsay
The reach of Sixth Amendment suppression of hearsay—the domain the Confrontation Clause governs—is defined entirely by the nature of the evidence at issue. As already noted, this constitutional exclusion doctrine is not grounded in unconstitutional or improper official conduct. Instead, it rests on the premise that the Sixth Amendment forbids the government's use of a certain kind of evidence to convict criminal defendants: unconfrontable testimonial hearsay.[258]

a. The Type of Evidence Barred: An Initial Constraint on Exclusion The first limitation on the Sixth Amendment's purview is its restriction to *hearsay*. Generally, hearsay is defined as an out-of-court statement that is offered to prove the truth of the matter asserted in that statement.[259] For purposes of this definition, a statement is made "out-of-court" when it is not made in the current courtroom proceeding. Consequently, if an individual testifies at a murder trial that "the person who fired the rifle was white and had curly red hair," this testimony is not hearsay. However, if the individual states, "My husband told me that the person who fired the rifle was white and had curly red hair," the husband's statement was not made at the trial and is hearsay *if* offered to prove that the shooter did fit that description. In addition, a transcript of the husband's testimony from a prior trial of the same or a different case that contains this same assertion, and is used for the same purpose, is hearsay because the husband did not testify live, at the current trial.

Oral or written assertions or nonverbal conduct can constitute "statements." A person's verbal declaration, "I saw Jenny shake her baby" or an e-mail containing the same statement can be hearsay. If the person is asked, "Who shook the baby?" and she points at Jenny, or if she is asked if Jenny shook the baby and she nods her head, these nonverbal expressions can also be hearsay. There has been some debate in evidence law about whether nonassertive conduct that reflects a belief can be hearsay when offered to prove that the belief is true. For example,

---

257. *See* Friedman, *Meaning of "Testimonial," supra* note 197, at 273 (stating that *Crawford*'s reform of Confrontation Clause hearsay law "will provide many interesting and perplexing issues over the next several years"); Michael J. Polelle, *The Death of Dying Declarations in a Post-*Crawford *World*, 71 Mo. L. Rev. 285, 285 (2006) [hereinafter Polelle, *Death of Dying Declarations*] (asserting that because *Crawford* "fundamentally altered [the] interpretation of the Confrontation Clause . . . the full reach of [its] doctrinal logic will take decades to unravel").

258. As will be seen, however, whether evidence qualifies as testimonial hearsay can depend on its source, and the involvement of government officials in generating the evidence is a relevant, though not necessary, criterion.

259. *See* Fed. R. Evid. 801(c); Graham C. Lilly, An Introduction to the Law of Evidence § 6.1 (3d ed. 1996).

suppose that a bar patron wrestles keys away from his stumbling friend while exclaiming, "Do not drive!" The patron did not assert that the friend was intoxicated, but his nonverbal act and his verbal command might well evince that belief. A prosecutor might offer a witness's description of the incident to prove that the friend was drunk when he drove his car immediately thereafter. Modern evidence law favors the view that such nonassertive conduct—verbal or nonverbal—is not hearsay even when offered to prove a belief of the actor that might logically be inferred.[260] For Confrontation Clause purposes, the Supreme Court is likely to adopt this position, holding that verbal or nonverbal conduct cannot qualify as hearsay unless the declarant *intended to assert* a belief and it is offered to prove the truth of that belief.[261]

Finally, no out-of-court assertion can be hearsay unless it is introduced into evidence for a specific purpose—to prove the truth of what it asserts. While the most common use of a statement, by far, is to prove the truth of what a declarant asserted, statements are sometimes offered for other relevant, probative purposes. For example, in a murder trial, a defendant who stabbed a deceased victim might claim that he did not kill the victim because the victim had already died before he stabbed her. Suppose that the prosecution calls a witness to testify that she heard the victim mumble, "You shot me" immediately before the accused stabbed her. If the victim's assertion is offered to prove that the accused shot the victim, it is hearsay. However, if the prosecutor offers the victim's statement to prove she was alive at the time (because dead people do not speak), and, therefore, that the accused did kill her by stabbing her, it is not hearsay. The statement has been offered for a nonhearsay purpose, not to prove the truth of the victim's assertion.

A statement might be offered as "legally operative conduct," another nonhearsay purpose. Suppose an accused is charged with automobile theft. The allegation is that he took a vehicle that he had allegedly sold to the supposed victim of the theft. The accused claims that he is not a thief because he did not sell the vehicle before taking it. The prosecutor then offers a videotape in which the accused states, "I will sell you my car for $1000," and the alleged victim replies, "I accept your offer." If contract law provides that a sale occurs and ownership is transferred whenever such words are spoken, and the prosecutor offers the videotaped statements to prove that the words that effect a sale were spoken—not

---

260. *See* Fed. R. Evid. 801(a) advisory committee's note; *see also* United States v. Zenni, 492 F.Supp. 464, 467–69 (D.C. Ky. 1980).

261. Under the Federal Rules of Evidence, "nothing is an assertion unless intended to be one." Fed. R. Evid. 801(a) advisory committee's note. Only assertions can be statements and only statements can be hearsay. *See* Fed. R. Evid. 801(a), (c). Thus, any conduct, verbal or nonverbal, that is not intended as an assertion cannot qualify as hearsay.

to prove the truth of any assertions in those statements—the statements are not hearsay.[262]

The Confrontation Clause does not impede the government's use of out-of-court statements for nonhearsay purposes. The Sixth Amendment excludes only hearsay evidence and does not regulate the admission of out-of-court assertions for purposes other than proving the truth of what they assert.[263] In essence, when an out-of-court statement is admitted for purposes other than proving the truth of what it asserts, the individual who made the statement is not a "witness." Consequently, the accused has no entitlement to confront him and no right to exclude his statement.

The justification for limiting this constitutional exclusion doctrine to hearsay is rooted not only in the text of the Sixth Amendment (i.e., the limiting term "witnesses") but in the purposes and objectives of the confrontation entitlement. An assertion of some fact might be unreliable and might jeopardize the accuracy of a verdict because the declarant perceived the matter inaccurately, had a faulty memory, was dishonest, or expressed what she knew in ambiguous or misleading language. The Constitution guarantees confrontation to afford the accused

---

262. Other nonhearsay purposes of statements include proving the state of mind of the declarant or proving the state of mind of someone who heard the statement. Whenever statements are used to prove something other than the truth of an assertion they contain, they do not constitute hearsay evidence. When statements are admitted for a nonhearsay purpose, but it is possible that a jury will misuse them for the forbidden hearsay purpose, the party against whom they are admitted is entitled to a limiting instruction in which the judge tells the jury how they may and may not use the statements.

263. In *Tennessee v. Street*, 471 U.S. 409 (1985), the prosecution was allowed to introduce a codefendant's confession not to prove that incriminating assertions he made about the defendant were true, but only to rebut the defendant's claim that his own confession had been coerced. According to the Supreme Court, this nonhearsay use "raise[d] no Confrontation Clause concerns." *Id.* at 414. The Court has reaffirmed the principle of *Street* on more than one occasion. *See* Crawford v. Washington, 541 U.S. 36, 60 n.9 (2004); United States v. Inadi, 475 U.S. 387, 398 n.11 (1986).

There was a risk in *Street* that the jury might misuse the evidence for its constitutionally forbidden hearsay purpose—that is, to prove that the accused was guilty because assertions the codefendant made in his confession were true. The Court was satisfied that the trial judge's instructions regarding the limited purpose for which the confession had been admitted were an adequate safeguard against any threat to the accused's Sixth Amendment right. *See Street*, 471 U.S. at 414–15, 417. The Court also stressed that the nonhearsay use of the confession had important probative value for the government. *See id.* at 415. In a different situation, where statements have powerful incriminating force and are not as valuable to the prosecution, an accused might have a valid claim that limiting instructions are inadequate and that exclusion of the evidence is the only constitutionally acceptable response. *See* Bruton v. United States, 391 U.S. 123, 135–37 (1968) (holding that limiting instructions could not adequately protect the accused against jury use of a codefendant's confession in a way that would violate his Sixth Amendment right to confront witnesses).

safeguards against these sources of unreliability and thereby to decrease the chances of erroneous conviction. Witnesses must make accusations under oath, in the presence of the defendant and the fact finder, and subject to cross-examination by the defense.

These procedural mechanisms are necessary only when the danger of evidentiary unreliability is sufficiently high, and the danger is sufficiently high only when a statement is relied upon to prove what it asserts. Only then is there a genuine need for concern about potential perceptual, memory, honesty, and expressive deficiencies. When there is sufficient danger of untrustworthiness and the Sixth Amendment's protections are not available—because the person did not make the inculpatory assertion in the courtroom—the fair trial objectives of the Confrontation Clause are jeopardized. For these reasons, hearsay evidence is the sole target of constitutional concern and the only kind of evidence that is barred.

The presumptive reach of the Sixth Amendment bar is restricted even further. *Only* hearsay is barred, but not *all* hearsay is subject to exclusion. According to the currently prevailing doctrine, the Confrontation Clause excludes only *testimonial* hearsay and poses no impediment to the prosecution's use of *nontestimonial* hearsay.[264] Nontestimonial hearsay, which was subject to suppression under the *Roberts* regime, is no longer excludable. The drastic difference in the treatment of testimonial and nontestimonial hearsay makes the distinction between these categories critical.[265] Although the Supreme Court has deliberately refused to prescribe a clear and comprehensive standard for making the distinction, it has offered significant guidance.[266]

---

264. *See* Davis v. Washington, 547 U.S. 813, 821, 824 (2006).

265. *See* Davies, *Not "The Framers' Design," supra* note 230, at 465 (stating that it is "plain that the testimonial/nontestimonial hearsay distinction is now a central feature of the law of the Confrontation Clause" and that it "is highly improbable that the Court will revisit" the legitimacy of this important dichotomy); Friedman, *Meaning of "Testimonial," supra* note 197, at 241 (asserting that under the presently controlling approach "[a] great deal . . . rides on the meaning of the word 'testimonial'"); *see also* Friedman, *Confrontation, supra* note 111, at 1025 (observing that the issue of what "out-of-court statements should be deemed to be 'testimony'"—that is, "what declarants of out-of-court statements should be deemed to be 'witnesses'" for Confrontation Clause purposes—is "difficult").

266. *Crawford v. Washington* introduced the critical distinction between testimonial and nontestimonial hearsay. The dichotomy had not appeared in prior decisions and has not been a part of the law of evidence. Because a "comprehensive definition of 'testimonial'" hearsay was unnecessary to resolve the *Crawford* case, the Court deliberately left "any effort" to furnish such a definition "for another day." *Crawford*, 541 U.S. at 68. The Court probably feared that any comprehensive definition it adopted could prove inadequate as unanticipated questions arose in future cases. While it might have been preferable to prescribe a clear, controlling standard to guide trial and appellate courts, any such effort was likely to prove deficient. *Crawford* did identify the core of the concept and specified certain types of hearsay that unquestionably qualify as testimonial. *See infra* text

According to the Court, "'[t]estimony' . . . is typically '[a] solemn declaration or affirmation made *for the purpose of establishing or proving some fact*.'"[267] Consequently, "[a]n accuser who makes a *formal statement to government officers* bears testimony in a sense that a person who makes a casual remark to an acquaintance does not."[268] General "formulations of [the] core class of 'testimonial' statements . . . all share a common nucleus."[269] These formulations include: "'ex parte in-court testimony or its functional equivalent—that is, material such as affidavits, custodial examinations, prior testimony . . . or similar pretrial statements that declarants would reasonably expect to be used prosecutorially'"; "'extrajudicial statements . . . contained in formalized testimonial materials, such as affidavits, depositions, prior testimony, or confessions'"; and "'statements that were made under circumstances which would lead an objective witness reasonably to believe that the statement would be available for use at a later trial.'"[270]

Two kinds of hearsay that unquestionably qualify as testimonial under any appropriate definition are "prior testimony" given in a formal courtroom proceeding—"at a preliminary hearing, before a grand jury, or at a former trial"—and some statements made in response "to police interrogations."[271] Statements in "affidavits" that have been prepared for use as evidence at trial also fall squarely

---

accompanying notes 271–72. Moreover, it indicated that the constitutional text and the historical purposes of the confrontation right should guide efforts to determine whether hearsay falls within that category. In subsequent opinions, the Court has persisted in its refusal to furnish a definition, preferring to answer narrow questions and provide incremental insights into the meaning of "testimonial." *See Davis*, 547 U.S. at 822; *see also* Melendez-Diaz v. Massachusetts, 557 U.S. ____, ____, 129 S.Ct. 2527, 2532, 2542 (2009) (finding that affidavits fell within the "'core class of testimonial statements'" described in *Crawford* and simply applying *Crawford*'s holding).

267. *Crawford*, 541 U.S. at 51 (emphasis added).

268. *Id.* (emphasis added). At one point, the Court indicated that one relevant consideration was the "[i]nvolvement of government officers in the production of [the hearsay statements] with an eye toward trial," but it did not decide whether such involvement is essential. *See id.* at 56 n.7. The two types of testimonial hearsay identified by the *Crawford* Court—prior courtroom testimony and responses to law enforcement interrogation—do share this common feature.

269. *Id.* at 51–52.

270. *Id.* While the *Crawford* Court implied that these general formulations were useful, it did not adopt or endorse any of them.

271. *Id.* at 68; *see also id.* at 52. *Crawford* intimated that business records and co-conspirator statements, two hearsay exceptions under the rules of evidence, would *not* qualify as testimonial hearsay. Later, the Court decided that a business record *could* qualify if it was prepared for purposes of proving a fact at trial. *See Melendez-Diaz*, 557 U.S. at ____, 129 S.Ct. at 2539–40.

within the testimonial hearsay category.[272] These varieties of hearsay qualify because they "are the modern practices with closest kinship to the abuses at which the Confrontation Clause was directed"—criminal prosecutions based on potentially unreliable ex parte accounts of unchallengeable witnesses.[273] Statements need not be "sworn"—made under oath—in order to be testimonial.[274] Thus, a police officer's notes or oral report of what an interrogated individual told him can be testimonial even though the individual did not answer the officer's questions while sworn to tell the truth.[275]

Although initially it appeared that all responses to official interrogation might be deemed testimonial,[276] post-*Crawford* refinements established that statements responding to official "interrogation" are not always testimonial. Responses "are testimonial when the circumstances objectively indicate that there is no . . . ongoing emergency, and that the primary purpose of the interrogation is to establish or prove past events potentially relevant to later criminal prosecution."[277] On the other hand, when hearsay "[s]tatements are . . . made in the course of police interrogation under circumstances objectively indicating that the primary purpose of the interrogation is to enable police assistance to meet an ongoing

---

272. *See Melendez-Diaz*, 557 U.S. at ____, 129 S.Ct. at 2532; *see also Crawford* at 51–52, 52–53 n.3 (referring to affidavits). In *Melendez-Diaz*, the Court ruled that "affidavits" prepared by government analysts that documented the nature and quantity of a contraband substance were testimonial hearsay. *See Melendez-Diaz*, 557 U.S. at ____, 129 S.Ct. at 2532.

273. *Crawford*, 541 U.S. at 68; *see also id.* at 51. For similar reasons, "depositions" of prospective witnesses taken by the government for use as evidence at trial surely constitute testimonial hearsay. *See id.* at 51–52; *see also* Davis v. Washington, 547 U.S. 813, 826 (2006) (observing that sworn "formal depositions" were barred by the "exclusionary rule" recognized in "English cases that were the progenitors of the Confrontation Clause").

274. *Crawford*, 541 U.S. at 52–53 n.3; *see also Davis*, 547 U.S. at 826 (deeming it not "conceivable" that Confrontation Clause protections "can readily be evaded by having a note-taking policeman *recite* the unsworn hearsay testimony of the declarant, instead of having the declarant sign a [sworn, formal] deposition") (emphasis in original).

275. *Davis*, 547 U.S. at 826.

276. *See Crawford*, 541 U.S. at 52 (asserting that "[s]tatements taken by police officers in the course of interrogations are . . . testimonial under even a narrow standard"); *id.* at 68 (stating that "the term" testimonial "applies at a minimum . . . to police interrogations"); *but see id.* at 53 n.4 (opining that responses to "'interrogation'" that took the form of "structured police questioning" were testimonial).

277. *Davis*, 547 U.S. at 822; *see also id.* at 826, 829–30. In *Crawford*, the Court observed that in this context, it "use[d] the term 'interrogation' in its colloquial, rather than any technical legal, sense" and that there were "various definitions" of that term. *Crawford*, 541 U.S. at 53 n.4. The intent was to reject the notion that the definition of interrogation under *Miranda* governs Sixth Amendment exclusion determinations. The *Miranda* doctrine definition is inappropriate because it is designed to identify situations involving official compulsion to speak, and compulsion is irrelevant to Confrontation Clause analysis.

emergency," they are "nontestimonial."[278] Interrogation by any "law enforcement personnel"—i.e., by regular police officers or any others acting as "agents of law enforcement"—can produce testimonial statements.[279] Whether "statements made to someone other than law enforcement personnel" can qualify as testimonial is uncertain.[280]

Interrogation is not essential for statements made to law enforcement officers and their agents to qualify as testimonial. "[S]tatements made in the absence of any interrogation are [not] necessarily nontestimonial."[281] In fact, "volunteered testimony or answers to open-ended questions" posed by officials can be testimonial

278. *Davis*, 547 U.S. at 822; *see also id.* at 827. One issue is whether a "subjective" or an "objective" approach is preferable for determining whether hearsay is testimonial. Should the classification of hearsay depend upon the purpose or the understanding of the actual individuals involved, or upon the purpose or understanding of "reasonable" persons in the particular situation? *See* Friedman, *Meaning of "Testimonial," supra* note 197, at 243, 253–54 (highlighting the question of whether a standard should be "subjective" or "objective," observing that there probably is not "very much difference" between these alternatives, and describing the advantages of each). The Court's objective standard for judging whether responses to interrogation are testimonial requires an assessment of the purpose of an interrogation from the viewpoint of reasonable law enforcement officers.

279. *See Davis*, 547 U.S. at 823 n.2. The Court has indicated that operators who respond to 911 calls "may . . . be agents of law enforcement" when they interrogate callers. *Id.* If so, 911 callers' responses are unquestionably testimonial when the primary purpose of an operator's inquiries "is to establish or prove past events potentially relevant to later criminal prosecution." *Id.* at 822.

280. *Id.* at 823 n.2; *see Crawford*, 541 U.S. at 56 n.7; *see also* Friedman, *Meaning of "Testimonial," supra* note 197, at 243, 255, 259–60 (discussing whether only statements made to government agents can be testimonial, asserting that "government involvement in the production of the statement is . . . [not] necessary to make the statement testimonial," and concluding "there is no requirement that the statement be made to [a government] agent"). *But see* Latimer, *Confrontation After* Crawford, *supra* note 111, at 364–70 (stating that the courts implementing *Crawford* generally have found statements nontestimonial when made to persons not connected to law enforcement).

The Court's conclusion in *Davis* that responses to law enforcement interrogations for the purpose of addressing emergency situations are not testimonial makes it clear that government involvement in the production of statements will not always make those statements testimonial hearsay. *See* Friedman, *Meaning of "Testimonial," supra* note 197, at 255 (contending that "government involvement in the production of the statement is [not] sufficient . . . to make the statement testimonial"); Friedman, *Confrontation, supra* note 111, at 1039–40 n.122 (asserting that "some statements procured by governmental agents are not testimonial" and citing a statement by a co-conspirator to an undercover agent as an example).

281. *Davis*, 547 U.S. at 822 n.1; *see* Friedman, *Meaning of "Testimonial," supra* note 197, at 263, 265 (calling an "interrogation requirement . . . entirely mistaken" and stating that "common sense tells us that there is no such requirement" for statements to be testimonial).

for Sixth Amendment purposes.[282] Moreover, even when government officials interrogate a witness, whether a response is testimonial depends upon an evaluation of "the declarant's statements, not the interrogator's questions."[283]

Although some amount of "formality is . . . essential to testimonial utterance,"[284] the kind and amount of formality necessary to satisfy this constitutional requisite are entirely uncertain. Whatever it entails, the "formality" demand would seem to be relatively modest, and not a significant hurdle. The kind of formality that characterized the "precise forms" of testimonial statements "against which" the Confrontation Clause "was originally directed" is not necessary.[285] Moreover,

---

282. *Davis*, 547 U.S. at 822–23 n.1; *see* Melendez-Diaz v. Massachusetts, 557 U.S. ____, ____, 129 S.Ct. 2527, 2535 (2009); Friedman, *Meaning of "Testimonial," supra* note 197, at 243.

283. *Davis*, 547 U.S. at 823 n.1. In formulating a general standard for identifying testimonial hearsay, another question is whose perspective should matter—i.e., whether the perspective of the declarant or the perspective of governmental authorities should be controlling. *See* Friedman, *Meaning of "Testimonial," supra* note 197, at 243, 255 (raising the issue and contending that "it is the perspective of the declarant—the witness—that matters"). The doctrine that has emerged since *Crawford* has not clearly resolved this issue. On the one hand, the standards announced in *Davis* refer to the "primary purpose of the interrogation," which would seem to endorse a law enforcement perspective. *Davis*, 547 U.S. at 822. On the other hand, the Court pointedly announced that whether or not interrogation has produced a statement, the determination of its testimonial character requires evaluation of "*the declarant's* statement, *not the interrogator's* questions." *Id.* at 823 n.1 (emphasis added). Moreover, in a subsequent opinion, the Court indicated that an important consideration was that the "*sole purpose*" of a statement was to provide evidence and deemed it significant that a statement was "'made under circumstances which would lead *an objective witness* reasonably to believe that the statement would be available for use at a later trial.'" *Melendez-Diaz*, 557 U.S. at ____, 129 S.Ct. at 2532 (emphasis added) (quoting Crawford v. Washington, 541 U.S. 36, 52 (2004)). These observations strongly suggest that the declarant's perspective is important. Suffice it to say that this unresolved issue requires further attention.

284. *Davis*, 547 U.S. at 831 n.5.

285. *Id.* Justice Thomas argued that the Court's view of testimonial hearsay is too expansive and that it should be restricted to statements that resemble the "formalized testimonial materials" that gave rise to a confrontation entitlement. *Id.* at 837 (Thomas, J., concurring in the judgment in part and dissenting in part). The majority resisted the proposal to limit the scope of Confrontation Clause protection to hearsay statements that possess the same "high degree of formality" that "characterized" the abusive, magistrate-taken "depositions" that were the target of that provision. *Id.* at 831 n.5. Justice Scalia observed that in our modern society when police officers interrogate witnesses they perform the same "investigative and testimonial functions" that magistrates used to perform by taking depositions. *Id.* According to the Court, "[r]estricting" the Sixth Amendment entitlement "to the precise forms against which it was originally directed" would be "a recipe for its extinction." *Id.*

statements made to police officers are sufficiently formal simply because "lies to . . . officers are criminal offenses."[286]

To determine whether hearsay statements are testimonial and, therefore, subject to Sixth Amendment exclusion, the general question is whether the declarant was "acting as a *witness*."[287] Statements are testimonial if they are a "substitute for live testimony, because they do precisely *what a witness does* on direct examination" at trial.[288] A hearsay statement is undoubtedly testimonial if its "*sole purpose*" is to provide evidence in a criminal prosecution.[289] Such a purpose, however, is not required. A statement will apparently qualify as testimonial whenever it is "'made under circumstances which would lead an objective witness reasonably to believe that the statement would be available for use at a later trial.'"[290]

In sum, the *Crawford* revolution restricted Sixth Amendment exclusion to testimonial hearsay. The Court has found it unnecessary and unwise to venture a comprehensive definition of that term. Consequently, there is no controlling doctrinal standard that readily separates the testimonial hearsay that is subject to suppression from the nontestimonial hearsay that escapes Confrontation Clause regulation. The Court has classified some varieties of hearsay statement as clearly

---

286. *Id.*

287. *Id.* at 828 (emphasis in original).

288. *Id.* at 830 (emphasis in original); *see also Melendez-Diaz*, 557 U.S. at ____, 129 S.Ct. at 2532. The *Davis* Court suggested that witnesses "deliberately recount[], in response to questioning, how potentially criminal past events . . . progressed." *Davis*, 547 U.S. at 830. Subsequently, the Court made it clear that a hearsay statement need not give an account of "'events observed in the past'" in order to qualify as testimonial, and that a statement reporting a declarant's "'near-contemporaneous observations'" can constitute testimonial hearsay. *See Melendez-Diaz*, 557 U.S. at ____, 129 S.Ct. at 2535.

Professor Richard Friedman has argued that "starting at a core of statements that includes trial testimony and then working outwards . . . is a bad approach" to the definitional task and that an approach "that depends on whether the statement has similar characteristics to trial testimony . . . lacks logic and historical foundation." *See* Friedman, *Meaning of "Testimonial," supra* note 197, at 243, 248.

289. *Melendez-Diaz*, 557 U.S. at ____, 129 S.Ct. at 2532 (emphasis in original).

290. *Id.* at 2532 (quoting Crawford v. Washington, 541 U.S. 36, 52 (2004)). In *Melendez-Diaz*, a slim five-Justice majority rejected a number of limiting criteria that would have narrowed the definition of testimonial hearsay and the scope of the Sixth Amendment's evidentiary bar. According to the Court, a declarant need not be an "'accusatory'" witness; it is sufficient if her hearsay statement is "helpful to the prosecution" in some way. *Id.* at ____, 129 S.Ct. at 2533–34. A declarant need not be a "'conventional'" witness of the kind that was historically objectionable and gave rise to a right of confrontation. *Id.* at ____, 129 S.Ct. at 2534–35. In addition, there is no need for hearsay statements to "recount[] historical events"; statements that document the "'resul[t] of neutral, scientific testing'" can constitute testimonial hearsay. *Id.* at ____, 129 S.Ct. at 2536. Finally, official records or business records "generally . . . are not testimonial," but they can be testimonial, and thus subject to exclusion, if they are "created for . . . the purpose of establishing or proving some fact at trial." *Id.* at ____, 129 S.Ct. at 2539–40.

testimonial and has offered some general and some specific insights into the considerations that are and are not relevant, but doctrinal ambiguities and uncertainties remain.

The roots of the "testimonial" hearsay restriction are clearly found in the text and history of the Sixth Amendment. The Supreme Court has intimated that the Framers' particular concern with and focus upon testimonial hearsay are logically defensible,[291] but has not elaborated upon the reasons that the Framers of the Sixth Amendment would have so confined the reach of the Confrontation Clause. While it is clear that judicial determinations of reliability are an inappropriate method of implementing the Sixth Amendment right,[292] it is also clear that the main objective of the confrontation guarantee is to ensure reliable evidence and accurate verdicts.[293] If the Framers of the Bill of Rights meant to provide a right to confront *only* those who make testimonial hearsay statements,[294] it must be because when a declarant is "acting as a witness" or "doing what a witness does"—that is, recounting facts relevant to proving a criminal offense with a purpose of providing evidence or under circumstances where it is reasonable to believe that statements will be available for use in a criminal prosecution—there are special risks of unreliability and, therefore, heightened needs for the confrontation safeguards that ensure fair criminal trials.

Testimonial hearsay might enable officials to discover other kinds of inculpatory evidence relevant to the same offense as the hearsay, to a related offense, or to an entirely distinct offense. A codefendant's confession might yield tangible evidence that an accused is guilty—a murder weapon with the defendant's fingerprints or clothing stained with the blood of a victim. An alleged victim of domestic violence might report the location of her abuser's narcotics or might direct investigators to his child pornography collection. The question is whether the Sixth Amendment right to exclusion, like some constitutional suppression mandates, includes a presumptive bar to such derivative evidence.

The answer is clear: The Sixth Amendment does not require the exclusion of derivative evidence. The Confrontation Clause grants a right to be confronted with adverse witnesses. Testimonial hearsay is the only type of evidence that the Sixth Amendment exclusion doctrine bars because only testimonial hearsay jeopardizes the confrontation entitlement. Other kinds of evidence, whether or

---

291. *See* Crawford v. Washington, 541 U.S. 36, 56 n.7 (2004) (referring to problems of prosecutorial abuse involved when the government is involved in generating witness accounts).

292. *See id.* at 62.

293. *See id.* at 61.

294. *See* Davies, *Not "The Framers' Design," supra* note 230, at 352–54, 372–73, 433–34, 465 (criticizing the Court's conclusion that history supports a restriction of the Sixth Amendment bar to testimonial hearsay).

not it is the product of testimonial hearsay, does not threaten the objectives of the Sixth Amendment, and, therefore, is not subject to its exclusion mandate.[295]

In sum, testimonial hearsay is presumptively barred whether or not it is acquired as a result of other testimonial hearsay. No other kind of evidence is excludable no matter what its relationship to testimonial hearsay. Neither the right to confront witnesses nor a need to deter official misconduct supports a derivative evidence rule.

b. Testifying Hearsay Declarants: A Second Restriction on the Scope of Exclusion Long before the current doctrine appeared, the Supreme Court held that hearsay evidence that would otherwise be subject to exclusion is admissible if the declarant testifies "as a witness" at the trial and is "subject to full and effective cross-examination" by the accused.[296] That principle remains valid today. "[W]hen the declarant appears for cross-examination at trial, the Confrontation Clause places no constraints at all on the use of his prior testimonial [hearsay] statements . . . The Clause does not bar admission of a statement so long as the declarant is present at trial to defend or explain it."[297] Put simply, the Sixth Amendment excludes only testimonial hearsay from a declarant who is "unconfrontable" at trial.

The reasoning beneath this limitation on the breadth of the suppression doctrine is clear. When a declarant is present and the accused has an opportunity to cross-examine her concerning her hearsay statement, confrontation is possible. In that situation, admission of the hearsay does not deprive an accused of his Sixth Amendment entitlement or undermine its objectives. The source of the hearsay testimony—the declarant-witness—must face the accused, is under oath, can be questioned about the hearsay, and is subject to observation by the jurors.[298]

---

295. The only premise that could justify the suppression of such derivative evidence is the need to deter unconstitutional or improper conduct. As discussed earlier, deterrence is not a basis for Confrontation Clause suppression because there is no out-of-court conduct to discourage. *See supra* text accompanying notes 247–50.

296. *See* California v. Green, 399 U.S. 149, 158 (1970). This principle appeared prior to the arrival of the first general framework—the *Ohio v. Roberts* reliability standards. During the *Roberts* era, the Court confirmed its validity. *See* United States v. Owens, 484 U.S. 554, 560 (1988).

297. *Crawford*, 541 U.S. at 60 n.9. The rules of evidence are more restrictive than the Sixth Amendment. In general, the fact that a declarant takes the witness stand at trial and is subject to cross-examination does not furnish a basis for admission of her hearsay. The witness herself cannot testify to her hearsay statement unless there it falls within an exception to the general ban on hearsay.

298. *See Owens*, 484 U.S. at 560 (stating that "[i]n that situation . . . the traditional protections of the oath, cross-examination, and opportunity for the jury to observe the witness's demeanor satisfy the constitutional requirements"); *Green*, 399 U.S. at 158–60

An opportunity to confront a testifying hearsay declarant, however, does not afford the identical protections available when an accused confronts a testifying witness about statements made on the witness stand.[299] At the time the declarant made the hearsay statement, she need not have been under oath or subject to cross-examination by the accused, and she was definitely not under the observing eyes of the jurors who will render the verdict.[300] Nonetheless, the safeguards that are available are thought adequate to satisfy the objectives of confrontation. Although the hearsay "statement may have been made under circumstances subject to none of the [constitutionally guaranteed] protections[,] . . . if the declarant is present and testifying at trial, the out-of-court statement for all practical purposes *regains* most of the lost protections."[301] The declarant-witness is now under oath, and now "must . . . assume a position as to the truth value of his prior statement, thus giving the jury a chance to observe and evaluate his demeanor."[302] In addition, the "belated cross-examination can . . . serve as a constitutionally adequate substitute for [the contemporaneous] cross-examination" that may not have been possible.[303]

To avoid the presumptive bar to testimonial hearsay, the prosecution must satisfy two requirements. First, the declarant must be present and testifying as a witness at trial—which means that the government must call her to the witness stand. The fact that the witness is available and could be called by the defense does not prevent exclusion. Government officials have the burden of complying

(citing oath, cross-examination, and jury observation of a testifying declarant as the bases for not barring hearsay).

299. *Green*, 399 U.S. at 158–60 (recognizing that the protections are diminished to some extent); Richard D. Friedman, *Prior Statements of a Witness: A Nettlesome Corner of the Hearsay Thicket*, 1995 SUP. CT. REV. 277, 289–92 (1995) [hereinafter Friedman, *Prior Statements*] (pointing out that "the inability of the jury to observe the [declarant's] demeanor" at the time of the statement, the lack of an oath at the time, and "most important" the lack of an opportunity for contemporaneous cross-examination by the accused can raise "serious concerns," and suggesting that, at least in some situations, the opportunity for cross-examination is "significantly hinder[ed]").

300. If the hearsay is former testimony given in a courtroom proceeding, the declarant will have been under oath and may have been subject to cross-examination by the accused.

301. *Green*, 399 U.S. at 158 (emphasis added).

302. *Id.* at 160.

303. *Id.* at 159. *But see* Friedman, *Prior Statements*, *supra* note 299, at 293–94, 321 (discussing the Court's decisions in *Green* and *Owens* and concluding that the Court's "analysis is misguided" and that it "should recognize that the mere fact that the declarant of a prior statement testifies at trial does not necessarily imply that the party opponent has had an adequate opportunity to cross-examine").

with the Sixth Amendment—that is, of assuring that the accused is afforded the right to confront a witness.[304]

A declarant's presence on the witness stand alone is not enough. The accused must also have "'"an *opportunity* for effective cross-examination"'" of the declarant.[305] An accused has no entitlement to "'"cross-examination that is effective in whatever way, and to whatever extent, [he] might wish."'"[306] The Confrontation Clause extends only "an adequate opportunity to cross-examine adverse witnesses."[307] The opportunity to cross-examine any witness, including a hearsay declarant, is not adequate if cross-examination is improperly restricted,[308] or if a declarant on the witness stand refuses to testify or asserts a privilege not to testify.[309] A memory loss (or a claimed memory loss) *may* preclude an adequate opportunity to cross-examine a declarant. If the declarant-witness cannot remember the underlying events or facts, but does remember making the hearsay statement about those events or facts, the accused's opportunity for cross-examination is constitutionally adequate.[310] However, if the witness has (or claims) a more profound loss of memory—for example, if she asserts that she cannot recall anything about the underlying events or facts or about the making of a prior

---

304. *See* Melendez-Diaz v. Massachusetts, 557 U.S. ____, ____, 129 S.Ct. 2527, 2540 (2009).

305. United States v. Owens, 484 U.S. 554, 559 (1988) (emphasis in original) (quoting Kentucky v. Stincer, 482 U.S. 730, 739 (1987) (quoting Delaware v. Fensterer, 474 U.S. 15, 20 (1985))).

306. *Id.*; *see also id.* at 560 ("successful cross-examination is not the constitutional guarantee"). In *California v. Green*, the Court had declared that hearsay could be admitted if the declarant was "subject to full and *effective* cross–examination," *Green*, 399 U.S. at 158 (emphasis added), or if "the defendant [was] assured of full and *effective* cross-examination at the time of trial." *Id.* at 159 (emphasis added). *Owens*, however, disavowed any entitlement to cross-examination that actually was "effective" or "successful."

307. *Owens*, 484 U.S. at 557.

308. *See id.* at 561–62 (indicating that trial court "limitations on the scope of examination" can "undermine" the adequacy of the accused's opportunity to cross-examine a witness); Davis v. Alaska, 415 U.S. 308, 315–18 (1974); Chambers v. Mississippi, 410 U.S. 284, 295–98 (1973); *see also* Latimer, *Confrontation After* Crawford, *supra* note 111, at 343 (observing that court restrictions on the scope of cross-examination can prevent a "meaningful opportunity to confront the witness").

309. *See Owens*, 484 U.S. at 561–62 (recognizing that for "meaningful cross-examination" to be possible a witness must "respond[] willingly to questions" and that "assertions of privilege" may preclude "meaningful cross-examination"); *Green*, 399 U.S. at 167–68 (indicating that a claim of privilege or "a simpl[e] refus[al] to answer" can render a witness unavailable at trial); Latimer, *Confrontation After* Crawford, *supra* note 111, at 343 (stating that a declarant who "refuses to answer questions propounded by the accused—or successfully asserts a privilege—would not be available for confrontation purposes").

310. *See Owens*, 484 U.S. at 559.

statement about those events or facts—an accused's opportunity for cross-examination might not be adequate.[311]

Whether there are other factors that might hinder effective cross-examination so much that the opportunity for confrontation would be inadequate, and the hearsay subject to exclusion, is uncertain. The decisive question is whether the accused has an adequate chance at trial to "afford the trier of fact a satisfactory basis for evaluating the truth of the [hearsay] statement."[312] If so, the hearsay is not subject to Sixth Amendment suppression. If not, the hearsay should be barred.

2. Proceedings in Which the Confrontation Clause Bars Hearsay

It is hardly surprising that every Supreme Court opinion exploring the relationship between the Confrontation Clause and hearsay has involved the prosecution's use of hearsay to prove an accused's guilt at *trial*. The Sixth Amendment grants a confrontation entitlement in "all criminal prosecutions," and the Court has acknowledged that the right to be confronted with adverse witnesses "is basically a trial right."[313] Testimonial hearsay is clearly barred from the trial phase of criminal proceedings. The question is whether the Sixth Amendment commands suppression from any other phase of the criminal process or in any civil proceedings.

There is no reason to believe that the trial right to confront witnesses extends to a grand jury hearing or to any other *pretrial* stage of the criminal process.[314] The use of testimonial hearsay before trial does not undermine the substantive or procedural fairness of the trial. There is no textual or historical basis for excluding evidence from any pretrial proceeding, and the purposes of the Sixth Amendment right do not support exclusion.

---

311. In both *Owens* and *Green*, the declarant-witnesses did not suffer total memory losses. Some of the reasoning in *Owens* could support a contention that even a total loss of memory does not render the opportunity for cross-examination inadequate. Still, the Court did not address that situation in *Owens* and has never ruled that a witness with no recollection whatsoever can satisfy the Confrontation Clause.

312. *Green*, 399 U.S. at 161.

313. *See* Barber v. Page, 390 U.S. 719, 725 (1968); *see also* Dutton v. Evans, 400 U.S. 74, 89 (1970) (plurality opinion) (stating that "the mission of the Confrontation Clause is to advance . . . the accuracy of the truth-determining process in criminal trials"); Pointer v. Texas, 380 U.S. 400, 404 (1965) (declaring that the Framers believed "that confrontation was a fundamental right essential to a fair trial in a criminal prosecution").

314. The Supreme Court has not extended any constitutional exclusion doctrine to grand jury proceedings or to any other pretrial proceeding. Before the conclusion of a grand jury proceeding, an individual may not even qualify as an "accused." Moreover, even if some prior event has made him an accused, he has no right to be present at grand jury hearings.

Post-trial sentencing proceedings are another matter. It is true that the use of hearsay at a sentencing hearing cannot jeopardize the fairness of the guilt determination. Nonetheless, the introduction of unreliable evidence into a sentencing process can lead directly to unjustifiable losses of liberty. A sentencing hearing is arguably both substantively and procedurally unfair if untrustworthy hearsay from an unconfrontable declarant induces a judge to impose a more severe sentence on a convicted defendant, and the injury to a defendant is similar to the injury suffered when hearsay skews a trial verdict. Nonetheless, it seems quite unlikely that the right to bar hearsay evidence extends to true sentencing hearings.

Over 50 years ago, in *Williams v. New York*,[315] the Supreme Court rejected a claim that a defendant had a constitutional entitlement to confront the sources of evidence relied upon by a judge who imposed a death sentence. The Court recognized an entitlement to "an opportunity to examine adverse witnesses" when "guilt" was at issue, but found both "historical" and "sound practical reasons" for "a distinction" when sentencing was involved.[316] To exercise the "broad discretion to decide the type and extent of punishment for convicted defendants," and to ensure "that the punishment . . . fit[s] the offender and not merely the crime," judges must take into account "the fullest information possible concerning the defendant's life and characteristics."[317] In light of prevailing policies and practices and the need for "the best available information," a requirement of "open court testimony with cross-examination" would be "totally impractical if not impossible" and "would hinder if not preclude . . . progressive efforts to improve the administration of criminal justice."[318] For these reasons, the Court concluded that the accused did not have a constitutional right to cross-examine those who furnished information for sentencing purposes.[319]

Although *Williams* was a state case decided before the Court held in *Pointer v. Texas*[320] that the confrontation guarantee applies in state prosecutions, its holding has been reaffirmed since *Pointer*.[321] In addition, the Supreme Court has not

---

315. 337 U.S. 241 (1949).

316. *Id.* at 245–46.

317. *Id.* at 245, 247.

318. *Id.* at 249–51.

319. *Id.* at 252.

320. 380 U.S. 400 (1965).

321. *See* Specht v. Patterson, 386 U.S. 605, 608 (1967); *see also* United States v. Tucker, 404 U.S. 443, 446–47 (1972). Although *Specht* did recognize a due process right to confrontation and cross-examination in a post-trial proceeding putatively for sentencing purposes, in fact the proceeding required a "new finding of fact . . . that was not an ingredient of the" crime for which the accused had been convicted, and that finding of fact justified "criminal punishment" not justified by the initial conviction. *Specht*, 386 U.S. at 608. Clearly, the proceeding at issue in *Specht* was not merely a sentencing; it was essentially a guilt-innocence determination that triggered trial rights.

been receptive to claims that Sixth Amendment fair trial rights extend to sentencing proceedings.[322] In sum, the Court has never held that the trial right to be confronted with witnesses extends to the sentencing phase, and it is unlikely that this Sixth Amendment right, and its inseparable entitlement to exclude testimonial hearsay, would apply in sentencing hearings today.

The Supreme Court has sometimes distinguished between capital and noncapital sentencing proceedings, recognizing a need for greater reliability when the ultimate sanction is at issue.[323] However, the Court has not distinguished between capital and noncapital sentencing processes when applying Sixth Amendment fair trial rights.[324] Therefore, there is no reason to believe that the Court would extend the guarantee of confrontation to capital sentencing proceedings and would bar sentencers from considering unconfronted testimonial hearsay.[325]

A jurisdiction's classification of a proceeding does not control constitutional analysis or the application of constitutional rights. For purposes of the jury trial guarantee and the requirement of proof beyond a reasonable doubt, proceedings labeled sentencings are considered trials—that is, determinations of guilt or innocence for criminal offenses—when they involve determinations of facts that increase the maximum punishment that otherwise could have been imposed.[326]

---

322. *See* John G. Douglass, *Confronting Death: Sixth Amendment Rights at Capital Sentencing*, 105 COLUM. L. REV. 1967, 1975 (2005) [hereinafter Douglass, *Confronting Death*] (observing that the Court has rejected "the right to jury sentencing" and "most aspects of the right of confrontation"). The one notable exception is the right to the assistance of counsel. *See* Mempa v. Rhay, 389 U.S. 128, 137 (1967) (acknowledging a right to counsel at sentencing); Douglass, *Confronting Death, supra* at 1975 (noting that the Court has "embrace[d] the right to counsel at sentencing").

323. *See* Monge v. California, 524 U.S. 721, 732 (1998); Strickland v. Washington, 466 U.S. 668, 704 (1984); Woodson v. North Carolina, 478 U.S. 280, 305 (1976).

324. "[W]ith regard to the rights listed in the Sixth Amendment, the Court's rules for capital sentencing are essentially the same as for noncapital sentencing." Douglass, *Confronting Death, supra* note 322, at 1993. As noted, *Williams v. New York* involved a capital sentencing proceeding. After concluding that there were historical and practical reasons not to extend the due process right to cross-examine witnesses at trial to sentencing hearings, the Court specifically rejected a claim that death sentence proceedings should be subject to a different constitutional rule. *Williams*, 337 U.S. at 251–52.

325. There is also no logical basis for extending the hearsay bar to any other kinds of post-trial proceedings such as motions for new trials or collateral attacks seeking to overturn convictions.

326. *See* Apprendi v. New Jersey, 530 U.S. 466 (2000). The *Apprendi* Court held that if a proceeding involves the determination of a fact, other than the existence of "a prior conviction[,] . . . that increases the penalty for a crime beyond the prescribed statutory maximum," for constitutional purposes that proceeding is a trial for a more serious offense and the fundamental guarantees of trial by jury and proof beyond a reasonable doubt are applicable. *Id.* at 490. This constitutional principle controls capital sentencing

Undoubtedly, the confrontation guarantee and its bar to testimonial hearsay would also operate in such proceedings. The government cannot deny a fundamental trial right in a proceeding that determines guilt or innocence for an offense.

The Sixth Amendment Confrontation Clause grants a trial right to accused individuals in *criminal* prosecutions, and the bar to hearsay evidence is an integral part of that right. There is no predicate for extending the right—textually and historically confined to criminal trials—to civil proceedings of any kind.[327] Accordingly, a judge need not exclude testimonial hearsay from a civil tax case, a civil deportation proceeding, or an administrative hearing for parole revocation purposes.[328]

Finally, the doctrine of *Stone v. Powell*[329] does not prevent state defendants who challenge their convictions in federal habeas corpus actions from raising claims that the Sixth Amendment required the exclusion of hearsay from their trials. *Stone* held that a defendant may not pursue a federal habeas claim that the Fourth Amendment exclusionary rule barred evidence from his state trial unless the state denied a "full and fair" hearing of that claim.[330] This restriction was premised on the fact that Fourth Amendment exclusion is a deterrent safeguard, not a constitutional right.[331] The logic of *Stone* does not apply to, and its holding does not limit, constitutional rights to exclude evidence.[332] Therefore, even if the state

---

proceedings involving factual determinations that are legally necessary for the imposition of a death sentence. *See* Ring v. Arizona, 536 U.S. 584 (2002). Fact determinations that are merely the basis for selecting a punishment *within* the range of sentences legally authorized by a jury verdict—not for elevating the maximum penalty that is authorized—are true sentencing proceedings and do not trigger the application of trial rights. *See* Blakely v. Washington, 542 U.S. 296, 308–09 (2004); *Apprendi*, 530 U.S. at 481–82.

327. The Confrontation Clause would not require suppression in a genuinely civil forfeiture proceeding. However, if a supposedly civil forfeiture proceeding was, in substance, a criminal case that could result in punishment for criminal acts, testimonial hearsay should be barred. *See* One 1958 Plymouth Sedan v. Pennsylvania, 380 U.S. 693, 700 (1965) (extending the Fourth Amendment exclusionary rule to a "quasi-criminal" forfeiture proceeding). Just as labels cannot dictate whether a proceeding is a sentencing proceeding or a trial, labels cannot control whether a proceeding is civil or criminal.

328. The Supreme Court has not extended other constitutional exclusion doctrines—both those that are deterrent safeguards and those that are constitutional rights—to civil proceedings. For a discussion of the inapplicability of the Fourth Amendment exclusionary rule in civil litigation, see *supra* Chapter 1, text accompanying notes 168–73.

329. 428 U.S. 465 (1976).

330. *Id.* at 481–82.

331. *Id.* at 492–95.

332. The Court refused to apply *Stone* to *Miranda* exclusion claims even though defendants have no right to exclusion under *Miranda*. *See* Withrow v. Williams, 507 U.S. 680 (1993). The ruling was based on the premise that *Miranda* exclusion protects against risks that a "'fundamental *trial* right'" will be violated by the admission of the evidence.

afforded a defendant an adequate opportunity to pursue his claim, in a federal habeas proceeding a convicted defendant is entitled to vindicate his Confrontation Clause right to exclude testimonial hearsay from a state trial.

3. "Standing" to Exclude Testimonial Hearsay

The right to confrontation is a personal trial right. This Sixth Amendment right to exclude evidence from criminal prosecutions—an integral part of the confrontation entitlement—belongs to every accused—that is, every individual whose guilt the prosecution seeks to prove with testimonial hearsay. Therefore, every accused person on trial has "standing" to claim that the government's use of such hearsay would violate his Sixth Amendment rights. It does not matter that the inculpatory testimonial hearsay was acquired by means unrelated to the defendant. A defendant is entitled to contest its admission simply because it is incriminating testimonial hearsay—that is, because the declarant is an adverse witness whom the accused has a constitutional right to confront.

4. Exceptions to the Sixth Amendment Right to Exclusion

Almost all of the exceptions to exclusionary doctrines discussed in earlier chapters are irrelevant here because Sixth Amendment suppression of testimonial hearsay is not based on the nature of the official conduct that acquired the evidence, but instead on the nature of the evidence at issue. The following discussion does not consider the independent source, inevitable discovery, attenuation, good faith, or public safety doctrines because all of them rest on the means used to obtain or produce contested evidence.[333] Nonetheless, there are

---

Id. at 691 (emphasis in original) (quoting United States v. Verdugo-Urquidez, 494 U.S. 259, 264 (1990)). Moreover, whenever defendants have sought habeas corpus relief for the denial of actual constitutional rights, the Court has rejected the government's claims that the *Stone* limitation should apply. *See* Kimmelman v. Morrison, 477 U.S. 365 (1986) (addressing the right to effective assistance of counsel); Jackson v. Virginia, 443 U.S. 307 (1979) (considering the due process right to a verdict based on sufficient evidence); Rose v. Mitchell, 443 U.S. 545 (1979) (discussing the equal protection right to nondiscriminatory selection of a grand jury foreperson).

333. Considering the nature and foundations of the Confrontation Clause right to suppression, it makes no sense to consider the admissibility of testimonial hearsay with an independent source, testimonial hearsay that would inevitably have been discovered, or testimonial hearsay with an attenuated connection to an illegality. Testimonial hearsay is excluded *because* it is testimonial hearsay. Moreover, it matters not that testimonial hearsay was acquired in "good faith" or that government officials obtained testimonial hearsay to defeat some threat to the public safety. Use at trial is forbidden because the Constitution entitles an accused to confront witnesses who are the source of testimonial hearsay even if the officials who gathered that hearsay lacked fault or were motivated by a compelling interest. Because the admission of the hearsay violates the accused's Sixth Amendment right, there is no "good faith" or "public safety" exception to the Confrontation Clause bar to unconfrontable testimonial hearsay.

a limited number of historically-accepted exceptions to the right to bar testimonial hearsay.[334] This section analyzes those exceptions—unavailability and a prior opportunity for cross-examination, forfeiture by wrongdoing, and dying declarations. It also considers whether the government may use testimonial hearsay to impeach defense witnesses.

a. Unavailability and a Prior Opportunity for Cross-Examination The government may introduce the testimonial hearsay of a declarant who is currently unavailable to testify at trial if the accused had a prior opportunity to cross-examine the declarant concerning the hearsay statements.[335] The history of the common law right of confrontation that informs the Sixth Amendment guarantee supports this significant exception to the accused's entitlement to exclude testimonial hearsay that cannot be confronted at trial.[336] Moreover, Confrontation Clause precedents have consistently recognized the validity of this exception.[337] The first requirement is that the declarant who is the source of the testimonial statement is currently unavailable to testify at the accused's trial. The prosecution must make "a good-faith effort to obtain [the declarant's] presence at trial,"[338] and "bears the burden of establishing" that "the witness is unavailable despite

---

334. In *Crawford*, the Court asserted that the Sixth Amendment's "text . . . does not suggest any open-ended exceptions from the confrontation requirement to be developed by the courts," but that the provision "is most naturally read as a reference to the right of confrontation at common law, admitting only those exceptions established at the time of the founding." Crawford v. Washington, 541 U.S. 36, 54 (2004). The *Crawford* Court described the few established exceptions it found. As long as the Court adheres to this understanding of the meaning of the Confrontation Clause, it seems clear that no additional exceptions are possible. Only those discussed here are legitimate.

335. *See id.* at 54, 57–59, 68.

336. *Id.* at 53–54. The *Crawford* Court analyzed whether the common law demanded a prior opportunity for cross-examination as a condition of admissibility and concluded that it did. *Id.* at 55–56 (stating that "a prior opportunity to cross-examine was [not] merely a sufficient, rather than a necessary, condition for admissibility" and that "this requirement was dispositive").

337. The Court first recognized the exception in *Mattox v. United States*, 156 U.S. 237, 243–44 (1895), allowing the admission of testimony given by two witnesses at an earlier murder trial when the witnesses had died before the subsequent trial. What started as a doctrine that applied when a declarant had died prior to trial evolved into a more general authority to introduce the testimony of unavailable declarants in *Barber v. Page*, 390 U.S. 719 (1968). Therein, the Court recognized an "exception to the confrontation requirement where a witness is unavailable and . . . was subject to cross-examination by th[e] defendant" in an earlier judicial proceeding. *Id.* at 722. In *California v. Green*, 399 U.S. 149 (1970), the Court again endorsed this general exception based upon showings of both unavailability and an earlier opportunity to cross-examine the witness. *See id.* at 165–66.

338. *Barber*, 390 U.S. at 724–25. The requirement is not met simply because the declarant-witness is incarcerated in another jurisdiction. The state must explore means of securing his presence and testimony. *See id.* at 720, 723–25.

good-faith efforts" to find him and have him testify.[339] Because there is no need for "futile" efforts to secure the testimony of the witness, if there is "no possibility" of success, "'good faith' demands nothing of the prosecution."[340] However, "good faith *may* demand" that the prosecution take "affirmative measures" if there is even a "remote" possibility that those measures will "produce the declarant" at trial.[341] Moreover, if the unavailability is "the fault of the [s]tate," the declarant is *not* unavailable.[342]

Death renders a witness unavailable.[343] Physical illness, mental illness, or a disability serious enough to prevent trial testimony suffices as well.[344] If a declarant disappears and cannot be located despite a good-faith exhaustion of the means available to find her, or if a witness moves to another jurisdiction and does not appear, despite the state's informal and formal good-faith efforts to secure her return for trial, the prosecution's burden is met.[345] Physically present witnesses can still be unavailable to testify for purposes of this exception. A memory loss that precludes an opportunity for meaningful cross-examination, the assertion of a privilege not to testify (for example, the Fifth Amendment privilege against compulsory self-incrimination), or a simple refusal to take the witness stand or respond to questions can render a witness unavailable.[346] Any other legitimate reason that the government cannot secure live testimony from

339. Ohio v. Roberts, 448 U.S. 56, 74–75 (1980).

340. *Id.* at 74.

341. *Id.* The unavailability demand is meaningful, requiring more than token efforts to secure a witness's presence because "[t]he right of confrontation" is a fundamental guarantee for a fair trial that "may not be dispensed with . . . lightly." *Barber,* 390 U.S. at 725.

342. *Green,* 399 U.S. at 166; *see also* Motes v. United States, 178 U.S. 458, 474 (1900) (holding that the government was not allowed to use a deposition statement of an absent witness because he had escaped from government custody and his absence, therefore, was due to "the negligence of the prosecution").

343. *See Green,* 399 U.S. at 166; *Motes,* 178 U.S. at 472; *Mattox,* 156 U.S. at 243.

344. *See Motes,* 178 U.S. at 472.

345. *See, e.g., Roberts,* 448 U.S. at 75–77 (finding that the government's use of subpoenas and a conversation with a witness's mother were sufficient efforts to locate and produce her); *Barber,* 390 U.S. at 723–24 (suggesting a need to use available legal process and to make requests for cooperation by others who had custody of a witness); *see also* Mancusi v. Stubbs, 408 U.S. 204, 212 (1972) (asserting that the witness's residence "in a foreign nation" rendered the state "powerless to compel his attendance at . . . trial" because there were no legal processes available to do so).

346. *See Green,* 399 U.S. at 167–68. Although a memory loss that is not total may not render a witness unavailable to testify, *see* United States v. Owens, 484 U.S. 554, 559 (1988), a more profound memory loss may suffice. *See Green,* 399 U.S. at 167–68, 168 n.17 (indicating that a "claimed . . . loss of memory" can suffice and noting that the rules of evidence do recognize that a "lapse of memory" can render a witness unavailable for hearsay rule exception purposes); *see also* Latimer, *Confrontation After* Crawford, *supra* note 111, at 347 (maintaining that unavailability is likely established if a "witness suffers a good

a declarant, despite genuine, good-faith efforts, satisfies the unavailability requirement.[347]

Unavailability is a necessary, but not sufficient, condition to admit testimonial hearsay under this exception. The government must also show that the accused had a prior opportunity to cross-examine the declarant—that is, cross-examination of the declarant must have been possible *at the time the hearsay statement was made.*[348] It is not necessary to show that the accused actually exploited the opportunity at that time, only that he could have done so.[349] Although cross-examination need not have been effective or successful, there must have been an adequate opportunity for effective questioning of the declarant concerning his hearsay statement. Restrictions on cross-examination by rule or judicial decision, a witness's refusal to testify or assertion of a privilege on the prior occasion, or possibly a sufficiently severe memory loss can prevent an accused from having a sufficient cross-examination opportunity to satisfy this exception.[350] Moreover, a prior opportunity for cross-examination might be

---

faith failure of recollection to the extent that he or she is virtually incompetent to testify to relevant matters").

347. *See* Latimer, *Confrontation After* Crawford, *supra* note 111, at 346 (maintaining that the meaning of unavailability under the current doctrine "will likely be governed by previously existing Confrontation Clause jurisprudence"). The Federal Rules of Evidence provide that, for purposes of the hearsay rules, a declarant is unavailable when she has a privilege, refuses to testify despite a court order, asserts a lack of memory, is dead or has a physical or mental illness or infirmity, or is absent and the party seeking to use the hearsay cannot, by process or other reasonable means, secure her attendance or testimony. FED. R. EVID. 804(a). It seems entirely possible that the meaning of unavailability for constitutional purposes may be informed and guided by this provision. *See Green*, 399 U.S. at 168 n.17 (referring to the recognition of memory lapse and privilege assertion as bases of unavailability under the rules of evidence).

348. *See, e.g.*, Pointer v. Texas, 380 U.S. 400, 407 (1965) (indicating that a prior statement of a witness who had moved to another state might well have been admissible at trial if it had been "taken at a full-fledged hearing" in which the defendant "had been given a complete and adequate opportunity to cross-examine" him, but holding the statement inadmissible because the defendant did not have such an opportunity).

349. *Ohio v. Roberts* observed that in *California v. Green* the Court had indicated that an "*opportunity* to cross-examine" was sufficient, "even absent actual cross-examination." *Roberts*, 448 U.S. at 70 (emphasis in original). The *Roberts* Court did not have to decide whether a "mere opportunity" is sufficient or "whether *de minimis* questioning is sufficient" because "significant [actual] cross-examination" had occurred in *Roberts*. *Id.* (emphasis in original). *Crawford*'s repeated references to the need for a "prior *opportunity*" for cross-examination, surely establishes that only an opportunity is needed, not actual cross-examination. *See* Crawford v. Washington, 541 U.S. 36, 50, 54, 55, 59, 68 (2004) (emphasis added); *see also Owens*, 484 U.S. at 559 (stressing that the Sixth Amendment ensures only an opportunity for effective cross-examination).

350. It seems likely that the adequacy of a prior opportunity to cross-examine a witness depends on the same variables that determine whether an accused has an adequate

inadequate if the nature of the earlier proceeding limited the chance to question the witness and expose infirmities in her testimony. Thus, if a defendant had an ample chance to cross-examine a declarant at an earlier trial for the very same offense, the prior opportunity would be adequate.[351] On the other hand, an opportunity to question a declarant at a hearing on a motion to suppress evidence might not suffice.[352] The adequacy of an opportunity to cross-examine a declarant at a preliminary hearing in the same criminal case is debatable and may depend on the particular circumstances of the case.[353]

The Confrontation Clause guarantees that testimony will be given under oath in the presence of the accused and the trier of fact and ensures that jurors will be able to observe a witness's demeanor during cross-examination by the defense. The confrontation right is premised on a belief that these mechanisms promote more reliable outcomes. When the testimonial hearsay of an absent declarant is admitted to prove the truth of the declarant's assertions, the trier of fact cannot observe the witness's behavior. Because valuable clues about the witness's credibility may be lost, and the reliability of the process may be undermined, it is arguable that the Sixth Amendment should not permit the admission of testimonial hearsay even when a declarant has died or is otherwise not available to testify.[354]

The Court long ago rejected this argument, concluding that the Framers of the Sixth Amendment did not provide an unqualified entitlement to confront witnesses at trial. Instead, they struck a balance that allowed the use of unconfrontable testimonial hearsay in certain limited circumstances—i.e., when the declarant is unavailable and the accused had a previous chance to confront

---

opportunity to cross-examine a hearsay declarant who is present and testifying at trial. *See supra* text accompanying notes 305–11.

351. *See* Mattox v. United States, 156 U.S. 237 (1895).

352. *See* Lee v. Illinois, 476 U.S. 530, 547 n.6 (1986) (rejecting a claim that the opportunity to cross-examine a witness during a suppression hearing was adequate because, in light of the limited "function of a suppression hearing," there was "no opportunity to cross-examine [the declarant] with respect to the reliability of the statement, especially as it may have related to" the accused).

353. *See* California v. Green, 399 U.S. 149, 165–66 (1970) (finding a prior opportunity to cross-examine at a preliminary hearing adequate to justify the admission of hearsay); *but see* Barber v. Page, 390 U.S. 719, 725 (1968) (suggesting that a preliminary hearing involves a "much less searching exploration" because it serves the "limited" purpose of "determining . . . probable cause," and evincing uncertainty about whether an opportunity to cross-examine a declarant at a preliminary hearing would satisfy the Sixth Amendment). In *Pointer v. Texas*, 380 U.S. at 407, the Court concluded that the accused did not have "an adequate opportunity to cross-examine" the victim-declarant at a preliminary hearing because he was not represented by counsel at the preliminary hearing.

354. *See Mattox*, 156 U.S. at 243 (noting the argument that an accused may "never lose the benefit of any of the[] safeguards" afforded by confrontation, including "personal presence of the witness before the jury").

the declarant.[355] The justification for this exception is evident in its twin requirements. The unavailability demand reflects a "necessity" predicate.[356] An accused is entitled to live testimony at trial and to all the available tools for combating unreliability *unless* there is a need to use testimonial hearsay. Society has an interest that can outweigh the accused's confrontation interests and tip the balance in favor of admission *only* when the unavailability of a witness makes it necessary to rely on the hearsay.[357]

However, the need engendered by unavailability alone is not enough to justify depriving an accused of *all* of the protections afforded by confrontation at trial. The "prior opportunity for cross-examination" requirement ensures that an accused will not suffer a total loss of confrontation safeguards. The declarant-witness will have testified under oath in the defendant's presence and the defendant will have had the chance to expose weaknesses and demonstrate infirmities in the hearsay.[358] To be sure, the accused will be deprived of the chance to have the jurors who will decide his fate observe the witness's demeanor, a facet of confrontation that is his presumptive entitlement.[359] Nonetheless, because this is the only element of confrontation that is missing, there is "substantial compliance" with the constitutional guarantee.[360] In other words, the deprivation is partial, sufficiently limited to be outweighed by society's need for the declarant's inculpatory hearsay testimony.

In sum, even limited, partial deprivations of the entitlement to confront witnesses are impermissible unless there is justification. Therefore, unavailability must be shown. Moreover, even in cases of serious need, substantial deprivations of the confrontation guarantee—and the resulting risks of unreliability—are impermissible.[361] Consequently, an adequate prior opportunity for

---

355. *See id.* (observing that "general rules" like the one prescribed by the Confrontation Clause "must occasionally give way to considerations of public policy and the necessities of the case," and that the "law . . . declares that the rights of the public shall not be wholly sacrificed in order that an incidental benefit may be preserved to the accused").

356. *See* Ohio v. Roberts, 448 U.S. 56, 65 (1980); *Barber*, 390 U.S. at 722.

357. *See Mattox*, 156 U.S. at 243.

358. *See id.* at 244 (noting that the "substance of the constitutional protection is preserved . . . in the advantage [the defendant] has once had of seeing the witness face to face, and of subjecting him to the ordeal of cross-examination").

359. *See id.* at 243 (acknowledging that the use of hearsay deprives the accused "of the advantage of th[e] personal presence of the witness before the jury").

360. California v. Green, 399 U.S. 149, 166 (1970); *Barber*, 390 U.S. at 722.

361. *See Mattox*, 156 U.S. at 244 (observing that it is permissible to introduce hearsay when the accused has had a prior opportunity for cross-examination because "the substance of the constitutional protection is preserved" insofar as the accused has had "the advantage . . . of seeing the witness face to face, and of subjecting him to . . . cross-examination," and suggesting that "under no circumstances" is it permissible to deprive the accused of those advantages).

cross-examination is essential. When both requisites are present—and only when both are established—the constitutional balance of interests supports an exception to the Sixth Amendment right to exclude testimonial hearsay.

b. Forfeiture by Wrongdoing The Sixth Amendment bar to testimonial hearsay is also qualified by a "forfeiture by wrongdoing" exception.[362] This exception, recognized in the Court's first opinion regarding the relationship between hearsay and the Confrontation Clause, applies whenever a declarant does not testify at trial as a result of the accused's "wrongful procurement."[363] When the exception applies, *any* inculpatory testimonial hearsay statement made by that declarant is admissible even "though [it is] unconfronted" at or before trial.[364]

To satisfy the exception, the witness "must have been wrongfully kept away" by the accused—that is, her absence or her refusal to give testimony at trial must be the result of "a wrong committed" by the defendant.[365] The prosecution must show that the defendant's wrongful acts were "*designed*" or "intended to prevent [the] witness from testifying."[366] The accused forfeits his confrontation entitlement only when the government proves that he engaged in the conduct that prevented the witness from testifying in court "for the purpose of preventing [the witness's] testimony."[367] It is not enough that the defendant did, in fact,

---

362. *See* Crawford v. Washington, 541 U.S. 36, 62 (2004) ("accept[ing]" the validity of the exception). One author has called forfeiture by wrongdoing "the most significant exception to the exclusion of testimonial hearsay." James F. Flanagan, *Foreshadowing the Future of Forfeiture/Estoppel By Wrongdoing:* Davis v. Washington *and the Necessity of the Defendant's Intent to Intimidate the Witness,* 15 J.L. & Pol'y 863, 863 (2007) [hereinafter Flanagan, *Foreshadowing Forfeiture*].

363. *See* Reynolds v. United States, 98 U.S. 145, 158 (1878).

364. Giles v. California, 554 U.S. ____, ____, 128 S.Ct. 2678, 2682–83 (2008); *see* Davis v. Washington, 547 U.S. 813, 833 (2006) (declaring that an accused "who obtains the absence of a witness by wrongdoing *forfeits the constitutional right to confrontation*") (emphasis added).

365. *Reynolds*, 98 U.S. at 159; *see Davis*, 547 U.S. at 833 (specifying the need to obtain "the absence of a witness by wrongdoing").

366. *Giles*, 554 U.S. at ____, 128 S.Ct. at 2683–84 (emphasis in original).

367. *Id.* at ____, 128 S.Ct. at 2688. To decide whether the exception renders testimonial hearsay admissible, a trial judge must make preliminary determinations of fact. *See Reynolds*, 98 U.S. at 159. There are unsettled questions of process, including whether a separate evidentiary hearing is necessary, the magnitude of the prosecution's burden of proof on the critical factual issues, and whether the declarant's hearsay statements alone can be sufficient to support the requisite findings of intent and causation. *See* Flanagan, *Foreshadowing Forfeiture, supra* note 362, at 885–86, 890–99 (highlighting and discussing these questions). In *Davis,* the Court opted to "take no position on the standards necessary to demonstrate . . . forfeiture," but observed that federal and state courts had "generally" required the government to meet "the preponderance-of-the-evidence standard," and had decided that "if a hearing on forfeiture is required," the trial judge may rely on hearsay, including hearsay from the witness at issue. *Davis,* 547 U.S. at 833.

cause the witness's failure to testify; the requisite purpose is essential.[368] However, the requisite purpose is established if the government proves that the accused acted with "the intent to isolate [a crime] victim and to stop her from reporting [a crime] to the authorities or cooperating with a criminal prosecution."[369] In that situation, the victim-declarant's "prior statements [are] admissible under the forfeiture doctrine."[370]

If a defendant kills a witness or injures her so severely that she is physically or mentally incapable of testifying, and the government establishes that he did so with the purpose of preventing her from reporting a crime, cooperating with the authorities, or testifying at his trial, he loses his entitlement to exclude her testimonial hearsay. An accused also forfeits his Sixth Amendment right to confront a witness, and, therefore, his right to exclude her trial testimony, if, with the necessary intent, he makes threats or offers incentives that cause a witness to disappear, refuse to testify, falsely claim a lack of memory, or assert a privilege

---

368. After *Crawford*, an issue arose over the breadth of the forfeiture exception. Some jurisdictions held that it was applicable in cases where an accused caused a witness's absence—by killing her, for example—even if there was no intent to prevent her cooperation in a criminal prosecution. *See* Flanagan, *Foreshadowing Forfeiture, supra* note 362, at 865, 877–78. In *Giles*, the Court addressed that expanded version of forfeiture, considering whether the right to confront an adverse witness is lost whenever "a judge determines that a wrongful act by the defendant made the witness unavailable to testify at trial." *Giles*, 554 U.S. at ___, 128 S.Ct. at 2681. The Court rejected that interpretation of the exception, concluding that it lacked common law roots and was not consistent with the underlying rationales for the forfeiture exception. *Id.* at ___, 128 S.Ct. at 2683–88. In response to concerns that domestic violence prosecutions might be impeded by a requirement of intent to prevent witness testimony, the Court noted that nontestimonial "[s]tatements to friends and neighbors" and "to [treating] physicians" were constitutionally admissible. The Court also pointed out that the evidence in a domestic violence case might well "support a finding that [a] crime expressed the intent to isolate the victim and to stop her from reporting abuse to the authorities or cooperating with a criminal prosecution—rendering her prior statements admissible under the forfeiture doctrine." *Id.* at ___, 128 S.Ct. at 2692–93. At least one author believes that the intent to prevent testimony, reporting, or cooperation should not be necessary where a "declarant has been killed" and there is evidence that the accused killed her. *See* Raeder, *Remember the Ladies, supra* note 230, at 363.

369. *Giles*, 554 U.S. at ___, 128 S.Ct. at 2693. In light of a concurrence joined by two Justices who were necessary for a majority in *Giles*, the government may have to show only that a defendant's treatment of a victim was "meant to isolate [her] from outside help, including the aid of law enforcement and the judicial process." *Id.* at ___, 128 S.Ct. at 2695 (Souter, J., concurring in part).

370. *Id.* at ___, 128 S.Ct. at 2693. It would seem that the government must show both that the required intent caused the accused's allegedly wrongful act and that the wrongful act caused the unavailability of the witness's testimony. *See* Flanagan, *Foreshadowing Forfeiture, supra* note 362, at 890–93 (discussing and proposing standards for these two causal showings).

she would not otherwise assert. Any improper act that prevents a witness's presence or testimony, if done with a design to thwart the effective operation of the criminal justice system, satisfies this simple doctrine and suspends the bar to testimonial hearsay.

The "forfeiture by wrongdoing" exception has deep historical roots. The doctrine "is a founding-era exception to the confrontation right" recognized and established "at common law."[371] The rationale for the exception is reflected in its name and character. It does not rest on the premise that confrontation is not necessary to ensure a fair trial because testimonial hearsay statements made by declarants wrongfully kept from trial are reliable.[372] Rather, it "extinguishes confrontation claims on essentially equitable grounds."[373] The exception is rooted in the principle that "no one shall be permitted to take advantage of his own wrong," which dictates that an accused "cannot complain if competent [hearsay] evidence is admitted to supply the place of that which he has kept away."[374] Moreover, without the exception's threat that unconfronted testimonial hearsay will be admissible if an accused wrongfully procures a witness's absence, defendants would have "an intolerable incentive . . . to bribe, intimidate, or even kill witnesses against them."[375] The exception is a necessary means of enabling "courts to protect the integrity of their proceedings."[376] Because a defendant should not be able to escape justice by suppressing probative evidence, because society has powerful interests in preventing the defeat of justice and the corruption of the adjudicative processes, and because it is imperative to discourage wrongful acts designed to thwart society's interests, testimonial hearsay from declarants improperly prevented from testifying is freely admissible. Although the admission of such unconfronted hearsay has the potential to inflict the fair trial injuries that are the concern of the Sixth Amendment guarantee, it is "reasonable to place the risk of untruth in an unconfronted, out-of-court statement on a defendant who meant to preclude the testing that confrontation provides."[377]

---

371. *Giles*, 554 U.S. at ____, 128 S.Ct. at 2682–83.

372. Crawford v. Washington, 541 U.S. 36, 62 (2004).

373. *Id.*

374. Reynolds v. United States, 98 U.S. 145, 158–59 (1878).

375. *Giles*, 554 U.S. at ____, 128 S.Ct. at 2686.

376. Davis v. Washington, 547 U.S. 813, 834 (2006).

377. *Giles*, 554 U.S. at ____, 128 S.Ct. at 2694 (Souter, J., concurring in part).

In *Diaz v. United States*, 223 U.S. 442, 452 (1912), the Court cited *Reynolds* as support for the principle that an accused can *waive* the confrontation right to bar out-of-court statements. The suggestion that forfeiture and waiver were the same concept was misguided. Forfeiture involves an undesired loss of rights due to wrongful conduct. Waiver is a choice to forego the exercise of an entitlement and occurs when an accused intentionally relinquishes a known right. *See* Johnson v. Zerbst, 304 U.S. 458, 464 (1938). An accused certainly can waive the Sixth Amendment right to confront witnesses. *See* Melendez-Diaz v. Massachusetts, 557 U.S. ____, ____, 129 S.Ct. 2527, 2534 n.3 (2009). He can validly

c. Dying Declarations The common law admitted one other "form[] of testimonial statement[]" even though the accused had no opportunity for confrontation—dying declarations.[378] Although early Supreme Court opinions explicitly endorsed a "dying declarations" exception to the Sixth Amendment right to exclude hearsay,[379] the current validity of the exception is uncertain. The *Crawford* Court, while acknowledging its historical credentials, pointedly refused to "decide . . . whether the Sixth Amendment incorporates an exception for testimonial dying declarations."[380]

On the one hand, history—the guiding light of the *Crawford* revolution—shows that at the time of the framing of the Bill of Rights, a testimonial hearsay statement that qualified as a dying declaration was admissible against an accused.[381] *Crawford* indicated that the Sixth Amendment "is most naturally read as a reference to the right of confrontation at common law, admitting only those exceptions established at the time of the founding."[382] On the other hand,

---

relinquish the constitutional right to bar hearsay by explicitly surrendering his right to confront the declarant, by consenting to the government's introduction of the hearsay, *see Diaz*, 223 U.S. at 451, or by introducing the hearsay at issue himself. *See id.* at 452–53. A "failure to object" to the government's efforts to introduce testimonial hearsay also can constitute a waiver. *Melendez-Diaz*, 557 U.S. at ____, 129 S.Ct. at 2534 n.3. Whether a valid assertion of a privilege that prevents a witness from testifying can constitute a waiver of the right to bar that witness's testimonial hearsay is uncertain. *See Crawford*, 541 U.S. at 42 n.1 (declining to "express [an] opinion on" that question).

378. *Giles*, 554 U.S. at ____, 128 S.Ct. at 2682; *see Crawford*, 541 U.S. at 56 n.6.

379. *See* Kirby v. United States, 174 U.S. 47, 61 (1899); Mattox v. United States, 156 U.S. 237, 243 (1895). Although both opinions recognized the validity of the exception, neither case actually involved the admission of a dying declaration against a defendant.

380. *Crawford*, 541 U.S. at 56 n.6. This stands in marked contrast to the Court's affirmative decision to "accept" the validity of the "forfeiture by wrongdoing" exception. *Id.* at 62. For some reason, the Court wanted to reserve judgment about the constitutional legitimacy of an exception for testimonial dying declarations. For discussions of the nature of the dying declarations exception and its constitutional status, see Stephen J. Cribari, *Is Death Different? Dying Declarations and the Confrontation Clause After* Crawford, 35 WM. MITCHELL L. REV. 1542 (2009) [hereinafter Cribari, *Is Death Different?*]; Peter Nicolas, *"I'm Dying To Tell You What Happened": The Admissibility of Testimonial Dying Declarations Post-*Crawford, 37 HASTINGS CONST. L.Q. 487 (2010) [hereinafter Nicolas, *Admissibility of Dying Declarations*]; Aviva Orenstein, *Her Last Words: Dying Declarations and Modern Confrontation Jurisprudence*, 2010 ILL. L. REV. 1411 (2010) [hereinafter Orenstein, *Her Last Words*].

381. *Crawford*, 541 U.S. at 56 n.6; *see* Reed, *Irretrievable Breakdown*, *supra* note 17, at 226 (asserting that *Crawford* "offered no plausible reason" for recognition of the exception "other than history"); *see also* Polelle, *Death of Dying Declarations*, *supra* note 257, at 291–93, 296–97, 313–14 (contesting the Court's reading of history and asserting that the "res gestae" exception was also recognized).

382. *Crawford*, 541 U.S. at 54; *see also Giles*, 554 U.S. at ____, 128 S.Ct. at 2682 (stating that the issue was whether the forfeiture doctrine under review was "a founding-era exception to the confrontation right"). It is noteworthy that the *Crawford* Court declared

the *Crawford* Court refused to give the exception its imprimatur—perhaps because this one-of-a-kind historical exception is anomalously inconsistent with, and threatens the protective aims of, the Confrontation Clause.[383] Although it seems likely that the Court will ultimately follow the guidance of history and endorse the exception, it has not yet done so.[384] Whether unconfronted and unconfrontable testimonial dying declarations are exempt from the Confrontation Clause under a unique and narrow historical exception is an open question.[385]

Should the Court accept a dying declaration exception to Sixth Amendment suppression as a historical relic embodied in the Confrontation Clause, it will be necessary to define its contours. The prevailing approach to Sixth Amendment interpretation indicates that history would guide the definitional endeavor—that is, that the details of the exception at the time the Sixth Amendment was adopted would govern.[386] The common law strictly limited the dying declaration exception to statements of *victims* in prosecutions for *homicide*—murder and

---

that "only" founding-era exceptions were legitimate, not that "all" founding-era exceptions were legitimate.

383. *Crawford* referred to the exception as a "deviation" from the general common law refusal to allow unconfronted testimonial hearsay to be admitted under other exceptions to the hearsay rule. *Crawford*, 541 U.S. at 56 n.6; *see also Mattox*, 156 U.S. at 243 (observing that "the admission of dying declarations" runs "directly contrary to the letter of the" Confrontation Clause because they are rarely made in the presence of the accused, there is no opportunity for cross-examination, and they are not made in the jury's presence); Orenstein, *Her Last Words, supra* note 380, at 1444–46 (arguing that the dying declarations exception "undermines the Court's entire originalist approach" and that it "makes no sense except for history and tradition"); Reed, *Irretrievable Breakdown, supra* note 17, at 226 (maintaining that "a dying declaration is an illogical exception to the rule" against unconfronted testimonial hearsay).

384. Scholars have predicted that the Court will eventually endorse the exception. *See* Nicolas, *Admissibility of Dying Declarations, supra* note 380, at 491–92; Orenstein, *Her Last Words, supra* note 380, at 1414, 1441.

385. *Crawford* observed that "many dying declarations may not be testimonial." *Crawford*, 541 U.S. at 56 n.6. Of course, nontestimonial dying declarations are immune from the constitutional bar.

386. The Court's strict adherence to the historical scope of the "forfeiture by wrongdoing" exception in *Giles*, and its rejection of the expanded version adopted by California, *see Giles*, 554 U.S. at ____, 128 S.Ct. at 2683–88, 2693, indicate that modern modifications of the dying declaration exception to the hearsay rule would not alter the scope of a Sixth Amendment exception. Identification and prescription of the details of a Sixth Amendment dying declarations exception will be anything but simple. For a thorough discussion of the issues the Court will need to address in specifying the details of this exception to Confrontation Clause exclusion and of the difficulties entailed in pinpointing the specifics of an exception that has contracted and expanded over time, see Nicolas, *Admissibility of Dying Declarations, supra* note 380, at 493–94, 504–38.

manslaughter cases.[387] It did not authorize the admission of hearsay statements made by any other person in homicide cases or encompass victim statements in prosecutions for other crimes or in civil lawsuits.[388] In addition, the declarant's state of mind was critical. At the time the statement was made, the declarant had to believe that she was going to die soon—that is, that death was "imminent" or "impending"—and that death was certain—that is, that there was no hope of surviving.[389] It was inherent in the exception for victim statements in homicide prosecutions that the content of the statements to be introduced would relate to the death the victim believed to be imminent.[390] For example, the statement would name the accused as the killer, or explain what the accused did to the victim or why or how the accused had brought about the victim's death.[391] Finally, because the declarant was an alleged victim of a homicide, by definition,

387. *See,* e.g., Rex v. Woodcock, 1 Leach 500, 500–01, 168 Eng. Rep. 352, 352–53 (K.B. 1789); *see also* FED. R. EVID. 804(b)(2) advisory committee's note; Orenstein, *Her Last Words, supra* note 380, at 1415.

388. The exception has undergone some expansion in modern times. The Federal Rules of Evidence, the most influential source of evidence law in the United States today, includes a dying declaration exception that applies in criminal homicide prosecutions and all civil cases. *See* FED. R. EVID. 804(b)(2). Moreover, the federal rule is not explicitly limited to statements by victims. It would allow the introduction of a statement that was made by someone other than the alleged victim of the homicide being prosecuted if the statement satisfied the other criteria for the exception. The rules in a number of jurisdictions allow the admission of dying declarations in *all* criminal cases, not just homicide prosecutions. *See* Nicolas, *Admissibility of Dying Declarations, supra* note 380, at 509, 509 n.124.

389. *See* Mattox v. United States, 146 U.S. 140, 151–52 (1892); *Woodcock,* 1 Leach at 502–04, 168 Eng.Rep. at 353–54; *see also* Orenstein, *Her Last Words, supra* note 380 at 1420–23. This state of mind requirement continues today, although it may be a bit less demanding than it was originally. *See, e.g.,* FED. R. EVID. 804(b)(2) (requiring a belief by the declarant "that death was imminent").

390. *See* Nicolas, *Admissibility of Dying Declarations, supra* note 380, at 528–34 (discussing the history of this limitation and potential rationales).

391. *See,* e.g., *Mattox,* 146 U.S. at 151 (asserting that the statements admissible under the exception were related "to the fact of the homicide and the person by whom it was committed"). Thus, a victim's statements accusing the defendant of stabbing her or asserting that the defendant had summoned her to his home and had attacked her once she entered would be admissible, but statements accusing the defendant of killing another individual would not be admissible. A statement in which the victim declared that another individual was *not* her attacker could be admitted against an accused insofar as it was relevant to disprove a defense claim that the other individual, not the accused, was the killer. Modern law has perpetuated this subject matter limitation. *See* FED. R. EVID. 804(b)(2) (including only statements "concerning the cause or circumstances of what the declarant believed to be impending death"). The common law also allowed defendants to introduce dying declarations to exculpate themselves in homicide prosecutions. *See Mattox,* 146 U.S. at 151 (stating that dying declarations were "admissible on a trial for murder . . . in favor of the defendant as well as against him").

he or she would have been unavailable to testify.[392] Consequently, if the Court remains true to the historical limitations of the exception, the dying declaration exception to Confrontation Clause exclusion could be limited to testimonial hearsay statements by alleged victims in homicide prosecutions that inculpate an accused in some way in the commission of that homicide. At the time of the statement, the declarant would have to believe that she was dying soon and have no hope of living.[393]

The requirements of the dying declarations exception reflect its dual rationales. First, dying declarations are admissible because of the *necessity* to prevent a killer from escaping justice. The common law believed that the need for this kind of hearsay counterbalanced the risks of admitting unconfronted hearsay.[394] Second, dying declarations were thought to have a guarantee of *reliability*.[395] The assumption was that a homicide victim who believed she would definitely die soon would have motivations—originally religious in nature—to be truthful. A person would be loathe to die—and face judgment—with an accusatory lie being one of her last earthly acts.[396] Together, the need for the evidence and the guarantee of sincerity were deemed sufficient to outweigh the accused's right to confront a witness in the courtroom. If history requires this unique exception, it will be because of a judgment made long ago by the Framers of the Sixth Amendment

---

392. *See* Nicolas, *Admissibility of Dying Declarations, supra* note 380, at 534–38 (discussing the common law "requirement that the declarant actually be dead"). Modern formulations of the dying declaration exception generally do require unavailability but do not require that the declarant be dead. *See id.* at 510 (stating that "most modern versions of the . . . exception . . . have eliminated" the need for the victim to "actually die," and that "it suffices that the declarant [is] 'unavailable' in one of a variety of ways").

393. It is not clear that all of these restrictions on the scope of the exception existed at the time the Sixth Amendment was adopted. *See* Nicolas, *Admissibility of Dying Declarations, supra* note 380, at 514–34 (suggesting that the exception was broader in some respects in 1791 and that some of the traditional restrictions appeared in the early nineteenth century). If the Court decides that the breadth of the exception at that time is dispositive, it will have to determine the requirements imposed by the common law in 1791.

394. *See* Mattox v. United States, 156 U.S. 237, 243 (1895); *Mattox*, 146 U.S. at 152; *see also* FED R. EVID. 804(b)(2) advisory committee's note; Orenstein, *Her Last Words, supra* note 380, at 1428, 1444.

395. *See Mattox*, 156 U.S. at 244; *Mattox*, 146 U.S. at 152; *see also* Cribari, *Is Death Different?, supra* note 380, at 1550; Orenstein, *Her Last Words, supra* note 380, at 1427–28, 1444.

396. *See* Rex v. Woodcock, 1 Leach 500, 502–03, 168 Eng. Rep. 352, 353–54 (K.B. 1789); *see also* FED. R. EVID. 804(b)(2) advisory committee's note (referring to the "original religious justification" which may have lost force for some, but observing that there still are "powerful psychological pressures" to make truthful statements); Orenstein, *Her Last Words, supra* note 380, at 106. Some have raised questions about the trustworthiness of dying declarations. *See* Nicolas, *Admissibility of Dying Declarations, supra* note 380, at 549; Orenstein, *Her Last Words, supra* note 380, at 1425–27.

that for a certain type of testimonial hearsay in a certain kind of case, suspension of the protection afforded by confrontation was justified.[397]

d. Impeachment Use of Testimonial Hearsay The last topic is impeachment use of testimonial hearsay—whether a prosecutor may introduce it to cast doubt on the credibility of a defense witness.[398] The history, nature, and objectives of the Confrontation Clause make it clear that there is no impeachment use exception to this exclusion doctrine. In general, the government may not introduce unconfrontable testimonial hearsay to inculpate an accused because such use at trial violates the Sixth Amendment right to confront adverse witnesses. When admitted to impeach a defense witness, hearsay is incriminating. It makes the witness less believable, thereby increasing the likelihood that the accused will be convicted. Consequently, the declarant of hearsay admitted for impeachment purposes is an adverse witness that the accused is entitled to confront. There is no historical exception for impeachment use of testimonial hearsay. Unless the testimonial hearsay falls within one of the exceptions to the confrontation entitlement, the Sixth Amendment bars impeachment use. Put simply, the use of testimonial hearsay to impeach defense witnesses is subject to the same constraints as its use for any other inculpatory purpose.

This does not mean that the prosecution may never introduce an out-of-court statement to impeach a defense witness. Because the Sixth Amendment bars only testimonial hearsay, if a statement is not hearsay, it is admissible for any purpose. Some out-of-court statements, when used to impeach witnesses, do not constitute hearsay. They can cast doubt on the credibility of the witness without being offered to prove the truth of anything they assert. For example, one type of impeachment that involves the use of out-of-court statements is the introduction of a statement made by the same witness that is inconsistent with her testimony. The prior statement can erode the witness's credibility merely because it shows that she made contradictory assertions. Whether or not the out-of-court assertion

397. Earlier cases suggested that the incentives to be truthful that justify the admission of dying declarations are equivalent to the incentives created by an "oath." *See Mattox*, 156 U.S. at 244; *Woodcock*, 1 Leach at 502, 168 Eng. Rep. at 353. If a dying declaration is trustworthy because of the source's motivation to be truthful, then its admission at trial without an opportunity for confrontation is less troubling because it is less likely to undermine the reliability of a trial's outcome.

398. The accused does not qualify as a "witness against" himself for Confrontation Clause purposes. Consequently, the use of a defendant's self-inculpatory hearsay statements at trial raises no Sixth Amendment issue. The Sixth Amendment grants him no right to confront himself and no right to exclude his own hearsay—whether it is introduced to prove his guilt directly or to impeach his own or another witness's testimony. *See* United States v. Nazemian, 948 F.2d 522, 525–26 (9th Cir. 1991).

is true, the self-contradiction makes the witness less believable and casts doubt on her trial testimony. The Sixth Amendment does not dictate suppression.[399]

In addition, if hearsay is nontestimonial—if it is not the kind of hearsay regulated by the Confrontation Clause—it is admissible for any purpose, including impeachment. A defense witness might be impeached by a government witness's testimony that an acquaintance told her that the defense witness has a grossly dishonest character. The acquaintance's out-of-court statement is hearsay because it is offered to prove the truth of what it asserts—that the defense witness has a dishonest character. The statement might be testimonial in nature. For example, it might have been made in response to questioning by a detective who was investigating the background of defense witnesses with an eye to trial, and the acquaintance might well have realized and intended that his character assessment would assist the government. In that case, the evidence would be barred. On the other hand, the acquaintance's character assessment might have been made to a fellow employee or a spouse under circumstances that clearly render it nontestimonial. In that case, there is no constitutional impediment to using it to impeach the witness.

Although illustrative examples could be multiplied, one more will suffice. Another mode of impeachment is to cast doubt on a witness's mental or physical capacities. Suppose that investigating officers question a defense witness's husband who reports that she has "awful eyesight and an even worse memory." The Sixth Amendment presumptively forbids the use of that assertion to impeach the witness—that is, to persuade the jury that she might not have seen what she claimed to have seen or that she might not be accurately remembering what she saw. However, if the husband made these assertions to a friend during a casual conversation at a bar and with no contemplation of its use in any litigation, it would be nontestimonial, and, therefore, beyond the reach of Sixth Amendment exclusion.

In sum, there is no impeachment use exception to the Confrontation Clause bar. Testimonial hearsay may not be used to impeach a defense witness unless the source of the hearsay testifies at trial and is subject to cross-examination or the hearsay falls within an exception to the Sixth Amendment rule. On the other hand, the government is free to use out-of-court statements to impeach witnesses if the statements cast doubt on the credibility of the witness through nonhearsay

---

399. There is another reason that most prior inconsistent statements would not be barred. A predicate for this type of impeachment is that the source of the hearsay has testified at the trial. If she is subject to cross-examination by the accused, there is an opportunity to confront her at the trial. The only time the government would need to rely on the "nonhearsay" nature of the prior inconsistent statement to justify its admission is when the defendant, for some reason, does not have an adequate opportunity for effective cross-examination.

means—i.e., without being used to prove the truth of what they assert—or if the statements are nontestimonial hearsay.

E. REFLECTIONS UPON CONFRONTATION CLAUSE EXCLUSION OF HEARSAY

The final chapter in this study of the constitutional bases for excluding evidence in criminal cases has proven to be the longest. In part, this is the result of the deep historical roots of the Confrontation Clause bar to hearsay evidence. This doctrine is the oldest of those that impede prosecutorial efforts to prove guilt by preventing the introduction of potentially probative evidence. It is one of only two suppression doctrines that emerged prior to the twentieth century. Moreover, its remarkable evolution has not slowed in modern times. Sixth Amendment regulation of hearsay has been a subject of considerable attention in recent years, and its development is likely to continue.

Unlike the opinions that address other constitutional exclusion doctrines, Supreme Court opinions contain little discussion of, and even less dispute over, the nature of and justifications for the Confrontation Clause bar to hearsay. The Justices have implicitly recognized that a personal right to bar certain hearsay evidence is necessary to prevent circumvention and violation of an accused's fundamental trial right to be confronted with adverse witnesses. Because this critical component of a constitutionally fair trial is not endangered by official pretrial conduct that produces the evidence at issue, but, instead, is jeopardized *only* by the courtroom use of a particular kind of evidence, deterrence—a major player in many exclusionary rule contexts—is not even a supplemental rationale in this domain. Confrontation Clause suppression is not entirely free of controversy, but the debates have been, and still are, over the scope and details of the exclusionary mandate, not its core or foundations.

The governing doctrinal framework is of quite recent origin. The trailblazing, rule-changing 2004 ruling in *Crawford v. Washington* contracted the territory governed by the Sixth Amendment to "testimonial hearsay." At the same time, it tightened the controls over the evidence that is subject to regulation. Today, there is a strong presumption in favor of an accused's right to confront "witnesses" who are the sources of testimonial hearsay in the courtroom, in front of the jurors, during the determination of guilt or innocence. If the accused does not have an opportunity to challenge the source of the hearsay testimony at his trial, the hearsay must be excluded except in three relatively limited situations.

First, a court may allow its introduction if the declarant is unavailable to testify—that is, if the government cannot produce the declarant for confrontation at trial—*and* if the accused had an adequate prior opportunity to cross-examine the declarant concerning the hearsay. In that case, the accused enjoys much of the constitutional protection guaranteed by the Sixth Amendment, and the partial deprivation that occurs is justified by society's legitimate interest in the effective prosecution of crimes.

Second, a court may admit any unconfronted and unconfrontable testimonial hearsay statements of a potential witness the accused has deliberately prevented from testifying at his trial. In that case, the defendant forfeits his right to confront the witness by wrongfully procuring her unavailability. Because equity demands that he not profit from this wrong and that the state not be impeded in its efforts to prove his guilt, the exclusionary bar is lifted.

Finally, it seems likely that the Court will recognize the unique, longstanding historical exception for "dying declarations" and will authorize the admission of testimonial hearsay that falls within this category. The breadth and details of this one-of-a-kind exception—which is apparently rooted in the need for and reliability of this narrow band of hearsay—have not been specified.

Although the future holds the promise of considerable doctrinal development—particularly in the difficult area of defining what constitutes testimonial hearsay—as long as the *Crawford* regime holds sway, the scope of Confrontation Clause exclusion will not extend beyond testimonial hearsay. Moreover, unless the Court discovers that it has misread the historical record, there will be no additional exceptions to the rule that an accused is entitled to confront testimonial hearsay declarants at trial. The prevailing wisdom holds that the exclusion of hearsay rooted in the Sixth Amendment must be guided, indeed determined, by the nature and specifics of the right of confrontation that the Framers of the Bill of Rights embodied in that provision. Future decisions will be devoted to interpreting the Framers' design and discerning the meaning of the guarantee they contemplated.

CONCLUSION: REFLECTIONS UPON CONSTITUTIONAL EXCLUSION

This study of constitutional mandates that exclude evidence of guilt began with the smallest of ideas. Years of studying Supreme Court opinions and reviewing scholarship pertaining to the topic led me to conclude that too often the rules of inadmissibility were treated as if they were all of one kind. To be sure, there were opinions acknowledging the significance of differences, and some insightful scholarship had highlighted distinctions and the need for separate analyses.[1] Nonetheless, a monolithic conception of suppression doctrines—reflected in the classification and labeling of all as "exclusionary rules"—frequently obscured differences with important theoretical and operational ramifications. Its misleading, distorting impact deserved attention.

At first, it seemed possible to accomplish my objectives—revealing the distinctions among the rules and identifying the implications of variations—in a relatively brief article. However, further reflection made it apparent that the project was much more expansive than first imagined and that only book-length treatment could suffice. Meaningful exploration of the differences required a comprehensive, detailed description and examination of each of the seven constitutional bases for excluding evidence. Thus was this text conceived. Now that the seed of my initial idea has ripened into intensive analyses of the seven exclusionary doctrines, a brief reflection upon the lessons learned is in order.

The preceding chapters have identified and explained noteworthy differences in the histories of the various suppression dictates—their origins and evolution. Four of the evidentiary bars have relatively short histories. These include the *Miranda*-Fifth Amendment self-incrimination privilege and *Massiah*-Sixth Amendment right to counsel rules regarding confessions and the *Wade-Gilbert* right to counsel and *Stovall* due process doctrines governing eyewitness identifications. These bars to government evidence did not appear until the mid-1960s, approximately 170 years after the adoption of our Bill of Rights. The Fourth Amendment exclusionary rule first appeared much earlier in the twentieth century. Still, the most significant event in its development—the extension of the rule to state prosecutions—was also a product of the revolutionary 1960s. In contrast, two suppression mandates have deep roots. The stories of the due process-Fifth Amendment privilege bar to coerced confessions and the

1. In my view, the best example of such scholarship is Arnold H. Loewy, *Police-Obtained Evidence and the Constitution: Distinguishing Unconstitutionally Obtained Evidence From Unconstitutionally Used Evidence*, 87 Mich. L. Rev. 907 (1989).

Confrontation Clause bar to hearsay began in the late nineteenth century and have continued to unfold in modern times. Moreover, unlike any of the other exclusion doctrines, both of these constitutional rules were the progeny of common law ancestors with pedigrees predating our Constitution. It is neither coincidental nor surprising that these two bars to evidence of guilt have been, and still are, the least controversial of the seven constitutional exclusion doctrines.

This text commenced with a study of the most prominent and best known of the exclusionary rules—the Fourth Amendment command that evidence obtained by means of unreasonable searches and seizures must be suppressed from trial. The Fourth Amendment exclusionary rule has been the most vigorously contested suppression sanction in part because the text of that provision says nothing about excluding illegally acquired evidence, in part because of its breadth, and in part because the illegalities that produce the evidence subject to suppression have no effect on the probative value of the barred evidence. The Fourth Amendment rule forces the justice system to ignore indisputably reliable proof of guilt. Although when it first appeared this exclusion doctrine appeared to be a courtroom right—an inseparable part of the guarantee against unreasonable searches and seizures—it was later transformed into a purely deterrent device designed to prevent future out-of-court deprivations of the right not to be searched or seized unreasonably. Unlike other exclusion doctrines, the Fourth Amendment bar extends to *every type of evidence*—not just confessions, identifications, or hearsay. In addition, it encompasses *all derivative evidence*—that is, it presumptively prevents the admission of any evidence with a causal connection to an unlawful search or seizure. Moreover, any official search or arrest might trigger this far-reaching doctrine and prevent the government from bringing a guilty individual to justice. It is understandable that there have long been challenges to the legitimacy of the Fourth Amendment exclusionary rule, and that in recent years the rule has been the target of a stealthy assault by the Supreme Court. It seems fair to predict that the force of the search and seizure exclusion doctrine will diminish even more in the near future.

The journey through the constitutional exclusion maze concluded with an analysis of the Sixth Amendment Confrontation Clause bar to hearsay evidence. In the very recent past, this suppression mandate has been the subject of more attention—and more dramatic revision—than any of the others. The contrasts between the Confrontation Clause rule and the Fourth Amendment rule could not be more stark. The Supreme Court has discerned firm support for the Confrontation Clause exclusion doctrine in both the history and the text of the right to be confronted with witnesses. The fundamental validity of this constitutional impediment to hearsay evidence has long been accepted. Debate has revolved around its scope and operation, not its validity. Moreover, unlike the Fourth Amendment bar, the Sixth Amendment rule is quite narrow, reaching only one variety of evidence—testimonial hearsay. It is unconcerned with the government's use of any other kind of evidence, no matter how clear and strong the causal connection between that evidence and forbidden testimonial hearsay.

In between the opening discussion of the Fourth Amendment rule and the closing analysis of the Confrontation Clause rule, this text addressed a diverse variety of suppression doctrines. Two of the exclusionary dictates encountered are similar in character to the Sixth Amendment bar to hearsay, one rule's nature resembles that of the Fourth Amendment exclusionary rule, one mandate is uniquely prophylactic in character, and the nature of one exclusionary command is somewhat uncertain. Like the Confrontation Clause doctrine, both the long-established due process-Fifth Amendment privilege bar to coerced confessions and the more recently-minted due process bar to identifications produced by unnecessarily suggestive official procedures are *constitutional trial rights.* They are essential to preserve the constitutional entitlements they are based upon. Although the conclusion is questionable and inconsistent with the *Massiah* rule's origins, the Supreme Court has determined that right to counsel-based suppression of confessions is not a courtroom right. Instead, like the Fourth Amendment exclusionary rule, the Sixth Amendment bar to confessions is a *deterrent device* aimed only at future enforcement of the pretrial right to the assistance of counsel.

On the other hand, two of the suppression rules are unlike either the Confrontation Clause or the Fourth Amendment mandate. *Miranda*'s (in)famous bar to voluntary confessions is a one-of-a-kind safeguard against unacceptably high risks that a trial right will be violated. While it most certainly is not a personal trial right of the accused individual, it is constitutionally-rooted prophylaxis designed to prevent courtroom deprivations of the entitlement not to be compelled to be a witness against oneself. Whether *Miranda*'s inadmissibility rule also serves deterrent purposes is currently uncertain. Finally, the right to counsel bar to eyewitness identification evidence seems to be a hybrid—both a necessary means of preventing courtroom violations of the Sixth Amendment entitlement and a necessary means of deterring future deprivations of assistance at pretrial identification confrontations. There is some uncertainty, however, about the true character of this exclusion doctrine. The only Supreme Court discussion of its underpinnings appears in the 1967 opinions that first announced its existence. Dramatic revisions of the premises for the other exclusionary rules that first emerged in the 1960s provide reason to suspect that if the occasion arose today, the *Wade-Gilbert* suppression doctrine for eyewitness identification evidence might well be recast as a mere deterrent sanction.

There are some similarities among the different doctrines. For example, all are limited by a "standing" restriction, and thus can be asserted only by a restricted group of individuals. Moreover, almost all operate only during criminal trials—that is, they do not bar evidence from other phases of the criminal process or from any kind of civil proceeding.[2]

However, because there are various kinds of constitutional exclusion doctrines, there is also great diversity in the doctrinal details that determine their scope and operation. Some have broad reach, barring both immediate products of government illegality and derivative fruits. Others are much narrower and pose no impediment to the prosecution's use of evidence acquired as a result of inadmissible evidence. Some claims that evidence should have been excluded from state criminal trials are subject to plenary review in federal habeas corpus proceedings, while others may be pursued in such post-trial challenges only in the rare instances where states have not fully and fairly considered those claims. Finally, it is difficult to generalize about the "exceptions" that qualify the different constitutional exclusion doctrines and authorize the admission of evidence that otherwise would be suppressed. While some rules are riddled with numerous exceptions, others have but a few. The issues raised by potential exceptions highlight and reinforce the need to analyze each exclusion doctrine individually and to interpret each in light of its nature and justifications.

Despite the differences in history, character, and doctrinal details, there is common ground—a shared core that makes it appropriate, even important, to juxtapose and analyze all seven constitutional exclusion doctrines in a single text. Each suppression mandate prevents a prosecutor from introducing relevant evidence that can assist efforts to prove that a defendant committed a criminal offense. By so doing, each rule of inadmissibility makes it more difficult for the government to meet the constitutional burden of proving guilt beyond a reasonable doubt. Insofar as the suppression rules diminish the chances of convicting a guilty, possibly dangerous, offender, they undermine individual security and threaten the social order. As a result, evidentiary exclusion doctrines generate resentment, hostility, and opposition.

The seven constitutional exclusion doctrines also share another significant facet. Each is essentially an effort to enforce a basic freedom embodied in our nation's fundamental charter. Some seek to preserve courtroom guarantees that are indispensable components of the Anglo-American conception of a fair trial. Others are mechanisms designed to prevent the erosion of basic liberties that operate outside the judicial process and are critical components of the free society our Founders envisioned. If the constitutional exclusion doctrines considered in this text did not exist, some of the core freedoms enshrined in our Constitution would have less force. Abolition of the evidentiary bars would diminish the fairness of criminal trials and lessen the security each of us enjoys against our government.

---

2. The exceptions are the rules that do or may apply to true sentencing proceedings in criminal cases. *See supra* Chapter 2, text accompanying notes 192–94; *supra* Chapter 3, text accompanying notes 137–43; *supra* Chapter 6, text accompanying notes 189–92.

There are defensible grounds for challenging the validity of constitutional exclusion doctrines and reasons to question whether they are worth the prices we pay. On the other hand, there are plausible grounds for celebrating the balances that evidentiary suppression doctrines strike between freedom and order and for concluding that the benefits they yield are worth the costs they impose. The debates over constitutional exclusion will surely continue in the coming years. My hope is that this text's accounts of the unique histories of the seven constitutional suppression doctrines, analyses of their underlying rationales, discussions of their similarities and differences, and explorations of their doctrinal nuances will facilitate more informed, more rational, and, ultimately, more productive debates.

TABLE OF CASES

C

D

J

K

L

N

O

Z

INDEX

www.ingramcontent.com/pod-product-compliance
Lightning Source LLC
Chambersburg PA
CBHW071353220926
51613CB00009B/195
* 9 7 8 0 1 9 5 3 6 9 2 4 3 *